AMERICAN INCOMES

AMERICAN INCOMES

Demographics of Who Has Money

BY THE EDITORS OF NEW STRATEGIST PRESS

New Strategist Press, LLC
Amityville, New York

New Strategist Press, LLC
P.O. Box 635, Amityville, New York 11701
800/848-0842; 631/608-8795
www.newstrategist.com

ISBN 978-1-940308-31-9 (hardcover)
ISBN 978-1-940308-37-1 (paper)

Printed in the United States of America

Table of Contents

Introduction 1

Chapter 1. Household Income 5
Household Income Trends 7
Income Inequality Has Grown 8
Many Households Have Incomes of $100,000 or More 10
Median Household Income Fell between 2000 and 2012 12
Every Household Type Lost Ground between 2000 and 2012 14
Every Racial and Ethnic Group Has Lost Ground 16
College Graduates Are Losing Ground 18
Incomes Fell in Households Large and Small 20
More Earners Did Little to Help Stabilize Incomes 22
Families with Children Are Losing Ground 24
Working Wives Are Keeping Families Afloat 28
Median Household Income Fell in Every Region 30
Many States Have Seen Double-Digit Percentage Declines in Income 32

Household Income, 2012 35
Dual-Earner Couples Dominate the Affluent 36
Married Couples Have the Highest Incomes 40
Household Income Peaks in the 45-to-54 Age Group 46
Among Couples, the Middle Aged Have the Highest Incomes 52
Incomes of Female-Headed Families Are below Average 58
Male-Headed Families Have Average Incomes 64
Women Who Live Alone Have the Lowest Incomes 70
Incomes Are Low for Men Who Live Alone 76
Two-Earner Households Have Above-Average Incomes 82
Married Couples with School-Aged Children Have the Highest Incomes 88
Dual-Earners Are the Majority of Married Couples 94
Female-Headed Families without Children Have Higher Incomes 99
Male-Headed Families with Children Have Below-Average Incomes 105
Household Incomes Rise with Education 111
Household Incomes Are Highest in New England 117
Among Blacks, Household Incomes Are Highest in the West 123
Suburban Households Have the Highest Incomes 128

Chapter 2. Men's Income 135
Men's Income Trends 137
Incomes Have Plummeted among Men under Age 65 138
Regardless of Race or Hispanic Origin, Men Lost Ground 140
In Every Region, Men Have Lost Ground since 2000 146
Men's Earnings Fell between 2000 and 2010 148
Asian Men Have Seen Their Earnings Rise 150

College Graduates Lost Ground between 2000 and 2012 152
Men in Most Occupations Have Seen Their Earnings Decline 154

Men's Income, 2012 157
Income Peaks among Men Aged 45 to 54 158
Men in the South Have the Lowest Incomes 165
Men in the Suburbs Have the Highest Incomes 171
Most Men Have Modest Earnings 173
Men's Earnings Rise with Education 179
Education Boosts Earnings of Asian, Black, Hispanic and Non-Hispanic White Men 186
Men's Earnings Vary Widely by Occupation 191
Most Men Receive Wage or Salary Income 194

Chapter 3. Women's Income 201
Women's Income Trends 203
Women's Incomes Were Growing until the Great Recession 204
The Great Recession Hurt Women in Every Race and Hispanic Origin Group 206
Women in the Every Region Lost Ground between 2007 and 2012 212
Earnings Have Declined among Women Who Work Full-Time 214
Among Full-Time Workers, Asian and Non-Hispanic White Women Made Gains 216
Education Does Not Guarantee Earnings Growth 218
Women in Most Occupations Have Seen Their Earnings Decline 220
Women Lost Ground during the Great Recession 222
Nine Million Wives Earn More than Their Husbands 224

Women's Income, 2012 227
Women's Incomes Peak in the 35-to-44 Age Group 228
Among Women Who Work Full-Time, Incomes are Highest in the Northeast 235
Women in Nonmetropolitan Areas Have Lower Incomes 241
Women Earn Little from Part-Time Work 243
Women with Professional Degrees Earn the Most 249
Education Boosts Earnings in Every Race and Hispanic Origin Group 256
Among Women, Lawyers Earn the Most 261
Two-Thirds of Women Receive Wage or Salary Income 264

Chapter 4. Discretional Income 271
Discretionary Income Peaks in Late Middle Age 276
More than 40 Percent of Households Have No Discretionary Income 278
Married Couples Control Most Discretionary Income 280
Asian Households Have the Most Discretionary Income 282
Discretionary Income Is Highest in the Midwest 284
The College Educated Control Most Discretionary Income 286

Chapter 5. Wealth
Net Worth Has Plunged 290
Married Couples Have the Greatest Wealth 292
Non-Hispanic Whites Have the Highest Net Worth 297
Homes Are the Most Important Asset 299

Homeownership Boosts the Net Worth of Non-Hispanic Whites 305

Most Households Are in Debt 307

Married Couples Have the Biggest Debts 310

Asians Are Most Likely to Be in Debt 314

Retirement Worries Are Growing 316

Chapter 6. Poverty 319

Poverty Trends 320

Women Head More than Half of the Nation's Poor Families 321

Family Poverty Increased between 2000 and 2012 323

Many More Families with Children Are in Poverty 329

Poverty Rate Has Increased since 2000 335

A Growing Share of Poor People Are Aged 18 to 64 337

Non-Hispanic Whites Are a Minority of the Poor 340

Poverty Has Grown in Every Region 343

Naturalized Citizens Have the Lowest Poverty Rate 346

The Poverty Rate Has Increased in Most States since 2007 348

A Growing Share of the Poor Lives in the Suburbs 353

Many of the Poor Have Jobs 356

Poverty, 2012 359

Few Households with Two Earners Are Poor 360

Poverty Rate Is Highest among Families in the South 365

Poverty Rate Is Highest in Central Cities 374

Non-Hispanic Whites Dominate the Elderly Poor 383

Poverty Rate Is Highest among Children 385

Poverty Rate Varies by Family Status and Age 391

Few College Graduates Are Poor 397

Many Young Adult Workers Are Poor 399

Many of the Nonworking Poor Are Ill or Disabled 405

Poverty Is Highest in the South 407

Poverty Is High in Nonmetropolitan Areas 410

More than One-Third of Nation's Poor Live in Four States 415

Glossary 419

Bibliography 425

Index 426

List of Tables

Chapter 1. Household Income

Household Income Trends

1.1   Share of Aggregate Income Received by Each Fifth and Top 5 Percent of Households, 2000 to 2012 9
1.2   Distribution of Households by Income, 2000 to 2012 11
1.3   Median Household Income by Age of Householder, 2000 to 2012 13
1.4   Median Household Income by Type of Household, 2000 to 2012 15
1.5   Median Household Income by Race and Hispanic Origin of Householder, 2000 to 2012 17
1.6   Median Household Income by Education of Householder, 2000 to 2012 19
1.7   Median Household Income by Size of Household, 2000 to 2012 21
1.8   Median Household Income by Number of Earners in Household, 2000 to 2012 23
1.9   Median Income of Married-Couple Families by Presence of Children, 2000 to 2012 25
1.10   Median Income of Female-Headed Families by Presence of Children, 2000 to 2012 26
1.11   Median Income of Male-Headed Families by Presence of Children, 2000 to 2012 27
1.12   Median Income of Married Couples by Work Experience of Husband and Wife, 2000 to 2012 29
1.13   Median Household Income by Region, 2000 to 2012 31
1.14   Median Household Income by State, 2007 and 2012 33

Household Income, 2012

1.15   Number of Households by Income Quintile and Household Characteristic, 2012 37
1.16   Distribution of Households within Income Quintile by Household Characteristic, 2012 38
1.17   Distribution of Household Characteristics by Income Quintile, 2012 39
1.18   Households by Income and Household Type, 2012: Total Households 41
1.19   Households by Income and Household Type, 2012: Asian Households 42
1.20   Households by Income and Household Type, 2012: Black Households 43
1.21   Households by Income and Household Type, 2012: Hispanic Households 44
1.22   Households by Income and Household Type, 2012: Non-Hispanic White Households 45
1.23   Households by Income and Age of Householder, 2012: Total Households 47
1.24   Households by Income and Age of Householder, 2012: Asian Households 48
1.25   Households by Income and Age of Householder, 2012: Black Households 49
1.26   Households by Income and Age of Householder, 2012: Hispanic Households 50
1.27   Households by Income and Age of Householder, 2012: Non-Hispanic White Households 51
1.28   Married Couples by Household Income and Age of Householder, 2012: Total Married Couples 53
1.29   Married Couples by Household Income and Age of Householder, 2012: Asian Married Couples 54
1.30   Married Couples by Household Income and Age of Householder, 2012: Black Married Couples 55
1.31   Married Couples by Household Income and Age of Householder, 2012: Hispanic Married Couples 56
1.32   Married Couples by Household Income and Age of Householder, 2012:
        Non-Hispanic White Married Couples 57
1.33   Female-Headed Families by Household Income and Age of Householder, 2012: Total Female-Headed Families . . 59
1.34   Female-Headed Families by Household Income and Age of Householder, 2012: Asian Female-Headed Families . . 60
1.35   Female-Headed Families by Household Income and Age of Householder, 2012: Black Female-Headed Families . 61
1.36   Female-Headed Families by Household Income and Age of Householder, 2012:
        Hispanic Female-Headed Families 62
1.37   Female-Headed Families by Household Income and Age of Householder, 2012:
        Non-Hispanic White Female-Headed Families 63
1.38   Male-Headed Families by Household Income and Age of Householder, 2012: Total Male-Headed Families 65
1.39   Male-Headed Families by Household Income and Age of Householder, 2012: Asian Male-Headed Families 66
1.40   Male-Headed Families by Household Income and Age of Householder, 2012: Black Male-Headed Families 67
1.41   Male-Headed Families by Household Income and Age of Householder, 2012: Hispanic Male-Headed Families . . 68
1.42   Male-Headed Families by Household Income and Age of Householder, 2012:
        Non-Hispanic White Male-Headed Families 69
1.43   Women Who Live Alone by Household Income and Age of Householder, 2012: Total Women Who Live Alone . . 71
1.44   Women Who Live Alone by Household Income and Age of Householder, 2012: Asian Women Who Live Alone . . 72
1.45   Women Who Live Alone by Household Income and Age of Householder, 2012: Black Women Who Live Alone . . 73
1.46   Women Who Live Alone by Household Income and Age of Householder, 2012:
        Hispanic Women Who Live Alone 74
1.47   Women Who Live Alone by Household Income and Age of Householder, 2012:
        Non-Hispanic White Women Who Live Alone 75

1.48   Men Who Live Alone by Household Income and Age of Householder, 2012: Total Men Who Live Alone 77
1.49   Men Who Live Alone by Household Income and Age of Householder, 2012: Asian Men Who Live Alone 78
1.50   Men Who Live Alone by Household Income and Age of Householder, 2012: Black Men Who Live Alone 79
1.51   Men Who Live Alone by Household Income and Age of Householder, 2012: Hispanic Men Who Live Alone 80
1.52   Men Who Live Alone by Household Income and Age of Householder, 2012:
       Non-Hispanic White Men Who Live Alone 81
1.53   Households by Income and Number of Earners, 2012: Total Households 83
1.54   Households by Income and Number of Earners, 2012: Asian Households 84
1.55   Households by Income and Number of Earners, 2012: Black Households 85
1.56   Households by Income and Number of Earners, 2012: Hispanic Households 86
1.57   Households by Income and Number of Earners, 2012: Non-Hispanic White Households 87
1.58   Married Couples by Family Income and Presence of Children, 2012: Total Married Couples 89
1.59   Married Couples by Family Income and Presence of Children, 2012: Asian Married Couples 90
1.60   Married Couples by Family Income and Presence of Children, 2012: Black Married Couples 91
1.61   Married Couples by Family Income and Presence of Children, 2012: Hispanic Married Couples 92
1.62   Married Couples by Family Income and Presence of Children, 2012: Non-Hispanic White Married Couples 93
1.63   Dual-Income Married Couples by Household Income and Presence of Children, 2012: Husband and Wife Work . . 95
1.64   Dual-Income Married Couples by Household Income and Presence of Children, 2012:
       Husband and Wife Work Full-Time 96
1.65   Married Couples by Work Status, Household Income, and Presence of Children, 2012:
       Husband Works Full-Time, Wife Does Not Work 97
1.66   Married Couples by Work Status, Household Income, and Presence of Children, 2012:
       Husband Does Not Work, Wife Does Not Work 98
1.67   Female-Headed Families by Family Income and Presence of Children, 2012: Total Female-Headed Families. . . . 100
1.68   Female-Headed Families by Family Income and Presence of Children, 2012: Asian Female-Headed Families. . . . 101
1.69   Female-Headed Families by Family Income and Presence of Children, 2012: Black Female-Headed Families. . . . 102
1.70   Female-Headed Families by Family Income and Presence of Children, 2012: Hispanic Female-Headed Families .103
1.71   Female-Headed Families by Family Income and Presence of Children, 2012:
       Non-Hispanic White Female-Headed Families 104
1.72   Male-Headed Families by Family Income and Presence of Children, 2012: Total Male-Headed Families 106
1.73   Male-Headed Families by Family Income and Presence of Children, 2012: Asian Male-Headed Families 107
1.74   Male-Headed Families by Family Income and Presence of Children, 2012: Black Male-Headed Families 108
1.75   Male-Headed Families by Family Income and Presence of Children, 2012: Hispanic Male-Headed Families 109
1.76   Male-Headed Families by Family Income and Presence of Children, 2012:
       Non-Hispanic White Male-Headed Families 110
1.77   Households by Income and Educational Attainment of Householder, 2012: Total Households 112
1.78   Households by Income and Educational Attainment of Householder, 2012: Asian Households 113
1.79   Households by Income and Educational Attainment of Householder, 2012: Black Households 114
1.80   Households by Income and Educational Attainment of Householder, 2012: Hispanic Households 115
1.81   Households by Income and Educational Attainment of Householder, 2012: Non-Hispanic White Households   116
1.82   Households by Income and Region, 2012 118
1.83   Households by Income, Region, and Division, 2012: Northeast 119
1.84   Households by Income, Region, and Division, 2012: Midwest 120
1.85   Households by Income, Region, and Division, 2012: South 121
1.86   Households by Income, Region, and Division, 2012: West 122
1.87   Households by Income, Region, Race, and Hispanic Origin, 2012: Northeast 124
1.88   Households by Income, Region, Race, and Hispanic Origin, 2012: Midwest 125
1.89   Households by Income, Region, Race, and Hispanic Origin, 2012: South 126
1.90   Households by Income, Region, Race, and Hispanic Origin, 2012: West 127
1.91   Median Household Income by State, 2012 129
1.92   Households by Income and Metropolitan Residence, 2012 131
1.93   Median Household Income in Large Metropolitan Areas, 2012 132

Chapter 2. Men's Income

Men's Income Trends

2.1   Median Income of Men by Age, 2000 to 2012 139
2.2   Median Income of Men by Race and Hispanic Origin, 2000 to 2012 141
2.3   Median Income of Asian Men by Age, 2002 to 2012 142
2.4   Median Income of Black Men by Age, 2000 to 2012 143
2.5   Median Income of Hispanic Men by Age, 2000 to 2012 144
2.6   Median Income of Non-Hispanic White Men by Age, 2000 to 2012 145
2.7   Median Income of Men by Region, 2000 to 2012 147

2.8   Median Earnings of Men by Employment Status, 2000 to 2012 149
2.9   Median Earnings of Men Who Work Full-Time by Race and Hispanic Origin, 2000 to 2012 151
2.10 Median Earnings of Men Who Work Full-Time by Education, 2000 to 2012 153
2.11 Median Earnings of Men Who Work Full-Time by Occupation, 2007 to 2012 155

Men's Income, 2012
2.12 Men by Income and Age, 2012: Total Men 159
2.13 Men by Income and Age, 2012: Asian Men 160
2.14 Men by Income and Age, 2012: Black Men 161
2.15 Men by Income and Age, 2012: Hispanic Men 162
2.16 Men by Income and Age, 2012: Non-Hispanic White Men 163
2.17 Men by Income, Race, and Hispanic Origin, 2012 164
2.18 Men by Income and Region, 2012: Total Men 166
2.19 Men by Income and Region, 2012: Asian Men 167
2.20 Men by Income and Region, 2012: Black Men 168
2.21 Men by Income and Region, 2012: Hispanic Men 169
2.22 Men by Income and Region, 2012: Non-Hispanic White Men 170
2.23 Men by Income and Metropolitan Residence, 2012 172
2.24 Men by Earnings and Employment Status, 2012: Total Men 174
2.25 Men by Earnings and Employment Status, 2012: Asian Men 175
2.26 Men by Earnings and Employment Status, 2012: Black Men 176
2.27 Men by Earnings and Employment Status, 2012: Hispanic Men 177
2.28 Men by Earnings and Employment Status, 2012: Non-Hispanic White Men 178
2.29 Men Who Work Full-Time by Earnings and Education, 2012: Total Men 180
2.30 Men Who Work Full-Time by Earnings and Education, 2012: Men Aged 25 to 34 181
2.31 Men Who Work Full-Time by Earnings and Education, 2012: Men Aged 35 to 44 182
2.32 Men Who Work Full-Time by Earnings and Education, 2012: Men Aged 45 to 54 183
2.33 Men Who Work Full-Time by Earnings and Education, 2012: Men Aged 55 to 64 184
2.34 Men Who Work Full-Time by Earnings and Education, 2012: Men Aged 65 or Older 185
2.35 Men Who Work Full-Time by Earnings and Education, 2012: Asian Men 187
2.36 Men Who Work Full-Time by Earnings and Education, 2012: Black Men 188
2.37 Men Who Work Full-Time by Earnings and Education, 2012: Hispanic Men 189
2.38 Men Who Work Full-Time by Earnings and Education, 2012: Non-Hispanic White Men 190
2.39 Median Earnings of Men by Occupation, 2013 192
2.40 Median Income of Men by Source of Income, 2012: Total Men 195
2.41 Median Income of Men by Source of Income, 2012: Asian Men 196
2.42 Median Income of Men by Source of Income, 2012: Black Men 197
2.43 Median Income of Men by Source of Income, 2012: Hispanic Men 198
2.44 Median Income of Men by Source of Income, 2012: Non-Hispanic White Men 199

Chapter 3. Women's Income

Women's Income Trends
3.1   Median Income of Women by Age, 2000 to 2012 205
3.2   Median Income of Women by Race and Hispanic Origin, 2000 to 2012 207
3.3   Median Income of Asian Women by Age, 2002 to 2012 208
3.4   Median Income of Black Women by Age, 2000 to 2012 209
3.5   Median Income of Hispanic Women by Age, 2000 to 2012 210
3.6   Median Income of Non-Hispanic White Women by Age, 2000 to 2012 211
3.7   Median Income of Women by Region, 2000 to 2012 213
3.8   Median Earnings of Women by Employment Status, 2000 to 2012 215
3.9   Median Earnings of Women Who Work Full-Time by Race and Hispanic Origin, 2000 to 2012 217
3.10 Median Earnings of Women Who Work Full-Time by Education, 2000 to 2012 219
3.11 Median Earnings of Women Who Work Full-Time by Occupation, 2007 to 2012 221
3.12 Median Earnings of Full-Time Workers by Sex, 2000 to 2012 223
3.13 Wives Who Earn More than Their Husbands, 2000 to 2012 225

Women's Income, 2012
3.14 Women by Income and Age, 2012: Total Women 229
3.15 Women by Income and Age, 2012: Asian Women 230
3.16 Women by Income and Age, 2012: Black Women 231
3.17 Women by Income and Age, 2012: Hispanic Women 232
3.18 Women by Income and Age, 2012: Non-Hispanic White Women 233

3.19   Women by Income, Race, and Hispanic Origin, 2012 234
3.20   Women by Income and Region, 2012: Total Women 236
3.21   Women by Income and Region, 2012: Asian Women 237
3.22   Women by Income and Region, 2012: Black Women 238
3.23   Women by Income and Region, 2012: Hispanic Women 239
3.24   Women by Income and Region, 2012: Non-Hispanic White Women 240
3.25   Women by Income and Metropolitan Residence, 2012 242
3.26   Women by Earnings and Employment Status, 2012: Total Women 244
3.27   Women by Earnings and Employment Status, 2012: Asian Women 245
3.28   Women by Earnings and Employment Status, 2012: Black Women 246
3.29   Women by Earnings and Employment Status, 2012: Hispanic Women 247
3.30   Women by Earnings and Employment Status, 2012: Non-Hispanic White Women 248
3.31   Women Who Work Full-Time by Earnings and Education, 2012: Total Women 250
3.32   Women Who Work Full-Time by Earnings and Education, 2012: Women Aged 25 to 34 251
3.33   Women Who Work Full-Time by Earnings and Education, 2012: Women Aged 35 to 44 252
3.34   Women Who Work Full-Time by Earnings and Education, 2012: Women Aged 45 to 54 253
3.35   Women Who Work Full-Time by Earnings and Education, 2012: Women Aged 55 to 64 254
3.36   Women Who Work Full-Time by Earnings and Education, 2012: Women Aged 65 or Older 255
3.37   Women Who Work Full-Time by Earnings and Education, 2012: Asian Women 257
3.38   Women Who Work Full-Time by Earnings and Education, 2012: Black Women 258
3.39   Women Who Work Full-Time by Earnings and Education, 2012: Hispanic Women 259
3.40   Women Who Work Full-Time by Earnings and Education, 2012: Non-Hispanic White Women 260
3.41   Median Earnings of Women by Occupation, 2012 262
3.42   Median Income of Women by Source of Income, 2012: Total Women 265
3.43   Median Income of Women by Source of Income, 2012: Asian Women 266
3.44   Median Income of Women by Source of Income, 2012: Black Women 267
3.45   Median Income of Women by Source of Income, 2012: Hispanic Women 268
3.46   Median Income of Women by Source of Income, 2012: Non-Hispanic White Women 269

Chapter 4. Discretionary Income

4.1   Top-10 Discretionary Expenditures, 2012 275
4.2   Discretionary Income by Age of Householder, 2012 277
4.3   Discretionary Income by Household Income, 2012 279
4.4   Discretionary Income by Type of Household, 2012 281
4.5   Discretionary Income by Race and Hispanic Origin of Householder, 2012 283
4.6   Discretionary Income by Region of Residence, 2012 285
4.7   Discretionary Income by Education of Householder, 2012 287

Chapter 5. Wealth

5.1   Median Household Net Worth by Age of Householder, 2005 and 2011 291
5.2   Distribution of Net Worth by Age of Householder, 2011 291
5.3   Median Household Net Worth by Type of Household and Age of Householder, 2005 and 2011 293
5.4   Distribution of Net Worth among Married-Couple Households by Age, 2011 294
5.5   Distribution of Net Worth among Female-Headed Households by Age, 2011 295
5.6   Distribution of Net Worth among Male-Headed Households by Age, 2011 296
5.7   Median Household Net Worth by Race and Hispanic Origin of Householder, 2005 and 2011 298
5.8   Distribution of Net Worth by Race and Hispanic Origin of Householder, 2011 298
5.9   Asset Ownership of Households by Age of Householder, 2011 300
5.10   Asset Ownership of Married-Couple Households by Age, 2011 302
5.11   Asset Ownership of Female-Headed Households by Age, 2011 303
5.12   Asset Ownership of Male-Headed Households by Age, 2011 304
5.13   Asset Ownership of Households by Race and Hispanic Origin of Householder, 2011 306
5.14   Debt of Households by Age of Householder, 2000 and 2011 308
5.15   Debt of Households by Type of Debt and Age of Householder, 2011 309
5.16   Debt of Married-Couple Households by Type of Debt and Age of Householder, 2011 311
5.17   Debt of Female-Headed Households by Type of Debt and Age of Householder, 2011 312
5.18   Debt of Male-Headed Households by Type of Debt and Age of Householder, 2011 313
5.19   Debt of Households by Type of Debt, Race, and Hispanic Origin of Householder, 2011 315
5.20   Retirement Confidence, 2007 to 2013 317
5.21   Expected Age of Retirement, 2007 and 2013 317
5.22   Retirement Savings by Age, 2013 318

Chapter 6. Poverty

Poverty Trends
6.1. Distribution of Families below Poverty Level by Family Type, 2000 to 2012 322
6.2 Number and Percent of Families below Poverty Level by Family Type, 2000 to 2012: Total Families 324
6.3 Number and Percent of Families below Poverty Level by Family Type, 2002 to 2012: Asian Families 325
6.4 Number and Percent of Families below Poverty Level by Family Type, 2000 to 2012: Black Families 326
6.5 Number and Percent of Families below Poverty Level by Family Type, 2000 to 2012: Hispanic Families 327
6.6 Number and Percent of Families below Poverty Level by Family Type, 2000 to 2012: Non-Hispanic White Families 328
6.7 Number and Percent of Families with Children below Poverty Level by Family Type, 2000 to 2012: Total Families with Children 330
6.8 Number and Percent of Families with Children below Poverty Level by Family Type, 2002 to 2012: Asian Families with Children 331
6.9 Number and Percent of Families with Children below Poverty Level by Family Type, 2000 to 2012: Black Families with Children 332
6.10 Number and Percent of Families with Children below Poverty Level by Family Type, 2000 to 2012: Hispanic Families with Children 333
6.11 Number and Percent of Families with Children below Poverty Level by Family Type, 2000 to 2012: Non-Hispanic White Families with Children 334
6.12 Number and Percent of People below Poverty Level by Sex, 2000 to 2012 336
6.13 Distribution of People below Poverty Level by Age, 2000 to 2012 338
6.14 Number and Percent of People below Poverty Level by Age, 2000 to 2012 339
6.15 Distribution of People below Poverty Level by Race and Hispanic Origin, 2000 to 2012 341
6.16 Number and Percent of People below Poverty Level by Race and Hispanic Origin, 2000 to 2012 342
6.17 Distribution of People below Poverty Level by Region, 2000 to 2012 344
6.18 Number and Percent of People below Poverty Level by Region, 2000 to 2012 345
6.19 Number and Percent of People below Poverty Level by Nativity Status, 2000 to 2012 347
6.20 Number of Poor by State, 2000 to 2012 349
6.21 Poverty Rate by State, 2000 to 2012 351
6.22 Distribution of People below Poverty Level by Metropolitan Residence, 2000 to 2012 354
6.23 Number and Percent of People below Poverty Level by Metropolitan Residence, 2000 to 2012 355
6.24 People below Poverty Level by Work Status, 2000 to 2012 357

Poverty, 2012
6.25 Families below Poverty Level by Work Status, Race, and Hispanic Origin, 2012 361
6.26 Married Couples below Poverty Level by Work Status, Race, and Hispanic Origin, 2012 362
6.27 Female-Headed Families below Poverty Level by Work Status, Race, and Hispanic Origin, 2012 363
6.28 Male-Headed Families below Poverty Level by Work Status, Race, and Hispanic Origin, 2012 364
6.29 Families below Poverty Level by Region, Race, and Hispanic Origin, 2012 366
6.30 Families with Children below Poverty Level by Region, Race, and Hispanic Origin, 2012 367
6.31 Married Couples below Poverty Level by Region, Race, and Hispanic Origin, 2012 368
6.32 Married Couples with Children below Poverty Level by Region, Race, and Hispanic Origin, 2012 369
6.33 Female-Headed Families below Poverty Level by Region, Race, and Hispanic Origin, 2012 370
6.34 Female-Headed Families with Children below Poverty Level by Region, Race, and Hispanic Origin, 2012 371
6.35 Male-Headed Families below Poverty Level by Region, Race, and Hispanic Origin, 2012 372
6.36 Male-Headed Families with Children below Poverty Level by Region, Race, and Hispanic Origin, 2012 373
6.37 Families below Poverty Level by Metropolitan Status, Race, and Hispanic Origin, 2012 375
6.38 Families with Children below Poverty Level by Metropolitan Status, Race, and Hispanic Origin, 2012 376
6.39 Married Couples below Poverty Level by Metropolitan Status, Race, and Hispanic Origin, 2012 377
6.40 Married Couples with Children below Poverty Level by Metropolitan Status, Race, and Hispanic Origin, 2012 .. 378
6.41 Female-Headed Families below Poverty Level by Metropolitan Status, Race, and Hispanic Origin, 2012 379
6.42 Female-Headed Families with Children below Poverty Level by Metropolitan Status, Race, and Hispanic Origin, 2012 380
6.43 Male-Headed Families below Poverty Level by Metropolitan Status, Race, and Hispanic Origin, 2012 381
6.44 Male-Headed Families with Children below Poverty Level by Metropolitan Status, Race, and Hispanic Origin, 2012 382
6.45 People below Poverty Level by Age, Race, and Hispanic Origin, 2012 384
6.46 People below Poverty Level by Age and Sex, 2012: Total People 386
6.47 People below Poverty Level by Age and Sex, 2012: Asians 387
6.48 People below Poverty Level by Age and Sex, 2012: Blacks 388
6.49 People below Poverty Level by Age and Sex, 2012: Hispanics 389

6.50 People below Poverty Level by Age and Sex, 2012: Non-Hispanic Whites 390
6.51 People below Poverty Level by Age and Family Status, 2012: Total People 392
6.52 People below Poverty Level by Age and Family Status, 2012: Asians 393
6.53 People below Poverty Level by Age and Family Status, 2012: Blacks 394
6.54 People below Poverty Level by Age and Family Status, 2012: Hispanics 395
6.55 People below Poverty Level by Age and Family Status, 2012: Non-Hispanic Whites 396
6.56 People below Poverty Level by Education, Race, and Hispanic Origin, 2012 398
6.57 Number and Percent of Workers below Poverty Level by Sex, Age, and Work Status, 2012: Total Workers 400
6.58 Number and Percent of Workers below Poverty Level by Sex, Age, and Work Status, 2012: Asian Workers 401
6.59 Number and Percent of Workers below Poverty Level by Sex, Age, and Work Status, 2012: Black Workers 402
6.60 Number and Percent of Workers below Poverty Level by Sex, Age, and Work Status, 2012: Hispanic Workers   403
6.61 Number and Percent of Workers below Poverty Level by Sex, Age, and Work Status, 2012:
     Non-Hispanic White Workers 404
6.62 People below Poverty Level by Reason for Not Working, 2012 406
6.63 People below Poverty Level by Age and Region, 2012 408
6.64 People below Poverty Level by Region, Race, and Hispanic Origin, 2012 409
6.65 People below Poverty Level by Age and Metropolitan Status, 2012 411
6.66 People below Poverty Level by Metropolitan Status, Race, and Hispanic Origin, 2012 412
6.67 Poor Population by Metropolitan Area, 2012 413
6.68 People below Poverty Level by State, 2012 416

List of Charts

Chapter 1. Household Income

Household Income Trends
The wealthiest households control more than half of the nation's income 8
There was little change in the proportion of households with incomes of $100,000 or more,
    despite the Great Recession 10
The oldest householders made gains between 2007 and 2012 12
Median income of married couples fell 6 percent between 2007 and 2012 14
Median income of non-Hispanic whites fell 6 percent between 2007 and 2012 16
Median income of college graduates fell between 2007 and 2012 18
Every household size has lost ground since the start of the Great Recession in 2007 20
Working households have lost ground since the start of the Great Recession in 2007 22
Among families with children under age 18, married couples have lost less than others 24
Single-earner couples have lost ground 28
Households in the Midwest have lost more than $8,000 30
Nevada has been the biggest loser 32

Household Income, 2012
More than one-third of households with two earners are in the top income quintile 36
Women who live alone have the lowest incomes 40
Incomes are lowest for the oldest householders 46
Asian couples have the highest median income 52
Incomes peak in middle age for female-headed families 58
Among male-headed families, Asians have the highest incomes 64
Among women who live alone, those aged 35 to 44 have the highest incomes 70
Among men who live alone, incomes peak in the 35-to-44 age group 76
Households with four or more earners have the highest incomes 82
Couples with school-aged children are the most affluent 88
Single-earner couples have much lower incomes 94
Female-headed families with children have lower incomes 99
Incomes vary for male-headed families 105
Education boosts income 111
Incomes are lowest in the South 117
Among households in the West, Asians have the highest median income 123
Nonmetropolitan households have the lowest incomes 128

Chapter 2. Men's Income

Men's Income Trends
Median income of men aged 45 to 54 fell 8 percent between 2007 and 2012 138
Asians experienced the smallest decline between 2007 and 2012 140
Between 2007 and 2012, men's incomes fell the most in the West 146
Men who work full-time, year-round are struggling to stay even 148
Non-Hispanic white men lost the most ground between 2007 and 2012 150
Premium paid to college graduates is holding steady 152
Recession hurt some men more than others 154

Men's Income, 2012
Among men who work full-time, incomes continue to rise into old age 158
Men's incomes are highest in the Northeast 165
Men in nonmetropolitan areas have the lowest incomes 171
Most men earn less than $50,000 per year 173
A college diploma adds to earning power 179
Among men with a bachelor's degree, non-Hispanic white men earn the most 186
Career choice affects earnings 191
Wage and salary income is most common 194

Chapter 3. Women's Income

Women's Income Trends
Median income of women grew in the first part of the decade 204
Asian women experienced the biggest income decline 206
Between 2000 and 2012, women's median income fell the most in the West 212
Among women with full-time jobs, earnings grew then fell 214
Hispanic women experienced the biggest earnings decline 216
Among women, the premium paid to college graduates held steady 218
Women's median earnings fell in most occupations 220
Earnings gap between women and men is no longer narrowing 222
A growing percentage of wives are earning more than their husbands 224

Women's Income, 2012
Among women who work full-time, income peaks in the older age groups 228
Women's median income tops $40,000 in the Northeast and West 235
Women in the suburbs have the highest incomes 241
Among women who work full-time, Asians have the highest median earnings 243
Women's earnings rise with education 249
Among women with a bachelor's degree, Hispanics earn the least 256
Women's earnings vary by occupation 261
Few women receive retirement income 264

Chapter 4. Discretionary Income

Discretionary income surpasses $20,000 among householders aged 55 to 64 276
Households with incomes of $100,000 or more control 73 percent of discretionary dollars 278
Married couples without children at home have the most discretionary income per household member 280
Hispanic households have the fewest discretionary dollars 282
Discretionary income is higher in the Northeast than in the West 284
Discretionary income rises with education 286

Chapter 5. Wealth

Net worth fell sharply between 2005 and 2011 290
The net worth of married couples exceeds $100,000 292
Net worth of Asians is well above average 297
Retirement accounts are modest, even among those approaching retirement age 299
Homeownership is an important asset for most households 301
Non-Hispanic whites have the highest rate of homeownership 305
Debt declines with advancing age 307
Most households have debt, including female- and male-headed households 310
Households headed by blacks are least likely to be in debt 314
More than two-thirds of workers are not planning on an early retirement 316

Chapter 6. Poverty

Poverty Trends
Married couples head a smaller share of poor families 321
Family poverty has grown since 2000 in every race and Hispanic origin group 323
Poverty has grown among families with children 329
Poverty rate is still close to its post-Great Recession high 335
Poverty rate has increased among people under age 65 337
Poverty rate has grown in every racial and ethnic group 340
Poverty rate has grown the most in the Midwest 343
Only 12 percent of naturalized citizens are poor 346
Among the 50 states, Nevada experienced one of the biggest increases in its poverty rate between 2007 and 2012 348
Poverty rate has grown both inside and outside of metro areas 353
Number of poor people who work has grown 356

Poverty, 2012

Poverty is less likely for families with two or more workers 360
Among married couples in the South, Hispanics have the highest poverty rate 365
Among families with children, the poverty rate peaks among black female-headed families in nonmetropolitan areas. . . 374
Non-Hispanic whites account for most of the elderly poor 383
Poverty rate is highest among children 385
Poverty rate declines as education increases 399
People who live alone or with nonrelatives account for a large share of the poor 391
Poverty rate declines as education increases 397
Many Hispanics who work full-time are poor 399
Many of the poor are too sick to work 405
More than 16 percent of people who live in the South are poor 407
Poverty rate is lowest in the suburbs 410
Poverty rate is highest in Mississippi and lowest in New Hampshire 415

Introduction

The United States is still recovering from the worst economic downturn since the Great Depression. Although the Great Recession is officially over, incomes are stuck well below what they were before the downturn, the poverty rate remains high, and net worth has declined. Americans are hurting. As the country adjusts to new economic realities, it is vital to stay on top of these socioeconomic trends. The ninth edition of *American Incomes: Demographics of Who Has Money* is your map to the changing consumer landscape.

Almost everywhere you look, the numbers are troubling. The $51,017 median household income of 2012 was 9 percent lower than the median of 2000, after adjusting for inflation. Men's median income fell by an even larger 10 percent during those years. Men aged 45 to 54—the nation's biggest earners—saw their median income decline by a stomach churning 15 percent, a loss of $8,253 after adjusting for inflation. The percentage of people in poverty was much higher in 2012 (15.0 percent) than in 2000 (11.3 percent). Although most households still have some discretionary income remaining after paying taxes and buying necessities, many are using that money to pay down debt rather than go out to eat or shop at the mall. The Census Bureau reports that median household net worth fell from to $107,344 in 2005 to just $68,828 in 2011 as the housing market collapsed.

As if the recession alone was not trouble enough, the aging of the enormous baby-boom generation out of the peak earning and spending age groups is dampening economic recovery. Boomer incomes and spending were a big factor behind the economic gains of the past two decades. Boomer retirees are likely to be a drag on the economy of the next two decades. The demographic trends that had been working in our favor are now working against us, making the determination of the real economic status of Americans much more complex. Researchers, businesses, and government policymakers will need to look beyond the averages to determine the trends. *American Incomes: Demographics of Who Has Money* can help them do just that.

The ninth edition of *American Incomes* explores and explains the economic status of Americans. It looks at household income trends by age, household type, race and ethnicity, education, region of residence, and work status. It examines trends in the incomes of men and women by a variety of demographic characteristics. It includes an analysis of hard-to-get discretionary income figures, produced by New Strategist's statisticians specifically for this book. It provides the latest data on the wealth of American households. The poverty population is also a focus of *American Incomes.*

American Incomes reveals the economic consequences of the many social, technological, and global changes that have transformed the workplace, families, the roles of men and women, and life in the United States. It reveals who is staying even and who is falling behind.

The raw ingredients of *American Incomes* are the massive spreadsheets of socioeconomic statistics housed on the government's web sites. Navigating these databases and making sense of them is a challenge for researchers who want to explore and analyze the trends. In some ways, the Internet has made it more time-consuming than ever to get no-nonsense answers to questions about the economic status of Americans. For those with questions, *American Incomes* has the answers. It has the numbers and the stories behind them. Thumbing (or scrolling) through these pages, you can gain more insight into the economic wellbeing of Americans than you could by spending all afternoon surfing databases on the Internet. By having *American Incomes* on your bookshelf or computer, you can get the answers to your questions faster than you can online.

How to Use This Book

American Incomes is designed for easy use. It is divided into six chapters, each of which provides an abundance of data about Americans and their money. The chapters are Household Income, Men's Income, Women's Income, Discretionary Income, Wealth, and Poverty.

• **Household Income** Chapter 1 examines trends in household income over the past 12 years. It also presents current household income statistics by age of householder, race and Hispanic origin of householder, type of household, and other important demographic characteristics.

• **Men's Income** Trends in men's incomes are examined in Chapter 2. Current income statistics for men are also shown by a variety of demographic characteristics.

• **Women's Income** Chapter 3 examines trends and the current status of women's income, which has become increasingly important to family economic well-being.

• **Discretionary Income** Presented only in *American Incomes*, the hard-to-find statistics in Chapter 4 show that even now most American households have some money to spend after paying taxes and buying necessities.

• **Wealth** The statistics shown in Chapter 5, from the Census Bureau's Survey of Income and Program Participation, provide a comprehensive portrait of the assets, debts, and net worth of American households by a variety of demographic characteristics.

• **Poverty** This chapter shows how poverty has grown and reveals the demographic characteristics of those who are falling behind.

Most of the tables in *American Incomes* are based on data from the March 2013 Current Population Survey. In this annual survey, the Census Bureau interviews the occupants of about 60,000 households, asking them for their demographic characteristics and their income in the preceding year. The Current Population Survey is the best source of up-to-date, reliable information on the incomes of Americans. While the Census Bureau produces most of the data published here, the tables in *American Incomes* are not reprints of Census Bureau spreadsheets. Instead, each has been individually compiled and created by New Strategist's editors, with calculations designed to reveal the stories behind the statistics. A page of text accompanies many of the tables, analyzing the data and highlighting the trends.

New Strategist's statisticians produced the discretionary income statistics in *American Incomes* using data from the Bureau of Labor Statistics' Consumer Expenditure Survey. These proprietary estimates give researchers a look at how much money households have left over after they pay their bills. The wealth statistics in Chapter 5 are from the Census Bureau's Survey of Income and Program Participation, providing a look at changes in household wealth between 2005 and 2011.

American Incomes contains a comprehensive list of tables to help you locate the information you need. For a more detailed search, use the index at the back of the book. Also at the back of the book is the glossary, which defines the terms commonly used in the tables and text.

American Incomes reveals the reality beneath the business headlines and political clichés, helping you prepare for the economic change that lies ahead.

1

Household Income

Household incomes have been falling not just because of the Great Recession, which began in December 2007 (and officially ended in June 2009), but because of the long-term decline in men's incomes. This decline was masked by the tremendous growth in women's incomes—until the Great Recession.

The $51,017 median household income of 2012 was well below the $55,987 of 2000, after adjusting for inflation. As the growth in women's incomes came to an end in the 2007-to-2012 time period, household incomes fell substantially and have yet to recover.

Despite the decline in median household income, more than one in five households (22.0 percent) had an income of $100,000 or more in 2012, only slightly below the 23.8 percent of 2000, after adjusting for inflation. Behind the near-record level of affluence is the baby-boom generation's continued presence in the peak earning age groups. Typically, householders aged 45 to 54 have the highest incomes. In 2012, householders aged 45 to 54 had a median income of $66,411—30 percent higher than the average household. These households have seen their median income decline by a substantial 13.6 percent since 2000.

■ As aging boomers remain in the workforce longer, the household incomes of 55-to-64-year-olds should grow.

Household Income Trends

Income Inequality Has Grown

The richest 20 percent of households control more than half of household income.

If you add up all the money going to American households, including earnings, interest, dividends, Social Security benefits, and so on, the result is called "aggregate household income." Year-to-year changes in how this aggregate is divided among the nation's households can reveal trends in income inequality. The numbers on the next page show how much aggregate income is received by each fifth of households, from poorest to richest. It also shows how much accrues to the 5 percent of households with the highest incomes.

For years, a growing share of income had been accruing to the most affluent households. The percentage of aggregate income received by the richest 20 percent of households (with an income above $104,096 in 2012) rose from 49.8 percent in 2000 to 51.0 percent in 2012. Despite the recession, the richest 20 percent of households have maintained their hold on the majority of aggregate household income.

■ A rise or fall in the amount of income accruing to each fifth of households reveals trends in the distribution of income among households, not the economic well-being of individual households.

The wealthiest households control more than half of the nation's income

(percent of aggregate household income accruing to the richest 20 percent of households, 2000 to 2012)

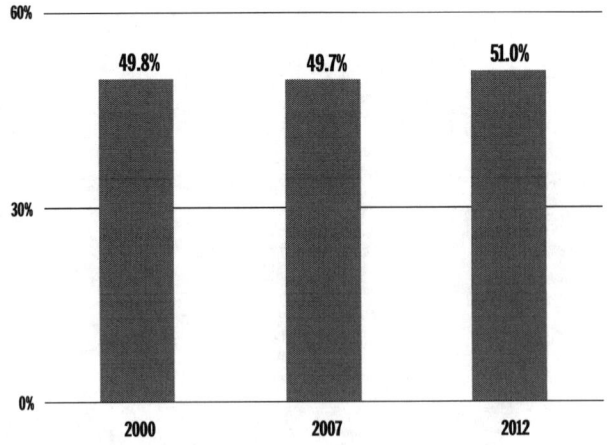

Table 1.1 Share of Aggregate Income Received by Each Fifth and Top 5 Percent of Households, 2000 to 2012

(distribution of aggregate income by household income quintile, 2000 to 2012; in 2012 dollars; households in thousands as of the following year)

INCOME LIMITS	total households	upper limit of each fifth				lower limit of top 5 percent
		bottom fifth	second fifth	third fifth	fourth fifth	
2012	122,459	$20,599	$39,764	$64,582	$104,096	$191,156
2011	121,084	20,262	38,520	62,434	101,582	186,000
2010	119,927	20,000	38,000	61,500	100,029	180,485
2009	117,538	20,453	38,550	61,801	100,000	180,001
2008	117,181	20,712	39,000	62,725	100,240	180,000
2007	116,783	20,291	39,100	62,000	100,000	177,000
2006	116,011	20,035	37,774	60,000	97,032	174,012
2005	114,384	19,178	36,000	57,660	91,705	166,000
2004	113,343	18,486	34,675	55,230	88,002	157,152
2003	112,000	17,984	34,000	54,453	86,867	154,120
2002	111,278	17,916	33,377	53,162	84,016	150,002
2001	109,297	17,970	33,314	53,000	83,500	150,499
2000	108,209	17,920	33,000	52,174	81,766	145,220

SHARE OF AGGREGATE INCOME	total households	bottom fifth	second fifth	third fifth	fourth fifth	top fifth	top 5 percent
2012	100.0%	3.2%	8.3%	14.4%	23.0%	51.0%	22.3%
2011	100.0	3.2	8.4	14.3	23.0	51.1	22.3
2010	100.0	3.3	8.5	14.6	23.4	50.3	21.3
2009	100.0	3.4	8.6	14.6	23.2	50.3	21.7
2008	100.0	3.4	8.6	14.7	23.3	50.0	21.5
2007	100.0	3.4	8.7	14.8	23.4	49.7	21.2
2006	100.0	3.4	8.6	14.5	22.9	50.5	22.3
2005	100.0	3.4	8.6	14.6	23.0	50.4	22.2
2004	100.0	3.4	8.7	14.7	23.2	50.1	21.8
2003	100.0	3.4	8.7	14.8	23.4	49.8	21.4
2002	100.0	3.5	8.8	14.8	23.3	49.7	21.7
2001	100.0	3.5	8.7	14.6	23.0	50.1	22.4
2000	100.0	3.6	8.9	14.8	23.0	49.8	22.1

Source: Bureau of the Census, Historical Income Data, Internet site http://www.census.gov/hhes/www/income/; calculations by New Strategist

Many Households Have Incomes of $100,000 or More

A larger share of households is at the lowest end of the income distribution.

Despite the Great Recession and its aftermath, the distribution of households by income has changed little over the past 12 years. Demographics explain the stability. The upper end of the income distribution is inflated by millions of dual-earner baby-boom couples in their peak earning years. The share of households with incomes of $100,000 or more is well above 20 percent, a proportion that fell only slightly during the Great Recession.

At the other extreme, the size of the lower end of the income distribution (with a household income below $25,000) has expanded somewhat because of the increasing share of households headed by retirees. Meanwhile, the share of households in the middle (with a household income between $25,000 and $100,000) has barely changed since 2000.

■ The proportion of households with incomes of $100,000 or more is likely to decline in the years ahead as boomers retire.

There was little change in the proportion of households with incomes of $100,000 or more, despite the Great Recession

(percent of households with incomes of $100,000 or more, 2000 to 2012; in 2012 dollars)

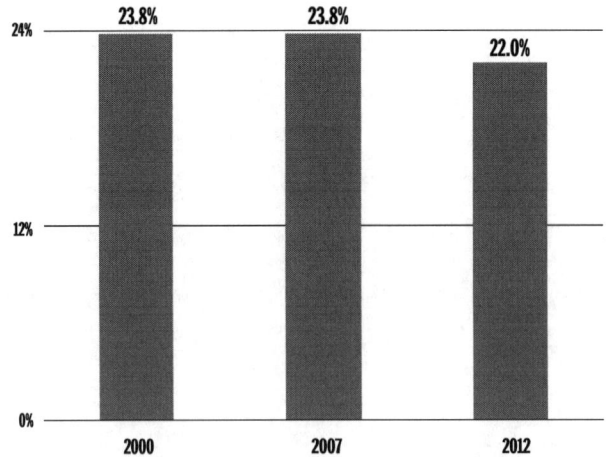

Table 1.2 Distribution of Households by Income, 2000 to 2012

(total number of households and percent distribution by income, 2000 to 2012, in 2012 dollars; households in thousands as of the following year)

| | total households | | under $25,000 | $25,000–$49,999 | $50,000–$74,999 | $75,000–$99,999 | $100,000 or more | | | |
	number	percent					total	$100,000–$149,999	$150,000–$199,999	$200,000 or more
2012	122,459	100.0%	24.7%	24.3%	17.5%	11.7%	22.0%	12.5%	5.0%	4.5%
2011	121,084	100.0	24.6	24.6	17.7	11.4	21.7	12.2	5.1	4.4
2010	119,927	100.0	24.4	24.2	17.6	11.6	22.1	12.8	4.9	4.4
2009	117,538	100.0	23.2	24.5	17.8	11.9	22.5	12.9	5.1	4.5
2008	117,181	100.0	23.2	24.2	17.7	12.3	22.7	13.1	5.1	4.5
2007	116,783	100.0	22.3	23.9	17.5	12.5	23.8	13.8	5.3	4.7
2006	116,011	100.0	21.9	24.3	18.0	12.1	23.7	13.5	5.3	4.9
2005	114,384	100.0	22.9	23.7	17.9	12.6	22.8	13.1	5.0	4.7
2004	113,343	100.0	23.0	24.3	17.6	12.6	22.6	13.0	5.2	4.4
2003	112,000	100.0	23.1	23.8	17.6	12.4	23.1	13.5	5.1	4.5
2002	111,278	100.0	22.3	24.3	17.7	13.0	22.9	13.6	4.9	4.4
2001	109,297	100.0	21.9	24.0	18.0	13.0	23.1	13.5	4.9	4.7
2000	108,209	100.0	21.2	23.9	18.4	12.7	23.8	13.9	5.3	4.6

Source: Bureau of the Census, Historical Income Data, Internet site http://www.census.gov/hhes/www/income/; calculations by New Strategist

Median Household Income Fell between 2000 and 2012

Householders under age 55 have experienced the biggest declines.

The $51,017 median household income of 2012 was a substantial 9 percent below the $55,987 of 2000, after adjusting for inflation. But trends in household income have varied significantly by age over the 12 years. Householders aged 65 or older saw their median household income rise 10 percent between 2000 and 2012. In contrast, householders under age 65 had a lower median household income in 2012 than their counterparts did in 2000.

Although many blame the Great Recession for the decline in household incomes, in fact incomes were declining in the years prior to the start of the Great Recession in 2007. Householders under age 55 saw their median household income fall by 4 to 6 percent between 2000 and 2007, after adjusting for inflation. The Great Recession exacerbated the decline, but did not initiate it. In contrast, the Great Recession did trigger the income decline among householders aged 55 to 64. Meanwhile, householders aged 65 or older made gains throughout the decade.

■ The median income of households headed by people aged 65 or older is at a record high.

The oldest householders made gains between 2007 and 2012

(percent change in median household income by age of householder, 2007 to 2012)

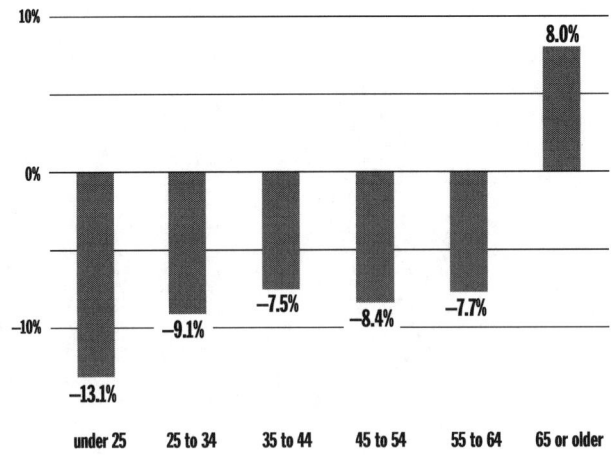

Table 1.3 Median Household Income by Age of Householder, 2000 to 2012

(median household income by age of householder, 2000 to 2012; percent change for selected years; in 2012 dollars)

| | total households | under 25 | 25 to 34 | 35 to 44 | 45 to 54 | 55 to 64 | 65 or older | | |
							total	65 to 74	75 or older
2012	$51,017	$30,604	$51,381	$63,629	$66,411	$58,626	$33,848	$42,343	$26,606
2011	51,100	31,096	51,835	63,209	65,195	57,106	33,810	42,467	26,826
2010	51,892	29,722	52,525	64,679	65,651	59,472	33,131	41,877	26,698
2009	53,285	32,899	53,737	65,388	68,762	60,988	33,564	41,636	27,504
2008	53,644	34,413	54,814	67,135	68,623	61,068	31,719	39,855	25,649
2007	55,627	35,204	56,495	68,795	72,507	63,549	31,345	39,901	25,725
2006	54,892	35,231	55,988	68,789	73,879	62,170	31,656	38,666	25,982
2005	54,486	33,838	55,724	68,315	73,420	61,465	30,622	37,248	25,689
2004	53,891	33,519	55,266	68,901	74,183	61,255	29,801	37,539	24,875
2003	54,079	33,774	55,903	68,718	75,208	61,441	29,696	37,003	24,307
2002	54,127	35,517	57,855	68,309	75,329	60,245	29,549	35,957	24,633
2001	54,766	36,568	58,465	69,152	75,280	59,482	29,982	36,537	24,867
2000	55,987	37,129	59,219	71,683	76,856	59,804	30,777	37,535	25,085

PERCENT CHANGE

	total households	under 25	25 to 34	35 to 44	45 to 54	55 to 64	total	65 to 74	75 or older
2007 to 2012	−8.3%	−13.1%	−9.1%	−7.5%	−8.4%	−7.7%	8.0%	6.1%	3.4%
2000 to 2007	−0.6	−5.2	−4.6	−4.0	−5.7	6.3	1.8	6.3	2.5
2000 to 2012	−8.9	−17.6	−13.2	−11.2	−13.6	−2.0	10.0	12.8	6.1

Source: Bureau of the Census, Historical Income Data, Internet site http://www.census.gov/hhes/www/income/; calculations by New Strategist

Every Household Type Lost Ground between 2000 and 2012

Most of the decline occurred during and after the Great Recession.

Every type of household saw its median income fall between 2007 and 2012, the biggest decline occurring among male-headed family households—a 12 percent loss, after adjusting for inflation. Women who live alone (most of them aged 55 or older) and married couples experienced the smallest loss in median household income between 2007 and 2012, with declines of 4.5 and 6.1 percent, respectively.

In the years leading up to the Great Recession, which began in 2007, median household income fell slightly for households overall (down 0.6 percent, after adjusting for inflation). Male- and female-headed families and men who live alone lost a larger 2 to 3 percent. Although many blame the Great Recession for the decline in American household incomes, in fact the losses for many households started well before the recession.

- Married couples have the highest incomes because most are dual-earners.

Median income of married couples fell 6 percent between 2007 and 2012

(percent change in median household income by household type, 2007 to 2012; in 2012 dollars)

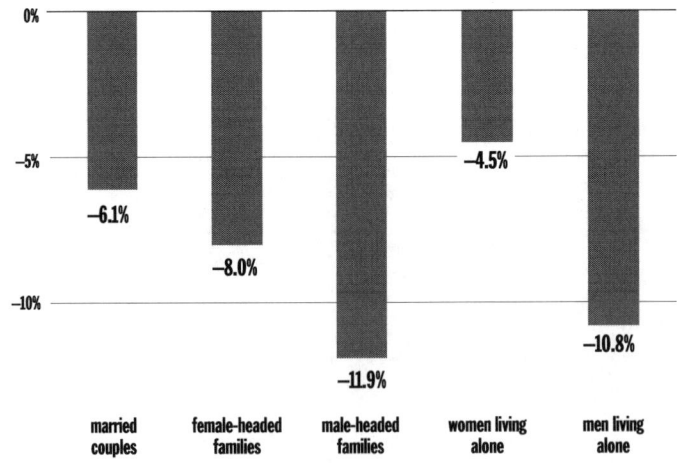

Table 1.4 Median Household Income by Type of Household, 2000 to 2012

(median household income by type of household, 2000 to 2012; percent change for selected years; in 2012 dollars)

	total households	family households			nonfamily households	
		married couples	female householder, no spouse present	male householder, no spouse present	women living alone	men living alone
2012	$51,017	$75,694	$34,002	$48,634	$22,794	$31,212
2011	51,100	75,679	34,340	50,602	22,727	31,263
2010	51,892	76,344	33,667	52,458	23,305	31,833
2009	53,285	76,892	34,894	51,473	23,897	33,822
2008	53,644	77,859	35,269	52,453	23,480	32,767
2007	55,627	80,601	36,954	55,191	23,860	35,000
2006	54,892	79,393	36,234	53,613	24,309	35,608
2005	54,486	77,704	36,049	54,992	23,718	35,308
2004	53,891	77,568	36,256	54,725	23,719	33,323
2003	54,079	77,908	36,588	52,383	23,316	34,254
2002	54,127	78,179	37,014	53,236	22,831	34,215
2001	54,766	78,426	36,498	52,804	23,173	36,681
2000	55,987	79,029	37,685	56,207	23,769	36,203
PERCENT CHANGE						
2007 to 2012	−8.3%	−6.1%	−8.0%	−11.9%	−4.5%	−10.8%
2000 to 2007	−0.6	2.0	−1.9	−1.8	0.4	−3.3
2000 to 2012	−8.9	−4.2	−9.8	−13.5	−4.1	−13.8

Source: Bureau of the Census, Historical Income Data, Internet site http://www.census.gov/hhes/www/income/; calculations by New Strategist

Every Racial and Ethnic Group Has Lost Ground

For most households, incomes were declining before the Great Recession.

Overall, median household income fell by a substantial 9 percent between 2000 and 2012, after adjusting for inflation. Asians, blacks, Hispanics, and non-Hispanic whites saw their median household income decline during those years.

The median household income of Asians, blacks, and Hispanics was in decline before the start of the Great Recession in 2007. The decline worsened once the Great Recession was under way. Median household income fell 8 percent overall between 2007 and 2012. By race and Hispanic origin, the decline ranged from 6 to 11 percent during those years.

■ Since 2000, blacks and Hispanics have lost more ground than Asians or non-Hispanic whites.

Median income of non-Hispanic whites fell 6 percent between 2007 and 2012

(percent change in median household income by race and Hispanic origin, 2007 to 2012; in 2012 dollars)

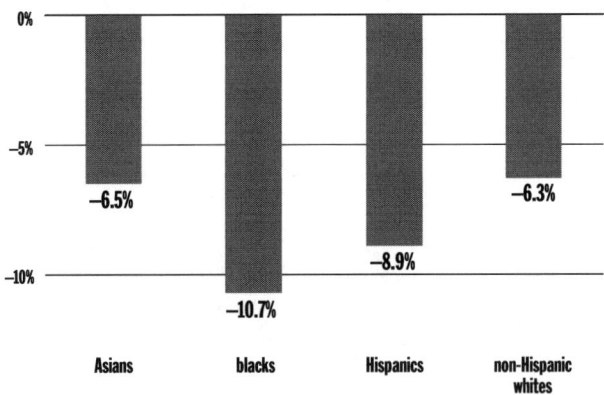

Table 1.5 Median Household Income by Race and Hispanic Origin of Householder, 2000 to 2012

(median household income by race and Hispanic origin of householder, 2000 to 2012; percent change in median for selected years; in 2012 dollars)

	total households	Asian	black	Hispanic	non-Hispanic white
2012	$51,017	$68,182	$33,718	$39,005	$57,009
2011	51,100	66,353	33,042	39,431	56,570
2010	51,892	66,900	33,863	39,629	57,351
2009	53,285	69,659	35,058	40,720	58,299
2008	53,644	69,922	36,626	40,431	59,218
2007	55,627	72,950	37,752	42,833	60,818
2006	54,892	72,770	36,592	43,025	59,700
2005	54,486	71,801	36,406	42,302	59,729
2004	53,891	69,833	36,753	41,659	59,454
2003	54,079	68,991	37,065	41,194	59,646
2002	54,127	66,732	37,239	42,250	59,859
2001	54,766	69,560	38,220	43,531	60,054
2000	55,987	74,343	39,556	44,224	60,831
PERCENT CHANGE					
2007 to 2012	−8.3%	−6.5%	−10.7%	−8.9%	−6.3%
2000 to 2007	−0.6	−1.9	−4.6	−3.1	0.0
2000 to 2012	−8.9	−8.3	−14.8	−11.8	−6.3

Note: Beginning in 2002, data for Asians and blacks are for those who identify themselves as being of the race alone and those who identify themselves as being of the race in combination with other races. Hispanics may be of any race. Beginning in 2002, data for non-Hispanic whites are for those who identify themselves as being white alone and not Hispanic.
Source: Bureau of the Census, Historical Income Data, Internet site http://www.census.gov/hhes/www/income/; calculations by New Strategist

College Graduates Are Losing Ground

Households headed by college graduates had a lower median income in 2012 than 2000.

Among households headed by people aged 25 or older, median income fell 10 percent between 2000 and 2012, after adjusting for inflation. Income declines have been steep for nearly every educational group, and they began well before the Great Recession.

Households headed by high school graduates saw their median income fall 18 percent between 2000 and 2012, after adjusting for inflation. Households headed by people with an associate's degree experienced a 15 percent decline. Households headed by college graduates saw their median household income fall 10 percent.

Between 2007 and 2012, median income declined by double-digit percentages for many households. Householders with a doctoral or professional degree made gains during those years.

■ A college education does not guarantee smooth sailing in today's slow-moving economy.

Median income of college graduates fell between 2007 and 2012

(median income of households headed by people aged 25 or older with a bachelor's degree or more education, 2007 and 2012; in 2012 dollars)

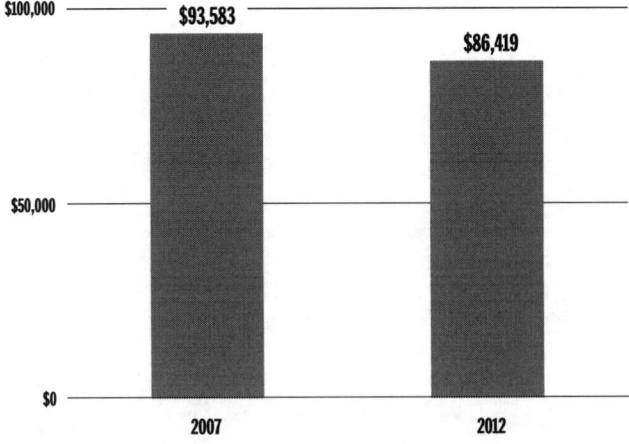

Table 1.6 Median Household Income by Education of Householder, 2000 to 2012

(median income of households headed by people aged 25 or older by educational attainment of householder, 2000 to 2012; percent change for selected years; in 2012 dollars)

	total households	less than 9th grade	9th to 12th grade, no diploma	high school graduate	some college	associate's degree	bachelor's degree or more				
							total	bachelor's degree	master's degree	professional degree	doctoral degree
2012	$52,119	$22,496	$23,347	$39,845	$48,987	$57,460	$86,419	$80,549	$92,362	$129,588	$116,983
2011	52,314	22,279	25,211	40,243	48,476	57,096	85,739	79,886	92,847	123,099	109,282
2010	53,391	22,410	26,074	40,947	51,289	59,777	86,410	79,498	95,546	126,172	124,789
2009	54,563	23,160	27,408	42,441	51,825	60,791	88,552	80,840	98,120	132,508	129,392
2008	54,801	22,653	27,003	42,616	53,665	63,092	90,781	83,490	98,795	106,641	106,641
2007	56,950	23,039	27,122	44,801	55,833	66,590	93,583	85,939	100,396	110,739	110,739
2006	56,945	23,802	29,509	44,899	56,588	63,792	93,067	86,391	100,695	113,880	113,880
2005	56,121	23,786	29,021	44,918	56,789	64,346	90,773	85,181	95,295	117,614	117,614
2004	55,859	23,711	27,337	45,377	57,557	65,532	90,321	83,166	97,406	121,557	121,557
2003	56,199	23,454	28,362	45,986	57,245	64,881	91,692	85,802	98,053	124,843	120,885
2002	56,207	23,459	29,696	45,495	57,859	65,166	93,936	88,264	97,599	127,631	125,885
2001	56,535	23,500	30,155	46,761	59,412	66,353	93,747	87,108	102,330	129,692	120,362
2000	57,707	23,340	30,229	48,701	59,497	67,335	95,789	88,821	104,440	133,333	126,771
PERCENT CHANGE											
2007 to 2012	−8.5%	−2.4%	−13.9%	−11.1%	−12.3%	−13.7%	−7.7%	−6.3%	−8.0%	17.0%	5.6%
2000 to 2007	−1.3	−1.3	−10.3	−8.0	−6.2	−1.1	−2.3	−3.2	−3.9	−16.9	−12.6
2000 to 2012	−9.7	−3.6	−22.8	−18.2	−17.7	−14.7	−9.8	−9.3	−11.6	−2.8	−7.7

Source: Bureau of the Census, Historical Income Data, Internet site http://www.census.gov/hhes/www/income/; calculations by New Strategist

Incomes Fell in Households Large and Small

Large households experienced some of the biggest declines.

Between 2000 and 2012, the median income of households large and small declined, after adjusting for inflation. The losses by household size ranged from 4 to 10 percent, with most of the decline occurring since 2007.

The median income of single-person households fell 8 percent between 2000 and 2012, after adjusting for inflation. Two-person households fared slightly better, with a 4 percent decline during those years. Many two-person households are empty-nest couples, some postponing retirement because of the Great Recession. Three- and four-person households saw their median income decline 6 to 9 percent. Many of these households are married couples with one or two children. Households with five people lost the most ground between 2000 and 2012, their median income falling by 10 percent.

■ Households of every size saw their incomes decline because of rising unemployment.

Every household size has lost ground since the start of the Great Recession in 2007

(median income of households by household size, 2007 to 2012; in 2012 dollars)

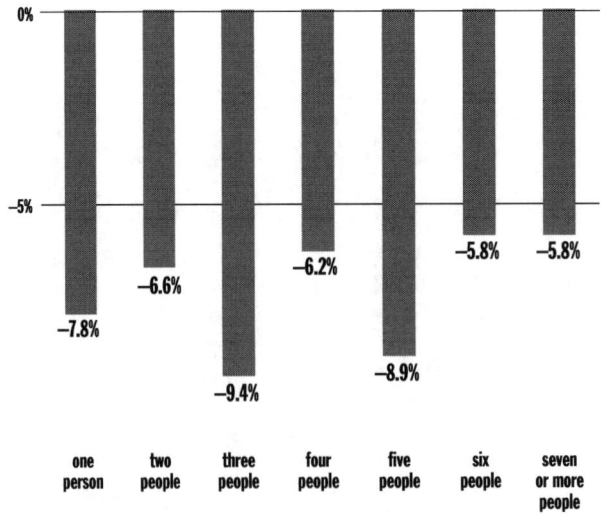

Table 1.7 Median Household Income by Size of Household, 2000 to 2012

(median income of households by size of household, 2000 to 2012; percent change for selected years; in 2012 dollars)

	total households	one person	two people	three people	four people	five people	six people	seven or more people
2012	$51,017	$26,251	$56,727	$64,614	$78,177	$71,585	$67,634	$66,612
2011	51,100	26,443	56,716	64,694	76,478	72,128	68,328	65,282
2010	51,892	26,804	57,401	65,933	77,344	72,512	69,262	63,579
2009	53,285	27,918	57,459	66,875	78,221	74,591	67,167	69,224
2008	53,644	27,345	59,099	68,069	80,777	73,872	71,618	71,762
2007	55,627	28,463	60,730	71,319	83,345	78,599	71,789	70,677
2006	54,892	29,044	58,689	69,964	82,985	76,098	70,445	69,312
2005	54,486	27,917	57,977	69,295	81,865	78,198	72,147	66,800
2004	53,891	27,425	57,326	70,402	79,968	75,779	69,457	70,896
2003	54,079	27,378	58,581	69,570	80,366	75,065	72,545	75,556
2002	54,127	27,470	58,143	69,920	79,727	78,650	71,597	71,922
2001	54,766	28,222	58,679	70,658	81,181	77,683	74,635	70,760
2000	55,987	28,612	59,279	70,796	83,132	79,585	71,701	72,177

PERCENT CHANGE

2007 to 2012	−8.3%	−7.8%	−6.6%	−9.4%	−6.2%	−8.9%	−5.8%	−5.8%
2000 to 2007	−0.6	−0.5	2.4	0.7	0.3	−1.2	0.1	−2.1
2000 to 2012	−8.9	−8.3	−4.3	−8.7	−6.0	−10.1	−5.7	−7.7

Source: Bureau of the Census, Historical Income Data, Internet site http://www.census.gov/hhes/www/income/; calculations by New Strategist

More Earners Did Little to Help Stabilize Incomes

Since 2007, no-earner households have fared better than everyone else.

Although the median income of the average household fell slightly between 2000 and 2007 (before the start of the Great Recession), the income decline was limited to households with no earners. The median income of households with one earner was stable during those years, and households with two or three earners saw their median income climb 4 percent.

Then the Great Recession set in. Between 2007 and 2012, households with no earners were the only ones to make gains in median income, after adjusting for inflation. Households with one, two, or three earners saw their median income fall by 3 to 4 percent during those years.

■ No-earner households have seen their incomes climb since 2007 because many are headed by the elderly who receive Social Security payments, which are guaranteed and indexed to inflation.

Working households have lost ground since the start of the Great Recession in 2007

(percent change in median income of households by number of earners, 2007 to 2012; in 2012 dollars)

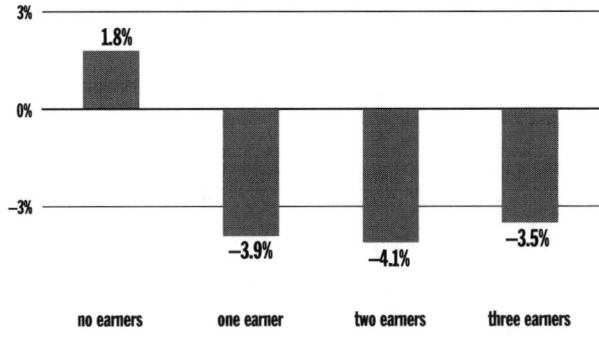

Table 1.8 Median Household Income by Number of Earners in Household, 2000 to 2012

(median income of households by number of earners, 2000 to 2012; percent change for selected years; in 2012 dollars)

	total households	no earners	one earner	two earners	three earners	four or more earners
2012	$51,017	$19,722	$43,335	$82,596	$101,561	$127,557
2011	51,100	19,718	43,054	82,961	100,934	124,465
2010	51,892	19,482	43,868	85,079	101,053	122,804
2009	53,285	20,889	44,032	84,003	100,448	124,896
2008	53,644	19,865	43,480	83,664	100,808	100,000+
2007	55,627	19,370	45,082	86,108	105,231	100,000+
2006	54,892	20,345	44,765	84,856	104,201	100,000+
2005	54,486	19,869	44,154	83,450	103,389	100,000+
2004	53,891	19,605	43,958	83,776	101,894	100,000+
2003	54,079	19,552	44,915	84,079	102,950	100,000+
2002	54,127	19,656	44,414	83,654	102,371	126,156
2001	54,766	20,040	44,230	83,719	100,194	122,675
2000	55,987	20,308	44,825	82,963	101,139	123,088
PERCENT CHANGE						
2007 to 2012	−8.3%	1.8%	−3.9%	−4.1%	−3.5%	−
2000 to 2007	−0.6	−4.6	0.6	3.8	4.0	−
2000 to 2012	−8.9	−2.9	−3.3	−0.4	0.4	3.6%

Note: "–" means data are not available.
Source: Bureau of the Census, Historical Income Data, Internet site http://www.census.gov/hhes/www/income/; calculations by New Strategist

Families with Children Are Losing Ground

Families without children at home also saw their median incomes decline.

Between 2000 and 2012, the median income of married couples with children under age 18 fell 3 percent, after adjusting for inflation. The median income of married couples without children at home fell 2 percent. The declines were even greater for male- and female-headed families with and without children.

Until 2007, the median income of married couples had been rising, with a 6 percent gain among those without children at home and a 0.9 percent increase among those with children under age 18. When the Great Recession hit, the incomes of married couples began to fall. In contrast, the median income of male-headed families was falling well before the Great Recession, which exacerbated the decline. The median income of female-headed families with children under age 18 also began to decline before the Great Recession, but the incomes of female-headed families without children at home had been rising until 2007.

■ The Great Recession hurt many families, but especially single parents.

Among families with children under age 18, married couples have lost less than others

(percent change in median income of families with children under age 18 at home by family type, 2007 to 2012; in 2012 dollars)

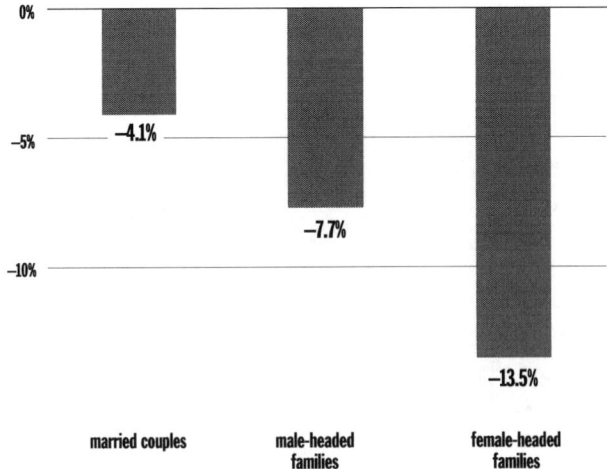

Table 1.9 Median Income of Married-Couple Families by Presence of Children, 2000 to 2012

(median income of married-couple families by presence of related children under age 18 at home, 2000 to 2012; percent change for selected years; in 2012 dollars)

	total married couples	no children under age 18	with children under age 18
2012	$75,535	$70,902	$81,455
2011	75,331	71,516	80,343
2010	76,076	72,156	81,484
2009	76,675	72,124	82,051
2008	77,574	73,091	82,876
2007	80,384	76,362	84,949
2006	79,038	73,296	84,327
2005	77,515	72,341	83,333
2004	77,342	72,358	82,437
2003	77,753	73,050	82,919
2002	78,021	72,615	83,469
2001	78,250	71,877	84,563
2000	78,799	72,349	84,168
PERCENT CHANGE			
2007 to 2012	−6.0%	−7.2%	−4.1%
2000 to 2007	2.0	5.5	0.9
2000 to 2012	−4.1	−2.0	−3.2

Note: Median incomes in this table are slightly different from the figures shown in the household income tables because these figures include the incomes of only the family members and not any unrelated members of the household.
Source: Bureau of the Census, Current Population Surveys, Annual Social and Economic Supplement, Internet site http://www .census.gov/hhes/www/income/data/historical/families/index.html; calculations by New Strategist

Table 1.10 Median Income of Female-Headed Families by Presence of Children, 2000 to 2012

(median income of female-headed families by presence of related children under age 18 at home, 2000 to 2012; percent change for selected years; in 2012 dollars)

	total female-headed families, no spouse present	no children under age 18	with children under age 18
2012	$30,686	$42,147	$25,493
2011	30,891	42,658	25,883
2010	30,703	41,319	25,664
2009	31,868	42,150	26,946
2008	32,130	44,064	27,260
2007	33,549	49,176	27,628
2006	32,831	47,280	27,780
2005	32,043	46,026	27,205
2004	32,783	45,035	28,454
2003	33,146	45,476	28,246
2002	33,724	45,851	28,892
2001	33,389	45,737	28,528
2000	34,288	45,895	29,220
PERCENT CHANGE			
2007 to 2012	–8.5%	–14.3%	–7.7%
2000 to 2007	–2.2	7.1	–5.4
2000 to 2012	–10.5	–8.2	–12.8

Note: Median incomes in this table are slightly different from the figures shown in the household income tables because these figures include the incomes of only the family members and not any unrelated members of the household.
Source: Bureau of the Census, Current Population Surveys, Annual Social and Economic Supplement, Internet site http://www .census.gov/hhes/www/income/data/historical/families/index.html; calculations by New Strategist

Table 1.11 Median Income of Male-Headed Families by Presence of Children, 2000 to 2012

(median income of male-headed families by presence of related children under age 18 at home, 2000 to 2012; percent change for selected years; in 2012 dollars)

	total male-headed families, no spouse present	no children under age 18	with children under age 18
2012	$42,358	$49,338	$36,471
2011	43,969	52,063	38,964
2010	45,500	54,534	38,289
2009	44,426	52,397	38,628
2008	46,465	52,956	40,811
2007	49,122	56,983	42,173
2006	47,652	55,272	42,578
2005	48,352	56,952	43,009
2004	49,062	55,055	44,246
2003	47,480	56,121	39,841
2002	48,167	56,588	41,038
2001	47,454	56,893	41,413
2000	50,303	59,416	43,311
PERCENT CHANGE			
2007 to 2012	−13.8%	−13.4%	−13.5%
2000 to 2007	−2.3	−4.1	−2.6
2000 to 2012	−15.8	−17.0	−15.8

Note: Median incomes in this table are slightly different from the figures shown in the household income tables because these figures include the incomes of only the family members and not any unrelated members of the household.
Source: Bureau of the Census, Current Population Surveys, Annual Social and Economic Supplement, Internet site http://www .census.gov/hhes/www/income/data/historical/families/index.html; calculations by New Strategist

Working Wives Are Keeping Families Afloat

Dual-income couples made gains between 2000 and 2012.

Between 2000 and 2012, the median income of the average married-couple household fell 4 percent, after adjusting for inflation. But some couples lost ground during those years, while others made gains. Among married couples with a husband who works full-time, median household income climbed by 0.7 percent between 2000 and 2012. Among couples in which both husband and wife worked full-time, median household income grew by a much greater 5.7 percent. Among couples in which the husband worked full-time and the wife did not work, median household income fell 2.8 percent during those years.

The benefit of the working wife disappeared between 2007 and 2012. Among couples in which both husband and wife work full-time, median income grew by a small 0.5 percent during those years, after adjusting for inflation. The median income of single-earner couples grew by 0.2 percent.

■ Working wives have long insulated their household from economic decline. That power may be eroding because the rapid growth in women's earnings came to a halt during the Great Recession.

Single-earner couples have lost ground

(median income of married couples in which the husband works full-time by work status of wife, 2000 and 2012; in 2012 dollars)

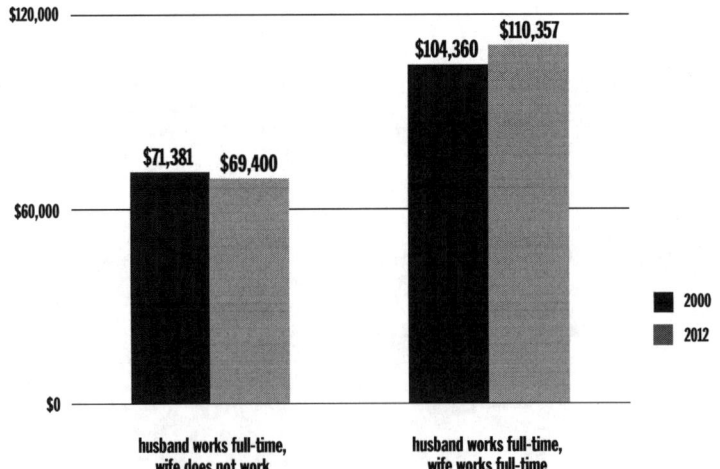

Table 1.12 Median Income of Married Couples by Work Experience of Husband and Wife, 2000 to 2012

(median income of total married couples and married couples in which the husband works full-time, by work experience of wife, 2000 to 2012; percent change for selected years; in 2012 dollars)

| | total married couples | husband works full-time, year-round | | | |
| | | total | wife works | | wife does not work |
			total	full-time	
2012	$75,535	$94,524	$103,196	$110,357	$69,400
2011	75,331	94,066	103,320	109,379	68,910
2010	76,076	96,291	104,793	109,255	70,493
2009	76,675	96,834	104,359	110,823	70,013
2008	77,574	94,333	101,866	106,641	68,719
2007	80,384	95,960	103,624	109,787	69,276
2006	79,038	94,336	102,781	108,207	69,035
2005	77,515	93,075	100,637	106,581	70,149
2004	77,342	93,284	100,533	106,741	68,083
2003	77,753	94,436	101,441	106,762	69,432
2002	78,021	94,671	100,582	106,980	71,100
2001	78,250	93,411	99,164	105,227	69,983
2000	78,799	93,831	99,189	104,360	71,381

PERCENT CHANGE

2007 to 2012	−6.0%	−1.5%	−0.4%	0.5%	0.2%
2000 to 2007	2.0	2.3	4.5	5.2	−2.9
2000 to 2012	−4.1	0.7	4.0	5.7	−2.8

Source: Bureau of the Census, Historical Income Data, Internet site http://www.census.gov/hhes/www/income/; calculations by New Strategist

Median Household Income Fell in Every Region

The decline has been greatest in the Midwest.

Median household income fell 6 to 8 percent in the Northeast, South, and West between 2000 and 2012, after adjusting for inflation. In the Midwest, the decline was a much greater 14 percent during those years.

Median household income in the Midwest was in decline well before the start of the Great Recession in 2007. Between 2000 and 2007, median household income in the Midwest fell 5.7 percent, after adjusting for inflation. The Great Recession accelerated the decline, with another 9.3 percent loss for the Midwest between 2007 and 2012. In the other regions, the decline in median household income did not begin in earnest until the Great Recession hit.

■ Since 2000, the Midwest has experienced the largest decline in median household income, but the South still has the lowest median.

Households in the Midwest have lost more than $8,000

(dollar loss in median household income by region, 2000 to 2012; in 2012 dollars)

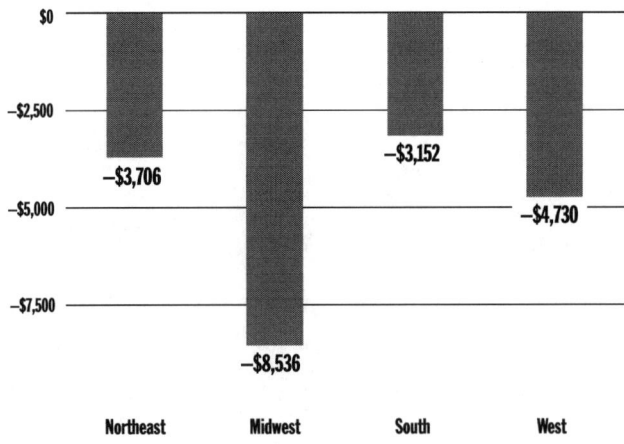

Table 1.13 Median Household Income by Region, 2000 to 2012

(median income of households by region, 2000 to 2012; percent change for selected years; in 2012 dollars)

	total households	Northeast	Midwest	South	West
2012	$51,017	$54,627	$50,479	$48,033	$55,157
2011	51,100	54,989	49,740	47,879	53,470
2010	51,892	55,810	50,802	47,855	55,771
2009	53,285	56,813	52,322	48,830	57,627
2008	53,644	57,955	53,440	48,618	58,743
2007	55,627	57,888	55,676	51,146	59,952
2006	54,892	59,283	54,476	49,975	59,501
2005	54,486	59,844	54,044	49,560	58,809
2004	53,891	58,179	54,264	49,529	57,923
2003	54,079	58,354	55,845	49,716	58,451
2002	54,127	58,534	55,675	50,442	57,616
2001	54,766	59,290	56,849	50,455	58,474
2000	55,987	58,333	59,015	51,185	59,887

PERCENT CHANGE

	total households	Northeast	Midwest	South	West
2007 to 2012	−8.3%	−5.6%	−9.3%	−6.1%	−8.0%
2000 to 2007	−0.6	−0.8	−5.7	−0.1	0.1
2000 to 2012	−8.9	−6.4	−14.5	−6.2	−7.9

Source: Bureau of the Census, Historical Income Data, Internet site http://www.census.gov/hhes/www/income/; calculations by New Strategist

Many States Have Seen Double-Digit Percentage Declines in Income

Between 2007 and 2012, median household income fell in all but five states and the District of Columbia.

The Great Recession had a devastating impact on households in most states, but some have suffered more than others. Nevada experienced the steepest decline in median household income between 2007 and 2012, a 21 percent drop after adjusting for inflation. In all, 16 states experienced double-digit percentage declines in median household income between 2007 and 2012. Only householders in North Dakota, Wyoming, Vermont, Texas, Oklahoma, and the District of Columbia saw their median income grow during those years.

In 2012, median household income was highest in Maryland ($71,836) and lowest in Mississippi ($36,641). The difference in median household income of the two states is more than $35,000.

■ Other states experiencing the largest declines in median household income were Hawaii, Delaware, Ohio, and Colorado.

Nevada has been the biggest loser

(median household income in Nevada, 2007 and 2012; in 2012 dollars)

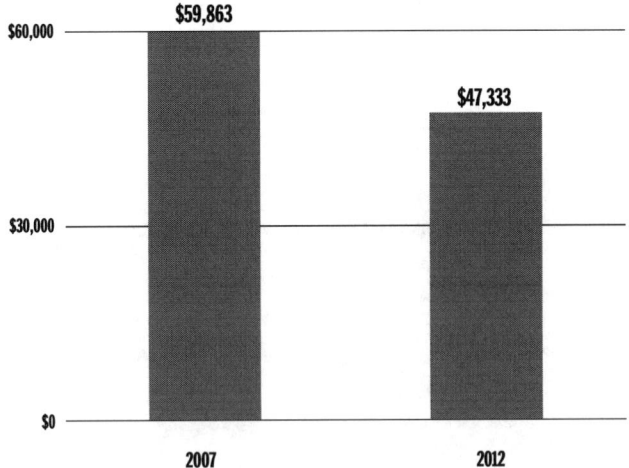

Table 1.14 Median Household Income by State, 2007 and 2012

(median income of households by state, 2007 and 2012; percent change, 2007–12; in 2012 dollars)

	2012	2007	percent change 2007–12
United States	**$51,017**	**$55,627**	**–8.3%**
Alabama	43,464	46,745	–7.0
Alaska	63,648	69,758	–8.8
Arizona	47,044	52,285	–10.0
Arkansas	39,018	45,176	–13.6
California	57,020	61,719	–7.6
Colorado	57,255	67,707	–15.4
Connecticut	64,247	71,029	–9.5
Delaware	48,972	60,451	–19.0
District of Columbia	65,246	56,237	16.0
Florida	46,071	50,712	–9.2
Georgia	48,121	53,865	–10.7
Hawaii	56,263	70,897	–20.6
Idaho	47,922	54,466	–12.0
Illinois	51,738	58,145	–11.0
Indiana	46,158	52,549	–12.2
Iowa	53,442	54,160	–1.3
Kansas	50,003	53,705	–6.9
Kentucky	41,086	43,689	–6.0
Louisiana	39,085	45,750	–14.6
Maine	49,158	53,037	–7.3
Maryland	71,836	72,678	–1.2
Massachusetts	63,656	64,741	–1.7
Michigan	50,015	54,672	–8.5
Minnesota	61,795	64,293	–3.9
Mississippi	36,641	41,282	–11.2
Missouri	49,764	50,945	–2.3
Montana	45,088	48,343	–6.7
Nebraska	52,196	54,455	–4.1
Nevada	47,333	59,863	–20.9
New Hampshire	67,819	74,833	–9.4
New Jersey	66,692	67,006	–0.5
New Mexico	43,424	49,119	–11.6
New York	47,680	54,200	–12.0
North Carolina	41,553	48,186	–13.8
North Dakota	55,766	52,274	6.7
Ohio	44,375	54,372	–18.4
Oklahoma	48,407	47,857	1.1
Oregon	51,775	55,631	–6.9
Pennsylvania	51,904	$53,639	–3.2

	2012	2007	percent change 2007–12
Rhode Island	$56,065	$60,032	–6.6%
South Carolina	44,401	48,961	–9.3
South Dakota	49,415	51,403	–3.9
Tennessee	42,995	45,619	–5.8
Texas	51,926	50,999	1.8
Utah	58,341	59,277	–1.6
Vermont	55,582	52,479	5.9
Virginia	64,632	65,514	–1.3
Washington	62,187	64,317	–3.3
West Virginia	43,553	46,611	–6.6
Wisconsin	53,079	56,784	–6.5
Wyoming	57,512	53,979	6.5

Source: Bureau of the Census, 2013 Current Population Survey, Internet site http://www.census.gov/hhes/www/income/data/incpovhlth/2012/dtables.html; calculations by New Strategist

Household Income, 2012

Dual-Earner Couples Dominate the Affluent

Householders aged 45 to 54 account for the largest share of those with incomes in the top quintile.

By examining the characteristics of households within income quintiles, or fifths, the requirements of affluence become apparent. Among households in the top quintile (with a household income of $104,096 or greater in 2012), married couples headed more than three out of four. Householders aged 35 to 54 were the 51 percent majority. And 75 percent have at least two earners. Households in the top 5 percent of the income distribution are even more likely to be headed by married couples (81 percent) and 35-to-54-year-olds (53 percent).

Looking at the distribution of households by income quintile confirms these findings. Among married couples, 32 percent are in the top fifth of the income distribution compared with only 8 percent of female-headed families. Well more than one-third of households with at least two earners are in the top income quintile versus just 12 percent of households with one earner.

■ Differences in household composition lead to unequal incomes, with dual-earner married couples making more money than other household types.

More than one-third of households with two earners are in the top income quintile

(percent distribution of two-earner households by household income quintile, 2012)

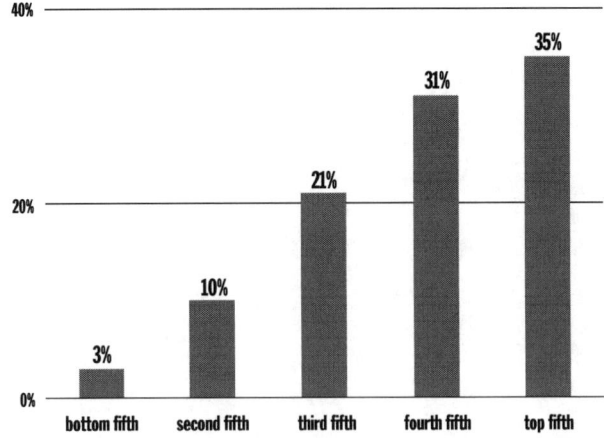

Table 1.15 Number of Households by Income Quintile and Household Characteristic, 2012

(total number of households, lower income limit of each income quintile and top 5 percent, and number of households by quintile and selected characteristics, 2012; households in thousands)

	total	bottom fifth	second fifth	third fifth	fourth fifth	top fifth	top 5 percent
Total households (in 000s)	122,459	24,492	24,492	24,492	24,492	24,492	6,126
Lower limit of income quintile	–	–	$20,599	$39,764	$64,582	$104,096	$191,156
AGE OF HOUSEHOLDER							
Total households	122,459	24,492	24,492	24,492	24,492	24,492	6,126
Under age 25	6,314	2,205	1,638	1,227	830	414	58
Aged 25 to 34	20,017	3,559	4,108	4,575	4,556	3,218	533
Aged 35 to 44	21,334	2,917	3,603	4,283	5,083	5,447	1,407
Aged 45 to 54	24,068	3,597	3,509	4,634	5,317	7,010	1,868
Aged 55 to 64	22,802	4,124	3,808	4,486	4,959	5,425	1,576
Aged 65 or older	27,924	8,081	7,822	5,286	3,751	2,984	684
Aged 65 to 74	15,349	3,357	3,853	3,281	2,622	2,235	538
Aged 75 or older	12,575	4,724	3,969	2,004	1,129	749	146
TYPE OF HOUSEHOLD							
Total households	122,459	24,492	24,492	24,492	24,492	24,492	6,126
Family households	80,902	9,870	14,323	16,594	19,033	21,082	5,356
Married couples	59,204	4,153	8,749	11,753	15,572	18,978	4,988
Female householder, no spouse present	15,469	4,667	4,121	3,234	2,239	1,208	202
Male householder, no spouse present	6,229	1,050	1,453	1,608	1,222	897	166
Nonfamily households	41,558	14,615	10,166	7,897	5,463	3,417	770
Female householder	21,810	8,910	5,467	3,737	2,379	1,317	259
Living alone	18,568	8,482	4,823	3,059	1,576	628	130
Male householder	19,747	5,705	4,699	4,160	3,084	2,099	511
Living alone	15,002	5,144	3,897	3,083	1,859	1,019	251
RACE AND HISPANIC ORIGIN OF HOUSEHOLDER							
Total households	122,459	24,492	24,492	24,492	24,492	24,492	6,126
Asian	5,872	847	849	1,101	1,256	1,819	544
Black	16,559	5,482	3,806	3,191	2,435	1,645	278
Hispanic	15,589	4,002	3,915	3,369	2,585	1,717	332
Non-Hispanic white	83,792	13,972	15,800	16,680	18,124	19,216	4,957
NUMBER OF EARNERS							
Total households	122,459	24,492	24,492	24,492	24,492	24,492	6,126
No earners	28,600	14,939	7,783	3,528	1,605	745	98
One earner	45,849	8,348	12,283	11,641	8,233	5,345	1,371
Two or more earners	48,010	1,198	4,423	9,323	14,658	18,409	4,656
Two earners	38,676	1,133	3,998	8,034	11,965	13,546	3,406
Three earners	7,053	56	381	1,115	2,102	3,399	805
Four earners	2,282	10	43	173	591	1,464	446
HOMEOWNERSHIP STATUS							
Total households	122,459	24,492	24,492	24,492	24,492	24,492	6,126
Owner-occupied	79,474	10,388	13,662	15,986	18,513	20,924	5,456
Renter-occupied	41,337	13,407	10,416	8,239	5,791	3,484	654
Occupier paid no cash rent	1,649	689	411	266	192	92	16

Note: Asians and blacks are those who identify themselves as being of the race alone and those who identify themselves as being of the race in combination with other races. Non-Hispanic whites are those who identify themselves as being white alone and not Hispanic. Hispanics may be of any race. "–" means not applicable.
Source: Bureau of the Census, 2013 Current Population Survey, Internet site http://www.census.gov/hhes/www/cpstables/ 032013/hhinc/toc.htm; calculations by New Strategist

Table 1.16 Distribution of Households within Income Quintile by Household Characteristic, 2012

(total number of households, lower income limit of each income quintile and top 5 percent, and percent distribution of households within quintile by selected characteristics, 2012)

	total	bottom fifth	second fifth	third fifth	fourth fifth	top fifth	top 5 percent
Total households (in 000s)	122,459	24,492	24,492	24,492	24,492	24,492	6,126
Lower limit of income quintile	–	–	$20,599	$39,764	$64,582	$104,096	$191,156
AGE OF HOUSEHOLDER							
Total households	100.0%	100.0%	100.0%	100.0%	100.0%	100.0%	100.0%
Under age 25	5.2	9.0	6.7	5.0	3.4	1.7	0.9
Aged 25 to 34	16.3	14.5	16.8	18.7	18.6	13.1	8.7
Aged 35 to 44	17.4	11.9	14.7	17.5	20.8	22.2	23.0
Aged 45 to 54	19.7	14.7	14.3	18.9	21.7	28.6	30.5
Aged 55 to 64	18.6	16.8	15.6	18.3	20.2	22.2	25.7
Aged 65 or older	22.8	33.0	31.9	21.6	15.3	12.2	11.2
Aged 65 to 74	12.5	13.7	15.7	13.4	10.7	9.1	8.8
Aged 75 or older	10.3	19.3	16.2	8.2	4.6	3.1	2.4
TYPE OF HOUSEHOLD							
Total households	100.0	100.0	100.0	100.0	100.0	100.0	100.0
Family households	66.1	40.3	58.5	67.8	77.7	86.1	87.4
Married couple	48.3	17.0	35.7	48.0	63.6	77.5	81.4
Female householder, no spouse present	12.6	19.1	16.8	13.2	9.1	4.9	3.3
Male householder, no spouse present	5.1	4.3	5.9	6.6	5.0	3.7	2.7
Nonfamily households	33.9	59.7	41.5	32.2	22.3	13.9	12.6
Female householder	17.8	36.4	22.3	15.3	9.7	5.4	4.2
Living alone	15.2	34.6	19.7	12.5	6.4	2.6	2.1
Male householder	16.1	23.3	19.2	17.0	12.6	8.6	8.3
Living alone	12.3	21.0	15.9	12.6	7.6	4.2	4.1
RACE AND HISPANIC ORIGIN OF HOUSEHOLDER							
Total households	100.0	100.0	100.0	100.0	100.0	100.0	100.0
Asian	4.8	3.5	3.5	4.5	5.1	7.4	8.9
Black	13.5	22.4	15.5	13.0	9.9	6.7	4.5
Hispanic	12.7	16.3	16.0	13.8	10.6	7.0	5.4
Non-Hispanic white	68.4	57.0	64.5	68.1	74.0	78.5	80.9
NUMBER OF EARNERS							
Total households	100.0	100.0	100.0	100.0	100.0	100.0	100.0
No earners	23.4	61.0	31.8	14.4	6.6	3.0	1.6
One earner	37.4	34.1	50.2	47.5	33.6	21.8	22.4
Two or more earners	39.2	4.9	18.1	38.1	59.8	75.2	76.0
Two earners	31.6	4.6	16.3	32.8	48.9	55.3	55.6
Three earners	5.8	0.2	1.6	4.6	8.6	13.9	13.1
Four earners	1.9	0.0	0.2	0.7	2.4	6.0	7.3
HOMEOWNERSHIP STATUS							
Total households	100.0	100.0	100.0	100.0	100.0	100.0	100.0
Owner-occupied	64.9	42.4	55.8	65.3	75.6	85.4	89.1
Renter-occupied	33.8	54.7	42.5	33.6	23.6	14.2	10.7
Occupier paid no cash rent	1.3	2.8	1.7	1.1	0.8	0.4	0.3

Note: Asians and blacks are those who identify themselves as being of the race alone and those who identify themselves as being of the race in combination with other races. Non-Hispanic whites are those who identify themselves as being white alone and not Hispanic. Hispanics may be of any race. "–" means not applicable.
Source: Bureau of the Census, 2013 Current Population Survey, Internet site http://www.census.gov/hhes/www/cpstables/ 032013/hhinc/toc.htm; calculations by New Strategist

Table 1.17 Distribution of Household Characteristics by Income Quintile, 2012

(total number of households, lower income limit of each income quintile and top 5 percent, and percent distribution of selected household characteristics by quintile, 2012)

	total	bottom fifth	second fifth	third fifth	fourth fifth	top fifth	top 5 percent
Total households (in 000s)	122,459	24,492	24,492	24,492	24,492	24,492	6,126
Lower limit of income quintile	–	–	$20,599	$39,764	$64,582	$104,096	$191,156
AGE OF HOUSEHOLDER							
Total households	100.0%	20.0%	20.0%	20.0%	20.0%	20.0%	5.0%
Under age 25	100.0	34.9	25.9	19.4	13.1	6.6	0.9
Aged 25 to 34	100.0	17.8	20.5	22.9	22.8	16.1	2.7
Aged 35 to 44	100.0	13.7	16.9	20.1	23.8	25.5	6.6
Aged 45 to 54	100.0	14.9	14.6	19.3	22.1	29.1	7.8
Aged 55 to 64	100.0	18.1	16.7	19.7	21.7	23.8	6.9
Aged 65 or older	100.0	28.9	28.0	18.9	13.4	10.7	2.5
Aged 65 to 74	100.0	21.9	25.1	21.4	17.1	14.6	3.5
Aged 75 or older	100.0	37.6	31.6	15.9	9.0	6.0	1.2
TYPE OF HOUSEHOLD							
Total households	100.0	20.0	20.0	20.0	20.0	20.0	5.0
Family households	100.0	12.2	17.7	20.5	23.5	26.1	6.6
Married couple	100.0	7.0	14.8	19.9	26.3	32.1	8.4
Female householder, no spouse present	100.0	30.2	26.6	20.9	14.5	7.8	1.3
Male householder, no spouse present	100.0	16.9	23.3	25.8	19.6	14.4	2.7
Nonfamily households	100.0	35.2	24.5	19.0	13.1	8.2	1.9
Female householder	100.0	40.9	25.1	17.1	10.9	6.0	1.2
Living alone	100.0	45.7	26.0	16.5	8.5	3.4	0.7
Male householder	100.0	28.9	23.8	21.1	15.6	10.6	2.6
Living alone	100.0	34.3	26.0	20.6	12.4	6.8	1.7
RACE AND HISPANIC ORIGIN OF HOUSEHOLDER							
Total households	100.0	20.0	20.0	20.0	20.0	20.0	5.0
Asian	100.0	14.4	14.5	18.7	21.4	31.0	9.3
Black	100.0	33.1	23.0	19.3	14.7	9.9	1.7
Hispanic	100.0	25.7	25.1	21.6	16.6	11.0	2.1
Non-Hispanic white	100.0	16.7	18.9	19.9	21.6	22.9	5.9
NUMBER OF EARNERS							
Total households	100.0	20.0	20.0	20.0	20.0	20.0	5.0
No earners	100.0	52.2	27.2	12.3	5.6	2.6	0.3
One earner	100.0	18.2	26.8	25.4	18.0	11.7	3.0
Two or more earners	100.0	2.5	9.2	19.4	30.5	38.3	9.7
Two earners	100.0	2.9	10.3	20.8	30.9	35.0	8.8
Three earners	100.0	0.8	5.4	15.8	29.8	48.2	11.4
Four earners	100.0	0.4	1.9	7.6	25.9	64.2	19.5
HOMEOWNERSHIP STATUS							
Total households	100.0	20.0	20.0	20.0	20.0	20.0	5.0
Owner-occupied	100.0	13.1	17.2	20.1	23.3	26.3	6.9
Renter-occupied	100.0	32.4	25.2	19.9	14.0	8.4	1.6
Occupier paid no cash rent	100.0	41.8	24.9	16.1	11.6	5.6	1.0

Note: Asians and blacks are those who identify themselves as being of the race alone and those who identify themselves as being of the race in combination with other races. Non-Hispanic whites are those who identify themselves as being white alone and not Hispanic. Hispanics may be of any race. "–" means not applicable.
Source: Bureau of the Census, 2013 Current Population Survey, Internet site http://www.census.gov/hhes/www/cpstables/032013/hhinc/toc.htm; calculations by New Strategist

Married Couples Have the Highest Incomes

Among the nation's married couples, more than one in three have an income of $100,000 or more.

With a median income of $75,694 in 2012, married couples are by far the most-affluent household type. Behind their higher incomes is the fact that most are dual-earners. Women who live alone have the lowest incomes, a median of just $22,794.

By race and Hispanic origin, Asian households have the highest incomes—a median of $68,182 in 2012 and well above the $57,009 non-Hispanic white median. Behind the higher incomes of Asians is their higher level of education. The $33,718 median income of black households is only 59 percent as high as that of non-Hispanic whites. Differences in household composition explain most of the gap. Married couples head the 52 percent majority of non-Hispanic white households. In contrast, couples head only 28 percent of black households and female-headed families account for another 27 percent.

The median household income of Hispanics is higher than that of blacks only because married couples head a larger share of Hispanic households (48 percent), which boosts their overall median to $39,005. In fact, Hispanic married couples have lower incomes than black couples (a median of $50,398 for Hispanics versus $64,954 for blacks).

■ The gap between the incomes of married couples and other household types may shrink in the years ahead as dual-income baby-boom couples retire.

Women who live alone have the lowest incomes

(median household income by household type, 2012)

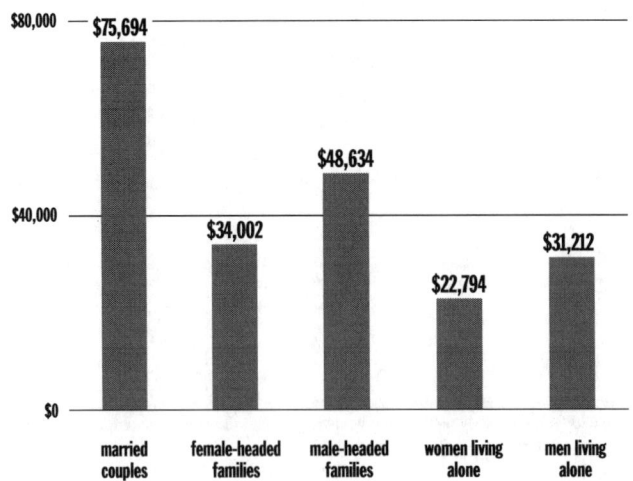

Table 1.18 Households by Income and Household Type, 2012: Total Households

(number and percent distribution of households by household income and household type, 2012; households in thousands as of 2013)

| | total households | family households | | | nonfamily households | | | |
| | | married couples | female householder, no spouse present | male householder, no spouse present | female householder | | male householder | |
					total	living alone	total	living alone
Total households	**122,459**	**59,204**	**15,469**	**6,229**	**21,810**	**18,568**	**19,747**	**15,002**
Under $5,000	4,204	754	979	155	1,278	1,192	1,039	939
$5,000 to $9,999	4,729	558	876	157	1,920	1,842	1,217	1,109
$10,000 to $14,999	6,982	1,009	1,261	277	2,844	2,746	1,591	1,445
$15,000 to $19,999	7,157	1,469	1,281	372	2,477	2,351	1,557	1,392
$20,000 to $24,999	7,131	2,009	1,296	391	2,033	1,849	1,403	1,196
$25,000 to $29,999	6,740	2,327	1,161	386	1,539	1,367	1,327	1,089
$30,000 to $34,999	6,354	2,389	1,037	434	1,304	1,082	1,189	1,026
$35,000 to $39,999	5,832	2,461	916	353	1,010	900	1,092	855
$40,000 to $44,999	5,547	2,320	866	340	936	766	1,085	871
$45,000 to $49,999	5,254	2,452	676	335	824	687	967	742
$50,000 to $54,999	5,102	2,456	630	348	768	622	899	651
$55,000 to $59,999	4,256	2,182	576	292	622	505	584	397
$60,000 to $64,999	4,356	2,366	488	277	589	482	636	430
$65,000 to $69,999	3,949	2,260	476	230	461	311	522	361
$70,000 to $74,999	3,756	2,227	376	158	447	299	548	377
$75,000 to $79,999	3,414	2,137	318	162	348	241	448	271
$80,000 to $84,999	3,326	2,113	288	187	282	209	455	259
$85,000 to $89,999	2,643	1,816	222	145	188	110	272	137
$90,000 to $94,999	2,678	1,743	216	121	260	165	338	174
$95,000 to $99,999	2,223	1,538	168	97	173	93	247	128
$100,000 or more	26,825	20,616	1,361	1,013	1,506	749	2,329	1,152
$100,000 to $124,999	9,490	6,913	642	437	639	351	859	467
$125,000 to $149,999	5,759	4,363	299	223	350	156	525	261
$150,000 to $174,999	3,870	3,096	164	144	171	87	295	130
$175,000 to $199,999	2,247	1,807	84	66	108	27	181	63
$200,000 or more	5,460	4,437	172	144	238	128	470	232
Median income	**$51,017**	**$75,694**	**$34,002**	**$48,634**	**$26,016**	**$22,794**	**$36,989**	**$31,212**
PERCENT DISTRIBUTION								
Total households	**100.0%**	**100.0%**	**100.0%**	**100.0%**	**100.0%**	**100.0%**	**100.0%**	**100.0%**
Under $25,000	24.7	9.8	36.8	21.7	48.4	53.7	34.5	40.5
$25,000 to $49,999	24.3	20.2	30.1	29.7	25.7	25.9	28.7	30.5
$50,000 to $74,999	17.5	19.4	16.5	20.9	13.2	11.9	16.2	14.8
$75,000 to $99,999	11.7	15.8	7.8	11.4	5.7	4.4	8.9	6.5
$100,000 or more	21.9	34.8	8.8	16.3	6.9	4.0	11.8	7.7

Source: Bureau of the Census, 2013 Current Population Survey, Internet site http://www.census.gov/hhes/www/cpstables/ 032013/hhinc/toc.htm; calculations by New Strategist

Table 1.19 Households by Income and Household Type, 2012: Asian Households

(number and percent distribution of Asian households by household income and household type, 2012; households in thousands as of 2013)

| | | family households | | | nonfamily households | | | |
| | | | female householder, no spouse present | male householder, no spouse present | female householder | | male householder | |
	total households	married couples			total	living alone	total	living alone
Asian households	**5,872**	**3,409**	**565**	**346**	**758**	**610**	**794**	**539**
Under $5,000	241	73	22	11	68	54	67	58
$5,000 to $9,999	152	27	22	8	59	57	35	32
$10,000 to $14,999	208	57	24	10	75	73	42	35
$15,000 to $19,999	201	74	28	13	57	54	30	26
$20,000 to $24,999	234	88	52	10	48	42	37	34
$25,000 to $29,999	219	98	28	14	46	44	34	29
$30,000 to $34,999	226	111	18	23	35	28	39	33
$35,000 to $39,999	225	118	23	17	30	26	37	16
$40,000 to $44,999	203	100	25	15	26	18	38	25
$45,000 to $49,999	228	104	49	15	22	19	39	22
$50,000 to $54,999	221	132	14	13	31	29	31	22
$55,000 to $59,999	214	115	24	21	26	22	28	21
$60,000 to $64,999	232	120	22	24	28	25	39	22
$65,000 to $69,999	183	97	22	18	17	9	30	19
$70,000 to $74,999	190	120	20	3	22	17	24	20
$75,000 to $79,999	172	109	15	5	17	11	26	15
$80,000 to $84,999	174	103	24	14	10	10	23	17
$85,000 to $89,999	116	83	4	11	7	6	12	10
$90,000 to $94,999	156	89	9	9	19	16	30	16
$95,000 to $99,999	104	78	6	4	6	6	10	8
$100,000 or more	1,970	1,514	116	88	109	46	143	58
$100,000 to $124,999	591	413	52	37	39	15	51	26
$125,000 to $149,999	364	277	29	12	26	13	19	7
$150,000 to $174,999	329	251	18	18	18	6	24	11
$175,000 to $199,999	185	160	0	3	13	4	9	2
$200,000 or more	500	412	17	19	12	8	40	12
Median income	**$68,182**	**$87,675**	**$49,010**	**$60,792**	**$32,409**	**$27,372**	**$49,928**	**$40,711**

PERCENT DISTRIBUTION

Asian households	**100.0%**	**100.0%**	**100.0%**	**100.0%**	**100.0%**	**100.0%**	**100.0%**	**100.0%**
Under $25,000	17.7	9.4	26.1	14.8	40.6	45.8	26.5	34.4
$25,000 to $49,999	18.8	15.6	25.3	24.2	20.9	22.0	23.6	23.3
$50,000 to $74,999	17.7	17.1	17.9	23.0	16.5	16.7	19.2	19.2
$75,000 to $99,999	12.3	13.5	10.2	12.6	7.7	8.0	12.8	12.2
$100,000 or more	33.5	44.4	20.5	25.5	14.4	7.5	18.0	10.8

Note: Asians are those who identify themselves as being of the race alone and those who identify themselves as being of the race in combination with other races.
Source: Bureau of the Census, 2013 Current Population Survey, Internet site http://www.census.gov/hhes/www/cpstables/ 032013/hhinc/toc.htm; calculations by New Strategist

Table 1.20 Households by Income and Household Type, 2012: Black Households

(number and percent distribution of black households by household income and household type, 2012; households in thousands as of 2013)

| | | family households | | | nonfamily households | | | |
| | | | female householder, no spouse present | male householder, no spouse present | female householder | | male householder | |
	total households	married couples			total	living alone	total	living alone
Black households	**16,559**	**4,700**	**4,473**	**1,105**	**3,424**	**3,042**	**2,856**	**2,370**
Under $5,000	1,108	100	392	60	317	301	240	218
$5,000 to $9,999	1,332	80	352	52	517	497	330	306
$10,000 to $14,999	1,503	121	477	79	480	455	346	323
$15,000 to $19,999	1,263	156	434	93	343	314	237	200
$20,000 to $24,999	1,262	220	437	78	294	268	233	194
$25,000 to $29,999	991	209	301	61	208	182	211	188
$30,000 to $34,999	996	201	317	74	200	177	205	174
$35,000 to $39,999	845	208	286	50	167	152	134	118
$40,000 to $44,999	759	188	220	60	150	126	141	115
$45,000 to $49,999	771	251	175	64	136	114	145	115
$50,000 to $54,999	635	221	144	54	112	78	104	80
$55,000 to $59,999	536	195	147	41	104	87	50	30
$60,000 to $64,999	495	201	119	46	59	51	71	52
$65,000 to $69,999	445	209	108	44	42	35	42	28
$70,000 to $74,999	364	179	82	31	28	23	44	30
$75,000 to $79,999	345	168	69	28	32	21	48	33
$80,000 to $84,999	349	171	63	23	54	42	38	20
$85,000 to $89,999	249	143	48	17	20	16	22	15
$90,000 to $94,999	218	123	40	10	17	12	27	21
$95,000 to $99,999	249	154	32	22	17	10	24	17
$100,000 or more	1,843	1,202	232	116	127	81	166	95
$100,000 to $124,999	786	491	123	60	50	31	62	34
$125,000 to $149,999	451	324	41	12	39	23	34	19
$150,000 to $174,999	220	139	30	18	11	9	22	10
$175,000 to $199,999	135	86	11	9	10	2	19	11
$200,000 or more	251	162	26	16	18	15	29	22
Median income	**$33,718**	**$64,954**	**$27,064**	**$40,301**	**$20,733**	**$19,165**	**$25,820**	**$23,163**
PERCENT DISTRIBUTION								
Black households	**100.0%**	**100.0%**	**100.0%**	**100.0%**	**100.0%**	**100.0%**	**100.0%**	**100.0%**
Under $25,000	39.1	14.4	46.8	32.8	57.0	60.3	48.5	52.4
$25,000 to $49,999	26.3	22.5	29.0	28.1	25.1	24.7	29.3	30.0
$50,000 to $74,999	14.9	21.4	13.4	19.6	10.1	9.0	10.8	9.3
$75,000 to $99,999	8.5	16.1	5.6	9.0	4.1	3.3	5.6	4.4
$100,000 or more	11.1	25.6	5.2	10.5	3.7	2.7	5.8	4.0

Note: Blacks are those who identify themselves as being of the race alone and those who identify themselves as being of the race in combination with other races.
Source: Bureau of the Census, 2013 Current Population Survey, Internet site http://www.census.gov/hhes/www/cpstables/032013/hhinc/toc.htm; calculations by New Strategist

Table 1.21 Households by Income and Household Type, 2012: Hispanic Households

(number and percent distribution of Hispanic households by household income and household type, 2012; households in thousands as of 2013)

| | | family households | | | nonfamily households | | | |
| | | | female householder, no spouse present | male householder, no spouse present | female householder | | male householder | |
	total households	married couples			total	living alone	total	living alone
Hispanic households	**15,589**	**7,455**	**3,106**	**1,391**	**1,683**	**1,367**	**1,954**	**1,345**
Under $5,000	716	127	268	29	166	159	127	118
$5,000 to $9,999	787	143	216	38	238	230	152	134
$10,000 to $14,999	1,112	302	276	64	295	275	176	155
$15,000 to $19,999	1,118	418	309	104	141	127	146	120
$20,000 to $24,999	1,154	489	291	88	144	113	142	106
$25,000 to $29,999	1,100	457	290	96	86	64	170	129
$30,000 to $34,999	1,020	471	230	102	97	69	120	104
$35,000 to $39,999	929	482	184	83	65	52	115	74
$40,000 to $44,999	805	404	150	92	46	36	112	80
$45,000 to $49,999	723	397	114	66	47	41	98	52
$50,000 to $54,999	689	350	112	71	59	38	98	66
$55,000 to $59,999	612	322	119	84	36	27	52	27
$60,000 to $64,999	534	313	70	61	29	20	61	24
$65,000 to $69,999	454	263	65	48	26	10	53	23
$70,000 to $74,999	383	249	38	41	29	11	26	15
$75,000 to $79,999	380	231	52	23	27	17	47	22
$80,000 to $84,999	355	214	46	47	13	9	35	16
$85,000 to $89,999	303	178	38	31	14	5	42	18
$90,000 to $94,999	260	176	28	21	15	8	21	11
$95,000 to $99,999	219	145	28	12	16	8	19	8
$100,000 or more	1,934	1,325	181	192	92	49	144	43
$100,000 to $124,999	836	541	98	94	33	21	69	23
$125,000 to $149,999	397	284	33	43	16	3	21	8
$150,000 to $174,999	269	194	26	21	11	6	17	3
$175,000 to $199,999	141	96	7	13	6	2	18	3
$200,000 or more	291	211	17	21	25	17	18	6
Median income	**$39,005**	**$50,398**	**$28,075**	**$45,015**	**$20,041**	**$15,675**	**$31,895**	**$26,517**

PERCENT DISTRIBUTION

Hispanic households	**100.0%**	**100.0%**	**100.0%**	**100.0%**	**100.0%**	**100.0%**	**100.0%**	**100.0%**
Under $25,000	31.4	19.8	43.8	23.2	58.5	66.2	38.0	47.1
$25,000 to $49,999	29.4	29.7	31.2	31.6	20.3	19.2	31.5	32.7
$50,000 to $74,999	17.1	20.1	13.0	21.8	10.7	7.7	14.8	11.5
$75,000 to $99,999	9.7	12.7	6.2	9.6	5.1	3.3	8.4	5.5
$100,000 or more	12.4	17.8	5.8	13.8	5.5	3.6	7.3	3.2

Source: Bureau of the Census, 2013 Current Population Survey, Internet site http://www.census.gov/hhes/www/cpstables/032013/hhinc/toc.htm; calculations by New Strategist

Table 1.22 Households by Income and Household Type, 2012: Non-Hispanic White Households

(number and percent distribution of non-Hispanic white households by household income and household type, 2012; households in thousands as of 2013)

| | | family households | | | nonfamily households | | | |
| | | married couples | female householder, no spouse present | male householder, no spouse present | female householder | | male householder | |
	total households				total	living alone	total	living alone
Non-Hispanic white households	83,792	43,299	7,317	3,388	15,833	13,476	13,955	10,609
Under $5,000	2,091	441	300	48	723	673	580	528
$5,000 to $9,999	2,452	301	291	61	1,105	1,057	694	627
$10,000 to $14,999	4,089	523	469	119	1,979	1,928	998	904
$15,000 to $19,999	4,516	810	504	163	1,922	1,844	1,117	1,026
$20,000 to $24,999	4,472	1,195	537	209	1,556	1,431	974	846
$25,000 to $29,999	4,392	1,571	530	209	1,177	1,059	905	742
$30,000 to $34,999	4,086	1,599	478	237	952	795	819	712
$35,000 to $39,999	3,788	1,629	421	200	744	665	794	639
$40,000 to $44,999	3,731	1,597	460	184	702	583	788	649
$45,000 to $49,999	3,517	1,686	344	186	611	511	691	547
$50,000 to $54,999	3,505	1,736	354	198	564	476	652	478
$55,000 to $59,999	2,890	1,537	298	148	461	375	445	311
$60,000 to $64,999	3,061	1,714	274	145	464	378	465	326
$65,000 to $69,999	2,859	1,683	278	127	374	257	397	286
$70,000 to $74,999	2,804	1,676	233	86	365	246	443	309
$75,000 to $79,999	2,491	1,602	186	105	271	195	328	202
$80,000 to $84,999	2,454	1,620	159	107	206	149	362	208
$85,000 to $89,999	1,959	1,408	129	84	143	82	195	95
$90,000 to $94,999	2,025	1,344	131	81	208	129	260	129
$95,000 to $99,999	1,649	1,162	104	58	133	69	192	97
$100,000 or more	20,963	16,465	837	635	1,172	570	1,854	949
$100,000 to $124,999	7,219	5,419	370	257	511	280	662	381
$125,000 to $149,999	4,519	3,447	198	155	267	117	451	226
$150,000 to $174,999	3,033	2,496	93	89	131	66	224	103
$175,000 to $199,999	1,787	1,471	64	41	77	19	134	48
$200,000 or more	4,404	3,632	112	92	185	89	383	191
Median income	**$57,009**	**$80,903**	**$41,206**	**$51,640**	**$27,414**	**$24,233**	**$40,457**	**$34,191**
PERCENT DISTRIBUTION								
Non-Hispanic white households	**100.0%**	**100.0%**	**100.0%**	**100.0%**	**100.0%**	**100.0%**	**100.0%**	**100.0%**
Under $25,000	21.0	7.6	28.7	17.7	46.0	51.5	31.3	37.1
$25,000 to $49,999	23.3	18.7	30.5	30.0	26.4	26.8	28.6	31.0
$50,000 to $74,999	18.0	19.3	19.6	20.8	14.1	12.9	17.2	16.1
$75,000 to $99,999	12.6	16.5	9.7	12.8	6.1	4.6	9.6	6.9
$100,000 or more	25.0	38.0	11.4	18.7	7.4	4.2	13.3	8.9

Note: Non-Hispanic whites are those who identify themselves as being white alone and not Hispanic.
Source: Bureau of the Census, 2013 Current Population Survey, Internet site http://www.census.gov/hhes/www/cpstables/ 032013/hhinc/toc.htm; calculations by New Strategist

Household Income Peaks in the 45-to-54 Age Group

Nearly half of Asian households headed by 45-to-54-year-olds have incomes of $100,000 or more.

Median household income stood at $51,017 in 2012. For householders aged 45 to 54, however, median income was a higher $66,411. Household incomes are highest in middle age because people in their thirties, forties, and fifties are usually at the height of their career. Nearly one-third of households headed by people aged 45 to 54 had an income of $100,000 or more in 2012.

By race and Hispanic origin, median income peaks among Asian households headed by 45-to-54-year-olds at $88,727. The median household income of their non-Hispanic white counterparts is a smaller $75,863. Hispanic household income peaks at just $47,653. Among black households, median income tops out in the 35-to-44 age group at $41,918. The black household income peak is relatively low because married couples—the most affluent household type—head few black households. The Hispanic household income peak is relatively low because many Hispanics have little education.

■ The incomes of householders aged 55 to 64 should grow in the years ahead as two-income baby-boom couples fill the age group and fewer opt for early retirement.

Incomes are lowest for the oldest householders

(median income of households by age of householder, 2012)

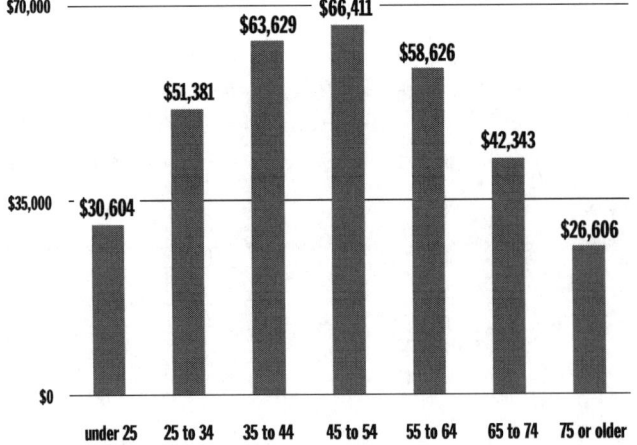

Table 1.23 Households by Income and Age of Householder, 2012: Total Households

(number and percent distribution of households by household income and age of householder, 2012; households in thousands as of 2013)

	total	15 to 24	25 to 34	35 to 44	45 to 54	55 to 64	65 or older total	65 to 74	75 or older
Total households	122,459	6,314	20,017	21,334	24,068	22,802	27,924	15,349	12,575
Under $5,000	4,204	557	752	670	784	759	683	322	361
$5,000 to $9,999	4,729	426	700	461	807	1,045	1,290	571	719
$10,000 to $14,999	6,982	557	861	746	915	1,139	2,764	1,089	1,675
$15,000 to $19,999	7,157	523	968	849	867	1,022	2,927	1,203	1,724
$20,000 to $24,999	7,131	584	1,128	908	940	1,099	2,473	1,091	1,382
$25,000 to $29,999	6,740	452	1,100	924	1,043	890	2,332	1,117	1,215
$30,000 to $34,999	6,354	402	1,051	1,025	945	1,024	1,908	1,000	908
$35,000 to $39,999	5,832	349	1,122	959	829	974	1,599	866	733
$40,000 to $44,999	5,547	299	936	898	1,055	997	1,363	790	573
$45,000 to $49,999	5,254	264	988	893	964	924	1,220	752	468
$50,000 to $54,999	5,102	292	1,041	858	928	924	1,060	647	414
$55,000 to $59,999	4,256	209	757	806	849	797	838	524	313
$60,000 to $64,999	4,356	158	855	837	852	856	798	565	233
$65,000 to $69,999	3,949	167	693	809	766	786	728	513	215
$70,000 to $74,999	3,756	156	705	724	823	762	586	417	169
$75,000 to $79,999	3,414	110	668	726	716	646	548	401	148
$80,000 to $84,999	3,326	124	611	684	696	690	522	339	183
$85,000 to $89,999	2,643	86	464	568	585	523	417	266	151
$90,000 to $94,999	2,678	67	567	554	575	583	332	247	85
$95,000 to $99,999	2,223	72	426	484	481	470	289	195	95
$100,000 or more	26,825	460	3,624	5,952	7,650	5,893	3,247	2,434	812
$100,000 to $124,999	9,490	219	1,581	2,112	2,474	1,883	1,221	868	352
$125,000 to $149,999	5,759	83	832	1,223	1,637	1,252	732	565	167
$150,000 to $174,999	3,870	62	483	874	1,166	846	440	317	124
$175,000 to $199,999	2,247	45	252	494	708	497	252	205	47
$200,000 or more	5,460	51	475	1,249	1,667	1,416	602	480	123
Median income	$51,017	$30,604	$51,381	$63,629	$66,411	$58,626	$33,848	$42,343	$26,606

PERCENT DISTRIBUTION

Total households	100.0%	100.0%	100.0%	100.0%	100.0%	100.0%	100.0%	100.0%	100.0%
Under $25,000	24.7	41.9	22.0	17.0	17.9	22.2	36.3	27.9	46.6
$25,000 to $49,999	24.3	28.0	26.0	22.0	20.1	21.1	30.2	29.5	31.0
$50,000 to $74,999	17.5	15.6	20.2	18.9	17.5	18.1	14.4	17.4	10.7
$75,000 to $99,999	11.7	7.3	13.7	14.1	12.7	12.8	7.5	9.4	5.3
$100,000 or more	21.9	7.3	18.1	27.9	31.8	25.8	11.6	15.9	6.5

Source: Bureau of the Census, 2013 Current Population Survey, Internet site http://www.census.gov/hhes/www/cpstables/032013/hhinc/toc.htm; calculations by New Strategist

Table 1.24 Households by Income and Age of Householder, 2012: Asian Households

(number and percent distribution of Asian households by household income and age of householder, 2012; households in thousands as of 2013)

	total	15 to 24	25 to 34	35 to 44	45 to 54	55 to 64	65 or older total	65 to 74	75 or older
Asian households	5,872	363	1,289	1,439	1,133	840	809	488	320
Under $5,000	241	59	60	26	43	28	25	12	13
$5,000 to $9,999	152	19	23	13	15	31	51	17	35
$10,000 to $14,999	208	11	31	37	27	28	75	31	44
$15,000 to $19,999	201	23	20	35	37	21	64	21	42
$20,000 to $24,999	234	21	48	36	36	29	65	37	28
$25,000 to $29,999	219	14	42	37	39	35	53	29	24
$30,000 to $34,999	226	7	48	64	35	24	48	22	27
$35,000 to $39,999	225	19	57	47	37	28	37	23	14
$40,000 to $44,999	203	19	45	48	32	28	31	23	8
$45,000 to $49,999	228	9	65	69	41	24	20	16	4
$50,000 to $54,999	221	25	54	45	35	37	25	19	6
$55,000 to $59,999	214	14	47	52	33	38	31	21	11
$60,000 to $64,999	232	17	56	69	37	34	19	13	6
$65,000 to $69,999	183	20	50	45	25	22	21	21	0
$70,000 to $74,999	190	12	45	62	17	32	22	19	3
$75,000 to $79,999	172	13	56	44	22	23	15	6	9
$80,000 to $84,999	174	8	53	36	38	25	14	9	4
$85,000 to $89,999	116	4	24	30	21	21	16	14	2
$90,000 to $94,999	156	8	60	26	34	19	8	6	2
$95,000 to $99,999	104	5	25	33	15	15	11	9	2
$100,000 or more	1,970	36	380	584	513	299	158	122	36
$100,000 to $124,999	591	17	143	144	145	86	56	37	18
$125,000 to $149,999	364	4	63	98	102	63	33	25	8
$150,000 to $174,999	329	5	61	113	87	42	21	15	6
$175,000 to $199,999	185	0	30	59	57	24	15	15	0
$200,000 or more	500	10	83	170	122	83	33	29	5
Median income	$68,182	$41,288	$69,698	$77,381	$88,727	$71,485	$38,109	$53,621	$24,484

PERCENT DISTRIBUTION

	total	15 to 24	25 to 34	35 to 44	45 to 54	55 to 64	65 or older total	65 to 74	75 or older
Asian households	100.0%	100.0%	100.0%	100.0%	100.0%	100.0%	100.0%	100.0%	100.0%
Under $25,000	17.7	36.7	14.1	10.2	14.0	16.4	34.5	24.0	50.5
$25,000 to $49,999	18.8	18.7	19.9	18.5	16.3	16.6	23.3	23.1	23.7
$50,000 to $74,999	17.7	24.1	19.5	19.0	13.0	19.3	14.7	19.0	8.2
$75,000 to $99,999	12.3	10.5	16.9	11.8	11.5	12.1	7.9	9.0	6.2
$100,000 or more	33.5	9.9	29.5	40.6	45.3	35.6	19.5	24.9	11.4

Note: Asians are those who identify themselves as being of the race alone and those who identify themselves as being of the race in combination with other races.
Source: Bureau of the Census, 2013 Current Population Survey, Internet site http://www.census.gov/hhes/www/cpstables/032013/hhinc/toc.htm; calculations by New Strategist

Table 1.25 Households by Income and Age of Householder, 2012: Black Households

(number and percent distribution of black households by household income and age of householder, 2012; households in thousands as of 2013)

	total	15 to 24	25 to 34	35 to 44	45 to 54	55 to 64	65 or older total	65 to 74	75 or older
Black households	**16,559**	**1,217**	**3,162**	**3,212**	**3,405**	**2,825**	**2,737**	**1,650**	**1,087**
Under $5,000	1,108	154	228	193	239	170	124	57	67
$5,000 to $9,999	1,332	155	235	147	239	290	265	139	126
$10,000 to $14,999	1,503	159	256	204	221	241	421	212	209
$15,000 to $19,999	1,263	124	220	216	220	199	284	162	122
$20,000 to $24,999	1,262	106	279	199	210	201	267	133	134
$25,000 to $29,999	991	64	230	165	192	137	201	123	78
$30,000 to $34,999	996	70	222	203	186	153	163	107	55
$35,000 to $39,999	845	35	211	190	153	123	134	96	38
$40,000 to $44,999	759	52	142	182	142	121	120	80	40
$45,000 to $49,999	771	60	154	186	165	118	89	59	29
$50,000 to $54,999	635	43	144	124	141	106	77	45	31
$55,000 to $59,999	536	41	102	132	106	88	68	52	16
$60,000 to $64,999	495	14	92	109	113	100	67	51	16
$65,000 to $69,999	445	19	74	112	106	93	41	26	15
$70,000 to $74,999	364	15	72	60	92	76	50	33	16
$75,000 to $79,999	345	10	59	82	85	56	51	27	24
$80,000 to $84,999	349	24	65	64	76	79	41	33	8
$85,000 to $89,999	249	8	34	68	62	43	33	25	9
$90,000 to $94,999	218	7	37	47	59	37	31	21	10
$95,000 to $99,999	249	2	52	67	72	35	21	15	6
$100,000 or more	1,843	53	254	462	527	358	189	150	39
$100,000 to $124,999	786	23	119	206	210	145	84	64	20
$125,000 to $149,999	451	10	63	103	142	91	42	32	11
$150,000 to $174,999	220	11	32	50	66	43	18	16	2
$175,000 to $199,999	135	2	17	48	29	25	13	13	0
$200,000 or more	251	8	23	56	79	54	31	26	6
Median income	**$33,718**	**$20,786**	**$32,142**	**$41,918**	**$41,197**	**$35,692**	**$25,157**	**$29,925**	**$20,613**

PERCENT DISTRIBUTION

	total	15 to 24	25 to 34	35 to 44	45 to 54	55 to 64	65 or older total	65 to 74	75 or older
Black households	**100.0%**	**100.0%**	**100.0%**	**100.0%**	**100.0%**	**100.0%**	**100.0%**	**100.0%**	**100.0%**
Under $25,000	39.1	57.4	38.6	29.8	33.1	39.0	49.8	42.6	60.6
$25,000 to $49,999	26.3	23.1	30.3	28.8	24.6	23.1	25.8	28.3	22.1
$50,000 to $74,999	14.9	10.8	15.3	16.7	16.4	16.4	11.0	12.6	8.6
$75,000 to $99,999	8.5	4.3	7.8	10.2	10.4	8.8	6.5	7.3	5.2
$100,000 or more	11.1	4.4	8.0	14.4	15.5	12.7	6.9	9.1	3.5

Note: Blacks are those who identify themselves as being of the race alone and those who identify themselves as being of the race in combination with other races.
Source: Bureau of the Census, 2013 Current Population Survey, Internet site http://www.census.gov/hhes/www/cpstables/032013/hhinc/toc.htm; calculations by New Strategist

Table 1.26 Households by Income and Age of Householder, 2012: Hispanic Households

(number and percent distribution of Hispanic households by household income and age of householder, 2012; households in thousands as of 2013)

	total	15 to 24	25 to 34	35 to 44	45 to 54	55 to 64	65 or older total	65 to 74	75 or older
Hispanic households	15,589	1,363	3,642	3,761	2,979	2,057	1,787	1,075	712
Under $5,000	716	104	145	148	118	114	88	49	39
$5,000 to $9,999	787	87	152	102	105	164	177	109	68
$10,000 to $14,999	1,112	107	214	203	147	159	282	135	147
$15,000 to $19,999	1,118	110	290	239	133	128	218	119	99
$20,000 to $24,999	1,154	139	280	264	189	125	158	87	71
$25,000 to $29,999	1,100	123	272	272	197	120	117	68	48
$30,000 to $34,999	1,020	113	236	249	173	148	102	61	42
$35,000 to $39,999	929	109	246	257	158	83	76	49	27
$40,000 to $44,999	805	62	204	199	182	93	66	42	24
$45,000 to $49,999	723	58	193	162	148	89	73	49	25
$50,000 to $54,999	689	56	176	161	153	88	55	38	18
$55,000 to $59,999	612	45	143	157	140	88	40	31	9
$60,000 to $64,999	534	24	153	140	110	67	41	26	14
$65,000 to $69,999	454	36	107	149	76	47	39	30	9
$70,000 to $74,999	383	26	75	103	103	52	25	19	5
$75,000 to $79,999	380	18	94	93	90	55	30	22	8
$80,000 to $84,999	355	19	106	101	70	34	25	20	5
$85,000 to $89,999	303	20	77	79	53	44	29	18	12
$90,000 to $94,999	260	9	64	71	60	44	13	10	3
$95,000 to $99,999	219	8	57	74	36	30	15	11	3
$100,000 or more	1,934	91	360	538	539	287	118	80	38
$100,000 to $124,999	836	46	178	238	220	105	47	30	18
$125,000 to $149,999	397	21	81	94	118	60	23	16	7
$150,000 to $174,999	269	14	35	86	66	50	18	12	6
$175,000 to $199,999	141	6	18	42	44	27	4	4	1
$200,000 or more	291	5	48	77	92	45	25	19	6
Median income	$39,005	$30,405	$39,648	$42,987	$47,653	$39,193	$24,122	$27,450	$20,363

PERCENT DISTRIBUTION

	total	15 to 24	25 to 34	35 to 44	45 to 54	55 to 64	65 or older total	65 to 74	75 or older
Hispanic households	100.0%	100.0%	100.0%	100.0%	100.0%	100.0%	100.0%	100.0%	100.0%
Under $25,000	31.4	40.2	29.7	25.4	23.2	33.5	51.6	46.5	59.4
$25,000 to $49,999	29.4	34.1	31.6	30.3	28.8	25.9	24.3	25.0	23.3
$50,000 to $74,999	17.1	13.7	18.0	18.9	19.5	16.6	11.2	13.4	7.8
$75,000 to $99,999	9.7	5.4	10.9	11.1	10.4	10.1	6.3	7.7	4.2
$100,000 or more	12.4	6.7	9.9	14.3	18.1	14.0	6.6	7.5	5.3

Source: Bureau of the Census, 2013 Current Population Survey, Internet site http://www.census.gov/hhes/www/cpstables/032013/hhinc/toc.htm; calculations by New Strategist

Table 1.27 Households by Income and Age of Householder, 2012: Non-Hispanic White Households

(number and percent distribution of non-Hispanic white households by household income and age of householder, 2012; households in thousands as of 2013)

	total	15 to 24	25 to 34	35 to 44	45 to 54	55 to 64	65 or older total	65 to 74	75 or older
Non-Hispanic white households	83,792	3,346	11,888	12,943	16,337	16,882	22,395	12,001	10,393
Under $5,000	2,091	221	294	312	378	441	446	203	243
$5,000 to $9,999	2,452	170	299	196	435	550	801	308	493
$10,000 to $14,999	4,089	287	348	292	500	702	1,959	692	1,267
$15,000 to $19,999	4,516	263	425	360	461	659	2,348	899	1,449
$20,000 to $24,999	4,472	315	534	423	502	741	1,956	813	1,143
$25,000 to $29,999	4,392	255	562	450	600	588	1,938	882	1,056
$30,000 to $34,999	4,086	208	555	511	549	684	1,579	797	782
$35,000 to $39,999	3,788	175	606	464	472	730	1,342	689	652
$40,000 to $44,999	3,731	166	543	467	681	740	1,133	638	496
$45,000 to $49,999	3,517	133	576	501	601	677	1,030	624	406
$50,000 to $54,999	3,505	161	665	515	583	685	896	541	355
$55,000 to $59,999	2,890	117	462	462	566	587	695	418	277
$60,000 to $64,999	3,061	103	555	518	580	641	664	470	194
$65,000 to $69,999	2,859	95	457	512	554	620	621	432	190
$70,000 to $74,999	2,804	104	517	500	609	591	482	340	143
$75,000 to $79,999	2,491	69	461	493	516	499	452	345	107
$80,000 to $84,999	2,454	70	396	487	514	544	443	277	165
$85,000 to $89,999	1,959	53	327	393	440	411	336	207	129
$90,000 to $94,999	2,025	42	400	408	418	486	270	201	69
$95,000 to $99,999	1,649	56	296	316	350	389	243	160	83
$100,000 or more	20,963	283	2,611	4,361	6,029	4,919	2,759	2,065	694
$100,000 to $124,999	7,219	140	1,126	1,518	1,882	1,530	1,022	730	292
$125,000 to $149,999	4,519	46	623	926	1,263	1,030	631	490	140
$150,000 to $174,999	3,033	31	356	628	940	705	373	264	109
$175,000 to $199,999	1,787	37	188	344	582	419	218	172	46
$200,000 or more	4,404	30	319	944	1,361	1,235	515	409	106
Median income	$57,009	$33,656	$60,504	$74,814	$75,863	$65,126	$35,559	$45,693	$27,605

PERCENT DISTRIBUTION

	total	15 to 24	25 to 34	35 to 44	45 to 54	55 to 64	65 or older total	65 to 74	75 or older
Non-Hispanic white households	100.0%	100.0%	100.0%	100.0%	100.0%	100.0%	100.0%	100.0%	100.0%
Under $25,000	21.0	37.5	16.0	12.2	13.9	18.3	33.5	24.3	44.2
$25,000 to $49,999	23.3	28.0	23.9	18.5	17.8	20.3	31.4	30.2	32.6
$50,000 to $74,999	18.0	17.3	22.3	19.4	17.7	18.5	15.0	18.3	11.1
$75,000 to $99,999	12.6	8.7	15.8	16.2	13.7	13.8	7.8	9.9	5.3
$200,000 or more	25.0	8.5	22.0	33.7	36.9	29.1	12.3	17.2	6.7

Note: Non-Hispanic whites are those who identify themselves as being white alone and not Hispanic.
Source: Bureau of the Census, 2013 Current Population Survey, Internet site http://www.census.gov/hhes/www/cpstables/032013/hhinc/toc.htm; calculations by New Strategist

Among Couples, the Middle Aged Have the Highest Incomes

Married couples aged 45 to 54 had a median income of $94,191 in 2012.

The incomes of married couples peak in the 45-to-54 age group. While most couples ranging in age from 35 to 64 have an income of $80,000 or more, those aged 45 to 54 have the highest income by a hefty margin. Nearly 47 percent of couples in the 45-to-54 age group had an income of $100,000 or more in 2012.

By race and Hispanic origin, the incomes of married couples peak among Asian households headed by 45-to-54-year-olds, at $105,266 in 2012. Their non-Hispanic white counterparts are not far behind, with a median income of $101,838. The median income of black couples in the age group far exceeds that of Hispanic couples—$75,397 versus $60,541.

■ The income of Hispanics will continue to lag because of their relatively low educational attainment.

Asian couples have the highest median income

(median income of married-couple households by race and Hispanic origin, 2012)

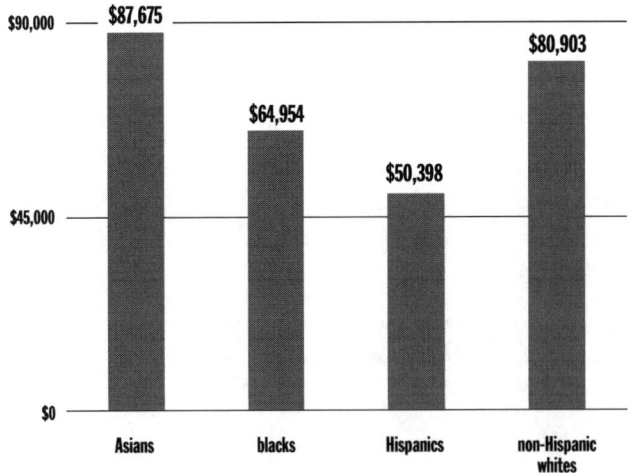

Table 1.28 Married Couples by Household Income and Age of Householder, 2012: Total Married Couples

(number and percent distribution of married couples by household income and age of householder, 2012; married couples in thousands as of 2013)

	total	15 to 24	25 to 34	35 to 44	45 to 54	55 to 64	65 or older total	65 to 74	75 or older
Total married couples	59,204	970	8,551	11,985	13,237	12,043	12,418	8,034	4,383
Under $5,000	754	19	136	139	152	165	143	83	60
$5,000 to $9,999	558	36	84	74	111	139	114	66	49
$10,000 to $14,999	1,009	58	174	155	160	195	267	134	133
$15,000 to $19,999	1,469	61	225	223	193	261	506	275	231
$20,000 to $24,999	2,009	77	303	290	290	326	723	338	385
$25,000 to $29,999	2,327	62	302	306	321	311	1,025	497	528
$30,000 to $34,999	2,389	90	315	359	297	362	967	519	448
$35,000 to $39,999	2,461	94	374	429	328	374	862	487	375
$40,000 to $44,999	2,320	52	362	379	445	422	660	417	243
$45,000 to $49,999	2,452	65	390	387	395	455	760	507	253
$50,000 to $54,999	2,456	67	439	444	433	470	604	404	200
$55,000 to $59,999	2,182	35	369	418	412	414	532	346	186
$60,000 to $64,999	2,366	33	455	457	502	462	457	336	120
$65,000 to $69,999	2,260	43	363	462	430	476	487	366	121
$70,000 to $74,999	2,227	27	402	447	462	493	396	286	110
$75,000 to $79,999	2,137	35	385	484	464	407	362	273	90
$80,000 to $84,999	2,113	20	358	498	439	445	353	251	102
$85,000 to $89,999	1,816	19	290	398	431	379	300	198	102
$90,000 to $94,999	1,743	21	308	397	404	402	211	166	45
$95,000 to $99,999	1,538	5	230	371	374	359	199	141	58
$100,000 or more	20,616	51	2,287	4,867	6,194	4,729	2,489	1,946	543
$100,000 to $124,999	6,913	31	1,004	1,655	1,875	1,446	902	674	228
$125,000 to $149,999	4,363	7	517	1,031	1,310	969	528	428	100
$150,000 to $174,999	3,096	7	314	728	986	716	346	245	101
$175,000 to $199,999	1,807	3	172	411	598	417	206	171	35
$200,000 or more	4,437	3	280	1,042	1,424	1,181	506	427	79
Median income	$75,694	$39,127	$69,727	$85,448	$94,191	$82,959	$51,416	$59,258	$39,727

PERCENT DISTRIBUTION

	total	15 to 24	25 to 34	35 to 44	45 to 54	55 to 64	65 or older total	65 to 74	75 or older
Total married couples	100.0%	100.0%	100.0%	100.0%	100.0%	100.0%	100.0%	100.0%	100.0%
Under $25,000	9.8	25.9	10.8	7.4	6.8	9.0	14.1	11.1	19.6
$25,000 to $49,999	20.2	37.5	20.4	15.5	13.5	16.0	34.4	30.2	42.1
$50,000 to $74,999	19.4	21.1	23.7	18.6	16.9	19.2	19.9	21.6	16.8
$75,000 to $99,999	15.8	10.3	18.4	17.9	16.0	16.5	11.5	12.8	9.1
$100,000 or more	34.8	5.2	26.7	40.6	46.8	39.3	20.0	24.2	12.4

Source: Bureau of the Census, 2013 Current Population Survey, Internet site http://www.census.gov/hhes/www/cpstables/032013/hhinc/toc.htm; calculations by New Strategist

Table 1.29 Married Couples by Household Income and Age of Householder, 2012: Asian Married Couples

(number and percent distribution of Asian married couples by household income and age of householder, 2012; married couples in thousands as of 2013)

	total	15 to 24	25 to 34	35 to 44	45 to 54	55 to 64	65 or older total	65 to 74	75 or older
Asian married couples	**3,409**	**27**	**584**	**1,000**	**792**	**543**	**463**	**325**	**138**
Under $5,000	73	4	16	9	22	9	14	9	5
$5,000 to $9,999	27	0	5	3	6	8	6	2	4
$10,000 to $14,999	57	0	15	10	6	6	20	10	9
$15,000 to $19,999	74	0	5	18	18	10	24	9	15
$20,000 to $24,999	88	0	18	12	17	15	26	12	14
$25,000 to $29,999	98	0	12	14	15	26	31	18	12
$30,000 to $34,999	111	0	18	35	18	10	29	16	13
$35,000 to $39,999	118	4	26	34	20	15	19	14	4
$40,000 to $44,999	100	0	17	36	20	10	18	14	4
$45,000 to $49,999	104	2	22	31	29	8	12	10	2
$50,000 to $54,999	132	3	18	38	28	25	20	14	6
$55,000 to $59,999	115	0	14	29	17	32	23	19	4
$60,000 to $64,999	120	0	26	43	22	16	12	7	6
$65,000 to $69,999	97	2	21	20	21	13	20	20	0
$70,000 to $74,999	120	0	25	39	12	28	15	13	2
$75,000 to $79,999	109	2	28	35	14	17	14	5	8
$80,000 to $84,999	103	0	23	25	27	18	10	9	1
$85,000 to $89,999	83	0	13	23	15	18	14	12	2
$90,000 to $94,999	89	4	30	11	25	12	6	6	0
$95,000 to $99,999	78	0	19	25	12	15	8	6	2
$100,000 or more	1,514	5	213	512	428	234	121	99	23
$100,000 to $124,999	413	2	75	124	111	64	37	26	11
$125,000 to $149,999	277	0	37	80	84	50	26	21	5
$150,000 to $174,999	251	0	35	101	69	31	15	13	2
$175,000 to $199,999	160	0	19	51	50	24	15	15	0
$200,000 or more	412	2	48	156	114	65	28	23	5
Median income	**$87,675**	**–**	**$81,238**	**$101,011**	**$105,266**	**$86,376**	**$58,065**	**$66,787**	**$32,441**

PERCENT DISTRIBUTION

	total	15 to 24	25 to 34	35 to 44	45 to 54	55 to 64	65 or older total	65 to 74	75 or older
Asian married couples	**100.0%**	**100.0%**	**100.0%**	**100.0%**	**100.0%**	**100.0%**	**100.0%**	**100.0%**	**100.0%**
Under $25,000	9.4	15.4	10.1	5.1	8.6	8.8	19.4	13.0	34.4
$25,000 to $49,999	15.6	25.0	16.3	15.0	12.8	12.7	23.4	22.2	26.2
$50,000 to $74,999	17.1	19.9	17.8	16.9	12.7	20.7	19.8	22.6	13.2
$75,000 to $99,999	13.5	22.4	19.2	11.9	11.7	14.6	11.2	11.8	9.9
$100,000 or more	44.4	17.3	36.5	51.2	54.1	43.1	26.2	30.4	16.3

Note: Asians are those who identify themselves as being of the race alone and those who identify themselves as being of the race in combination with other races. "–" means sample is too small to make a reliable estimate.
Source: Bureau of the Census, 2013 Current Population Survey, Internet site http://www.census.gov/hhes/www/cpstables/ 032013/hhinc/toc.htm; calculations by New Strategist

Table 1.30 Married Couples by Household Income and Age of Householder, 2012: Black Married Couples

(number and percent distribution of black married couples by household income and age of householder, 2012; married couples in thousands as of 2013)

	total	15 to 24	25 to 34	35 to 44	45 to 54	55 to 64	65 or older total	65 to 74	75 or older
Black married couples	**4,700**	**68**	**662**	**1,082**	**1,194**	**908**	**787**	**524**	**263**
Under $5,000	100	2	7	27	27	16	20	13	8
$5,000 to $9,999	80	7	19	10	17	17	10	6	4
$10,000 to $14,999	121	7	18	18	18	26	33	11	22
$15,000 to $19,999	156	4	16	21	34	38	43	20	22
$20,000 to $24,999	220	5	27	24	43	51	71	36	34
$25,000 to $29,999	209	1	35	35	44	31	62	39	23
$30,000 to $34,999	201	10	27	40	39	34	50	36	14
$35,000 to $39,999	208	2	32	39	44	37	54	40	14
$40,000 to $44,999	188	3	34	33	41	40	37	23	14
$45,000 to $49,999	251	9	38	71	44	55	34	22	12
$50,000 to $54,999	221	6	47	43	60	31	33	19	14
$55,000 to $59,999	195	6	33	49	42	36	29	20	9
$60,000 to $64,999	201	0	29	53	45	41	33	29	4
$65,000 to $69,999	209	2	28	54	52	50	23	17	6
$70,000 to $74,999	179	0	41	30	39	44	25	15	11
$75,000 to $79,999	168	0	27	32	50	28	30	14	16
$80,000 to $84,999	171	5	21	46	41	33	24	20	5
$85,000 to $89,999	143	0	21	39	34	29	20	16	4
$90,000 to $94,999	123	0	13	37	28	20	24	18	6
$95,000 to $99,999	154	0	27	43	54	15	15	11	4
$100,000 or more	1,202	0	121	336	395	235	115	99	16
$100,000 to $124,999	491	0	60	149	144	87	50	41	9
$125,000 to $149,999	324	0	34	86	115	61	28	22	5
$150,000 to $174,999	139	0	12	30	52	34	11	11	0
$175,000 to $199,999	86	0	5	31	21	18	10	10	0
$200,000 or more	162	0	10	40	61	35	17	15	2
Median income	**$64,954**	**–**	**$59,141**	**$72,460**	**$75,397**	**$65,024**	**$46,983**	**$53,393**	**$36,486**

PERCENT DISTRIBUTION

	total	15 to 24	25 to 34	35 to 44	45 to 54	55 to 64	65 or older total	65 to 74	75 or older
Black married couples	**100.0%**	**100.0%**	**100.0%**	**100.0%**	**100.0%**	**100.0%**	**100.0%**	**100.0%**	**100.0%**
Under $25,000	14.4	36.9	13.2	9.2	11.7	16.4	22.5	16.4	34.6
$25,000 to $49,999	22.5	35.7	25.1	20.2	17.8	21.8	30.2	30.6	29.3
$50,000 to $74,999	21.4	20.2	26.8	21.2	20.0	22.1	18.2	19.0	16.7
$75,000 to $99,999	16.1	7.2	16.6	18.2	17.4	13.8	14.5	15.0	13.3
$100,000 or more	25.6	0.0	18.2	31.1	33.1	25.9	14.7	19.0	6.1

Note: Blacks are those who identify themselves as being of the race alone and those who identify themselves as being of the race in combination with other races. "–" means sample is too small to make a reliable estimate.
Source: Bureau of the Census, 2013 Current Population Survey, Internet site http://www.census.gov/hhes/www/cpstables/032013/hhinc/toc.htm; calculations by New Strategist

Table 1.31 Married Couples by Household Income and Age of Householder, 2012: Hispanic Married Couples

(number and percent distribution of Hispanic married couples by household income and age of householder, 2012; married couples in thousands as of 2013)

	total	15 to 24	25 to 34	35 to 44	45 to 54	55 to 64	65 or older total	65 to 74	75 or older
Hispanic married couples	**7,455**	**310**	**1,677**	**2,053**	**1,651**	**984**	**780**	**526**	**254**
Under $5,000	127	6	22	31	33	22	13	8	5
$5,000 to $9,999	143	10	34	19	24	29	27	16	11
$10,000 to $14,999	302	27	78	59	46	32	61	41	20
$15,000 to $19,999	418	28	119	107	41	37	86	43	43
$20,000 to $24,999	489	38	115	133	73	51	79	43	36
$25,000 to $29,999	457	22	105	138	75	45	72	48	24
$30,000 to $34,999	471	36	120	120	87	58	50	28	22
$35,000 to $39,999	482	46	127	147	84	38	41	30	10
$40,000 to $44,999	404	14	91	120	100	54	26	20	5
$45,000 to $49,999	397	16	113	76	87	57	48	36	12
$50,000 to $54,999	350	8	85	90	89	41	37	25	12
$55,000 to $59,999	322	5	73	97	75	44	28	22	6
$60,000 to $64,999	313	6	76	85	82	41	23	15	8
$65,000 to $69,999	263	14	59	89	45	33	23	21	2
$70,000 to $74,999	249	11	48	66	63	41	20	17	3
$75,000 to $79,999	231	3	55	66	57	34	16	11	5
$80,000 to $84,999	214	2	52	72	51	17	20	17	4
$85,000 to $89,999	178	7	33	50	39	29	20	13	7
$90,000 to $94,999	176	2	37	52	49	31	5	4	1
$95,000 to $99,999	145	0	29	56	33	16	11	9	2
$100,000 or more	1,325	9	207	380	419	235	76	61	15
$100,000 to $124,999	541	5	95	163	163	84	31	23	8
$125,000 to $149,999	284	3	45	80	92	48	15	13	2
$150,000 to $174,999	194	0	29	55	56	39	14	9	4
$175,000 to $199,999	96	0	11	22	35	25	2	2	1
$200,000 or more	211	0	26	61	73	39	13	13	0
Median income	**$50,398**	**$32,905**	**$46,073**	**$53,444**	**$60,541**	**$58,022**	**$35,515**	**$41,183**	**$27,279**

PERCENT DISTRIBUTION

	total	15 to 24	25 to 34	35 to 44	45 to 54	55 to 64	65 or older total	65 to 74	75 or older
Hispanic married couples	**100.0%**	**100.0%**	**100.0%**	**100.0%**	**100.0%**	**100.0%**	**100.0%**	**100.0%**	**100.0%**
Under $25,000	19.8	35.2	21.9	17.0	13.1	17.3	34.0	28.6	45.0
$25,000 to $49,999	29.7	43.0	33.1	29.2	26.3	25.6	30.3	30.9	29.1
$50,000 to $74,999	20.1	14.3	20.3	20.8	21.5	20.3	16.7	18.8	12.3
$75,000 to $99,999	12.7	4.5	12.3	14.4	13.8	12.9	9.4	10.1	7.7
$100,000 or more	17.8	3.0	12.3	18.5	25.4	23.9	9.7	11.5	5.9

Source: Bureau of the Census, 2013 Current Population Survey, Internet site http://www.census.gov/hhes/www/cpstables/ 032013/hhinc/toc.htm; calculations by New Strategist

Table 1.32 Married Couples by Household Income and Age of Householder, 2012: Non-Hispanic White Married Couples

(number and percent distribution of non-Hispanic white married couples by household income and age of householder, 2012; married couples in thousands as of 2013)

	total	15 to 24	25 to 34	35 to 44	45 to 54	55 to 64	65 or older total	65 to 74	75 or older
Non-Hispanic white married couples	43,299	550	5,616	7,828	9,478	9,513	10,314	6,611	3,702
Under $5,000	441	7	80	72	69	118	95	54	41
$5,000 to $9,999	301	16	31	42	59	79	74	42	32
$10,000 to $14,999	523	28	62	66	86	129	152	72	79
$15,000 to $19,999	810	28	82	77	101	170	353	200	153
$20,000 to $24,999	1,195	33	142	123	148	211	538	240	298
$25,000 to $29,999	1,571	38	159	125	183	208	857	392	466
$30,000 to $34,999	1,599	43	157	158	155	254	832	436	396
$35,000 to $39,999	1,629	35	195	207	174	276	742	397	345
$40,000 to $44,999	1,597	34	221	187	268	316	571	355	216
$45,000 to $49,999	1,686	38	221	210	230	328	659	436	223
$50,000 to $54,999	1,736	49	288	268	249	370	511	344	167
$55,000 to $59,999	1,537	24	242	242	273	304	451	285	166
$60,000 to $64,999	1,714	27	321	280	342	358	385	285	101
$65,000 to $69,999	1,683	24	253	300	310	377	419	307	112
$70,000 to $74,999	1,676	16	297	309	347	375	332	239	93
$75,000 to $79,999	1,602	30	270	337	341	320	303	243	60
$80,000 to $84,999	1,620	13	261	357	324	368	297	205	93
$85,000 to $89,999	1,408	12	224	290	337	301	243	155	89
$90,000 to $94,999	1,344	15	223	297	299	341	170	133	37
$95,000 to $99,999	1,162	5	160	250	270	311	165	115	50
$100,000 or more	16,465	34	1,726	3,631	4,913	3,999	2,163	1,677	486
$100,000 to $124,999	5,419	21	763	1,219	1,448	1,194	774	577	197
$125,000 to $149,999	3,447	4	396	780	1,006	803	459	372	87
$150,000 to $174,999	2,496	6	238	541	801	609	301	206	95
$175,000 to $199,999	1,471	2	136	307	498	350	179	145	34
$200,000 or more	3,632	1	194	784	1,161	1,043	450	378	72
Median income	$80,903	$46,497	$75,839	$94,252	$101,838	$87,891	$52,751	$60,914	$40,852

PERCENT DISTRIBUTION

Non-Hispanic white married couples	100.0%	100.0%	100.0%	100.0%	100.0%	100.0%	100.0%	100.0%	100.0%
Under $25,000	7.6	20.2	7.1	4.8	4.9	7.4	11.8	9.2	16.3
$25,000 to $49,999	18.7	34.3	17.0	11.3	10.7	14.5	35.5	30.5	44.5
$50,000 to $74,999	19.3	25.7	24.9	17.9	16.0	18.8	20.4	22.1	17.3
$75,000 to $99,999	16.5	13.7	20.3	19.6	16.6	17.2	11.4	12.9	8.9
$100,000 or more	38.0	6.1	30.7	46.4	51.8	42.0	21.0	25.4	13.1

Note: Non-Hispanic whites are those who identify themselves as being white alone and not Hispanic.
Source: Bureau of the Census, 2013 Current Population Survey, Internet site http://www.census.gov/hhes/www/cpstables/032013/hhinc/toc.htm; calculations by New Strategist

Incomes of Female-Headed Families Are below Average

The youngest are the poorest.

The median income of female-headed families was just $34,002 in 2012. Householders under age 25 have the lowest incomes, a median of just $24,445. Those aged 25 to 34 have a median income that is only slightly higher, at $25,525. Among householders ranging in age from 45 to 64, median income rises above $40,000. Female-headed families headed by younger women typically include children. Many of these households have only one earner or even no earners, which explains their low incomes. Female-headed families headed by older women typically include other adults—such as grown children or siblings. These households often have two or more earners, which explains their higher incomes.

The poorest female-headed families are those headed by black women. Black female family householders had a median income of just $27,064 in 2012. In contrast, Asian female family householders have the highest incomes, a median income of $49,010 in 2012 and close to the all-household median of $51,017.

■ Female-headed families have low incomes because their households are likely to have just one earner, and many have no earners.

Incomes peak in middle age for female-headed families

(median household income of female-headed families by age of householder, 2012)

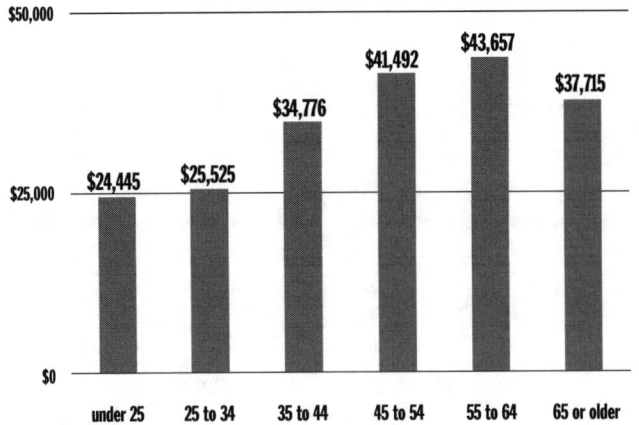

Table 1.33 Female-Headed Families by Household Income and Age of Householder, 2012: Total Female-Headed Families

(number and percent distribution of female-headed families by household income and age of householder, 2012; female-headed families in thousands as of 2013)

	total	15 to 24	25 to 34	35 to 44	45 to 54	55 to 64	65 or older total	65 to 74	75 or older
Total female-headed families	**15,469**	**1,394**	**3,373**	**3,605**	**3,099**	**1,969**	**2,029**	**1,086**	**943**
Under $5,000	979	199	303	240	123	72	42	21	21
$5,000 to $9,999	876	141	274	179	146	80	56	26	30
$10,000 to $14,999	1,261	140	365	292	194	125	145	70	75
$15,000 to $19,999	1,281	120	368	301	214	113	166	84	81
$20,000 to $24,999	1,296	107	337	296	213	154	188	81	108
$25,000 to $29,999	1,161	102	301	250	229	107	172	80	92
$30,000 to $34,999	1,037	64	231	251	188	135	168	97	71
$35,000 to $39,999	916	74	194	232	156	116	144	74	69
$40,000 to $44,999	866	52	157	216	211	101	129	73	56
$45,000 to $49,999	676	40	121	170	134	112	100	48	52
$50,000 to $54,999	630	44	107	147	151	87	94	45	49
$55,000 to $59,999	576	40	91	139	144	84	77	35	43
$60,000 to $64,999	488	24	79	138	101	74	72	51	21
$65,000 to $69,999	476	20	72	143	118	69	55	29	26
$70,000 to $74,999	376	30	50	82	112	54	47	33	15
$75,000 to $79,999	318	18	28	64	89	54	64	41	23
$80,000 to $84,999	288	35	32	47	77	65	32	12	20
$85,000 to $89,999	222	11	38	43	50	34	45	32	14
$90,000 to $94,999	216	13	29	41	56	37	41	30	11
$95,000 to $99,999	168	10	25	51	30	28	24	17	7
$100,000 or more	1,361	108	170	282	363	268	170	110	60
$100,000 to $124,999	642	51	85	128	172	122	85	42	43
$125,000 to $149,999	299	13	44	47	80	68	46	35	11
$150,000 to $174,999	164	14	30	36	42	23	19	15	4
$175,000 to $199,999	84	12	4	21	22	16	9	8	0
$200,000 or more	172	18	8	50	46	38	11	10	1
Median income	**$34,002**	**$24,445**	**$25,525**	**$34,776**	**$41,492**	**$43,657**	**$37,715**	**$40,518**	**$34,587**

PERCENT DISTRIBUTION

	total	15 to 24	25 to 34	35 to 44	45 to 54	55 to 64	65 or older total	65 to 74	75 or older
Total female-headed families	**100.0%**	**100.0%**	**100.0%**	**100.0%**	**100.0%**	**100.0%**	**100.0%**	**100.0%**	**100.0%**
Under $25,000	36.8	50.8	48.8	36.3	28.7	27.6	29.4	26.0	33.4
$25,000 to $49,999	30.1	23.8	29.8	31.0	29.6	29.0	35.1	34.3	36.0
$50,000 to $74,999	16.5	11.4	11.9	18.0	20.2	18.7	17.0	17.7	16.3
$75,000 to $99,999	7.8	6.3	4.5	6.8	9.7	11.1	10.1	12.0	7.9
$100,000 or more	8.8	7.7	5.0	7.8	11.7	13.6	8.4	10.1	6.4

Source: Bureau of the Census, 2013 Current Population Survey, Internet site http://www.census.gov/hhes/www/cpstables/032013/hhinc/toc.htm; calculations by New Strategist

Table 1.34 Female-Headed Families by Household Income and Age of Householder, 2012: Asian Female-Headed Families

(number and percent distribution of Asian female-headed families by household income and age of householder, 2012; female-headed families in thousands as of 2013)

	total	under age 45	aged 45 or older
Asian female-headed families	565	309	256
Under $5,000	22	12	10
$5,000 to $9,999	22	14	8
$10,000 to $14,999	24	11	13
$15,000 to $19,999	28	18	9
$20,000 to $24,999	52	29	23
$25,000 to $29,999	28	20	9
$30,000 to $34,999	18	6	12
$35,000 to $39,999	23	9	14
$40,000 to $44,999	25	12	13
$45,000 to $49,999	49	27	22
$50,000 to $54,999	14	3	11
$55,000 to $59,999	24	14	10
$60,000 to $64,999	22	17	5
$65,000 to $69,999	22	15	7
$70,000 to $74,999	20	14	6
$75,000 to $79,999	15	8	7
$80,000 to $84,999	24	16	8
$85,000 to $89,999	4	2	2
$90,000 to $94,999	9	6	3
$95,000 to $99,999	6	5	0
$100,000 or more	116	52	64
$100,000 to $124,999	52	23	29
$125,000 to $149,999	29	10	19
$150,000 to $174,999	18	10	8
$175,000 to $199,999	0	0	0
$200,000 or more	17	9	8
Median income	**$49,010**	**$49,352**	**$48,864**
PERCENT DISTRIBUTION			
Asian female-headed families	**100.0%**	**100.0%**	**100.0%**
Under $25,000	26.1	27.4	24.5
$25,000 to $49,999	25.3	23.7	27.3
$50,000 to $74,999	17.9	20.0	15.3
$75,000 to $99,999	10.2	12.0	8.0
$100,000 or more	20.5	16.9	24.8

Note: Asians are those who identify themselves as being of the race alone and those who identify themselves as being of the race in combination with other races.
Source: Bureau of the Census, 2013 Current Population Survey, Internet site http://www.census.gov/hhes/www/cpstables/032013/hhinc/toc.htm; calculations by New Strategist

Table 1.35 Female-Headed Families by Household Income and Age of Householder, 2012: Black Female-Headed Families

(number and percent distribution of black female-headed families by household income and age of householder, 2012; female-headed families in thousands as of 2013)

	total	15 to 24	25 to 34	35 to 44	45 to 54	55 to 64	65 or older total	65 to 74	75 or older
Black female-headed families	4,473	445	1,152	1,108	834	512	422	251	171
Under $5,000	392	77	134	96	47	18	19	10	10
$5,000 to $9,999	352	54	112	71	60	32	24	11	13
$10,000 to $14,999	477	62	157	113	68	40	36	27	10
$15,000 to $19,999	434	46	128	113	70	39	37	18	19
$20,000 to $24,999	437	45	132	102	73	46	39	17	21
$25,000 to $29,999	301	23	82	70	61	30	35	24	11
$30,000 to $34,999	317	20	91	71	52	45	37	24	13
$35,000 to $39,999	286	12	84	81	52	31	26	13	12
$40,000 to $44,999	220	15	49	75	34	19	28	18	10
$45,000 to $49,999	175	19	21	48	46	17	25	12	12
$50,000 to $54,999	144	5	29	34	41	22	13	7	5
$55,000 to $59,999	147	18	26	35	28	25	15	11	4
$60,000 to $64,999	119	6	17	32	23	25	16	12	3
$65,000 to $69,999	108	6	15	35	28	13	11	6	5
$70,000 to $74,999	82	1	12	17	35	11	6	5	1
$75,000 to $79,999	69	4	9	19	18	8	10	4	6
$80,000 to $84,999	63	8	10	10	14	15	5	3	2
$85,000 to $89,999	48	1	2	17	11	7	8	5	3
$90,000 to $94,999	40	7	3	3	17	7	3	1	2
$95,000 to $99,999	32	0	6	16	1	6	3	2	1
$100,000 or more	232	14	33	49	53	56	27	20	6
$100,000 to $124,999	123	3	18	21	35	35	11	6	5
$125,000 to $149,999	41	3	5	8	7	15	3	2	1
$150,000 to $174,999	30	4	8	8	6	2	2	2	0
$175,000 to $199,999	11	2	0	4	2	0	3	3	0
$200,000 or more	26	3	2	9	2	3	7	7	0
Median income	$27,064	$18,502	$21,298	$29,106	$32,823	$36,147	$32,244	$33,618	$30,336

PERCENT DISTRIBUTION

	total	15 to 24	25 to 34	35 to 44	45 to 54	55 to 64	65 or older total	65 to 74	75 or older
Black female-headed families	100.0%	100.0%	100.0%	100.0%	100.0%	100.0%	100.0%	100.0%	100.0%
Under $25,000	46.8	64.0	57.6	44.6	38.2	34.1	37.0	32.9	43.0
$25,000 to $49,999	29.0	19.8	28.4	31.2	29.4	27.9	35.5	36.2	34.5
$50,000 to $74,999	13.4	8.4	8.6	13.8	18.6	18.6	14.3	16.8	10.4
$75,000 to $99,999	5.6	4.7	2.6	5.9	7.5	8.5	6.9	6.0	8.3
$100,000 or more	5.2	3.2	2.9	4.4	6.3	10.9	6.4	8.1	3.8

Note: Blacks are those who identify themselves as being of the race alone and those who identify themselves as being of the race in combination with other races.
Source: Bureau of the Census, 2013 Current Population Survey, Internet site http://www.census.gov/hhes/www/cpstables/032013/hhinc/toc.htm; calculations by New Strategist

Table 1.36 Female-Headed Families by Household Income and Age of Householder, 2012: Hispanic Female-Headed Families

(number and percent distribution of Hispanic female-headed families by household income and age of householder, 2012; female-headed families in thousands as of 2013)

	total	15 to 24	25 to 34	35 to 44	45 to 54	55 to 64	65 or older total	65 to 74	75 or older
Hispanic female-headed families	**3,106**	**384**	**820**	**840**	**519**	**323**	**219**	**135**	**85**
Under $5,000	268	54	83	68	31	22	10	9	1
$5,000 to $9,999	216	34	66	47	35	26	9	8	1
$10,000 to $14,999	276	37	87	86	30	22	14	9	5
$15,000 to $19,999	309	40	92	83	48	25	23	13	11
$20,000 to $24,999	291	34	85	69	49	33	22	12	10
$25,000 to $29,999	290	39	85	64	56	26	20	12	8
$30,000 to $34,999	230	14	54	68	47	33	15	13	2
$35,000 to $39,999	184	25	46	58	27	15	14	5	8
$40,000 to $44,999	150	11	44	27	35	22	12	4	8
$45,000 to $49,999	114	10	21	44	17	11	11	4	7
$50,000 to $54,999	112	11	29	29	20	13	11	7	4
$55,000 to $59,999	119	12	21	35	29	15	6	4	2
$60,000 to $64,999	70	10	26	18	3	3	11	8	3
$65,000 to $69,999	65	4	11	28	7	8	5	4	2
$70,000 to $74,999	38	5	5	11	13	3	1	1	0
$75,000 to $79,999	52	7	10	14	11	5	6	3	3
$80,000 to $84,999	46	6	7	12	13	8	0	0	0
$85,000 to $89,999	38	3	15	6	4	7	5	5	0
$90,000 to $94,999	28	1	8	11	1	4	3	3	0
$95,000 to $99,999	28	4	4	13	2	3	3	2	1
$100,000 or more	181	25	24	50	42	20	19	9	10
$100,000 to $124,999	98	11	15	24	25	11	12	4	8
$125,000 to $149,999	33	5	4	6	9	6	3	1	2
$150,000 to $174,999	26	8	3	10	3	2	1	1	0
$175,000 to $199,999	7	0	0	4	1	0	1	1	0
$200,000 or more	17	1	2	6	4	1	2	2	0
Median income	**$28,075**	**$23,479**	**$24,935**	**$30,164**	**$31,124**	**$30,975**	**$33,284**	**$31,438**	**$37,327**

PERCENT DISTRIBUTION

	total	15 to 24	25 to 34	35 to 44	45 to 54	55 to 64	65 or older total	65 to 74	75 or older
Hispanic female-headed families	**100.0%**	**100.0%**	**100.0%**	**100.0%**	**100.0%**	**100.0%**	**100.0%**	**100.0%**	**100.0%**
Under $25,000	43.8	51.7	50.1	42.0	37.1	39.5	35.5	37.6	32.2
$25,000 to $49,999	31.2	25.6	30.4	31.0	35.0	33.1	32.7	28.7	39.1
$50,000 to $74,999	13.0	10.8	11.3	14.4	13.8	13.1	15.6	17.9	12.0
$75,000 to $99,999	6.2	5.3	5.3	6.6	6.0	8.2	7.4	9.1	4.7
$100,000 or more	5.8	6.5	2.9	6.0	8.1	6.1	8.8	6.7	12.0

Source: Bureau of the Census, 2013 Current Population Survey, Internet site http://www.census.gov/hhes/www/cpstables/ 032013/hhinc/toc.htm; calculations by New Strategist

Table 1.37 Female-Headed Families by Household Income and Age of Householder, 2012: Non-Hispanic White Female-Headed Families

(number and percent distribution of non-Hispanic white female-headed families by household income and age of householder, 2012; female-headed families in thousands as of 2013)

Non-Hispanic white female-headed families	total	15 to 24	25 to 34	35 to 44	45 to 54	55 to 64	65 or older total	65 to 74	75 or older
Non-Hispanic white female-headed families	**7,317**	**513**	**1,299**	**1,562**	**1,619**	**1,023**	**1,301**	**646**	**654**
Under $5,000	300	62	79	74	44	26	15	4	11
$5,000 to $9,999	291	54	89	58	48	22	20	4	15
$10,000 to $14,999	469	51	114	81	80	55	88	36	52
$15,000 to $19,999	504	29	140	105	84	44	102	53	50
$20,000 to $24,999	537	30	112	125	86	68	114	42	72
$25,000 to $29,999	530	39	126	102	106	48	109	39	70
$30,000 to $34,999	478	32	84	118	85	56	104	53	50
$35,000 to $39,999	421	31	67	87	69	64	103	54	49
$40,000 to $44,999	460	20	59	112	133	54	82	44	38
$45,000 to $49,999	344	9	64	74	69	65	63	28	35
$50,000 to $54,999	354	28	50	79	83	45	70	30	40
$55,000 to $59,999	298	10	46	62	82	46	53	19	34
$60,000 to $64,999	274	7	36	75	72	40	44	31	13
$65,000 to $69,999	278	2	43	76	80	41	36	16	20
$70,000 to $74,999	233	20	31	47	60	38	37	24	14
$75,000 to $79,999	186	4	7	35	54	39	47	33	14
$80,000 to $84,999	159	14	14	24	41	40	26	9	18
$85,000 to $89,999	129	5	21	20	34	19	30	19	11
$90,000 to $94,999	131	5	12	25	33	25	32	23	9
$95,000 to $99,999	104	5	15	23	24	20	18	14	4
$100,000 or more	837	59	92	161	252	166	107	72	35
$100,000 to $124,999	370	33	41	71	111	62	51	26	26
$125,000 to $149,999	198	4	30	30	54	44	36	30	6
$150,000 to $174,999	93	0	13	20	30	17	14	12	2
$175,000 to $199,999	64	10	4	12	19	15	4	4	0
$200,000 or more	112	12	4	27	39	29	1	0	1
Median income	**$41,206**	**$28,760**	**$29,597**	**$41,342**	**$50,199**	**$51,335**	**$39,767**	**$44,136**	**$35,767**

PERCENT DISTRIBUTION

Non-Hispanic white female-headed families									
Non-Hispanic white female-headed families	**100.0%**	**100.0%**	**100.0%**	**100.0%**	**100.0%**	**100.0%**	**100.0%**	**100.0%**	**100.0%**
Under $25,000	28.7	44.0	41.1	28.4	21.2	21.1	26.1	21.5	30.6
$25,000 to $49,999	30.5	25.3	30.8	31.6	28.6	28.0	35.5	33.8	37.1
$50,000 to $74,999	19.6	13.0	15.8	21.7	23.2	20.6	18.5	18.4	18.5
$75,000 to $99,999	9.7	6.3	5.2	8.1	11.5	14.0	11.8	15.1	8.5
$100,000 or more	11.4	11.5	7.1	10.3	15.6	16.3	8.2	11.1	5.4

Note: Non-Hispanic whites are those who identify themselves as being white alone and not Hispanic.
Source: Bureau of the Census, 2013 Current Population Survey, Internet site http://www.census.gov/hhes/www/cpstables/032013/hhinc/toc.htm; calculations by New Strategist

Male-Headed Families Have Average Incomes

The median income of male-headed families is slightly below the national median.

Male-headed families are the least-common household type and account for only 5 percent of the nation's households. In 2012, there were 6 million male-headed families versus 15 million families headed by women. The median income of male-headed families stood at $48,634 in 2012, a substantial 43 percent higher than the median income of female-headed families and not far below the $51,017 national median.

Black male-headed families had a median income of $40,301 in 2012, and Hispanic male-headed families had a median income of $45,015. Both black and Hispanic male-headed families have incomes well below the $51,640 of their non-Hispanic white counterparts. Asian male-headed families have the highest incomes—a median of $60,792.

■ Male-headed families are more likely than female-headed families to include two or more earners, which explains their higher incomes.

Among male-headed families, Asians have the highest incomes

(median income of male-headed families by race and Hispanic origin, 2012)

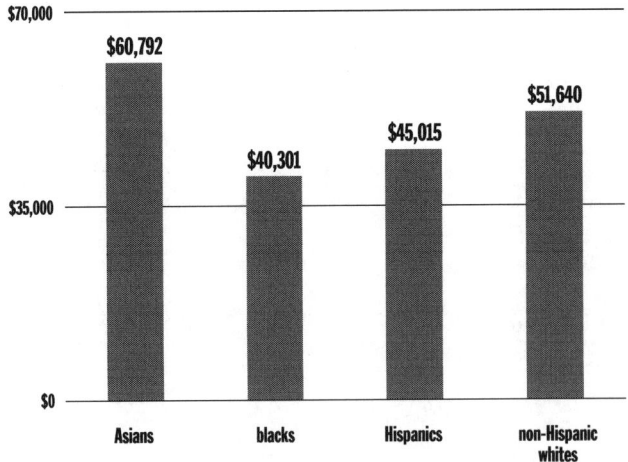

Table 1.38 Male-Headed Families by Household Income and Age of Householder, 2012: Total Male-Headed Families

(number and percent distribution of male-headed families by household income and age of householder, 2012; male-headed families in thousands as of 2013)

	total	15 to 24	25 to 34	35 to 44	45 to 54	55 to 64	65 or older total	65 to 74	75 or older
Total male-headed families	**6,229**	**921**	**1,416**	**1,258**	**1,204**	**812**	**619**	**304**	**316**
Under $5,000	155	23	35	37	30	25	5	5	0
$5,000 to $9,999	157	30	24	22	38	32	10	9	2
$10,000 to $14,999	277	43	57	53	63	35	27	13	13
$15,000 to $19,999	372	66	78	83	54	39	52	19	33
$20,000 to $24,999	391	64	99	60	69	39	59	28	31
$25,000 to $29,999	386	60	66	80	78	45	56	29	28
$30,000 to $34,999	434	73	72	107	95	45	41	21	20
$35,000 to $39,999	353	37	111	67	67	43	27	11	17
$40,000 to $44,999	340	61	77	73	45	49	36	16	19
$45,000 to $49,999	335	54	75	61	83	39	21	9	12
$50,000 to $54,999	348	52	84	54	73	31	54	28	26
$55,000 to $59,999	292	43	60	62	48	56	22	17	5
$60,000 to $64,999	277	32	81	63	48	33	20	12	8
$65,000 to $69,999	230	40	41	53	41	39	17	10	7
$70,000 to $74,999	158	26	31	39	28	18	15	8	7
$75,000 to $79,999	162	10	38	46	22	31	15	6	9
$80,000 to $84,999	187	27	46	40	38	20	17	2	15
$85,000 to $89,999	145	24	36	34	29	15	8	4	4
$90,000 to $94,999	121	10	34	24	23	16	13	8	5
$95,000 to $99,999	97	18	34	15	14	8	8	3	5
$100,000 or more	1,013	127	237	184	216	154	96	45	51
$100,000 to $124,999	437	49	107	90	90	61	41	19	21
$125,000 to $149,999	223	29	57	37	47	27	26	12	14
$150,000 to $174,999	144	18	27	22	36	25	16	9	7
$175,000 to $199,999	66	14	14	13	15	7	3	3	0
$200,000 or more	144	17	33	22	28	34	10	2	9
Median income	**$48,634**	**$45,184**	**$50,660**	**$48,828**	**$48,389**	**$51,458**	**$44,566**	**$45,562**	**$43,687**

PERCENT DISTRIBUTION

	total	15 to 24	25 to 34	35 to 44	45 to 54	55 to 64	65 or older total	65 to 74	75 or older
Total male-headed families	**100.0%**	**100.0%**	**100.0%**	**100.0%**	**100.0%**	**100.0%**	**100.0%**	**100.0%**	**100.0%**
Under $25,000	36.8	50.8	48.8	36.3	28.7	27.6	29.4	26.0	33.4
$25,000 to $49,999	30.1	23.8	29.8	31.0	29.6	29.0	35.1	34.3	36.0
$50,000 to $74,999	16.5	11.4	11.9	18.0	20.2	18.7	17.0	17.7	16.3
$75,000 to $99,999	7.8	6.3	4.5	6.8	9.7	11.1	10.1	12.0	7.9
$100,000 or more	8.8	7.7	5.0	7.8	11.7	13.6	8.4	10.1	6.4

Source: Bureau of the Census, 2013 Current Population Survey, Internet site http://www.census.gov/hhes/www/cpstables/032013/hhinc/toc.htm; calculations by New Strategist

Table 1.39 Male-Headed Families by Household Income and Age of Householder, 2012: Asian Male-Headed Families

(number and percent distribution of Asian male-headed families by household income and age of householder, 2012; male-headed families in thousands as of 2013)

	total	under age 45	aged 45 or older
Asian male-headed families	**346**	**221**	**125**
Under $5,000	11	5	5
$5,000 to $9,999	8	6	2
$10,000 to $14,999	10	9	1
$15,000 to $19,999	13	12	1
$20,000 to $24,999	10	8	1
$25,000 to $29,999	14	9	5
$30,000 to $34,999	23	14	9
$35,000 to $39,999	17	9	8
$40,000 to $44,999	15	3	12
$45,000 to $49,999	15	10	5
$50,000 to $54,999	13	9	4
$55,000 to $59,999	21	16	5
$60,000 to $64,999	24	17	7
$65,000 to $69,999	18	13	5
$70,000 to $74,999	3	3	0
$75,000 to $79,999	5	5	0
$80,000 to $84,999	14	8	6
$85,000 to $89,999	11	6	4
$90,000 to $94,999	9	8	1
$95,000 to $99,999	4	3	1
$100,000 or more	88	46	42
$100,000 to $124,999	37	24	13
$125,000 to $149,999	12	6	7
$150,000 to $174,999	18	4	13
$175,000 to $199,999	3	3	0
$200,000 or more	19	10	9
Median income	**$60,792**	**$59,844**	**$62,500**
PERCENT DISTRIBUTION			
Asian male-headed families	**100.0%**	**100.0%**	**100.0%**
Under $25,000	14.8	18.5	8.3
$25,000 to $49,999	24.2	20.4	30.9
$50,000 to $74,999	23.0	26.0	17.6
$75,000 to $99,999	12.6	14.1	9.9
$100,000 or more	25.5	21.0	33.3

Note: Asians are those who identify themselves as being of the race alone and those who identify themselves as being of the race in combination with other races.
Source: Bureau of the Census, 2013 Current Population Survey, Internet site http://www.census.gov/hhes/www/cpstables/032013/hhinc/toc.htm; calculations by New Strategist

Table 1.40 Male-Headed Families by Household Income and Age of Householder, 2012: Black Male-Headed Families

(number and percent distribution of black male-headed families by household income and age of householder, 2012; male-headed families in thousands as of 2013)

	total	15 to 24	25 to 34	35 to 44	45 to 54	55 to 64	65 or older
Black male-headed families	**1,105**	**176**	**280**	**237**	**187**	**124**	**101**
Under $5,000	60	7	16	10	18	9	0
$5,000 to $9,999	52	6	10	5	16	14	2
$10,000 to $14,999	79	11	23	6	21	9	9
$15,000 to $19,999	93	15	20	31	10	10	7
$20,000 to $24,999	78	6	27	15	14	6	10
$25,000 to $29,999	61	9	8	19	11	6	9
$30,000 to $34,999	74	12	10	24	8	9	11
$35,000 to $39,999	50	6	22	11	4	5	3
$40,000 to $44,999	60	13	15	19	5	2	6
$45,000 to $49,999	64	10	22	7	22	3	0
$50,000 to $54,999	54	4	13	8	12	7	10
$55,000 to $59,999	41	8	7	12	3	5	6
$60,000 to $64,999	46	5	18	7	7	3	6
$65,000 to $69,999	44	11	10	8	6	6	2
$70,000 to $74,999	31	9	6	2	2	6	7
$75,000 to $79,999	28	0	6	16	2	2	1
$80,000 to $84,999	23	9	8	3	0	3	0
$85,000 to $89,999	17	0	2	2	6	3	3
$90,000 to $94,999	10	0	1	2	3	2	2
$95,000 to $99,999	22	0	10	4	2	5	0
$100,000 or more	116	33	27	26	13	9	8
$100,000 to $124,999	60	16	13	17	8	2	5
$125,000 to $149,999	12	5	3	2	1	1	0
$150,000 to $174,999	18	7	4	5	1	0	2
$175,000 to $199,999	9	0	4	2	3	0	0
$200,000 or more	16	5	2	0	1	6	2
Median income	**$40,301**	**$45,478**	**$41,236**	**$38,562**	**$31,980**	**$34,085**	**$39,533**

PERCENT DISTRIBUTION

	total	15 to 24	25 to 34	35 to 44	45 to 54	55 to 64	65 or older
Black male-headed families	**100.0%**	**100.0%**	**100.0%**	**100.0%**	**100.0%**	**100.0%**	**100.0%**
Under $25,000	32.8	26.0	33.8	28.5	42.3	38.7	27.8
$25,000 to $49,999	28.1	28.4	27.8	33.0	27.0	19.8	28.7
$50,000 to $74,999	19.6	21.6	19.1	15.5	16.2	21.9	30.2
$75,000 to $99,999	9.0	5.1	9.8	12.0	7.3	12.6	5.3
$100,000 or more	10.5	18.9	9.5	11.0	7.1	7.0	8.1

Note: Blacks are those who identify themselves as being of the race alone and those who identify themselves as being of the race in combination with other races.
Source: Bureau of the Census, 2013 Current Population Survey, Internet site http://www.census.gov/hhes/www/cpstables/ 032013/hhinc/toc.htm; calculations by New Strategist

Table 1.41 Male-Headed Families by Household Income and Age of Householder, 2012: Hispanic Male-Headed Families

(number and percent distribution of Hispanic male-headed families by household income and age of householder, 2012; male-headed families in thousands as of 2013)

	total	15 to 24	25 to 34	35 to 44	45 to 54	55 to 64	65 or older
Hispanic male-headed families	**1,391**	**335**	**404**	**277**	**220**	**96**	**59**
Under $5,000	29	8	6	9	3	2	1
$5,000 to $9,999	38	11	7	6	4	4	5
$10,000 to $14,999	64	20	14	8	9	9	4
$15,000 to $19,999	104	29	34	13	10	8	9
$20,000 to $24,999	88	27	21	12	22	5	1
$25,000 to $29,999	96	27	22	15	17	11	6
$30,000 to $34,999	102	29	21	21	12	9	9
$35,000 to $39,999	83	21	30	18	12	3	0
$40,000 to $44,999	92	23	27	23	15	1	3
$45,000 to $49,999	66	15	16	15	18	3	0
$50,000 to $54,999	71	16	18	18	13	5	0
$55,000 to $59,999	84	23	23	14	11	9	2
$60,000 to $64,999	61	6	21	20	7	6	1
$65,000 to $69,999	48	13	12	11	8	2	3
$70,000 to $74,999	41	10	5	13	10	0	2
$75,000 to $79,999	23	1	7	4	5	6	0
$80,000 to $84,999	47	8	26	6	3	3	1
$85,000 to $89,999	31	10	11	5	3	1	2
$90,000 to $94,999	21	5	7	5	1	1	1
$95,000 to $99,999	12	0	7	3	0	1	0
$100,000 or more	192	34	70	39	35	6	8
$100,000 to $124,999	94	18	36	23	16	1	0
$125,000 to $149,999	43	9	18	3	8	2	3
$150,000 to $174,999	21	1	3	8	6	1	2
$175,000 to $199,999	13	4	2	4	2	2	0
$200,000 or more	21	3	11	1	2	0	3
Median income	**$45,015**	**$37,382**	**$51,245**	**$49,897**	**$46,537**	**$37,646**	–

PERCENT DISTRIBUTION

	total	15 to 24	25 to 34	35 to 44	45 to 54	55 to 64	65 or older
Hispanic male-headed families	**100.0%**	**100.0%**	**100.0%**	**100.0%**	**100.0%**	**100.0%**	**100.0%**
Under $25,000	23.2	28.3	20.3	17.2	22.1	29.3	35.3
$25,000 to $49,999	31.6	34.2	28.6	32.9	33.3	28.1	31.1
$50,000 to $74,999	21.8	20.3	19.7	27.4	22.9	23.5	13.2
$75,000 to $99,999	9.6	7.1	14.1	8.3	5.9	12.8	6.7
$100,000 or more	13.8	10.2	17.3	14.3	15.9	6.3	13.6

Note: "–" means sample is too small to make a reliable estimate.
Source: Bureau of the Census, 2013 Current Population Survey, Internet site http://www.census.gov/hhes/www/cpstables/032013/hhinc/toc.htm; calculations by New Strategist

Table 1.42 Male-Headed Families by Household Income and Age of Householder, 2012: Non-Hispanic White Male-Headed Families

(number and percent distribution of non-Hispanic white male-headed families by household income and age of householder, 2012; male-headed families in thousands as of 2013)

	total	15 to 24	25 to 34	35 to 44	45 to 54	55 to 64	65 or older total	65 to 74	75 or older
Non-Hispanic white male-headed families	**3,388**	**357**	**646**	**695**	**720**	**531**	**438**	**217**	**221**
Under $5,000	48	4	10	16	7	10	3	3	0
$5,000 to $9,999	61	11	6	10	18	12	4	4	0
$10,000 to $14,999	119	9	18	29	31	20	12	4	8
$15,000 to $19,999	163	16	25	33	32	21	36	11	25
$20,000 to $24,999	209	21	52	34	33	23	46	21	25
$25,000 to $29,999	209	24	29	44	46	25	41	24	17
$30,000 to $34,999	237	31	37	58	70	23	20	14	6
$35,000 to $39,999	200	11	49	37	45	33	24	9	15
$40,000 to $44,999	184	25	40	34	20	38	27	13	13
$45,000 to $49,999	186	28	33	38	35	31	21	9	12
$50,000 to $54,999	198	20	49	28	43	16	43	20	23
$55,000 to $59,999	148	9	23	33	32	40	12	11	1
$60,000 to $64,999	145	17	36	29	30	22	11	6	5
$65,000 to $69,999	127	15	15	32	23	29	11	9	3
$70,000 to $74,999	86	9	20	22	16	12	7	4	3
$75,000 to $79,999	105	7	24	22	16	22	14	6	8
$80,000 to $84,999	107	6	14	28	32	12	14	2	12
$85,000 to $89,999	84	11	19	24	17	9	4	3	0
$90,000 to $94,999	81	6	22	14	18	12	10	5	5
$95,000 to $99,999	58	14	16	8	11	1	8	3	5
$100,000 or more	635	63	110	121	146	122	72	38	35
$100,000 to $124,999	257	22	37	54	53	55	36	17	18
$125,000 to $149,999	155	15	32	31	37	19	22	11	10
$150,000 to $174,999	89	8	20	11	22	20	8	6	2
$175,000 to $199,999	41	11	6	6	11	5	3	3	0
$200,000 or more	92	8	14	21	22	23	4	0	4
Median income	**$51,640**	**$49,797**	**$52,057**	**$52,223**	**$52,028**	**$57,285**	**$46,812**	**$48,879**	**$45,395**

PERCENT DISTRIBUTION

Non-Hispanic white male-headed families	**100.0%**	**100.0%**	**100.0%**	**100.0%**	**100.0%**	**100.0%**	**100.0%**	**100.0%**	**100.0%**
Under $25,000	17.7	17.0	17.1	17.5	16.9	16.0	22.7	19.2	26.2
$25,000 to $49,999	30.0	33.4	29.0	30.3	29.9	28.2	30.2	31.7	28.8
$50,000 to $74,999	20.8	19.6	22.1	20.8	19.9	22.2	19.4	23.0	15.8
$75,000 to $99,999	12.8	12.2	14.7	13.8	13.1	10.6	11.2	8.8	13.6
$100,000 or more	18.7	17.8	17.0	17.5	20.2	22.9	16.5	17.3	15.6

Note: Non-Hispanic whites are those who identify themselves as being white alone and not Hispanic.
Source: Bureau of the Census, 2013 Current Population Survey, Internet site http://www.census.gov/hhes/www/cpstables/ 032013/hhinc/toc.htm; calculations by New Strategist

Women Who Live Alone Have the Lowest Incomes

Most of them are older, which is why their incomes are low.

Households headed by people who live alone are the second-most-common household type in the United States, second only to married couples without children at home. Among single-person households, those headed by women are more numerous than those headed by men—19 million versus 15 million.

The median income of women who live alone was just $22,794 in 2012, but there is great variation by age. Two out of three women who live alone are aged 55 or older. Many are widows and not in the workforce. Consequently, their incomes are low. In contrast, younger women who live alone have incomes almost as high as their male counterparts. Among 35-to-44-year-olds who live by themselves, for example, the $37,517 median income of women was not much lower than the $39,579 median income of men.

Older Hispanic women who live alone have the lowest incomes of any households in the nation. The median income of Hispanic women aged 75 or older who live alone was below $12,000 in 2012.

■ The incomes of older women who live alone should rise as the working women of the baby-boom generation enter the older age groups.

Among women who live alone, those aged 35 to 44 have the highest incomes

(median household income of women who live alone by age, 2012)

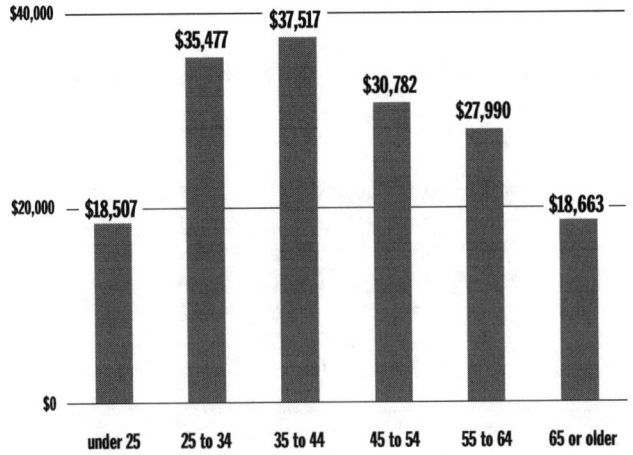

Table 1.43 Women Who Live Alone by Household Income and Age of Householder, 2012: Total Women Who Live Alone

(number and percent distribution of women who live alone by household income and age of householder, 2012; women who live alone in thousands as of 2013)

	total	15 to 24	25 to 34	35 to 44	45 to 54	55 to 64	65 or older total	65 to 74	75 or older
Total women who live alone	18,568	788	1,818	1,296	2,432	3,805	8,429	3,534	4,895
Under $5,000	1,192	109	127	113	207	275	361	149	212
$5,000 to $9,999	1,842	75	137	79	251	432	868	324	544
$10,000 to $14,999	2,746	113	105	76	272	429	1,751	603	1,147
$15,000 to $19,999	2,351	142	96	79	146	288	1,601	542	1,059
$20,000 to $24,999	1,849	129	141	79	158	327	1,015	380	635
$25,000 to $29,999	1,367	58	142	69	152	231	715	315	401
$30,000 to $34,999	1,082	35	139	84	133	264	427	205	222
$35,000 to $39,999	900	32	159	104	94	205	305	170	136
$40,000 to $44,999	766	28	88	50	135	180	284	136	148
$45,000 to $49,999	687	14	133	75	119	163	184	110	74
$50,000 to $54,999	622	16	112	74	88	153	179	102	76
$55,000 to $59,999	505	11	72	77	129	120	96	58	38
$60,000 to $64,999	482	8	66	54	80	137	137	102	35
$65,000 to $69,999	311	6	40	39	71	67	87	61	26
$70,000 to $74,999	299	2	27	52	76	71	70	43	27
$75,000 to $79,999	241	3	52	22	46	72	47	36	11
$80,000 to $84,999	209	0	18	22	45	62	61	41	20
$85,000 to $89,999	110	4	11	15	16	27	38	19	18
$90,000 to $94,999	165	0	41	13	35	56	20	16	4
$95,000 to $99,999	93	0	16	8	16	36	17	16	1
$100,000 or more	749	4	95	111	162	210	166	106	60
$100,000 to $124,999	351	2	48	44	79	96	82	45	38
$125,000 to $149,999	156	2	24	23	20	49	39	23	16
$150,000 to $174,999	87	0	10	12	24	17	23	21	2
$175,000 to $199,999	27	0	0	2	10	8	7	5	2
$200,000 or more	128	0	14	30	29	41	14	12	2
Median income	$22,794	$18,507	$35,477	$37,517	$30,782	$27,990	$18,663	$21,712	$17,392

PERCENT DISTRIBUTION

	total	15 to 24	25 to 34	35 to 44	45 to 54	55 to 64	65 or older total	65 to 74	75 or older
Total women who live alone	100.0%	100.0%	100.0%	100.0%	100.0%	100.0%	100.0%	100.0%	100.0%
Under $25,000	53.7	72.0	33.4	32.9	42.5	46.0	66.4	56.5	73.5
$25,000 to $49,999	25.9	21.1	36.3	29.5	26.0	27.4	22.7	26.5	20.0
$50,000 to $74,999	11.9	5.5	17.5	22.8	18.3	14.4	6.7	10.4	4.1
$75,000 to $99,999	4.4	0.9	7.6	6.2	6.5	6.6	2.2	3.6	1.1
$100,000 or more	4.0	0.5	5.2	8.6	6.6	5.5	2.0	3.0	1.2

Source: Bureau of the Census, 2013 Current Population Survey, Internet site http://www.census.gov/hhes/www/cpstables/032013/hhinc/toc.htm; calculations by New Strategist

Table 1.44 Women Who Live Alone by Household Income and Age of Householder, 2012: Asian Women Who Live Alone

(number and percent distribution of Asian women who live alone by household income and age of householder, 2012; women who live alone in thousands as of 2013)

	total	15 to 24	25 to 34	35 to 44	45 to 54	55 to 64	65 or older
Asian women who live alone	**610**	**46**	**130**	**83**	**92**	**83**	**176**
Under $5,000	54	10	14	3	12	10	6
$5,000 to $9,999	57	3	4	2	2	14	31
$10,000 to $14,999	73	6	3	3	15	7	39
$15,000 to $19,999	54	5	2	2	7	8	29
$20,000 to $24,999	42	2	2	7	3	1	27
$25,000 to $29,999	44	5	8	4	10	6	11
$30,000 to $34,999	28	0	7	10	1	3	6
$35,000 to $39,999	26	3	2	4	3	6	8
$40,000 to $44,999	18	2	4	2	0	5	5
$45,000 to $49,999	19	0	6	8	3	0	1
$50,000 to $54,999	29	3	17	5	1	2	1
$55,000 to $59,999	22	0	7	5	7	0	3
$60,000 to $64,999	25	4	7	6	5	3	0
$65,000 to $69,999	9	0	7	0	0	2	0
$70,000 to $74,999	17	2	3	6	1	0	4
$75,000 to $79,999	11	0	8	0	3	0	0
$80,000 to $84,999	10	0	3	0	2	4	1
$85,000 to $89,999	6	0	2	2	0	1	0
$90,000 to $94,999	16	0	5	3	4	4	0
$95,000 to $99,999	6	0	4	0	2	0	1
$100,000 or more	46	0	15	9	11	8	3
$100,000 to $124,999	15	0	6	1	6	0	3
$125,000 to $149,999	13	0	4	4	2	4	0
$150,000 to $174,999	6	0	2	2	0	2	0
$175,000 to $199,999	4	0	0	0	3	0	0
$200,000 or more	8	0	3	2	0	3	0
Median income	**$27,372**	–	**$53,641**	**$46,027**	**$28,266**	**$27,742**	**$17,149**

PERCENT DISTRIBUTION

	total	15 to 24	25 to 34	35 to 44	45 to 54	55 to 64	65 or older
Asian women who live alone	**100.0%**	**100.0%**	**100.0%**	**100.0%**	**100.0%**	**100.0%**	**100.0%**
Under $25,000	45.8	57.4	19.5	21.6	42.1	47.0	74.8
$25,000 to $49,999	22.0	23.1	20.9	34.6	19.1	23.1	17.7
$50,000 to $74,999	16.7	19.5	31.4	26.7	15.3	8.6	4.9
$75,000 to $99,999	8.0	0.0	16.7	6.3	11.9	11.0	1.1
$100,000 or more	7.5	0.0	11.6	10.8	11.6	10.2	1.5

Note: Asians are those who identify themselves as being of the race alone and those who identify themselves as being of the race in combination with other races. "–" means sample is too small to make a reliable estimate.
Source: Bureau of the Census, 2013 Current Population Survey, Internet site http://www.census.gov/hhes/www/cpstables/ 032013/hhinc/toc.htm; calculations by New Strategist

Table 1.45 Women Who Live Alone by Household Income and Age of Householder, 2012: Black Women Who Live Alone

(number and percent distribution of black women who live alone by household income and age of householder, 2012; women who live alone in thousands as of 2013)

	total	15 to 24	25 to 34	35 to 44	45 to 54	55 to 64	65 or older total	65 to 74	75 or older
Black women who live alone	3,042	194	391	307	560	674	917	486	430
Under $5,000	301	36	31	22	68	89	56	17	38
$5,000 to $9,999	497	36	50	23	90	125	173	82	91
$10,000 to $14,999	455	17	21	19	64	83	252	113	139
$15,000 to $19,999	314	42	19	17	48	66	123	74	48
$20,000 to $24,999	268	22	44	25	38	59	79	33	46
$25,000 to $29,999	182	6	40	9	30	35	62	37	25
$30,000 to $34,999	177	7	24	31	34	36	44	28	16
$35,000 to $39,999	152	5	38	30	27	23	28	20	8
$40,000 to $44,999	126	10	24	19	26	27	20	16	4
$45,000 to $49,999	114	4	37	26	20	15	13	12	0
$50,000 to $54,999	78	2	17	16	7	23	13	7	6
$55,000 to $59,999	87	0	13	24	23	15	13	13	0
$60,000 to $64,999	51	0	2	10	18	15	6	6	0
$65,000 to $69,999	35	0	2	4	14	13	2	2	0
$70,000 to $74,999	23	0	3	3	6	8	4	2	2
$75,000 to $79,999	21	0	4	7	4	4	2	2	0
$80,000 to $84,999	42	0	6	2	12	16	6	5	2
$85,000 to $89,999	16	4	2	3	2	2	2	2	0
$90,000 to $94,999	12	0	3	0	5	4	0	0	0
$95,000 to $99,999	10	0	2	1	4	2	1	1	0
$100,000 or more	81	2	10	16	20	15	19	14	5
$100,000 to $124,999	31	0	2	6	7	4	12	9	3
$125,000 to $149,999	23	2	8	2	6	3	3	2	1
$150,000 to $174,999	9	0	0	2	2	2	4	3	1
$175,000 to $199,999	2	0	0	2	0	0	0	0	0
$200,000 or more	15	0	0	4	6	6	0	0	0
Median income	$19,165	$16,287	$27,422	$36,038	$21,052	$17,695	$14,413	$16,433	$12,460

PERCENT DISTRIBUTION

Black women who live alone	100.0%	100.0%	100.0%	100.0%	100.0%	100.0%	100.0%	100.0%	100.0%
Under $25,000	60.3	79.3	42.0	34.5	55.0	62.5	74.4	65.8	84.1
$25,000 to $49,999	24.7	16.6	41.9	37.4	24.6	20.1	18.2	23.3	12.5
$50,000 to $74,999	9.0	1.1	9.4	18.5	12.2	11.0	4.0	5.9	1.9
$75,000 to $99,999	3.3	2.0	4.2	4.5	4.6	4.3	1.3	2.1	0.4
$100,000 or more	2.7	1.0	2.5	5.1	3.6	2.2	2.1	2.9	1.1

Note: Blacks are those who identify themselves as being of the race alone and those who identify themselves as being of the race in combination with other races.
Source: Bureau of the Census, 2013 Current Population Survey, Internet site http://www.census.gov/hhes/www/cpstables/032013/hhinc/toc.htm; calculations by New Strategist

Table 1.46 Women Who Live Alone by Household Income and Age of Householder, 2012: Hispanic Women Who Live Alone

(number and percent distribution of Hispanic women who live alone by household income and age of householder, 2012; women who live alone in thousands as of 2013)

	total	15 to 24	25 to 34	35 to 44	45 to 54	55 to 64	65 or older total	65 to 74	75 or older
Hispanic women who live alone	**1,367**	**64**	**176**	**129**	**204**	**324**	**469**	**227**	**242**
Under $5,000	159	17	19	15	18	39	50	27	23
$5,000 to $9,999	230	7	20	12	29	66	97	47	49
$10,000 to $14,999	275	4	11	19	38	51	152	58	95
$15,000 to $19,999	127	7	10	12	16	22	59	29	30
$20,000 to $24,999	113	3	20	11	18	19	41	18	23
$25,000 to $29,999	64	4	16	5	14	15	10	2	8
$30,000 to $34,999	69	12	5	5	6	30	10	5	5
$35,000 to $39,999	52	6	11	8	9	9	9	7	2
$40,000 to $44,999	36	3	10	6	3	5	9	7	3
$45,000 to $49,999	41	0	10	4	9	10	8	7	1
$50,000 to $54,999	38	2	8	3	6	14	4	4	0
$55,000 to $59,999	27	0	8	1	9	10	0	0	0
$60,000 to $64,999	20	0	3	4	4	6	2	0	2
$65,000 to $69,999	10	0	1	3	3	0	3	1	1
$70,000 to $74,999	11	0	2	2	4	2	1	1	0
$75,000 to $79,999	17	0	4	1	6	1	4	4	0
$80,000 to $84,999	9	0	3	2	0	1	3	3	0
$85,000 to $89,999	5	0	2	0	0	2	1	0	1
$90,000 to $94,999	8	0	1	0	2	4	0	0	0
$95,000 to $99,999	8	0	2	0	0	6	0	0	0
$100,000 or more	49	0	9	16	8	12	4	4	0
$100,000 to $124,999	21	0	4	12	0	4	0	0	0
$125,000 to $149,999	3	0	3	0	0	1	0	0	0
$150,000 to $174,999	6	0	0	3	0	3	0	0	0
$175,000 to $199,999	2	0	0	0	1	1	0	0	0
$200,000 or more	17	0	2	1	7	3	4	4	0
Median income	**$15,675**	**–**	**$27,111**	**$22,041**	**$19,995**	**$16,421**	**$12,297**	**$13,150**	**$11,932**

PERCENT DISTRIBUTION

	total	15 to 24	25 to 34	35 to 44	45 to 54	55 to 64	65 or older total	65 to 74	75 or older
Hispanic women who live alone	**100.0%**	**100.0%**	**100.0%**	**100.0%**	**100.0%**	**100.0%**	**100.0%**	**100.0%**	**100.0%**
Under $25,000	66.2	59.0	45.4	53.1	58.9	61.0	85.2	79.3	90.8
$25,000 to $49,999	19.2	37.9	29.9	21.4	20.1	21.4	10.0	12.6	7.5
$50,000 to $74,999	7.7	2.8	12.6	10.9	13.0	9.7	2.1	3.1	1.2
$75,000 to $99,999	3.3	0.0	7.0	2.0	4.1	4.2	1.8	3.2	0.5
$100,000 or more	3.6	0.2	5.1	12.6	3.8	3.6	0.9	1.8	0.0

Note: "–" means sample is too small to make a reliable estimate.
Source: Bureau of the Census, 2013 Current Population Survey, Internet site http://www.census.gov/hhes/www/cpstables/032013/hhinc/toc.htm; calculations by New Strategist

Table 1.47 Women Who Live Alone by Household Income and Age of Householder, 2012: Non-Hispanic White Women Who Live Alone

(number and percent distribution of non-Hispanic white women who live alone by household income and age of householder, 2012; women who live alone in thousands as of 2013)

	total	15 to 24	25 to 34	35 to 44	45 to 54	55 to 64	65 or older total	65 to 74	75 or older
Non-Hispanic white women who live alone	13,476	478	1,116	785	1,560	2,703	6,835	2,734	4,101
Under $5,000	673	45	58	73	108	141	249	100	149
$5,000 to $9,999	1,057	27	65	42	124	226	573	190	384
$10,000 to $14,999	1,928	86	69	34	157	286	1,296	408	888
$15,000 to $19,999	1,844	86	64	46	76	190	1,382	431	951
$20,000 to $24,999	1,431	98	80	35	105	247	866	310	556
$25,000 to $29,999	1,059	43	76	52	91	172	625	267	358
$30,000 to $34,999	795	16	101	36	87	189	366	170	196
$35,000 to $39,999	665	17	104	66	53	169	256	137	119
$40,000 to $44,999	583	15	50	27	101	140	250	113	136
$45,000 to $49,999	511	9	78	39	87	136	162	91	71
$50,000 to $54,999	476	9	70	51	74	115	158	89	69
$55,000 to $59,999	375	11	47	49	92	95	81	45	36
$60,000 to $64,999	378	4	51	34	52	109	128	95	33
$65,000 to $69,999	257	6	30	31	54	52	83	58	25
$70,000 to $74,999	246	0	19	41	65	62	59	36	24
$75,000 to $79,999	195	3	40	14	33	65	41	30	11
$80,000 to $84,999	149	0	7	18	31	41	52	34	18
$85,000 to $89,999	82	0	5	9	12	22	34	17	17
$90,000 to $94,999	129	0	32	10	24	43	20	15	4
$95,000 to $99,999	69	0	9	6	10	28	15	15	0
$100,000 or more	570	2	62	70	124	174	139	84	55
$100,000 to $124,999	280	2	36	23	65	86	69	34	35
$125,000 to $149,999	117	0	10	19	12	41	35	20	14
$150,000 to $174,999	66	0	8	6	22	10	19	18	1
$175,000 to $199,999	19	0	0	0	6	7	6	4	2
$200,000 or more	89	0	8	23	19	29	10	8	2
Median income	$24,233	$19,712	$36,439	$40,986	$37,030	$31,865	$19,652	$23,654	$18,158

PERCENT DISTRIBUTION

Non-Hispanic white women who live alone	100.0%	100.0%	100.0%	100.0%	100.0%	100.0%	100.0%	100.0%	100.0%
Under $25,000	51.5	71.6	30.1	29.3	36.5	40.3	63.9	52.6	71.4
$25,000 to $49,999	26.8	21.0	36.7	28.0	26.8	29.8	24.3	28.5	21.5
$50,000 to $74,999	12.9	6.4	19.4	26.3	21.6	16.1	7.4	11.8	4.5
$75,000 to $99,999	4.6	0.7	8.3	7.5	7.1	7.3	2.4	4.1	1.2
$100,000 or more	4.2	0.4	5.5	8.9	7.9	6.4	2.0	3.1	1.3

Note: Non-Hispanic whites are those who identify themselves as being white alone and not Hispanic.
Source: Bureau of the Census, 2013 Current Population Survey, Internet site http://www.census.gov/hhes/www/cpstables/032013/hhinc/toc.htm; calculations by New Strategist

Incomes Are Low for Men Who Live Alone

The median income of men who live alone is well below the national average.

Both men and women who live alone have below-average incomes. The median income of men who live alone is considerably higher than that of women who live alone, however—$31,212 versus $22,794 in 2012.

Most of the income gap between men and women who live alone is explained by their differing ages. While two-thirds of women who live alone are aged 55 or older, most men who live alone are under age 55. Many women who live alone are widows and not in the labor force. Most men who live alone have a job, which is why their overall median is substantially higher. Among men and women under age 55 who live alone, the incomes of men and women are similar.

The median income of black men who live alone was just $23,163 in 2012, while the figure was slightly higher for Hispanic men at $26,517. The median income of non-Hispanic white men who live alone stood at $34,191, while their Asian counterparts had a higher median of $40,711.

■ The incomes of older men who live alone may rise in the years ahead as fewer opt for early retirement.

Among men who live alone, incomes peak in the 35-to-44 age group

(median household income of men who live alone by age, 2012)

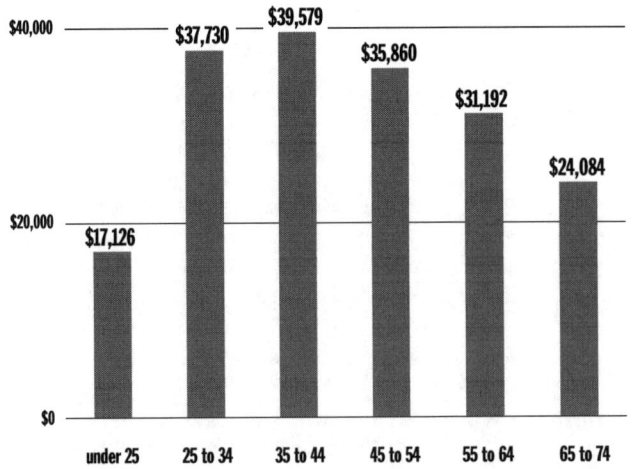

Table 1.48 Men Who Live Alone by Household Income and Age of Householder, 2012: Total Men Who Live Alone

(number and percent distribution of men who live alone by household income and age of householder, 2012; men who live alone in thousands as of 2013)

	total	15 to 24	25 to 34	35 to 44	45 to 54	55 to 64	65 or older total	65 to 74	75 or older
Total men who live alone	15,002	760	2,433	2,161	2,880	3,110	3,658	1,888	1,770
Under $5,000	939	127	98	134	245	213	122	61	61
$5,000 to $9,999	1,109	98	143	85	228	325	230	138	93
$10,000 to $14,999	1,445	112	133	141	198	304	556	256	300
$15,000 to $19,999	1,392	78	134	128	204	283	564	251	313
$20,000 to $24,999	1,196	90	173	137	174	210	413	209	204
$25,000 to $29,999	1,089	55	211	171	207	169	276	144	132
$30,000 to $34,999	1,026	37	207	195	154	165	269	134	135
$35,000 to $39,999	855	40	166	95	149	187	217	99	118
$40,000 to $44,999	871	37	154	131	150	204	195	114	81
$45,000 to $49,999	742	11	164	135	177	129	126	65	61
$50,000 to $54,999	651	28	152	106	126	141	98	49	49
$55,000 to $59,999	397	7	72	74	71	95	77	49	28
$60,000 to $64,999	430	1	79	76	78	116	81	48	33
$65,000 to $69,999	361	2	73	74	78	79	55	29	27
$70,000 to $74,999	377	11	102	64	93	61	45	35	9
$75,000 to $79,999	271	3	58	76	52	45	37	31	6
$80,000 to $84,999	259	7	50	39	63	56	44	24	20
$85,000 to $89,999	137	4	20	27	22	38	26	13	13
$90,000 to $94,999	174	2	49	32	40	24	27	13	14
$95,000 to $99,999	128	3	20	23	27	28	28	10	18
$100,000 or more	1,152	5	175	217	346	236	172	117	55
$100,000 to $124,999	467	3	86	103	143	78	53	44	10
$125,000 to $149,999	261	1	24	31	76	65	64	43	21
$150,000 to $174,999	130	1	20	29	38	23	19	12	7
$175,000 to $199,999	63	0	12	13	20	17	1	1	0
$200,000 or more	232	0	34	40	69	54	34	17	17
Median income	$31,212	$17,126	$37,730	$39,579	$35,860	$31,192	$24,084	$25,996	$22,078

PERCENT DISTRIBUTION

	total	15 to 24	25 to 34	35 to 44	45 to 54	55 to 64	65 or older total	65 to 74	75 or older
Total men who live alone	100.0%	100.0%	100.0%	100.0%	100.0%	100.0%	100.0%	100.0%	100.0%
Under $25,000	40.5	66.5	28.0	28.9	36.4	42.9	51.6	48.4	54.9
$25,000 to $49,999	30.5	23.8	37.1	33.6	29.1	27.5	29.6	29.4	29.7
$50,000 to $74,999	14.8	6.5	19.6	18.3	15.5	15.8	9.7	11.2	8.2
$75,000 to $99,999	6.5	2.6	8.1	9.1	7.1	6.2	4.4	4.8	4.0
$100,000 or more	7.7	0.7	7.2	10.1	12.0	7.6	4.7	6.2	3.1

Source: Bureau of the Census, 2013 Current Population Survey, Internet site http://www.census.gov/hhes/www/cpstables/032013/hhinc/toc.htm; calculations by New Strategist

Table 1.49 Men Who Live Alone by Household Income and Age of Householder, 2012:
Asian Men Who Live Alone

(number and percent distribution of Asian men who live alone by household income and age of householder, 2012; men who live alone in thousands as of 2013)

	total	under age 45	aged 45 or older
Asian men who live alone	**539**	**363**	**176**
Under $5,000	58	50	8
$5,000 to $9,999	32	14	18
$10,000 to $14,999	35	12	23
$15,000 to $19,999	26	10	16
$20,000 to $24,999	34	20	15
$25,000 to $29,999	29	16	12
$30,000 to $34,999	33	19	15
$35,000 to $39,999	16	8	8
$40,000 to $44,999	25	21	5
$45,000 to $49,999	22	17	5
$50,000 to $54,999	22	17	5
$55,000 to $59,999	21	18	3
$60,000 to $64,999	22	13	9
$65,000 to $69,999	19	19	0
$70,000 to $74,999	20	18	2
$75,000 to $79,999	15	15	0
$80,000 to $84,999	17	17	0
$85,000 to $89,999	10	7	3
$90,000 to $94,999	16	14	2
$95,000 to $99,999	8	5	3
$100,000 or more	58	34	25
$100,000 to $124,999	26	18	8
$125,000 to $149,999	7	4	2
$150,000 to $174,999	11	6	6
$175,000 to $199,999	2	0	2
$200,000 or more	12	5	7
Median income	**$40,711**	**$48,382**	**$28,333**
PERCENT DISTRIBUTION			
Asian men who live alone	**100.0%**	**100.0%**	**100.0%**
Under $25,000	34.4	29.1	45.6
$25,000 to $49,999	23.3	22.4	25.2
$50,000 to $74,999	19.2	23.4	10.5
$75,000 to $99,999	12.2	15.9	4.6
$100,000 or more	10.8	9.3	14.1

Note: Asians are those who identify themselves as being of the race alone and those who identify themselves as being of the race in combination with other races.
Source: Bureau of the Census, 2013 Current Population Survey, Internet site http://www.census.gov/hhes/www/cpstables/ 032013/hhinc/toc.htm; calculations by New Strategist

Table 1.50 Men Who Live Alone by Household Income and Age of Householder, 2012: Black Men Who Live Alone

(number and percent distribution of black men who live alone by household income and age of householder, 2012; men who live alone in thousands as of 2013)

| | total | 15 to 24 | 25 to 34 | 35 to 44 | 45 to 54 | 55 to 64 | 65 or older | | |
							total	65 to 74	75 or older
Black men who live alone	**2,370**	**150**	**444**	**357**	**479**	**481**	**459**	**294**	**165**
Under $5,000	218	26	22	36	68	38	28	17	11
$5,000 to $9,999	306	36	36	32	50	96	56	39	17
$10,000 to $14,999	323	37	36	39	50	71	90	53	36
$15,000 to $19,999	200	8	27	29	39	33	65	36	28
$20,000 to $24,999	194	18	39	17	37	27	55	29	26
$25,000 to $29,999	188	9	58	25	38	30	27	18	10
$30,000 to $34,999	174	3	51	33	42	27	18	14	4
$35,000 to $39,999	118	2	26	26	19	24	21	19	2
$40,000 to $44,999	115	2	15	30	19	23	27	18	9
$45,000 to $49,999	115	6	24	24	25	23	14	9	5
$50,000 to $54,999	80	2	20	19	11	19	8	5	3
$55,000 to $59,999	30	0	12	6	4	4	4	4	0
$60,000 to $64,999	52	0	12	6	16	12	5	0	5
$65,000 to $69,999	28	0	7	7	4	8	2	2	1
$70,000 to $74,999	30	0	7	3	10	3	8	8	0
$75,000 to $79,999	33	0	4	6	7	8	7	6	1
$80,000 to $84,999	20	0	2	0	6	8	4	4	0
$85,000 to $89,999	15	0	4	4	4	2	0	0	0
$90,000 to $94,999	21	0	13	2	5	0	0	0	0
$95,000 to $99,999	17	0	2	2	5	6	2	1	0
$100,000 or more	95	0	28	11	18	20	18	13	5
$100,000 to $124,999	34	0	12	4	5	7	6	6	0
$125,000 to $149,999	19	0	2	2	4	5	7	3	3
$150,000 to $174,999	10	0	0	1	4	4	0	0	0
$175,000 to $199,999	11	0	4	3	2	2	0	0	0
$200,000 or more	22	0	10	2	4	1	5	4	2
Median income	**$23,163**	**$11,678**	**$30,290**	**$29,811**	**$24,209**	**$20,547**	**$19,185**	**$20,208**	**$17,358**

PERCENT DISTRIBUTION

Black men who live alone	**100.0%**	**100.0%**	**100.0%**	**100.0%**	**100.0%**	**100.0%**	**100.0%**	**100.0%**	**100.0%**
Under $25,000	52.4	83.4	36.0	43.1	51.0	54.9	64.0	59.1	72.7
$25,000 to $49,999	30.0	15.1	38.8	38.6	29.8	26.3	23.4	26.4	18.0
$50,000 to $74,999	9.3	1.3	13.1	11.3	9.5	9.6	5.9	6.2	5.4
$75,000 to $99,999	4.4	0.0	5.8	4.0	5.9	5.0	2.8	3.8	1.0
$100,000 or more	4.0	0.2	6.2	3.0	3.8	4.1	3.9	4.5	2.9

Note: Blacks are those who identify themselves as being of the race alone and those who identify themselves as being of the race in combination with other races.
Source: Bureau of the Census, 2013 Current Population Survey, Internet site http://www.census.gov/hhes/www/cpstables/032013/hhinc/toc.htm; calculations by New Strategist

Table 1.51 Men Who Live Alone by Household Income and Age of Householder, 2012: Hispanic Men Who Live Alone

(number and percent distribution of Hispanic men who live alone by household income and age of householder, 2012; men who live alone in thousands as of 2013)

	total	15 to 24	25 to 34	35 to 44	45 to 54	55 to 64	65 or older total	65 to 74	75 or older
Hispanic men who live alone	**1,345**	**81**	**265**	**289**	**269**	**246**	**194**	**115**	**78**
Under $5,000	118	12	13	24	28	27	15	4	11
$5,000 to $9,999	134	14	19	13	12	37	37	32	5
$10,000 to $14,999	155	8	19	20	20	39	49	24	24
$15,000 to $19,999	120	6	24	21	14	28	27	18	8
$20,000 to $24,999	106	13	22	28	24	14	7	6	0
$25,000 to $29,999	129	12	31	38	30	16	4	3	1
$30,000 to $34,999	104	9	24	27	10	18	17	7	9
$35,000 to $39,999	74	1	18	16	19	14	6	3	3
$40,000 to $44,999	80	0	22	16	23	7	12	7	5
$45,000 to $49,999	52	0	19	10	14	3	6	1	4
$50,000 to $54,999	66	4	18	13	19	10	1	1	0
$55,000 to $59,999	27	0	1	7	11	6	2	0	2
$60,000 to $64,999	24	0	3	7	5	5	3	1	2
$65,000 to $69,999	23	2	5	8	5	3	1	1	0
$70,000 to $74,999	15	0	6	5	2	2	1	0	1
$75,000 to $79,999	22	0	3	6	7	4	2	2	0
$80,000 to $84,999	16	0	5	5	2	4	0	0	0
$85,000 to $89,999	18	1	5	6	4	2	1	0	1
$90,000 to $94,999	11	0	0	3	6	0	2	2	0
$95,000 to $99,999	8	0	5	1	2	0	0	0	0
$100,000 or more	43	0	3	16	13	8	3	1	1
$100,000 to $124,999	23	0	3	7	7	4	3	1	1
$125,000 to $149,999	8	0	0	1	3	3	0	0	0
$150,000 to $174,999	3	0	0	3	0	0	0	0	0
$175,000 to $199,999	3	0	0	1	2	0	0	0	0
$200,000 or more	6	0	0	3	2	2	0	0	0
Median income	**$26,517**	**$20,242**	**$30,696**	**$30,066**	**$32,863**	**$18,602**	**$14,641**	**$14,501**	**$14,827**

PERCENT DISTRIBUTION

	total	15 to 24	25 to 34	35 to 44	45 to 54	55 to 64	65 or older total	65 to 74	75 or older
Hispanic men who live alone	**100.0%**	**100.0%**	**100.0%**	**100.0%**	**100.0%**	**100.0%**	**100.0%**	**100.0%**	**100.0%**
Under $25,000	47.1	65.5	36.6	36.8	36.6	59.0	68.8	73.5	61.9
$25,000 to $49,999	32.7	26.2	42.8	36.9	35.5	23.4	23.1	18.7	29.6
$50,000 to $74,999	11.5	7.4	12.7	13.9	15.5	10.4	4.0	3.3	5.0
$75,000 to $99,999	5.5	0.9	6.8	7.1	7.5	3.9	2.7	3.4	1.8
$100,000 or more	3.2	0.0	1.1	5.4	4.9	3.3	1.4	1.2	1.7

Source: Bureau of the Census, 2013 Current Population Survey, Internet site http://www.census.gov/hhes/www/cpstables/ 032013/hhinc/toc.htm; calculations by New Strategist

Table 1.52 Men Who Live Alone by Household Income and Age of Householder, 2012: Non-Hispanic White Men Who Live Alone

(number and percent distribution of non-Hispanic white men who live alone by household income and age of householder, 2012; men who live alone in thousands as of 2013)

	total	15 to 24	25 to 34	35 to 44	45 to 54	55 to 64	65 or older total	65 to 74	75 or older
Non-Hispanic white men who live alone	**10,609**	**455**	**1,508**	**1,406**	**2,069**	**2,286**	**2,886**	**1,401**	**1,484**
Under $5,000	528	61	38	72	142	141	74	39	35
$5,000 to $9,999	627	39	83	37	159	183	125	63	62
$10,000 to $14,999	904	63	72	74	122	177	397	163	234
$15,000 to $19,999	1,026	63	76	76	139	215	457	190	267
$20,000 to $24,999	846	48	102	88	105	163	340	163	177
$25,000 to $29,999	742	35	119	103	132	120	233	117	116
$30,000 to $34,999	712	23	124	128	98	113	226	105	121
$35,000 to $39,999	639	34	116	48	112	146	183	73	110
$40,000 to $44,999	649	29	103	81	116	166	152	87	66
$45,000 to $49,999	547	6	103	100	138	102	100	49	50
$50,000 to $54,999	478	17	108	70	92	108	84	40	44
$55,000 to $59,999	311	7	43	54	56	82	69	43	26
$60,000 to $64,999	326	1	49	59	55	91	71	45	26
$65,000 to $69,999	286	0	49	50	69	68	50	25	26
$70,000 to $74,999	309	8	74	54	81	55	36	27	9
$75,000 to $79,999	202	0	46	56	39	32	28	23	5
$80,000 to $84,999	208	7	30	30	55	47	40	20	20
$85,000 to $89,999	95	4	8	11	12	34	25	13	12
$90,000 to $94,999	129	2	28	21	31	22	25	11	13
$95,000 to $99,999	97	3	12	16	20	22	23	5	17
$100,000 or more	949	5	124	178	295	201	146	98	48
$100,000 to $124,999	381	3	59	86	124	66	44	37	7
$125,000 to $149,999	226	1	21	25	67	55	57	38	18
$150,000 to $174,999	103	0	17	22	28	17	18	11	7
$175,000 to $199,999	48	0	8	9	15	15	1	1	0
$200,000 or more	191	0	19	36	60	49	27	11	16
Median income	**$34,191**	**$20,139**	**$40,908**	**$44,523**	**$40,624**	**$35,832**	**$25,853**	**$28,411**	**$23,365**

PERCENT DISTRIBUTION

Non-Hispanic white men who live alone	**100.0%**	**100.0%**	**100.0%**	**100.0%**	**100.0%**	**100.0%**	**100.0%**	**100.0%**	**100.0%**
Under $25,000	37.1	60.3	24.6	24.7	32.2	38.4	48.3	44.2	52.2
$25,000 to $49,999	31.0	27.9	37.4	32.8	28.8	28.3	31.0	30.7	31.1
$50,000 to $74,999	16.1	7.3	21.4	20.4	17.1	17.6	10.8	12.9	8.8
$75,000 to $99,999	6.9	3.4	8.3	9.6	7.6	6.9	4.9	5.2	4.6
$100,000 or more	8.9	1.1	8.2	12.7	14.2	8.8	5.1	7.0	3.2

Note: Non-Hispanic whites are those who identify themselves as being white alone and not Hispanic.
Source: Bureau of the Census, 2013 Current Population Survey, Internet site http://www.census.gov/hhes/www/cpstables/
032013/hhinc/toc.htm; calculations by New Strategist

Two-Earner Households Have Above-Average Incomes

Households with only one earner have incomes well below average.

The 48 million households with two or more earners account for 39 percent of the nation's total households. Those with only one earner are another 37 percent, while households with no earners—many of them headed by retirees—account for the remaining 23 percent.

The median income of households with one earner stood at $43,335 in 2012, a substantial 15 percent below the national median of $51,017. Households with two earners had a much larger median of $82,596, 62 percent higher than average. Households with no earners had a median income of $19,722.

The median income of black households is only 59 percent as high as that of non-Hispanic white households, but among households with two earners the black median is 75 percent of the non-Hispanic white median. The black household median is lower than the non-Hispanic white median because only 29 percent of black households have two or more earners versus a larger 40 percent of non-Hispanic white households. Among two-earner households, blacks have a higher median income than Hispanics, $67,185 versus $57,193. Asian two-earner households have the highest incomes—a median of $99,000 in 2012.

■ The number of households with no earners should grow as the oldest boomers begin to retire.

Households with four or more earners have the highest incomes

(median income of households by number of earners, 2012)

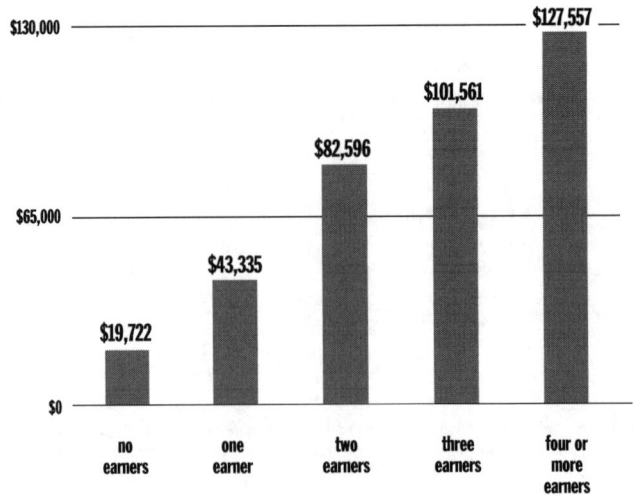

Table 1.53 Households by Income and Number of Earners, 2012: Total Households

(number and percent distribution of total households by household income and number of earners, 2012; households in thousands as of 2013)

	total	no earners	one earner	two or more earners			
				total	two earners	three earners	four or more earners
Total households	**122,459**	**28,600**	**45,849**	**48,010**	**38,676**	**7,053**	**2,282**
Under $5,000	4,204	3,305	839	61	56	5	0
$5,000 to $9,999	4,729	3,181	1,414	134	123	4	7
$10,000 to $14,999	6,982	4,245	2,403	334	320	13	1
$15,000 to $19,999	7,157	3,759	2,873	525	490	33	2
$20,000 to $24,999	7,131	2,823	3,471	837	781	53	3
$25,000 to $29,999	6,740	2,344	3,343	1,053	943	103	8
$30,000 to $34,999	6,354	1,765	3,317	1,272	1,142	115	15
$35,000 to $39,999	5,832	1,346	3,041	1,445	1,311	118	16
$40,000 to $44,999	5,547	1,036	2,881	1,630	1,426	187	18
$45,000 to $49,999	5,254	903	2,608	1,744	1,531	185	27
$50,000 to $54,999	5,102	712	2,406	1,984	1,707	236	41
$55,000 to $59,999	4,256	495	1,849	1,912	1,609	247	56
$60,000 to $64,999	4,356	378	1,902	2,075	1,775	269	32
$65,000 to $69,999	3,949	382	1,471	2,096	1,763	276	58
$70,000 to $74,999	3,756	301	1,452	2,003	1,673	263	67
$75,000 to $79,999	3,414	204	1,183	2,027	1,691	256	80
$80,000 to $84,999	3,326	206	1,145	1,975	1,642	268	66
$85,000 to $89,999	2,643	165	779	1,699	1,318	302	80
$90,000 to $94,999	2,678	98	838	1,742	1,399	267	76
$95,000 to $99,999	2,223	97	596	1,530	1,193	244	93
$100,000 or more	26,825	855	6,040	19,931	14,782	3,612	1,537
$100,000 to $124,999	9,490	441	2,294	6,755	5,173	1,213	369
$125,000 to $149,999	5,759	200	1,185	4,374	3,205	837	332
$150,000 to $174,999	3,870	83	874	2,913	2,114	524	275
$175,000 to $199,999	2,247	50	415	1,781	1,288	337	156
$200,000 or more	5,460	81	1,272	4,107	3,002	701	405
Median income	**$51,017**	**$19,722**	**$43,335**	**$87,338**	**$82,596**	**$101,561**	**$127,557**

PERCENT DISTRIBUTION

	total	no earners	one earner	total	two earners	three earners	four or more earners
Total households	**100.0%**	**100.0%**	**100.0%**	**100.0%**	**100.0%**	**100.0%**	**100.0%**
Under $25,000	24.7	60.5	24.0	3.9	4.6	1.5	0.6
$25,000 to $49,999	24.3	25.9	33.1	14.9	16.4	10.0	3.7
$50,000 to $74,999	17.5	7.9	19.8	21.0	22.0	18.3	11.1
$75,000 to $99,999	11.7	2.7	9.9	18.7	18.7	19.0	17.2
$100,000 or more	21.9	3.0	13.2	41.5	38.2	51.2	67.3

Source: Bureau of the Census, 2013 Current Population Survey, Internet site http://www.census.gov/hhes/www/cpstables/032013/hhinc/toc.htm; calculations by New Strategist

Table 1.54 Households by Income and Number of Earners, 2012: Asian Households

(number and percent distribution of Asian households by household income and number of earners, 2012; households in thousands as of 2013)

	total	no earners	one earner	two or more earners total	two earners	three earners	four or more earners
Asian households	**5,872**	**798**	**2,331**	**2,742**	**2,118**	**421**	**203**
Under $5,000	241	201	39	2	2	0	0
$5,000 to $9,999	152	91	57	4	4	0	0
$10,000 to $14,999	208	103	92	14	14	0	0
$15,000 to $19,999	201	84	92	25	25	0	0
$20,000 to $24,999	234	69	123	42	40	2	0
$25,000 to $29,999	219	48	131	40	36	4	0
$30,000 to $34,999	226	39	118	69	67	2	0
$35,000 to $39,999	225	29	118	78	72	5	1
$40,000 to $44,999	203	21	90	92	71	19	2
$45,000 to $49,999	228	17	130	81	69	10	2
$50,000 to $54,999	221	24	111	86	71	11	4
$55,000 to $59,999	214	8	105	101	80	20	1
$60,000 to $64,999	232	8	128	96	74	22	1
$65,000 to $69,999	183	8	72	103	79	13	10
$70,000 to $74,999	190	9	94	88	74	14	0
$75,000 to $79,999	172	12	81	79	70	6	4
$80,000 to $84,999	174	3	88	83	62	15	6
$85,000 to $89,999	116	3	49	65	48	14	3
$90,000 to $94,999	156	0	66	90	70	10	10
$95,000 to $99,999	104	3	44	57	41	11	5
$100,000 or more	1,970	18	504	1,448	1,050	244	155
$100,000 to $124,999	591	10	194	387	277	70	40
$125,000 to $149,999	364	5	97	262	178	52	32
$150,000 to $174,999	329	2	98	229	159	39	31
$175,000 to $199,999	185	0	30	155	119	25	11
$200,000 or more	500	1	85	415	316	58	41
Median income	**$68,182**	**$15,233**	**$57,522**	**$103,566**	**$99,000**	**$110,535**	**$137,277**

PERCENT DISTRIBUTION

	total	no earners	one earner	two or more earners total	two earners	three earners	four or more earners
Asian households	**100.0%**	**100.0%**	**100.0%**	**100.0%**	**100.0%**	**100.0%**	**100.0%**
Under $25,000	17.7	68.6	17.3	3.1	4.0	0.5	0.0
$25,000 to $49,999	18.8	19.2	25.2	13.2	14.9	9.7	2.4
$50,000 to $74,999	17.7	7.2	21.9	17.3	17.8	19.1	7.8
$75,000 to $99,999	12.3	2.7	14.0	13.6	13.7	12.9	13.6
$100,000 or more	33.5	2.3	21.6	52.8	49.6	57.9	76.2

Note: Asians are those who identify themselves as being of the race alone and those who identify themselves as being of the race in combination with other races.
Source: Bureau of the Census, 2013 Current Population Survey, Internet site http://www.census.gov/hhes/www/cpstables/ 032013/hhinc/toc.htm; calculations by New Strategist

Table 1.55 Households by Income and Number of Earners, 2012: Black Households

(number and percent distribution of black households by household income and number of earners, 2012; households in thousands as of 2013)

	total	no earners	one earner	two or more earners total	two earners	three earners	four or more earners
Black households	**16,559**	**4,303**	**7,396**	**4,861**	**3,949**	**754**	**158**
Under $5,000	1,108	895	197	16	16	0	0
$5,000 to $9,999	1,332	908	386	37	34	0	3
$10,000 to $14,999	1,503	810	607	85	82	3	0
$15,000 to $19,999	1,263	468	708	87	83	4	0
$20,000 to $24,999	1,262	338	796	129	124	5	0
$25,000 to $29,999	991	232	615	144	122	21	1
$30,000 to $34,999	996	156	676	164	156	7	0
$35,000 to $39,999	845	116	549	181	163	16	2
$40,000 to $44,999	759	73	472	214	183	31	0
$45,000 to $49,999	771	65	444	262	233	27	1
$50,000 to $54,999	635	56	303	275	244	28	3
$55,000 to $59,999	536	31	251	254	225	29	0
$60,000 to $64,999	495	30	230	235	198	35	2
$65,000 to $69,999	445	16	174	255	208	39	7
$70,000 to $74,999	364	17	147	200	157	39	3
$75,000 to $79,999	345	19	111	215	175	36	4
$80,000 to $84,999	349	8	124	217	180	31	6
$85,000 to $89,999	249	18	70	161	118	36	6
$90,000 to $94,999	218	5	77	135	92	38	6
$95,000 to $99,999	249	2	76	172	119	46	6
$100,000 or more	1,843	37	383	1,423	1,034	282	107
$100,000 to $124,999	786	24	160	601	442	122	37
$125,000 to $149,999	451	8	76	368	277	72	18
$150,000 to $174,999	220	4	45	172	107	36	29
$175,000 to $199,999	135	0	34	101	76	17	8
$200,000 or more	251	2	68	182	132	34	16
Median income	**$33,718**	**$11,826**	**$32,102**	**$71,992**	**$67,185**	**$88,360**	**$116,822**

PERCENT DISTRIBUTION

	total	no earners	one earner	two or more earners total	two earners	three earners	four or more earners
Black households	**100.0%**	**100.0%**	**100.0%**	**100.0%**	**100.0%**	**100.0%**	**100.0%**
Under $25,000	39.1	79.5	36.4	7.3	8.6	1.6	2.1
$25,000 to $49,999	26.3	14.9	37.3	19.8	21.7	13.6	2.4
$50,000 to $74,999	14.9	3.5	14.9	25.1	26.2	22.6	9.7
$75,000 to $99,999	8.5	1.2	6.2	18.5	17.3	24.8	18.0
$100,000 or more	11.1	0.9	5.2	29.3	26.2	37.4	67.8

Note: Blacks are those who identify themselves as being of the race alone and those who identify themselves as being of the race in combination with other races.
Source: Bureau of the Census, 2013 Current Population Survey, Internet site http://www.census.gov/hhes/www/cpstables/ 032013/hhinc/toc.htm; calculations by New Strategist

Table 1.56 Households by Income and Number of Earners, 2012: Hispanic Households

(number and percent distribution of Hispanic households by household income and number of earners, 2012; households in thousands as of 2013)

	total	no earners	one earner	two or more earners total	two earners	three earners	four or more earners
Hispanic households	**15,589**	**2,375**	**6,283**	**6,930**	**5,154**	**1,265**	**511**
Under $5,000	716	541	171	5	5	0	0
$5,000 to $9,999	787	441	315	32	32	0	0
$10,000 to $14,999	1,112	476	522	114	111	3	0
$15,000 to $19,999	1,118	293	674	150	145	5	0
$20,000 to $24,999	1,154	177	701	277	258	18	1
$25,000 to $29,999	1,100	119	653	328	282	42	5
$30,000 to $34,999	1,020	95	549	376	317	52	7
$35,000 to $39,999	929	43	469	417	366	47	5
$40,000 to $44,999	805	39	373	394	319	66	9
$45,000 to $49,999	723	41	307	375	307	55	14
$50,000 to $54,999	689	28	281	380	269	96	14
$55,000 to $59,999	612	12	169	430	313	82	35
$60,000 to $64,999	534	11	163	361	273	67	21
$65,000 to $69,999	454	12	108	333	250	65	19
$70,000 to $74,999	383	11	111	261	176	57	28
$75,000 to $79,999	380	5	109	266	179	55	31
$80,000 to $84,999	355	5	96	254	164	68	23
$85,000 to $89,999	303	7	68	228	159	53	15
$90,000 to $94,999	260	2	59	198	152	30	17
$95,000 to $99,999	219	3	41	175	104	46	25
$100,000 or more	1,934	13	344	1,577	974	360	243
$100,000 to $124,999	836	11	163	661	422	154	85
$125,000 to $149,999	397	2	61	334	189	82	64
$150,000 to $174,999	269	0	40	229	147	46	35
$175,000 to $199,999	141	0	19	122	62	31	29
$200,000 or more	291	0	60	231	155	46	30
Median income	**$39,005**	**$11,833**	**$30,689**	**$62,140**	**$57,193**	**$72,373**	**$97,519**

PERCENT DISTRIBUTION

	total	no earners	one earner	two or more earners total	two earners	three earners	four or more earners
Hispanic households	**100.0%**	**100.0%**	**100.0%**	**100.0%**	**100.0%**	**100.0%**	**100.0%**
Under $25,000	31.4	81.1	37.9	8.3	10.7	2.0	0.2
$25,000 to $49,999	29.4	14.2	37.4	27.3	30.8	20.7	7.6
$50,000 to $74,999	17.1	3.1	13.3	25.5	24.9	29.0	22.9
$75,000 to $99,999	9.7	1.0	5.9	16.2	14.7	19.8	21.8
$100,000 or more	12.4	0.6	5.5	22.8	18.9	28.4	47.6

Source: Bureau of the Census, 2013 Current Population Survey, Internet site http://www.census.gov/hhes/www/cpstables/ 032013/hhinc/toc.htm; calculations by New Strategist

Table 1.57 Households by Income and Number of Earners, 2012: Non-Hispanic White Households

(number and percent distribution of non-Hispanic white households by household income and number of earners, 2012; households in thousands as of 2013)

	total	no earners	one earner	two or more earners total	two earners	three earners	four or more earners
Non-Hispanic white households	**83,792**	**20,878**	**29,630**	**33,284**	**27,280**	**4,597**	**1,407**
Under $5,000	2,091	1,646	409	36	31	5	0
$5,000 to $9,999	2,452	1,736	651	65	57	4	3
$10,000 to $14,999	4,089	2,806	1,162	121	114	7	1
$15,000 to $19,999	4,516	2,871	1,384	261	238	21	2
$20,000 to $24,999	4,472	2,201	1,870	400	370	28	3
$25,000 to $29,999	4,392	1,929	1,935	528	490	35	4
$30,000 to $34,999	4,086	1,466	1,967	653	594	51	8
$35,000 to $39,999	3,788	1,148	1,868	771	711	52	9
$40,000 to $44,999	3,731	892	1,929	910	835	67	8
$45,000 to $49,999	3,517	767	1,741	1,009	908	90	10
$50,000 to $54,999	3,505	594	1,692	1,219	1,099	99	20
$55,000 to $59,999	2,890	442	1,317	1,131	994	117	19
$60,000 to $64,999	3,061	326	1,353	1,382	1,230	144	8
$65,000 to $69,999	2,859	341	1,100	1,418	1,235	162	20
$70,000 to $74,999	2,804	263	1,104	1,437	1,253	149	34
$75,000 to $79,999	2,491	166	879	1,446	1,251	155	39
$80,000 to $84,999	2,454	190	847	1,417	1,230	154	33
$85,000 to $89,999	1,959	137	588	1,233	986	195	52
$90,000 to $94,999	2,025	89	632	1,304	1,074	187	43
$95,000 to $99,999	1,649	89	437	1,123	930	139	55
$100,000 or more	20,963	778	4,766	15,419	11,648	2,735	1,036
$100,000 to $124,999	7,219	392	1,752	5,075	3,990	875	209
$125,000 to $149,999	4,519	183	950	3,386	2,541	632	213
$150,000 to $174,999	3,033	74	678	2,281	1,691	408	182
$175,000 to $199,999	1,787	50	327	1,410	1,033	263	113
$200,000 or more	4,404	78	1,060	3,267	2,393	557	318
Median income	**$57,009**	**$23,004**	**$49,673**	**$94,516**	**$90,046**	**$111,547**	**$140,098**

PERCENT DISTRIBUTION

	total	no earners	one earner	two or more earners total	two earners	three earners	four or more earners
Non-Hispanic white households	**100.0%**	**100.0%**	**100.0%**	**100.0%**	**100.0%**	**100.0%**	**100.0%**
Under $25,000	21.0	53.9	18.5	2.7	3.0	1.4	0.6
$25,000 to $49,999	23.3	29.7	31.9	11.6	13.0	6.4	2.7
$50,000 to $74,999	18.0	9.4	22.2	19.8	21.3	14.6	7.3
$75,000 to $99,999	12.6	3.2	11.4	19.6	20.1	18.1	15.8
$100,000 or more	25.0	3.7	16.1	46.3	42.7	59.5	73.6

Note: Non-Hispanic whites are those who identify themselves as being white alone and not Hispanic.
Source: Bureau of the Census, 2013 Current Population Survey, Internet site http://www.census.gov/hhes/www/cpstables/032013/hhinc/toc.htm; calculations by New Strategist

Married Couples with School-Aged Children Have the Highest Incomes

Empty-nesters have lower incomes than couples with children.

Married couples with children aged 6 to 17 and none younger had a median income of $87,102 in 2012, much higher than the median income of couples with younger or no children at home. Behind these income differences are the differing ages of the couples. Those with only school-aged children at home are generally older and more likely to be in their peak earning years than those with younger children. Many couples without children at home are empty-nesters and retired, which accounts for their lower incomes.

The income pattern is the same for Asians, blacks, Hispanics, and non-Hispanic whites, although there are substantial income differences among them. Non-Hispanic white couples with children aged 6 to 17 and none younger had a median income of $96,884 in 2012. The median income of black couples with children aged 6 to 17 and none younger stood at $73,919, while their Hispanic counterparts had a much lower median income of $52,623. Among Asian couples, the median income of couples with school-aged children exceeded $100,000.

■ Many of the nation's affluent couples saw their incomes decline during the Great Recession.

Couples with school-aged children are the most affluent

(median income of married couples by presence and age of children under age 18 at home, 2012)

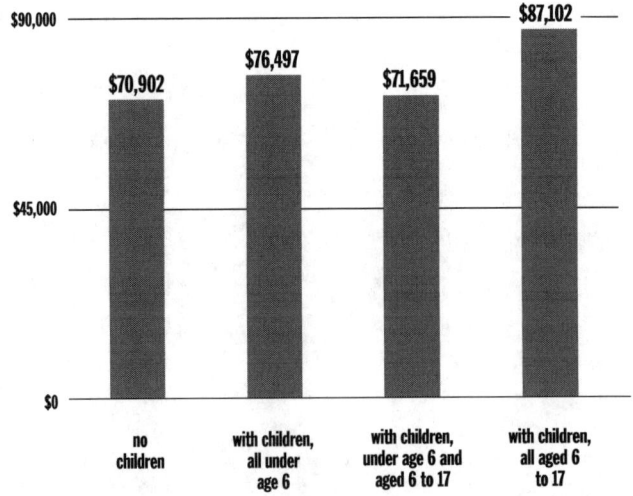

Table 1.58 Married Couples by Family Income and Presence of Children, 2012: Total Married Couples

(number and percent distribution of married couples by family income and presence and age of related children under age 18 at home, 2012; married couples in thousands as of 2013)

	total	no children	one or more children under age 18			
			total	all under 6	some under 6, some 6 to 17	all 6 to 17
Total married couples	59,224	33,955	25,269	5,915	5,358	13,996
Under $5,000	758	456	302	75	77	150
$5,000 to $9,999	560	344	216	61	63	92
$10,000 to $14,999	1,023	600	423	126	112	186
$15,000 to $19,999	1,486	928	557	120	190	248
$20,000 to $24,999	2,021	1,317	704	186	205	314
$25,000 to $29,999	2,332	1,582	750	167	228	354
$30,000 to $34,999	2,415	1,579	836	229	217	390
$35,000 to $39,999	2,460	1,482	977	244	230	503
$40,000 to $44,999	2,324	1,413	912	219	218	474
$45,000 to $49,999	2,469	1,562	908	243	192	473
$50,000 to $54,999	2,460	1,462	997	235	249	513
$55,000 to $59,999	2,176	1,291	885	228	180	477
$60,000 to $64,999	2,366	1,327	1,039	263	237	539
$65,000 to $69,999	2,259	1,355	904	206	189	508
$70,000 to $74,999	2,223	1,264	959	263	179	517
$75,000 to $79,999	2,136	1,201	935	219	194	522
$80,000 to $84,999	2,108	1,164	943	230	199	514
$85,000 to $89,999	1,816	983	833	207	157	469
$90,000 to $94,999	1,738	915	823	196	177	449
$95,000 to $99,999	1,534	828	707	147	139	421
$100,000 or more	20,560	10,900	9,660	2,051	1,725	5,883
$100,000 to $124,999	6,921	3,655	3,266	756	605	1,906
$125,000 to $149,999	4,340	2,319	2,022	411	343	1,267
$150,000 to $174,999	3,081	1,631	1,449	327	253	869
$175,000 to $199,999	1,795	945	850	158	155	538
$200,000 or more	4,422	2,350	2,072	399	369	1,303
Median income	**$75,535**	**$70,902**	**$81,455**	**$76,497**	**$71,659**	**$87,102**
Total married couples	**100.0%**	**100.0%**	**100.0%**	**100.0%**	**100.0%**	**100.0%**
Under $25,000	9.9	10.7	8.7	9.6	12.1	7.1
$25,000 to $49,999	20.3	22.4	17.3	18.6	20.3	15.7
$50,000 to $74,999	19.4	19.7	18.9	20.2	19.3	18.3
$75,000 to $99,999	15.8	15.0	16.8	16.9	16.2	17.0
$100,000 or more	34.7	32.1	38.2	34.7	32.2	42.0

Note: The median income of married couples in this table is slightly different from the figure shown in the household income tables because this figure includes the incomes of only family members and not any unrelated members of the household.
Source: Bureau of the Census, 2013 Current Population Survey, Internet site http://www.census.gov/hhes/www/cpstables/032013/faminc/toc.htm; calculations by New Strategist

Table 1.59 Married Couples by Family Income and Presence of Children, 2012: Asian Married Couples

(number and percent distribution of Asian married couples by family income and presence and age of related children under age 18 at home, 2012; married couples in thousands as of 2013)

	total	no children	one or more children under age 18 total	all under 6	some under 6, some 6 to 17	all 6 to 17
Asian married couples	**3,411**	**1,578**	**1,832**	**502**	**383**	**948**
Under $5,000	73	33	40	17	9	15
$5,000 to $9,999	27	14	13	3	5	5
$10,000 to $14,999	57	36	21	9	5	8
$15,000 to $19,999	74	38	35	4	9	23
$20,000 to $24,999	88	44	44	10	10	24
$25,000 to $29,999	98	60	37	12	5	21
$30,000 to $34,999	116	57	59	14	14	31
$35,000 to $39,999	118	60	58	21	10	27
$40,000 to $44,999	100	36	63	4	20	39
$45,000 to $49,999	105	49	56	17	11	28
$50,000 to $54,999	130	67	63	14	9	40
$55,000 to $59,999	118	69	48	14	5	30
$60,000 to $64,999	119	50	69	23	19	27
$65,000 to $69,999	99	51	48	11	10	27
$70,000 to $74,999	121	68	53	13	16	24
$75,000 to $79,999	108	50	59	22	14	23
$80,000 to $84,999	103	43	59	13	15	31
$85,000 to $89,999	82	49	33	20	2	11
$90,000 to $94,999	91	50	41	15	9	17
$95,000 to $99,999	81	34	46	17	6	23
$100,000 or more	1,504	618	886	231	181	4743
$100,000 to $124,999	411	177	235	80	34	121
$125,000 to $149,999	273	112	161	32	33	96
$150,000 to $174,999	249	110	139	37	24	79
$175,000 to $199,999	158	63	95	15	27	53
$200,000 or more	412	157	256	67	63	125
Median income	**$87,285**	**$80,731**	**$97,438**	**$93,292**	**$91,877**	**$100,025**
Asian married couples	**100.0%**	**100.0%**	**100.0%**	**100.0%**	**100.0%**	**100.0%**
Under $25,000	9.4	10.5	8.4	8.5	9.8	7.8
$25,000 to $49,999	15.7	16.6	14.9	13.6	15.5	15.4
$50,000 to $74,999	17.2	19.3	15.4	14.7	15.4	15.7
$75,000 to $99,999	13.6	14.3	13.0	17.1	12.2	11.1
$100,000 or more	44.1	39.2	48.3	46.0	47.1	50.0

Note: Asians are those who identify themselves as being of the race alone and those who identify themselves as being of the race in combination with other races. The median income of married couples in this table is slightly different from the figure shown in the household income tables because this figure includes the incomes of only family members and not any unrelated members of the household.
Source: Bureau of the Census, 2013 Current Population Survey, Internet site http://www.census.gov/hhes/www/cpstables/032013/faminc/toc.htm; calculations by New Strategist

Table 1.60 Married Couples by Family Income and Presence of Children, 2012: Black Married Couples

(number and percent distribution of black married couples by family income and presence and age of related children under age 18 at home, 2012; married couples in thousands as of 2013)

	total	no children	one or more children under age 18			
			total	all under 6	some under 6, some 6 to 17	all 6 to 17
Black married couples	**4,703**	**2,412**	**2,291**	**445**	**586**	**1,259**
Under $5,000	100	55	45	10	14	20
$5,000 to $9,999	80	41	39	9	15	15
$10,000 to $14,999	124	75	49	14	11	24
$15,000 to $19,999	157	98	59	14	20	26
$20,000 to $24,999	218	139	78	20	16	42
$25,000 to $29,999	213	133	80	7	35	38
$30,000 to $34,999	203	108	96	24	24	48
$35,000 to $39,999	210	123	87	18	27	41
$40,000 to $44,999	188	97	90	21	26	44
$45,000 to $49,999	251	131	120	36	33	52
$50,000 to $54,999	224	120	104	18	37	49
$55,000 to $59,999	192	95	97	13	22	62
$60,000 to $64,999	196	101	95	13	21	61
$65,000 to $69,999	211	99	112	27	20	65
$70,000 to $74,999	180	92	89	25	13	50
$75,000 to $79,999	166	77	90	11	28	51
$80,000 to $84,999	175	94	81	18	21	42
$85,000 to $89,999	143	75	68	7	13	47
$90,000 to $94,999	120	60	60	14	16	31
$95,000 to $99,999	150	69	81	10	28	43
$100,000 or more	1,199	529	670	117	145	408
$100,000 to $124,999	495	203	293	51	56	186
$125,000 to $149,999	320	146	174	29	40	104
$150,000 to $174,999	135	71	64	19	6	39
$175,000 to $199,999	87	32	54	9	12	33
$200,000 or more	161	76	85	9	31	46
Median income	**$64,812**	**$59,519**	**$69,646**	**$65,915**	**$61,929**	**$73,919**
Black married couples	**100.0%**	**100.0%**	**100.0%**	**100.0%**	**100.0%**	**100.0%**
Under $25,000	14.4	16.9	11.8	15.1	13.1	10.1
$25,000 to $49,999	22.7	24.6	20.7	23.7	24.7	17.7
$50,000 to $74,999	21.3	21.0	21.7	21.5	19.4	22.8
$75,000 to $99,999	16.1	15.6	16.6	13.4	18.1	17.0
$100,000 or more	25.5	21.9	29.2	26.2	24.8	32.4

Note: Blacks are those who identify themselves as being of the race alone and those who identify themselves as being of the race in combination with other races. The median income of married couples in this table is slightly different from the figure shown in the household income tables because this figure includes the incomes of only family members and not any unrelated members of the household.
Source: Bureau of the Census, 2013 Current Population Survey, Internet site http://www.census.gov/hhes/www/cpstables/ 032013/faminc/toc.htm; calculations by New Strategist

Table 1.61 Married Couples by Family Income and Presence of Children, 2012: Hispanic Married Couples

(number and percent distribution of Hispanic married couples by family income and presence and age of related children under age 18 at home, 2012; married couples in thousands as of 2013)

			one or more children under age 18			
	total	no children	total	all under 6	some under 6, some 6 to 17	all 6 to 17
Hispanic married couples	**7,460**	**2,794**	**4,666**	**977**	**1,355**	**2,334**
Under $5,000	128	57	71	14	25	32
$5,000 to $9,999	146	70	76	21	29	26
$10,000 to $14,999	314	122	192	61	53	78
$15,000 to $19,999	426	150	276	58	109	109
$20,000 to $24,999	497	189	308	70	110	128
$25,000 to $29,999	459	167	292	52	102	139
$30,000 to $34,999	469	150	319	80	92	147
$35,000 to $39,999	481	129	351	76	104	171
$40,000 to $44,999	405	123	282	51	88	143
$45,000 to $49,999	404	145	259	56	70	133
$50,000 to $54,999	353	144	209	42	65	101
$55,000 to $59,999	317	109	207	44	47	117
$60,000 to $64,999	312	124	188	34	52	102
$65,000 to $69,999	256	102	154	32	47	75
$70,000 to $74,999	251	93	158	36	42	80
$75,000 to $79,999	224	89	135	23	38	75
$80,000 to $84,999	209	80	129	30	31	67
$85,000 to $89,999	178	76	102	14	32	56
$90,000 to $94,999	174	58	116	21	30	66
$95,000 to $99,999	143	45	98	23	29	46
$100,000 or more	1,313	572	742	138	157	446
$100,000 to $124,999	537	227	309	63	58	189
$125,000 to $149,999	279	104	175	31	43	102
$150,000 to $174,999	193	79	113	16	24	73
$175,000 to $199,999	94	45	49	15	14	20
$200,000 or more	211	116	95	13	19	62
Median income	**$50,012**	**$52,397**	**$47,770**	**$45,328**	**$42,404**	**$52,623**
Hispanic married couples	**100.0%**	**100.0%**	**100.0%**	**100.0%**	**100.0%**	**100.0%**
Under $25,000	20.3	21.1	19.8	22.9	24.1	15.9
$25,000 to $49,999	29.7	25.5	32.2	32.3	33.7	31.4
$50,000 to $74,999	20.0	20.5	19.6	19.3	18.7	20.3
$75,000 to $99,999	12.4	12.4	12.5	11.3	11.9	13.3
$100,000 or more	17.6	20.5	15.9	14.2	11.6	19.1

Note: The median income of married couples in this table is slightly different from the figure shown in the household income tables because this figure includes the incomes of only family members and not any unrelated members of the household.
Source: Bureau of the Census, 2013 Current Population Survey, Internet site http://www.census.gov/hhes/www/cpstables/ 032013/faminc/toc.htm; calculations by New Strategist

Table 1.62 Married Couples by Family Income and Presence of Children, 2012: Non-Hispanic White Married Couples

(number and percent distribution of non-Hispanic white married couples by family income and presence and age of related children under age 18 at home, 2012; married couples in thousands as of 2013)

| | total | no children | one or more children under age 18 | | | |
			total	all under 6	some under 6, some 6 to 17	all 6 to 17
Non-Hispanic white married couples	**43,309**	**26,938**	**16,371**	**3,963**	**3,055**	**9,353**
Under $5,000	442	311	132	26	26	79
$5,000 to $9,999	301	211	90	28	20	43
$10,000 to $14,999	525	363	162	47	41	74
$15,000 to $19,999	816	635	182	48	51	83
$20,000 to $24,999	1,200	928	272	85	66	121
$25,000 to $29,999	1,570	1,222	348	99	92	158
$30,000 to $34,999	1,620	1,254	366	112	91	163
$35,000 to $39,999	1,628	1,156	472	129	89	254
$40,000 to $44,999	1,601	1,134	467	143	87	238
$45,000 to $49,999	1,695	1,220	475	136	79	260
$50,000 to $54,999	1,735	1,127	608	155	135	319
$55,000 to $59,999	1,534	1,002	531	157	105	270
$60,000 to $64,999	1,719	1,037	682	189	146	348
$65,000 to $69,999	1,686	1,101	585	136	113	336
$70,000 to $74,999	1,670	1,004	666	189	110	367
$75,000 to $79,999	1,607	969	638	161	112	365
$80,000 to $84,999	1,615	942	673	172	132	369
$85,000 to $89,999	1,407	780	627	162	109	356
$90,000 to $94,999	1,341	740	601	147	124	331
$95,000 to $99,999	1,161	677	484	96	84	305
$100,000 or more	16,435	9,127	7,308	1,548	1,245	4,515
$100,000 to $124,999	5,426	3,025	2,401	549	459	1,394
$125,000 to $149,999	3,440	1,944	1,496	316	228	952
$150,000 to $174,999	2,488	1,357	1,131	257	199	675
$175,000 to $199,999	1,462	807	655	120	104	431
$200,000 or more	3,619	1,993	1,625	306	255	1,064
Median income	**$80,789**	**$73,518**	**$91,362**	**$83,940**	**$86,240**	**$96,884**
Non-Hispanic white married couples	**100.0%**	**100.0%**	**100.0%**	**100.0%**	**100.0%**	**100.0%**
Under $25,000	7.6	9.1	5.1	5.9	6.7	4.3
$25,000 to $49,999	18.7	22.2	13.0	15.6	14.3	11.5
$50,000 to $74,999	19.3	19.6	18.8	20.8	19.9	17.5
$75,000 to $99,999	16.5	15.2	18.5	18.6	18.3	18.5
$100,000 or more	37.9	33.9	44.6	39.1	40.8	48.3

Note: Non-Hispanic whites are those who identify themselves as being white alone and not Hispanic. The median income of married couples in this table is slightly different from the figure shown in the household income tables because this figure includes the incomes of only family members and not any unrelated members of the household.
Source: Bureau of the Census, 2013 Current Population Survey, Internet site http://www.census.gov/hhes/www/cpstables/ 032013/faminc/toc.htm; calculations by New Strategist

Dual Earners Are the Majority of Married Couples

Single-earner couples account for a much smaller share of total couples.

Most of the nation's married couples are dual-earner, which means both husband and wife are in the labor force. Of the nation's 59 million married couples, 32 million are dual-earner. In 17 million of those dual-earner couples, both husband and wife work full-time. The full-time, dual-earner couples greatly outnumber the 10 million traditional couples in which the husband works full-time and the wife does not work.

The median income of dual-earner couples in which both husband and wife work full-time was a substantial $110,357 in 2012. In contrast, traditional single-earner couples had a median income of $69,400. Among couples with no earners—most of them retirees—median income was just $34,803.

■ Couples with no earners are almost as numerous as traditional, single-earner couples.

Single-earner couples have much lower incomes

(median income of married couples by work status of husband and wife, 2012)

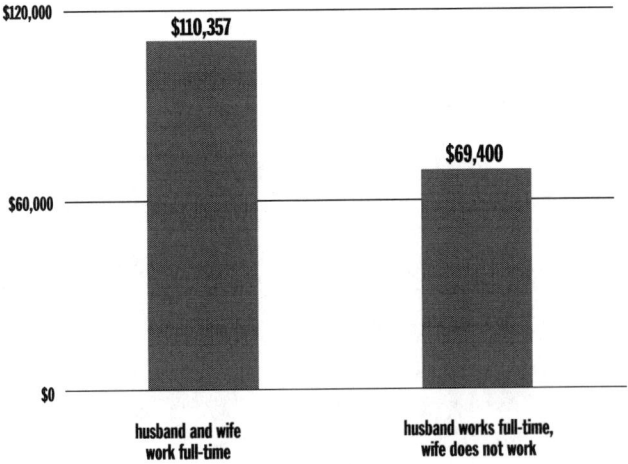

Table 1.63 Dual-Income Married Couples by Household Income and Presence of Children, 2012: Husband and Wife Work

(number and percent distribution of married couples in which both husband and wife work by household income and presence and age of related children under age 18 at home, 2012; married couples in thousands as of 2013)

	total	no children	one or more children under age 18			
			total	all under 6	some under 6, some 6 to 17	all 6 to 17
Husband and wife work	**31,608**	**15,460**	**16,148**	**3,793**	**2,992**	**9,363**
Under $5,000	26	21	5	1	4	1
$5,000 to $9,999	47	14	33	8	9	16
$10,000 to $14,999	125	43	83	39	21	23
$15,000 to $19,999	191	77	114	31	31	53
$20,000 to $24,999	307	133	173	51	36	85
$25,000 to $29,999	458	191	267	63	86	118
$30,000 to $34,999	592	267	326	98	78	150
$35,000 to $39,999	674	284	390	100	69	222
$40,000 to $44,999	812	373	439	104	84	251
$45,000 to $49,999	931	458	473	119	80	275
$50,000 to $54,999	1,091	534	557	135	137	285
$55,000 to $59,999	1,066	490	576	139	109	328
$60,000 to $64,999	1,211	590	620	154	146	321
$65,000 to $69,999	1,281	634	647	145	133	369
$70,000 to $74,999	1,279	646	633	182	97	354
$75,000 to $79,999	1,364	677	687	158	140	389
$80,000 to $84,999	1,330	656	674	160	136	379
$85,000 to $89,999	1,115	494	620	147	111	362
$90,000 to $94,999	1,200	585	615	153	118	345
$95,000 to $99,999	1,103	552	551	113	104	334
$100,000 or more	15,404	7,742	7,663	1,695	1,263	4,705
$100,000 to $124,999	5,032	2,458	2,575	616	436	1,523
$125,000 to $149,999	3,347	1,678	1,669	343	263	1,063
$150,000 to $174,999	2,295	1,188	1,107	265	186	657
$175,000 to $199,999	1,398	687	712	133	109	470
$200,000 or more	3,331	1,731	1,600	339	270	991
Median income	**$97,854**	**$100,076**	**$96,114**	**$91,432**	**$89,401**	**$100,250**
Husband and wife work	**100.0%**	**100.0%**	**100.0%**	**100.0%**	**100.0%**	**100.0%**
Under $25,000	9.9	10.7	8.7	9.6	12.1	7.1
$25,000 to $49,999	20.3	22.4	17.3	18.6	20.3	15.7
$50,000 to $74,999	19.4	19.7	18.9	20.2	19.3	18.3
$75,000 to $99,999	15.8	15.0	16.8	16.9	16.2	17.0
$100,000 or more	34.7	32.1	38.2	34.7	32.2	42.0

Source: Bureau of the Census, 2013 Current Population Survey, Internet site http://www.census.gov/hhes/www/cpstables/ 032013/faminc/toc.htm; calculations by New Strategist

Table 1.64 Dual-Income Married Couples by Household Income and Presence of Children, 2012: Husband and Wife Work Full-Time

(number and percent distribution of married couples in which both husband and wife work full-time, year-round by household income and presence and age of related children under age 18 at home, 2012; married couples in thousands as of 2013)

			one or more children under age 18			
	total	no children	total	all under 6	some under 6, some 6 to 17	all 6 to 17
Husband and wife work full-time	**16,868**	**8,550**	**8,319**	**1,900**	**1,474**	**4,945**
Under $5,000	5	5	0	0	0	0
$5,000 to $9,999	1	1	0	0	0	0
$10,000 to $14,999	8	7	1	0	0	1
$15,000 to $19,999	13	5	8	2	2	3
$20,000 to $24,999	39	27	13	0	1	11
$25,000 to $29,999	69	42	27	6	7	14
$30,000 to $34,999	111	61	50	16	8	25
$35,000 to $39,999	147	60	88	27	11	50
$40,000 to $44,999	271	115	156	25	37	94
$45,000 to $49,999	353	184	169	39	29	101
$50,000 to $54,999	436	225	210	54	48	108
$55,000 to $59,999	419	195	223	52	40	132
$60,000 to $64,999	573	285	288	72	67	149
$65,000 to $69,999	618	318	300	62	65	173
$70,000 to $74,999	647	346	301	95	46	160
$75,000 to $79,999	751	371	379	83	68	228
$80,000 to $84,999	764	386	378	77	79	222
$85,000 to $89,999	600	260	341	87	67	186
$90,000 to $94,999	663	327	336	94	60	182
$95,000 to $99,999	616	311	305	72	53	180
$100,000 or more	9,765	5,018	4,747	1,033	788	2,927
$100,000 to $124,999	2,998	1,514	1,485	342	235	907
$125,000 to $149,999	2,126	1,081	1,045	211	171	663
$150,000 to $174,999	1,482	788	694	178	118	397
$175,000 to $199,999	975	486	489	79	82	327
$200,000 or more	2,184	1,149	1,035	222	181	632
Median income	**$110,357**	**$111,124**	**$109,070**	**$106,591**	**$103,148**	**$111,254**
Husband and wife work full-time	**100.0%**	**100.0%**	**100.0%**	**100.0%**	**100.0%**	**100.0%**
Under $25,000	0.4	0.5	0.3	0.1	0.2	0.3
$25,000 to $49,999	5.6	5.4	5.9	6.0	6.2	5.7
$50,000 to $74,999	16.0	16.0	15.9	17.7	17.9	14.6
$75,000 to $99,999	20.1	19.4	20.9	21.8	22.2	20.2
$100,000 or more	57.9	58.7	57.1	54.4	53.5	59.2

Source: Bureau of the Census, 2013 Current Population Survey, Internet site http://www.census.gov/hhes/www/cpstables/ 032013/faminc/toc.htm; calculations by New Strategist

Table 1.65 Married Couples by Work Status, Household Income, and Presence of Children, 2012: Husband Works Full-Time, Wife Does Not Work

(number and percent distribution of married couples in which the husband works full-time and the wife does not work, by household income and presence and age of related children under age 18 at home, 2012; married couples in thousands as of 2013)

	total	no children	one or more children under age 18			
			total	all under 6	some under 6, some 6 to 17	all 6 to 17
Husband works full-time, wife does not work	**10,052**	**4,000**	**6,051**	**1,469**	**1,652**	**2,930**
Under $5,000	38	11	27	10	6	11
$5,000 to $9,999	34	4	30	13	9	8
$10,000 to $14,999	135	34	101	30	21	50
$15,000 to $19,999	264	68	195	43	89	63
$20,000 to $24,999	408	116	292	75	113	104
$25,000 to $29,999	395	125	269	76	84	110
$30,000 to $34,999	447	133	315	95	87	133
$35,000 to $39,999	518	140	378	105	109	163
$40,000 to $44,999	482	172	310	80	92	138
$45,000 to $49,999	510	203	307	86	91	130
$50,000 to $54,999	541	225	316	76	90	149
$55,000 to $59,999	390	176	214	69	50	95
$60,000 to $64,999	526	208	318	87	78	152
$65,000 to $69,999	367	176	191	46	40	105
$70,000 to $74,999	425	181	245	65	70	110
$75,000 to $79,999	352	148	204	56	44	104
$80,000 to $84,999	362	144	219	53	54	112
$85,000 to $89,999	334	172	162	44	38	80
$90,000 to $94,999	266	114	153	40	47	66
$95,000 to $99,999	220	93	127	26	32	69
$100,000 or more	3,038	1,357	1,681	293	409	978
$100,000 to $124,999	1,007	422	585	125	155	304
$125,000 to $149,999	503	230	273	50	70	153
$150,000 to $174,999	534	225	309	48	62	199
$175,000 to $199,999	229	115	114	18	41	55
$200,000 or more	766	366	400	52	81	267
Median income	**$69,400**	**$75,663**	**$63,345**	**$57,440**	**$57,464**	**$71,669**
Husband works full-time, wife does not work	**100.0%**	**100.0%**	**100.0%**	**100.0%**	**100.0%**	**100.0%**
Under $25,000	8.7	5.8	10.7	11.6	14.4	8.1
$25,000 to $49,999	23.4	19.3	26.1	30.1	28.0	23.0
$50,000 to $74,999	22.4	24.2	21.2	23.3	19.9	20.9
$75,000 to $99,999	15.3	16.7	14.3	15.0	13.0	14.7
$100,000 or more	30.2	33.9	27.8	20.0	24.8	33.4

Source: Bureau of the Census, 2013 Current Population Survey, Internet site http://www.census.gov/hhes/www/cpstables/ 032013/faminc/toc.htm; calculations by New Strategist

Table 1.66 Married Couples by Work Status, Household Income, and Presence of Children, 2012: Husband Does Not Work, Wife Does Not Work

(number and percent distribution of married couples in which neither husband nor wife works, by household income and presence and age of related children under age 18 at home, 2012; married couples in thousands as of 2013)

			one or more children under age 18			
	total	no children	total	all under 6	some under 6, some 6 to 17	all 6 to 17
Husband does not work, wife does not work	**9,916**	**9,063**	**852**	**175**	**182**	**495**
Under $5,000	599	381	217	49	55	114
$5,000 to $9,999	310	238	72	16	17	38
$10,000 to $14,999	472	398	74	21	14	39
$15,000 to $19,999	679	620	58	13	13	33
$20,000 to $24,999	899	842	58	7	12	39
$25,000 to $29,999	1,084	1,030	54	8	13	34
$30,000 to $34,999	949	918	32	5	5	22
$35,000 to $39,999	773	728	45	9	9	27
$40,000 to $44,999	521	487	34	7	5	22
$45,000 to $49,999	588	564	24	9	1	14
$50,000 to $54,999	445	418	27	4	5	18
$55,000 to $59,999	367	350	17	5	5	7
$60,000 to $64,999	279	255	24	3	2	19
$65,000 to $69,999	299	288	11	2	2	8
$70,000 to $74,999	237	227	10	1	2	7
$75,000 to $79,999	171	161	9	2	4	4
$80,000 to $84,999	170	154	16	4	4	8
$85,000 to $89,999	151	136	15	3	4	8
$90,000 to $94,999	86	78	8	1	0	6
$95,000 to $99,999	89	86	3	0	0	3
$100,000 or more	747	703	45	9	10	26
$100,000 to $124,999	384	362	22	3	4	15
$125,000 to $149,999	171	162	10	3	2	5
$150,000 to $174,999	72	69	3	1	2	0
$175,000 to $199,999	41	37	4	2	1	2
$200,000 or more	79	73	6	0	2	4
Median income	**$34,803**	**$35,569**	**$20,465**	**$17,832**	**$16,334**	**$23,087**
Husband does not work, wife does not work	**100.0%**	**100.0%**	**100.0%**	**100.0%**	**100.0%**	**100.0%**
Under $25,000	29.8	27.4	56.2	60.1	60.9	53.1
$25,000 to $49,999	39.5	41.1	22.1	21.4	18.2	23.8
$50,000 to $74,999	16.4	17.0	10.5	8.2	8.7	11.9
$75,000 to $99,999	6.7	6.8	6.0	5.4	6.7	5.9
$100,000 or more	7.5	7.8	5.3	4.9	5.6	5.3

Source: Bureau of the Census, 2013 Current Population Survey, Internet site http://www.census.gov/hhes/www/cpstables/032013/faminc/toc.htm; calculations by New Strategist

Female-Headed Families without Children Have Higher Incomes

Those with preschoolers have the lowest incomes.

The median income of female-headed families stood at $30,686 in 2012. Women who head families that include children under age 18 have lower incomes (a median of $25,493) than those who head families without children ($42,147). Behind this income difference is the fact that female-headed families without children under age 18 include adult relatives and are more likely to have an additional earner in the home.

Black and Hispanic female-headed families with children have the lowest incomes—a median of $21,709 for Hispanics and $21,745 for blacks in 2012. The median income of non-Hispanic white female-headed families with children was a higher $30,072, and their Asian counterparts had the highest median income—$36,246 in 2012.

■ The incomes of female-headed families dropped sharply during the Great Recession and its aftermath.

Female-headed families with children have lower incomes

(median income of female-headed families by presence and age of children under age 18 at home, 2012)

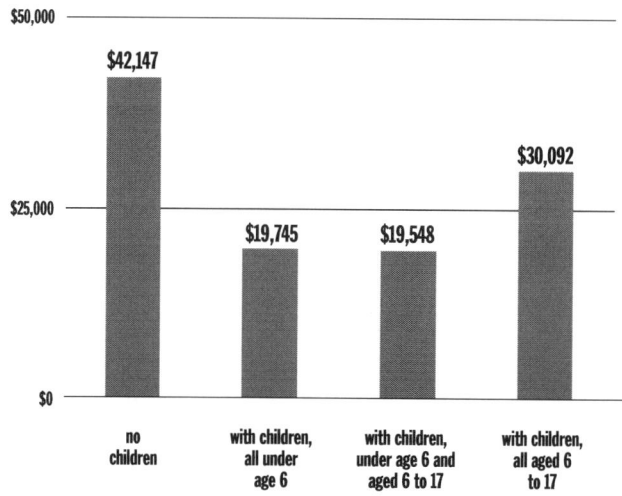

Table 1.67 Female-Headed Families by Family Income and Presence of Children, 2012: Total Female-Headed Families

(number and percent distribution of total female-headed families by family income and presence and age of related children under age 18 at home, 2012; female-headed families in thousands as of 2013)

			one or more children under age 18			
	total	no children	total	all under 6	some under 6, some 6 to 17	all 6 to 17
Total female-headed families	**15,489**	**5,456**	**10,033**	**2,141**	**2,118**	**5,774**
Under $5,000	1,288	166	1,122	344	329	449
$5,000 to $9,999	1,012	180	832	244	227	361
$10,000 to $14,999	1,434	306	1,128	283	274	571
$15,000 to $19,999	1,345	377	968	209	246	513
$20,000 to $24,999	1,301	420	881	183	210	488
$25,000 to $29,999	1,189	403	786	148	144	494
$30,000 to $34,999	1,053	365	688	117	127	444
$35,000 to $39,999	898	328	570	118	99	353
$40,000 to $44,999	881	345	535	70	111	354
$45,000 to $49,999	627	280	348	51	43	254
$50,000 to $54,999	578	268	310	54	44	212
$55,000 to $59,999	529	217	312	42	57	213
$60,000 to $64,999	434	196	238	42	32	164
$65,000 to $69,999	425	228	197	21	18	158
$70,000 to $74,999	328	160	168	25	22	121
$75,000 to $79,999	295	168	127	28	18	81
$80,000 to $84,999	257	142	114	27	17	71
$85,000 to $89,999	180	103	77	17	6	54
$90,000 to $94,999	177	105	72	8	16	48
$95,000 to $99,999	136	75	62	6	13	44
$100,000 or more	1,122	626	496	103	65	329
$100,000 to $124,999	531	289	242	59	29	154
$125,000 to $149,999	261	161	100	22	12	66
$150,000 to $174,999	115	59	57	9	11	36
$175,000 to $199,999	72	45	27	4	3	20
$200,000 or more	143	73	70	8	10	52
Median income	**$30,686**	**$42,147**	**$25,493**	**$19,745**	**$19,548**	**$30,092**
Total female-headed families	**100.0%**	**100.0%**	**100.0%**	**100.0%**	**100.0%**	**100.0%**
Under $25,000	41.2	26.6	49.2	59.0	60.7	41.3
$25,000 to $49,999	30.0	31.5	29.2	23.6	24.8	32.9
$50,000 to $74,999	14.8	19.6	12.2	8.6	8.2	15.0
$75,000 to $99,999	6.7	10.9	4.5	4.0	3.3	5.2
$100,000 or more	7.2	11.5	4.9	4.8	3.1	5.7

Note: The median income of female-headed families in this table is slightly different from the figure shown in the household income tables because this figure includes the incomes of only family members and not any unrelated members of the household. Source: Bureau of the Census, 2013 Current Population Survey, Internet site http://www.census.gov/hhes/www/cpstables/032013/faminc/toc.htm; calculations by New Strategist

Table 1.68 Female-Headed Families by Family Income and Presence of Children, 2012: Asian Female-Headed Families

(number and percent distribution of Asian female-headed families by family income and presence of related children under age 18 at home, 2012; female-headed families in thousands as of 2013)

	total	no children	with one or more children
Asian female-headed families	**568**	**269**	**299**
Under $5,000	34	10	24
$5,000 to $9,999	20	9	12
$10,000 to $14,999	26	9	18
$15,000 to $19,999	32	14	18
$20,000 to $24,999	52	9	44
$25,000 to $29,999	28	9	19
$30,000 to $34,999	19	11	8
$35,000 to $39,999	33	12	20
$40,000 to $44,999	27	17	10
$45,000 to $49,999	45	23	22
$50,000 to $54,999	18	7	11
$55,000 to $59,999	20	10	10
$60,000 to $64,999	23	7	16
$65,000 to $69,999	20	11	9
$70,000 to $74,999	20	10	10
$75,000 to $79,999	10	8	2
$80,000 to $84,999	23	14	9
$85,000 to $89,999	4	4	0
$90,000 to $94,999	9	6	3
$95,000 to $99,999	3	0	3
$100,000 or more	101	72	29
$100,000 to $124,999	48	34	14
$125,000 to $149,999	20	17	4
$150,000 to $174,999	15	12	3
$175,000 to $199,999	2	0	2
$200,000 or more	15	9	6
Median income	**$46,164**	**$58,929**	**$36,246**
PERCENT DISTRIBUTION			
Asian female-headed families	**100.0%**	**100.0%**	**100.0%**
Under $25,000	28.9	18.3	38.6
$25,000 to $49,999	26.7	26.7	26.7
$50,000 to $74,999	17.9	16.6	19.1
$75,000 to $99,999	8.7	11.8	6.0
$100,000 or more	17.7	26.6	9.7

Note: Asians are those who identify themselves as being of the race alone and those who identify themselves as being of the race in combination with other races. The median income of female-headed families in this table is slightly different from the figure shown in the household income tables because this figure includes the incomes of only family members and not any unrelated members of the household.
Source: Bureau of the Census, 2013 Current Population Survey, Internet site http://www.census.gov/hhes/www/cpstables/032013/hhinc/toc.htm; calculations by New Strategist

Table 1.69 Female-Headed Families by Family Income and Presence of Children, 2012: Black Female-Headed Families

(number and percent distribution of black female-headed families by family income and presence and age of related children under age 18 at home, 2012; female-headed families in thousands as of 2013)

	total	no children	total	all under 6	some under 6, some 6 to 17	all 6 to 17
			one or more children under age 18			
Black female-headed families	**4,485**	**1,327**	**3,158**	**665**	**781**	**1,713**
Under $5,000	429	55	374	92	121	161
$5,000 to $9,999	377	72	305	96	77	132
$10,000 to $14,999	518	84	433	101	121	211
$15,000 to $19,999	446	110	337	77	86	174
$20,000 to $24,999	432	119	313	73	88	151
$25,000 to $29,999	304	98	206	35	51	120
$30,000 to $34,999	319	105	214	31	51	132
$35,000 to $39,999	294	78	216	47	36	133
$40,000 to $44,999	230	76	154	20	38	96
$45,000 to $49,999	171	82	90	16	14	59
$50,000 to $54,999	125	56	69	14	7	48
$55,000 to $59,999	133	51	82	13	13	56
$60,000 to $64,999	108	52	56	10	13	33
$65,000 to $69,999	100	52	48	6	2	40
$70,000 to $74,999	66	27	39	6	9	25
$75,000 to $79,999	67	31	36	3	8	24
$80,000 to $84,999	55	20	35	5	12	18
$85,000 to $89,999	43	20	23	6	5	12
$90,000 to $94,999	40	19	21	1	7	13
$95,000 to $99,999	29	12	17	1	3	12
$100,000 or more	200	108	92	12	18	62
$100,000 to $124,999	108	54	54	10	11	33
$125,000 to $149,999	40	19	21	0	7	14
$150,000 to $174,999	18	8	10	0	1	9
$175,000 to $199,999	10	10	0	0	0	0
$200,000 or more	24	17	7	2	0	6
Median income	**$25,581**	**$36,175**	**$21,745**	**$17,595**	**$18,651**	**$26,042**
Black female-headed families	**100.0%**	**100.0%**	**100.0%**	**100.0%**	**100.0%**	**100.0%**
Under $25,000	49.1	33.1	55.8	66.1	63.3	48.4
$25,000 to $49,999	29.4	33.1	27.8	22.4	24.3	31.5
$50,000 to $74,999	11.9	17.9	9.3	7.3	5.5	11.8
$75,000 to $99,999	5.2	7.7	4.1	2.3	4.6	4.6
$100,000 or more	4.4	8.1	2.9	1.9	2.3	3.6

Note: Blacks are those who identify themselves as being of the race alone and those who identify themselves as being of the race in combination with other races. The median income of female-headed families in this table is slightly different from the figure shown in the household income tables because this figure includes the incomes of only family members and not any unrelated members of the household.
Source: Bureau of the Census, 2013 Current Population Survey, Internet site http://www.census.gov/hhes/www/cpstables/ 032013/faminc/toc.htm; calculations by New Strategist

Table 1.70 Female-Headed Families by Family Income and Presence of Children, 2012: Hispanic Female-Headed Families

(number and percent distribution of Hispanic female-headed families by family income and presence and age of related children under age 18 at home, 2012; female-headed families in thousands as of 2013)

| | total | no children | one or more children under age 18 | | | |
			total	all under 6	some under 6, some 6 to 17	all 6 to 17
Hispanic female-headed families	**3,109**	**780**	**2,329**	**519**	**598**	**1,211**
Under $5,000	377	38	339	104	106	129
$5,000 to $9,999	253	42	211	51	66	94
$10,000 to $14,999	305	35	270	70	77	123
$15,000 to $19,999	312	66	246	58	62	126
$20,000 to $24,999	287	65	221	54	58	110
$25,000 to $29,999	288	68	220	41	46	134
$30,000 to $34,999	228	67	160	26	40	95
$35,000 to $39,999	162	43	119	22	23	74
$40,000 to $44,999	152	46	107	17	35	54
$45,000 to $49,999	108	46	62	8	5	49
$50,000 to $54,999	99	44	54	11	16	28
$55,000 to $59,999	103	38	65	9	18	38
$60,000 to $64,999	56	22	34	6	5	22
$65,000 to $69,999	49	21	28	2	6	21
$70,000 to $74,999	39	12	27	3	5	19
$75,000 to $79,999	51	18	32	4	10	19
$80,000 to $84,999	37	11	26	8	3	16
$85,000 to $89,999	27	18	9	3	0	6
$90,000 to $94,999	14	5	9	2	2	5
$95,000 to $99,999	18	14	4	2	1	1
$100,000 or more	144	60	84	20	15	49
$100,000 to $124,999	86	34	51	11	8	32
$125,000 to $149,999	28	18	10	6	0	4
$150,000 to $174,999	13	2	11	1	5	5
$175,000 to $199,999	1	1	0	0	0	0
$200,000 or more	17	5	11	2	2	7
Median income	**$25,318**	**$35,867**	**$21,709**	**$17,321**	**$18,517**	**$25,784**
Hispanic female-headed families	**100.0%**	**100.0%**	**100.0%**	**100.0%**	**100.0%**	**100.0%**
Under $25,000	49.3	31.5	55.3	65.0	61.6	48.0
$25,000 to $49,999	30.2	34.6	28.7	21.8	24.9	33.6
$50,000 to $74,999	11.1	17.7	8.9	5.9	8.2	10.6
$75,000 to $99,999	4.7	8.5	3.5	3.5	2.7	3.8
$100,000 or more	4.6	7.7	3.6	3.8	2.5	4.0

Note: The median income of female-headed families in this table is slightly different from the figure shown in the household income tables because this figure includes the incomes of only family members and not any unrelated members of the household. Source: Bureau of the Census, 2013 Current Population Survey, Internet site http://www.census.gov/hhes/www/cpstables/032013/faminc/toc.htm; calculations by New Strategist

Table 1.71 Female-Headed Families by Family Income and Presence of Children, 2012: Non-Hispanic White Female-Headed Families

(number and percent distribution of non-Hispanic white female-headed families by family income and presence and age of related children under age 18 at home, 2012; female-headed families in thousands as of 2013)

	total	no children	one or more children under age 18			
			total	all under 6	some under 6, some 6 to 17	all 6 to 17
Non-Hispanic white female-headed families	**7,321**	**3,046**	**4,275**	**927**	**694**	**2,653**
Under $5,000	440	68	372	132	95	144
$5,000 to $9,999	372	59	313	104	81	128
$10,000 to $14,999	572	162	409	121	73	215
$15,000 to $19,999	550	181	370	77	84	210
$20,000 to $24,999	550	221	329	60	60	209
$25,000 to $29,999	560	222	338	67	50	221
$30,000 to $34,999	495	178	317	60	36	221
$35,000 to $39,999	408	197	211	40	39	132
$40,000 to $44,999	458	202	257	30	40	187
$45,000 to $49,999	313	138	175	23	19	132
$50,000 to $54,999	333	163	170	28	18	124
$55,000 to $59,999	282	125	157	18	25	114
$60,000 to $64,999	247	115	131	25	11	95
$65,000 to $69,999	247	143	105	14	7	84
$70,000 to $74,999	204	108	96	16	10	70
$75,000 to $79,999	176	111	65	19	4	42
$80,000 to $84,999	143	94	49	13	2	34
$85,000 to $89,999	101	57	43	8	0	35
$90,000 to $94,999	110	71	39	3	7	28
$95,000 to $99,999	83	48	34	2	3	30
$100,000 or more	675	382	293	66	29	199
$100,000 to $124,999	290	167	122	33	10	79
$125,000 to $149,999	171	105	66	16	5	45
$150,000 to $174,999	70	37	34	8	6	20
$175,000 to $199,999	56	31	25	4	1	20
$200,000 or more	89	42	47	4	7	35
Median income	**$36,324**	**$45,926**	**$30,072**	**$21,558**	**$21,122**	**$34,424**
Non-Hispanic white female-headed families	**100.0%**	**100.0%**	**100.0%**	**100.0%**	**100.0%**	**100.0%**
Under $25,000	33.9	22.7	42.0	53.3	56.7	34.1
$25,000 to $49,999	30.5	30.7	30.4	23.8	26.7	33.6
$50,000 to $74,999	17.9	21.5	15.4	10.9	10.3	18.3
$75,000 to $99,999	8.4	12.5	5.4	4.9	2.2	6.4
$100,000 or more	9.2	12.6	6.9	7.1	4.1	7.5

Note: Non-Hispanic whites are those who identify themselves as being of the race alone and not Hispanic. The median income of female-headed families in this table is slightly different from the figure shown in the household income tables because this figure includes the incomes of only family members and not any unrelated members of the household.
Source: Bureau of the Census, 2013 Current Population Survey, Internet site http://www.census.gov/hhes/www/cpstables/032013/faminc/toc.htm; calculations by New Strategist

Male-Headed Families with Children Have Below-Average Incomes

Those with preschoolers have the lowest incomes.

The median income of male-headed families stood at $42,358 in 2012, well above the $30,686 median of their female counterparts. Male-headed families without children under age 18 have incomes close to the average, with a median of $49,338 in 2012. These men live with relatives such as adult children, siblings, or parents, and many of their families have more than one wage earner. Of the nation's 6.2 million male-headed families, only half include children under age 18. A much larger 65 percent of female-headed families include children.

The incomes of black and Hispanic male-headed families are well below those of non-Hispanic whites or Asians. Black male-headed families had a median income of $33,932 in 2012, while the Hispanic median was $38,130. The non-Hispanic white median was a higher $46,137, and the Asian median of $57,680 was the highest of all.

■ Male-headed families are the least-common household type and account for only 5 percent of households, a status that is unlikely to change in the years ahead.

Incomes vary for male-headed families

(median income of male-headed families by presence and age of children under age 18 at home, 2012)

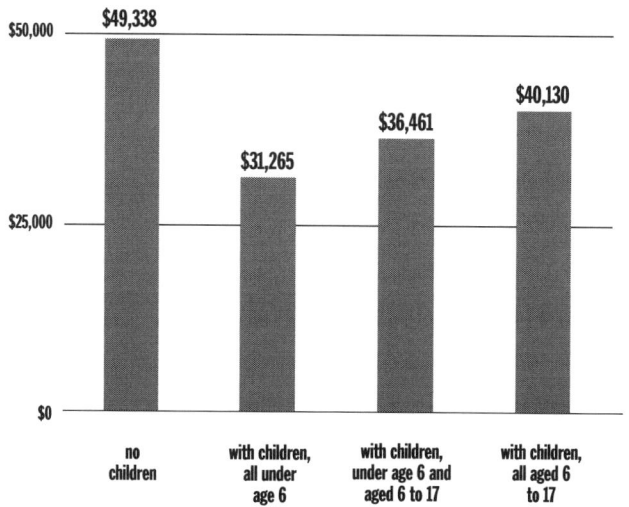

Table 1.72 Male-Headed Families by Family Income and Presence of Children, 2012: Total Male-Headed Families

(number and percent distribution of total male-headed families by family income and presence and age of related children under age 18 at home, 2012; male-headed families in thousands as of 2013)

	total	no children	one or more children under age 18 total	all under 6	some under 6, some 6 to 17	all 6 to 17
Total male-headed families	**6,231**	**3,062**	**3,169**	**921**	**466**	**1,782**
Under $5,000	231	76	155	61	26	68
$5,000 to $9,999	208	82	126	47	14	66
$10,000 to $14,999	320	129	191	77	22	92
$15,000 to $19,999	462	189	273	88	58	127
$20,000 to $24,999	446	195	251	84	36	131
$25,000 to $29,999	431	189	242	76	23	143
$30,000 to $34,999	451	207	244	83	33	128
$35,000 to $39,999	398	153	245	68	44	133
$40,000 to $44,999	329	171	158	40	23	95
$45,000 to $49,999	315	162	153	49	19	85
$50,000 to $54,999	340	201	139	24	22	93
$55,000 to $59,999	257	143	114	19	20	74
$60,000 to $64,999	253	106	147	37	24	86
$65,000 to $69,999	214	135	79	19	8	52
$70,000 to $74,999	150	97	52	19	7	27
$75,000 to $79,999	136	84	52	11	10	32
$80,000 to $84,999	146	79	68	18	11	38
$85,000 to $89,999	133	66	67	19	8	40
$90,000 to $94,999	119	66	53	8	8	36
$95,000 to $99,999	90	48	42	15	8	19
$100,000 or more	800	483	317	60	41	216
$100,000 to $124,999	336	201	134	27	27	81
$125,000 to $149,999	163	115	49	7	3	38
$150,000 to $174,999	122	69	52	5	2	45
$175,000 to $199,999	58	37	21	5	3	13
$200,000 or more	122	61	61	16	6	39
Median income	**$42,358**	**$49,338**	**$36,471**	**$31,265**	**$36,461**	**$40,130**
Total male-headed families	**100.0%**	**100.0%**	**100.0%**	**100.0%**	**100.0%**	**100.0%**
Under $25,000	26.8	21.9	31.4	38.7	33.5	27.2
$25,000 to $49,999	30.9	28.8	32.9	34.3	30.5	32.8
$50,000 to $74,999	19.5	22.3	16.7	12.7	17.6	18.6
$75,000 to $99,999	10.0	11.2	8.9	7.8	9.7	9.3
$100,000 or more	12.8	15.8	10.0	6.5	8.7	12.1

Note: The median income of male-headed families in this table is slightly different from the figure shown in the household income tables because this figure includes the incomes of only family members and not any unrelated members of the household. Source: Bureau of the Census, 2013 Current Population Survey, Internet site http://www.census.gov/hhes/www/cpstables/ 032013/faminc/toc.htm; calculations by New Strategist

Table 1.73 Male-Headed Families by Family Income and Presence of Children, 2012: Asian Male-Headed Families

(number and percent distribution of Asian male-headed families by family income and presence of related children under age 18 at home, 2012; male-headed families in thousands as of 2013)

	total	no children	with one or more children
Asian male-headed families	**346**	**229**	**117**
Under $5,000	12	8	3
$5,000 to $9,999	11	3	8
$10,000 to $14,999	12	6	6
$15,000 to $19,999	13	4	8
$20,000 to $24,999	17	9	8
$25,000 to $29,999	13	5	9
$30,000 to $34,999	21	17	5
$35,000 to $39,999	19	16	2
$40,000 to $44,999	14	11	3
$45,000 to $49,999	16	6	10
$50,000 to $54,999	12	9	2
$55,000 to $59,999	21	17	5
$60,000 to $64,999	21	12	9
$65,000 to $69,999	17	11	6
$70,000 to $74,999	3	3	0
$75,000 to $79,999	6	4	2
$80,000 to $84,999	12	11	1
$85,000 to $89,999	11	8	3
$90,000 to $94,999	11	9	3
$95,000 to $99,999	6	4	2
$100,000 or more	79	57	22
$100,000 to $124,999	31	24	7
$125,000 to $149,999	10	10	1
$150,000 to $174,999	17	8	9
$175,000 to $199,999	2	2	0
$200,000 or more	19	14	5
Median income	**$57,680**	**$62,505**	**$46,783**
PERCENT DISTRIBUTION			
Asian male-headed families	**100.0%**	**100.0%**	**100.0%**
Under $25,000	18.4	13.2	28.7
$25,000 to $49,999	24.1	23.9	24.5
$50,000 to $74,999	21.4	22.6	19.0
$75,000 to $99,999	13.2	15.3	9.1
$100,000 or more	22.9	25.0	18.8

Note: Asians are those who identify themselves as being of the race alone and those who identify themselves as being of the race in combination with other races. The median income of male-headed families in this table is slightly different from the figure shown in the household income tables because this figure includes the incomes of only family members and not any unrelated members of the household.
Source: Bureau of the Census, 2013 Current Population Survey, Internet site http://www.census.gov/hhes/www/cpstables/032013/hhinc/toc.htm; calculations by New Strategist

Table 1.74 Male-Headed Families by Family Income and Presence of Children, 2012: Black Male-Headed Families

(number and percent distribution of black male-headed families by family income and presence and age of related children under age 18 at home, 2012; male-headed families in thousands as of 2013)

	total	no children	total	all under 6	some under 6, some 6 to 17	all 6 to 17
			one or more children under age 18			
Black male-headed families	**1,105**	**499**	**606**	**214**	**104**	**289**
Under $5,000	91	30	60	24	15	22
$5,000 to $9,999	54	24	30	12	4	14
$10,000 to $14,999	73	37	36	19	3	14
$15,000 to $19,999	110	48	63	25	9	28
$20,000 to $24,999	92	37	56	25	7	24
$25,000 to $29,999	62	32	30	11	3	15
$30,000 to $34,999	83	33	50	21	6	23
$35,000 to $39,999	59	7	52	21	10	21
$40,000 to $44,999	52	23	29	8	7	15
$45,000 to $49,999	66	27	39	12	0	27
$50,000 to $54,999	49	34	14	1	2	11
$55,000 to $59,999	39	19	20	5	5	9
$60,000 to $64,999	36	15	22	6	5	11
$65,000 to $69,999	36	28	8	0	4	4
$70,000 to $74,999	29	21	8	3	3	2
$75,000 to $79,999	23	14	9	3	2	4
$80,000 to $84,999	10	5	6	3	0	3
$85,000 to $89,999	17	5	13	5	2	6
$90,000 to $94,999	13	8	6	0	2	4
$95,000 to $99,999	14	5	8	2	3	4
$100,000 or more	97	49	48	8	12	29
$100,000 to $124,999	54	22	32	4	12	16
$125,000 to $149,999	12	8	3	1	0	2
$150,000 to $174,999	10	6	4	0	0	4
$175,000 to $199,999	5	2	2	0	0	2
$200,000 or more	16	10	6	2	0	4
Median income	**$33,932**	**$40,724**	**$32,196**	**$25,748**	**$38,004**	**$35,784**
Black male-headed families	**100.0%**	**100.0%**	**100.0%**	**100.0%**	**100.0%**	**100.0%**
Under $25,000	38.0	35.1	40.4	48.9	37.0	35.2
$25,000 to $49,999	29.1	24.3	33.1	34.2	25.7	34.8
$50,000 to $74,999	17.1	23.5	11.9	7.3	18.1	13.0
$75,000 to $99,999	7.0	7.2	6.8	6.0	8.1	7.0
$100,000 or more	8.8	9.8	7.9	3.5	11.1	9.9

Note: Blacks are those who identify themselves as being of the race alone and those who identify themselves as being of the race in combination with other races. The median income of male-headed families in this table is slightly different from the figure shown in the household income tables because this figure includes the incomes of only family members and not any unrelated members of the household.
Source: Bureau of the Census, 2013 Current Population Survey, Internet site http://www.census.gov/hhes/www/cpstables/032013/faminc/toc.htm; calculations by New Strategist

Table 1.75 Male-Headed Families by Family Income and Presence of Children, 2012: Hispanic Male-Headed Families

(number and percent distribution of Hispanic male-headed families by family income and presence and age of related children under age 18 at home, 2012; male-headed families in thousands as of 2013)

			one or more children under age 18			
	total	no children	total	all under 6	some under 6, some 6 to 17	all 6 to 17
Hispanic male-headed families	**1,392**	**611**	**781**	**236**	**166**	**379**
Under $5,000	46	14	31	8	8	15
$5,000 to $9,999	65	21	44	17	6	22
$10,000 to $14,999	82	28	54	23	9	22
$15,000 to $19,999	136	39	97	28	28	41
$20,000 to $24,999	117	37	80	25	15	40
$25,000 to $29,999	96	31	66	20	9	37
$30,000 to $34,999	89	39	50	16	13	21
$35,000 to $39,999	91	34	57	18	9	31
$40,000 to $44,999	84	45	39	11	8	20
$45,000 to $49,999	67	35	32	17	4	11
$50,000 to $54,999	66	27	39	6	8	25
$55,000 to $59,999	76	49	27	8	6	13
$60,000 to $64,999	47	20	27	9	6	12
$65,000 to $69,999	33	14	18	4	0	14
$70,000 to $74,999	41	25	16	6	5	5
$75,000 to $79,999	19	7	12	2	5	5
$80,000 to $84,999	28	18	11	5	2	4
$85,000 to $89,999	31	23	9	0	1	7
$90,000 to $94,999	18	14	5	2	2	1
$95,000 to $99,999	15	5	10	4	4	1
$100,000 or more	145	85	60	10	18	32
$100,000 to $124,999	72	35	37	8	10	19
$125,000 to $149,999	31	22	9	1	2	7
$150,000 to $174,999	13	8	5	0	0	5
$175,000 to $199,999	11	9	2	0	2	0
$200,000 or more	19	12	7	1	4	2
Median income	**$38,130**	**$47,690**	**$31,841**	**$29,113**	**$32,274**	**$33,438**
Hispanic male-headed families	**100.0%**	**100.0%**	**100.0%**	**100.0%**	**100.0%**	**100.0%**
Under $25,000	32.0	22.8	39.1	42.3	40.1	36.8
$25,000 to $49,999	30.7	30.1	31.2	34.4	25.4	31.7
$50,000 to $74,999	18.8	22.3	16.1	13.8	15.3	17.9
$75,000 to $99,999	8.1	10.9	5.9	5.4	8.3	5.1
$100,000 or more	10.4	14.0	7.7	4.1	10.9	8.5

Note: The median income of male-headed families in this table is slightly different from the figure shown in the household income tables because this figure includes the incomes of only family members and not any unrelated members of the household. Source: Bureau of the Census, 2013 Current Population Survey, Internet site http://www.census.gov/hhes/www/cpstables/ 032013/faminc/toc.htm; calculations by New Strategist

Table 1.76 Male-Headed Families by Family Income and Presence of Children, 2012: Non-Hispanic White Male-Headed Families

(number and percent distribution of non-Hispanic white male-headed families by family income and presence and age of related children under age 18 at home, 2012; male-headed families in thousands as of 2013)

			one or more children under age 18			
	total	no children	total	all under 6	some under 6, some 6 to 17	all 6 to 17
Non-Hispanic white male-headed families	**3,388**	**1,702**	**1,686**	**455**	**185**	**1,047**
Under $5,000	76	17	59	27	4	28
$5,000 to $9,999	70	35	35	11	2	23
$10,000 to $14,999	151	58	93	32	5	57
$15,000 to $19,999	208	100	107	39	16	52
$20,000 to $24,999	217	106	111	33	11	66
$25,000 to $29,999	258	121	137	43	10	84
$30,000 to $34,999	258	116	142	46	13	82
$35,000 to $39,999	228	92	136	34	25	77
$40,000 to $44,999	188	95	94	23	12	59
$45,000 to $49,999	167	91	76	22	14	39
$50,000 to $54,999	200	122	78	16	9	53
$55,000 to $59,999	127	62	65	5	11	49
$60,000 to $64,999	143	58	85	20	10	55
$65,000 to $69,999	131	85	46	12	4	30
$70,000 to $74,999	81	48	33	11	2	19
$75,000 to $79,999	87	56	30	6	3	21
$80,000 to $84,999	96	47	49	10	9	30
$85,000 to $89,999	75	31	44	12	4	28
$90,000 to $94,999	76	36	40	7	4	29
$95,000 to $99,999	56	34	22	7	1	14
$100,000 or more	495	290	204	38	15	152
$100,000 to $124,999	190	121	69	15	8	46
$125,000 to $149,999	111	75	35	5	2	28
$150,000 to $174,999	82	43	39	3	2	33
$175,000 to $199,999	41	24	17	5	1	11
$200,000 or more	72	27	44	10	2	33
Median income	**$46,137**	**$50,679**	**$40,957**	**$34,320**	**$41,486**	**$44,514**
Non-Hispanic white male-headed families	**100.0%**	**100.0%**	**100.0%**	**100.0%**	**100.0%**	**100.0%**
Under $25,000	21.3	18.6	24.1	31.2	20.7	21.6
$25,000 to $49,999	32.4	30.3	34.6	37.0	40.3	32.6
$50,000 to $74,999	20.1	22.1	18.2	14.3	19.0	19.7
$75,000 to $99,999	11.5	12.0	11.0	9.2	12.2	11.6
$100,000 or more	14.6	17.1	12.1	8.4	7.9	14.5

Note: Non-Hispanic whites are those who identify themselves as being of the race alone and not Hispanic. The median income of male-headed families in this table is slightly different from the figure shown in the household income tables because this figure includes the incomes of only family members and not any unrelated members of the household.
Source: Bureau of the Census, 2013 Current Population Survey, Internet site http://www.census.gov/hhes/www/cpstables/032013/faminc/toc.htm; calculations by New Strategist

Household Income Rises with Education

Householders with a bachelor's degree had a median income of $80,549 in 2012.

Education largely determines household income. Householders with an associate's degree or more education have above-average incomes, while those with only some college or less education have average or below-average incomes. Household income peaks among those with a professional degree, a category that includes physicians and lawyers. The 61 percent majority of this group has an income of $100,000 or more.

The pattern is the same regardless of race and Hispanic origin, with better-educated householders commanding higher incomes. Black householders with a bachelor's degree had a median income of $60,925 in 2012, while Hispanic householders with a bachelor's degree had a median income of $70,607. Among non-Hispanic whites with a bachelor's degree, median household income is a higher $83,181, and the figure peaks among Asians at $87,302.

■ The financial rewards of a college degree appear to be worth the cost, but many blacks and Hispanics cannot afford the cost regardless of the benefits.

Education boosts income

(median household income of householders aged 25 or older by educational attainment, 2012)

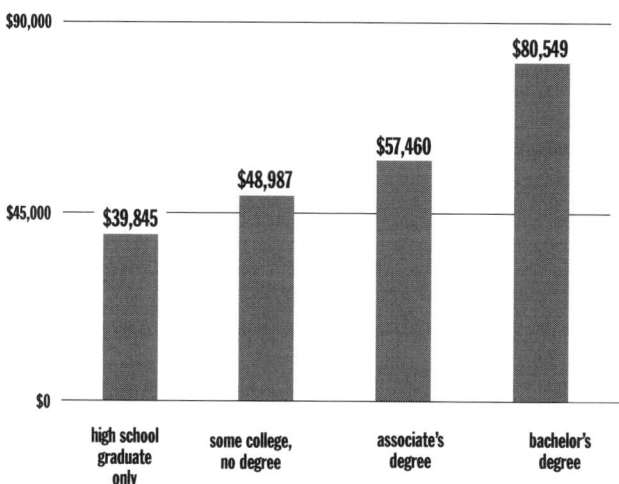

Table 1.77 Households by Income and Educational Attainment of Householder, 2012: Total Households

(number and percent distribution of total households headed by people aged 25 or older by household income and educational attainment of householder, 2012; households in thousands as of 2013)

	total	less than 9th grade	9th to 12th grade, no diploma	high school graduate	some college, no degree	associate's degree	bachelor's degree or more total	bachelor's degree	master's degree	professional degree	doctoral degree
Total households	116,145	4,903	8,054	32,308	21,211	11,760	37,910	23,782	10,247	1,826	2,055
Under $5,000	3,647	298	546	1,265	625	252	662	445	162	31	25
$5,000 to $9,999	4,303	549	842	1,404	739	274	495	335	128	16	18
$10,000 to $14,999	6,426	733	1,055	2,345	1,080	489	723	516	144	33	30
$15,000 to $19,999	6,633	583	1,002	2,471	1,227	527	823	554	214	26	28
$20,000 to $24,999	6,547	512	839	2,383	1,320	590	903	650	184	31	39
$25,000 to $29,999	6,289	453	585	2,300	1,211	620	1,119	815	228	27	49
$30,000 to $34,999	5,952	319	463	2,144	1,218	584	1,224	856	285	46	36
$35,000 to $39,999	5,483	258	411	1,887	1,180	572	1,175	878	247	22	28
$40,000 to $44,999	5,248	208	338	1,756	1,085	590	1,271	882	306	25	58
$45,000 to $49,999	4,990	160	333	1,507	1,128	604	1,258	877	289	43	50
$50,000 to $54,999	4,810	157	289	1,537	960	541	1,326	868	345	48	65
$55,000 to $59,999	4,046	110	172	1,192	871	489	1,213	802	330	37	44
$60,000 to $64,999	4,198	103	181	1,136	846	588	1,343	867	406	30	39
$65,000 to $69,999	3,782	68	135	1,090	755	438	1,297	834	370	46	47
$70,000 to $74,999	3,600	56	147	980	780	434	1,203	712	383	53	56
$75,000 to $79,999	3,303	68	119	787	579	425	1,324	888	335	32	69
$80,000 to $84,999	3,202	31	108	788	589	412	1,274	818	343	54	59
$85,000 to $89,999	2,557	42	68	614	485	333	1,014	685	256	45	28
$90,000 to $94,999	2,612	35	64	587	456	290	1,180	761	314	46	59
$95,000 to $99,999	2,151	22	65	399	404	279	982	649	268	23	42
$100,000 or more	26,366	136	295	3,735	3,671	2,428	16,099	9,090	4,709	1,112	1,188
$100,000 to $124,999	9,271	62	162	1,820	1,593	1,091	4,542	2,860	1,284	168	230
$125,000 to $149,999	5,676	31	59	835	909	571	3,271	1,970	941	157	203
$150,000 to $174,999	3,808	10	33	449	498	335	2,482	1,418	734	150	180
$175,000 to $199,999	2,202	6	15	222	229	177	1,552	812	507	106	126
$200,000 or more	5,409	26	27	409	442	253	4,252	2,030	1,243	531	449
Median income	$52,119	$22,496	$23,347	$39,845	$48,987	$57,460	$86,419	$80,549	$92,362	$129,588	$116,983

PERCENT DISTRIBUTION

	total	less than 9th grade	9th to 12th grade, no diploma	high school graduate	some college, no degree	associate's degree	bachelor's degree or more total	bachelor's degree	master's degree	professional degree	doctoral degree
Total households	100.0%	100.0%	100.0%	100.0%	100.0%	100.0%	100.0%	100.0%	100.0%	100.0%	100.0%
Under $25,000	23.7	54.6	53.2	30.5	23.5	18.1	9.5	10.5	8.1	7.5	6.8
$25,000 to $49,999	24.1	28.5	26.4	29.7	27.4	25.3	16.0	18.1	13.2	8.9	10.7
$50,000 to $74,999	17.6	10.1	11.5	18.4	19.9	21.2	16.8	17.2	17.9	11.7	12.2
$75,000 to $99,999	11.9	4.1	5.3	9.8	11.8	14.8	15.2	16.0	14.8	11.0	12.5
$100,000 or more	22.7	2.8	3.7	11.6	17.3	20.6	42.5	38.2	46.0	60.9	57.8

Source: Bureau of the Census, 2013 Current Population Survey, Internet site http://www.census.gov/hhes/www/income/data/incpovhlth/2012/dtables.html; calculations by New Strategist

Table 1.78 Households by Income and Educational Attainment of Householder, 2012: Asian Households

(number and percent distribution of Asian households headed by people aged 25 or older by household income and educational attainment of householder, 2012; households in thousands as of 2013)

	total	less than 9th grade	9th to 12th grade, no diploma	high school graduate	some college, no degree	associate's degree	bachelor's degree or more				
							total	bachelor's degree	master's degree	professional degree	doctoral degree
Asian households	5,509	193	210	882	600	414	3,210	1,691	973	237	309
Under $5,000	182	16	9	29	25	7	97	56	26	4	11
$5,000 to $9,999	133	25	11	18	24	9	46	22	16	4	5
$10,000 to $14,999	197	31	15	72	23	15	42	21	9	6	5
$15,000 to $19,999	178	27	21	49	23	9	48	30	14	0	4
$20,000 to $24,999	213	21	24	66	33	20	49	22	22	0	5
$25,000 to $29,999	206	10	22	60	26	17	71	48	11	0	11
$30,000 to $34,999	220	4	6	64	22	18	105	67	28	4	6
$35,000 to $39,999	206	6	13	53	39	15	80	58	18	2	2
$40,000 to $44,999	184	11	8	40	32	11	82	44	22	9	7
$45,000 to $49,999	219	3	11	51	26	39	89	51	16	14	8
$50,000 to $54,999	196	8	12	38	16	18	105	69	17	7	12
$55,000 to $59,999	200	4	11	36	39	15	96	65	20	6	5
$60,000 to $64,999	215	2	7	37	40	19	111	64	28	9	10
$65,000 to $69,999	163	2	5	42	15	17	82	50	24	4	3
$70,000 to $74,999	179	4	1	30	29	19	96	44	33	9	10
$75,000 to $79,999	160	5	1	12	18	12	112	63	35	4	10
$80,000 to $84,999	165	0	2	25	19	14	106	48	48	7	2
$85,000 to $89,999	112	0	2	16	11	11	71	39	26	4	2
$90,000 to $94,999	148	1	5	9	5	14	115	68	30	2	15
$95,000 to $99,999	99	0	3	13	6	8	68	45	13	2	8
$100,000 or more	1,934	13	21	123	130	107	1,540	717	516	140	167
$100,000 to $124,999	574	5	15	51	52	37	414	225	121	31	38
$125,000 to $149,999	360	0	4	22	35	25	274	129	102	16	26
$150,000 to $174,999	324	2	2	16	16	23	265	138	88	14	26
$175,000 to $199,999	185	3	0	15	13	8	146	71	51	8	17
$200,000 or more	491	3	1	18	14	14	441	155	154	71	61
Median income	$70,894	$19,663	$31,734	$42,476	$56,347	$63,446	$95,247	$87,302	$105,746	$121,102	$105,546

PERCENT DISTRIBUTION

	total	less than 9th grade	9th to 12th grade, no diploma	high school graduate	some college, no degree	associate's degree	bachelor's degree or more				
							total	bachelor's degree	master's degree	professional degree	doctoral degree
Asian households	100.0%	100.0%	100.0%	100.0%	100.0%	100.0%	100.0%	100.0%	100.0%	100.0%	100.0%
Under $25,000	16.4	61.7	38.4	26.6	21.2	14.7	8.8	8.9	8.9	5.7	9.8
$25,000 to $49,999	18.8	17.7	28.6	30.4	24.3	24.1	13.3	15.9	9.8	12.4	11.0
$50,000 to $74,999	17.3	10.6	16.9	20.6	23.0	21.3	15.2	17.2	12.7	14.6	13.0
$75,000 to $99,999	12.4	3.2	6.1	8.5	9.8	14.1	14.7	15.6	15.7	8.0	12.1
$100,000 or more	35.1	6.8	9.9	14.0	21.6	25.8	48.0	42.4	53.0	59.3	54.1

Note: Asians are those who identify themselves as being of the race alone and those who identify themselves as being of the race in combination with other races.
Source: Bureau of the Census, 2013 Current Population Survey, Internet site http://www.census.gov/hhes/www/income/data/ incpovhlth/2012/dtables.html; calculations by New Strategist

Table 1.79 Households by Income and Educational Attainment of Householder, 2012: Black Households

(number and percent distribution of black households headed by people aged 25 or older by household income and educational attainment of householder, 2012; households in thousands as of 2013)

	total	less than 9th grade	9th to 12th grade, no diploma	high school graduate	some college, no degree	associate's degree	bachelor's degree or more total	bachelor's degree	master's degree	professional degree	doctoral degree
Black households	15,342	589	1,701	4,671	3,311	1,587	3,483	2,247	970	127	139
Under $5,000	955	52	234	388	168	41	72	55	16	0	1
$5,000 to $9,999	1,177	108	295	438	184	81	71	58	12	0	2
$10,000 to $14,999	1,344	118	297	498	228	100	102	78	18	2	4
$15,000 to $19,999	1,139	75	181	428	247	103	106	72	29	2	2
$20,000 to $24,999	1,156	62	168	446	285	112	83	58	23	0	1
$25,000 to $29,999	926	43	102	353	211	100	117	88	28	1	0
$30,000 to $34,999	926	26	107	339	218	91	145	96	46	2	1
$35,000 to $39,999	810	20	57	261	223	108	141	111	25	4	0
$40,000 to $44,999	707	16	47	210	169	81	183	135	45	2	1
$45,000 to $49,999	711	3	47	185	179	95	201	145	39	10	7
$50,000 to $54,999	591	9	27	169	132	66	188	126	53	3	6
$55,000 to $59,999	495	9	14	122	138	70	142	79	56	4	2
$60,000 to $64,999	482	6	26	119	118	86	127	89	34	2	1
$65,000 to $69,999	426	9	15	103	86	57	157	94	47	6	10
$70,000 to $74,999	349	2	21	91	81	40	114	65	40	0	10
$75,000 to $79,999	335	7	14	66	89	44	115	82	25	2	6
$80,000 to $84,999	325	4	8	81	68	51	113	75	30	7	1
$85,000 to $89,999	241	3	4	53	47	22	111	68	42	2	0
$90,000 to $94,999	210	9	5	44	39	23	90	53	32	3	2
$95,000 to $99,999	247	2	4	22	51	31	138	98	31	4	5
$100,000 or more	1,790	5	27	256	349	185	968	522	298	72	76
$100,000 to $124,999	763	4	15	129	176	98	340	209	95	9	26
$125,000 to $149,999	441	1	1	59	96	43	241	131	79	16	14
$150,000 to $174,999	210	0	5	26	34	22	123	63	39	4	16
$175,000 to $199,999	133	0	0	21	15	9	88	40	30	14	4
$200,000 or more	243	0	6	21	28	13	176	78	54	28	161
Median income	$35,239	$16,125	$15,574	$26,699	$37,227	$42,258	$66,610	$60,925	$71,388	$121,512	$107,696

PERCENT DISTRIBUTION

	total	less than 9th grade	9th to 12th grade, no diploma	high school graduate	some college, no degree	associate's degree	bachelor's degree or more total	bachelor's degree	master's degree	professional degree	doctoral degree
Black households	100.0%	100.0%	100.0%	100.0%	100.0%	100.0%	100.0%	100.0%	100.0%	100.0%	100.0%
Under $25,000	37.6	70.4	69.1	47.1	33.6	27.5	12.5	14.3	10.2	3.4	7.1
$25,000 to $49,999	26.6	18.5	21.2	28.9	30.2	29.9	22.6	25.6	18.9	14.9	6.3
$50,000 to $74,999	15.3	5.8	6.1	12.9	16.8	20.1	20.9	20.2	23.8	11.7	21.2
$75,000 to $99,999	8.8	4.3	2.0	5.7	8.9	10.8	16.3	16.7	16.4	13.6	10.9
$100,000 or more	11.7	0.9	1.6	5.5	10.5	11.7	27.8	23.2	30.7	56.5	54.5

Note: Blacks are those who identify themselves as being of the race alone and those who identify themselves as being of the race in combination with other races.
Source: Bureau of the Census, 2013 Current Population Survey, Internet site http://www.census.gov/hhes/www/income/data/incpovhlth/2012/dtables.html; calculations by New Strategist

Table 1.80 Households by Income and Educational Attainment of Householder, 2012: Hispanic Households

(number and percent distribution of Hispanic households headed by people aged 25 or older by household income and educational attainment of householder, 2012; households in thousands as of 2013)

	total	less than 9th grade	9th to 12th grade, no diploma	high school graduate	some college, no degree	associate's degree	bachelor's degree or more total	bachelor's degree	master's degree	professional degree	doctoral degree
Hispanic households	14,225	2,514	2,027	3,984	2,245	1,112	2,344	1,674	506	85	79
Under $5,000	612	158	100	210	64	27	52	41	8	3	0
$5,000 to $9,999	700	226	153	179	74	19	48	44	4	0	0
$10,000 to $14,999	1,005	300	191	285	111	51	66	52	13	2	0
$15,000 to $19,999	1,007	246	230	314	114	57	47	40	5	0	2
$20,000 to $24,999	1,016	243	194	303	144	64	68	55	12	1	0
$25,000 to $29,999	977	248	163	283	143	68	71	59	6	3	3
$30,000 to $34,999	907	194	138	282	129	59	106	88	17	1	0
$35,000 to $39,999	820	164	131	267	140	50	67	54	11	2	0
$40,000 to $44,999	743	123	97	215	153	66	90	73	16	0	1
$45,000 to $49,999	665	103	96	222	100	59	84	65	14	2	4
$50,000 to $54,999	633	94	89	196	96	71	87	71	15	0	2
$55,000 to $59,999	567	74	78	153	122	47	94	67	21	3	3
$60,000 to $64,999	511	79	61	128	112	55	75	55	20	0	0
$65,000 to $69,999	418	47	57	117	77	41	79	67	9	1	2
$70,000 to $74,999	357	36	38	124	58	35	66	52	14	0	0
$75,000 to $79,999	362	37	39	75	57	49	106	74	27	0	5
$80,000 to $84,999	336	16	37	92	54	44	93	58	29	4	3
$85,000 to $89,999	283	30	18	56	77	27	74	59	10	5	1
$90,000 to $94,999	252	16	15	68	29	31	93	58	23	5	7
$95,000 to $99,999	212	18	13	44	42	17	77	66	9	1	2
$100,000 or more	1,843	63	88	369	348	174	800	478	223	55	45
$100,000 to $124,999	789	33	37	188	161	91	279	185	72	14	8
$125,000 to $149,999	376	20	23	68	86	31	148	92	37	8	12
$150,000 to $174,999	255	2	15	48	44	22	123	75	36	8	5
$175,000 to $199,999	135	0	5	24	26	10	71	42	19	9	2
$200,000 or more	286	8	8	41	31	20	179	85	59	16	19
Median income	$40,356	$26,634	$29,241	$37,005	$46,963	$52,055	$77,983	$70,607	$90,231	$122,609	$112,957

PERCENT DISTRIBUTION

	total	less than 9th grade	9th to 12th grade, no diploma	high school graduate	some college, no degree	associate's degree	bachelor's degree or more total	bachelor's degree	master's degree	professional degree	doctoral degree
Hispanic households	100.0%	100.0%	100.0%	100.0%	100.0%	100.0%	100.0%	100.0%	100.0%	100.0%	100.0%
Under $25,000	30.5	46.7	42.8	32.4	22.6	19.6	12.0	13.9	8.4	6.2	2.0
$25,000 to $49,999	28.9	33.1	30.8	31.9	29.6	27.2	17.8	20.2	12.6	8.4	10.4
$50,000 to $74,999	17.5	13.1	15.9	18.0	20.7	22.4	17.1	18.6	15.6	4.5	8.8
$75,000 to $99,999	10.2	4.6	6.1	8.4	11.5	15.1	18.9	18.8	19.2	16.6	22.0
$100,000 or more	13.0	2.5	4.3	9.3	15.5	15.7	34.1	28.5	44.1	64.2	56.8

Source: Bureau of the Census, 2013 Current Population Survey, Internet site http://www.census.gov/hhes/www/income/data/ incpovhlth/2012/dtables.html; calculations by New Strategist

Table 1.81 **Households by Income and Educational Attainment of Householder, 2012: Non-Hispanic White Households**

(number and percent distribution of non-Hispanic white households headed by people aged 25 or older by household income and educational attainment of householder, 2012; households in thousands as of 2013)

	total	less than 9th grade	9th to 12th grade, no diploma	high school graduate	some college, no degree	associate's degree	bachelor's degree or more total	bachelor's degree	master's degree	professional degree	doctoral degree
Non-Hispanic white households	80,445	1,636	4,111	22,532	14,862	8,537	28,767	18,100	7,768	1,377	1,523
Under $5,000	1,870	76	194	621	361	171	447	298	111	25	13
$5,000 to $9,999	2,281	198	385	759	452	158	331	214	94	12	10
$10,000 to $14,999	3,801	296	540	1,455	688	315	507	361	102	23	20
$15,000 to $19,999	4,253	232	558	1,673	817	358	616	409	163	24	20
$20,000 to $24,999	4,157	186	461	1,568	842	398	702	515	124	30	33
$25,000 to $29,999	4,137	161	303	1,587	807	421	858	621	178	24	35
$30,000 to $34,999	3,878	97	214	1,453	834	414	866	606	193	37	29
$35,000 to $39,999	3,613	70	206	1,283	782	389	883	652	192	12	26
$40,000 to $44,999	3,564	59	188	1,264	716	426	911	624	225	14	49
$45,000 to $49,999	3,385	44	181	1,049	810	413	888	617	220	20	31
$50,000 to $54,999	3,344	49	160	1,111	701	377	945	605	257	38	45
$55,000 to $59,999	2,772	26	67	875	573	357	876	585	233	24	33
$60,000 to $64,999	2,958	14	87	842	578	429	1,008	645	317	20	26
$65,000 to $69,999	2,764	9	66	829	574	313	972	620	286	35	31
$70,000 to $74,999	2,700	15	89	722	609	337	926	552	296	43	36
$75,000 to $79,999	2,422	17	65	626	407	315	991	671	244	26	50
$80,000 to $84,999	2,384	11	60	589	453	305	966	636	240	38	52
$85,000 to $89,999	1,906	9	43	486	347	268	753	510	186	34	23
$90,000 to $94,999	1,982	9	36	460	378	216	882	579	232	36	35
$95,000 to $99,999	1,593	2	45	321	298	220	708	445	217	16	29
$100,000 or more	20,680	55	162	2,961	2,835	1,936	12,732	7,334	3,656	847	894
$100,000 to $124,999	7,079	19	97	1,437	1,195	856	3,474	2,218	986	114	156
$125,000 to $149,999	4,473	10	33	674	695	464	2,597	1,611	721	115	150
$150,000 to $174,999	3,002	6	10	360	400	267	1,959	1,141	564	124	130
$175,000 to $199,999	1,750	3	11	162	177	145	1,252	661	409	77	105
$200,000 or more	4,375	16	11	328	367	204	3,449	1,703	976	417	353
Median income	$58,354	$20,408	$24,108	$42,868	$51,948	$60,727	$89,565	$83,181	$94,767	$132,164	$121,398

PERCENT DISTRIBUTION

Non-Hispanic white households	100.0%	100.0%	100.0%	100.0%	100.0%	100.0%	100.0%	100.0%	100.0%	100.0%	100.0%
Under $25,000	20.3	60.3	52.0	27.0	21.3	16.4	9.1	9.9	7.7	8.3	6.4
$25,000 to $49,999	23.1	26.4	26.6	29.5	26.6	24.2	15.3	17.2	13.0	7.7	11.1
$50,000 to $74,999	18.1	7.0	11.4	19.4	20.4	21.2	16.4	16.6	17.9	11.6	11.3
$75,000 to $99,999	12.8	3.0	6.1	11.0	12.7	15.5	14.9	15.7	14.4	10.9	12.4
$100,000 or more	25.7	3.3	3.9	13.1	19.1	22.7	44.3	40.5	47.1	61.5	58.7

Note: Non-Hispanic whites are those who identify themselves as white alone and not Hispanic.
Source: Bureau of the Census, 2013 Current Population Survey, Internet site http://www.census.gov/hhes/www/income/data/incpovhlth/2012/dtables.html; calculations by New Strategist

Household Incomes Are Highest in New England

Incomes are lowest in the East South Central states.

Among the country's four geographical regions, only the South—which is home to 37 percent of the nation's households—has a median household income significantly below the national average. In 2012, median household income in the South was $48,033 versus $51,017 nationally. In the Midwest, median household income is about average ($50,479), and it is well above average in the Northeast ($54,627) and West ($55,157).

In the New England states, the $61,175 median household income is 20 percent above the national median. The Pacific states rank second, with a median income of $57,398. The lowest household incomes are in the East South Central states of Alabama, Kentucky, Mississippi, and Tennessee. Median household income in that area was just $41,551 in 2012, 19 percent below the national figure.

■ The Great Recession reduced incomes in every region, the biggest losses occurring in the Midwest.

Incomes are lowest in the South

(median household income by region, 2012)

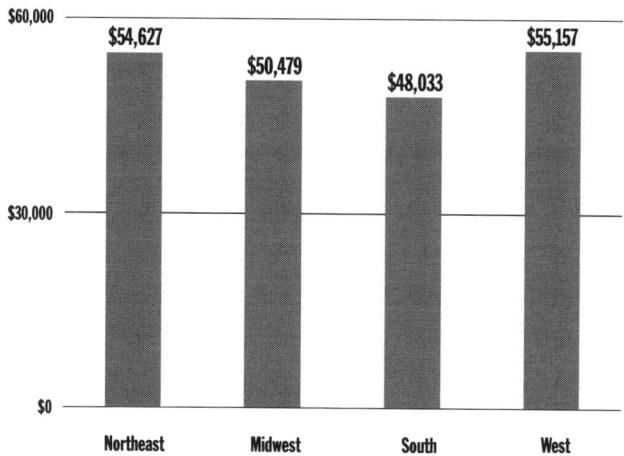

Table 1.82 Households by Income and Region, 2012

(number and percent distribution of households by household income and region of residence, 2012; households in thousands as of 2013)

	total	Northeast	Midwest	South	West
Total households	**122,459**	**22,125**	**27,093**	**45,938**	**27,303**
Under $5,000	4,204	752	820	1,693	939
$5,000 to $9,999	4,729	876	1,026	1,949	878
$10,000 to $14,999	6,982	1,289	1,363	2,818	1,512
$15,000 to $19,999	7,157	1,312	1,649	2,791	1,405
$20,000 to $24,999	7,131	1,171	1,572	2,810	1,578
$25,000 to $29,999	6,740	1,085	1,578	2,698	1,379
$30,000 to $34,999	6,354	1,087	1,435	2,557	1,275
$35,000 to $39,999	5,832	880	1,394	2,267	1,292
$40,000 to $44,999	5,547	975	1,308	2,069	1,195
$45,000 to $49,999	5,254	888	1,255	2,069	1,042
$50,000 to $54,999	5,102	786	1,247	1,946	1,122
$55,000 to $59,999	4,256	769	950	1,576	960
$60,000 to $64,999	4,356	630	1,077	1,677	972
$65,000 to $69,999	3,949	717	823	1,539	870
$70,000 to $74,999	3,756	676	850	1,440	789
$75,000 to $79,999	3,414	586	727	1,317	783
$80,000 to $84,999	3,326	641	755	1,224	706
$85,000 to $89,999	2,643	460	622	1,021	540
$90,000 to $94,999	2,678	481	610	959	629
$95,000 to $99,999	2,223	410	512	764	537
$100,000 or more	26,825	5,653	5,518	8,753	6,901
$100,000 to $124,999	9,490	1,886	2,098	3,196	2,310
$125,000 to $149,999	5,759	1,156	1,259	1,909	1,435
$150,000 to $174,999	3,870	769	813	1,221	1,066
$175,000 to $199,999	2,247	543	358	731	615
$200,000 or more	5,460	1,299	991	1,697	1,474
Median income	**$51,017**	**$54,627**	**$50,479**	**$48,033**	**$55,157**

PERCENT DISTRIBUTION

	total	Northeast	Midwest	South	West
Total households	**100.0%**	**100.0%**	**100.0%**	**100.0%**	**100.0%**
Under $25,000	24.7	24.4	23.7	26.3	23.1
$25,000 to $49,999	24.3	22.2	25.7	25.4	22.6
$50,000 to $74,999	17.5	16.2	18.3	17.8	17.3
$75,000 to $99,999	11.7	11.6	11.9	11.5	11.7
$100,000 or more	21.9	25.5	20.4	19.1	25.3

Source: Bureau of the Census, 2013 Current Population Survey, Internet site http://www.census.gov/hhes/www/cpstables/032013/hhinc/toc.htm; calculations by New Strategist

Table 1.83 Households by Income, Region, and Division, 2012: Northeast

(number and percent distribution of total households and households in the Northeast region and divisions by household income, 2012; households in thousands as of 2013)

	total	Northeast total	New England	Middle Atlantic
Total households	122,459	22,125	5,777	16,348
Under $5,000	4,204	752	128	625
$5,000 to $9,999	4,729	876	213	663
$10,000 to $14,999	6,982	1,289	308	981
$15,000 to $19,999	7,157	1,312	308	1,005
$20,000 to $24,999	7,131	1,171	233	938
$25,000 to $29,999	6,740	1,085	286	800
$30,000 to $34,999	6,354	1,087	290	797
$35,000 to $39,999	5,832	880	219	660
$40,000 to $44,999	5,547	975	219	756
$45,000 to $49,999	5,254	888	257	631
$50,000 to $54,999	5,102	786	198	588
$55,000 to $59,999	4,256	769	184	585
$60,000 to $64,999	4,356	630	166	464
$65,000 to $69,999	3,949	717	207	510
$70,000 to $74,999	3,756	676	196	480
$75,000 to $79,999	3,414	586	151	436
$80,000 to $84,999	3,326	641	174	467
$85,000 to $89,999	2,643	460	118	342
$90,000 to $94,999	2,678	481	135	346
$95,000 to $99,999	2,223	410	106	304
$100,000 or more	26,825	5,653	1,682	3,971
$100,000 to $124,999	9,490	1,886	552	1,335
$125,000 to $149,999	5,759	1,156	351	805
$150,000 to $174,999	3,870	769	224	546
$175,000 to $199,999	2,247	543	154	389
$200,000 or more	5,460	1,299	401	898
Median income	$51,017	$54,627	$61,175	$52,075
PERCENT DISTRIBUTION				
Total households	100.0%	100.0%	100.0%	100.0%
Under $25,000	24.7	24.4	20.6	25.8
$25,000 to $49,999	24.3	22.2	22.0	22.3
$50,000 to $74,999	17.5	16.2	16.5	16.1
$75,000 to $99,999	11.7	11.6	11.8	11.6
$100,000 or more	21.9	25.5	29.1	24.3

Source: Bureau of the Census, 2013 Current Population Survey, Internet site http://www.census.gov/hhes/www/cpstables/ 032013/hhinc/toc.htm; calculations by New Strategist

Table 1.84 Households by Income, Region, and Division, 2012: Midwest

(number and percent distribution of total households and households in the Midwest region and divisions by household income, 2012; households in thousands as of 2013)

	total	Midwest total	East North Central	West North Central
Total households	**122,459**	**27,093**	**18,701**	**8,392**
Under $5,000	4,204	820	606	214
$5,000 to $9,999	4,729	1,026	748	278
$10,000 to $14,999	6,982	1,363	932	431
$15,000 to $19,999	7,157	1,649	1,161	488
$20,000 to $24,999	7,131	1,572	1,119	453
$25,000 to $29,999	6,740	1,578	1,157	422
$30,000 to $34,999	6,354	1,435	1,022	414
$35,000 to $39,999	5,832	1,394	974	420
$40,000 to $44,999	5,547	1,308	910	397
$45,000 to $49,999	5,254	1,255	854	401
$50,000 to $54,999	5,102	1,247	857	391
$55,000 to $59,999	4,256	950	656	294
$60,000 to $64,999	4,356	1,077	699	379
$65,000 to $69,999	3,949	823	535	289
$70,000 to $74,999	3,756	850	590	260
$75,000 to $79,999	3,414	727	477	250
$80,000 to $84,999	3,326	755	514	241
$85,000 to $89,999	2,643	622	440	182
$90,000 to $94,999	2,678	610	435	175
$95,000 to $99,999	2,223	512	330	182
$100,000 or more	26,825	5,518	3,685	1,833
$100,000 to $124,999	9,490	2,098	1,374	724
$125,000 to $149,999	5,759	1,259	846	413
$150,000 to $174,999	3,870	813	549	265
$175,000 to $199,999	2,247	358	235	123
$200,000 or more	5,460	991	681	309
Median income	**$51,017**	**$50,479**	**$49,139**	**$53,041**

PERCENT DISTRIBUTION

	total	total	East North Central	West North Central
Total households	**100.0%**	**100.0%**	**100.0%**	**100.0%**
Under $25,000	24.7	23.7	24.4	22.2
$25,000 to $49,999	24.3	25.7	26.3	24.5
$50,000 to $74,999	17.5	18.3	17.8	19.2
$75,000 to $99,999	11.7	11.9	11.7	12.3
$100,000 or more	21.9	20.4	19.7	21.8

Source: Bureau of the Census, 2013 Current Population Survey, Internet site http://www.census.gov/hhes/www/cpstables/032013/hhinc/toc.htm; calculations by New Strategist

Table 1.85 Households by Income, Region, and Division, 2012: South

(number and percent distribution of total households and households in the South region and divisions by household income, 2012; households in thousands as of 2013)

		South			
	total	total	South Atlantic	East South Central	West South Central
Total households	**122,459**	**45,938**	**24,424**	**7,489**	**14,025**
Under $5,000	4,204	1,693	889	284	520
$5,000 to $9,999	4,729	1,949	988	433	528
$10,000 to $14,999	6,982	2,818	1,425	552	841
$15,000 to $19,999	7,157	2,791	1,492	496	802
$20,000 to $24,999	7,131	2,810	1,414	526	870
$25,000 to $29,999	6,740	2,698	1,406	488	804
$30,000 to $34,999	6,354	2,557	1,344	445	768
$35,000 to $39,999	5,832	2,267	1,124	393	751
$40,000 to $44,999	5,547	2,069	1,112	338	620
$45,000 to $49,999	5,254	2,069	1,121	337	611
$50,000 to $54,999	5,102	1,946	1,028	338	581
$55,000 to $59,999	4,256	1,576	767	249	559
$60,000 to $64,999	4,356	1,677	902	247	528
$65,000 to $69,999	3,949	1,539	828	244	468
$70,000 to $74,999	3,756	1,440	782	198	460
$75,000 to $79,999	3,414	1,317	720	179	417
$80,000 to $84,999	3,326	1,224	660	193	371
$85,000 to $89,999	2,643	1,021	540	185	297
$90,000 to $94,999	2,678	959	504	157	298
$95,000 to $99,999	2,223	764	430	124	211
$100,000 or more	26,825	8,753	4,949	1,085	2,720
$100,000 to $124,999	9,490	3,196	1,790	433	973
$125,000 to $149,999	5,759	1,909	1,047	267	595
$150,000 to $174,999	3,870	1,221	697	155	369
$175,000 to $199,999	2,247	731	438	62	231
$200,000 or more	5,460	1,697	977	168	551
Median income	**$51,017**	**$48,033**	**$49,532**	**$41,551**	**$49,020**

PERCENT DISTRIBUTION

Total households	**100.0%**	**100.0%**	**100.0%**	**100.0%**	**100.0%**
Under $25,000	24.7	26.3	25.4	30.6	25.4
$25,000 to $49,999	24.3	25.4	25.0	26.7	25.3
$50,000 to $74,999	17.5	17.8	17.6	17.0	18.5
$75,000 to $99,999	11.7	11.5	11.7	11.2	11.4
$100,000 or more	21.9	19.1	20.3	14.5	19.4

Source: Bureau of the Census, 2013 Current Population Survey, Internet site http://www.census.gov/hhes/www/cpstables/ 032013/hhinc/toc.htm; calculations by New Strategist

Table 1.86 Households by Income, Region, and Division, 2012: West

(number and percent distribution of total households and households in the West region and divisions by household income, 2012; households in thousands as of 2013)

	total	West total	Mountain	Pacific
Total households	122,459	27,303	8,817	18,486
Under $5,000	4,204	939	340	599
$5,000 to $9,999	4,729	878	331	547
$10,000 to $14,999	6,982	1,512	466	1,046
$15,000 to $19,999	7,157	1,405	500	905
$20,000 to $24,999	7,131	1,578	573	1,005
$25,000 to $29,999	6,740	1,379	498	881
$30,000 to $34,999	6,354	1,275	416	859
$35,000 to $39,999	5,832	1,292	448	843
$40,000 to $44,999	5,547	1,195	400	795
$45,000 to $49,999	5,254	1,042	369	673
$50,000 to $54,999	5,102	1,122	363	760
$55,000 to $59,999	4,256	960	347	613
$60,000 to $64,999	4,356	972	316	656
$65,000 to $69,999	3,949	870	282	588
$70,000 to $74,999	3,756	789	237	552
$75,000 to $79,999	3,414	783	250	533
$80,000 to $84,999	3,326	706	234	472
$85,000 to $89,999	2,643	540	182	358
$90,000 to $94,999	2,678	629	211	418
$95,000 to $99,999	2,223	537	177	360
$100,000 or more	26,825	6,901	1,878	5,023
$100,000 to $124,999	9,490	2,310	700	1,610
$125,000 to $149,999	5,759	1,435	369	1,066
$150,000 to $174,999	3,870	1,066	280	786
$175,000 to $199,999	2,247	615	185	430
$200,000 or more	5,460	1,474	343	1,130
Median income	$51,017	$55,157	$50,705	$57,398
PERCENT DISTRIBUTION				
Total households	100.0%	100.0%	100.0%	100.0%
Under $25,000	24.7	23.1	25.1	22.2
$25,000 to $49,999	24.3	22.6	24.2	21.9
$50,000 to $74,999	17.5	17.3	17.5	17.1
$75,000 to $99,999	11.7	11.7	11.9	11.6
$100,000 or more	21.9	25.3	21.3	27.2

Source: Bureau of the Census, 2013 Current Population Survey, Internet site http://www.census.gov/hhes/www/cpstables/032013/hhinc/toc.htm; calculations by New Strategist

Among Blacks, Household Incomes Are Highest in the West

Hispanic household incomes also peak in the West.

In every region, the median income of Asian households surpasses that of non-Hispanic whites. Asian household income is highest in the West, at $71,894 in 2012. The non-Hispanic white median is also highest in the West, at $62,376.

Among black households, median income is higher in the West than in the other regions, at $38,337 in 2012. This compares with a median household income of more than $60,000 for non-Hispanic white households in the region and more than $70,000 for Asian households there. In the South, which is home to the majority of black households, the median income of black households is only $33,947, and the median is an even lower $30,889 in the Midwest. Household composition is one of the primary reasons for the lower incomes of blacks. Black households are much less likely than average to be headed by married couples, the most affluent household type.

■ Income disparities by race and Hispanic origin will continue as long as differences in household composition persist.

Among households in the West, Asians have the highest median income

(median income of households in the West by race and Hispanic origin of householder, 2012)

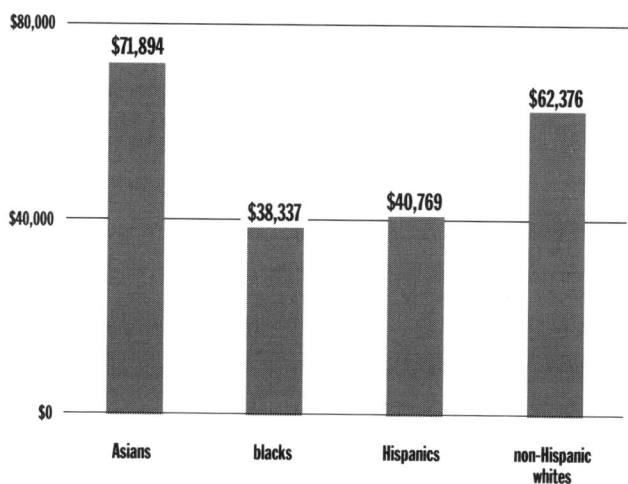

Table 1.87 Households by Income, Region, Race, and Hispanic Origin, 2012: Northeast

(number and percent distribution of households in the Northeast by household income and race and Hispanic origin of householder, 2012; households in thousands as of 2013)

	total	Asian	black	Hispanic	non-Hispanic white
Households in the Northeast	**22,125**	**1,174**	**2,880**	**2,295**	**16,036**
Under $5,000	752	75	199	123	385
$5,000 to $9,999	876	36	233	165	475
$10,000 to $14,999	1,289	38	289	223	778
$15,000 to $19,999	1,312	50	192	200	879
$20,000 to $24,999	1,171	37	212	174	775
$25,000 to $29,999	1,085	52	166	152	744
$30,000 to $34,999	1,087	50	179	134	732
$35,000 to $39,999	880	48	113	136	594
$40,000 to $44,999	975	27	137	102	729
$45,000 to $49,999	888	47	113	88	654
$50,000 to $54,999	786	28	91	64	602
$55,000 to $59,999	769	36	103	101	544
$60,000 to $64,999	630	34	74	51	470
$65,000 to $69,999	717	43	76	42	556
$70,000 to $74,999	676	36	43	42	559
$75,000 to $79,999	586	34	68	55	431
$80,000 to $84,999	641	30	90	37	492
$85,000 to $89,999	460	26	46	35	348
$90,000 to $94,999	481	43	34	40	367
$95,000 to $99,999	410	16	48	37	312
$100,000 or more	5,653	388	373	296	4,610
$100,000 to $124,999	1,886	101	157	132	1,503
$125,000 to $149,999	1,156	49	98	53	956
$150,000 to $174,999	769	58	39	49	624
$175,000 to $199,999	543	54	26	22	443
$200,000 or more	1,299	126	53	40	1,084
Median income	**$54,627**	**$67,894**	**$33,874**	**$34,066**	**$61,047**
PERCENT DISTRIBUTION					
Households in the Northeast	**100.0%**	**100.0%**	**100.0%**	**100.0%**	**100.0%**
Under $25,000	24.4	20.1	39.1	38.5	20.5
$25,000 to $49,999	22.2	19.1	24.6	26.6	21.5
$50,000 to $74,999	16.2	15.2	13.4	13.1	17.0
$75,000 to $99,999	11.6	12.6	9.9	8.9	12.2
$100,000 or more	25.5	33.0	12.9	12.9	28.8

Note: Asians and blacks are those who identify themselves as being of the race alone and those who identify themselves as being of the race in combination with other races. Non-Hispanic whites are those who identify themselves as being white alone and not Hispanic. Numbers do not add to total because some people identify themselves as being of more than one race, not all races are shown, and Hispanics may be of any race.
Source: Bureau of the Census, 2013 Current Population Survey, Internet site http://www.census.gov/hhes/www/cpstables/032013/hhinc/toc.htm; calculations by New Strategist

Table 1.88 Households by Income, Region, Race, and Hispanic Origin, 2012: Midwest

(number and percent distribution of households in the Midwest by household income and race and Hispanic origin of householder, 2012; households in thousands as of 2013)

	total	Asian	black	Hispanic	non-Hispanic white
Households in the Midwest	27,093	687	2,971	1,310	21,933
Under $5,000	820	32	232	46	486
$5,000 to $9,999	1,026	20	251	52	688
$10,000 to $14,999	1,363	30	255	91	960
$15,000 to $19,999	1,649	21	280	90	1,239
$20,000 to $24,999	1,572	28	247	89	1,203
$25,000 to $29,999	1,578	20	177	84	1,275
$30,000 to $34,999	1,435	19	181	89	1,139
$35,000 to $39,999	1,394	28	146	77	1,134
$40,000 to $44,999	1,308	33	156	82	1,023
$45,000 to $49,999	1,255	26	139	82	994
$50,000 to $54,999	1,247	51	130	59	995
$55,000 to $59,999	950	19	89	56	787
$60,000 to $64,999	1,077	36	99	56	879
$65,000 to $69,999	823	21	68	39	703
$70,000 to $74,999	850	26	71	38	715
$75,000 to $79,999	727	25	49	24	626
$80,000 to $84,999	755	23	39	38	655
$85,000 to $89,999	622	12	57	23	530
$90,000 to $94,999	610	15	46	18	532
$95,000 to $99,999	512	16	40	24	430
$100,000 or more	5,518	185	219	153	4,940
$100,000 to $124,999	2,098	72	88	55	1,873
$125,000 to $149,999	1,259	38	46	39	1,127
$150,000 to $174,999	813	28	27	23	737
$175,000 to $199,999	358	9	13	11	323
$200,000 or more	991	39	46	26	880
Median income	**$50,479**	**$61,613**	**$30,889**	**$41,734**	**$53,964**

PERCENT DISTRIBUTION

	total	Asian	black	Hispanic	non-Hispanic white
Households in the Midwest	100.0%	100.0%	100.0%	100.0%	100.0%
Under $25,000	23.7	18.9	42.6	28.1	20.9
$25,000 to $49,999	25.7	18.5	26.8	31.6	25.4
$50,000 to $74,999	18.3	22.3	15.4	18.9	18.6
$75,000 to $99,999	11.9	13.3	7.8	9.7	12.6
$100,000 or more	20.4	27.0	7.4	11.7	22.5

Note: Asians and blacks are those who identify themselves as being of the race alone and those who identify themselves as being of the race in combination with other races. Non-Hispanic whites are those who identify themselves as being white alone and not Hispanic. Numbers do not add to total because some people identify themselves as being of more than one race, not all races are shown, and Hispanics may be of any race.
Source: Bureau of the Census, 2013 Current Population Survey, Internet site http://www.census.gov/hhes/www/cpstables/ 032013/hhinc/toc.htm; calculations by New Strategist

Table 1.89 Households by Income, Region, Race, and Hispanic Origin, 2012: South

(number and percent distribution of households in the South by household income and race and Hispanic origin of householder, 2012; households in thousands as of 2013)

	total	Asian	black	Hispanic	non-Hispanic white
Households in the South	**45,938**	**1,342**	**9,059**	**5,899**	**29,369**
Under $5,000	1,693	45	576	255	802
$5,000 to $9,999	1,949	39	704	287	908
$10,000 to $14,999	2,818	24	798	397	1,552
$15,000 to $19,999	2,791	44	703	417	1,609
$20,000 to $24,999	2,810	57	703	442	1,602
$25,000 to $29,999	2,698	55	577	454	1,589
$30,000 to $34,999	2,557	67	543	403	1,537
$35,000 to $39,999	2,267	42	495	379	1,335
$40,000 to $44,999	2,069	52	396	297	1,294
$45,000 to $49,999	2,069	47	451	273	1,302
$50,000 to $54,999	1,946	55	334	257	1,290
$55,000 to $59,999	1,576	64	286	230	981
$60,000 to $64,999	1,677	70	282	221	1,102
$65,000 to $69,999	1,539	45	265	198	1,036
$70,000 to $74,999	1,440	52	209	139	1,034
$75,000 to $79,999	1,317	36	209	150	913
$80,000 to $84,999	1,224	34	185	134	872
$85,000 to $89,999	1,021	30	125	120	743
$90,000 to $94,999	959	43	115	104	687
$95,000 to $99,999	764	17	138	69	544
$100,000 or more	8,753	425	965	674	6,637
$100,000 to $124,999	3,196	118	431	290	2,320
$125,000 to $149,999	1,909	88	245	133	1,439
$150,000 to $174,999	1,221	68	118	99	929
$175,000 to $199,999	731	54	63	55	558
$200,000 or more	1,697	96	109	96	1,390
Median income	**$48,033**	**$65,863**	**$33,947**	**$38,585**	**$54,326**

PERCENT DISTRIBUTION

	total	Asian	black	Hispanic	non-Hispanic white
Households in the South	**100.0%**	**100.0%**	**100.0%**	**100.0%**	**100.0%**
Under $25,000	26.3	15.6	38.5	30.5	22.0
$25,000 to $49,999	25.4	19.6	27.2	30.6	24.0
$50,000 to $74,999	17.8	21.3	15.2	17.7	18.5
$75,000 to $99,999	11.5	11.8	8.5	9.8	12.8
$100,000 or more	19.1	31.7	10.7	11.4	22.6

Note: Asians and blacks are those who identify themselves as being of the race alone and those who identify themselves as being of the race in combination with other races. Non-Hispanic whites are those who identify themselves as being white alone and not Hispanic. Numbers do not add to total because some people identify themselves as being of more than one race, not all races are shown, and Hispanics may be of any race.
Source: Bureau of the Census, 2013 Current Population Survey, Internet site http://www.census.gov/hhes/www/cpstables/032013/hhinc/toc.htm; calculations by New Strategist

Table 1.90 Households by Income, Region, Race, and Hispanic Origin, 2012: West

(number and percent distribution of households in the West by household income and race and Hispanic origin of householder, 2012; households in thousands as of 2013)

	total	Asian	black	Hispanic	non-Hispanic white
Households in the West	27,303	2,669	1,649	6,085	16,454
Under $5,000	939	90	102	292	419
$5,000 to $9,999	878	57	143	283	381
$10,000 to $14,999	1,512	116	161	402	798
$15,000 to $19,999	1,405	86	88	410	789
$20,000 to $24,999	1,578	113	100	449	892
$25,000 to $29,999	1,379	92	71	410	784
$30,000 to $34,999	1,275	90	93	394	678
$35,000 to $39,999	1,292	107	92	338	725
$40,000 to $44,999	1,195	91	70	325	684
$45,000 to $49,999	1,042	108	69	280	567
$50,000 to $54,999	1,122	87	79	309	618
$55,000 to $59,999	960	94	58	225	578
$60,000 to $64,999	972	92	40	207	610
$65,000 to $69,999	870	75	36	175	563
$70,000 to $74,999	789	75	41	164	496
$75,000 to $79,999	783	78	19	152	520
$80,000 to $84,999	706	87	35	147	436
$85,000 to $89,999	540	48	20	125	338
$90,000 to $94,999	629	55	23	99	438
$95,000 to $99,999	537	55	23	89	363
$100,000 or more	6,901	972	286	811	4,775
$100,000 to $124,999	2,310	300	109	358	1,522
$125,000 to $149,999	1,435	189	62	172	997
$150,000 to $174,999	1,066	176	37	98	744
$175,000 to $199,999	615	68	33	53	462
$200,000 or more	1,474	239	44	129	1,050
Median income	**$55,157**	**$71,894**	**$38,337**	**$40,769**	**$62,376**

PERCENT DISTRIBUTION

	total	Asian	black	Hispanic	non-Hispanic white
Households in the West	100.0%	100.0%	100.0%	100.0%	100.0%
Under $25,000	23.1	17.3	36.0	30.2	19.9
$25,000 to $49,999	22.6	18.3	23.9	28.7	20.9
$50,000 to $74,999	17.3	15.9	15.4	17.7	17.4
$75,000 to $99,999	11.7	12.1	7.3	10.1	12.7
$100,000 or more	25.3	36.4	17.4	13.3	29.0

Note: Asians and blacks are those who identify themselves as being of the race alone and those who identify themselves as being of the race in combination with other races. Non-Hispanic whites are those who identify themselves as being white alone and not Hispanic. Numbers do not add to total because some people identify themselves as being of more than one race, not all races are shown, and Hispanics may be of any race.
Source: Bureau of the Census, 2013 Current Population Survey, Internet site http://www.census.gov/hhes/www/cpstables/ 032013/hhinc/toc.htm; calculations by New Strategist

Suburban Households Have the Highest Incomes

Households in nonmetropolitan areas have below-average incomes.

Median household income was highest in Maryland ($71,836) and lowest in Mississippi ($36,641) in 2012, according to the Census Bureau's Current Population Survey. The difference in the median income of households in the two states is more than $35,000.

By metropolitan status, suburban households have the highest incomes—a median of $58,780 in 2012. Twenty-six percent have incomes of $100,000 or more. In the nation's central cities (called principal cities), median household income was $45,902 in 2012, surpassing the $41,198 median in nonmetropolitan areas.

Among the 52 metropolitan areas with at least 1 million residents, median household income was highest in San Jose, according to the Census Bureau's 2012 American Community Survey. San Jose's household median of $90,737 was 77 percent above the national figure. Other large metros with a relatively high median household income are Washington, D.C., San Francisco, and Boston. The median household income of New Orleans—$44,379—was at the bottom of the list in 2012. Other large metros with a relatively low median household income are Tampa, Memphis, Orlando, and Miami.

■ More than 80 percent of Americans now live in a metropolitan area.

Nonmetropolitan households have the lowest incomes

(median household income by metropolitan residence, 2012)

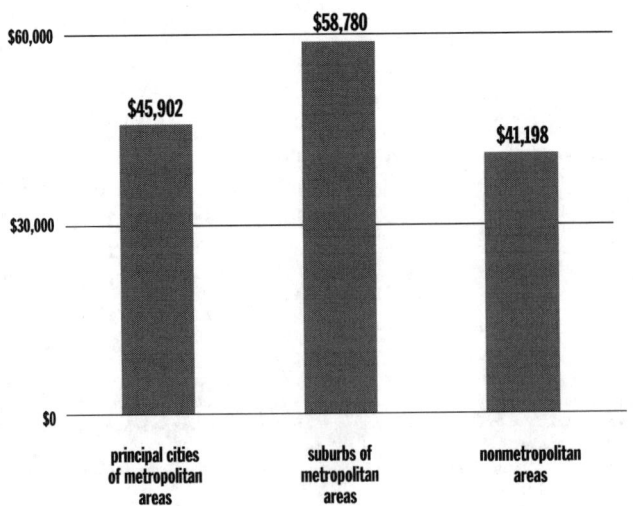

Table 1.91 Median Household Income by State, 2012

(median income of households by state, state rank, and index to national median, 2012)

	median household income	rank among 50 states	index to national median
United States	**$51,017**	–	**100**
Alabama	43,464	44	85
Alaska	63,648	8	125
Arizona	47,044	37	92
Arkansas	39,018	50	76
California	57,020	14	112
Colorado	57,255	13	112
Connecticut	64,247	6	126
Delaware	48,972	31	96
District of Columbia	65,246	4	128
Florida	46,071	39	90
Georgia	48,121	33	94
Hawaii	56,263	15	110
Idaho	47,922	34	94
Illinois	51,738	25	101
Indiana	46,158	38	90
Iowa	53,442	19	105
Kansas	50,003	27	98
Kentucky	41,086	48	81
Louisiana	39,085	49	77
Maine	49,158	30	96
Maryland	71,836	1	141
Massachusetts	63,656	7	125
Michigan	50,015	26	98
Minnesota	61,795	10	121
Mississippi	36,641	51	72
Missouri	49,764	28	98
Montana	45,088	40	88
Nebraska	52,196	21	102
Nevada	47,333	36	93
New Hampshire	67,819	2	133
New Jersey	66,692	3	131
New Mexico	43,424	45	85
New York	47,680	35	93
North Carolina	41,553	47	81
North Dakota	55,766	17	109
Ohio	44,375	42	87
Oklahoma	48,407	32	95
Oregon	51,775	24	101
Pennsylvania	51,904	23	102

	median household income	rank among 50 states	index to national median
Rhode Island	$56,065	16	110
South Carolina	44,401	41	87
South Dakota	49,415	29	97
Tennessee	42,995	46	84
Texas	51,926	22	102
Utah	58,341	11	114
Vermont	55,582	18	109
Virginia	64,632	5	127
Washington	62,187	9	122
West Virginia	43,553	43	85
Wisconsin	53,079	20	104
Wyoming	57,512	12	113

Note: The index is calculated by dividing the median income of each state by the national median and multiplying by 100. "–" means not applicable.
Source: Bureau of the Census, 2013 Current Population Survey, Internet site http://www.census.gov/hhes/www/income/data/incpovhlth/2012/dtables.html; calculations by New Strategist

Table 1.92 Households by Income and Metropolitan Residence, 2012

(number and percent distribution of households by household income and metropolitan residence, 2012; households in thousands as of 2013)

| | | in metropolitan area | | | |
	total	total	inside principal cities	outside principal cities	not in metropolitan area
Total households	**122,459**	**102,784**	**41,152**	**61,631**	**19,676**
Under $5,000	4,204	3,533	1,980	1,552	672
$5,000 to $9,999	4,729	3,704	1,958	1,746	1,025
$10,000 to $14,999	6,982	5,581	2,672	2,909	1,402
$15,000 to $19,999	7,157	5,720	2,620	3,100	1,437
$20,000 to $24,999	7,131	5,773	2,686	3,086	1,359
$25,000 to $29,999	6,740	5,358	2,382	2,976	1,382
$30,000 to $34,999	6,354	5,143	2,182	2,960	1,212
$35,000 to $39,999	5,832	4,743	1,982	2,761	1,089
$40,000 to $44,999	5,547	4,582	1,774	2,807	966
$45,000 to $49,999	5,254	4,327	1,691	2,636	927
$50,000 to $54,999	5,102	4,165	1,588	2,577	937
$55,000 to $59,999	4,256	3,563	1,395	2,168	693
$60,000 to $64,999	4,356	3,693	1,398	2,295	663
$65,000 to $69,999	3,949	3,342	1,248	2,093	607
$70,000 to $74,999	3,756	3,123	1,129	1,994	633
$75,000 to $79,999	3,414	2,872	1,048	1,824	542
$80,000 to $84,999	3,326	2,850	1,042	1,809	476
$85,000 to $89,999	2,643	2,186	751	1,435	457
$90,000 to $94,999	2,678	2,309	775	1,534	370
$95,000 to $99,999	2,223	1,908	650	1,258	316
$100,000 or more	26,825	24,313	8,202	16,110	2,513
$100,000 to $124,999	9,490	8,289	2,757	5,533	1,201
$125,000 to $149,999	5,759	5,220	1,729	3,491	539
$150,000 to $174,999	3,870	3,575	1,164	2,411	294
$175,000 to $199,999	2,247	2,079	679	1,399	168
$200,000 or more	5,460	5,150	1,873	3,277	310
Median income	**$51,017**	**$52,988**	**$45,902**	**$58,780**	**$41,198**

PERCENT DISTRIBUTION

Total households	**100.0%**	**100.0%**	**100.0%**	**100.0%**	**100.0%**
Under $25,000	24.7	23.7	29.0	20.1	30.0
$25,000 to $49,999	24.3	23.5	24.3	22.9	28.3
$50,000 to $74,999	17.5	17.4	16.4	18.1	18.0
$75,000 to $99,999	11.7	11.8	10.4	12.8	11.0
$100,000 or more	21.9	23.7	19.9	26.1	12.8

Source: Bureau of the Census, 2013 Current Population Survey, Internet site http://www.census.gov/hhes/www/cpstables/ 032013/hhinc/toc.htm; calculations by New Strategist

Table 1.93 Median Household Income in Large Metropolitan Areas, 2012

(median household income in metropolitan areas with at least 1 million residents, rank among large metropolitan areas, and index to national median, 2012)

	median household income	rank among top metro areas	index to national median
United States	**$51,371**	–	**100**
Atlanta–Sandy Springs–Marietta, GA	54,628	24	106
Austin–Round Rock–San Marcos, TX	59,433	15	116
Baltimore–Towson, MD	66,970	5	130
Birmingham–Hoover, AL	46,763	47	91
Boston–Cambridge–Quincy, MA–NH	71,738	4	140
Buffalo–Niagara Falls, NY	50,269	41	98
Charlotte–Gastonia–Rock Hill, NC–SC	52,470	29	102
Chicago–Joliet–Naperville, IL–IN–WI	59,261	16	115
Cincinnati–Middletown, OH–KY–IN	52,439	30	102
Cleveland–Elyria–Mentor, OH	46,944	46	91
Columbus, OH	53,699	27	105
Dallas–Fort Worth–Arlington, TX	56,954	19	111
Denver–Aurora–Broomfield, CO	61,453	10	120
Detroit–Warren–Livonia, MI	50,310	40	98
Grand Rapids–Wyoming, MI	50,658	38	99
Hartford–West Hartford–East Hartford, CT	66,732	6	130
Houston–Sugar Land–Baytown, TX	55,910	23	109
Indianapolis–Carmel, IN	51,808	32	101
Jacksonville, FL	48,118	45	94
Kansas City, MO–KS	54,519	25	106
Las Vegas–Paradise, NV	49,546	42	96
Los Angeles–Long Beach–Santa Ana, CA	57,271	17	111
Louisville/Jefferson County, KY–IN	48,895	43	95
Memphis, TN–MS–AR	45,687	50	89
Miami–Fort Lauderdale–Pompano Beach, FL	46,648	48	91
Milwaukee–Waukesha–West Allis, WI	52,605	28	102
Minneapolis–St. Paul–Bloomington, MN–WI	66,282	7	129
Nashville-Davidson–Murfreesboro–Franklin, TN	51,500	34	100
New Orleans–Metairie–Kenner, LA	44,379	52	86
New York–Northern New Jersey–Long Island, NY–NJ–PA	63,982	9	125
Oklahoma City, OK	48,557	44	95
Orlando–Kissimmee–Sanford, FL	46,020	49	90
Philadelphia–Camden–Wilmington, PA–NJ–DE–MD	60,105	13	117
Phoenix–Mesa–Glendale, AZ	51,359	36	100
Pittsburgh, PA	50,489	39	98
Portland–Vancouver–Hillsboro, OR–WA	56,978	18	111
Providence–New Bedford–Fall River, RI–MA	54,243	26	106
Raleigh–Cary, NC	60,319	12	117

	median household income	rank among top metro areas	index to national median
Richmond, VA	$56,769	21	111
Riverside–San Bernardino–Ontario, CA	51,695	33	101
Rochester, NY	50,701	37	99
Sacramento–Arden-Arcade–Roseville, CA	56,813	20	111
Salt Lake City, UT	60,061	14	117
San Antonio–New Braunfels, TX	51,486	35	100
San Diego–Carlsbad–San Marcos, CA	60,330	11	117
San Francisco–Oakland–Fremont, CA	74,922	3	146
San Jose–Sunnyvale–Santa Clara, CA	90,737	1	177
Seattle–Tacoma–Bellevue, WA	65,677	8	128
St. Louis, MO–IL	52,243	31	102
Tampa–St. Petersburg–Clearwater, FL	44,402	51	86
Virginia Beach–Norfolk–Newport News, VA–NC	55,997	22	109
Washington–Arlington–Alexandria, DC–VA–MD–WV	88,233	2	172

Source: Bureau of the Census, 2013 Current Population Survey, Internet site http://www.census.gov/hhes/www/cpstables/ 032013/hhinc/toc.htm; calculations by New Strategist

2

Men's Income

American men under age 55 have experienced a steep decline in their income that began well before the Great Recession. The overall median income of men fell 2.7 percent between 2000 and 2007 then dropped by an even larger 7.8 percent between 2007 and 2012, after adjusting for inflation. Among men under age 55, the decline in median income between 2000 and 2012 was in the double digits. For years, the growing incomes of women kept households from falling behind, but women's income growth came to a halt with the Great Recession.

In contrast to their younger counterparts, men aged 65 or older have gained ground since 2000. Behind their growing income is Social Security, with guaranteed benefits indexed to inflation. The greater labor force participation of older men is also a reason for their income growth.

The median income of men in every racial and ethnic group fell between 2000 and 2012, after adjusting for inflation. Among men with full-time jobs, median earnings were lower in 2012 than in 2000 for blacks and non-Hispanic whites. Even college graduates with full-time jobs experienced a steep decline in earnings between 2000 and 2012.

■ Men's incomes are likely to continue to decline in the years ahead because of structural changes in the economy.

Men's Income Trends

Incomes Have Plummeted among Men under Age 65

Older men made gains, even during the Great Recession.

Men's incomes were declining well before the Great Recession. The median income of men under age 55 was lower in 2007 than in 2000, after adjusting for inflation. Then the Great Recession hit and dragged incomes even lower. Between 2000 and 2012, men under age 55 experienced double-digit percentage declines in median income. Among men aged 45 to 54—the nation's peak earners—median income fell by more than $8,000 during those years, after adjusting for inflation.

In contrast to the experience of their younger counterparts, men aged 65 or older made gains before and after the Great Recession. Their median income climbed 4.1 percent between 2000 and 2007 and then by another 2.5 percent between 2007 and 2012, after adjusting for inflation. In 2012, the $27,612 median income of men aged 65 or older was close to its record high.

■ Men aged 55 to 64 had growing incomes until the Great Recession, then experienced a 10 percent decline between 2007 and 2012.

Median income of men aged 45 to 54 fell 8 percent between 2007 and 2012

(median income of men aged 25 to 64 by age, 2007 and 2012; in 2012 dollars)

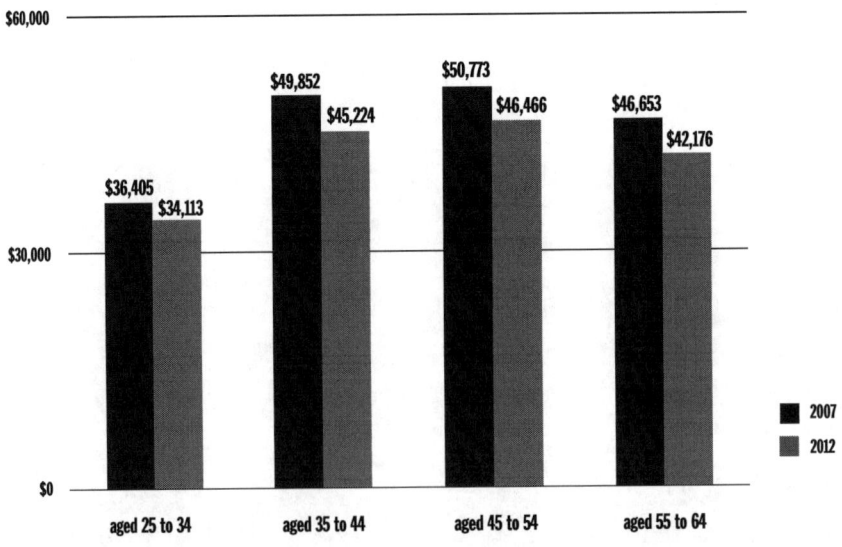

Table 2.1 Median Income of Men by Age, 2000 to 2012

(median income of men aged 15 or older with income by age, 2000 to 2012; percent change for selected years; in 2012 dollars)

	total men	15 to 24	25 to 34	35 to 44	45 to 54	55 to 64	65 or older total	65 to 74	75 or older
2012	$33,904	$10,869	$34,113	$45,224	$46,466	$42,176	$27,612	$31,762	$23,570
2011	33,675	10,738	33,262	44,885	46,910	42,418	28,286	31,888	24,115
2010	33,915	10,433	33,637	44,474	47,861	43,432	27,096	30,878	23,165
2009	34,452	10,743	34,163	45,200	47,883	44,206	27,701	30,992	24,366
2008	35,363	11,494	35,634	47,124	48,564	44,530	27,197	30,919	23,366
2007	36,761	12,413	36,405	49,852	50,773	46,653	26,935	30,770	23,033
2006	36,744	12,486	36,591	48,555	52,035	47,234	26,762	29,920	23,504
2005	36,784	12,313	36,650	48,179	51,312	47,815	25,621	28,605	22,867
2004	37,094	12,255	37,673	49,272	50,890	47,757	25,686	29,433	22,763
2003	37,367	12,436	38,154	48,932	52,533	48,583	25,422	28,915	22,197
2002	37,317	12,306	39,153	48,362	52,289	46,301	24,806	27,174	22,346
2001	37,742	12,063	39,569	49,724	53,309	46,218	25,534	28,137	22,723
2000	37,791	12,728	40,339	50,563	54,719	45,585	25,881	28,621	22,925

PERCENT CHANGE

	total men	15 to 24	25 to 34	35 to 44	45 to 54	55 to 64	65 or older total	65 to 74	75 or older
2007 to 2012	−7.8%	−12.4%	−6.3%	−9.3%	−8.5%	−9.6%	2.5%	3.2%	2.3%
2000 to 2007	−2.7	−2.5	−9.8	−1.4	−7.2	2.3	4.1	7.5	0.5
2000 to 2012	−10.3	−14.6	−15.4	−10.6	−15.1	−7.5	6.7	11.0	2.8

Source: Bureau of the Census, Current Population Survey, Historical Tables, Internet site http://www.census.gov/hhes/www/income/data/historical/people/; calculations by New Strategist

Regardless of Race or Hispanic Origin, Men Lost Ground

Older men made gains, however.

The median income of men in every race and Hispanic origin group fell between 2000 and 2012, after adjusting for inflation. Most of the decline occurred after the start of the Great Recession, but Asian and non-Hispanic white men saw their median income begin to decline before the Great Recession.

Among men of working age, only Asians aged 35 to 44 saw their median income rise in the 2007-to-2012 time period, after adjusting for inflation. Among Hispanic men under age 25, median income fell by a stunning 25 percent during those years. Among black men aged 45 to 54, the decline was 20 percent. In contrast, men aged 65 or older made gains in every racial and ethnic group. The increase ranged from a low of 1 percent among Hispanic men to a high of 19 percent among black men.

■ Asian men have the highest median income, Hispanic men the lowest.

Asians experienced the smallest decline between 2007 and 2012

(percent change in median income of men aged 15 or older, by race and Hispanic origin, 2007 to 2012; in 2012 dollars)

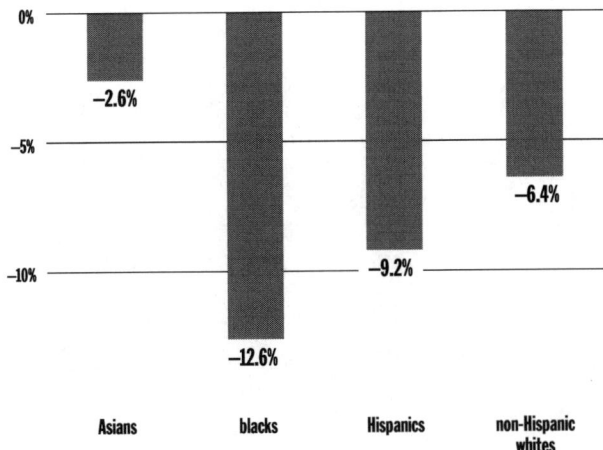

Table 2.2 Median Income of Men by Race and Hispanic Origin, 2000 to 2012

(median income of men aged 15 or older with income by race and Hispanic origin, 2000 to 2012; percent change for selected years; in 2012 dollars)

	total men	Asian	black	Hispanic	non-Hispanic white
2012	$33,904	$39,606	$24,959	$24,592	$38,751
2011	33,675	36,584	24,077	24,227	38,945
2010	33,915	36,986	24,312	23,610	39,127
2009	34,452	39,486	25,342	23,825	39,377
2008	35,363	38,608	26,786	25,597	39,893
2007	36,761	40,673	28,562	27,077	41,386
2006	36,744	42,255	28,556	26,707	41,639
2005	36,784	38,855	26,591	25,980	41,571
2004	37,094	39,465	27,609	26,203	40,938
2003	37,367	39,621	27,384	26,283	40,363
2002	37,317	39,360	27,452	26,422	40,885
2001	37,742	40,329	27,840	26,184	41,230
2000	37,791	41,111	28,457	25,997	42,011
PERCENT CHANGE					
2007 to 2012	−7.8%	−2.6%	−12.6%	−9.2%	−6.4%
2000 to 2007	−2.7	−1.1	0.4	4.2	−1.5
2000 to 2012	−10.3	−3.7	−12.3	−5.4	−7.8

Note: Beginning in 2002, Asians and blacks are those who identify themselves as being of the race alone and those who identify themselves as being of the race in combination with other races. Hispanics may be of any race. Beginning in 2002, non-Hispanic whites are those who identify themselves as being white alone and not Hispanic.
Source: Bureau of the Census, Current Population Survey, Historical Tables, Internet site http://www.census.gov/hhes/www/income/data/historical/people/; calculations by New Strategist

Table 2.3 Median Income of Asian Men by Age, 2002 to 2012

(median income of Asian men aged 15 or older with income by age, 2002 to 2012; percent change for selected years; in 2012 dollars)

	total Asian men	15 to 24	25 to 34	35 to 44	45 to 54	55 to 64	65 or older
2012	$39,606	$11,290	$45,381	$61,424	$50,935	$38,207	$21,716
2011	36,584	9,472	38,632	57,423	51,355	36,854	22,212
2010	36,986	11,603	38,043	58,020	48,982	43,447	22,111
2009	39,486	8,288	40,017	61,523	47,437	39,540	23,178
2008	38,608	10,585	44,098	55,092	52,201	43,444	19,712
2007	40,673	11,796	46,095	57,776	53,040	44,064	20,991
2006	42,255	8,325	47,330	58,020	52,599	48,325	21,226
2005	38,855	10,675	43,709	56,875	48,254	45,890	22,428
2004	39,465	11,751	41,272	58,135	50,095	44,644	19,725
2003	39,621	8,563	45,749	55,031	52,180	49,857	17,665
2002	39,360	12,486	44,856	53,167	52,580	40,222	19,559

PERCENT CHANGE

2007 to 2012	−2.6%	−4.3%	−1.5%	6.3%	−4.0%	−13.3%	3.5%
2002 to 2007	3.3	−5.5	2.8	8.7	0.9	9.6	7.3
2002 to 2012	0.6	−9.6	1.2	15.5	−3.1	−5.0	11.0

Note: Asians are those who identify themselves as being of the race alone and those who identify themselves as being of the race in combination with other races.
Source: Bureau of the Census, Current Population Survey, Historical Tables, Internet site http://www.census.gov/hhes/www/income/data/historical/people/; calculations by New Strategist

Table 2.4 Median Income of Black Men by Age, 2000 to 2012

(median income of black men aged 15 or older with income by age, 2000 to 2012; percent change for selected years; in 2012 dollars)

	total black men	15 to 24	25 to 34	35 to 44	45 to 54	55 to 64	65 or older
2012	$24,959	$9,411	$26,338	$34,555	$31,421	$29,389	$21,130
2011	24,077	8,869	26,606	32,606	31,578	26,716	20,574
2010	24,312	9,572	24,837	33,381	32,363	29,076	19,451
2009	25,342	9,208	26,172	36,573	32,906	31,550	19,358
2008	26,786	10,081	28,077	34,239	33,979	30,730	20,311
2007	28,562	11,069	29,791	35,944	39,227	33,485	17,775
2006	28,556	11,267	30,396	36,810	35,828	32,987	17,868
2005	26,591	10,928	27,933	37,128	36,038	31,646	16,001
2004	27,609	9,387	30,872	37,138	36,884	31,706	18,228
2003	27,384	10,062	30,770	37,644	37,544	32,498	17,945
2002	27,452	9,678	31,591	36,816	34,386	32,679	18,075
2001	27,840	9,718	33,193	38,137	36,086	30,924	17,866
2000	28,457	10,137	31,301	36,293	36,229	32,207	18,536

PERCENT CHANGE

2007 to 2012	−12.6%	−15.0%	−11.6%	−3.9%	−19.9%	−12.2%	18.9%
2000 to 2007	0.4	9.2	−4.8	−1.0	8.3	4.0	−4.1
2000 to 2012	−12.3	−7.2	−15.9	−4.8	−13.3	−8.7	14.0

Note: Beginning in 2002, blacks are those who identify themselves as being of the race alone and those who identify themselves as being of the race in combination with other races.
Source: Bureau of the Census, Current Population Survey, Historical Tables, Internet site http://www.census.gov/hhes/www/income/data/historical/people/; calculations by New Strategist

Table 2.5 Median Income of Hispanic Men by Age, 2000 to 2012

(median income of Hispanic men aged 15 or older with income by age, 2000 to 2012; percent change for selected years; in 2012 dollars)

	total Hispanic men	15 to 24	25 to 34	35 to 44	45 to 54	55 to 64	65 or older
2012	$24,592	$12,420	$26,096	$29,340	$31,299	$27,768	$17,348
2011	24,227	12,076	26,199	30,801	30,028	27,047	17,405
2010	23,610	12,587	23,967	29,986	29,930	27,853	16,669
2009	23,825	12,605	24,276	30,069	31,087	28,713	17,023
2008	25,597	13,680	27,033	32,410	32,253	29,738	16,389
2007	27,077	16,485	28,009	33,702	33,489	32,393	17,115
2006	26,707	17,088	27,870	34,254	34,872	28,895	16,471
2005	25,980	16,481	26,848	31,816	33,736	30,433	16,323
2004	26,203	14,900	27,082	32,738	33,302	32,067	16,481
2003	26,283	15,438	27,674	32,730	32,938	31,805	15,866
2002	26,422	15,895	28,100	32,663	33,109	28,582	14,841
2001	26,184	15,909	27,993	32,855	32,222	27,949	16,001
2000	25,997	16,308	28,119	33,136	33,936	26,633	14,948

PERCENT CHANGE

2007 to 2012	−9.2%	−24.7%	−6.8%	−12.9%	−6.5%	−14.3%	1.4%
2000 to 2007	4.2	1.1	−0.4	1.7	−1.3	21.6	14.5
2000 to 2012	−5.4	−23.8	−7.2	−11.5	−7.8	4.3	16.1

Source: Bureau of the Census, Current Population Survey, Historical Tables, Internet site http://www.census.gov/hhes/www/income/data/historical/people/; calculations by New Strategist

Table 2.6 Median Income of Non-Hispanic White Men by Age, 2000 to 2012

(median income of non-Hispanic white men aged 15 or older with income by age, 2000 to 2012; percent change for selected years; in 2012 dollars)

	total non-Hispanic white men	15 to 24	25 to 34	35 to 44	45 to 54	55 to 64	65 or older
2012	$38,751	$10,661	$39,120	$51,263	$52,111	$47,195	$30,010
2011	38,945	10,828	38,297	52,174	52,987	48,165	30,278
2010	39,127	9,916	39,086	52,801	54,020	48,301	28,932
2009	39,377	10,700	40,855	52,922	53,780	48,912	29,577
2008	39,893	11,322	40,832	54,462	54,112	49,282	29,036
2007	41,386	11,830	41,623	56,334	56,207	51,488	29,046
2006	41,639	11,962	41,750	57,067	57,988	51,672	28,748
2005	41,571	11,605	41,715	54,441	58,131	51,293	27,441
2004	40,938	11,556	43,454	55,164	57,121	51,279	27,258
2003	40,363	11,765	42,166	53,813	58,489	51,549	27,292
2002	40,885	11,304	43,719	54,076	57,872	50,552	26,528
2001	41,230	11,233	43,216	54,432	58,231	49,655	27,049
2000	42,011	11,863	43,963	55,748	60,155	49,229	27,552
PERCENT CHANGE							
2007 to 2012	–6.4%	–9.9%	–6.0%	–9.0%	–7.3%	–8.3%	3.3%
2000 to 2007	–1.5	–0.3	–5.3	1.1	–6.6	4.6	5.4
2000 to 2012	–7.8	–10.1	–11.0	–8.0	–13.4	–4.1	8.9

Note: Beginning in 2002, data are for those who identify themselves as being white alone and not Hispanic.
Source: Bureau of the Census, Current Population Survey, Historical Tables, Internet site http://www.census.gov/hhes/www/income/data/historical/people/; calculations by New Strategist

In Every Region, Men Have Lost Ground since 2000

In most regions, the decline began before the Great Recession.

In every region, men saw their income decline between 2000 and 2012. The greatest loss occurred among men in the Midwest (down 13 percent, after adjusting for inflation). The smallest decline was in the South (down 9 percent). Men in the West saw their median income decline by 11 percent, and in the Northeast they experienced a 10 percent drop in median income.

Men in the West were the only ones who saw their median income rise between 2000 and 2007—up 2 percent, after adjusting for inflation. In the other regions, men's median income was in decline before the Great Recession.

■ Men in the South have the lowest median income ($32,181), and men in the Northeast have the highest ($36,342).

Between 2007 and 2012, men's incomes fell the most in the West

(percent change in median income of men aged 15 or older by region, 2007 to 2012; in 2012 dollars)

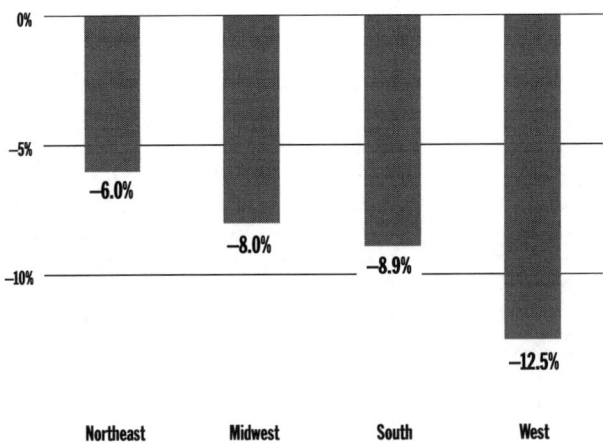

Table 2.7 Median Income of Men by Region, 2000 to 2012

(median income of men aged 15 or older with income by region, 2000 to 2012; percent change for selected years; in 2012 dollars)

	total men	Northeast	Midwest	South	West
2012	$33,904	$36,342	$34,978	$32,181	$33,546
2011	33,675	36,499	34,745	32,787	32,884
2010	33,915	37,341	34,000	32,950	34,150
2009	34,452	37,910	34,319	33,235	35,530
2008	35,363	38,143	35,472	33,779	37,385
2007	36,761	38,671	38,010	35,311	38,326
2006	36,744	40,109	37,425	35,474	37,337
2005	36,784	38,369	37,622	35,265	37,150
2004	37,094	38,834	37,855	34,985	37,268
2003	37,367	39,216	37,814	34,473	37,985
2002	37,317	39,117	38,593	35,129	37,133
2001	37,742	39,733	39,273	35,464	37,200
2000	37,791	40,451	40,145	35,475	37,667
PERCENT CHANGE					
2007 to 2012	−7.8%	−6.0%	−8.0%	−8.9%	−12.5%
2000 to 2007	−2.7	−4.4	−5.3	−0.5	1.7
2000 to 2012	−10.3	−10.2	−12.9	−9.3	−10.9

Source: Bureau of the Census, Current Population Survey, Historical Tables, Internet site http://www.census.gov/hhes/www/ income/data/historical/people/; calculations by New Strategist

Men's Earnings Fell between 2000 and 2012

Men who work full-time, year-round barely stayed even.

Between 2000 and 2012, the median earnings of men fell 8 percent, to $37,916 after adjusting for inflation. But men who managed to hold on to a full-time job saw their median earnings fall by a much smaller 0.5 percent during those years—to $49,398 in 2012.

Most of the decline in men's earnings has occurred since 2007. Among men who work full-time, year-round, median earnings grew by 0.6 percent between 2000 and 2007, after adjusting for inflation. Between 2007 and 2012, however, their median earnings fell by 1.1 percent.

■ Men who had a full-time job during the Great Recession barely maintained their standard of living.

Men who work full-time, year-round are struggling to stay even

*(median income of men aged 15 or older who work full-time,
year-round, 2000, 2007, and 2012; in 2012 dollars)*

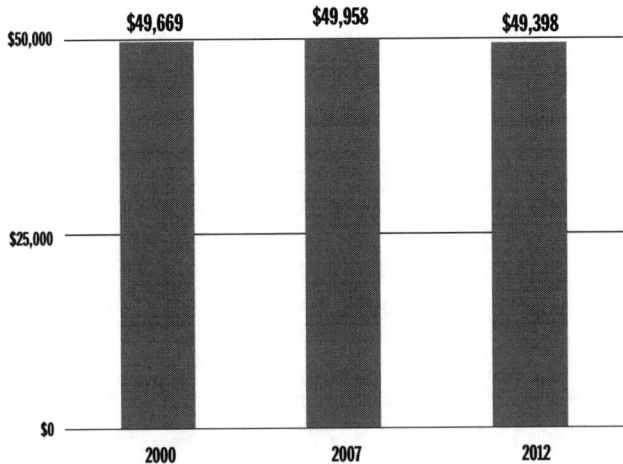

Table 2.8 Median Earnings of Men by Employment Status, 2000 to 2012

(median earnings of men aged 15 or older with earnings by employment status, 2000 to 2012; percent change for selected years; in 2012 dollars)

	total men with earnings	worked full-time		worked part-time	
		total	year-round	total	year-round
2012	$37,916	$43,963	$49,398	$9,912	$14,215
2011	38,121	43,346	49,209	9,449	14,067
2010	38,737	44,268	50,497	9,176	13,375
2009	38,891	44,492	50,448	9,503	14,036
2008	38,997	44,119	49,446	8,507	13,096
2007	40,569	45,393	49,958	8,297	13,604
2006	40,859	45,886	48,127	8,178	13,494
2005	40,399	44,850	48,676	8,137	13,814
2004	39,485	45,020	49,591	7,981	13,455
2003	40,010	45,809	50,771	8,131	13,754
2002	40,391	45,744	50,323	8,062	13,672
2001	40,677	45,802	49,640	7,376	13,502
2000	41,268	46,085	49,669	7,676	13,791
PERCENT CHANGE					
2007 to 2012	−6.5%	−3.2%	−1.1%	19.5%	4.5%
2000 to 2007	−1.7	−1.5	0.6	8.1	−1.4
2000 to 2012	−8.1	−4.6	−0.5	29.1	3.1

Note: Earnings include wages and salaries only.
Source: Bureau of the Census, Current Population Survey, Historical Tables, Internet site http://www.census.gov/hhes/www/income/data/historical/people/; calculations by New Strategist

Asian Men Have Seen Their Earnings Rise

Black and non-Hispanic white men have lost ground since 2000.

Between 2000 and 2012, Asian men with full-time jobs gained the most ground. Their median earnings climbed 6 percent during those years, after adjusting for inflation. The median earnings of Hispanic men grew by 1.7 percent. In contrast, black men experienced a 3.6 percent decline in earnings, and non-Hispanic white men saw their median earnings fall by an even larger 4.5 percent.

The earnings of men who work full-time had been either growing or stable before the Great Recession. Once the Great Recession set in, the earnings of black, Hispanic, and non-Hispanic white men fell. Non-Hispanic white men experienced the biggest decline. Their earnings fell 5.7 percent between 2007 and 2012, after adjusting for inflation. In contrast, Asian men who work full-time saw their earnings grow during those years.

■ Despite the decline between 2000 and 2012, black men who work full-time still earn substantially more than their Hispanic counterparts.

Non-Hispanic white men lost the most ground between 2007 and 2012

(percent change in median earnings of men aged 15 or older who work full-time, year-round, by race and Hispanic origin, 2007 to 2012; in 2012 dollars)

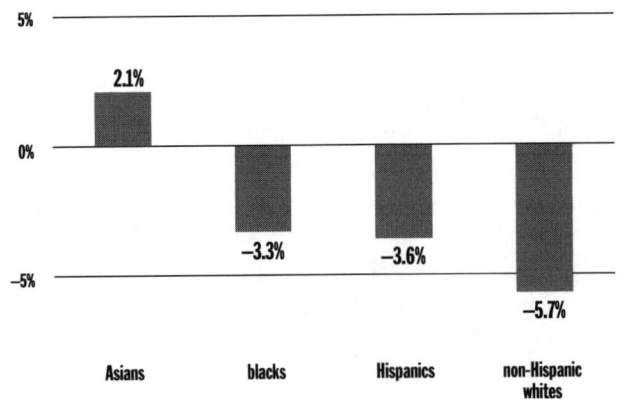

Table 2.9 Median Earnings of Men Who Work Full-Time by Race and Hispanic Origin, 2000 to 2012

(median earnings of men aged 15 or older who work full-time, year-round, by race and Hispanic origin, 2000 to 2012; percent change for selected years; in 2012 dollars)

	total men working full-time	Asian	black	Hispanic	non-Hispanic white
2012	$49,398	$57,148	$38,670	$32,243	$52,535
2011	49,209	55,894	39,911	32,508	53,411
2010	50,497	54,184	38,880	33,255	54,719
2009	50,448	55,279	40,140	33,605	55,028
2008	49,446	54,562	39,727	33,014	54,647
2007	49,958	55,955	39,988	33,441	55,735
2006	48,127	58,224	39,757	33,095	55,141
2005	48,676	55,399	38,784	31,484	54,617
2004	49,591	55,597	38,021	32,402	55,358
2003	50,771	56,299	40,269	32,563	55,876
2002	50,323	53,274	40,136	33,147	54,215
2001	49,640	54,280	40,660	32,531	54,057
2000	49,669	54,075	40,135	31,704	54,997

PERCENT CHANGE

2007 to 2012	–1.1%	2.1%	–3.3%	–3.6%	–5.7%
2000 to 2007	0.6	3.5	–0.4	5.5	1.3
2000 to 2012	–0.5	5.7	–3.6	1.7	–4.5

Note: Beginning in 2002, Asians and blacks are those who identify themselves as being of the race alone and those who identify themselves as being of the race in combination with other races. Hispanics may be of any race. Beginning in 2002, non-Hispanic whites are those who identify themselves as being white alone and not Hispanic. Earnings include wages and salaries only.

Source: Bureau of the Census, Current Population Survey, Historical Tables, Internet site http://www.census.gov/hhes/www/ income/data/historical/people/; calculations by New Strategist

College Graduates Lost Ground between 2000 and 2012

Since 2007, men with graduate degrees are the only ones who have made gains.

Between 2000 and 2012, the median earnings of men aged 25 or older who work full-time, year-round fell 4.7 percent, after adjusting for inflation. College graduates saw their median earnings fall almost as much as those with less education. Among men with at least a bachelor's degree, median earnings fell 6.4 percent. Among men with less education, the earnings decline ranged from 6.7 to 7.7 percent.

The decline in the earnings of men who work full-time began well before the Great Recession. In the 2000-to-2007 time period, men with at least a bachelor's degree who worked full-time saw their median earnings fall by 3.1 percent. The Great Recession added to the loss, with another 3.4 percent decline between 2007 and 2012. The story is similar for men with less education. Men with a graduate degree were the only ones who made gains in the 2007-to-2012 time period.

■ Despite the decline in earnings, the premium paid to college graduates held steady between 2000 and 2012.

Premium paid to college graduates is holding steady

(median earnings of men aged 25 or older who work full-time, year-round, by selected educational attainment, 2000 and 2012; in 2012 dollars)

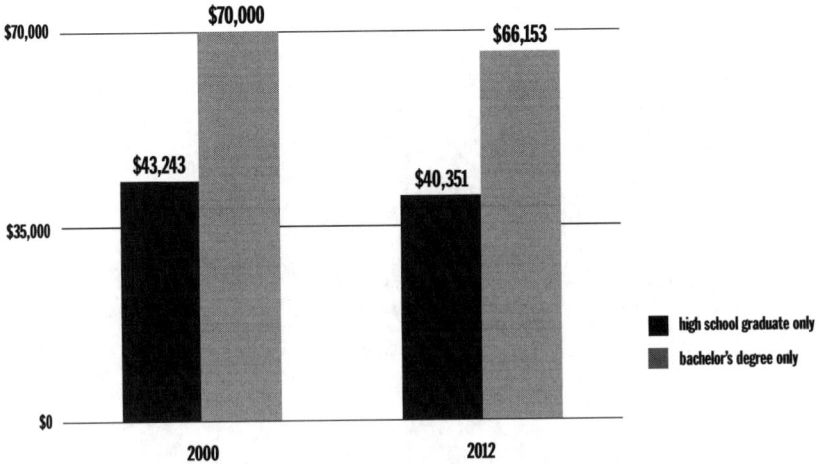

Table 2.10 Median Earnings of Men Who Work Full-Time by Education, 2000 to 2012

(median income of households by educational attainment of householders aged 25 or older, 2000 to 2012; percent change for selected years; in 2012 dollars)

	total men	less than 9th grade	9th to 12th grade, no diploma	high school graduate	some college	associate's degree	bachelor's degree or more				
							total	bachelor's degree	master's degree	professional degree	doctoral degree
2012	$50,955	$25,131	$30,329	$40,351	$47,187	$50,961	$75,320	$66,153	$85,116	$116,355	$106,467
2011	51,713	25,750	31,059	41,292	48,055	51,992	75,397	67,579	84,761	121,970	102,871
2010	53,099	26,324	31,372	42,210	49,051	53,026	75,755	67,575	85,363	121,732	106,606
2009	53,517	25,633	29,998	42,260	50,416	53,848	76,503	66,845	84,934	131,929	107,840
2008	52,254	25,866	31,649	41,600	48,864	53,477	77,011	70,170	86,339	–	–
2007	52,052	25,885	32,465	41,920	49,721	54,309	77,961	68,754	84,476	–	101,978
2006	52,111	25,860	31,491	42,171	49,918	53,606	76,224	69,360	85,902	–	–
2005	50,947	26,263	31,978	42,696	49,890	55,490	77,821	70,592	88,240	–	100,988
2004	51,156	26,312	31,945	43,428	50,940	53,965	76,195	69,530	86,833	–	100,160
2003	52,358	26,488	33,043	44,209	51,620	53,521	77,496	70,539	88,189	–	108,777
2002	52,523	26,699	33,060	42,381	52,138	54,697	78,748	71,571	85,871	–	106,323
2001	52,793	27,416	33,535	42,846	52,083	54,027	78,533	68,877	86,808	–	105,151
2000	53,451	27,000	32,861	43,243	50,900	54,644	80,468	70,000	87,040	124,368	100,488

PERCENT CHANGE

2007 to 2012	–2.1%	–2.9%	–6.6%	–3.7%	–5.1%	–6.2%	–3.4%	–3.8%	0.8%	–	4.4%
2000 to 2007	–2.6	–4.1	–1.2	–3.1	–2.3	–0.6	–3.1	–1.8	–2.9	–	1.5
2000 to 2012	–4.7	–6.9	–7.7	–6.7	–7.3	–6.7	–6.4	–5.5	–2.2	–6.4%	5.9

Note: Earnings include wages and salaries only. "–" means data are not available.
Source: Bureau of the Census, Current Population Survey, Historical Tables, Internet site http://www.census.gov/hhes/www/income/data/historical/people/; calculations by New Strategist

Men in Most Occupations Have Seen Their Earnings Decline

Some men have gained ground, however.

Among all men who work full-time, year-round, median earnings fell 1.1 percent between 2007 and 2012, after adjusting for inflation. Only three occupational groups saw earnings grow during the time period. Men in health care support experienced the biggest gain—up 5.2 percent. The median earnings of men in professional occupations climbed 3.1 percent, and men in production occupations held their ground with a 0.3 percent rise in median earnings.

The biggest earnings decline occurred among men working in personal care and service occupations, with a loss of 9.0 percent in median earnings between 2007 and 2012 after adjusting for inflation. Men in sales occupations saw their earnings fall by 7.4 percent, and those in management lost 7.3 percent.

■ The earnings of men who work in health care support occupations increased between 2007 and 2012, while the earnings of their female counterparts declined.

Recession hurt some men more than others

(percent change in median earnings of men aged 15 or older who work full-time, year-round, by selected occupation, 2007 to 2012; in 2012 dollars)

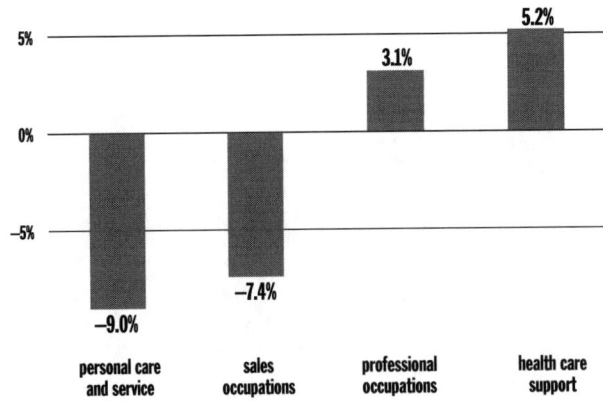

Table 2.11 Median Earnings of Men Who Work Full-Time by Occupation, 2007 to 2012

(median earnings of men aged 15 or older who work full-time, year-round, by occupation of longest job held, 2007 to 2012; percent change, 2007–12; in 2012 dollars)

	2012	2010	2007	percent change 2007–12
Total men who work full-time	**$49,398**	**$50,497**	**$49,958**	**–1.1%**
Management, business and financial occupations	71,837	75,971	77,526	–7.3
Professional and related occupations	71,298	71,314	69,130	3.1
Health care support occupations	30,586	35,173	29,062	5.2
Protective service occupations	53,836	54,016	55,186	–2.4
Food preparation occupations	23,672	24,650	24,134	–1.9
Building and grounds occupations	28,340	30,295	28,895	–1.9
Personal care and service occupations	31,544	33,012	34,669	–9.0
Sales and related occupations	47,401	49,733	51,178	–7.4
Office and administrative support occupations	40,696	39,308	40,734	–0.1
Farming, fishing, and forestry occupations	25,711	25,460	26,121	–1.6
Construction and extraction occupations	38,295	42,316	39,341	–2.7
Installation, maintenance, and repair occupations	43,100	45,185	45,619	–5.5
Production occupations	40,595	39,194	40,477	0.3
Transportation and material moving occupations	38,405	37,736	39,254	–2.2
Armed Forces	45,977	49,535	46,581	–1.3

Note: Earnings include wages and salaries only.
Source: Bureau of the Census, Current Population Survey, Historical Tables, Internet site http://www.census.gov/hhes/www/income/data/historical/people/; calculations by New Strategist

Men's Income, 2012

Income Peaks among Men Aged 45 to 54

Asian men have the highest incomes, Hispanics the lowest.

The median income of men stood at $33,904 in 2012, meaning half of men had incomes above that amount and half below. Men's income rises with age to a peak of $46,466 in the 45-to-54 age group. Sixty-nine percent of men aged 45 to 54 work full-time, year-round, and those who do have a median income of $57,954. Median income surpasses $60,000 for men aged 55 or older with full-time jobs.

Among full-time workers, the $59,531 median income of Asian men is higher than that of their black, Hispanic, or non-Hispanic white counterparts. The median income of non-Hispanic white men who work full-time was a lower $56,247. Among blacks, the figure was $39,975. Hispanic men who work full-time had the lowest median income, just $32,516.

■ When the economy begins to recover, men's median income may rise as growing numbers of highly paid older men postpone retirement.

Among men working full-time, incomes continue to rise into old age

(median income of men aged 15 or older who work full-time, year-round, by age, 2012)

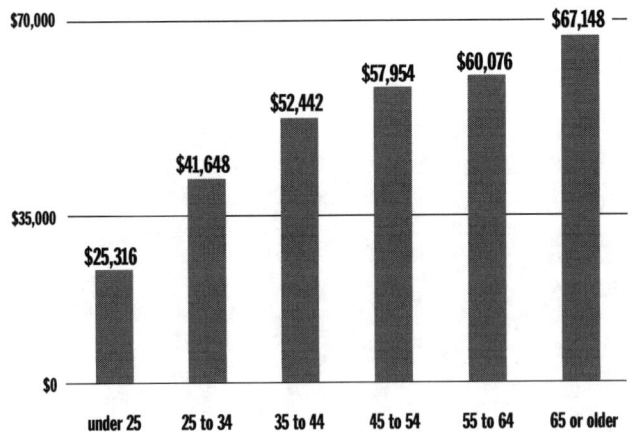

Table 2.12 Men by Income and Age, 2012: Total Men

(number and percent distribution of men aged 15 or older by income and age, 2012; median income of men with income and of men working full-time, year-round; percent working full-time, year-round; men in thousands as of 2013)

	total	15 to 24	25 to 34	35 to 44	45 to 54	55 to 64	65 or older total	65 to 74	75 or older
Total men	**121,111**	**21,806**	**20,816**	**19,623**	**21,244**	**18,323**	**19,298**	**11,604**	**7,693**
Without income	13,577	8,534	1,634	1,040	1,061	808	500	285	214
With income	107,534	13,271	19,183	18,583	20,183	17,515	18,798	11,319	7,479
Under $5,000	7,050	3,884	870	549	688	676	383	232	151
$5,000 to $9,999	7,122	2,344	1,128	662	964	945	1,078	624	454
$10,000 to $14,999	8,706	1,814	1,359	1,029	1,149	1,211	2,144	1,090	1,053
$15,000 to $19,999	9,103	1,442	1,446	1,161	1,088	1,261	2,705	1,325	1,380
$20,000 to $24,999	8,370	1,153	1,637	1,218	1,209	1,007	2,146	1,204	942
$25,000 to $29,999	7,276	768	1,618	1,086	1,198	1,059	1,547	853	694
$30,000 to $34,999	7,032	542	1,683	1,314	1,230	990	1,273	738	536
$35,000 to $39,999	5,975	327	1,375	1,096	1,073	1,016	1,088	671	417
$40,000 to $44,999	5,584	273	1,213	1,121	1,141	988	847	559	288
$45,000 to $49,999	4,666	160	1,065	954	961	817	709	478	231
$50,000 to $54,999	4,886	168	1,024	1,021	1,050	932	691	472	219
$55,000 to $59,999	3,028	68	629	642	615	580	494	376	118
$60,000 to $64,999	3,640	71	737	761	827	734	509	359	150
$65,000 to $69,999	2,653	26	434	621	652	563	357	231	127
$70,000 to $74,999	2,627	43	512	561	668	509	334	240	95
$75,000 to $79,999	2,112	29	374	550	506	360	293	212	81
$80,000 to $84,999	2,113	21	338	507	551	482	215	167	48
$85,000 to $89,999	1,447	17	211	323	391	314	191	127	64
$90,000 to $94,999	1,684	27	279	427	460	292	200	136	64
$95,000 to $99,999	929	7	148	269	221	151	133	98	35
$100,000 or more	11,531	88	1,103	2,711	3,541	2,628	1,459	1,126	333

MEDIAN INCOME

	total	15 to 24	25 to 34	35 to 44	45 to 54	55 to 64	65 or older total	65 to 74	75 or older
Men with income	$33,904	$10,869	$34,113	$45,224	$46,466	$42,176	$27,612	$31,762	$23,570
Men working full-time	50,683	25,316	41,648	52,442	57,954	60,076	67,148	69,024	63,969
Percent working full-time	48.7%	17.5%	65.0%	72.2%	69.2%	55.5%	13.7%	18.7%	6.1%

PERCENT DISTRIBUTION

	total	15 to 24	25 to 34	35 to 44	45 to 54	55 to 64	65 or older total	65 to 74	75 or older
Total men	**100.0%**	**100.0%**	**100.0%**	**100.0%**	**100.0%**	**100.0%**	**100.0%**	**100.0%**	**100.0%**
Without income	11.2	39.1	7.8	5.3	5.0	4.4	2.6	2.5	2.8
With income	88.8	60.9	92.2	94.7	95.0	95.6	97.4	97.5	97.2
Under $15,000	18.9	36.9	16.1	11.4	13.2	15.5	18.7	16.8	21.6
$15,000 to $24,999	14.4	11.9	14.8	12.1	10.8	12.4	25.1	21.8	30.2
$25,000 to $34,999	11.8	6.0	15.9	12.2	11.4	11.2	14.6	13.7	16.0
$35,000 to $49,999	13.4	3.5	17.5	16.2	14.9	15.4	13.7	14.7	12.2
$50,000 to $74,999	13.9	1.7	16.0	18.4	17.9	18.1	12.4	14.5	9.2
$75,000 to $99,999	6.8	0.5	6.5	10.6	10.0	8.7	5.3	6.4	3.8
$100,000 or more	9.5	0.4	5.3	13.8	16.7	14.3	7.6	9.7	4.3

Source: Bureau of the Census, 2013 Current Population Survey Annual Social and Economic Supplement, Internet site http:// www.census.gov/hhes/www/cpstables/032013/perinc/toc.htm; calculations by New Strategist

Table 2.13 Men by Income and Age, 2012: Asian Men

(number and percent distribution of Asian men aged 15 or older by income and age, 2012; median income of men with income and of men working full-time, year-round; percent working full-time, year-round; men in thousands as of 2013)

	total	15 to 24	25 to 34	35 to 44	45 to 54	55 to 64	65 or older total	65 to 74	75 or older
Total Asian men	**6,729**	**1,310**	**1,444**	**1,350**	**1,084**	**806**	**735**	**475**	**260**
Without income	920	570	116	55	53	60	66	35	31
With income	5,810	740	1,328	1,295	1,032	745	669	440	229
Under $5,000	422	224	66	21	31	50	29	10	19
$5,000 to $9,999	392	114	52	26	47	31	122	63	59
$10,000 to $14,999	405	88	58	50	65	65	78	46	32
$15,000 to $19,999	420	78	87	62	46	65	81	50	31
$20,000 to $24,999	382	54	112	61	53	35	67	44	23
$25,000 to $29,999	334	49	91	56	54	42	43	31	12
$30,000 to $34,999	335	29	66	85	68	55	32	20	12
$35,000 to $39,999	228	18	49	64	32	34	31	21	10
$40,000 to $44,999	275	18	74	67	56	38	22	18	3
$45,000 to $49,999	225	12	79	47	50	24	14	13	1
$50,000 to $54,999	229	16	66	51	40	34	22	18	3
$55,000 to $59,999	169	4	60	36	27	24	19	16	3
$60,000 to $64,999	201	4	57	42	55	31	13	11	2
$65,000 to $69,999	127	6	34	33	32	16	5	2	2
$70,000 to $74,999	171	6	67	41	21	30	7	2	6
$75,000 to $79,999	131	3	34	52	22	10	10	7	3
$80,000 to $84,999	138	2	38	52	24	14	7	7	0
$85,000 to $89,999	86	2	18	28	18	15	5	3	2
$90,000 to $94,999	136	6	36	50	27	11	7	5	2
$95,000 to $99,999	91	0	23	37	13	3	15	12	2
$100,000 or more	913	8	162	335	251	118	40	38	2

MEDIAN INCOME

	total	15 to 24	25 to 34	35 to 44	45 to 54	55 to 64	65 or older total	65 to 74	75 or older
Men with income	$39,606	$11,290	$45,381	$61,424	$50,935	$38,207	$21,716	$25,566	$15,625
Men working full-time	59,531	28,777	55,250	75,193	61,604	54,717	50,803	50,780	–
Percent working full-time	54.0%	14.9%	66.1%	79.1%	75.0%	60.1%	16.2%	23.4%	3.1%

PERCENT DISTRIBUTION

	total	15 to 24	25 to 34	35 to 44	45 to 54	55 to 64	65 or older total	65 to 74	75 or older
Total Asian men	**100.0%**	**100.0%**	**100.0%**	**100.0%**	**100.0%**	**100.0%**	**100.0%**	**100.0%**	**100.0%**
Without income	13.7	43.5	8.0	4.0	4.9	7.5	9.0	7.4	12.0
With income	86.3	56.5	92.0	96.0	95.1	92.5	91.0	92.6	88.0
Under $15,000	18.1	32.5	12.2	7.2	13.2	18.2	31.2	25.3	42.0
$15,000 to $24,999	11.9	10.1	13.8	9.2	9.2	12.5	20.1	19.8	20.7
$25,000 to $34,999	10.0	6.0	10.8	10.4	11.2	12.0	10.3	10.8	9.4
$35,000 to $49,999	10.8	3.7	14.0	13.2	12.7	11.8	9.0	11.1	5.3
$50,000 to $74,999	13.3	2.7	19.7	15.0	16.1	16.7	9.0	10.5	6.2
$75,000 to $99,999	8.6	1.0	10.3	16.2	9.6	6.7	5.9	7.2	3.5
$100,000 or more	13.6	0.6	11.2	24.8	23.1	14.6	5.5	7.9	0.9

Note: Asians are those who identify themselves as being of the race alone and those who identify themselves as being of the race in combination with other races. "–" means sample is too small to make a reliable estimate.
Source: Bureau of the Census, 2013 Current Population Survey Annual Social and Economic Supplement, Internet site http://www.census.gov/hhes/www/cpstables/032013/perinc/toc.htm; calculations by New Strategist

Table 2.14 Men by Income and Age, 2012: Black Men

(number and percent distribution of black men aged 15 or older by income and age, 2012; median income of men with income and of men working full-time, year-round; percent working full-time, year-round; men in thousands as of 2013)

	total	15 to 24	25 to 34	35 to 44	45 to 54	55 to 64	65 or older total	65 to 74	75 or older
Total black men	14,895	3,572	2,771	2,447	2,555	1,885	1,665	1,057	608
Without income	2,934	1,727	416	266	281	155	89	58	31
With income	11,961	1,845	2,355	2,181	2,273	1,730	1,576	999	577
Under $5,000	1,070	529	173	125	134	73	37	26	11
$5,000 to $9,999	1,475	448	255	128	221	229	193	119	74
$10,000 to $14,999	1,343	274	218	168	205	200	278	151	127
$15,000 to $19,999	1,128	176	212	192	168	144	237	137	100
$20,000 to $24,999	971	146	223	149	175	111	167	107	60
$25,000 to $29,999	904	94	252	148	163	121	126	87	40
$30,000 to $34,999	853	56	229	188	174	104	100	55	45
$35,000 to $39,999	636	22	162	131	144	119	58	50	8
$40,000 to $44,999	574	44	109	157	118	82	63	34	29
$45,000 to $49,999	444	16	111	118	69	76	53	40	13
$50,000 to $54,999	458	15	74	125	109	95	40	25	15
$55,000 to $59,999	266	3	47	74	71	36	35	27	8
$60,000 to $64,999	277	2	53	70	79	42	31	22	9
$65,000 to $69,999	257	5	34	78	55	57	29	16	13
$70,000 to $74,999	206	0	54	28	74	28	23	16	7
$75,000 to $79,999	151	4	21	47	42	19	18	15	3
$80,000 to $84,999	144	0	18	32	51	27	14	14	1
$85,000 to $89,999	105	0	17	24	33	21	10	8	2
$90,000 to $94,999	117	0	27	41	23	19	7	5	2
$95,000 to $99,999	81	2	10	43	15	8	4	4	0
$100,000 or more	504	9	58	113	151	120	52	41	11

MEDIAN INCOME

	total	15 to 24	25 to 34	35 to 44	45 to 54	55 to 64	65 or older total	65 to 74	75 or older
Men with income	$24,959	$9,411	$26,338	$34,555	$31,421	$29,389	$21,130	$22,689	$18,478
Men working full-time	39,975	21,775	34,311	42,899	42,299	45,606	51,448	55,518	–
Percent working full-time	39.5%	12.3%	52.7%	63.2%	55.0%	44.6%	11.7%	14.5%	6.9%

PERCENT DISTRIBUTION

	total	15 to 24	25 to 34	35 to 44	45 to 54	55 to 64	65 or older total	65 to 74	75 or older
Total black men	100.0%	100.0%	100.0%	100.0%	100.0%	100.0%	100.0%	100.0%	100.0%
Without income	19.7	48.3	15.0	10.9	11.0	8.2	5.3	5.5	5.1
With income	80.3	51.7	85.0	89.1	89.0	91.8	94.7	94.5	94.9
Under $15,000	26.1	35.0	23.3	17.3	21.9	26.6	30.5	28.0	34.9
$15,000 to $24,999	14.1	9.0	15.7	14.0	13.4	13.5	24.2	23.0	26.4
$25,000 to $34,999	11.8	4.2	17.4	13.7	13.2	11.9	13.6	13.4	13.9
$35,000 to $49,999	11.1	2.3	13.8	16.6	13.0	14.7	10.5	11.7	8.2
$50,000 to $74,999	9.8	0.7	9.4	15.3	15.2	13.7	9.5	10.1	8.4
$75,000 to $99,999	4.0	0.2	3.4	7.7	6.4	4.9	3.2	4.4	1.2
$100,000 or more	3.4	0.3	2.1	4.6	5.9	6.4	3.2	3.9	1.8

Note: Blacks are those who identify themselves as being of the race alone and those who identify themselves as being of the race in combination with other races. "–" means sample is too small to make a reliable estimate.
Source: Bureau of the Census, 2013 Current Population Survey Annual Social and Economic Supplement, Internet site http://www.census.gov/hhes/www/cpstables/032013/perinc/toc.htm; calculations by New Strategist

Table 2.15 Men by Income and Age, 2012: Hispanic Men

(number and percent distribution of Hispanic men aged 15 or older by income and age, 2012; median income of men with income and of men working full-time, year-round; percent working full-time, year-round; men in thousands as of 2013)

	total	15 to 24	25 to 34	35 to 44	45 to 54	55 to 64	65 or older total	65 to 74	75 or older
Total Hispanic men	**19,187**	**4,688**	**4,492**	**3,862**	**2,979**	**1,789**	**1,378**	**836**	**541**
Without income	3,182	2,141	373	258	187	124	99	54	44
With income	16,005	2,547	4,119	3,604	2,792	1,664	1,279	782	497
Under $5,000	1,130	610	184	99	102	78	56	29	26
$5,000 to $9,999	1,403	408	293	208	137	161	196	123	72
$10,000 to $14,999	1,897	409	426	350	236	185	291	161	130
$15,000 to $19,999	1,933	339	532	425	285	174	178	103	75
$20,000 to $24,999	1,738	290	506	420	269	144	110	76	34
$25,000 to $29,999	1,373	168	394	329	259	137	87	51	36
$30,000 to $34,999	1,225	109	390	279	265	123	59	33	26
$35,000 to $39,999	1,033	55	335	266	208	115	55	39	16
$40,000 to $44,999	790	67	207	199	202	81	33	23	10
$45,000 to $49,999	548	26	165	132	110	80	34	24	11
$50,000 to $54,999	544	20	139	136	142	76	31	18	13
$55,000 to $59,999	259	9	69	71	45	51	15	8	7
$60,000 to $64,999	335	4	87	112	65	38	28	23	5
$65,000 to $69,999	232	8	53	85	38	27	20	13	8
$70,000 to $74,999	201	2	57	47	53	24	18	12	6
$75,000 to $79,999	204	3	56	70	41	24	10	6	4
$80,000 to $84,999	193	3	55	63	42	24	5	3	1
$85,000 to $89,999	123	1	24	36	36	17	9	4	4
$90,000 to $94,999	137	5	37	47	32	10	5	2	3
$95,000 to $99,999	90	0	19	30	28	9	3	3	0
$100,000 or more	617	9	88	201	197	87	35	26	10

MEDIAN INCOME

	total	15 to 24	25 to 34	35 to 44	45 to 54	55 to 64	65 or older total	65 to 74	75 or older
Men with income	$24,592	$12,420	$26,096	$29,340	$31,299	$27,768	$17,348	$18,636	$16,042
Men working full-time	32,516	22,078	31,800	35,668	36,904	37,724	51,282	51,006	–
Percent working full-time	49.1%	20.3%	61.7%	66.6%	66.9%	52.3%	14.0%	17.8%	8.2%

PERCENT DISTRIBUTION

	total	15 to 24	25 to 34	35 to 44	45 to 54	55 to 64	65 or older total	65 to 74	75 or older
Total Hispanic men	**100.0%**	**100.0%**	**100.0%**	**100.0%**	**100.0%**	**100.0%**	**100.0%**	**100.0%**	**100.0%**
Without income	16.6	45.7	8.3	6.7	6.3	6.9	7.2	6.5	8.2
With income	83.4	54.3	91.7	93.3	93.7	93.1	92.8	93.5	91.8
Under $15,000	23.1	30.4	20.1	17.0	15.9	23.7	39.4	37.5	42.3
$15,000 to $24,999	19.1	13.4	23.1	21.9	18.6	17.8	20.9	21.4	20.2
$25,000 to $34,999	13.5	5.9	17.4	15.7	17.6	14.5	10.6	10.0	11.5
$35,000 to $49,999	12.4	3.2	15.7	15.5	17.4	15.4	8.9	10.2	6.8
$50,000 to $74,999	8.2	0.9	9.1	11.6	11.5	12.0	8.2	8.9	6.9
$75,000 to $99,999	3.9	0.3	4.3	6.4	6.0	4.7	2.4	2.4	2.3
$100,000 or more	3.2	0.2	1.9	5.2	6.6	4.9	2.6	3.1	1.8

Note: "–" means sample is too small to make a reliable estimate.
Source: Bureau of the Census, 2013 Current Population Survey Annual Social and Economic Supplement, Internet site http://www.census.gov/hhes/www/cpstables/032013/perinc/toc.htm; calculations by New Strategist

6ort>5

Table 2.16 Men by Income and Age, 2012: Non-Hispanic White Men

(number and percent distribution of non-Hispanic white men aged 15 or older by income and age, 2012; median income of men with income and of men working full-time, year-round; percent working full-time, year-round; men in thousands as of 2013)

	total	15 to 24	25 to 34	35 to 44	45 to 54	55 to 64	65 or older total	65 to 74	75 or older
Total non-Hispanic white men	**79,740**	**12,170**	**12,110**	**11,922**	**14,478**	**13,683**	**15,377**	**9,136**	**6,241**
Without income	6,500	4,087	743	447	526	452	245	143	103
With income	73,240	8,084	11,367	11,475	13,952	13,231	15,132	8,993	6,139
Under $5,000	4,385	2,528	431	300	399	469	258	163	95
$5,000 to $9,999	3,816	1,345	541	301	548	513	568	322	246
$10,000 to $14,999	5,033	1,019	680	460	633	757	1,485	721	763
$15,000 to $19,999	5,582	852	612	493	581	859	2,185	1,017	1,167
$20,000 to $24,999	5,220	650	787	591	698	708	1,787	970	816
$25,000 to $29,999	4,657	455	889	556	728	748	1,281	673	608
$30,000 to $34,999	4,593	342	999	760	718	707	1,067	616	451
$35,000 to $39,999	4,061	227	832	649	676	741	936	558	377
$40,000 to $44,999	3,929	160	809	695	773	771	722	479	243
$45,000 to $49,999	3,423	102	711	652	720	633	603	400	203
$50,000 to $54,999	3,618	117	752	688	750	724	587	404	183
$55,000 to $59,999	2,313	55	449	456	472	457	424	323	102
$60,000 to $64,999	2,798	60	535	531	627	616	428	296	131
$65,000 to $69,999	2,023	7	304	426	520	462	303	196	107
$70,000 to $74,999	2,041	35	341	444	519	418	284	208	76
$75,000 to $79,999	1,615	20	261	375	401	304	254	183	71
$80,000 to $84,999	1,635	15	221	363	431	416	189	143	46
$85,000 to $89,999	1,123	14	154	234	298	257	167	112	56
$90,000 to $94,999	1,284	15	181	290	373	251	175	120	56
$95,000 to $99,999	660	5	93	156	165	131	110	78	32
$100,000 or more	9,430	62	786	2,054	2,922	2,289	1,318	1,009	309

MEDIAN INCOME

	total	15 to 24	25 to 34	35 to 44	45 to 54	55 to 64	65 or older total	65 to 74	75 or older
Men with income	$38,751	$10,661	$39,120	$51,263	$52,111	$47,195	$30,010	$35,113	$24,871
Men working full-time	56,247	26,719	46,216	60,547	65,028	63,718	72,278	73,496	66,934
Percent working full-time	50.1%	18.2%	68.8%	75.4%	72.1%	57.5%	13.8%	19.1%	6.0%

PERCENT DISTRIBUTION

	total	15 to 24	25 to 34	35 to 44	45 to 54	55 to 64	65 or older total	65 to 74	75 or older
Total non-Hispanic white men	**100.0%**	**100.0%**	**100.0%**	**100.0%**	**100.0%**	**100.0%**	**100.0%**	**100.0%**	**100.0%**
Without income	8.2	33.6	6.1	3.7	3.6	3.3	1.6	1.6	1.6
With income	91.8	66.4	93.9	96.3	96.4	96.7	98.4	98.4	98.4
Under $15,000	16.6	40.2	13.6	8.9	10.9	12.7	15.0	13.2	17.7
$15,000 to $24,999	13.5	12.3	11.5	9.1	8.8	11.5	25.8	21.8	31.8
$25,000 to $34,999	11.6	6.5	15.6	11.0	10.0	10.6	15.3	14.1	17.0
$35,000 to $49,999	14.3	4.0	19.4	16.7	15.0	15.7	14.7	15.7	13.2
$50,000 to $74,999	16.0	2.3	19.7	21.4	19.9	19.6	13.2	15.6	9.6
$75,000 to $99,999	7.9	0.6	7.5	11.9	11.5	9.9	5.8	7.0	4.2
$100,000 or more	11.8	0.5	6.5	17.2	20.2	16.7	8.6	11.0	4.9

Note: Non-Hispanic whites are those who identify themselves as being white alone and not Hispanic.
Source: Bureau of the Census, 2013 Current Population Survey Annual Social and Economic Supplement, Internet site http://www.census.gov/hhes/www/cpstables/032013/perinc/toc.htm; calculations by New Strategist

Table 2.17 Men by Income, Race, and Hispanic Origin, 2012

(number and percent distribution of men aged 15 or older by income, race, and Hispanic origin, 2012; median income of men with income and of men working full-time, year-round; percent working full-time, year-round; men in thousands as of 2013)

	total	Asian	black	Hispanic	non-Hispanic white
Total men	**121,111**	**6,729**	**14,895**	**19,187**	**79,740**
Without income	13,577	920	2,934	3,182	6,500
With income	107,534	5,810	11,961	16,005	73,240
Under $5,000	7,050	422	1,070	1,130	4,385
$5,000 to $9,999	7,122	392	1,475	1,403	3,816
$10,000 to $14,999	8,706	405	1,343	1,897	5,033
$15,000 to $19,999	9,103	420	1,128	1,933	5,582
$20,000 to $24,999	8,370	382	971	1,738	5,220
$25,000 to $29,999	7,276	334	904	1,373	4,657
$30,000 to $34,999	7,032	335	853	1,225	4,593
$35,000 to $39,999	5,975	228	636	1,033	4,061
$40,000 to $44,999	5,584	275	574	790	3,929
$45,000 to $49,999	4,666	225	444	548	3,423
$50,000 to $54,999	4,886	229	458	544	3,618
$55,000 to $59,999	3,028	169	266	259	2,313
$60,000 to $64,999	3,640	201	277	335	2,798
$65,000 to $69,999	2,653	127	257	232	2,023
$70,000 to $74,999	2,627	171	206	201	2,041
$75,000 to $79,999	2,112	131	151	204	1,615
$80,000 to $84,999	2,113	138	144	193	1,635
$85,000 to $89,999	1,447	86	105	123	1,123
$90,000 to $94,999	1,684	136	117	137	1,284
$95,000 to $99,999	929	91	81	90	660
$100,000 or more	11,531	913	504	617	9,430

MEDIAN INCOME

	total	Asian	black	Hispanic	non-Hispanic white
Men with income	$33,904	$39,606	$24,959	$24,592	$38,751
Men working full-time	50,683	59,531	39,975	32,516	56,247
Percent working full-time	48.7%	54.0%	39.5%	49.1%	50.1%

PERCENT DISTRIBUTION

	total	Asian	black	Hispanic	non-Hispanic white
Total men	**100.0%**	**100.0%**	**100.0%**	**100.0%**	**100.0%**
Without income	11.2	13.7	19.7	16.6	8.2
With income	88.8	86.3	80.3	83.4	91.8
Under $15,000	18.9	18.1	26.1	23.1	16.6
$15,000 to $24,999	14.4	11.9	14.1	19.1	13.5
$25,000 to $34,999	11.8	10.0	11.8	13.5	11.6
$35,000 to $49,999	13.4	10.8	11.1	12.4	14.3
$50,000 to $74,999	13.9	13.3	9.8	8.2	16.0
$75,000 to $99,999	6.8	8.6	4.0	3.9	7.9
$100,000 or more	9.5	13.6	3.4	3.2	11.8

Note: Asians and blacks are those who identify themselves as being of the race alone and those who identify themselves as being of the race in combination with other races. Non-Hispanic whites are those who identify themselves as white alone and not Hispanic. Numbers do not add to total because some people identify themselves as being of more than one race, not all races are shown, and Hispanics may be of any race.
Source: Bureau of the Census, 2013 Current Population Survey Annual Social and Economic Supplement, Internet site http://www.census.gov/hhes/www/cpstables/032013/perinc/toc.htm; calculations by New Strategist

Men in the South Have the Lowest Incomes

Among full-time workers, incomes are highest in the Northeast.

The median income of men in the South was $32,181 in 2012, less than the median income of their counterparts in the other three regions. In the West, men's median income was a higher $33,546, and in the Midwest $34,978. Men's median income was highest in the Northeast, at $36,342 in 2012. Among full-time workers, men in the Northeast are ahead of those in the other regions, with a median income of $55,412. In the South, the median income of men who work full-time was just $47,761.

Among Asian men who work full-time, incomes are highest in the Northeast, at $63,207 in 2012. Among their non-Hispanic white counterparts, median income is highest in the West, at $61,888. The median income of black men who work full-time is also highest in the West, at $45,330. Hispanic men who work full-time have lower incomes than Asians, blacks, and non-Hispanic whites. Their median income peaks at $35,450 in the Northeast.

■ Hispanic men have low incomes because many are poorly educated, with little earning power.

Men's incomes are highest in the Northeast

(median income of men aged 15 or older who work full-time, year-round, by region, 2012)

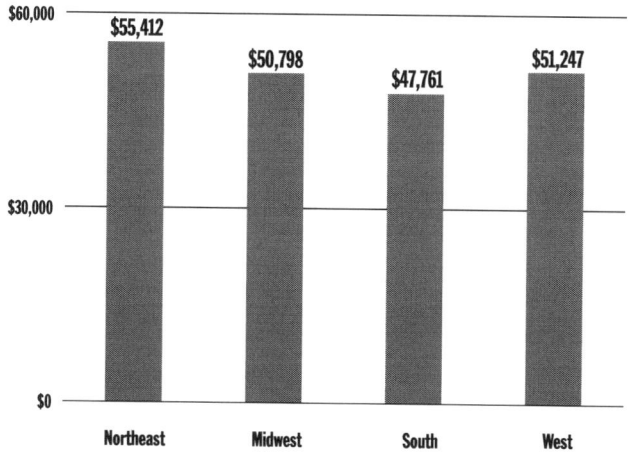

Table 2.18 Men by Income and Region, 2012: Total Men

(number and percent distribution of men aged 15 or older by income and region, 2012; median income of men with income and of men working full-time, year-round; percent working full-time, year-round; men in thousands as of 2013)

	total	Northeast	Midwest	South	West
Total men	**121,111**	**21,653**	**25,879**	**44,634**	**28,945**
Without income	13,577	2,415	2,431	5,304	3,427
With income	107,534	19,238	23,449	39,330	25,518
Under $5,000	7,050	1,361	1,604	2,363	1,721
$5,000 to $9,999	7,122	1,187	1,538	2,655	1,743
$10,000 to $14,999	8,706	1,432	1,701	3,518	2,055
$15,000 to $19,999	9,103	1,538	1,869	3,586	2,110
$20,000 to $24,999	8,370	1,345	1,832	3,094	2,099
$25,000 to $29,999	7,276	1,192	1,681	2,778	1,624
$30,000 to $34,999	7,032	1,210	1,504	2,646	1,672
$35,000 to $39,999	5,975	1,017	1,455	2,188	1,315
$40,000 to $44,999	5,584	1,016	1,286	2,082	1,200
$45,000 to $49,999	4,666	786	1,147	1,682	1,051
$50,000 to $54,999	4,886	858	1,135	1,774	1,119
$55,000 to $59,999	3,028	568	681	1,104	675
$60,000 to $64,999	3,640	654	825	1,366	796
$65,000 to $69,999	2,653	540	607	961	545
$70,000 to $74,999	2,627	508	589	918	612
$75,000 to $79,999	2,112	370	454	797	491
$80,000 to $84,999	2,113	439	478	667	529
$85,000 to $89,999	1,447	246	326	514	361
$90,000 to $94,999	1,684	334	372	594	384
$95,000 to $99,999	929	188	195	308	238
$100,000 or more	11,531	2,448	2,170	3,736	3,178
MEDIAN INCOME					
Men with income	$33,904	$36,342	$34,978	$32,181	$33,546
Men working full-time	50,683	55,412	50,798	47,761	51,247
Percent working full-time	48.7%	48.9%	48.5%	49.7%	47.4%
PERCENT DISTRIBUTION					
Total men	**100.0%**	**100.0%**	**100.0%**	**100.0%**	**100.0%**
Without income	11.2	11.2	9.4	11.9	11.8
With income	88.8	88.8	90.6	88.1	88.2
Under $15,000	18.9	18.4	18.7	19.1	19.1
$15,000 to $24,999	14.4	13.3	14.3	15.0	14.5
$25,000 to $34,999	11.8	11.1	12.3	12.2	11.4
$35,000 to $49,999	13.4	13.0	15.0	13.3	12.3
$50,000 to $74,999	13.9	14.4	14.8	13.7	12.9
$75,000 to $99,999	6.8	7.3	7.1	6.5	6.9
$100,000 or more	9.5	11.3	8.4	8.4	11.0

Source: Bureau of the Census, 2013 Current Population Survey Annual Social and Economic Supplement, Internet site http://www.census.gov/hhes/www/cpstables/032013/perinc/toc.htm; calculations by New Strategist

Table 2.19 Men by Income and Region, 2012: Asian Men

(number and percent distribution of Asian men aged 15 or older by income and region, 2012; median income of men with income and of men working full-time, year-round; percent working full-time, year-round; men in thousands as of 2013)

	total	Northeast	Midwest	South	West
Total Asian men	**6,729**	**1,348**	**855**	**1,452**	**3,075**
Without income	920	183	130	180	426
With income	5,810	1,164	725	1,272	2,649
Under $5,000	422	84	73	99	165
$5,000 to $9,999	392	73	51	75	193
$10,000 to $14,999	405	65	62	69	209
$15,000 to $19,999	420	89	60	90	181
$20,000 to $24,999	382	67	40	87	189
$25,000 to $29,999	334	62	34	87	152
$30,000 to $34,999	335	68	44	67	158
$35,000 to $39,999	228	51	32	29	116
$40,000 to $44,999	275	43	35	76	121
$45,000 to $49,999	225	32	31	54	108
$50,000 to $54,999	229	44	29	57	98
$55,000 to $59,999	169	32	15	34	88
$60,000 to $64,999	201	36	31	47	87
$65,000 to $69,999	127	29	13	28	57
$70,000 to $74,999	171	40	28	28	75
$75,000 to $79,999	131	27	16	36	52
$80,000 to $84,999	138	36	20	31	51
$85,000 to $89,999	86	15	8	19	45
$90,000 to $94,999	136	34	18	35	50
$95,000 to $99,999	91	28	9	26	28
$100,000 or more	913	210	76	199	428

MEDIAN INCOME

	total	Northeast	Midwest	South	West
Men with income	$39,606	$41,826	$34,935	$41,726	$38,214
Men working full-time	59,531	63,207	55,179	57,002	59,329
Percent working full-time	54.0%	57.4%	50.3%	59.2%	51.1%

PERCENT DISTRIBUTION

	total	Northeast	Midwest	South	West
Total Asian men	**100.0%**	**100.0%**	**100.0%**	**100.0%**	**100.0%**
Without income	13.7	13.6	15.2	12.4	13.9
With income	86.3	86.4	84.8	87.6	86.1
Under $15,000	18.1	16.5	21.7	16.7	18.5
$15,000 to $24,999	11.9	11.6	11.7	12.2	12.0
$25,000 to $34,999	10.0	9.6	9.1	10.6	10.1
$35,000 to $49,999	10.8	9.4	11.6	11.0	11.2
$50,000 to $74,999	13.3	13.5	13.6	13.4	13.1
$75,000 to $99,999	8.6	10.3	8.3	10.0	7.3
$100,000 or more	13.6	15.6	8.9	13.7	13.9

Note: Asians are those who identify themselves as being of the race alone and those who identify themselves as being of the race in combination with other races.
Source: Bureau of the Census, 2013 Current Population Survey Annual Social and Economic Supplement, Internet site http://www.census.gov/hhes/www/cpstables/032013/perinc/toc.htm; calculations by New Strategist

Table 2.20 Men by Income and Region, 2012: Black Men

(number and percent distribution of black men aged 15 or older by income and region, 2012; median income of men with income and of men working full-time, year-round; percent working full-time, year-round; men in thousands as of 2013)

	total	Northeast	Midwest	South	West
Total black men	**14,895**	**2,655**	**2,498**	**8,174**	**1,569**
Without income	2,934	618	514	1,543	259
With income	11,961	2,037	1,984	6,630	1,310
Under $5,000	1,070	194	203	578	95
$5,000 to $9,999	1,475	251	295	762	166
$10,000 to $14,999	1,343	213	222	756	152
$15,000 to $19,999	1,128	177	153	688	111
$20,000 to $24,999	971	158	164	541	108
$25,000 to $29,999	904	141	162	542	58
$30,000 to $34,999	853	143	120	482	108
$35,000 to $39,999	636	112	86	349	89
$40,000 to $44,999	574	126	93	301	54
$45,000 to $49,999	444	56	79	275	33
$50,000 to $54,999	458	61	71	253	73
$55,000 to $59,999	266	47	51	146	22
$60,000 to $64,999	277	54	41	154	28
$65,000 to $69,999	257	55	41	132	29
$70,000 to $74,999	206	39	18	127	23
$75,000 to $79,999	151	14	16	97	24
$80,000 to $84,999	144	46	13	63	21
$85,000 to $89,999	105	7	22	57	18
$90,000 to $94,999	117	11	30	65	11
$95,000 to $99,999	81	28	9	39	5
$100,000 or more	504	103	94	225	82

MEDIAN INCOME

	total	Northeast	Midwest	South	West
Men with income	$24,959	$25,634	$23,246	$24,879	$26,909
Men working full-time	39,975	39,994	40,959	38,099	45,330
Percent working full-time	39.5%	37.8%	36.2%	41.3%	38.4%

PERCENT DISTRIBUTION

	total	Northeast	Midwest	South	West
Total black men	**100.0%**	**100.0%**	**100.0%**	**100.0%**	**100.0%**
Without income	19.7	23.3	20.6	18.9	16.5
With income	80.3	76.7	79.4	81.1	83.5
Under $15,000	26.1	24.8	28.8	25.6	26.3
$15,000 to $24,999	14.1	12.6	12.7	15.0	13.9
$25,000 to $34,999	11.8	10.7	11.3	12.5	10.6
$35,000 to $49,999	11.1	11.1	10.3	11.3	11.2
$50,000 to $74,999	9.8	9.7	8.9	9.9	11.2
$75,000 to $99,999	4.0	4.0	3.6	3.9	5.1
$100,000 or more	3.4	3.9	3.8	2.8	5.2

Note: Blacks are those who identify themselves as being of the race alone and those who identify themselves as being of the race in combination with other races.
Source: Bureau of the Census, 2013 Current Population Survey Annual Social and Economic Supplement, Internet site http://www.census.gov/hhes/www/cpstables/032013/perinc/toc.htm; calculations by New Strategist

Table 2.21 Men by Income and Region, 2012: Hispanic Men

(number and percent distribution of Hispanic men aged 15 or older by income and region, 2012; median income of men with income and of men working full-time, year-round; percent working full-time, year-round; men in thousands as of 2013)

	total	Northeast	Midwest	South	West
Total Hispanic men	**19,187**	**2,536**	**1,707**	**7,074**	**7,869**
Without income	3,182	475	217	1,118	1,371
With income	16,005	2,061	1,490	5,956	6,498
Under $5,000	1,130	183	137	345	465
$5,000 to $9,999	1,403	217	130	465	590
$10,000 to $14,999	1,897	226	175	749	747
$15,000 to $19,999	1,933	233	174	780	746
$20,000 to $24,999	1,738	194	152	678	714
$25,000 to $29,999	1,373	152	133	505	582
$30,000 to $34,999	1,225	137	125	449	514
$35,000 to $39,999	1,033	139	100	385	409
$40,000 to $44,999	790	117	68	287	318
$45,000 to $49,999	548	66	51	214	218
$50,000 to $54,999	544	65	46	200	233
$55,000 to $59,999	259	45	17	99	98
$60,000 to $64,999	335	43	21	122	148
$65,000 to $69,999	232	34	26	92	80
$70,000 to $74,999	201	27	18	76	79
$75,000 to $79,999	204	19	17	85	83
$80,000 to $84,999	193	28	19	67	79
$85,000 to $89,999	123	13	9	49	52
$90,000 to $94,999	137	21	26	49	41
$95,000 to $99,999	90	14	9	31	37
$100,000 or more	617	87	37	230	263

MEDIAN INCOME

	total	Northeast	Midwest	South	West
Men with income	$24,592	$24,283	$23,857	$24,581	$24,866
Men working full-time	32,516	35,450	31,778	31,848	33,858
Percent working full-time	49.1%	46.3%	49.4%	52.8%	46.5%

PERCENT DISTRIBUTION

	total	Northeast	Midwest	South	West
Total Hispanic men	**100.0%**	**100.0%**	**100.0%**	**100.0%**	**100.0%**
Without income	16.6	18.7	12.7	15.8	17.4
With income	83.4	81.3	87.3	84.2	82.6
Under $15,000	23.1	24.7	25.9	22.0	22.9
$15,000 to $24,999	19.1	16.9	19.1	20.6	18.5
$25,000 to $34,999	13.5	11.4	15.1	13.5	13.9
$35,000 to $49,999	12.4	12.7	12.8	12.5	12.0
$50,000 to $74,999	8.2	8.4	7.5	8.3	8.1
$75,000 to $99,999	3.9	3.7	4.6	4.0	3.7
$100,000 or more	3.2	3.4	2.2	3.2	3.3

Source: Bureau of the Census, 2013 Current Population Survey Annual Social and Economic Supplement, Internet site http:// www.census.gov/hhes/www/cpstables/032013/perinc/toc.htm; calculations by New Strategist

Table 2.22 Men by Income and Region, 2012: Non-Hispanic White Men

(number and percent distribution of non-Hispanic white men aged 15 or older by income and region, 2012; median income of men with income and of men working full-time, year-round; percent working full-time, year-round; men in thousands as of 2013)

	total	Northeast	Midwest	South	West
Total non-Hispanic white men	**79,740**	**15,353**	**20,677**	**27,783**	**15,927**
Without income	6,500	1,226	1,537	2,454	1,282
With income	73,240	14,127	19,140	25,329	14,644
Under $5,000	4,385	916	1,192	1,340	937
$5,000 to $9,999	3,816	687	1,048	1,328	754
$10,000 to $14,999	5,033	936	1,249	1,958	890
$15,000 to $19,999	5,582	1,060	1,463	2,019	1,040
$20,000 to $24,999	5,220	931	1,453	1,776	1,061
$25,000 to $29,999	4,657	849	1,354	1,643	811
$30,000 to $34,999	4,593	872	1,206	1,640	876
$35,000 to $39,999	4,061	722	1,232	1,425	682
$40,000 to $44,999	3,929	760	1,079	1,395	695
$45,000 to $49,999	3,423	627	987	1,137	671
$50,000 to $54,999	3,618	689	977	1,253	699
$55,000 to $59,999	2,313	442	598	813	460
$60,000 to $64,999	2,798	526	725	1,028	520
$65,000 to $69,999	2,023	423	525	702	373
$70,000 to $74,999	2,041	402	524	696	419
$75,000 to $79,999	1,615	307	401	578	330
$80,000 to $84,999	1,635	333	427	508	367
$85,000 to $89,999	1,123	210	281	389	244
$90,000 to $94,999	1,284	269	298	449	269
$95,000 to $99,999	660	118	167	209	165
$100,000 or more	9,430	2,051	1,953	3,044	2,382

MEDIAN INCOME					
Men with income	$38,751	$40,435	$36,892	$37,666	$41,366
Men working full-time	56,247	60,914	52,144	53,688	61,888
Percent working full-time	50.1%	50.2%	50.0%	51.0%	48.6%

PERCENT DISTRIBUTION					
Total non-Hispanic white men	**100.0%**	**100.0%**	**100.0%**	**100.0%**	**100.0%**
Without income	8.2	8.0	7.4	8.8	8.1
With income	91.8	92.0	92.6	91.2	91.9
Under $15,000	16.6	16.5	16.9	16.6	16.2
$15,000 to $24,999	13.5	13.0	14.1	13.7	13.2
$25,000 to $34,999	11.6	11.2	12.4	11.8	10.6
$35,000 to $49,999	14.3	13.7	16.0	14.2	12.9
$50,000 to $74,999	16.0	16.2	16.2	16.2	15.5
$75,000 to $99,999	7.9	8.1	7.6	7.7	8.6
$100,000 or more	11.8	13.4	9.4	11.0	15.0

Note: Non-Hispanic whites are those who identify themselves as being white alone and not Hispanic.
Source: Bureau of the Census, 2013 Current Population Survey Annual Social and Economic Supplement, Internet site http:// www.census.gov/hhes/www/cpstables/032013/perinc/toc.htm; calculations by New Strategist

Men in the Suburbs Have the Highest Incomes

They are also most likely to work full-time.

Men who live outside the principal cities of the nation's metropolitan areas (in other words, in the suburbs) have the highest incomes. Their median income stood at $37,132 in 2012. Half have full-time jobs, and among those who do median income was $53,779.

At the other extreme, men who live in nonmetropolitan areas have the lowest incomes, a median of just $30,036 in 2012. The 44 percent of men who work full-time had a median income of $42,069—only 78 percent as much as their suburban counterparts. The cost of living is often lower in nonmetropolitan areas than in the suburbs, making the gap in spending power smaller than the gap in income.

■ The Great Recession has lowered men's incomes regardless of where they live.

Men in nonmetropolitan areas have the lowest incomes

(median income of men aged 15 or older who work full-time, year-round, by metropolitan status, 2012)

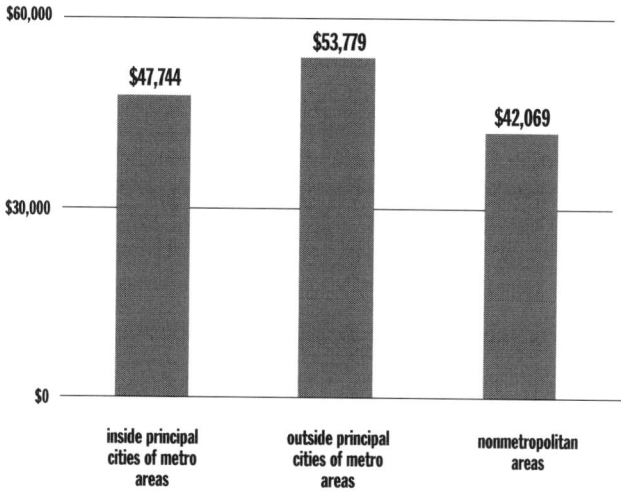

Table 2.23 Men by Income and Metropolitan Residence, 2012

(number and percent distribution of men aged 15 or older by income and metropolitan residence, 2012; median income of men with income and of men working full-time, year-round; percent working full-time, year-round; men in thousands as of 2013)

	total	in metropolitan area total	in metropolitan area inside principal cities	in metropolitan area outside principal cities	not in metropolitan area
Total men	**121,111**	**102,443**	**39,206**	**63,237**	**18,668**
Without income	13,577	11,704	4,881	6,823	1,873
With income	107,534	90,739	34,325	56,415	16,795
Under $5,000	7,050	5,941	2,323	3,619	1,108
$5,000 to $9,999	7,122	5,851	2,621	3,230	1,272
$10,000 to $14,999	8,706	7,091	3,067	4,024	1,615
$15,000 to $19,999	9,103	7,419	2,973	4,446	1,683
$20,000 to $24,999	8,370	6,950	2,876	4,074	1,420
$25,000 to $29,999	7,276	5,990	2,359	3,631	1,286
$30,000 to $34,999	7,032	5,721	2,289	3,432	1,311
$35,000 to $39,999	5,975	4,840	1,757	3,083	1,135
$40,000 to $44,999	5,584	4,632	1,630	3,003	951
$45,000 to $49,999	4,666	3,937	1,395	2,542	729
$50,000 to $54,999	4,886	4,144	1,406	2,738	741
$55,000 to $59,999	3,028	2,570	955	1,616	458
$60,000 to $64,999	3,640	3,137	1,037	2,100	503
$65,000 to $69,999	2,653	2,303	768	1,535	350
$70,000 to $74,999	2,627	2,274	784	1,490	353
$75,000 to $79,999	2,112	1,839	590	1,249	272
$80,000 to $84,999	2,113	1,860	615	1,244	254
$85,000 to $89,999	1,447	1,249	407	843	198
$90,000 to $94,999	1,684	1,503	505	997	181
$95,000 to $99,999	929	838	285	553	91
$100,000 or more	11,531	10,649	3,684	6,965	882
MEDIAN INCOME					
Men with income	$33,904	$35,313	$31,419	$37,132	$30,036
Men working full-time	50,683	51,579	47,744	53,779	42,069
Percent working full-time	48.7%	49.5%	48.5%	50.2%	44.5%
PERCENT DISTRIBUTION					
Total men	**100.0%**	**100.0%**	**100.0%**	**100.0%**	**100.0%**
Without income	11.2	11.4	12.5	10.8	10.0
With income	88.8	88.6	87.5	89.2	90.0
Under $15,000	18.9	18.4	20.4	17.2	21.4
$15,000 to $24,999	14.4	14.0	14.9	13.5	16.6
$25,000 to $34,999	11.8	11.4	11.9	11.2	13.9
$35,000 to $49,999	13.4	13.1	12.2	13.6	15.1
$50,000 to $74,999	13.9	14.1	12.6	15.0	12.9
$75,000 to $99,999	6.8	7.1	6.1	7.7	5.3
$100,000 or more	9.5	10.4	9.4	11.0	4.7

Source: Bureau of the Census, 2013 Current Population Survey Annual Social and Economic Supplement, Internet site http://www.census.gov/hhes/www/cpstables/032013/perinc/toc.htm; calculations by New Strategist

Most Men Have Modest Earnings

Only 16 percent of those who work full-time, year-round earn $100,000 or more.

Among the nation's 83 million men with earnings in 2012, about 59 million work full-time, year-round. Fewer than 13 million men work part-time. Among men with full-time, year-round jobs, median earnings stood at $49,398 in 2012.

Asian men who work full-time, year-round earned a median of $57,148 in 2012. This is well above the $52,535 median earnings of their non-Hispanic white counterparts. The median earnings of black men who work full-time, year-round was $38,670 in 2012, substantially higher than the $32,243 median earnings of Hispanic men with full-time jobs. The Hispanic median is just 56 percent as high as the Asian median.

■ The earnings of black men should rise in the years ahead because they are making gains in educational attainment.

Most men earn less than $50,000 per year

*(percent distribution of men aged 15 or older who work
full-time, year-round, by earnings, 2012)*

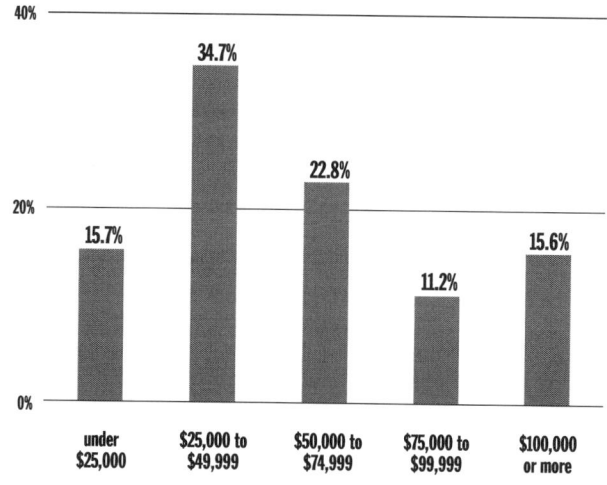

Table 2.24 Men by Earnings and Employment Status, 2012: Total Men

(number and percent distribution of men aged 15 or older with earnings by employment status and median earnings, 2012; men in thousands as of 2013)

	total	worked full-time		worked part-time	
		total	year-round	total	year-round
Total men with earnings	**121,111**	**102,443**	**39,206**	**63,237**	**18,668**
Under $5,000	7,050	5,941	2,323	3,619	1,108
$5,000 to $9,999	7,122	5,851	2,621	3,230	1,272
$10,000 to $14,999	8,706	7,091	3,067	4,024	1,615
$15,000 to $19,999	9,103	7,419	2,973	4,446	1,683
$20,000 to $24,999	8,370	6,950	2,876	4,074	1,420
$25,000 to $29,999	7,276	5,990	2,359	3,631	1,286
$30,000 to $34,999	7,032	5,721	2,289	3,432	1,311
$35,000 to $39,999	5,975	4,840	1,757	3,083	1,135
$40,000 to $44,999	5,584	4,632	1,630	3,003	951
$45,000 to $49,999	4,666	3,937	1,395	2,542	729
$50,000 to $54,999	4,886	4,144	1,406	2,738	741
$55,000 to $59,999	3,028	2,570	955	1,616	458
$60,000 to $64,999	3,640	3,137	1,037	2,100	503
$65,000 to $69,999	2,653	2,303	768	1,535	350
$70,000 to $74,999	2,627	2,274	784	1,490	353
$75,000 to $79,999	2,112	1,839	590	1,249	272
$80,000 to $84,999	2,113	1,860	615	1,244	254
$85,000 to $89,999	1,447	1,249	407	843	198
$90,000 to $94,999	1,684	1,503	505	997	181
$95,000 to $99,999	929	838	285	553	91
$100,000 or more	11,531	10,649	3,684	6,965	882
Median earnings	**$51,017**	**$52,988**	**$45,902**	**$58,780**	**$41,198**

PERCENT DISTRIBUTION

	total	worked full-time		worked part-time	
		total	year-round	total	year-round
Total men with earnings	**100.0%**	**100.0%**	**100.0%**	**100.0%**	**100.0%**
Under $15,000	18.9	18.4	20.4	17.2	21.4
$15,000 to $24,999	14.4	14.0	14.9	13.5	16.6
$25,000 to $34,999	11.8	11.4	11.9	11.2	13.9
$35,000 to $49,999	13.4	13.1	12.2	13.6	15.1
$50,000 to $74,999	13.9	14.1	12.6	15.0	12.9
$75,000 to $99,999	6.8	7.1	6.1	7.7	5.3
$100,000 or more	9.5	10.4	9.4	11.0	4.7

Source: Bureau of the Census, 2013 Current Population Survey Annual Social and Economic Supplement, Internet site http://www.census.gov/hhes/www/cpstables/032013/perinc/toc.htm; calculations by New Strategist

Table 2.25 Men by Earnings and Employment Status, 2012: Asian Men

(number and percent distribution of Asian men aged 15 or older with earnings by employment status and median earnings, 2012; men in thousands as of 2013)

	total	worked full-time		worked part-time	
		total	year-round	total	year-round
Asian men with earnings	**4,796**	**4,138**	**3,629**	**658**	**346**
Under $5,000	261	74	20	187	33
$5,000 to $9,999	197	86	21	111	63
$10,000 to $14,999	292	175	94	117	70
$15,000 to $19,999	294	206	162	88	60
$20,000 to $24,999	262	225	183	37	31
$25,000 to $29,999	271	246	226	25	17
$30,000 to $34,999	302	283	254	19	19
$35,000 to $39,999	221	209	184	11	7
$40,000 to $44,999	246	238	223	7	6
$45,000 to $49,999	208	206	180	2	2
$50,000 to $54,999	223	211	195	12	12
$55,000 to $59,999	130	125	108	5	3
$60,000 to $64,999	202	202	194	0	0
$65,000 to $69,999	119	117	114	2	0
$70,000 to $74,999	157	156	142	1	0
$75,000 to $79,999	133	129	120	4	4
$80,000 to $84,999	145	140	136	5	3
$85,000 to $89,999	73	71	71	2	2
$90,000 to $94,999	128	126	120	3	3
$95,000 to $99,999	64	61	59	3	3
$100,000 or more	868	850	825	17	9
Median earnings	**$45,837**	**$51,619**	**$57,148**	**$11,030**	**$15,520**
PERCENT DISTRIBUTION					
Asian men with earnings	**100.0%**	**100.0%**	**100.0%**	**100.0%**	**100.0%**
Under $15,000	15.6	8.1	3.7	62.9	47.8
$15,000 to $24,999	11.6	10.4	9.5	19.0	26.3
$25,000 to $34,999	12.0	12.8	13.2	6.7	10.4
$35,000 to $49,999	14.1	15.8	16.2	3.1	4.2
$50,000 to $74,999	17.3	19.6	20.7	3.0	4.4
$75,000 to $99,999	11.3	12.7	13.9	2.6	4.4
$100,000 or more	18.1	20.5	22.7	2.6	2.5

Note: Asians are those who identify themselves as being of the race alone and those who identify themselves as being of the race in combination with other races. Earnings include wages and salary only.
Source: Bureau of the Census, 2013 Current Population Survey Annual Social and Economic Supplement, Internet site http://www.census.gov/hhes/www/cpstables/032013/perinc/toc.htm; calculations by New Strategist

Table 2.26 Men by Earnings and Employment Status, 2012: Black Men

(number and percent distribution of black men aged 15 or older with earnings by employment status and median earnings, 2012; men in thousands as of 2013)

	total	worked full-time		worked part-time	
		total	year-round	total	year-round
Black men with earnings	**8,871**	**7,359**	**5,882**	**1,512**	**730**
Under $5,000	849	364	52	485	66
$5,000 to $9,999	677	315	54	362	161
$10,000 to $14,999	707	431	236	276	202
$15,000 to $19,999	707	534	405	173	135
$20,000 to $24,999	774	696	562	78	57
$25,000 to $29,999	729	670	581	60	39
$30,000 to $34,999	724	701	625	23	22
$35,000 to $39,999	568	553	495	15	14
$40,000 to $44,999	528	518	447	9	9
$45,000 to $49,999	370	363	338	7	3
$50,000 to $54,999	410	405	374	5	4
$55,000 to $59,999	227	224	214	3	3
$60,000 to $64,999	275	271	251	4	2
$65,000 to $69,999	214	214	203	0	0
$70,000 to $74,999	181	179	173	2	2
$75,000 to $79,999	116	115	109	1	1
$80,000 to $84,999	128	128	121	0	0
$85,000 to $89,999	83	83	83	0	0
$90,000 to $94,999	117	117	112	0	0
$95,000 to $99,999	68	68	64	0	0
$100,000 or more	419	409	384	10	10
Median earnings	**$29,910**	**$34,506**	**$38,670**	**$8,662**	**$12,851**

PERCENT DISTRIBUTION

	total	total	year-round	total	year-round
Black men with earnings	**100.0%**	**100.0%**	**100.0%**	**100.0%**	**100.0%**
Under $15,000	25.2	15.1	5.8	74.2	58.8
$15,000 to $24,999	16.7	16.7	16.4	16.6	26.3
$25,000 to $34,999	16.4	18.6	20.5	5.5	8.3
$35,000 to $49,999	16.5	19.5	21.8	2.1	3.6
$50,000 to $74,999	14.7	17.6	20.7	0.9	1.5
$75,000 to $99,999	5.8	7.0	8.3	0.0	0.1
$100,000 or more	4.7	5.6	6.5	0.7	1.4

Note: Blacks are those who identify themselves as being of the race alone and those who identify themselves as being of the race in combination with other races. Earnings include wages and salary only.
Source: Bureau of the Census, 2013 Current Population Survey Annual Social and Economic Supplement, Internet site http:// www.census.gov/hhes/www/cpstables/032013/perinc/toc.htm; calculations by New Strategist

Table 2.27 Men by Earnings and Employment Status, 2012: Hispanic Men

(number and percent distribution of Hispanic men aged 15 or older with earnings by employment status and median earnings, 2012; men in thousands as of 2013)

	total	worked full-time		worked part-time	
		total	year-round	total	year-round
Hispanic men with earnings	**13,747**	**11,600**	**9,410**	**2,147**	**1,147**
Under $5,000	859	320	37	538	67
$5,000 to $9,999	929	473	147	457	234
$10,000 to $14,999	1,414	912	587	502	364
$15,000 to $19,999	1,636	1,341	994	295	211
$20,000 to $24,999	1,550	1,436	1,212	114	82
$25,000 to $29,999	1,290	1,221	1,066	69	50
$30,000 to $34,999	1,161	1,105	955	55	42
$35,000 to $39,999	942	894	796	48	43
$40,000 to $44,999	757	744	664	13	10
$45,000 to $49,999	504	497	462	7	4
$50,000 to $54,999	522	513	474	9	8
$55,000 to $59,999	230	228	221	2	2
$60,000 to $64,999	327	310	285	17	16
$65,000 to $69,999	208	208	199	0	0
$70,000 to $74,999	182	182	163	0	0
$75,000 to $79,999	198	197	182	2	2
$80,000 to $84,999	177	174	162	3	2
$85,000 to $89,999	85	83	80	2	2
$90,000 to $94,999	136	133	123	3	2
$95,000 to $99,999	81	77	76	4	4
$100,000 or more	559	552	523	7	4
Median earnings	**$26,360**	**$30,282**	**$32,243**	**$10,537**	**$12,823**

PERCENT DISTRIBUTION

	total	worked full-time		worked part-time	
Hispanic men with earnings	**100.0%**	**100.0%**	**100.0%**	**100.0%**	**100.0%**
Under $15,000	23.3	14.7	8.2	69.8	58.0
$15,000 to $24,999	23.2	23.9	23.4	19.0	25.5
$25,000 to $34,999	17.8	20.1	21.5	5.8	8.0
$35,000 to $49,999	16.0	18.4	20.4	3.2	5.0
$50,000 to $74,999	10.7	12.4	14.3	1.3	2.2
$75,000 to $99,999	4.9	5.7	6.6	0.6	1.0
$100,000 or more	4.1	4.8	5.6	0.3	0.3

Note: Earnings include wages and salary only.
Source: Bureau of the Census, 2013 Current Population Survey Annual Social and Economic Supplement, Internet site http://www.census.gov/hhes/www/cpstables/032013/perinc/toc.htm; calculations by New Strategist

Table 2.28 Men by Earnings and Employment Status, 2012: Non-Hispanic White Men

(number and percent distribution of non-Hispanic white men aged 15 or older with earnings by employment status and median earnings, 2012; men in thousands as of 2013)

	total	worked full-time total	worked full-time year-round	worked part-time total	worked part-time year-round
Non-Hispanic white men with earnings	**55,332**	**46,886**	**39,948**	**8,446**	**3,978**
Under $5,000	3,816	1,121	244	2,695	396
$5,000 to $9,999	2,692	1,139	257	1,553	717
$10,000 to $14,999	2,831	1,466	778	1,365	868
$15,000 to $19,999	2,698	1,900	1,216	798	535
$20,000 to $24,999	3,195	2,743	2,048	452	303
$25,000 to $29,999	3,160	2,792	2,288	368	274
$30,000 to $34,999	3,525	3,255	2,873	270	183
$35,000 to $39,999	2,994	2,870	2,552	124	76
$40,000 to $44,999	3,292	3,173	2,833	119	95
$45,000 to $49,999	2,671	2,614	2,429	57	35
$50,000 to $54,999	3,250	3,133	2,878	117	78
$55,000 to $59,999	1,844	1,806	1,663	38	25
$60,000 to $64,999	2,548	2,488	2,312	60	45
$65,000 to $69,999	1,683	1,668	1,564	15	15
$70,000 to $74,999	1,825	1,766	1,633	58	50
$75,000 to $79,999	1,422	1,385	1,326	37	34
$80,000 to $84,999	1,395	1,365	1,294	29	22
$85,000 to $89,999	893	871	830	22	22
$90,000 to $94,999	1,084	1,077	1,026	7	7
$95,000 to $99,999	508	503	478	5	5
$100,000 or more	8,004	7,748	7,427	256	193
Median earnings	**$42,749**	**$50,345**	**$52,535**	**$9,902**	**$15,053**

PERCENT DISTRIBUTION					
Non-Hispanic white men with earnings	**100.0%**	**100.0%**	**100.0%**	**100.0%**	**100.0%**
Under $15,000	16.9	7.9	3.2	66.5	49.8
$15,000 to $24,999	10.7	9.9	8.2	14.8	21.1
$25,000 to $34,999	12.1	12.9	12.9	7.6	11.5
$35,000 to $49,999	16.2	18.5	19.6	3.6	5.2
$50,000 to $74,999	20.2	23.2	25.2	3.4	5.4
$75,000 to $99,999	9.6	11.1	12.4	1.2	2.2
$100,000 or more	14.5	16.5	18.6	3.0	4.9

Note: Non-Hispanic whites are those who identify themselves as being white alone and not Hispanic. Earnings include wages and salary only.
Source: Bureau of the Census, 2013 Current Population Survey Annual Social and Economic Supplement, Internet site http:// www.census.gov/hhes/www/cpstables/032013/perinc/toc.htm; calculations by New Strategist

Men's Earnings Rise with Education

Those with a professional degree earn the most.

Earnings rise in lockstep with education. Among full-time workers, the least-educated men earned a median of just $25,131 in 2012, well below the $50,955 median of all men aged 25 or older. Median earnings are a larger $40,351 among high school graduates and rise to $75,320 for men with a bachelor's degree or more education. Men holding a professional degree have the highest earnings, with a median exceeding $116,000.

Education pays off almost immediately. Among men aged 25 to 34 who work full-time, the median earnings of those with a bachelor's degree are 57 percent higher than the median earnings of men with no more than a high school diploma—$51,716 versus $32,845 in 2012. Among men aged 45 to 54, those with a bachelor's degree earn 91 percent more than those with no more than a high school diploma.

■ The Great Recession affected men at every level of education, but men with a college degree still earn more than those with less education.

A college diploma adds to earning power

(median earnings of men aged 25 or older who work full-time, year-round, by educational attainment, 2012)

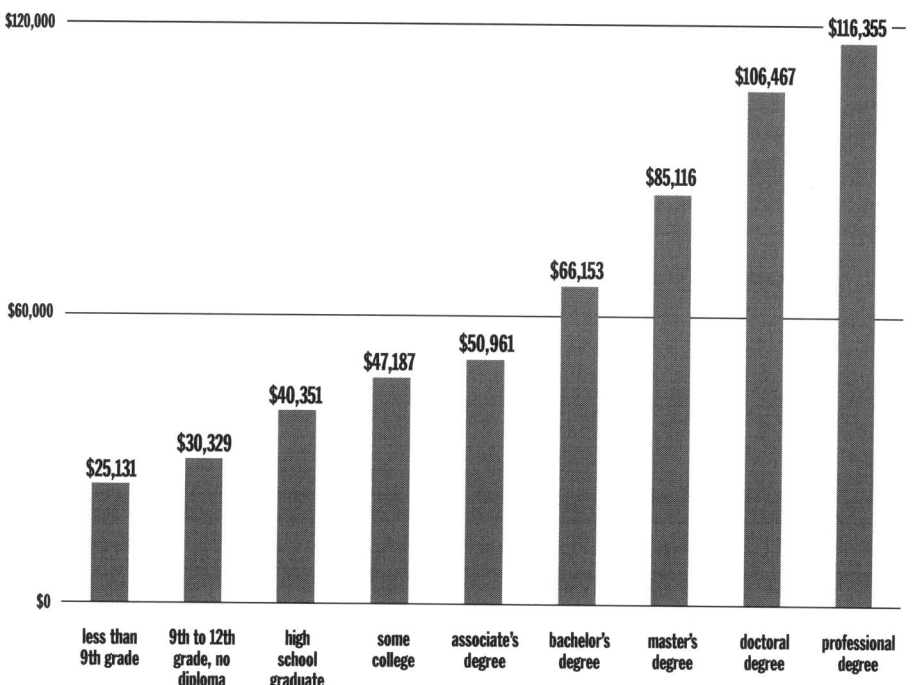

Table 2.29 Men Who Work Full-Time by Earnings and Education, 2012: Total Men

(number and percent distribution of men aged 25 or older who work full-time, year-round, by earnings and educational attainment, 2012; median earnings of men with earnings; men in thousands as of 2013)

	total	less than 9th grade	9th to 12th grade, no diploma	high school graduate	some college, no degree	associate's degree	bachelor's degree or more total	bachelor's degree	master's degree	professional degree	doctoral degree
Total men who work full-time	**55,208**	**1,793**	**2,671**	**15,295**	**8,974**	**5,423**	**21,052**	**13,315**	**5,003**	**1,301**	**1,433**
Under $5,000	325	18	25	85	65	50	82	51	17	4	11
$5,000 to $9,999	334	32	49	117	40	25	71	55	13	2	1
$10,000 to $14,999	1,237	167	156	510	146	75	183	120	46	10	7
$15,000 to $19,999	2,130	334	357	814	264	121	240	187	39	5	9
$20,000 to $24,999	3,332	336	427	1,329	576	232	432	355	60	9	8
$25,000 to $29,999	3,631	292	290	1,404	740	344	561	420	110	12	18
$30,000 to $34,999	4,343	174	312	1,753	796	457	850	674	131	24	22
$35,000 to $39,999	3,765	111	241	1,466	739	394	813	686	103	18	7
$40,000 to $44,999	3,989	96	225	1,442	718	445	1,063	833	160	21	48
$45,000 to $49,999	3,278	59	94	985	665	411	1,064	779	209	34	42
$50,000 to $54,999	3,818	52	124	1,205	682	505	1,250	920	245	35	50
$55,000 to $59,999	2,171	25	68	574	414	247	843	589	178	26	50
$60,000 to $64,999	3,000	18	68	774	545	423	1,170	802	259	51	59
$65,000 to $69,999	2,066	22	53	519	385	268	818	522	223	31	41
$70,000 to $74,999	2,089	14	49	440	356	237	994	646	236	49	62
$75,000 to $79,999	1,719	7	28	299	317	216	851	592	211	20	28
$80,000 to $84,999	1,704	11	17	321	301	167	888	527	254	51	55
$85,000 to $89,999	1,070	5	15	174	146	115	615	382	171	30	33
$90,000 to $94,999	1,377	2	14	241	155	152	815	519	214	32	49
$95,000 to $99,999	675	2	11	97	113	77	374	220	97	32	26
$100,000 or more	9,156	17	48	745	810	463	7,073	3,436	2,027	806	805
Median earnings	**$50,955**	**$25,131**	**$30,329**	**$40,351**	**$47,187**	**$50,961**	**$75,320**	**$66,153**	**$85,116**	**$116,355**	**$106,467**

PERCENT DISTRIBUTION

	total	less than 9th grade	9th to 12th grade, no diploma	high school graduate	some college, no degree	associate's degree	bachelor's degree or more total	bachelor's degree	master's degree	professional degree	doctoral degree
Total men who work full-time	**100.0%**	**100.0%**	**100.0%**	**100.0%**	**100.0%**	**100.0%**	**100.0%**	**100.0%**	**100.0%**	**100.0%**	**100.0%**
Under $15,000	3.4	12.1	8.6	4.7	2.8	2.7	1.6	1.7	1.5	1.1	1.4
$15,000 to $24,999	9.9	37.3	29.3	14.0	9.4	6.5	3.2	4.1	2.0	1.1	1.2
$25,000 to $34,999	14.4	26.0	22.5	20.6	17.1	14.8	6.7	8.2	4.8	2.8	2.8
$35,000 to $49,999	20.0	14.9	21.0	25.5	23.6	23.0	14.0	17.3	9.4	5.6	6.8
$50,000 to $74,999	23.8	7.3	13.5	23.0	26.5	31.0	24.1	26.1	22.8	14.8	18.3
$75,000 to $99,999	11.9	1.5	3.2	7.4	11.5	13.4	16.8	16.8	18.9	12.7	13.4
$100,000 or more	16.6	0.9	1.8	4.9	9.0	8.5	33.6	25.8	40.5	61.9	56.2

Note: Earnings include wages and salary only.
Source: Bureau of the Census, 2013 Current Population Survey Annual Social and Economic Supplement, Internet site http://www.census.gov/hhes/www/cpstables/032013/perinc/toc.htm; calculations by New Strategist

Table 2.30 Men Who Work Full-Time by Earnings and Education, 2012: Men Aged 25 to 34

(number and percent distribution of men aged 25 to 34 who work full-time, year-round, by earnings and educational attainment, 2012; median earnings of men with earnings; men in thousands as of 2013)

Men aged 25 to 34 who work full-time	total	less than 9th grade	9th to 12th grade, no diploma	high school graduate	some college, no degree	associate's degree	bachelor's degree or more				
							total	bachelor's degree	master's degree	professional degree	doctoral degree
Men aged 25 to 34 who work full-time	13,522	419	769	3,738	2,346	1,319	4,930	3,697	862	185	186
Under $5,000	73	5	6	24	16	11	11	11	0	0	0
$5,000 to $9,999	105	5	30	28	23	7	12	12	0	0	0
$10,000 to $14,999	418	64	62	170	51	22	49	38	12	0	0
$15,000 to $19,999	718	68	112	302	120	42	75	63	12	0	0
$20,000 to $24,999	1,136	103	130	454	208	76	164	148	12	3	2
$25,000 to $29,999	1,267	65	70	483	291	139	219	191	21	0	7
$30,000 to $34,999	1,422	45	89	524	303	144	316	269	36	9	2
$35,000 to $39,999	1,146	22	59	403	202	127	333	303	28	1	0
$40,000 to $44,999	1,084	17	65	306	189	107	400	337	43	7	14
$45,000 to $49,999	916	5	31	200	179	114	387	271	84	20	12
$50,000 to $54,999	942	4	41	220	137	114	426	349	56	5	16
$55,000 to $59,999	555	3	10	118	69	64	290	227	41	7	16
$60,000 to $64,999	730	0	18	128	152	101	331	234	65	17	15
$65,000 to $69,999	378	4	6	50	70	56	192	120	52	5	15
$70,000 to $74,999	448	1	13	67	57	32	278	205	51	11	11
$75,000 to $79,999	344	2	12	32	59	36	204	145	42	8	9
$80,000 to $84,999	302	3	4	51	46	30	168	125	37	5	1
$85,000 to $89,999	182	2	0	13	24	23	119	95	13	11	0
$90,000 to $94,999	267	0	0	59	31	20	157	107	42	4	4
$95,000 to $99,999	113	0	0	16	16	10	71	41	22	2	6
$100,000 or more	976	2	11	90	103	43	727	405	196	70	56
Median earnings	$41,303	$22,392	$27,005	$32,845	$38,437	$42,683	$55,767	$51,716	$66,501	$80,079	$66,545

PERCENT DISTRIBUTION

Men aged 25 to 34 who work full-time	total	less than 9th grade	9th to 12th grade, no diploma	high school graduate	some college, no degree	associate's degree	bachelor's degree or more				
							total	bachelor's degree	master's degree	professional degree	doctoral degree
Men aged 25 to 34 who work full-time	100.0%	100.0%	100.0%	100.0%	100.0%	100.0%	100.0%	100.0%	100.0%	100.0%	100.0%
Under $15,000	4.4	17.6	12.7	5.9	3.8	3.0	1.5	1.6	1.4	0.0	0.0
$15,000 to $24,999	13.7	40.7	31.5	20.2	14.0	9.0	4.8	5.7	2.7	1.6	1.1
$25,000 to $34,999	19.9	26.3	20.7	26.9	25.3	21.5	10.9	12.4	6.6	4.8	5.0
$35,000 to $49,999	23.3	10.7	20.1	24.3	24.3	26.4	22.7	24.6	17.9	15.1	14.1
$50,000 to $74,999	22.6	2.7	11.5	15.6	20.7	27.8	30.8	30.7	30.7	24.3	38.8
$75,000 to $99,999	8.9	1.6	2.1	4.6	7.5	9.1	14.6	13.9	17.9	16.3	10.7
$100,000 or more	7.2	0.4	1.4	2.4	4.4	3.3	14.8	11.0	22.7	37.9	30.2

Note: Earnings include wages and salary only.
Source: Bureau of the Census, 2013 Current Population Survey Annual Social and Economic Supplement, Internet site http://www.census.gov/hhes/www/cpstables/032013/perinc/toc.htm; calculations by New Strategist

(number and percent distribution of men aged 35 to 44 who work full-time, year-round, by earnings and educational attainment, 2012; median earnings of men with earnings; men in thousands as of 2013)

	total	less than 9th grade	9th to 12th grade, no diploma	high school graduate	some college, no degree	associate's degree	bachelor's degree or more				
							total	bachelor's degree	master's degree	professional degree	doctoral degree
Men aged 35 to 44 who work full-time	14,168	538	713	3,667	2,348	1,404	5,499	3,397	1,423	336	343
Under $5,000	58	2	8	14	12	7	16	10	1	2	4
$5,000 to $9,999	63	15	2	22	4	9	11	9	2	0	0
$10,000 to $14,999	276	47	39	120	29	13	28	17	9	0	2
$15,000 to $19,999	551	126	118	196	39	26	48	39	8	0	0
$20,000 to $24,999	825	109	102	329	133	59	92	78	14	0	0
$25,000 to $29,999	814	93	66	289	155	89	122	87	25	6	4
$30,000 to $34,999	1,093	41	86	452	193	131	190	144	37	4	5
$35,000 to $39,999	915	24	75	353	199	99	165	150	11	4	0
$40,000 to $44,999	1,008	22	54	376	198	101	257	199	40	4	14
$45,000 to $49,999	827	10	15	255	185	116	246	173	48	8	18
$50,000 to $54,999	944	16	34	273	209	117	295	218	60	9	9
$55,000 to $59,999	576	10	30	123	150	62	202	131	54	5	12
$60,000 to $64,999	719	5	21	172	126	112	282	189	72	10	11
$65,000 to $69,999	570	3	16	115	130	72	235	163	53	11	9
$70,000 to $74,999	513	1	8	72	104	55	274	176	69	17	13
$75,000 to $79,999	522	3	13	81	102	55	267	184	69	4	10
$80,000 to $84,999	491	4	6	107	70	49	255	147	76	15	16
$85,000 to $89,999	318	3	5	48	41	40	181	114	59	0	8
$90,000 to $94,999	397	2	5	25	44	41	280	164	81	10	25
$95,000 to $99,999	228	2	4	25	26	23	149	99	31	17	2
$100,000 or more	2,461	2	6	220	200	129	1,904	906	605	212	181
Median earnings	**$51,990**	**$23,012**	**$30,821**	**$40,450**	**$50,369**	**$51,239**	**$80,226**	**$71,511**	**$90,204**	**$120,271**	**$101,337**

PERCENT DISTRIBUTION

Men aged 35 to 44 who work full-time	100.0%	100.0%	100.0%	100.0%	100.0%	100.0%	100.0%	100.0%	100.0%	100.0%	100.0%
Under $15,000	2.8	11.9	6.8	4.2	1.9	2.1	1.0	1.1	0.8	0.5	1.7
$15,000 to $24,999	9.7	43.6	30.9	14.3	7.3	6.0	2.5	3.5	1.6	0.0	0.0
$25,000 to $34,999	13.5	24.8	21.4	20.2	14.8	15.7	5.7	6.8	4.4	3.0	2.5
$35,000 to $49,999	19.4	10.5	20.1	26.8	24.8	22.5	12.2	15.4	7.0	4.5	9.4
$50,000 to $74,999	23.4	6.4	15.4	20.6	30.6	29.7	23.4	25.8	21.6	15.2	15.6
$75,000 to $99,999	13.8	2.5	4.7	7.8	12.0	14.8	20.6	20.8	22.2	13.8	18.0
$100,000 or more	17.4	0.3	0.9	6.0	8.5	9.2	34.6	26.7	42.5	63.0	52.9

Note: Earnings include wages and salary only.
Source: Bureau of the Census, 2013 Current Population Survey Annual Social and Economic Supplement, Internet site http://www.census.gov/hhes/www/cpstables/032013/perinc/toc.htm; calculations by New Strategist

Table 2.32 Men Who Work Full-Time by Earnings and Education, 2012: Men Aged 45 to 54

(number and percent distribution of men aged 45 to 54 who work full-time, year-round, by earnings and educational attainment, 2012; median earnings of men with earnings; men in thousands as of 2013)

	total	less than 9th grade	9th to 12th grade, no diploma	high school graduate	some college, no degree	associate's degree	bachelor's degree or more total	bachelor's degree	master's degree	professional degree	doctoral degree
Men aged 45 to 54 who work full-time	14,705	452	724	4,327	2,237	1,520	5,445	3,402	1,381	311	351
Under $5,000	78	0	5	27	14	4	28	13	11	2	2
$5,000 to $9,999	52	4	2	28	4	4	10	10	0	0	0
$10,000 to $14,999	275	33	25	109	33	21	54	35	13	3	2
$15,000 to $19,999	463	87	64	187	61	30	34	27	5	0	2
$20,000 to $24,999	756	64	131	314	127	49	72	62	8	0	1
$25,000 to $29,999	845	78	111	355	165	63	74	64	8	0	2
$30,000 to $34,999	992	64	92	433	147	103	152	112	25	5	9
$35,000 to $39,999	920	33	67	394	170	120	136	107	25	4	0
$40,000 to $44,999	1,023	31	69	440	169	123	191	144	36	5	6
$45,000 to $49,999	807	17	23	291	168	102	207	159	38	5	5
$50,000 to $54,999	972	14	28	389	155	117	270	185	58	15	12
$55,000 to $59,999	520	3	14	174	93	70	166	112	36	7	11
$60,000 to $64,999	801	8	19	228	145	124	276	214	43	8	12
$65,000 to $69,999	592	4	11	196	107	84	190	124	56	5	6
$70,000 to $74,999	583	5	18	137	94	88	241	157	58	10	16
$75,000 to $79,999	468	3	1	109	80	65	210	143	61	3	3
$80,000 to $84,999	496	0	8	97	93	42	256	149	82	14	11
$85,000 to $89,999	355	0	8	76	48	40	183	115	51	5	11
$90,000 to $94,999	425	0	1	88	38	60	238	163	55	15	5
$95,000 to $99,999	185	0	7	34	30	23	91	51	30	10	1
$100,000 or more	3,095	4	20	222	296	189	2,365	1,254	683	195	233
Median earnings	$56,073	$26,621	$30,773	$42,247	$51,172	$56,272	$88,080	$80,590	$98,270	$122,725	$130,240

PERCENT DISTRIBUTION

	total	less than 9th grade	9th to 12th grade, no diploma	high school graduate	some college, no degree	associate's degree	bachelor's degree or more total	bachelor's degree	master's degree	professional degree	doctoral degree
Men aged 45 to 54 who work full-time	100.0%	100.0%	100.0%	100.0%	100.0%	100.0%	100.0%	100.0%	100.0%	100.0%	100.0%
Under $15,000	2.8	8.2	4.5	3.8	2.3	1.9	1.7	1.7	1.8	1.7	1.1
$15,000 to $24,999	8.3	33.3	27.0	11.6	8.4	5.2	1.9	2.6	1.0	0.0	1.0
$25,000 to $34,999	12.5	31.5	28.0	18.2	13.9	10.9	4.2	5.2	2.4	1.7	3.3
$35,000 to $49,999	18.7	18.0	22.0	26.0	22.6	22.7	9.8	12.1	7.1	4.5	3.2
$50,000 to $74,999	23.6	7.4	12.4	26.0	26.6	31.8	21.0	23.3	18.0	14.2	16.0
$75,000 to $99,999	13.1	0.6	3.4	9.3	12.9	15.1	18.0	18.3	20.2	15.2	9.0
$100,000 or more	21.0	0.9	2.7	5.1	13.2	12.4	43.4	36.9	49.4	62.7	66.4

Note: Earnings include wages and salary only.
Source: Bureau of the Census, 2013 Current Population Survey Annual Social and Economic Supplement, Internet site http:// www.census.gov/hhes/www/cpstables/032013/perinc/toc.htm; calculations by New Strategist

Table 2.33 Men Who Work Full-Time by Earnings and Education, 2012: Men Aged 55 to 64

(number and percent distribution of men aged 55 to 64 who work full-time, year-round, by earnings and educational attainment, 2012; median earnings of men with earnings; men in thousands as of 2013)

	total	less than 9th grade	9th to 12th grade, no diploma	high school graduate	some college, no degree	associate's degree	bachelor's degree or more				
							total	bachelor's degree	master's degree	professional degree	doctoral degree
Men aged 55 to 64 who work full-time	10,174	276	332	2,942	1,697	979	3,947	2,206	1,055	337	349
Under $5,000	72	8	5	10	4	24	20	14	3	0	3
$5,000 to $9,999	92	7	11	38	6	4	25	15	7	2	1
$10,000 to $14,999	195	18	23	83	21	10	39	24	11	0	3
$15,000 to $19,999	298	38	44	103	41	18	54	40	14	1	0
$20,000 to $24,999	461	45	43	181	75	41	77	49	24	1	3
$25,000 to $29,999	559	40	28	234	111	48	98	53	42	1	2
$30,000 to $34,999	665	18	35	276	123	68	145	115	23	6	2
$35,000 to $39,999	617	27	30	251	132	40	136	97	29	9	2
$40,000 to $44,999	715	18	25	266	141	102	163	118	29	6	9
$45,000 to $49,999	572	13	17	208	105	59	170	140	27	1	2
$50,000 to $54,999	759	10	17	265	149	131	188	130	52	2	4
$55,000 to $59,999	439	8	10	144	84	42	151	98	40	4	9
$60,000 to $64,999	607	4	7	205	109	72	211	118	64	15	13
$65,000 to $69,999	440	3	9	141	77	51	160	90	55	8	6
$70,000 to $74,999	463	7	7	134	91	55	169	96	48	11	15
$75,000 to $79,999	290	0	3	62	71	41	112	81	25	2	4
$80,000 to $84,999	358	4	0	64	72	39	180	94	42	16	27
$85,000 to $89,999	180	0	2	33	33	11	101	48	39	12	3
$90,000 to $94,999	253	0	7	60	40	28	119	73	34	3	9
$95,000 to $99,999	94	0	0	17	31	10	35	19	12	0	4
$100,000 or more	2,045	10	10	165	182	85	1,594	693	435	237	228
Median earnings	**$55,663**	**$26,549**	**$31,624**	**$45,558**	**$51,810**	**$51,970**	**$80,811**	**$70,057**	**$82,037**	**$135,035**	**$122,309**

PERCENT DISTRIBUTION

Men aged 55 to 64 who work full-time	100.0%	100.0%	100.0%	100.0%	100.0%	100.0%	100.0%	100.0%	100.0%	100.0%	100.0%
Under $15,000	3.5	12.1	11.9	4.5	1.9	3.9	2.1	2.4	2.0	0.4	2.3
$15,000 to $24,999	7.5	30.0	26.2	9.7	6.8	6.0	3.3	4.0	3.6	0.6	0.8
$25,000 to $34,999	12.0	21.0	18.8	17.4	13.8	11.9	6.2	7.6	6.2	2.0	1.0
$35,000 to $49,999	18.7	20.9	21.9	24.7	22.3	20.5	11.9	16.1	8.0	4.8	3.8
$50,000 to $74,999	26.6	11.2	14.9	30.2	30.0	35.9	22.3	24.1	24.7	11.7	13.5
$75,000 to $99,999	11.5	1.3	3.3	8.0	14.6	13.2	13.9	14.3	14.3	9.9	13.3
$100,000 or more	20.1	3.5	3.0	5.6	10.7	8.6	40.4	31.4	41.2	70.5	65.4

Note: Earnings include wages and salary only.
Source: Bureau of the Census, 2013 Current Population Survey Annual Social and Economic Supplement, Internet site http://www.census.gov/hhes/www/cpstables/032013/perinc/toc.htm; calculations by New Strategist

Table 2.34 Men Who Work Full-Time by Earnings and Education, 2012: Men Aged 65 or Older

(number and percent distribution of men aged 65 or older who work full-time, year-round, by earnings and educational attainment, 2012; median earnings of men with earnings; men in thousands as of 2013)

	total	less than 9th grade	9th to 12th grade, no diploma	high school graduate	some college, no degree	associate's degree	bachelor's degree or more				
							total	bachelor's degree	master's degree	professional degree	doctoral degree
Men aged 65 or older who work full-time	2,639	108	133	621	345	201	1,231	613	282	132	204
Under $5,000	43	2	1	10	18	5	7	3	2	0	2
$5,000 to $9,999	22	2	3	1	3	0	12	8	5	0	0
$10,000 to $14,999	73	4	7	28	12	9	13	6	0	6	0
$15,000 to $19,999	100	16	18	27	4	6	29	17	0	5	7
$20,000 to $24,999	154	15	21	51	33	7	27	18	3	4	2
$25,000 to $29,999	146	16	16	43	18	4	48	26	14	5	4
$30,000 to $34,999	171	6	9	67	30	12	47	34	10	0	3
$35,000 to $39,999	168	5	10	66	36	7	44	29	10	0	5
$40,000 to $44,999	158	8	13	53	22	11	52	35	12	0	5
$45,000 to $49,999	155	14	8	31	27	21	53	36	12	0	5
$50,000 to $54,999	201	9	5	58	32	27	71	38	19	5	10
$55,000 to $59,999	81	2	4	15	18	9	34	21	7	4	2
$60,000 to $64,999	144	1	3	41	13	14	71	47	15	1	8
$65,000 to $69,999	86	9	10	18	2	5	42	25	8	3	6
$70,000 to $74,999	81	0	3	30	11	8	30	12	11	0	7
$75,000 to $79,999	96	0	0	14	6	18	58	39	14	3	2
$80,000 to $84,999	58	0	0	1	20	7	29	12	17	0	0
$85,000 to $89,999	35	0	0	4	0	0	31	10	8	1	11
$90,000 to $94,999	35	0	0	8	3	3	21	12	3	0	5
$95,000 to $99,999	55	0	0	6	9	12	29	9	2	4	13
$100,000 or more	579	0	2	48	29	17	484	177	109	91	106
Median earnings	**$51,924**	**$29,253**	**$30,002**	**$40,939**	**$43,365**	**$51,861**	**$76,651**	**$62,304**	**$77,336**	**$132,260**	**$101,101**

PERCENT DISTRIBUTION

Men aged 65 or older who work full-time	100.0%	100.0%	100.0%	100.0%	100.0%	100.0%	100.0%	100.0%	100.0%	100.0%	100.0%
Under $15,000	5.2	7.3	8.7	6.3	9.8	6.8	2.6	2.7	2.4	4.8	1.0
$15,000 to $24,999	9.6	28.5	29.4	12.5	10.8	6.3	4.5	5.8	1.0	6.7	4.4
$25,000 to $34,999	12.0	20.4	18.8	17.8	13.9	8.0	7.7	9.8	8.3	3.6	3.5
$35,000 to $49,999	18.2	24.3	23.3	24.2	24.6	19.6	12.1	16.3	12.2	0.0	7.2
$50,000 to $74,999	22.5	19.6	18.3	26.0	21.7	31.0	20.2	23.2	21.4	9.8	16.1
$75,000 to $99,999	10.5	0.0	0.0	5.4	10.9	19.8	13.6	13.4	16.0	5.8	15.9
$100,000 or more	21.9	0.0	1.5	7.7	8.3	8.5	39.3	28.9	38.7	69.4	51.9

Note: Earnings include wages and salary only.
Source: Bureau of the Census, 2013 Current Population Survey Annual Social and Economic Supplement, Internet site http://www.census.gov/hhes/www/cpstables/032013/perinc/toc.htm; calculations by New Strategist

Education Boosts Earnings of Asian, Black, Hispanic, and Non-Hispanic White Men

Among men with a bachelor's degree, non-Hispanic whites earn the most.

Education lifts earnings in every racial and ethnic group. Among full-time workers, non-Hispanic white men with a bachelor's degree earned a median of $70,021 in 2012. This figure was 65 percent greater than the $42,558 median of non-Hispanic white men with no more than a high school diploma.

Among Asian men who work full-time, those with a bachelor's degree earned a median of $68,322 in 2012, more than double the $33,501 median of their counterparts with a high school diploma. The story is similar for blacks and Hispanics. Among black men who work full-time, those with a bachelor's degree earned a median of $53,649 in 2012 versus the $32,438 of those with no more than a high school diploma. Hispanic men who work full-time are least likely to have a bachelor's degree, but those with a degree have median earnings 64 percent higher than their counterparts with no more than a high school diploma.

■ Among men with a bachelor's degree who work full-time, the earnings of blacks and Hispanics are substantially lower than the earnings of Asians and non-Hispanic whites.

Among men with a bachelor's degree, non-Hispanic white men earn the most

(median earnings of men aged 25 or older with a bachelor's degree who work full-time, year-round, by race and Hispanic origin, 2012)

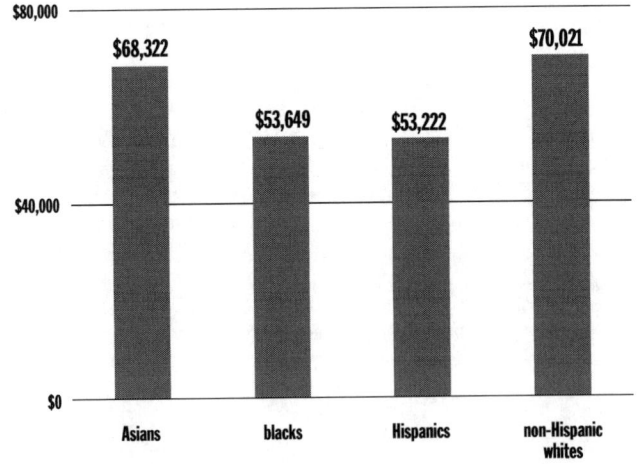

Table 2.35 Men Who Work Full-Time by Earnings and Education, 2012: Asian Men

(number and percent distribution of Asian men aged 25 or older who work full-time, year-round, by earnings and educational attainment, 2012; median earnings of men with earnings; men in thousands as of 2013)

	total	less than 9th grade	9th to 12th grade, no diploma	high school graduate	some college, no degree	associate's degree	bachelor's degree or more total	bachelor's degree	master's degree	professional degree	doctoral degree
Asian men who work full-time	**3,436**	**56**	**109**	**546**	**322**	**245**	**2,158**	**1,100**	**656**	**159**	**244**
Under $5,000	20	0	0	3	4	1	12	6	4	0	2
$5,000 to $9,999	17	1	1	5	1	4	5	5	0	0	0
$10,000 to $14,999	78	4	9	30	2	7	26	14	10	2	0
$15,000 to $19,999	129	11	15	48	19	9	28	24	4	0	0
$20,000 to $24,999	162	8	17	60	26	18	33	25	6	1	0
$25,000 to $29,999	195	11	13	68	31	15	57	41	13	0	2
$30,000 to $34,999	233	7	15	64	49	26	72	54	12	4	3
$35,000 to $39,999	172	4	14	45	29	17	62	60	2	0	0
$40,000 to $44,999	209	0	14	50	26	18	102	60	19	8	15
$45,000 to $49,999	174	5	3	41	26	11	89	48	21	12	8
$50,000 to $54,999	182	1	0	31	27	30	93	62	11	6	14
$55,000 to $59,999	106	3	2	13	6	11	70	46	11	5	9
$60,000 to $64,999	190	0	2	26	20	16	126	81	34	2	9
$65,000 to $69,999	111	0	0	16	15	12	67	29	32	3	3
$70,000 to $74,999	139	0	0	9	12	9	108	48	45	8	7
$75,000 to $79,999	118	0	0	7	10	3	98	56	31	4	7
$80,000 to $84,999	136	0	0	3	9	7	117	61	38	11	7
$85,000 to $89,999	69	0	2	0	1	4	62	22	26	6	8
$90,000 to $94,999	117	0	0	5	0	9	103	60	31	0	12
$95,000 to $99,999	59	0	0	8	0	5	46	27	16	0	3
$100,000 or more	821	0	1	12	10	16	782	272	290	86	135
Median earnings	**$60,616**	**–**	**$28,765**	**$33,501**	**$40,073**	**$48,662**	**$80,805**	**$68,322**	**$91,023**	**$102,047**	**$101,344**

PERCENT DISTRIBUTION

Asian men who work full-time	total	less than 9th grade	9th to 12th grade, no diploma	high school graduate	some college, no degree	associate's degree	bachelor's degree or more total	bachelor's degree	master's degree	professional degree	doctoral degree
	100.0%	100.0%	100.0%	100.0%	100.0%	100.0%	100.0%	100.0%	100.0%	100.0%	100.0%
Under $15,000	3.3	8.6	9.5	7.1	2.0	4.6	2.0	2.3	2.1	1.1	0.9
$15,000 to $24,999	8.5	34.2	29.5	19.8	14.0	11.1	2.8	4.4	1.5	1.1	0.0
$25,000 to $34,999	12.5	31.9	25.9	24.3	24.9	16.6	6.0	8.6	3.8	2.3	2.0
$35,000 to $49,999	16.1	16.3	28.1	25.0	25.0	18.5	11.7	15.2	6.4	12.8	9.3
$50,000 to $74,999	21.2	9.1	3.8	17.4	24.9	31.7	21.6	24.1	20.2	15.5	17.5
$75,000 to $99,999	14.5	0.0	2.0	4.3	6.2	11.1	19.8	20.6	21.7	13.1	15.0
$100,000 or more	23.9	0.0	1.1	2.1	3.0	6.4	36.3	24.7	44.2	54.1	55.3

Note: Asians are those who identify themselves as being of the race alone and those who identify themselves as being of the race in combination with other races. Earnings include wages and salary only. "–" means sample is too small to make a reliable estimate.
Source: Bureau of the Census, 2013 Current Population Survey Annual Social and Economic Supplement, Internet site http://www.census.gov/hhes/www/cpstables/032013/perinc/toc.htm; calculations by New Strategist

Table 2.36 Men Who Work Full-Time by Earnings and Education, 2012: Black Men

(number and percent distribution of black men aged 25 or older who work full-time, year-round, by earnings and educational attainment, 2012; median earnings of men with earnings; men in thousands as of 2013)

	total	less than 9th grade	9th to 12th grade, no diploma	high school graduate	some college, no degree	associate's degree	bachelor's degree or more total	bachelor's degree	master's degree	professional degree	doctoral degree
Black men who work full-time	**5,447**	**110**	**295**	**1,771**	**1,206**	**579**	**1,486**	**988**	**360**	**62**	**76**
Under $5,000	37	1	10	9	4	5	8	7	0	2	0
$5,000 to $9,999	25	0	12	3	2	4	5	5	0	0	0
$10,000 to $14,999	167	12	29	72	24	6	25	13	10	0	2
$15,000 to $19,999	326	43	41	151	64	9	18	16	2	0	0
$20,000 to $24,999	479	10	47	209	124	45	44	42	3	0	0
$25,000 to $29,999	520	11	31	236	126	48	68	44	21	0	2
$30,000 to $34,999	595	11	44	262	138	56	85	70	12	2	1
$35,000 to $39,999	475	5	16	200	121	50	82	65	14	3	0
$40,000 to $44,999	434	7	21	173	93	54	85	71	12	0	2
$45,000 to $49,999	328	0	8	96	92	47	84	63	14	3	4
$50,000 to $54,999	367	1	2	83	84	46	150	110	35	5	0
$55,000 to $59,999	210	0	3	43	43	36	84	55	21	2	6
$60,000 to $64,999	249	4	9	54	54	35	94	76	12	3	2
$65,000 to $69,999	201	5	6	23	39	38	91	47	32	4	8
$70,000 to $74,999	173	0	14	42	24	19	74	46	16	2	9
$75,000 to $79,999	107	0	2	20	36	12	38	28	10	0	0
$80,000 to $84,999	121	0	0	31	29	23	38	19	12	2	5
$85,000 to $89,999	83	0	0	13	20	3	46	27	13	1	6
$90,000 to $94,999	112	0	0	23	18	10	61	32	21	1	7
$95,000 to $99,999	62	2	0	7	9	8	37	25	8	3	0
$100,000 or more	377	0	0	22	62	25	269	129	89	28	22
Median earnings	**$40,668**	**$20,076**	**$26,044**	**$32,438**	**$40,038**	**$46,102**	**$60,087**	**$53,649**	**$67,195**	**–**	**$81,306**

PERCENT DISTRIBUTION

	total	less than 9th grade	9th to 12th grade, no diploma	high school graduate	some college, no degree	associate's degree	bachelor's degree or more total	bachelor's degree	master's degree	professional degree	doctoral degree
Black men who work full-time	**100.0%**	**100.0%**	**100.0%**	**100.0%**	**100.0%**	**100.0%**	**100.0%**	**100.0%**	**100.0%**	**100.0%**	**100.0%**
Under $15,000	4.2	11.2	17.1	4.7	2.5	2.6	2.6	2.4	3.0	2.7	2.7
$15,000 to $24,999	14.8	47.6	29.9	20.3	15.6	9.3	4.2	5.8	1.3	0.3	0.0
$25,000 to $34,999	20.5	20.2	25.5	28.1	21.8	17.9	10.3	11.6	9.3	3.9	3.9
$35,000 to $49,999	22.7	10.9	15.2	26.5	25.4	26.1	16.9	20.0	11.4	11.1	7.7
$50,000 to $74,999	22.0	8.5	11.7	13.8	20.2	30.2	33.2	33.9	32.5	25.3	33.8
$75,000 to $99,999	8.9	1.7	0.6	5.3	9.4	9.6	14.7	13.2	17.8	11.2	23.0
$100,000 or more	6.9	0.0	0.0	1.2	5.1	4.2	18.1	13.1	24.8	45.4	29.0

Note: Blacks are those who identify themselves as being of the race alone and those who identify themselves as being of the race in combination with other races. Earnings include wages and salary only. "–" means sample is too small to make a reliable estimate.
Source: Bureau of the Census, 2013 Current Population Survey Annual Social and Economic Supplement, Internet site http://www.census.gov/hhes/www/cpstables/032013/perinc/toc.htm; calculations by New Strategist

Table 2.37 Men Who Work Full-Time by Earnings and Education, 2012: Hispanic Men

(number and percent distribution of Hispanic men aged 25 or older who work full-time, year-round, by earnings and educational attainment, 2012; median earnings of men with earnings; men in thousands as of 2013)

	total	less than 9th grade	9th to 12th grade, no diploma	high school graduate	some college, no degree	associate's degree	bachelor's degree or more total	bachelor's degree	master's degree	professional degree	doctoral degree
Hispanic men who work full-time	8,458	1,407	1,213	2,744	1,119	528	1,448	1,009	316	50	73
Under $5,000	32	14	5	8	3	0	2	1	1	0	0
$5,000 to $9,999	111	29	31	38	4	4	5	4	0	0	1
$10,000 to $14,999	452	145	80	156	29	16	25	19	6	0	0
$15,000 to $19,999	809	281	188	249	43	21	27	26	1	0	0
$20,000 to $24,999	1,011	292	212	345	84	31	47	40	6	1	0
$25,000 to $29,999	926	224	143	321	116	42	78	60	14	1	3
$30,000 to $34,999	863	136	138	331	113	59	86	72	12	0	1
$35,000 to $39,999	748	91	115	305	111	47	79	71	6	0	1
$40,000 to $44,999	625	68	92	225	104	36	100	80	14	0	5
$45,000 to $49,999	437	38	40	123	75	58	102	73	23	3	3
$50,000 to $54,999	459	31	53	166	84	38	87	66	16	1	4
$55,000 to $59,999	213	10	18	73	52	17	43	28	7	1	6
$60,000 to $64,999	281	9	16	80	74	28	75	58	17	0	0
$65,000 to $69,999	195	9	17	50	32	17	70	54	13	1	3
$70,000 to $74,999	161	7	17	44	28	11	53	29	20	2	4
$75,000 to $79,999	179	7	14	33	35	24	66	41	19	2	4
$80,000 to $84,999	161	7	5	46	29	11	63	45	15	3	1
$85,000 to $89,999	80	2	4	18	9	17	30	22	6	0	2
$90,000 to $94,999	123	2	2	36	15	15	54	35	13	4	3
$95,000 to $99,999	76	0	2	22	13	5	34	26	6	1	1
$100,000 or more	514	4	21	75	63	31	320	159	101	29	31
Median earnings	**$35,110**	**$23,609**	**$27,149**	**$32,473**	**$41,520**	**$45,391**	**$61,881**	**$53,222**	**$75,170**	–	–

PERCENT DISTRIBUTION

Hispanic men who work full-time	100.0%	100.0%	100.0%	100.0%	100.0%	100.0%	100.0%	100.0%	100.0%	100.0%	100.0%
Under $15,000	7.0	13.4	9.5	7.4	3.3	3.7	2.3	2.4	2.4	0.0	1.7
$15,000 to $24,999	21.5	40.8	33.0	21.6	11.3	9.9	5.1	6.5	2.2	3.0	0.0
$25,000 to $34,999	21.1	25.6	23.2	23.8	20.5	19.1	11.3	13.1	8.3	2.9	6.0
$35,000 to $49,999	21.4	14.0	20.4	23.8	26.0	26.8	19.4	22.3	13.7	6.4	12.3
$50,000 to $74,999	15.5	4.7	9.8	15.1	24.2	21.1	22.7	23.3	22.9	9.5	23.2
$75,000 to $99,999	7.3	1.3	2.3	5.6	9.1	13.4	17.1	16.7	18.5	19.8	14.9
$100,000 or more	6.1	0.3	1.7	2.7	5.7	5.9	22.1	15.8	31.9	58.5	42.0

Note: Earnings include wages and salary only. "–" means sample is too small to make a reliable estimate.
Source: Bureau of the Census, 2013 Current Population Survey Annual Social and Economic Supplement, Internet site http://www.census.gov/hhes/www/cpstables/032013/perinc/toc.htm; calculations by New Strategist

Table 2.38 Men Who Work Full-Time by Earnings and Education, 2012: Non-Hispanic White Men

(number and percent distribution of non-Hispanic white men aged 25 or older who work full-time, year-round, by earnings and educational attainment, 2012; median earnings of men with earnings; men in thousands as of 2013)

	total	less than 9th grade	9th to 12th grade, no diploma	high school graduate	some college, no degree	associate's degree	bachelor's degree or more total	bachelor's degree	master's degree	professional degree	doctoral degree
Non-Hispanic white men who work full-time	37,734	260	1,095	10,210	6,277	4,004	15,889	10,163	3,659	1,027	1,039
Under $5,000	230	3	10	62	51	44	60	38	12	2	9
$5,000 to $9,999	188	3	13	70	33	13	55	41	13	2	0
$10,000 to $14,999	574	11	53	260	93	46	112	73	25	8	5
$15,000 to $19,999	876	19	109	377	128	79	163	117	33	5	9
$20,000 to $24,999	1,683	31	148	731	341	127	306	245	46	6	8
$25,000 to $29,999	2,008	51	105	791	467	235	359	276	61	11	11
$30,000 to $34,999	2,633	20	123	1,088	492	311	598	471	94	17	15
$35,000 to $39,999	2,368	14	101	904	482	273	594	496	77	15	6
$40,000 to $44,999	2,705	21	104	986	491	336	767	613	114	13	27
$45,000 to $49,999	2,333	17	46	719	464	292	796	598	154	17	28
$50,000 to $54,999	2,782	18	68	914	489	377	916	680	182	23	31
$55,000 to $59,999	1,626	12	44	451	305	182	633	452	135	17	28
$60,000 to $64,999	2,265	5	38	604	402	344	872	587	192	45	48
$65,000 to $69,999	1,550	9	30	428	296	199	588	392	147	24	25
$70,000 to $74,999	1,614	7	25	344	284	196	759	518	157	38	46
$75,000 to $79,999	1,303	0	12	237	234	176	644	466	147	14	17
$80,000 to $84,999	1,285	4	12	241	234	125	670	406	186	35	43
$85,000 to $89,999	826	3	8	137	113	91	474	309	124	22	18
$90,000 to $94,999	1,020	0	11	174	127	115	593	387	150	28	29
$95,000 to $99,999	473	0	9	60	90	59	255	141	66	28	20
$100,000 or more	7,392	13	26	631	663	385	5,675	2,859	1,543	659	614
Median earnings	$55,989	$31,552	$33,949	$42,558	$50,570	$52,014	$76,708	$70,021	$86,330	$120,517	$115,964

PERCENT DISTRIBUTION

	total	less than 9th grade	9th to 12th grade, no diploma	high school graduate	some college, no degree	associate's degree	bachelor's degree or more total	bachelor's degree	master's degree	professional degree	doctoral degree
Non-Hispanic white men who work full-time	100.0%	100.0%	100.0%	100.0%	100.0%	100.0%	100.0%	100.0%	100.0%	100.0%	100.0%
Under $15,000	2.6	6.2	7.0	3.8	2.8	2.6	1.4	1.5	1.4	1.1	1.4
$15,000 to $24,999	6.8	19.3	23.4	10.9	7.5	5.2	3.0	3.6	2.2	1.0	1.6
$25,000 to $34,999	12.3	27.4	20.8	18.4	15.3	13.6	6.0	7.3	4.3	2.8	2.6
$35,000 to $49,999	19.6	19.9	22.9	25.6	22.9	22.5	13.6	16.8	9.4	4.3	5.8
$50,000 to $74,999	26.1	19.6	18.8	26.8	28.3	32.4	23.7	25.9	22.2	14.3	17.2
$75,000 to $99,999	13.0	2.6	4.7	8.3	12.7	14.1	16.6	16.8	18.4	12.4	12.3
$100,000 or more	19.6	4.9	2.4	6.2	10.6	9.6	35.7	28.1	42.2	64.1	59.1

Note: Non-Hispanic whites are those who identify themselves as being of the race alone and not Hispanic. Earnings include wages and salary only.
Source: Bureau of the Census, 2013 Current Population Survey Annual Social and Economic Supplement, Internet site http://www.census.gov/hhes/www/cpstables/032013/perinc/toc.htm; calculations by New Strategist

Men's Earnings Vary Widely by Occupation

Men in several occupations have median earnings exceeding $100,000.

The median earnings of men aged 15 or older who work full-time stood at $49,398 in 2012. By occupation, men's earnings vary widely. The highest-paid men are, not surprisingly, doctors, lawyers, and CEOs, with median earnings of more than $100,000 in 2012. Doctors had the highest median earnings of all ($162,129). Other highly paid men are engineers ($86,959), computer scientists ($80,262), and college teachers ($76,212).

The occupation with the lowest earnings for men is cashier ($21,947). Other low-paying occupations are chefs and cooks ($23,288); and farming, fishing, and forestry occupations ($25,711).

■ Some of the men in low-paying occupations are young adults working their way up the career ladder.

Career choice affects earnings

(median earnings of men aged 15 or older who work full-time, year-round, by selected occupation, 2012)

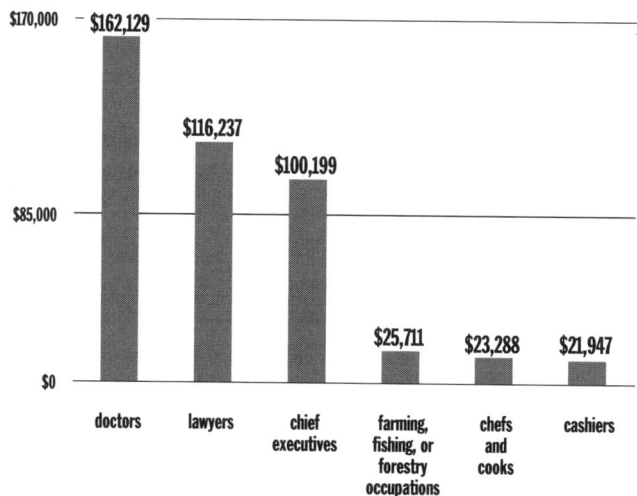

Table 2.39 Median Earnings of Men by Occupation, 2013

(number of men aged 15 or older who work full-time, year-round, and median earnings, by occupation of longest job held, 2012; men in thousands as of 2013)

	number with earnings	median earnings
TOTAL MEN WORKING FULL-TIME, YEAR-ROUND	**59,009**	**$49,398**
Management, science, and arts occupations	**22,244**	**71,550**
Management, business and financial operations occupations	11,050	71,837
Management occupations	8,639	72,811
Chief executives, general and operations managers	1,761	100,199
All other managers	6,875	69,906
Business and financial operations occupations	2,410	67,413
Business operations specialists	1,181	66,847
Financial specialists	1,229	68,628
Professional and related occupations	11,195	71,298
Computer and mathematical occupations	2,615	80,068
Computer scientists, analysts, programmers, engineers, and administrators	2,487	80,262
Mathematicians, statisticians, operations research, and other math occupations	107	76,004
Architecture and engineering occupations	2,103	79,163
Architects, except naval	108	71,151
Engineers	1,570	86,959
Drafters, engineering technicians, and surveying and mapping technicians	395	58,807
Life, physical, and social science occupations	637	71,675
All other scientists	417	75,467
Science technicians	133	49,042
Community and social services occupations	747	42,297
Legal occupations	788	102,216
Lawyers, judges, and magistrates	705	116,237
Paralegals, legal assistants, and legal support workers	83	50,532
Education, training, and library occupations	1,510	56,306
Postsecondary teachers	433	76,212
All other teachers	945	51,783
Archivists, curators, museum technicians, librarians, and other technicians and assistants	132	38,563
Arts, design, entertainment, sports, and media occupations	997	55,805
Health care practitioner and technical occupations	1,797	79,339
Doctors	706	162,129
Nurses	346	64,037
All other health and technical occupations	746	51,962
Service occupations	**7,369**	**31,331**
Health care support occupations	275	30,586
Protective service occupations	2,054	53,836
Supervisors	235	63,524
Firefighters and police	995	67,764
All other protective service occupations	823	35,097
Food preparation and serving related occupations	2,088	23,672
Supervisors	194	31,676
Chefs and cooks	1,055	23,288
All other food preparation occupations	839	21,933
Building and grounds cleaning and maintenance occupations	2,257	28,340
Supervisors	368	45,062
All other maintenance occupations	1,890	26,890

	number with earnings	median earnings
Personal care and service occupations	694	$31,544
Supervisors	129	41,365
All other personal care and service occupations	565	29,610
Sales and office occupations	**9,396**	**45,117**
Sales and related occupations	5,942	47,401
Supervisors	2,413	47,360
Cashiers	379	21,947
Insurance sales agents	288	61,920
Real estate brokers and sales agents	275	50,804
All other sales and related occupations	2,588	50,984
Office and administrative support occupations	3,454	40,696
Supervisors	435	51,395
Postal workers	283	58,429
All other office and administrative support occupations	2,736	36,905
Natural resources, construction, and maintenance occupations	**9,279**	**40,421**
Farming, fishing, and forestry occupations	468	25,711
Farming, fishing, and forestry occupations, except supervisors	447	25,404
Construction and extraction occupations	4,771	38,295
Construction	4,567	37,360
Supervisors	558	50,685
Brickmasons, blockmasons, and stonemasons	109	30,986
Carpenters	701	32,215
Electricians	594	53,993
Painters and paperhangers	306	31,849
All other construction trades	2,194	34,467
Extraction workers	204	62,399
Installation, maintenance, and repair occupations	4,040	43,100
Supervisors	219	56,873
Aircraft mechanics and service	164	57,730
Auto, bus, truck, heavy equipment mechanics	1,232	41,021
Heating, air conditioning, and refrigeration mechanics and installers	265	41,059
Electrical power-line and telecommunications line installers and repairers	282	51,455
All other installation, maintenance, and repair occupations	1,877	42,142
Production, transportation, and material moving occupations	**10,099**	**40,100**
Production occupations	4,921	40,595
Supervisors	548	52,177
All other production occupations	4,372	38,624
Transportation and material moving occupations	5,178	38,405
Supervisors	134	56,708
Auto, bus, truck, ambulance, taxi drivers	2,783	41,454
Rail and subway workers	91	65,901
All other transportation occupations	2,025	31,585
Armed Forces	**622**	**45,977**

Note: Number of workers does not add to total because only occupations with data on median earnings are shown. Earnings include wages and salary only.
Source: Bureau of the Census, 2013 Current Population Survey Annual Social and Economic Supplement, Internet site http://www.census.gov/hhes/www/cpstables/032013/perinc/toc.htm; calculations by New Strategist

Most Men Receive Wage or Salary Income

One in five receives Social Security income.

Seventy-two percent of men received income from wages or salary in 2012, making it the most common source of income. Interest income ranks second as a source, with 40 percent of men receiving interest. Eleven percent of men receive retirement income and 20 percent Social Security. The median amount of Social Security income received by recipients stood at $15,710 in 2012.

Asian and Hispanic men are more likely to receive wage or salary income, but less likely to receive Social Security or interest income, than non-Hispanic white men and black men. Eighty-one percent of Hispanics and 78 percent of Asians receive wage or salary income versus 70 percent of non-Hispanic whites and 71 percent of blacks. But 23 percent of non-Hispanic white men receive Social Security income compared with 17 percent of blacks and 10 percent of Asians and Hispanics.

■ Non-Hispanic white men are more likely to receive Social Security income because they are older, on average, than Asian, black, or Hispanic men.

Wage or salary income is most common

(percent of men aged 15 or older receiving income, by source, 2012)

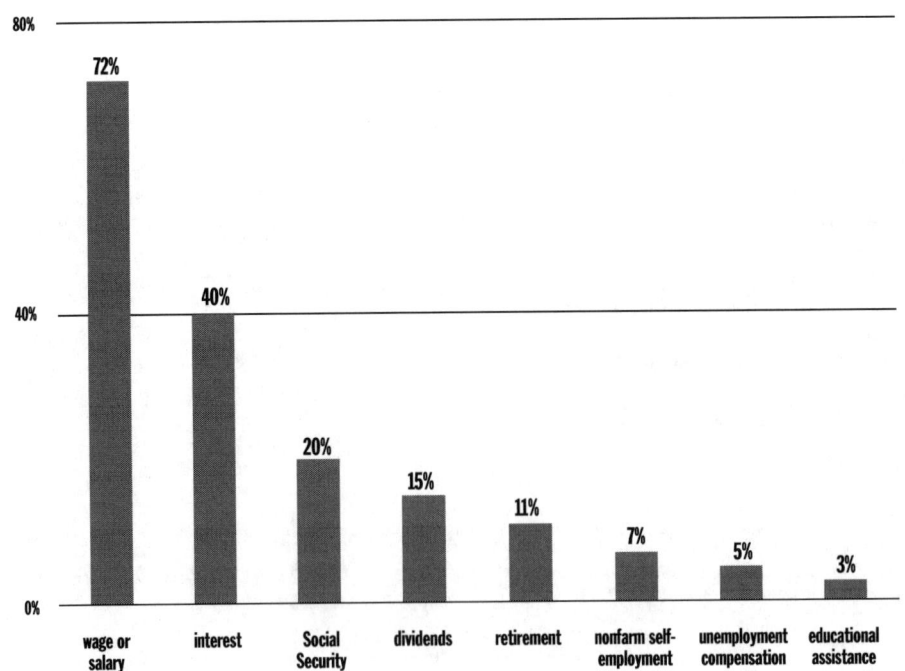

Table 2.40 Median Income of Men by Source of Income, 2012: Total Men

(number and percent of men aged 15 or older with income, and median income of those with income, 2012; men in thousands as of 2013)

	number	percent receiving	median income
Men with income	**107,534**	**100.0%**	**$33,904**
Earnings	83,003	77.2	37,916
Wages or salary	77,550	72.1	38,747
Nonfarm self-employment	7,150	6.6	21,071
Farm self-employment	1,209	1.1	2,428
Social Security	21,286	19.8	15,710
SSI (Supplemental Security)	2,549	2.4	8,163
Public Assistance	424	0.4	1,913
Veteran's benefits	2,638	2.5	9,379
Survivor's benefits	696	0.6	7,271
Disability benefits	892	0.8	10,436
Unemployment compensation	4,874	4.5	4,722
Worker's compensation	931	0.9	3,418
Property income	46,613	43.3	1,635
Interest	43,243	40.2	1,420
Dividends	16,379	15.2	1,722
Rents, royalties, estates, trusts	6,100	5.7	2,307
Retirement income	11,630	10.8	16,443
Company or union retirement	6,574	6.1	11,714
Federal government retirement	1,018	0.9	31,733
Military retirement	976	0.9	21,240
State or local government retirement	2,096	1.9	23,612
Railroad retirement	136	0.1	24,374
Annuities	264	0.2	7,454
IRA or Keogh, or 401(k)	490	0.5	11,425
Pension income	10,183	9.5	17,194
Company or union retirement	6,242	5.8	11,744
Federal government retirement	889	0.8	33,894
Military retirement	921	0.9	21,266
State or local government retirement	1,888	1.8	24,716
Railroad retirement	117	0.1	23,747
Annuities	126	0.1	8,799
Alimony	23	0.0	–
Child support	390	0.4	2,220
Educational assistance	3,753	3.5	4,827
Financial assistance from outside the household	1034	1.0	4,052
Other income	408	0.4	1,684

Note: IRA and 401(k) income includes only withdrawals taken in the form of annuities. "–" means sample is too small to make a reliable estimate.
Source: Bureau of the Census, 2013 Current Population Survey Annual Social and Economic Supplement, Internet site http:// www.census.gov/hhes/www/cpstables/032013/perinc/toc.htm; calculations by New Strategist

Table 2.41 Median Income of Men by Source of Income, 2012: Asian Men

(number and percent of Asian men aged 15 or older with income, and median income of those with income, 2012; men in thousands as of 2013)

	number	percent receiving	median income
Asian men with income	**5,810**	**100.0%**	**$39,606**
Earnings	4,796	82.5	45,837
Wages or salary	4,533	78.0	46,860
Nonfarm self-employment	335	5.8	22,087
Farm self-employment	33	0.6	–
Social Security	598	10.3	14,326
SSI (Supplemental Security)	136	2.3	8,116
Public Assistance	35	0.6	–
Veteran's benefits	59	1.0	–
Survivor's benefits	12	0.2	–
Disability benefits	31	0.5	–
Unemployment compensation	171	2.9	7,097
Worker's compensation	39	0.7	–
Property income	2,590	44.6	1,540
Interest	2,406	41.4	1,379
Dividends	891	15.3	1,555
Rents, royalties, estates, trusts	317	5.5	2,086
Retirement income	261	4.5	15,586
Company or union retirement	130	2.2	9,359
Federal government retirement	23	0.4	–
Military retirement	35	0.6	–
State or local government retirement	44	0.8	–
Railroad retirement	2	0.0	–
Annuities	4	0.1	–
IRA or Keogh, or 401(k)	22	0.4	–
Pension income	217	3.7	16,644
Company or union retirement	121	2.1	9,889
Federal government retirement	21	0.4	–
Military retirement	32	0.6	–
State or local government retirement	40	0.7	–
Railroad retirement	2	0.0	–
Annuities	0	0.0	–
Alimony	0	0.0	–
Child support	10	0.2	–
Educational assistance	327	5.6	4,871
Financial assistance from outside the household	105	1.8	7,014
Other income	15	0.3	–

Note: IRA and 401(k) income includes only withdrawals taken in the form of annuities. Asians are those who identify themselves as being of the race alone and those who identify themselves as being of the race in combination with other races. "–" means sample is too small to make a reliable estimate.
Source: Bureau of the Census, 2013 Current Population Survey Annual Social and Economic Supplement, Internet site http://www.census.gov/hhes/www/cpstables/032013/perinc/toc.htm; calculations by New Strategist

Table 2.42 Median Income of Men by Source of Income, 2012: Black Men

(number and percent of black men aged 15 or older with income, and median income of those with income, 2012; men in thousands as of 2013)

	number	percent receiving	median income
Black men with income	**11,961**	**100.0%**	**$24,959**
Earnings	8,871	74.2	29,910
Wages or salary	8,462	70.7	29,965
Nonfarm self-employment	566	4.7	16,263
Farm self-employment	44	0.4	–
Social Security	2,058	17.2	12,852
SSI (Supplemental Security)	669	5.6	7,858
Public Assistance	120	1.0	1,759
Veteran's benefits	385	3.2	9,635
Survivor's benefits	26	0.2	–
Disability benefits	149	1.2	9,312
Unemployment compensation	644	5.4	4,750
Worker's compensation	91	0.8	2,430
Property income	2,844	23.8	1,509
Interest	2,580	21.6	1,370
Dividends	659	5.5	1,594
Rents, royalties, estates, trusts	344	2.9	2,347
Retirement income	998	8.3	13,823
Company or union retirement	533	4.5	11,067
Federal government retirement	95	0.8	27,927
Military retirement	127	1.1	19,394
State or local government retirement	164	1.4	15,650
Railroad retirement	10	0.1	–
Annuities	11	0.1	–
IRA or Keogh, or 401(k)	23	0.2	–
Pension income	857	7.2	14,656
Company or union retirement	502	4.2	11,069
Federal government retirement	77	0.6	31,522
Military retirement	125	1.0	19,229
State or local government retirement	138	1.2	20,256
Railroad retirement	10	0.1	–
Annuities	4	0.0	–
Alimony	0	0.0	–
Child support	66	0.6	–
Educational assistance	574	4.8	5,165
Financial assistance from outside the household	138	1.2	2,677
Other income	36	0.3	–

Note: IRA and 401(k) income includes only withdrawals taken in the form of annuities. Blacks are those who identify themselves as being of the race alone and those who identify themselves as being of the race in combination with other races. "–" means sample is too small to make a reliable estimate.
Source: Bureau of the Census, 2013 Current Population Survey Annual Social and Economic Supplement, Internet site http://www.census.gov/hhes/www/cpstables/032013/perinc/toc.htm; calculations by New Strategist

Table 2.43 Median Income of Men by Source of Income, 2012: Hispanic Men

(number and percent of Hispanic men aged 15 or older with income, and median income of those with income, 2012; men in thousands as of 2013)

	number	percent receiving	median income
Hispanic men with income	**16,005**	**100.0%**	**$24,592**
Earnings	13,747	85.9	26,360
Wages or salary	12,908	80.6	26,580
Nonfarm self-employment	1028	6.4	17,148
Farm self-employment	87	0.5	1748
Social Security	1,562	9.8	11,936
SSI (Supplemental Security)	369	2.3	7,977
Public Assistance	93	0.6	1,846
Veteran's benefits	168	1.0	9,884
Survivor's benefits	30	0.2	–
Disability benefits	97	0.6	9,937
Unemployment compensation	739	4.6	4,775
Worker's compensation	166	1.0	3,478
Property income	3,294	20.6	1,465
Interest	2,981	18.6	1,334
Dividends	670	4.2	1,614
Rents, royalties, estates, trusts	402	2.5	2,291
Retirement income	548	3.4	14,548
Company or union retirement	280	1.7	11,341
Federal government retirement	53	0.3	–
Military retirement	39	0.2	–
State or local government retirement	102	0.6	17,667
Railroad retirement	5	0.0	–
Annuities	2	0.0	–
IRA or Keogh, or 401(k)	24	0.1	–
Pension income	436	2.7	17,812
Company or union retirement	250	1.6	11,232
Federal government retirement	49	0.3	–
Military retirement	37	0.2	–
State or local government retirement	73	0.5	–
Railroad retirement	5	0.0	–
Annuities	2	0.0	–
Alimony	3	0.0	–
Child support	51	0.3	–
Educational assistance	542	3.4	4,153
Financial assistance from outside the household	125	0.8	4,434
Other income	30	0.2	–

Note: IRA and 401(k) income includes only withdrawals taken in the form of annuities. "–" means sample is too small to make a reliable estimate.
Source: Bureau of the Census, 2013 Current Population Survey Annual Social and Economic Supplement, Internet site http:// www.census.gov/hhes/www/cpstables/032013/perinc/toc.htm; calculations by New Strategist

Table 2.44 Median Income of Men by Source of Income, 2012: Non-Hispanic White Men

(number and percent of non-Hispanic white men aged 15 or older with income, and median income of those with income, 2012; men in thousands as of 2013)

	number	percent receiving	median income
Non-Hispanic white men with income	**73,240**	**100.0%**	**$38,751**
Earnings	55,332	75.5	42,749
Wages or salary	51,427	70.2	44,201
Nonfarm self-employment	5,182	7.1	22,039
Farm self-employment	1,029	1.4	3,186
Social Security	16,854	23.0	16,326
SSI (Supplemental Security)	1,338	1.8	8,406
Public Assistance	164	0.2	2,012
Veteran's benefits	1,978	2.7	9,267
Survivor's benefits	608	0.8	7,189
Disability benefits	595	0.8	11,037
Unemployment compensation	3,275	4.5	4,628
Worker's compensation	620	0.8	3,428
Property income	37,586	51.3	1,668
Interest	35,010	47.8	1,434
Dividends	14,054	19.2	1,744
Rents, royalties, estates, trusts	4,997	6.8	2,323
Retirement income	9,706	13.3	16,840
Company or union retirement	5,597	7.6	11,844
Federal government retirement	832	1.1	32,415
Military retirement	756	1.0	21,772
State or local government retirement	1,759	2.4	24,648
Railroad retirement	116	0.2	23,559
Annuities	245	0.3	7,550
IRA or Keogh, or 401(k)	417	0.6	11,958
Pension income	8,593	11.7	17,375
Company or union retirement	5,340	7.3	11,874
Federal government retirement	731	1.0	34,103
Military retirement	710	1.0	21,835
State or local government retirement	1,613	2.2	25,861
Railroad retirement	98	0.1	22,587
Annuities	119	0.2	8,971
Alimony	21	0.0	–
Child support	271	0.4	2,324
Educational assistance	2,266	3.1	4,965
Financial assistance from outside the household	655	0.9	3,745
Other income	299	0.4	1,608

Note: IRA and 401(k) income includes only withdrawals taken in the form of annuities. Non-Hispanic whites are those who identify themselves as white alone and not Hispanic. "–" means sample is too small to make a reliable estimate.
Source: Bureau of the Census, 2013 Current Population Survey Annual Social and Economic Supplement, Internet site http://www.census.gov/hhes/www/cpstables/032013/perinc/toc.htm; calculations by New Strategist

3

Women's Income

Women's incomes had been growing rapidly, but those gains came to a halt with the Great Recession. The median income of women rose 8.2 percent between 2000 and 2007, after adjusting for inflation. Between 2007 and 2012, however, most women saw their incomes decline.

Women's rising labor force participation was behind their income growth before the Great Recession. An ever-larger percentage of women were working full-time, and the educational attainment and career aspirations of those who worked full-time were also increasing. This shift can be seen in the 24 percent rise in the median income of women aged 55 to 64 between 2000 and 2007. Behind the increase was the entry of the career-oriented baby-boom generation into the age group.

The Great Recession brought an end to the tremendous growth in women's incomes. This growth masked the long-term decline in men's incomes. As the growth in women's incomes came to a halt, household incomes fell substantially and have yet to recover.

■ Because women's incomes are no longer growing, American households are struggling to maintain their standard of living.

Women's Income Trends

Women's Incomes Were Growing until the Great Recession

Women aged 65 to 74 made gains even during the 2007 to 2012 time period.

The median income of women grew by a substantial 8.2 percent between 2000 and 2007, after adjusting for inflation. Women in every age group made gains, with the biggest increase (up 24 percent) among women aged 55 to 64. Then the Great Recession set in. The median income of women fell 7.1 percent between 2007 and 2012. Women aged 65 to 74 were the only ones who continued to experience income growth during the time period, their median income rising by a substantial 7.8 percent.

Women had a median income of $21,520 in 2012, well below the $33,904 median income of men. Men's incomes are higher than women's in part because men are more likely to work full-time. Incomes peak among men aged 45 to 54 at $46,466. In 2012, women's income peak was in the 35-to-44 age group at $30,061—including both full- and part-time workers.

■ The median income of women aged 55 to 64 grew rapidly between 2000 and 2007 because career-oriented baby boomers were filling the age group.

Median income of women grew in the first part of the decade

(percent change in median income of women aged 15 or older, 2000–07 and 2007–12; in 2012 dollars)

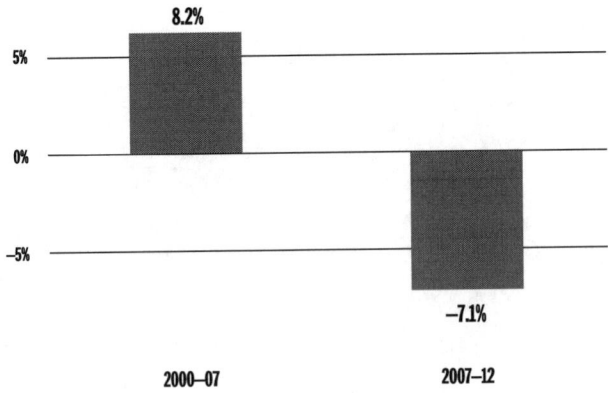

Table 3.1 Median Income of Women by Age, 2000 to 2012

(median income of women aged 15 or older with income by age, 2000 to 2012; percent change for selected years; in 2012 dollars)

	total women	15 to 24	25 to 34	35 to 44	45 to 54	55 to 64	65 or older total	65 to 74	75 or older
2012	$21,520	$9,581	$26,173	$30,061	$29,784	$26,684	$16,040	$17,236	$14,916
2011	21,543	9,297	26,260	29,703	29,055	26,465	15,683	16,818	14,895
2010	21,878	9,159	26,919	30,826	29,142	26,817	15,888	16,961	15,157
2009	22,434	9,581	27,015	29,860	30,634	26,882	16,359	17,243	15,750
2008	22,253	9,492	27,250	29,189	30,111	27,210	15,526	15,816	15,333
2007	23,169	9,921	28,664	30,677	32,616	27,975	15,527	15,993	15,168
2006	22,792	9,854	27,535	30,028	31,709	27,543	15,491	16,033	15,148
2005	21,848	9,668	26,834	29,915	31,140	26,019	14,696	15,102	14,456
2004	21,476	9,364	26,824	29,662	31,887	25,286	14,685	14,936	14,516
2003	21,547	9,282	27,455	29,303	32,292	25,428	14,788	15,160	14,524
2002	21,457	9,677	27,631	28,490	32,118	24,460	14,558	14,395	14,681
2001	21,547	9,684	27,849	29,143	31,301	23,115	14,672	14,527	14,780
2000	21,417	9,813	28,065	29,436	31,643	22,560	14,697	14,544	14,813

PERCENT CHANGE

2007 to 2012	−7.1%	−3.4%	−8.7%	−2.0%	−8.7%	−4.6%	3.3%	7.8%	−1.7%
2000 to 2007	8.2	1.1	2.1	4.2	3.1	24.0	5.6	10.0	2.4
2000 to 2012	0.5	−2.4	−6.7	2.1	−5.9	18.3	9.1	18.5	0.7

Source: Bureau of the Census, Current Population Survey, Historical Tables, Internet site http://www.census.gov/hhes/www/income/data/historical/people/; calculations by New Strategist

The Great Recession Hurt Women in Every Race and Hispanic Origin Group

All were making gains before the Great Recession.

No race or Hispanic origin group was immune from the Great Recession. The median income of Asian women fell 13 percent between 2007 and 2012, after adjusting for inflation. The median income of Hispanic women fell 10 percent, black women lost 9 percent, and non-Hispanic white women 5 percent. This was a reversal of the pattern earlier in the decade. Between 2000 and 2007, women in every race and Hispanic origin group made gains.

Among women, Hispanics have the lowest median income—just $16,725 in 2012. Asians have the highest median income, $23,290 in 2012.

■ The median income of black women was lower in 2012 than in 2000, after adjusting for inflation.

Asian women experienced the biggest income decline

(percent change in median income of women aged 15 or older, by race and Hispanic origin, 2007 to 2012; in 2012 dollars)

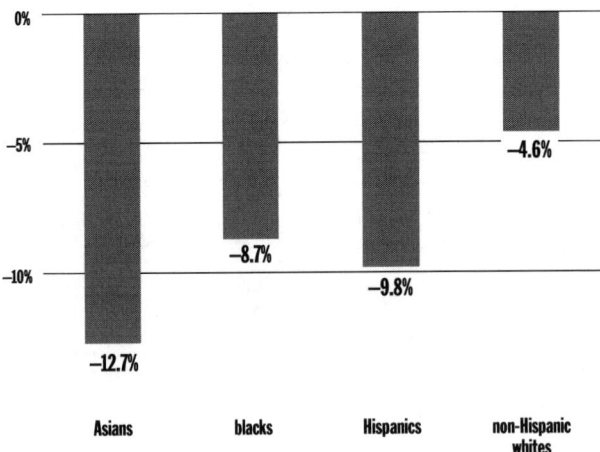

Table 3.2 Median Income of Women by Race and Hispanic Origin, 2000 to 2012

(median income of women aged 15 or older with income by race and Hispanic origin, 2000 to 2012; percent change for selected years; in 2012 dollars)

	total women	Asian	black	Hispanic	non-Hispanic white
2012	$21,520	$23,290	$19,925	$16,725	$22,902
2011	21,543	22,473	19,970	17,181	22,690
2010	21,878	24,802	20,586	17,157	22,868
2009	22,434	25,873	20,781	17,352	23,485
2008	22,253	24,544	21,545	17,507	23,193
2007	23,169	26,683	21,829	18,547	24,016
2006	22,792	25,147	21,711	17,945	23,604
2005	21,848	25,432	20,694	17,684	22,877
2004	21,476	25,060	21,087	17,567	22,409
2003	21,547	22,321	20,649	17,031	22,847
2002	21,457	22,843	21,277	17,057	22,194
2001	21,547	24,026	21,117	16,319	22,345
2000	21,417	23,141	21,175	16,331	22,220

PERCENT CHANGE

	total women	Asian	black	Hispanic	non-Hispanic white
2007 to 2012	−7.1%	−12.7%	−8.7%	−9.8%	−4.6%
2000 to 2007	8.2	15.3	3.1	13.6	8.1
2000 to 2012	0.5	0.6	−5.9	2.4	3.1

Note: Beginning in 2002, Asians and blacks are those who identify themselves as being of the race alone and those who identify themselves as being of the race in combination with other races. Hispanics may be of any race. Beginning in 2002, non-Hispanic whites are those who identify themselves as being white alone and not Hispanic.
Source: Bureau of the Census, Current Population Survey, Historical Tables, Internet site http://www.census.gov/hhes/www/ income/data/historical/people/; calculations by New Strategist

Table 3.3 Median Income of Asian Women by Age, 2002 to 2012

(median income of Asian women aged 15 or older with income by age, 2002 to 2012; percent change for selected years; in 2012 dollars)

	total Asian women	15 to 24	25 to 34	35 to 44	45 to 54	55 to 64	65 or older
2012	$23,290	$9,813	$35,504	$33,233	$31,020	$24,219	$13,134
2011	22,473	7,781	30,711	30,936	29,198	24,738	12,302
2010	24,802	7,935	32,971	33,613	31,570	28,084	12,643
2009	25,873	7,887	32,832	34,383	32,929	27,421	12,586
2008	24,544	10,990	34,612	33,743	31,275	25,124	12,365
2007	26,683	9,804	35,729	32,798	38,104	26,437	13,557
2006	25,147	10,546	33,747	35,873	30,964	25,427	12,732
2005	25,432	10,362	32,452	35,116	30,427	27,462	14,354
2004	25,060	9,417	31,867	35,089	31,909	26,538	11,637
2003	22,321	12,168	31,932	29,344	28,352	25,183	11,399
2002	22,843	9,905	28,509	29,019	31,831	26,271	11,796
PERCENT CHANGE							
2007 to 2012	−12.7%	0.1%	−0.6%	1.3%	−18.6%	−8.4%	−3.1%
2002 to 2007	16.8	−1.0	25.3	13.0	19.7	0.6	14.9
2002 to 2012	2.0	−0.9	24.5	14.5	−2.5	−7.8	11.3

Note: Asians are those who identify themselves as being of the race alone and those who identify themselves as being of the race in combination with other races.
Source: Bureau of the Census, Current Population Survey, Historical Tables, Internet site http://www.census.gov/hhes/www/income/data/historical/people/; calculations by New Strategist

Table 3.4 Median Income of Black Women by Age, 2000 to 2012

(median income of black women aged 15 or older with income by age, 2000 to 2012; percent change for selected years; in 2012 dollars)

	total black women	15 to 24	25 to 34	35 to 44	45 to 54	55 to 64	65 or older
2012	$19,925	$9,948	$21,820	$29,284	$25,182	$21,225	$14,215
2011	19,970	8,965	21,665	28,928	25,824	22,794	14,216
2010	20,586	8,952	22,881	30,408	26,286	22,535	13,827
2009	20,781	9,542	23,738	29,033	28,479	21,623	13,780
2008	21,545	9,143	23,822	29,074	27,917	22,492	13,359
2007	21,829	8,947	24,600	31,697	28,697	23,486	12,816
2006	21,711	8,896	24,522	30,157	29,468	23,488	12,619
2005	20,694	9,481	23,983	30,402	28,371	23,391	12,579
2004	21,087	8,439	25,825	29,097	29,107	22,396	12,060
2003	20,649	8,609	25,425	28,811	28,826	22,939	12,243
2002	21,277	9,081	26,214	28,261	29,356	23,157	12,098
2001	21,117	9,854	26,429	29,868	28,585	20,783	11,738
2000	21,175	9,635	27,004	29,403	29,067	19,680	11,760

PERCENT CHANGE

	total black women	15 to 24	25 to 34	35 to 44	45 to 54	55 to 64	65 or older
2007 to 2012	−8.7%	11.2%	−11.3%	−7.6%	−12.2%	−9.6%	10.9%
2000 to 2007	3.1	−7.1	−8.9	7.8	−1.3	19.3	9.0
2000 to 2012	−5.9	3.3	−19.2	−0.4	−13.4	7.9	20.9

Note: Beginning in 2002, blacks are those who identify themselves as being of the race alone and those who identify themselves as being of the race in combination with other races.
Source: Bureau of the Census, Current Population Survey, Historical Tables, Internet site http://www.census.gov/hhes/www/income/data/historical/people/; calculations by New Strategist

Table 3.5 Median Income of Hispanic Women by Age, 2000 to 2012

(median income of Hispanic women aged 15 or older with income by age, 2000 to 2012; percent change for selected years; in 2012 dollars)

	total Hispanic women	15 to 24	25 to 34	35 to 44	45 to 54	55 to 64	65 or older
2012	$16,725	$9,306	$20,312	$21,351	$21,550	$18,549	$11,046
2011	17,181	9,917	20,101	22,159	22,195	17,971	11,544
2010	17,157	9,438	21,181	22,228	21,856	17,178	11,041
2009	17,352	10,253	20,947	21,570	21,547	19,373	10,817
2008	17,507	10,192	21,337	21,698	22,003	18,741	10,600
2007	18,547	10,772	23,099	23,597	23,501	18,591	10,837
2006	17,945	11,140	21,879	22,134	23,478	18,059	10,879
2005	17,684	10,712	20,380	21,380	22,163	19,130	10,281
2004	17,567	10,605	20,746	21,924	22,177	17,271	10,927
2003	17,031	10,835	19,814	21,786	21,554	15,618	10,397
2002	17,057	10,952	20,986	21,517	21,558	15,163	9,754
2001	16,319	10,910	20,685	21,583	21,231	15,024	9,837
2000	16,331	10,305	20,393	21,404	21,471	15,708	9,920
PERCENT CHANGE							
2007 to 2012	−9.8%	−13.6%	−12.1%	−9.5%	−8.3%	−0.2%	1.9%
2000 to 2007	13.6	4.5	13.3	10.2	9.5	18.4	9.2
2000 to 2012	2.4	−9.7	−0.4	−0.2	0.4	18.1	11.4

Source: Bureau of the Census, Current Population Survey, Historical Tables, Internet site http://www.census.gov/hhes/www/ income/data/historical/people/; calculations by New Strategist

Table 3.6 Median Income of Non-Hispanic White Women by Age, 2000 to 2012

(median income of non-Hispanic white women aged 15 or older with income by age, 2000 to 2012; percent change for selected years; in 2012 dollars)

	total non-Hispanic white women	15 to 24	25 to 34	35 to 44	45 to 54	55 to 64	65 or older
2012	$22,902	$9,598	$28,974	$31,963	$31,753	$29,524	$16,851
2011	22,690	9,418	29,391	32,116	31,745	28,362	16,532
2010	22,868	9,204	29,883	32,907	32,062	28,489	16,740
2009	23,485	9,545	28,991	32,815	32,942	28,562	17,372
2008	23,193	9,379	29,123	31,918	32,491	28,736	16,398
2007	24,016	10,034	30,442	32,915	34,236	29,671	16,307
2006	23,604	9,706	29,867	31,502	34,541	29,322	16,361
2005	22,877	9,449	29,419	31,128	33,860	27,608	15,455
2004	22,409	9,416	29,280	31,143	33,551	26,367	15,413
2003	22,847	9,223	30,238	31,369	34,100	26,792	15,569
2002	22,194	9,686	29,860	30,229	33,677	25,539	15,285
2001	22,345	9,504	30,313	30,751	33,275	24,389	15,471
2000	22,220	9,753	29,948	30,963	33,743	23,820	15,505

PERCENT CHANGE

2007 to 2012	−4.6%	−4.3%	−4.8%	−2.9%	−7.3%	−0.5%	3.3%
2000 to 2007	8.1	2.9	1.6	6.3	1.5	24.6	5.2
2000 to 2012	3.1	−1.6	−3.3	3.2	−5.9	23.9	8.7

Note: Beginning in 2002, data are for those who identify themselves as being white alone and not Hispanic.
Source: Bureau of the Census, Current Population Survey, Historical Tables, Internet site http://www.census.gov/hhes/www/income/data/historical/people/; calculations by New Strategist

Women in Every Region Lost Ground between 2007 and 2012

Women's incomes were growing between 2000 and 2007.

Between 2000 and 2007, women's median income grew in every region, after adjusting for inflation. The smallest increase was in the Midwest, with a 3.6 percent rise. In the other regions, the gains ranged from 9 to 11 percent.

Between 2007 and 2012, women's median income fell in every region, after adjusting for inflation. The decline was greatest in the West, where women's median income dropped by 12.1 percent. The decline was smallest in the Midwest, a 3.8 percent loss.

■ Women's median income does not vary much by region.

Between 2007 and 2012, women's median income fell the most in the West

(percent change in median income of women aged 15 or older by region, 2007 to 2012; in 2012 dollars)

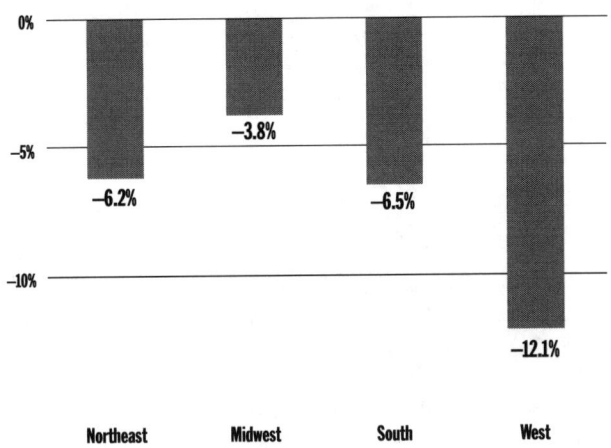

Table 3.7 Median Income of Women by Region, 2000 to 2012

(median income of women aged 15 or older with income by region, 2000 to 2012; percent change for selected years; in 2012 dollars)

	total women	Northeast	Midwest	South	West
2012	$21,520	$22,539	$21,900	$21,049	$21,086
2011	21,543	22,328	21,296	21,265	21,652
2010	21,878	22,556	21,819	21,600	21,870
2009	22,434	23,622	22,466	21,689	22,620
2008	22,253	23,386	22,200	21,463	22,830
2007	23,169	24,020	22,765	22,521	24,000
2006	22,792	23,100	22,941	21,961	23,431
2005	21,848	22,896	22,179	21,183	21,840
2004	21,476	22,241	21,750	20,869	21,828
2003	21,547	22,411	21,845	20,803	21,846
2002	21,457	22,007	21,596	20,706	22,058
2001	21,547	22,136	21,900	20,656	22,022
2000	21,439	21,735	21,977	20,704	21,844
PERCENT CHANGE					
2007 to 2012	−7.1%	−6.2%	−3.8%	−6.5%	−12.1%
2000 to 2007	8.1	10.5	3.6	8.8	9.9
2000 to 2012	0.4	3.7	−0.4	1.7	−3.5

Source: Bureau of the Census, Current Population Survey, Historical Tables, Internet site http://www.census.gov/hhes/www/income/data/historical/people/; calculations by New Strategist

Earnings Have Declined among Women Who Work Full-Time

The Great Recession halted the growth in women's earnings.

Women who work full-time, year-round, saw their median earnings rise 6 percent between 2000 and 2007, after adjusting for inflation. This increase dwarfed the 0.6 percent rise in the earnings of their male counterparts during that time period. This pattern shifted once the Great Recession set in.

Between 2007 and 2012, women who work full-time, year-round saw their median earnings fall by 2.8 percent, after adjusting for inflation. Among their male counterparts, earnings fell by a smaller 1.1 percent. Consequently, progress in closing the earnings gap between women and men has stopped.

■ Women's earnings are no longer sheltering households from economic decline.

Among women with full-time jobs, earnings grew then fell

(median earnings of women aged 15 or older who work full-time, year-round, 2000, 2007, and 2012; in 2012 dollars)

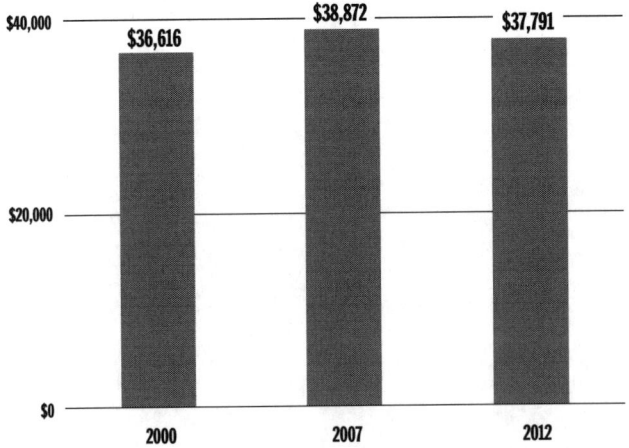

Table 3.8 Median Earnings of Women by Employment Status, 2000 to 2012

(median earnings of women aged 15 or older with earnings by employment status, 2000 to 2012; percent change for selected years; in 2012 dollars)

	total women with earnings	worked full-time		worked part-time	
		total	year-round	total	year-round
2012	$26,882	$35,388	$37,791	$10,120	$14,478
2011	27,105	35,604	37,893	10,244	14,027
2010	27,910	36,057	38,846	10,303	14,521
2009	27,864	34,923	38,835	10,196	13,691
2008	27,354	34,196	38,119	9,693	13,558
2007	28,657	35,269	38,872	9,930	13,900
2006	27,862	35,067	37,028	10,044	14,193
2005	27,138	35,321	37,470	9,369	14,432
2004	27,054	34,948	37,975	9,097	14,203
2003	27,470	34,651	38,357	9,437	14,500
2002	27,350	34,497	38,548	9,321	14,620
2001	27,042	34,157	37,890	9,158	14,348
2000	27,023	33,969	36,616	8,840	14,164
PERCENT CHANGE					
2007 to 2012	–6.2%	0.3%	–2.8%	1.9%	4.2%
2000 to 2007	6.0	3.8	6.2	12.3	–1.9
2000 to 2012	–0.5	4.2	3.2	14.5	2.2

Note: Earnings include wages and salaries only.

Source: Bureau of the Census, Current Population Survey, Historical Tables, Internet site http://www.census.gov/hhes/www/income/data/historical/people/; calculations by New Strategist

Among Full-Time Workers, Asian and Non-Hispanic White Women Made Gains

The earnings of black and Hispanic women who work full-time fell between 2007 and 2012.

Among women who work full-time, every racial and ethnic group saw their earnings grow between 2000 and 2007, after adjusting for inflation. The increase ranged from a low of 3 percent among black women to a high of 10 percent among Asian women.

Between 2007 and 2012, the median earnings of black and Hispanic women who work full-time fell, while the earnings of Asian and non-Hispanic white women continued to grow. Asian women who work full-time had the highest median earnings in 2012, at $45,439. Hispanic women had the lowest earnings, a median of $28,424.

■ The earnings of Asian women are above average because most are college graduates. The earnings of Hispanic women are below average because many are poorly educated.

Hispanic women experienced the biggest earnings decline

(percent change in median earnings of women aged 15 or older who work full-time, year-round, by race and Hispanic origin, 2007 to 2012; in 2012 dollars)

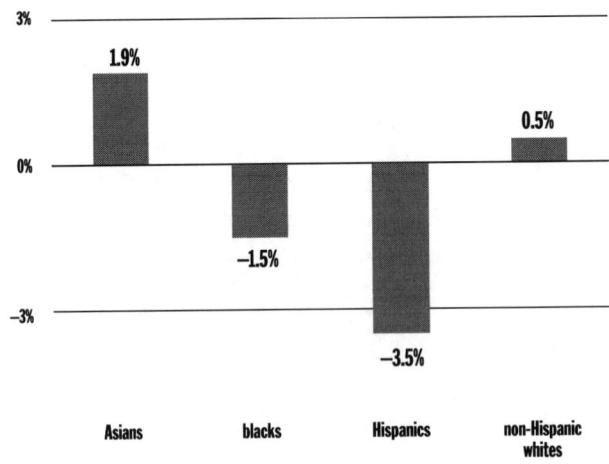

Table 3.9 Median Earnings of Women Who Work Full-Time by Race and Hispanic Origin, 2000 to 2012

(median earnings of women aged 15 or older who work full-time, year-round, by race and Hispanic origin, 2000 to 2012; percent change for selected years; in 2012 dollars)

	total women working full-time	Asian	black	Hispanic	non-Hispanic white
2012	$37,791	$45,439	$33,903	$28,424	$40,912
2011	37,893	41,892	34,077	29,626	41,178
2010	38,846	43,313	33,998	29,678	42,426
2009	38,835	45,358	34,145	29,097	41,249
2008	38,119	44,989	33,602	28,629	39,872
2007	38,872	44,599	34,405	29,470	40,691
2006	37,028	45,014	34,622	28,696	40,694
2005	37,470	42,318	34,908	28,479	40,123
2004	37,975	43,639	33,770	28,536	39,538
2003	38,357	40,506	33,694	27,919	40,020
2002	38,548	40,153	34,348	27,964	40,079
2001	37,890	39,796	34,492	27,875	39,947
2000	36,616	40,633	33,452	27,545	39,783
PERCENT CHANGE					
2007 to 2012	−2.8%	1.9%	−1.5%	−3.5%	0.5%
2000 to 2007	6.2	9.8	2.9	7.0	2.3
2000 to 2012	3.2	11.8	1.3	3.2	2.8

Note: Beginning in 2002, Asians and blacks are those who identify themselves as being of the race alone and those who identify themselves as being of the race in combination with other races. Hispanics may be of any race. Beginning in 2002, non-Hispanic whites are those who identify themselves as being white alone and not Hispanic. Earnings include wages and salaries only.

Source: Bureau of the Census, Current Population Survey, Historical Tables, Internet site http://www.census.gov/hhes/www/income/data/historical/people/; calculations by New Strategist

Education Does Not Guarantee Earnings Growth

Women with a bachelor's degree who work full-time had lower earnings in 2012 than in 2000.

Between 2000 and 2012, the median earnings of women aged 25 or older who work full-time, year-round, increased by 2.8 percent, after adjusting for inflation. But among women with at least a bachelor's degree, median earnings in 2012 were 2.7 percent lower than in 2000. Among women with less education, the earnings decline ranged from 3.3 to 8.8 percent.

The decline in the earnings of educated women who work full-time began well before the Great Recession. In the 2000-to-2007 time period, women with a bachelor's degree who worked full-time saw their median earnings fall by 1.1 percent. The Great Recession added to the loss, with another 1.0 percent decline between 2007 and 2012. Women with a professional or doctoral degree were the only ones who made gains in the 2007-to-2012 time period.

■ Despite the decline in earnings, the premium paid to college graduates is holding steady.

Among women, the premium paid to college graduates held steady

(median earnings of women aged 25 or older who work full-time, year-round, by selected educational attainment, 2000 and 2012; in 2012 dollars)

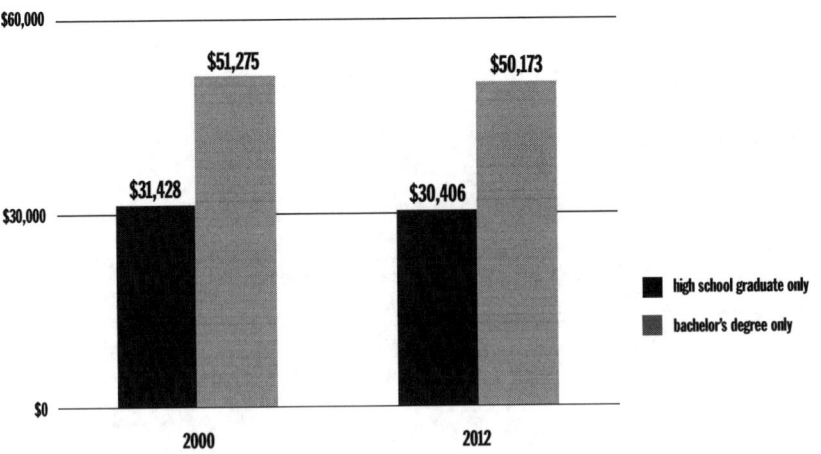

high school graduate only
bachelor's degree only

Table 3.10 Median Earnings of Women Who Work Full-Time by Education, 2000 to 2012

(median earnings of women aged 25 or older who work full-time, year-round, by educational attainment, 2000 to 2012; percent change for selected years; in 2012 dollars)

	total women	less than 9th grade	9th to 12th grade, no diploma	high school graduate	some college	associate's degree	bachelor's degree or more				
							total	bachelor's degree	master's degree	professional degree	doctoral degree
2012	$39,977	$20,060	$21,387	$30,406	$35,058	$37,321	$53,686	$50,173	$60,927	$94,473	$77,902
2011	39,722	20,522	21,554	30,638	35,315	40,107	53,225	50,134	61,564	82,404	79,076
2010	40,205	19,170	21,942	31,427	35,246	39,732	54,726	49,966	62,443	80,942	81,540
2009	39,890	19,782	22,722	31,204	36,489	39,893	55,534	50,133	65,372	89,818	81,978
2008	39,134	19,872	21,760	30,267	34,793	39,201	54,823	50,149	61,332	76,032	78,941
2007	39,961	20,222	22,589	30,165	36,363	40,235	55,810	50,689	61,378	78,733	76,398
2006	39,966	20,650	22,924	30,448	36,389	40,039	56,452	51,711	59,717	86,825	80,307
2005	38,901	18,985	23,670	30,920	36,930	39,917	55,218	49,600	60,468	94,630	78,627
2004	38,908	20,683	23,299	31,660	37,466	40,708	55,840	50,693	62,382	91,290	83,129
2003	39,407	21,107	23,643	32,551	37,630	40,266	56,324	51,594	62,625	83,009	83,912
2002	39,578	21,072	24,642	32,140	37,523	40,363	55,194	52,141	62,399	72,772	83,872
2001	39,486	20,971	23,263	31,408	37,402	40,456	54,530	51,641	62,610	77,936	78,367
2000	38,895	20,829	22,915	31,428	36,405	40,935	55,187	51,275	62,649	80,641	76,468

PERCENT CHANGE

2007 to 2012	0.0%	−0.8%	−5.3%	0.8%	−3.6%	−7.2%	−3.8%	−1.0%	−0.7%	20.0%	2.0%
2000 to 2007	2.7	−2.9	−1.4	−4.0	−0.1	−1.7	1.1	−1.1	−2.0	−2.4	−0.1
2000 to 2012	2.8	−3.7	−6.7	−3.3	−3.7	−8.8	−2.7	−2.1	−2.7	17.2	1.9

Note: Earnings include wages and salaries only.
Source: Bureau of the Census, Current Population Survey, Historical Tables, Internet site http://www.census.gov/hhes/www/income/data/historical/people/; calculations by New Strategist

Women in Most Occupations Have Seen Their Earnings Decline

Some women have gained ground, however.

Among women who work full-time, year-round, median earnings fell 2.8 percent between 2007 and 2012, after adjusting for inflation. Only two occupational groups saw earnings grow during the time period. Women in protective services experienced the biggest gain—up 8.9 percent. The median earnings of women in office and administrative support occupations climbed 0.9 percent.

The biggest earnings decline occurred among the few women who work in construction and extraction occupations—a 38 percent decline in median earnings between 2007 and 2012, after adjusting for inflation. The few women in farming, fishing, and forestry occupations saw their median earnings fall by 23 percent. In the occupations in which many women work, the decline in median earnings was smaller. Among women who work in health care support occupations, median earnings fell 3.4 percent.

■ Women in professional occupations had fairly stable earnings, with a decline of just 0.3 percent between 2007 and 2012, after adjusting for inflation.

Women's median earnings fell in most occupations

(percent change in median earnings of women aged 15 or older who work full-time, year-round, by selected occupation, 2007 to 2012; in 2012 dollars)

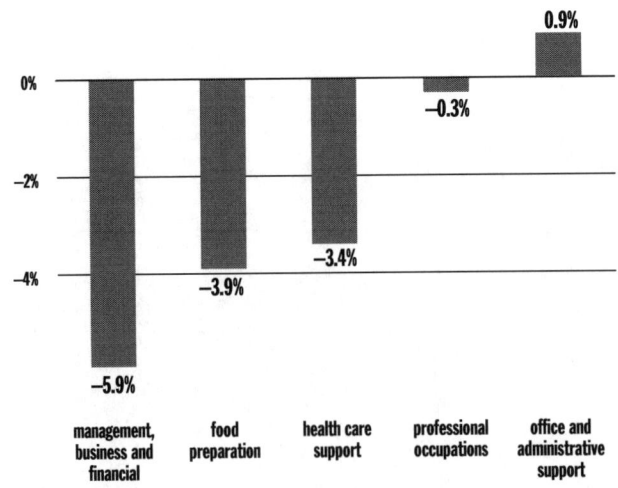

Table 3.11 Median Earnings of Women Who Work Full-Time by Occupation, 2007 to 2012

(median earnings of women aged 15 or older who work full-time, year-round, by occupation of longest job held, 2007 to 2012; percent change, 2007–12; in 2012 dollars)

	2012	2010	2007	percent change 2007–12
Total women who work full-time	**$37,791**	**$38,846**	**$38,872**	**−2.8%**
Management, business and financial occupations	52,438	55,026	55,705	−5.9
Professional and related occupations	50,605	51,875	50,765	−0.3
Health care support occupations	26,624	27,734	27,551	−3.4
Protective service occupations	42,215	41,362	38,771	8.9
Food preparation occupations	20,739	20,354	21,582	−3.9
Building and grounds occupations	21,078	21,782	21,834	−3.5
Personal care and service occupations	22,824	23,329	24,684	−7.5
Sales and related occupations	30,495	32,564	31,762	−4.0
Office and administrative support occupations	35,084	34,420	34,782	0.9
Farming, fishing, and forestry occupations	20,587	21,746	26,685	−22.9
Construction and extraction occupations	27,494	33,546	44,599	−38.4
Installation, maintenance, and repair occupations	42,773	43,577	46,370	−7.8
Production occupations	27,324	27,035	28,509	−4.2
Transportation and material moving occupations	27,511	26,357	30,048	−8.4
Armed Forces	–	53,542	–	–

Note: Earnings include wages and salaries only. "–" means data are not available.
Source: Bureau of the Census, Current Population Survey, Historical Tables, Internet site http://www.census.gov/hhes/www/ income/data/historical/people/; calculations by New Strategist

Women Lost Ground during the Great Recession

Women's earnings fell more than men's between 2007 and 2012.

Among those who worked full-time, year-round in 2012, men's median earnings stood at $49,398. Among their female counterparts, median earnings were a smaller $37,791—or 77 percent as high as men's. The earnings gap between women and men narrowed somewhat between 2000 and 2007, but since then women have made no progress.

The earnings gap between women and men had been closing because women's earnings were growing faster than men's. Among full-time workers, women's median earnings grew 6 percent between 2000 and 2007, after adjusting for inflation. Men's earnings grew by a tiny 0.6 percent during those years. Between 2007 and 2012, however, women's earnings fell 2.8 percent, which was more than double the 1.1 percent loss experienced by men.

■ With women's earnings declining, households are feeling the pinch.

Earnings gap between women and men is no longer narrowing

(women's median earnings as a percent of men's median earnings among full-time, year-round workers, 2000 to 2012)

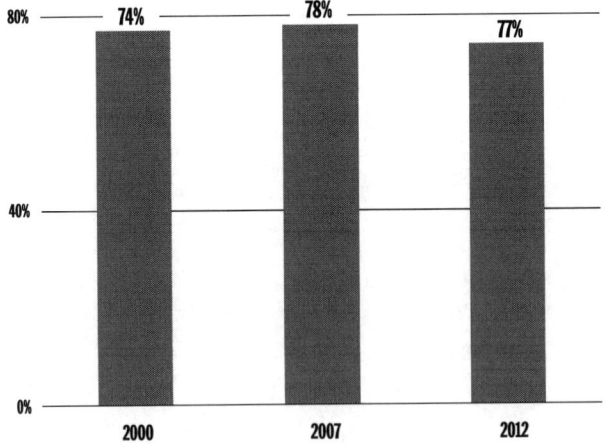

Table 3.12 Median Earnings of Full-Time Workers by Sex, 2000 to 2012

(median earnings of people aged 15 or older who work full-time, year-round, by sex, and and women's earnings as a percent of men's earnings, 2000 to 2012; percent change for selected years; in 2012 dollars)

	men	women	women's earnings as a percent of men's
2012	$49,398	$37,791	77%
2011	49,209	37,893	77
2010	50,497	38,846	77
2009	50,448	38,835	77
2008	49,446	38,119	77
2007	49,958	38,872	78
2006	48,127	37,028	77
2005	48,676	37,470	77
2004	49,591	37,975	77
2003	50,771	38,357	76
2002	50,323	38,548	77
2001	49,640	37,890	76
2000	49,669	36,616	74
PERCENT CHANGE			
2007 to 2012	–1.1%	–2.8%	–
2000 to 2007	0.6	6.2	–
2000 to 2012	–0.5	3.2	–

Note: Earnings include wages and salaries only. "–" means not applicable.
Source: Bureau of the Census, Historical Income Data, Internet site http://www.census.gov/hhes/www/income/; calculations by New Strategist

Nine Million Wives Earn More than Their Husbands

Nearly 3 out of 10 wives are the primary breadwinner.

Among the nation's 32 million dual-earner couples, 9 million wives earn more than their husbands—accounting for a substantial 29 percent of all dual-earner couples. The percentage of couples in which the wife earns more than the husband grew strongly during the past few years, in part because of the Great Recession. Between 2000 and 2007, the share of dual-earner couples in which the wife earns more than the husband climbed 2.5 percentage points. Between 2007 and 2012, it grew by a larger 3.2 percentage points.

In 2012, only 53 percent of married couples were dual-earners, down from 60 percent in 2000. Behind the decline is the aging of the population as well as unemployment during the Great Recession, which turned dual-earners into single-earner or even no-earner households.

■ The incomes of working wives are critical to family well-being, especially when husbands are unemployed.

A growing percentage of wives are earning more than their husbands

(percent of dual-earner couples in which the wife earns more than the husband, 2000 and 2012)

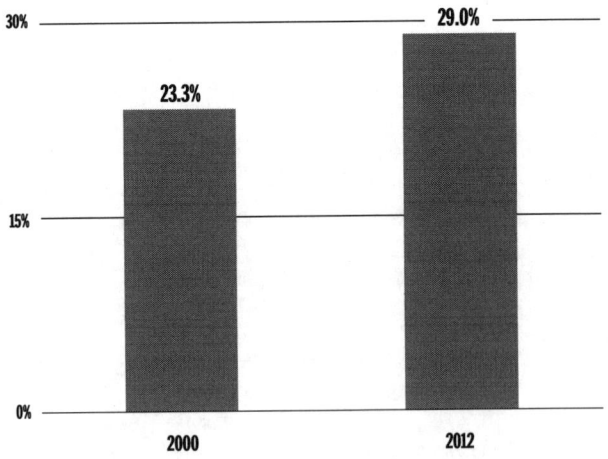

Table 3.13 Wives Who Earn More than Their Husbands, 2000 to 2012

(number of married couples, dual-earner couples, and wives who earn more than their husbands, and wives who earn more than their husbands as a percent of all dual-earner couples, 2000 to 2012; couples in thousands as of the following year)

	total married couples	dual-earner couples	wives who earn more than their husbands	percent of dual-earner couples with wives earning more
2012	59,224	31,549	9,137	29.0%
2011	58,963	31,165	8,755	28.1
2010	58,667	31,573	9,215	29.2
2009	58,428	32,285	9,291	28.8
2008	59,137	33,905	9,002	26.6
2007	58,395	33,678	8,700	25.8
2006	58,964	33,838	8,688	25.7
2005	58,189	33,364	8,521	25.5
2004	57,983	33,110	8,387	25.3
2003	57,725	33,189	8,355	25.2
2002	57,327	33,531	8,394	25.0
2001	56,755	33,666	8,109	24.1
2000	56,598	33,876	7,906	23.3

Source: Bureau of the Census, Current Population Survey, Historical Tables, Internet site http://www.census.gov/hhes/www/income/data/historical/families/; calculations by New Strategist

Women's Income, 2012

Women's Incomes Peak in the 35-to-44 Age Group

Among full-time workers, however, income peaks among older women.

The incomes of women peak in the 35-to-44 age group, at $30,061 in 2012—40 percent greater than the $21,520 median of all women aged 15 or older. Among full-time workers aged 35 to 44, median income was a much larger $41,682, and it was an even higher $46,718 among women aged 65 or older who work full-time. Only 7 percent of women aged 65 or older are full-time workers, however.

Asian women are most likely to work full time, with 37 percent doing so in 2012. Hispanic women are least likely to be full-time workers, at 31 percent. Among women who work full-time, the median income of black women stood at $35,105, substantially more than the $29,508 of their Hispanic counterparts. Asian women who work full-time have the highest incomes, a median of $46,241, while their non-Hispanic white counterparts have a median income of $42,171.

■ Asian women have higher incomes than others because they are most likely to be college graduates.

Among women who work full-time, incomes peak in the older age groups

(median income of women aged 15 or older who work full-time, year-round, by age, 2012)

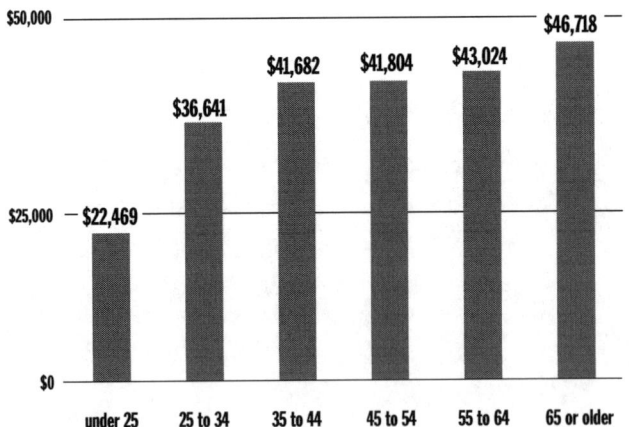

Table 3.14 Women by Income and Age, 2012: Total Women

(number and percent distribution of women aged 15 or older by income and age, 2012; median income of women with income and of women working full-time, year-round; percent working full-time, year-round; women in thousands as of 2013)

	total	15 to 24	25 to 34	35 to 44	45 to 54	55 to 64	65 or older total	65 to 74	75 or older
Total women	**128,912**	**21,318**	**20,981**	**20,254**	**22,202**	**20,168**	**23,990**	**13,098**	**10,892**
Without income	19,529	8,191	3,165	2,712	2,445	2,071	945	561	384
With income	109,383	13,127	17,815	17,542	19,757	18,097	23,045	12,537	10,508
Under $5,000	12,544	4,186	1,877	1,872	1,806	1,632	1,171	599	571
$5,000 to $9,999	13,589	2,553	1,628	1,381	1,722	1,885	4,420	2,185	2,235
$10,000 to $14,999	13,957	1,926	1,727	1,452	1,758	2,025	5,070	2,581	2,489
$15,000 to $19,999	10,988	1,437	1,601	1,410	1,547	1,408	3,585	1,662	1,923
$20,000 to $24,999	9,643	1,067	1,628	1,442	1,718	1,588	2,200	1,149	1,052
$25,000 to $29,999	7,488	678	1,528	1,193	1,367	1,225	1,497	844	654
$30,000 to $34,999	6,840	396	1,455	1,241	1,450	1,242	1,056	663	393
$35,000 to $39,999	5,504	244	1,271	1,125	1,186	952	725	506	219
$40,000 to $44,999	4,849	207	988	1,029	1,110	879	637	391	246
$45,000 to $49,999	3,756	146	834	774	824	748	430	287	143
$50,000 to $54,999	3,687	84	778	826	886	668	445	306	140
$55,000 to $59,999	2,223	58	410	528	513	453	261	194	67
$60,000 to $64,999	2,496	32	405	565	612	588	295	224	71
$65,000 to $69,999	1,688	36	333	391	355	351	221	158	63
$70,000 to $74,999	1,677	17	223	400	499	373	166	122	44
$75,000 to $79,999	1,193	8	239	219	331	278	118	92	26
$80,000 to $84,999	1,144	1	144	235	336	301	126	97	29
$85,000 to $89,999	698	6	99	163	171	165	94	69	25
$90,000 to $94,999	735	4	118	157	203	183	71	59	12
$95,000 to $99,999	488	4	67	118	129	115	55	48	7
$100,000 or more	4,196	38	462	1,023	1,233	1,039	401	300	101

MEDIAN INCOME

	total	15 to 24	25 to 34	35 to 44	45 to 54	55 to 64	65 or older total	65 to 74	75 or older
Women with income	$21,520	$9,581	$26,173	$30,061	$29,784	$26,684	$16,040	$17,236	$14,916
Women working full-time	40,019	22,469	36,641	41,682	41,804	43,024	46,718	47,957	41,357
Percent working full-time	34.2%	12.8%	47.0%	49.7%	51.4%	41.4%	6.9%	10.8%	2.2%

PERCENT DISTRIBUTION

	total	15 to 24	25 to 34	35 to 44	45 to 54	55 to 64	65 or older total	65 to 74	75 or older
Total women	**100.0%**	**100.0%**	**100.0%**	**100.0%**	**100.0%**	**100.0%**	**100.0%**	**100.0%**	**100.0%**
Without income	15.1	38.4	15.1	13.4	11.0	10.3	3.9	4.3	3.5
With income	84.9	61.6	84.9	86.6	89.0	89.7	96.1	95.7	96.5
Under $15,000	31.1	40.6	24.9	23.2	23.8	27.5	44.4	41.0	48.6
$15,000 to $24,999	16.0	11.7	15.4	14.1	14.7	14.9	24.1	21.5	27.3
$25,000 to $34,999	11.1	5.0	14.2	12.0	12.7	12.2	10.6	11.5	9.6
$35,000 to $49,999	10.9	2.8	14.7	14.5	14.1	12.8	7.5	9.0	5.6
$50,000 to $74,999	9.1	1.1	10.2	13.4	12.9	12.1	5.8	7.7	3.5
$75,000 to $99,999	3.3	0.1	3.2	4.4	5.3	5.2	1.9	2.8	0.9
$100,000 or more	3.3	0.2	2.2	5.0	5.6	5.2	1.7	2.3	0.9

Source: Bureau of the Census, 2013 Current Population Survey Annual Social and Economic Supplement, Internet site http:// www.census.gov/hhes/www/cpstables/032013/perinc/toc.htm; calculations by New Strategist

Table 3.15 Women by Income and Age, 2012: Asian Women

(number and percent distribution of Asian women aged 15 or older by income and age, 2012; median income of women with income and of women working full-time, year-round; percent working full-time, year-round; women in thousands as of 2013)

	total	15 to 24	25 to 34	35 to 44	45 to 54	55 to 64	65 or older total	65 to 74	75 or older
Total Asian women	7,649	1,333	1,545	1,531	1,245	1,027	968	558	410
Without income	1,677	553	339	261	222	177	126	82	44
With income	5,972	781	1,206	1,270	1,022	851	842	475	367
Under $5,000	820	253	125	171	113	93	65	45	20
$5,000 to $9,999	726	142	69	92	79	96	249	113	136
$10,000 to $14,999	567	109	74	67	75	89	153	81	72
$15,000 to $19,999	502	81	77	94	76	72	101	49	52
$20,000 to $24,999	483	51	87	110	83	86	66	37	29
$25,000 to $29,999	323	44	75	55	72	42	35	21	15
$30,000 to $34,999	291	22	87	53	53	44	31	24	7
$35,000 to $39,999	267	16	66	56	63	45	21	16	5
$40,000 to $44,999	256	18	63	60	44	44	27	22	4
$45,000 to $49,999	218	17	75	54	33	32	7	6	1
$50,000 to $54,999	207	8	68	41	48	31	10	3	8
$55,000 to $59,999	138	1	34	40	37	15	10	6	5
$60,000 to $64,999	193	5	40	64	36	39	9	6	2
$65,000 to $69,999	118	6	52	28	14	13	6	6	0
$70,000 to $74,999	111	4	30	38	18	15	6	6	1
$75,000 to $79,999	77	0	26	18	20	6	7	6	1
$80,000 to $84,999	79	0	17	16	29	13	5	2	3
$85,000 to $89,999	48	0	15	14	5	7	6	4	2
$90,000 to $94,999	74	1	16	29	14	13	0	0	0
$95,000 to $99,999	49	0	16	8	18	6	1	0	0
$100,000 or more	426	4	94	163	92	48	25	21	4

MEDIAN INCOME

	total	15 to 24	25 to 34	35 to 44	45 to 54	55 to 64	65 or older total	65 to 74	75 or older
Women with income	$23,290	$9,813	$35,504	$33,233	$31,020	$24,219	$13,134	$14,921	$11,546
Women working full-time	46,241	25,574	50,553	52,058	45,098	40,256	43,425	42,289	–
Percent working full-time	36.6%	10.6%	45.9%	50.7%	52.1%	41.8%	10.3%	16.2%	2.3%

PERCENT DISTRIBUTION

	total	15 to 24	25 to 34	35 to 44	45 to 54	55 to 64	65 or older total	65 to 74	75 or older
Total Asian women	100.0%	100.0%	100.0%	100.0%	100.0%	100.0%	100.0%	100.0%	100.0%
Without income	21.9	41.4	22.0	17.0	17.9	17.2	13.0	14.7	10.6
With income	78.1	58.6	78.0	83.0	82.1	82.8	87.0	85.3	89.4
Under $15,000	27.6	37.8	17.3	21.5	21.4	27.1	48.3	42.8	55.7
$15,000 to $24,999	12.9	9.9	10.6	13.3	12.8	15.4	17.2	15.4	19.6
$25,000 to $34,999	8.0	5.0	10.5	7.0	10.0	8.4	6.9	8.0	5.4
$35,000 to $49,999	9.7	3.8	13.2	11.1	11.2	11.8	5.6	8.0	2.4
$50,000 to $74,999	10.0	1.7	14.5	13.8	12.3	11.0	4.3	4.8	3.7
$75,000 to $99,999	4.3	0.1	5.8	5.6	7.0	4.4	2.0	2.4	1.5
$100,000 or more	5.6	0.3	6.1	10.6	7.4	4.7	2.6	3.8	1.0

Note: Asians are those who identify themselves as being of the race alone and those who identify themselves as being of the race in combination with other races. "–" means sample is too small to make a reliable estimate.
Source: Bureau of the Census, 2013 Current Population Survey Annual Social and Economic Supplement, Internet site http:// www.census.gov/hhes/www/cpstables/032013/perinc/toc.htm; calculations by New Strategist

Table 3.16 Women by Income and Age, 2012: Black Women

(number and percent distribution of black women aged 15 or older by income and age, 2012; median income of women with income and of women working full-time, year-round; percent working full-time, year-round; women in thousands as of 2013)

	total	15 to 24	25 to 34	35 to 44	45 to 54	55 to 64	65 or older total	65 to 74	75 or older
Total black women	17,837	3,744	3,232	2,998	3,048	2,486	2,328	1,337	991
Without income	3,115	1,595	429	333	295	310	153	80	73
With income	14,722	2,149	2,803	2,666	2,753	2,176	2,176	1,257	918
Under $5,000	1,523	624	280	162	201	131	123	48	75
$5,000 to $9,999	2,214	455	324	236	363	356	480	233	248
$10,000 to $14,999	2,085	326	339	268	283	315	554	298	256
$15,000 to $19,999	1,558	259	307	248	250	221	274	163	111
$20,000 to $24,999	1,396	173	319	250	270	205	179	102	77
$25,000 to $29,999	1,039	91	279	190	193	137	150	98	52
$30,000 to $34,999	990	62	228	233	215	147	106	65	40
$35,000 to $39,999	782	38	204	216	188	76	59	42	17
$40,000 to $44,999	608	45	127	153	139	94	51	39	12
$45,000 to $49,999	471	27	94	132	107	72	38	35	3
$50,000 to $54,999	418	25	70	119	98	78	29	21	8
$55,000 to $59,999	281	4	55	91	60	46	25	24	1
$60,000 to $64,999	252	5	28	64	78	59	18	17	1
$65,000 to $69,999	184	0	30	42	57	46	8	6	2
$70,000 to $74,999	162	1	29	45	38	34	15	11	4
$75,000 to $79,999	111	0	22	29	32	23	4	3	2
$80,000 to $84,999	125	0	17	28	34	35	12	10	2
$85,000 to $89,999	79	4	5	36	22	9	2	2	0
$90,000 to $94,999	73	0	8	19	21	19	5	3	2
$95,000 to $99,999	48	0	6	17	12	9	5	5	0
$100,000 or more	324	11	33	88	91	62	38	32	6

MEDIAN INCOME

	total	15 to 24	25 to 34	35 to 44	45 to 54	55 to 64	65 or older total	65 to 74	75 or older
Women with income	$19,925	$9,948	$21,820	$29,284	$25,182	$21,225	$14,215	$16,211	$12,209
Women working full-time	35,105	22,384	31,846	37,338	36,472	39,705	41,496	43,443	–
Percent working full-time	35.0%	12.8%	44.0%	54.8%	52.4%	37.1%	8.0%	11.8%	2.7%

PERCENT DISTRIBUTION

	total	15 to 24	25 to 34	35 to 44	45 to 54	55 to 64	65 or older total	65 to 74	75 or older
Total black women	100.0%	100.0%	100.0%	100.0%	100.0%	100.0%	100.0%	100.0%	100.0%
Without income	17.5	42.6	13.3	11.1	9.7	12.5	6.6	6.0	7.4
With income	82.5	57.4	86.7	88.9	90.3	87.5	93.4	94.0	92.6
Under $15,000	32.6	37.5	29.2	22.2	27.8	32.3	49.7	43.3	58.4
$15,000 to $24,999	16.6	11.5	19.4	16.6	17.1	17.2	19.4	19.8	18.9
$25,000 to $34,999	11.4	4.1	15.7	14.1	13.4	11.4	11.0	12.2	9.3
$35,000 to $49,999	10.4	2.9	13.1	16.7	14.2	9.7	6.4	8.6	3.3
$50,000 to $74,999	7.3	0.9	6.6	12.1	10.8	10.6	4.1	5.9	1.6
$75,000 to $99,999	2.4	0.1	1.8	4.3	4.0	3.8	1.2	1.7	0.5
$100,000 or more	1.8	0.3	1.0	2.9	3.0	2.5	1.6	2.4	0.6

Note: Blacks are those who identify themselves as being of the race alone and those who identify themselves as being of the race in combination with other races. "–" means sample is too small to make a reliable estimate.
Source: Bureau of the Census, 2013 Current Population Survey Annual Social and Economic Supplement, Internet site http://www.census.gov/hhes/www/cpstables/032013/perinc/toc.htm; calculations by New Strategist

Table 3.17 Women by Income and Age, 2012: Hispanic Women

(number and percent distribution of Hispanic women aged 15 or older by income and age, 2012; median income of women with income and of women working full-time, year-round; percent working full-time, year-round; women in thousands as of 2013)

	total	15 to 24	25 to 34	35 to 44	45 to 54	55 to 64	65 or older total	65 to 74	75 or older
Total Hispanic women	**19,039**	**4,409**	**4,105**	**3,767**	**2,976**	**1,948**	**1,835**	**1,080**	**755**
Without income	5,350	2,103	1,081	906	603	443	215	121	94
With income	13,689	2,306	3,024	2,861	2,373	1,505	1,620	959	661
Under $5,000	1,896	706	347	304	220	153	166	112	55
$5,000 to $9,999	2,170	503	353	256	280	254	524	302	222
$10,000 to $14,999	2,110	345	407	385	300	230	443	227	216
$15,000 to $19,999	1,602	275	378	378	265	153	152	90	62
$20,000 to $24,999	1,411	208	335	318	300	154	96	61	35
$25,000 to $29,999	939	117	279	219	171	105	48	28	20
$30,000 to $34,999	771	54	194	206	178	100	38	23	15
$35,000 to $39,999	585	46	169	165	120	63	23	13	10
$40,000 to $44,999	442	21	143	127	89	37	26	14	12
$45,000 to $49,999	350	10	105	87	89	45	14	12	2
$50,000 to $54,999	333	5	83	96	78	45	26	22	3
$55,000 to $59,999	202	10	61	54	48	17	12	12	0
$60,000 to $64,999	187	2	53	43	48	34	8	5	3
$65,000 to $69,999	91	2	24	31	19	8	7	3	5
$70,000 to $74,999	111	0	16	44	25	18	7	7	0
$75,000 to $79,999	89	0	14	17	31	18	9	9	0
$80,000 to $84,999	66	0	12	24	22	6	3	3	0
$85,000 to $89,999	34	0	9	9	14	2	1	0	1
$90,000 to $94,999	51	3	7	16	8	16	1	1	0
$95,000 to $99,999	14	0	3	3	1	6	1	1	0
$100,000 or more	235	0	33	81	69	42	11	11	0

MEDIAN INCOME

	total	15 to 24	25 to 34	35 to 44	45 to 54	55 to 64	65 or older total	65 to 74	75 or older
Women with income	$16,725	$9,306	$20,312	$21,351	$21,550	$18,549	$11,046	$11,077	$11,012
Women working full-time	29,508	20,683	29,485	30,851	31,101	31,279	40,750	41,730	–
Percent working full-time	31.2%	12.8%	38.9%	42.7%	45.1%	36.0%	6.9%	9.8%	2.9%

PERCENT DISTRIBUTION

	total	15 to 24	25 to 34	35 to 44	45 to 54	55 to 64	65 or older total	65 to 74	75 or older
Total Hispanic women	**100.0%**	**100.0%**	**100.0%**	**100.0%**	**100.0%**	**100.0%**	**100.0%**	**100.0%**	**100.0%**
Without income	28.1	47.7	26.3	24.0	20.3	22.7	11.7	11.2	12.4
With income	71.9	52.3	73.7	76.0	79.7	77.3	88.3	88.8	87.6
Under $15,000	32.4	35.2	27.0	25.1	26.9	32.7	61.8	59.4	65.2
$15,000 to $24,999	15.8	11.0	17.4	18.5	19.0	15.8	13.5	14.0	12.8
$25,000 to $34,999	9.0	3.9	11.5	11.3	11.7	10.5	4.7	4.7	4.7
$35,000 to $49,999	7.2	1.7	10.2	10.1	10.0	7.4	3.5	3.6	3.3
$50,000 to $74,999	4.8	0.4	5.8	7.1	7.3	6.3	3.3	4.6	1.4
$75,000 to $99,999	1.3	0.1	1.1	1.8	2.5	2.5	0.9	1.4	0.2
$100,000 or more	1.2	0.0	0.8	2.1	2.3	2.1	0.6	1.0	0.0

Note: "–" means sample is too small to make a reliable estimate.
Source: Bureau of the Census, 2013 Current Population Survey Annual Social and Economic Supplement, Internet site http://www.census.gov/hhes/www/cpstables/032013/perinc/toc.htm; calculations by New Strategist

Table 3.18 Women by Income and Age, 2012: Non-Hispanic White Women

(number and percent distribution of non-Hispanic white women aged 15 or older by income and age, 2012; median income of women with income and of women working full-time, year-round; percent working full-time, year-round; women in thousands as of 2013)

	total	15 to 24	25 to 34	35 to 44	45 to 54	55 to 64	65 or older total	65 to 74	75 or older
Total non-Hispanic white women	**83,919**	**11,804**	**12,060**	**11,957**	**14,773**	**14,571**	**18,754**	**10,048**	**8,706**
Without income	9,390	3,934	1,334	1,228	1,306	1,124	464	282	182
With income	74,529	7,870	10,726	10,729	13,467	13,446	18,290	9,766	8,525
Under $5,000	8,186	2,591	1,096	1,215	1,241	1,237	805	383	422
$5,000 to $9,999	8,374	1,436	863	768	983	1,171	3,153	1,524	1,629
$10,000 to $14,999	9,156	1,146	909	737	1,081	1,384	3,899	1,958	1,941
$15,000 to $19,999	7,307	824	834	725	942	943	3,039	1,354	1,686
$20,000 to $24,999	6,363	644	909	774	1,059	1,137	1,840	935	905
$25,000 to $29,999	5,138	433	891	717	923	923	1,250	689	561
$30,000 to $34,999	4,768	247	946	755	1,002	942	876	547	328
$35,000 to $39,999	3,840	144	824	688	802	767	616	432	183
$40,000 to $44,999	3,511	123	657	684	821	695	531	315	217
$45,000 to $49,999	2,708	96	560	505	591	588	368	232	136
$50,000 to $54,999	2,724	46	551	569	670	512	376	256	120
$55,000 to $59,999	1,607	43	263	349	368	371	212	151	61
$60,000 to $64,999	1,854	20	283	393	443	456	258	194	64
$65,000 to $69,999	1,273	29	218	284	265	280	198	141	56
$70,000 to $74,999	1,282	12	146	271	410	309	135	96	39
$75,000 to $79,999	918	8	184	151	249	227	99	76	23
$80,000 to $84,999	877	1	97	169	257	245	108	83	25
$85,000 to $89,999	531	0	70	104	126	146	84	63	21
$90,000 to $94,999	543	0	85	96	159	138	65	54	10
$95,000 to $99,999	371	4	38	91	98	91	49	43	7
$100,000 or more	3,200	23	303	685	979	882	329	238	91

MEDIAN INCOME

	total	15 to 24	25 to 34	35 to 44	45 to 54	55 to 64	65 or older total	65 to 74	75 or older
Women with income	$22,902	$9,598	$28,974	$31,963	$31,753	$29,524	$16,851	$18,463	$15,724
Women working full-time	42,171	24,027	38,684	45,859	45,575	46,224	48,716	49,498	42,749
Percent working full-time	34.5%	13.2%	50.8%	50.5%	52.3%	42.9%	6.6%	10.5%	2.1%

PERCENT DISTRIBUTION

	total	15 to 24	25 to 34	35 to 44	45 to 54	55 to 64	65 or older total	65 to 74	75 or older
Total non-Hispanic white women	**100.0%**	**100.0%**	**100.0%**	**100.0%**	**100.0%**	**100.0%**	**100.0%**	**100.0%**	**100.0%**
Without income	11.2	33.3	11.1	10.3	8.8	7.7	2.5	2.8	2.1
With income	88.8	66.7	88.9	89.7	91.2	92.3	97.5	97.2	97.9
Under $15,000	30.6	43.8	23.8	22.7	22.4	26.0	41.9	38.5	45.9
$15,000 to $24,999	16.3	12.4	14.5	12.5	13.5	14.3	26.0	22.8	29.8
$25,000 to $34,999	11.8	5.8	15.2	12.3	13.0	12.8	11.3	12.3	10.2
$35,000 to $49,999	12.0	3.1	16.9	15.7	15.0	14.1	8.1	9.7	6.2
$50,000 to $74,999	10.4	1.3	12.1	15.6	14.6	13.2	6.3	8.3	3.9
$75,000 to $99,999	3.9	0.1	3.9	5.1	6.0	5.8	2.2	3.2	1.0
$100,000 or more	3.8	0.2	2.5	5.7	6.6	6.1	1.8	2.4	1.0

Note: Non-Hispanic whites are those who identify themselves as being white alone and not Hispanic.
Source: Bureau of the Census, 2013 Current Population Survey Annual Social and Economic Supplement, Internet site http://www.census.gov/hhes/www/cpstables/032013/perinc/toc.htm; calculations by New Strategist

Table 3.19 Women by Income, Race, and Hispanic Origin, 2012

(number and percent distribution of women aged 15 or older by income, race, and Hispanic origin, 2012; median income of women with income and of women working full-time, year-round; percent working full-time, year-round; women in thousands as of 2013)

	total	Asian	black	Hispanic	non-Hispanic white
Total women	**128,912**	**7,649**	**17,837**	**19,039**	**83,919**
Without income	19,529	1,677	3,115	5,350	9,390
With income	109,383	5,972	14,722	13,689	74,529
Under $5,000	12,544	820	1,523	1,896	8,186
$5,000 to $9,999	13,589	726	2,214	2,170	8,374
$10,000 to $14,999	13,957	567	2,085	2,110	9,156
$15,000 to $19,999	10,988	502	1,558	1,602	7,307
$20,000 to $24,999	9,643	483	1,396	1,411	6,363
$25,000 to $29,999	7,488	323	1,039	939	5,138
$30,000 to $34,999	6,840	291	990	771	4,768
$35,000 to $39,999	5,504	267	782	585	3,840
$40,000 to $44,999	4,849	256	608	442	3,511
$45,000 to $49,999	3,756	218	471	350	2,708
$50,000 to $54,999	3,687	207	418	333	2,724
$55,000 to $59,999	2,223	138	281	202	1,607
$60,000 to $64,999	2,496	193	252	187	1,854
$65,000 to $69,999	1,688	118	184	91	1,273
$70,000 to $74,999	1,677	111	162	111	1,282
$75,000 to $79,999	1,193	77	111	89	918
$80,000 to $84,999	1,144	79	125	66	877
$85,000 to $89,999	698	48	79	34	531
$90,000 to $94,999	735	74	73	51	543
$95,000 to $99,999	488	49	48	14	371
$100,000 or more	4,196	426	324	235	3,200
MEDIAN INCOME					
Women with income	$21,520	$23,290	$19,925	$16,725	$22,902
Women working full-time	40,019	46,241	35,105	29,508	42,171
Percent working full-time	34.2%	36.6%	35.0%	31.2%	34.5%
PERCENT DISTRIBUTION					
Total women	**100.0%**	**100.0%**	**100.0%**	**100.0%**	**100.0%**
Without income	15.1	21.9	17.5	28.1	11.2
With income	84.9	78.1	82.5	71.9	88.8
Under $15,000	31.1	27.6	32.6	32.4	30.6
$15,000 to $24,999	16.0	12.9	16.6	15.8	16.3
$25,000 to $34,999	11.1	8.0	11.4	9.0	11.8
$35,000 to $49,999	10.9	9.7	10.4	7.2	12.0
$50,000 to $74,999	9.1	10.0	7.3	4.8	10.4
$75,000 to $99,999	3.3	4.3	2.4	1.3	3.9
$100,000 or more	3.3	5.6	1.8	1.2	3.8

Note: Asians and blacks are those who identify themselves as being of the race alone and those who identify themselves as being of the race in combination with other races. Non-Hispanic whites are those who identify themselves as white alone and not Hispanic. Numbers do not add to total because some people identify themselves as being of more than one race, not all races are shown, and Hispanics may be of any race.
Source: Bureau of the Census, 2013 Current Population Survey Annual Social and Economic Supplement, Internet site http://www.census.gov/hhes/www/cpstables/032013/perinc/toc.htm; calculations by New Strategist

Among Women Who Work Full-Time, Incomes Are Highest in the Northeast

Women in the South have the lowest incomes.

The median income of all women aged 15 or older does not vary much by geographical region, falling between about $21,000 and $23,000 in every region in 2012. Among full-time workers, median income ranges from a low of $37,118 in the South to a high of $44,554 in the Northeast.

Women's income patterns differ somewhat by race and Hispanic origin. Among Asian women who work full-time, median income is highest in the Northeast at $54,098. Among black women who work full-time, median income peaks in the West at $39,286. For Hispanic women with full-time jobs, median income is much lower, ranging from $28,109 in the South to a peak of $31,608 in the Northeast. For non-Hispanic white women who work full-time, incomes peak in the Northeast at a median of $47,460.

■ The incomes of Hispanic women are lower than those of Asian, non-Hispanic white, or black women because Hispanics are less educated.

Women's median income tops $40,000 in the Northeast and West

(median income of women aged 15 or older who work full-time, year-round, by region, 2012)

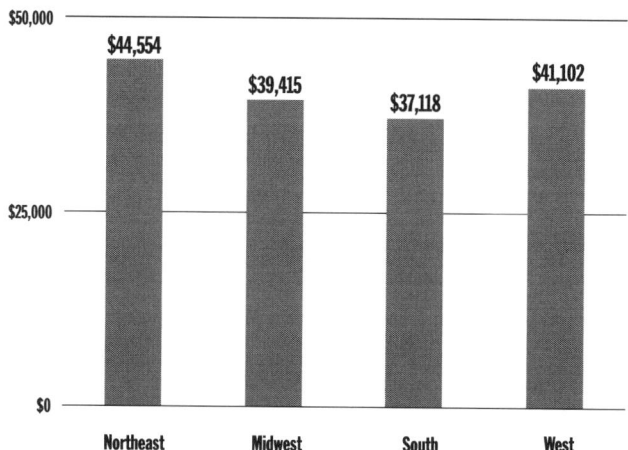

Table 3.20 Women by Income and Region, 2012: Total Women

(number and percent distribution of women aged 15 or older by income and region, 2012; median income of women with income and of women working full-time, year-round; percent working full-time, year-round; women in thousands as of 2013)

	total	Northeast	Midwest	South	West
Total women	**128,912**	**23,577**	**27,527**	**48,172**	**29,636**
Without income	19,529	3,183	3,290	7,901	5,156
With income	109,383	20,394	24,238	40,271	24,481
Under $5,000	12,544	2,352	2,681	4,398	3,114
$5,000 to $9,999	13,589	2,319	2,915	5,410	2,945
$10,000 to $14,999	13,957	2,429	2,985	5,420	3,123
$15,000 to $19,999	10,988	1,999	2,514	4,012	2,463
$20,000 to $24,999	9,643	1,744	2,187	3,566	2,146
$25,000 to $29,999	7,488	1,350	1,810	2,807	1,521
$30,000 to $34,999	6,840	1,229	1,620	2,616	1,375
$35,000 to $39,999	5,504	956	1,282	2,060	1,206
$40,000 to $44,999	4,849	947	1,138	1,841	923
$45,000 to $49,999	3,756	702	847	1,394	813
$50,000 to $54,999	3,687	700	876	1,295	816
$55,000 to $59,999	2,223	466	497	771	489
$60,000 to $64,999	2,496	527	557	864	549
$65,000 to $69,999	1,688	328	381	590	389
$70,000 to $74,999	1,677	412	370	541	355
$75,000 to $79,999	1,193	259	246	407	281
$80,000 to $84,999	1,144	240	276	348	280
$85,000 to $89,999	698	133	141	230	195
$90,000 to $94,999	735	180	131	229	195
$95,000 to $99,999	488	133	100	130	125
$100,000 or more	4,196	988	685	1,343	1,180
MEDIAN INCOME					
Women with income	$21,520	$22,539	$21,900	$21,049	$21,086
Women working full-time	40,019	44,554	39,415	37,118	41,102
Percent working full-time	34.2%	34.2%	34.8%	35.3%	31.7%
PERCENT DISTRIBUTION					
Total women	**100.0%**	**100.0%**	**100.0%**	**100.0%**	**100.0%**
Without income	15.1	13.5	12.0	16.4	17.4
With income	84.9	86.5	88.0	83.6	82.6
Under $15,000	31.1	30.1	31.2	31.6	31.0
$15,000 to $24,999	16.0	15.9	17.1	15.7	15.6
$25,000 to $34,999	11.1	10.9	12.5	11.3	9.8
$35,000 to $49,999	10.9	11.1	11.9	11.0	9.9
$50,000 to $74,999	9.1	10.3	9.7	8.4	8.8
$75,000 to $99,999	3.3	4.0	3.2	2.8	3.6
$100,000 or more	3.3	4.2	2.5	2.8	4.0

Source: Bureau of the Census, 2013 Current Population Survey Annual Social and Economic Supplement, Internet site http:// www.census.gov/hhes/www/cpstables/032013/perinc/toc.htm; calculations by New Strategist

Table 3.21 Women by Income and Region, 2012: Asian Women

(number and percent distribution of Asian women aged 15 or older by income and region, 2012; median income of women with income and of women working full-time, year-round; percent working full-time, year-round; women in thousands as of 2013)

	total	Northeast	Midwest	South	West
Total Asian women	**7,649**	**1,447**	**863**	**1,723**	**3,617**
Without income	1,677	387	218	414	658
With income	5,972	1,060	645	1,308	2,959
Under $5,000	820	178	100	174	368
$5,000 to $9,999	726	126	75	165	360
$10,000 to $14,999	567	87	60	113	308
$15,000 to $19,999	502	80	61	92	269
$20,000 to $24,999	483	76	54	109	245
$25,000 to $29,999	323	54	37	78	154
$30,000 to $34,999	291	50	32	57	152
$35,000 to $39,999	267	36	21	66	143
$40,000 to $44,999	256	30	31	77	118
$45,000 to $49,999	218	48	30	34	106
$50,000 to $54,999	207	31	21	53	102
$55,000 to $59,999	138	26	8	36	68
$60,000 to $64,999	193	49	17	30	98
$65,000 to $69,999	118	16	18	33	50
$70,000 to $74,999	111	25	5	29	51
$75,000 to $79,999	77	20	16	15	26
$80,000 to $84,999	79	10	11	16	42
$85,000 to $89,999	48	0	4	16	28
$90,000 to $94,999	74	13	9	14	38
$95,000 to $99,999	49	14	2	7	26
$100,000 or more	426	93	31	95	208

MEDIAN INCOME

	total	Northeast	Midwest	South	West
Women with income	$23,290	$22,673	$21,580	$25,088	$22,982
Women working full-time	46,241	54,098	44,920	42,215	45,863
Percent working full-time	36.6%	34.0%	34.1%	40.5%	36.5%

PERCENT DISTRIBUTION

	total	Northeast	Midwest	South	West
Total Asian women	**100.0%**	**100.0%**	**100.0%**	**100.0%**	**100.0%**
Without income	21.9	26.7	25.3	24.1	18.2
With income	78.1	73.3	74.7	75.9	81.8
Under $15,000	27.6	27.0	27.3	26.2	28.6
$15,000 to $24,999	12.9	10.7	13.3	11.7	14.2
$25,000 to $34,999	8.0	7.1	8.0	7.8	8.5
$35,000 to $49,999	9.7	7.9	9.5	10.3	10.1
$50,000 to $74,999	10.0	10.1	8.2	10.6	10.2
$75,000 to $99,999	4.3	4.0	4.9	3.9	4.4
$100,000 or more	5.6	6.4	3.6	5.5	5.7

Note: Asians are those who identify themselves as being of the race alone and those who identify themselves as being of the race in combination with other races.
Source: Bureau of the Census, 2013 Current Population Survey Annual Social and Economic Supplement, Internet site http:// www.census.gov/hhes/www/cpstables/032013/perinc/toc.htm; calculations by New Strategist

Table 3.22 Women by Income and Region, 2012: Black Women

(number and percent distribution of black women aged 15 or older by income and region, 2012; median income of women with income and of women working full-time, year-round; percent working full-time, year-round; women in thousands as of 2013)

	total	Northeast	Midwest	South	West
Total black women	**17,837**	**3,239**	**3,024**	**9,855**	**1,719**
Without income	3,115	597	500	1,683	334
With income	14,722	2,641	2,524	8,172	1,384
Under $5,000	1,523	239	320	796	168
$5,000 to $9,999	2,214	362	358	1,297	197
$10,000 to $14,999	2,085	354	332	1,199	200
$15,000 to $19,999	1,558	277	302	833	146
$20,000 to $24,999	1,396	280	240	770	106
$25,000 to $29,999	1,039	163	175	605	95
$30,000 to $34,999	990	216	172	523	81
$35,000 to $39,999	782	127	139	449	67
$40,000 to $44,999	608	124	97	347	40
$45,000 to $49,999	471	99	69	263	40
$50,000 to $54,999	418	81	77	214	47
$55,000 to $59,999	281	60	52	138	31
$60,000 to $64,999	252	49	48	136	20
$65,000 to $69,999	184	36	11	118	19
$70,000 to $74,999	162	32	36	77	18
$75,000 to $79,999	111	21	14	59	16
$80,000 to $84,999	125	23	17	68	18
$85,000 to $89,999	79	14	7	51	7
$90,000 to $94,999	73	17	15	30	11
$95,000 to $99,999	48	11	8	21	9
$100,000 or more	324	56	36	182	50

MEDIAN INCOME

	total	Northeast	Midwest	South	West
Women with income	$19,925	$21,157	$18,900	$19,712	$19,060
Women working full-time	35,105	35,756	34,530	34,219	39,286
Percent working full-time	35.0%	36.0%	31.9%	36.4%	30.9%

PERCENT DISTRIBUTION

	total	Northeast	Midwest	South	West
Total black women	**100.0%**	**100.0%**	**100.0%**	**100.0%**	**100.0%**
Without income	17.5	18.4	16.5	17.1	19.4
With income	82.5	81.6	83.5	82.9	80.6
Under $15,000	32.6	29.5	33.4	33.4	32.9
$15,000 to $24,999	16.6	17.2	17.9	16.3	14.7
$25,000 to $34,999	11.4	11.7	11.5	11.4	10.2
$35,000 to $49,999	10.4	10.8	10.1	10.7	8.6
$50,000 to $74,999	7.3	7.9	7.4	6.9	7.8
$75,000 to $99,999	2.4	2.7	2.0	2.3	3.5
$100,000 or more	1.8	1.7	1.2	1.8	2.9

Note: Blacks are those who identify themselves as being of the race alone and those who identify themselves as being of the race in combination with other races.
Source: Bureau of the Census, 2013 Current Population Survey Annual Social and Economic Supplement, Internet site http:// www.census.gov/hhes/www/cpstables/032013/perinc/toc.htm; calculations by New Strategist

Table 3.23 Women by Income and Region, 2012: Hispanic Women

(number and percent distribution of Hispanic women aged 15 or older by income and region, 2012; median income of women with income and of women working full-time, year-round; percent working full-time, year-round; women in thousands as of 2013)

	total	Northeast	Midwest	South	West
Total Hispanic women	**19,039**	**2,796**	**1,552**	**7,035**	**7,657**
Without income	5,350	641	436	2,060	2,214
With income	13,689	2,155	1,116	4,975	5,443
Under $5,000	1,896	290	175	606	826
$5,000 to $9,999	2,170	346	162	835	827
$10,000 to $14,999	2,110	344	158	743	864
$15,000 to $19,999	1,602	261	126	575	640
$20,000 to $24,999	1,411	209	135	514	554
$25,000 to $29,999	939	126	85	357	372
$30,000 to $34,999	771	99	71	312	288
$35,000 to $39,999	585	92	49	225	219
$40,000 to $44,999	442	72	33	169	168
$45,000 to $49,999	350	59	20	136	135
$50,000 to $54,999	333	55	39	107	132
$55,000 to $59,999	202	27	7	87	81
$60,000 to $64,999	187	35	13	73	65
$65,000 to $69,999	91	11	3	29	48
$70,000 to $74,999	111	24	10	27	49
$75,000 to $79,999	89	18	6	36	29
$80,000 to $84,999	66	16	2	27	21
$85,000 to $89,999	34	7	4	13	11
$90,000 to $94,999	51	13	3	14	22
$95,000 to $99,999	14	4	0	5	5
$100,000 or more	235	45	18	85	87

MEDIAN INCOME

	total	Northeast	Midwest	South	West
Women with income	$16,725	$16,547	$16,869	$17,202	$16,337
Women working full-time	29,508	31,608	28,455	28,109	29,834
Percent working full-time	31.2%	30.8%	31.6%	33.7%	28.9%

PERCENT DISTRIBUTION

	total	Northeast	Midwest	South	West
Total Hispanic women	**100.0%**	**100.0%**	**100.0%**	**100.0%**	**100.0%**
Without income	28.1	22.9	28.1	29.3	28.9
With income	71.9	77.1	71.9	70.7	71.1
Under $15,000	32.4	35.1	31.9	31.0	32.9
$15,000 to $24,999	15.8	16.8	16.8	15.5	15.6
$25,000 to $34,999	9.0	8.0	10.1	9.5	8.6
$35,000 to $49,999	7.2	8.0	6.6	7.5	6.8
$50,000 to $74,999	4.8	5.5	4.6	4.6	4.9
$75,000 to $99,999	1.3	2.1	0.9	1.3	1.1
$100,000 or more	1.2	1.6	1.1	1.2	1.1

Source: Bureau of the Census, 2013 Current Population Survey Annual Social and Economic Supplement, Internet site http://www.census.gov/hhes/www/cpstables/032013/perinc/toc.htm; calculations by New Strategist

Table 3.24 Women by Income and Region, 2012: Non-Hispanic White Women

(number and percent distribution of non-Hispanic white women aged 15 or older by income and region, 2012; median income of women with income and of women working full-time, year-round; percent working full-time, year-round; women in thousands as of 2013)

	total	Northeast	Midwest	South	West
Total non-Hispanic white women	**83,919**	**16,486**	**21,934**	**29,347**	**16,153**
Without income	9,390	1,646	2,132	3,745	1,867
With income	74,529	14,840	19,801	25,601	14,286
Under $5,000	8,186	1,675	2,054	2,789	1,667
$5,000 to $9,999	8,374	1,531	2,281	3,073	1,488
$10,000 to $14,999	9,156	1,708	2,415	3,312	1,720
$15,000 to $19,999	7,307	1,422	2,010	2,499	1,377
$20,000 to $24,999	6,363	1,215	1,753	2,168	1,227
$25,000 to $29,999	5,138	1,016	1,505	1,749	867
$30,000 to $34,999	4,768	888	1,338	1,713	830
$35,000 to $39,999	3,840	710	1,074	1,310	745
$40,000 to $44,999	3,511	728	969	1,239	574
$45,000 to $49,999	2,708	511	721	962	514
$50,000 to $54,999	2,724	539	743	925	517
$55,000 to $59,999	1,607	361	428	509	308
$60,000 to $64,999	1,854	396	476	620	361
$65,000 to $69,999	1,273	262	343	404	264
$70,000 to $74,999	1,282	331	318	402	232
$75,000 to $79,999	918	203	212	293	209
$80,000 to $84,999	877	193	246	241	197
$85,000 to $89,999	531	109	125	148	148
$90,000 to $94,999	543	142	104	170	127
$95,000 to $99,999	371	103	88	94	85
$100,000 or more	3,200	795	597	981	827
MEDIAN INCOME					
Women with income	$22,902	$24,333	$22,803	$22,199	$23,140
Women working full-time	42,171	47,460	40,660	40,584	46,930
Percent working full-time	34.5%	34.4%	35.6%	35.1%	32.0%
PERCENT DISTRIBUTION					
Total non-Hispanic white women	**100.0%**	**100.0%**	**100.0%**	**100.0%**	**100.0%**
Without income	11.2	10.0	9.7	12.8	11.6
With income	88.8	90.0	90.3	87.2	88.4
Under $15,000	30.6	29.8	30.8	31.3	30.2
$15,000 to $24,999	16.3	16.0	17.2	15.9	16.1
$25,000 to $34,999	11.8	11.5	13.0	11.8	10.5
$35,000 to $49,999	12.0	11.8	12.6	12.0	11.3
$50,000 to $74,999	10.4	11.5	10.5	9.7	10.4
$75,000 to $99,999	3.9	4.6	3.5	3.2	4.7
$100,000 or more	3.8	4.8	2.7	3.3	5.1

Note: Non-Hispanic whites are those who identify themselves as being white alone and not Hispanic.
Source: Bureau of the Census, 2013 Current Population Survey Annual Social and Economic Supplement, Internet site http:// www.census.gov/hhes/www/cpstables/032013/perinc/toc.htm; calculations by New Strategist

Women in Nonmetropolitan Areas Have Lower Incomes

Those in metropolitan areas have higher incomes.

Women who live in nonmetropolitan areas—the countryside and small towns of America—have the lowest incomes. The median income of women in nonmetropolitan areas who work full-time stood at $32,211 in 2011. The $41,873 median income of their counterparts living in the suburbs of the nation's metropolitan areas (outside principal cities) is 30 percent higher. Among women with full-time jobs who live in the principal cities of metropolitan areas, median income is a slightly lower $39,392.

The proportion of women who work full-time varies somewhat by metropolitan status. Among women who live in nonmetropolitan areas, only 31 percent have full-time jobs. Among women who live in the principal cities or suburbs of metropolitan areas, 35 percent work full-time.

■ The nation's metropolitan areas attract the best-educated and most-career-oriented women, which is one reason why women who live there have higher incomes.

Women in the suburbs have the highest incomes

(median income of women aged 15 or older who work full-time, year-round, by metropolitan residence, 2012)

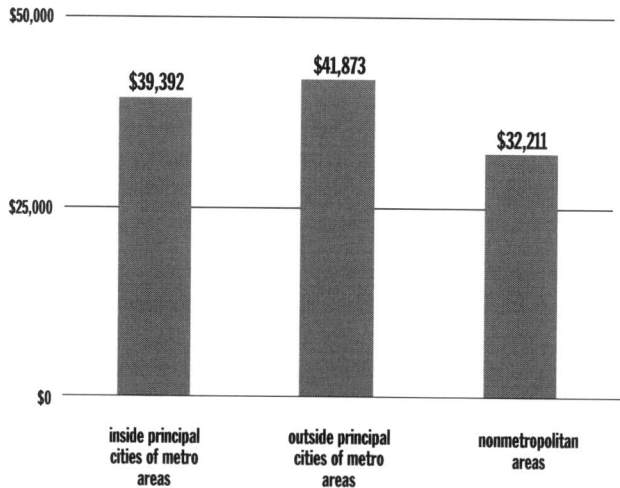

Table 3.25 Women by Income and Metropolitan Residence, 2012

(number and percent distribution of women aged 15 or older by income and metropolitan residence, 2012; median income of women with income and of women working full-time, year-round; percent working full-time, year-round; women in thousands as of 2013)

		in metropolitan area			
			inside	outside	not in
			principal	principal	metropolitan
	total	total	cities	cities	area
Total women	**128,912**	**108,931**	**41,848**	**67,083**	**19,981**
Without income	19,529	16,767	7,037	9,730	2,762
With income	109,383	92,164	34,811	57,353	17,219
Under $5,000	12,544	10,596	3,893	6,703	1,948
$5,000 to $9,999	13,589	10,914	4,337	6,578	2,675
$10,000 to $14,999	13,957	11,354	4,392	6,962	2,602
$15,000 to $19,999	10,988	9,005	3,637	5,369	1,982
$20,000 to $24,999	9,643	7,919	3,033	4,886	1,724
$25,000 to $29,999	7,488	6,143	2,312	3,831	1,346
$30,000 to $34,999	6,840	5,750	2,140	3,610	1,090
$35,000 to $39,999	5,504	4,614	1,713	2,901	890
$40,000 to $44,999	4,849	4,155	1,451	2,704	695
$45,000 to $49,999	3,756	3,266	1,148	2,118	491
$50,000 to $54,999	3,687	3,266	1,182	2,084	421
$55,000 to $59,999	2,223	1,984	727	1,257	239
$60,000 to $64,999	2,496	2,258	849	1,409	238
$65,000 to $69,999	1,688	1,537	638	900	151
$70,000 to $74,999	1,677	1,536	485	1,051	141
$75,000 to $79,999	1,193	1,109	381	729	84
$80,000 to $84,999	1,144	1,048	342	705	96
$85,000 to $89,999	698	624	226	398	74
$90,000 to $94,999	735	688	238	450	47
$95,000 to $99,999	488	447	157	289	42
$100,000 or more	4,196	3,952	1,531	2,420	245
MEDIAN INCOME					
Women with income	$21,520	$22,147	$21,499	$22,596	$18,069
Women working full-time	40,019	41,109	39,392	41,873	32,211
Percent working full-time	34.2%	34.7%	34.6%	34.8%	31.2%
PERCENT DISTRIBUTION					
Total women	**100.0%**	**100.0%**	**100.0%**	**100.0%**	**100.0%**
Without income	15.1	15.4	16.8	14.5	13.8
With income	84.9	84.6	83.2	85.5	86.2
Under $15,000	31.1	30.2	30.2	30.2	36.2
$15,000 to $24,999	16.0	15.5	15.9	15.3	18.5
$25,000 to $34,999	11.1	10.9	10.6	11.1	12.2
$35,000 to $49,999	10.9	11.0	10.3	11.5	10.4
$50,000 to $74,999	9.1	9.7	9.3	10.0	6.0
$75,000 to $99,999	3.3	3.6	3.2	3.8	1.7
$100,000 or more	3.3	3.6	3.7	3.6	1.2

Source: Bureau of the Census, 2013 Current Population Survey Annual Social and Economic Supplement, Internet site http:// www.census.gov/hhes/www/cpstables/032013/perinc/toc.htm; calculations by New Strategist

Women Earn Little from Part-Time Work

Because women's earnings are increasingly important to their families, most women workers have full-time jobs.

Among the nation's nearly 74 million women with earnings in 2012, more than 44 million worked full-time, year-round (59 percent). The median earnings of full-time, year-round workers stood at $37,791—41 percent higher than the $26,882 median earnings of all women. The 21 million women with part-time jobs earned a median of just $10,120.

Among Asian women who work full-time, year-round, median earnings stood at $45,439 in 2012. Their non-Hispanic white counterparts had lower median earnings of $40,912. The median earnings of black women who work full-time, year-round were $33,903, and the median earnings of Hispanic women were just $28,424. Among women with earnings, the proportion who work full time ranges from a low of 58 percent among Hispanics to a high of 64 percent among Asians.

■ Among working women, most have full-time jobs because part-time work pays little and offers few benefits.

Among women who work full-time, Asians have the highest median earnings

*(median earnings of women aged 15 or older working full-time,
year-round, by race and Hispanic origin, 2012)*

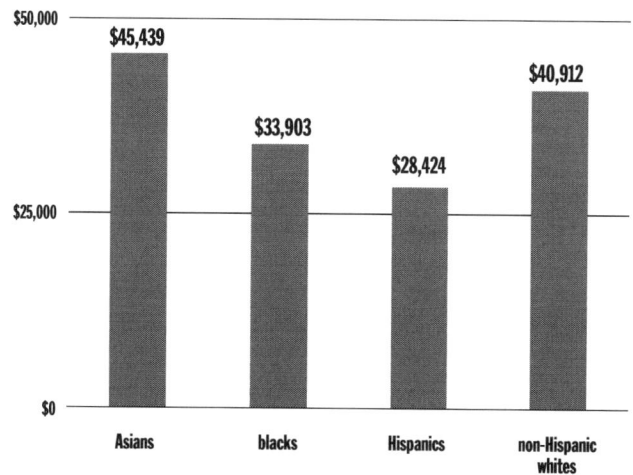

Table 3.26 Women by Earnings and Employment Status, 2012: Total Women

(number and percent distribution of women aged 15 or older with earnings by employment status and median earnings, 2012; women in thousands as of 2013)

	total	worked full-time total	worked full-time year-round	worked part-time total	worked part-time year-round
Total women with earnings	**74,188**	**53,045**	**44,042**	**21,143**	**11,277**
Under $5,000	7,867	1,908	296	5,959	1,000
$5,000 to $9,999	6,410	1,926	640	4,485	2,166
$10,000 to $14,999	6,957	3,206	1,949	3,751	2,640
$15,000 to $19,999	6,280	4,204	3,195	2,076	1,494
$20,000 to $24,999	6,711	5,226	4,424	1,485	1,160
$25,000 to $29,999	5,489	4,637	4,125	852	705
$30,000 to $34,999	5,645	4,937	4,407	708	556
$35,000 to $39,999	4,726	4,349	3,987	377	286
$40,000 to $44,999	3,994	3,716	3,380	278	239
$45,000 to $49,999	3,221	3,020	2,786	201	178
$50,000 to $54,999	3,274	3,072	2,815	201	172
$55,000 to $59,999	1,716	1,608	1,487	108	100
$60,000 to $64,999	2,263	2,123	1,964	140	116
$65,000 to $69,999	1,318	1,258	1,166	59	55
$70,000 to $74,999	1,469	1,381	1,279	87	72
$75,000 to $79,999	962	902	854	60	57
$80,000 to $84,999	999	940	903	60	50
$85,000 to $89,999	511	474	449	37	37
$90,000 to $94,999	627	594	564	33	31
$95,000 to $99,999	357	345	328	13	13
$100,000 or more	3,395	3,220	3,045	175	151
Median earnings	**$26,882**	**$35,388**	**$37,791**	**$10,120**	**$14,478**

PERCENT DISTRIBUTION

	total	worked full-time total	worked full-time year-round	worked part-time total	worked part-time year-round
Total women with earnings	**100.0%**	**100.0%**	**100.0%**	**100.0%**	**100.0%**
Under $15,000	28.6	13.3	6.5	67.1	51.5
$15,000 to $24,999	17.5	17.8	17.3	16.8	23.5
$25,000 to $34,999	15.0	18.0	19.4	7.4	11.2
$35,000 to $49,999	16.1	20.9	23.1	4.0	6.2
$50,000 to $74,999	13.5	17.8	19.8	2.8	4.6
$75,000 to $99,999	4.7	6.1	7.0	1.0	1.7
$100,000 or more	4.6	6.1	6.9	0.8	1.3

Source: Bureau of the Census, 2013 Current Population Survey Annual Social and Economic Supplement, Internet site http://www.census.gov/hhes/www/cpstables/032013/perinc/toc.htm; calculations by New Strategist

Table 3.27 Women by Earnings and Employment Status, 2012: Asian Women

(number and percent distribution of Asian women aged 15 or older with earnings by employment status and median earnings, 2012; women in thousands as of 2013)

	total	worked full-time		worked part-time	
		total	year-round	total	year-round
Asian women with earnings	**4,368**	**3,258**	**2,802**	**1,110**	**614**
Under $5,000	371	78	17	293	71
$5,000 to $9,999	355	92	25	263	128
$10,000 to $14,999	334	167	98	167	111
$15,000 to $19,999	347	218	177	129	89
$20,000 to $24,999	381	289	255	92	79
$25,000 to $29,999	271	235	212	36	30
$30,000 to $34,999	269	230	194	39	28
$35,000 to $39,999	244	232	212	13	10
$40,000 to $44,999	223	209	186	14	12
$45,000 to $49,999	195	186	171	9	7
$50,000 to $54,999	193	183	164	10	8
$55,000 to $59,999	128	118	112	10	10
$60,000 to $64,999	161	155	149	6	4
$65,000 to $69,999	105	100	95	4	4
$70,000 to $74,999	98	95	93	3	1
$75,000 to $79,999	70	70	67	0	0
$80,000 to $84,999	80	74	71	6	6
$85,000 to $89,999	39	37	35	2	2
$90,000 to $94,999	71	69	68	2	2
$95,000 to $99,999	43	43	38	0	0
$100,000 or more	390	379	363	11	11
Median earnings	**$31,393**	**$41,327**	**$45,439**	**$9,966**	**$14,703**
PERCENT DISTRIBUTION					
Asian women with earnings	**100.0%**	**100.0%**	**100.0%**	**100.0%**	**100.0%**
Under $15,000	24.3	10.3	5.0	65.2	50.5
$15,000 to $24,999	16.7	15.6	15.4	19.9	27.4
$25,000 to $34,999	12.4	14.3	14.5	6.7	9.4
$35,000 to $49,999	15.2	19.2	20.3	3.2	4.8
$50,000 to $74,999	15.7	20.0	21.9	3.0	4.4
$75,000 to $99,999	6.9	9.0	10.0	0.9	1.6
$100,000 or more	8.9	11.6	12.9	1.0	1.8

Note: Asians are those who identify themselves as being of the race alone and those who identify themselves as being of the race in combination with other races. Earnings include wages and salary only.
Source: Bureau of the Census, 2013 Current Population Survey Annual Social and Economic Supplement, Internet site http:// www.census.gov/hhes/www/cpstables/032013/perinc/toc.htm; calculations by New Strategist

Table 3.28 Women by Earnings and Employment Status, 2012: Black Women

(number and percent distribution of black women aged 15 or older with earnings by employment status and median earnings, 2012; women in thousands as of 2013)

	total	worked full-time		worked part-time	
		total	year-round	total	year-round
Black women with earnings	**10,152**	**7,673**	**6,249**	**2,478**	**1,259**
Under $5,000	974	271	18	703	97
$5,000 to $9,999	915	348	108	567	245
$10,000 to $14,999	1,068	559	333	509	362
$15,000 to $19,999	1,064	823	642	241	176
$20,000 to $24,999	1,080	890	744	190	165
$25,000 to $29,999	780	705	634	75	54
$30,000 to $34,999	859	783	731	76	65
$35,000 to $39,999	691	659	606	31	20
$40,000 to $44,999	531	513	468	18	17
$45,000 to $49,999	409	400	375	8	7
$50,000 to $54,999	382	368	330	13	9
$55,000 to $59,999	219	215	194	4	4
$60,000 to $64,999	248	242	229	6	6
$65,000 to $69,999	155	147	140	8	6
$70,000 to $74,999	160	158	140	3	2
$75,000 to $79,999	71	69	68	2	1
$80,000 to $84,999	117	114	103	3	3
$85,000 to $89,999	79	77	76	2	2
$90,000 to $94,999	52	52	52	0	0
$95,000 to $99,999	36	36	36	0	0
$100,000 or more	262	244	223	18	18
Median earnings	**$24,824**	**$31,027**	**$33,903**	**$9,691**	**$13,556**

PERCENT DISTRIBUTION					
Black women with earnings	**100.0%**	**100.0%**	**100.0%**	**100.0%**	**100.0%**
Under $15,000	29.1	15.4	7.4	71.8	55.9
$15,000 to $24,999	21.1	22.3	22.2	17.4	27.1
$25,000 to $34,999	16.1	19.4	21.8	6.1	9.4
$35,000 to $49,999	16.1	20.5	23.2	2.3	3.5
$50,000 to $74,999	11.5	14.7	16.5	1.4	2.2
$75,000 to $99,999	3.5	4.5	5.3	0.3	0.5
$100,000 or more	2.6	3.2	3.6	0.7	1.4

Note: Blacks are those who identify themselves as being of the race alone and those who identify themselves as being of the race in combination with other races. Earnings include wages and salary only.
Source: Bureau of the Census, 2013 Current Population Survey Annual Social and Economic Supplement, Internet site http:// www.census.gov/hhes/www/cpstables/032013/perinc/toc.htm; calculations by New Strategist

Table 3.29 Women by Earnings and Employment Status, 2012: Hispanic Women

(number and percent distribution of Hispanic women aged 15 or older with earnings by employment status and median earnings, 2012; women in thousands as of 2013)

	total	worked full-time		worked part-time	
		total	year-round	total	year-round
Hispanic women with earnings	**10,293**	**7,313**	**5,936**	**2,980**	**1,655**
Under $5,000	1,146	354	53	793	140
$5,000 to $9,999	1,173	396	140	777	409
$10,000 to $14,999	1,427	771	531	656	493
$15,000 to $19,999	1,279	972	804	307	233
$20,000 to $24,999	1,242	1,061	912	181	141
$25,000 to $29,999	805	712	654	93	89
$30,000 to $34,999	702	629	594	73	54
$35,000 to $39,999	558	519	481	39	36
$40,000 to $44,999	391	376	344	15	15
$45,000 to $49,999	303	299	283	5	5
$50,000 to $54,999	324	317	300	7	7
$55,000 to $59,999	149	137	127	12	9
$60,000 to $64,999	165	164	158	1	1
$65,000 to $69,999	89	89	81	0	0
$70,000 to $74,999	103	96	82	7	6
$75,000 to $79,999	73	69	67	5	5
$80,000 to $84,999	65	62	60	2	2
$85,000 to $89,999	22	22	22	0	0
$90,000 to $94,999	52	51	45	2	2
$95,000 to $99,999	9	9	9	0	0
$100,000 or more	215	208	188	7	7
Median earnings	**$20,369**	**$25,528**	**$28,424**	**$9,379**	**$11,941**
PERCENT DISTRIBUTION					
Hispanic women with earnings	**100.0%**	**100.0%**	**100.0%**	**100.0%**	**100.0%**
Under $15,000	36.4	20.8	12.2	74.7	63.0
$15,000 to $24,999	24.5	27.8	28.9	16.4	22.6
$25,000 to $34,999	14.6	18.3	21.0	5.6	8.7
$35,000 to $49,999	12.2	16.3	18.7	2.0	3.4
$50,000 to $74,999	8.1	11.0	12.6	0.9	1.4
$75,000 to $99,999	2.2	2.9	3.4	0.3	0.5
$100,000 or more	2.1	2.8	3.2	0.2	0.4

Note: Earnings include wages and salary only.
Source: Bureau of the Census, 2013 Current Population Survey Annual Social and Economic Supplement, Internet site http:// www.census.gov/hhes/www/cpstables/032013/perinc/toc.htm; calculations by New Strategist

Table 3.30 Women by Earnings and Employment Status, 2012: Non-Hispanic White Women

(number and percent distribution of non-Hispanic white women aged 15 or older with earnings by employment status and median earnings, 2012; women in thousands as of 2013)

	total	worked full-time		worked part-time	
		total	year-round	total	year-round
Non-Hispanic white women with earnings	**49,134**	**34,639**	**28,923**	**14,495**	**7,723**
Under $5,000	5,290	1,190	208	4,100	686
$5,000 to $9,999	3,947	1,088	366	2,860	1,367
$10,000 to $14,999	4,107	1,679	971	2,428	1,679
$15,000 to $19,999	3,615	2,210	1,584	1,405	995
$20,000 to $24,999	4,033	3,012	2,522	1,020	777
$25,000 to $29,999	3,584	2,932	2,577	652	538
$30,000 to $34,999	3,790	3,259	2,856	532	411
$35,000 to $39,999	3,209	2,921	2,674	288	214
$40,000 to $44,999	2,826	2,598	2,368	228	193
$45,000 to $49,999	2,301	2,130	1,957	171	154
$50,000 to $54,999	2,384	2,217	2,033	167	144
$55,000 to $59,999	1,214	1,132	1,045	82	76
$60,000 to $64,999	1,683	1,556	1,423	127	104
$65,000 to $69,999	956	909	838	47	44
$70,000 to $74,999	1,106	1,031	959	75	63
$75,000 to $79,999	747	693	654	53	51
$80,000 to $84,999	739	690	670	48	38
$85,000 to $89,999	365	332	313	33	33
$90,000 to $94,999	454	424	403	29	27
$95,000 to $99,999	263	251	240	12	12
$100,000 or more	2,523	2,385	2,264	138	115
Median earnings	**$29,978**	**$37,421**	**$40,912**	**$10,420**	**$15,478**

PERCENT DISTRIBUTION

	total	total	year-round	total	year-round
Non-Hispanic white women with earnings	**100.0%**	**100.0%**	**100.0%**	**100.0%**	**100.0%**
Under $15,000	27.2	11.4	5.3	64.8	48.3
$15,000 to $24,999	15.6	15.1	14.2	16.7	22.9
$25,000 to $34,999	15.0	17.9	18.8	8.2	12.3
$35,000 to $49,999	17.0	22.1	24.2	4.7	7.3
$50,000 to $74,999	14.9	19.8	21.8	3.4	5.6
$75,000 to $99,999	5.2	6.9	7.9	1.2	2.1
$100,000 or more	5.1	6.9	7.8	1.0	1.5

Note: Non-Hispanic whites are those who identify themselves as being white alone and not Hispanic. Earnings include wages and salary only.
Source: Bureau of the Census, 2013 Current Population Survey Annual Social and Economic Supplement, Internet site http://www.census.gov/hhes/www/cpstables/032013/perinc/toc.htm; calculations by New Strategist

Women with Professional Degrees Earn the Most

Those who did not complete high school earn the least.

The more highly educated a woman, the more she earns. Among women with at least a bachelor's degree who work full-time, median earnings were $53,686 in 2012. For full-time workers who went no further than high school, median earnings stood at a much lower $30,406. Women with a professional degree (such as doctors and lawyers) earned a median of $94,473, with 48 percent earning $100,000 or more.

By age and education, women aged 35 to 44 with a professional degree have the highest earnings, a median of $110,786 in 2012. Even the youngest women benefit from getting more education. Women aged 25 to 34 with at least a bachelor's degree earned $46,989. Their counterparts who went no further than high school earned just $25,820.

■ Among 25-to-34-year-old full-time workers, 49 percent of women and a smaller 36 percent of men have a bachelor's degree.

Women's earnings rise with education

(median earnings of women aged 25 or older who work full-time, year-round, by educational attainment, 2012)

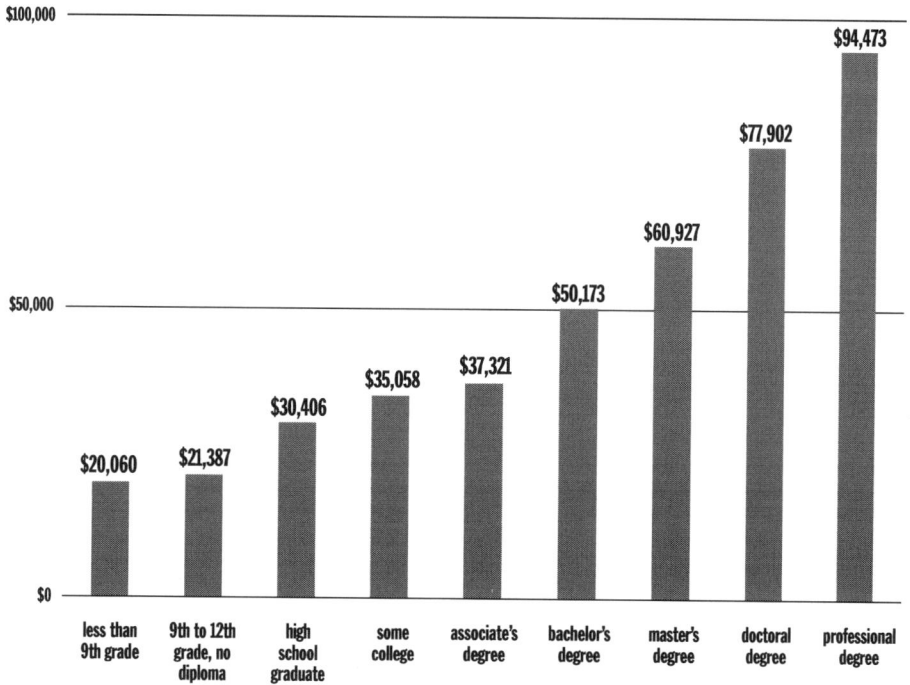

Table 3.31 Women Who Work Full-Time by Earnings and Education, 2012: Total Women

(number and percent distribution of women aged 25 or older who work full-time, year-round, by earnings and educational attainment, 2012; median earnings of women with earnings; women in thousands as of 2013)

	total	less than 9th grade	9th to 12th grade, no diploma	high school graduate	some college, no degree	associate's degree	bachelor's degree or more total	bachelor's degree	master's degree	professional degree	doctoral degree
Total women who work full-time	41,319	690	1,351	9,870	6,899	5,246	17,263	10,961	4,887	670	745
Under $5,000	266	18	10	77	60	31	70	51	15	0	3
$5,000 to $9,999	497	34	66	172	68	36	121	101	19	1	0
$10,000 to $14,999	1,621	123	225	587	314	163	208	176	26	4	3
$15,000 to $19,999	2,624	167	262	1,044	509	313	329	266	52	7	4
$20,000 to $24,999	3,890	164	310	1,470	771	527	648	539	88	12	9
$25,000 to $29,999	3,784	79	179	1,414	793	542	777	637	112	12	15
$30,000 to $34,999	4,174	43	101	1,334	921	651	1,125	892	201	13	18
$35,000 to $39,999	3,813	23	67	1,052	846	533	1,292	961	294	14	22
$40,000 to $44,999	3,242	9	43	784	551	481	1,375	977	345	19	34
$45,000 to $49,999	2,695	12	30	458	446	425	1,324	825	433	26	40
$50,000 to $54,999	2,779	8	9	491	406	354	1,510	958	466	44	42
$55,000 to $59,999	1,462	0	4	244	178	180	856	540	281	20	15
$60,000 to $64,999	1,932	3	16	227	289	219	1,178	702	395	24	57
$65,000 to $69,999	1,150	0	0	93	142	191	724	444	223	27	31
$70,000 to $74,999	1,274	1	7	101	138	158	870	488	310	25	47
$75,000 to $79,999	851	0	4	60	55	72	660	406	184	33	37
$80,000 to $84,999	902	0	0	67	103	102	630	326	232	30	42
$85,000 to $89,999	449	0	0	26	52	37	333	184	122	9	19
$90,000 to $94,999	561	0	2	15	35	45	464	258	160	16	30
$95,000 to $99,999	328	0	1	11	39	39	238	126	83	13	16
$100,000 or more	3,027	6	14	143	182	150	2,532	1,104	845	322	262
Median earnings	$39,977	$20,060	$21,387	$30,406	$35,058	$37,321	$53,686	$50,173	$60,927	$94,473	$77,902

PERCENT DISTRIBUTION

	total	less than 9th grade	9th to 12th grade, no diploma	high school graduate	some college, no degree	associate's degree	bachelor's degree or more total	bachelor's degree	master's degree	professional degree	doctoral degree
Total women who work full-time	100.0%	100.0%	100.0%	100.0%	100.0%	100.0%	100.0%	100.0%	100.0%	100.0%	100.0%
Under $15,000	5.8	25.4	22.3	8.5	6.4	4.4	2.3	3.0	1.2	0.8	0.8
$15,000 to $24,999	15.8	47.9	42.3	25.5	18.6	16.0	5.7	7.3	2.9	2.8	1.7
$25,000 to $34,999	19.3	17.6	20.8	27.8	24.8	22.7	11.0	14.0	6.4	3.7	4.5
$35,000 to $49,999	23.6	6.5	10.4	23.2	26.7	27.4	23.1	25.2	22.0	8.8	12.8
$50,000 to $74,999	20.8	1.8	2.7	11.7	16.7	21.0	29.8	28.6	34.3	20.9	25.8
$75,000 to $99,999	7.5	0.0	0.5	1.8	4.1	5.6	13.5	11.9	16.0	15.0	19.3
$100,000 or more	7.3	0.9	1.0	1.4	2.6	2.9	14.7	10.1	17.3	48.1	35.2

Note: Earnings include wages and salary only.
Source: Bureau of the Census, 2013 Current Population Survey Annual Social and Economic Supplement, Internet site http://www.census.gov/hhes/www/cpstables/032013/perinc/toc.htm; calculations by New Strategist

Table 3.32 Women Who Work Full-Time by Earnings and Education, 2012: Women Aged 25 to 34

(number and percent distribution of women aged 25 to 34 who work full-time, year-round, by earnings and educational attainment, 2012; median earnings of women with earnings; women in thousands as of 2013)

	total	less than 9th grade	9th to 12th grade, no diploma	high school graduate	some college, no degree	associate's degree	bachelor's degree or more				
							total	bachelor's degree	master's degree	professional degree	doctoral degree
Women aged 25 to 34 who work full-time	9,868	101	307	1,779	1,627	1,205	4,848	3,315	1,243	134	155
Under $5,000	66	6	4	15	20	4	18	14	2	0	2
$5,000 to $9,999	129	7	21	52	9	8	32	31	1	0	0
$10,000 to $14,999	510	23	67	178	126	58	59	54	5	0	0
$15,000 to $19,999	735	29	63	276	182	99	85	75	10	0	0
$20,000 to $24,999	1,000	14	60	305	245	159	215	189	22	4	0
$25,000 to $29,999	1,095	10	48	280	252	188	318	276	30	2	10
$30,000 to $34,999	1,090	0	13	211	234	175	458	371	76	5	6
$35,000 to $39,999	1,022	3	8	190	198	118	503	371	121	7	5
$40,000 to $44,999	763	0	8	117	104	81	452	330	114	0	8
$45,000 to $49,999	698	1	6	39	71	94	487	304	159	9	16
$50,000 to $54,999	670	7	3	40	68	52	500	334	144	15	8
$55,000 to $59,999	304	0	0	26	28	22	228	125	86	9	8
$60,000 to $64,999	365	0	3	16	18	42	286	184	91	2	8
$65,000 to $69,999	265	0	0	4	17	29	215	144	64	4	4
$70,000 to $74,999	216	0	2	5	10	26	174	101	63	4	7
$75,000 to $79,999	201	0	0	6	4	13	178	118	38	16	7
$80,000 to $84,999	127	0	0	3	12	10	102	56	40	3	3
$85,000 to $89,999	76	0	0	1	3	0	72	41	25	0	6
$90,000 to $94,999	111	0	0	0	13	12	85	34	39	6	6
$95,000 to $99,999	44	0	0	0	5	3	36	16	16	0	4
$100,000 or more	382	0	0	17	8	13	343	148	98	48	50
Median earnings	$36,017	$16,613	$19,823	$25,820	$29,391	$31,691	$46,989	$43,306	$51,795	$76,541	$71,323

PERCENT DISTRIBUTION

	total	less than 9th grade	9th to 12th grade, no diploma	high school graduate	some college, no degree	associate's degree	bachelor's degree or more				
							total	bachelor's degree	master's degree	professional degree	doctoral degree
Women aged 25 to 34 who work full-time	100.0%	100.0%	100.0%	100.0%	100.0%	100.0%	100.0%	100.0%	100.0%	100.0%	100.0%
Under $15,000	7.1	35.6	29.8	13.8	9.5	5.8	2.2	3.0	0.6	0.0	1.5
$15,000 to $24,999	17.6	43.5	40.2	32.7	26.3	21.4	6.2	8.0	2.6	2.8	0.0
$25,000 to $34,999	22.1	9.9	19.8	27.6	29.9	30.1	16.0	19.5	8.5	5.4	10.0
$35,000 to $49,999	25.2	4.4	7.4	19.4	23.0	24.2	29.8	30.3	31.7	12.2	18.3
$50,000 to $74,999	18.4	6.7	2.7	5.1	8.6	14.2	29.0	26.8	36.0	24.8	22.3
$75,000 to $99,999	5.7	0.0	0.0	0.6	2.3	3.1	9.8	8.0	12.7	19.3	15.8
$100,000 or more	3.9	0.0	0.1	0.9	0.5	1.1	7.1	4.5	7.9	35.5	32.1

Note: Earnings include wages and salary only.
Source: Bureau of the Census, 2013 Current Population Survey Annual Social and Economic Supplement, Internet site http:// www.census.gov/hhes/www/cpstables/032013/perinc/toc.htm; calculations by New Strategist

Table 3.33 Women Who Work Full-Time by Earnings and Education, 2012: Women Aged 35 to 44

(number and percent distribution of women aged 35 to 44 who work full-time, year-round, by earnings and educational attainment, 2012; median earnings of women with earnings; women in thousands as of 2013)

	total	less than 9th grade	9th to 12th grade, no diploma	high school graduate	some college, no degree	associate's degree	bachelor's degree or more				
							total	bachelor's degree	master's degree	professional degree	doctoral degree
Women aged 35 to 44 who work full-time	10,051	178	371	2,226	1,576	1,262	4,438	2,699	1,347	185	207
Under $5,000	52	1	2	12	15	9	14	11	3	0	0
$5,000 to $9,999	109	6	19	34	20	14	17	12	4	0	0
$10,000 to $14,999	317	39	50	95	62	34	37	28	6	2	0
$15,000 to $19,999	670	37	86	296	106	60	85	67	12	5	0
$20,000 to $24,999	912	44	97	323	167	147	135	102	24	3	7
$25,000 to $29,999	834	24	38	326	161	124	161	137	20	2	2
$30,000 to $34,999	946	11	31	310	206	164	224	176	45	0	3
$35,000 to $39,999	986	6	22	276	213	122	347	240	96	2	9
$40,000 to $44,999	799	5	5	188	126	118	356	245	97	7	7
$45,000 to $49,999	632	3	3	88	110	108	320	194	115	3	8
$50,000 to $54,999	710	0	4	115	109	92	390	243	120	8	19
$55,000 to $59,999	380	0	2	38	40	61	239	161	73	4	0
$60,000 to $64,999	511	0	2	45	65	55	344	203	110	8	23
$65,000 to $69,999	322	0	0	13	47	54	209	119	62	12	16
$70,000 to $74,999	314	0	0	18	31	38	228	118	91	10	10
$75,000 to $79,999	165	0	0	13	16	4	132	67	51	5	8
$80,000 to $84,999	194	0	0	6	16	15	157	84	61	5	6
$85,000 to $89,999	125	0	0	6	10	10	100	61	34	0	4
$90,000 to $94,999	128	0	2	2	5	6	113	56	50	0	7
$95,000 to $99,999	100	0	0	1	11	6	82	47	23	6	7
$100,000 or more	843	1	8	22	40	22	750	327	249	102	71
Median earnings	**$40,759**	**$20,360**	**$21,306**	**$30,289**	**$35,875**	**$37,656**	**$56,867**	**$51,654**	**$61,839**	**$110,786**	**$74,697**

PERCENT DISTRIBUTION

	total	less than 9th grade	9th to 12th grade, no diploma	high school graduate	some college, no degree	associate's degree	bachelor's degree or more				
							total	bachelor's degree	master's degree	professional degree	doctoral degree
Women aged 35 to 44 who work full-time	100.0%	100.0%	100.0%	100.0%	100.0%	100.0%	100.0%	100.0%	100.0%	100.0%	100.0%
Under $15,000	4.8	26.1	19.0	6.3	6.2	4.5	1.5	1.9	1.0	1.2	0.1
$15,000 to $24,999	15.7	45.7	49.3	27.8	17.3	16.4	5.0	6.3	2.7	4.7	3.3
$25,000 to $34,999	17.7	19.7	18.6	28.6	23.3	22.8	8.7	11.6	4.8	0.9	2.4
$35,000 to $49,999	24.0	8.0	8.2	24.8	28.5	27.5	23.1	25.2	22.9	6.1	11.6
$50,000 to $74,999	22.3	0.0	2.1	10.3	18.5	23.7	31.7	31.3	33.9	22.4	32.7
$75,000 to $99,999	7.1	0.0	0.6	1.2	3.6	3.3	13.1	11.7	16.3	9.4	15.4
$100,000 or more	8.4	0.6	2.2	1.0	2.5	1.8	16.9	12.1	18.5	55.4	34.5

Note: Earnings include wages and salary only.
Source: Bureau of the Census, 2013 Current Population Survey Annual Social and Economic Supplement, Internet site http://www.census.gov/hhes/www/cpstables/032013/perinc/toc.htm; calculations by New Strategist

Table 3.34 Women Who Work Full-Time by Earnings and Education, 2012: Women Aged 45 to 54

(number and percent distribution of women aged 45 to 54 who work full-time, year-round, by earnings and educational attainment, 2012; median earnings of women with earnings; women in thousands as of 2013)

	total	less than 9th grade	9th to 12th grade, no diploma	high school graduate	some college, no degree	associate's degree	bachelor's degree or more				
							total	bachelor's degree	master's degree	professional degree	doctoral degree
Women aged 45 to 54 who work full-time	**11,397**	**202**	**353**	**3,076**	**1,912**	**1,523**	**4,331**	**2,825**	**1,165**	**168**	**173**
Under $5,000	44	5	3	14	3	5	14	12	3	0	0
$5,000 to $9,999	146	13	21	41	19	10	42	32	8	1	0
$10,000 to $14,999	400	22	53	175	54	45	52	40	7	1	3
$15,000 to $19,999	670	56	62	275	138	77	62	52	7	2	2
$20,000 to $24,999	1,048	44	83	437	192	118	174	147	21	2	3
$25,000 to $29,999	1,000	26	60	443	200	107	165	127	33	2	3
$30,000 to $34,999	1,125	17	23	444	233	181	227	183	33	4	7
$35,000 to $39,999	992	11	21	342	204	162	251	206	41	2	2
$40,000 to $44,999	929	1	9	254	170	161	333	249	70	6	7
$45,000 to $49,999	701	4	7	130	142	127	291	193	83	7	8
$50,000 to $54,999	785	0	0	165	127	128	364	229	121	7	7
$55,000 to $59,999	421	0	1	87	58	66	209	150	53	2	5
$60,000 to $64,999	507	1	3	62	113	63	265	167	82	6	10
$65,000 to $69,999	277	0	0	30	30	69	148	85	42	10	11
$70,000 to $74,999	416	0	0	38	59	51	268	177	78	5	8
$75,000 to $79,999	257	0	4	24	18	28	183	129	35	8	10
$80,000 to $84,999	290	0	0	31	37	36	187	102	70	3	12
$85,000 to $89,999	145	0	0	13	21	16	95	49	39	5	2
$90,000 to $94,999	159	0	0	11	12	11	125	77	37	1	9
$95,000 to $99,999	97	0	0	6	8	10	72	44	22	3	4
$100,000 or more	988	2	3	54	74	52	803	374	278	91	61
Median earnings	**$40,892**	**$20,451**	**$21,423**	**$31,109**	**$37,017**	**$41,220**	**$59,244**	**$52,286**	**$66,289**	**$105,940**	**$80,347**

PERCENT DISTRIBUTION

Women aged 45 to 54 who work full-time	**100.0%**	**100.0%**	**100.0%**	**100.0%**	**100.0%**	**100.0%**	**100.0%**	**100.0%**	**100.0%**	**100.0%**	**100.0%**
Under $15,000	5.2	19.9	21.7	7.5	4.0	3.9	2.5	3.0	1.6	1.5	1.6
$15,000 to $24,999	15.1	49.4	41.0	23.2	17.3	12.8	5.4	7.0	2.4	2.2	2.7
$25,000 to $34,999	18.6	21.1	23.4	28.8	22.6	18.9	9.1	11.0	5.7	3.3	5.7
$35,000 to $49,999	23.0	8.1	10.7	23.6	27.0	29.6	20.2	22.9	16.7	9.1	9.9
$50,000 to $74,999	21.1	0.4	1.3	12.4	20.2	24.8	29.0	28.6	32.3	17.7	23.3
$75,000 to $99,999	8.3	0.0	1.1	2.8	5.0	6.7	15.3	14.2	17.5	12.1	21.5
$100,000 or more	8.7	1.1	0.9	1.8	3.9	3.4	18.6	13.2	23.8	53.9	35.2

Note: Earnings include wages and salary only.
Source: Bureau of the Census, 2013 Current Population Survey Annual Social and Economic Supplement, Internet site http://www.census.gov/hhes/www/cpstables/032013/perinc/toc.htm; calculations by New Strategist

Table 3.35 Women Who Work Full-Time by Earnings and Education, 2012: Women Aged 55 to 64

(number and percent distribution of women aged 55 to 64 who work full-time, year-round, by earnings and educational attainment, 2012; median earnings of women with earnings; women in thousands as of 2013)

	total	less than 9th grade	9th to 12th grade, no diploma	high school graduate	some college, no degree	associate's degree	bachelor's degree or more total	bachelor's degree	master's degree	professional degree	doctoral degree
Women aged 55 to 64 who work full-time	8,346	170	224	2,289	1,483	1,065	3,116	1,841	963	153	158
Under $5,000	66	7	1	20	14	9	15	10	4	0	1
$5,000 to $9,999	84	6	3	32	19	0	25	21	3	0	0
$10,000 to $14,999	278	29	33	98	58	24	36	32	4	0	0
$15,000 to $19,999	441	38	32	149	68	65	90	70	20	0	0
$20,000 to $24,999	769	51	57	336	137	88	101	83	17	1	0
$25,000 to $29,999	716	14	22	307	152	109	112	84	24	4	0
$30,000 to $34,999	804	12	20	316	183	104	170	137	29	4	0
$35,000 to $39,999	718	3	15	215	205	115	166	127	31	4	4
$40,000 to $44,999	631	2	11	192	115	109	204	142	54	5	3
$45,000 to $49,999	563	3	13	176	100	78	192	122	56	6	8
$50,000 to $54,999	505	2	2	130	81	72	218	135	65	14	4
$55,000 to $59,999	314	0	0	73	48	26	166	98	63	6	0
$60,000 to $64,999	466	0	7	76	85	48	250	126	100	7	16
$65,000 to $69,999	240	0	0	43	40	31	126	76	48	1	0
$70,000 to $74,999	270	0	5	29	34	38	164	83	62	5	14
$75,000 to $79,999	216	0	0	18	17	24	157	86	57	3	11
$80,000 to $84,999	247	0	0	25	38	35	148	66	54	14	14
$85,000 to $89,999	90	0	0	6	18	11	55	26	20	1	7
$90,000 to $94,999	148	0	0	1	6	12	128	83	31	6	8
$95,000 to $99,999	74	0	1	1	15	17	41	16	20	3	2
$100,000 or more	706	3	2	48	53	49	551	218	201	68	64
Median earnings	$41,403	$20,364	$23,329	$31,979	$37,030	$40,452	$60,852	$51,968	$65,862	$90,649	$87,024

PERCENT DISTRIBUTION

	total	less than 9th grade	9th to 12th grade, no diploma	high school graduate	some college, no degree	associate's degree	bachelor's degree or more total	bachelor's degree	master's degree	professional degree	doctoral degree
Women aged 55 to 64 who work full-time	100.0%	100.0%	100.0%	100.0%	100.0%	100.0%	100.0%	100.0%	100.0%	100.0%	100.0%
Under $15,000	5.1	24.5	16.4	6.5	6.1	3.1	2.4	3.5	1.2	0.3	0.4
$15,000 to $24,999	14.5	52.5	39.7	21.2	13.8	14.3	6.1	8.3	3.8	0.4	0.2
$25,000 to $34,999	18.2	15.4	18.7	27.2	22.6	20.0	9.1	12.0	5.5	5.1	0.2
$35,000 to $49,999	22.9	4.6	17.5	25.4	28.3	28.4	18.0	21.2	14.6	9.9	9.8
$50,000 to $74,999	21.5	1.4	6.3	15.3	19.4	20.2	29.7	28.1	35.1	21.9	21.9
$75,000 to $99,999	9.3	0.0	0.5	2.2	6.3	9.4	17.0	15.1	18.9	17.9	27.1
$100,000 or more	8.5	1.6	1.0	2.1	3.6	4.6	17.7	11.8	20.9	44.6	40.4

Note: Earnings include wages and salary only.
Source: Bureau of the Census, 2013 Current Population Survey Annual Social and Economic Supplement, Internet site http://www.census.gov/hhes/www/cpstables/032013/perinc/toc.htm; calculations by New Strategist

Table 3.36 Women Who Work Full-Time by Earnings and Education, 2012: Women Aged 65 or Older

(number and percent distribution of women aged 65 or older who work full-time, year-round, by earnings and educational attainment, 2012; median earnings of women with earnings; women in thousands as of 2013)

	total	less than 9th grade	9th to 12th grade, no diploma	high school graduate	some college, no degree	associate's degree	bachelor's degree or more				
							total	bachelor's degree	master's degree	professional degree	doctoral degree
Women aged 65 or older who work full-time	1,657	39	97	500	302	190	530	281	168	29	52
Under $5,000	38	0	0	16	9	4	9	4	5	0	0
$5,000 to $9,999	29	1	3	14	1	3	6	5	1	0	0
$10,000 to $14,999	116	9	23	42	14	3	24	21	3	0	0
$15,000 to $19,999	108	7	19	49	15	12	6	2	3	0	1
$20,000 to $24,999	161	9	13	69	30	16	24	18	4	2	0
$25,000 to $29,999	138	4	12	59	28	14	21	13	5	3	0
$30,000 to $34,999	209	3	15	54	64	28	46	25	18	0	3
$35,000 to $39,999	95	0	1	28	26	16	24	18	5	0	2
$40,000 to $44,999	120	1	10	33	36	12	30	12	10	0	8
$45,000 to $49,999	101	1	0	26	23	18	33	12	20	1	0
$50,000 to $54,999	110	0	0	41	21	11	38	17	16	1	4
$55,000 to $59,999	43	0	2	19	5	5	13	5	7	0	2
$60,000 to $64,999	82	2	0	28	9	10	33	21	12	0	0
$65,000 to $69,999	44	0	0	4	8	8	26	19	6	0	0
$70,000 to $74,999	57	1	0	12	4	6	36	10	16	1	9
$75,000 to $79,999	12	0	0	0	0	3	9	7	2	0	0
$80,000 to $84,999	44	0	0	2	1	5	35	17	6	5	7
$85,000 to $89,999	13	0	0	0	0	0	13	7	3	3	0
$90,000 to $94,999	15	0	0	0	0	3	12	8	3	1	0
$95,000 to $99,999	13	0	0	3	1	2	7	4	3	0	0
$100,000 or more	108	0	0	3	8	13	84	36	19	13	16
Median earnings	**$36,427**	–	**$21,601**	**$30,090**	**$33,288**	**$40,140**	**$55,815**	**$51,605**	**$51,562**	–	–

PERCENT DISTRIBUTION

Women aged 65 or older who work full-time	100.0%	100.0%	100.0%	100.0%	100.0%	100.0%	100.0%	100.0%	100.0%	100.0%	100.0%
Under $15,000	11.0	28.0	27.0	14.4	8.0	5.1	7.4	10.8	5.4	0.0	0.0
$15,000 to $24,999	16.2	42.3	33.2	23.6	14.9	14.4	5.7	7.1	4.2	6.6	2.0
$25,000 to $34,999	21.0	19.4	27.6	22.6	30.6	22.0	12.5	13.4	13.7	9.5	5.3
$35,000 to $49,999	19.1	4.0	10.6	17.3	28.0	24.2	16.5	14.8	20.7	2.7	20.1
$50,000 to $74,999	20.3	6.3	1.6	20.5	15.1	20.4	27.5	25.8	33.9	6.1	27.9
$75,000 to $99,999	5.9	0.0	0.0	1.1	0.6	6.9	14.5	15.2	10.8	31.4	13.7
$100,000 or more	6.5	0.0	0.0	0.5	2.7	7.0	15.8	12.8	11.3	43.7	30.9

Note: Earnings include wages and salary only. "–" means sample is too small to make a reliable estimate.
Source: Bureau of the Census, 2013 Current Population Survey Annual Social and Economic Supplement, Internet site http://www.census.gov/hhes/www/cpstables/032013/perinc/toc.htm; calculations by New Strategist

Education Boosts Earnings in Every Race and Hispanic Origin Group

Among women with a bachelor's degree who work full-time, Asians earn the most.

The earnings of women vary much more by education than they do by race and Hispanic origin. Among full-time workers with a bachelor's degree, Asian women have the highest earnings. Their median earnings stood at $54,528 in 2012. Non-Hispanic white women rank second, with median earnings of $50,621. Black women with a bachelor's degree earned a median of $46,198, and their Hispanic counterparts earned $45,344.

Regardless of race or Hispanic origin, earnings are lowest among women with the least education. Among women who have no more than a high school diploma, median earnings ranged from a low of $26,330 for Hispanics to a high of $31,623 for non-Hispanic whites.

■ Among women with a bachelor's degree who work full-time, blacks and Hispanics have lower earnings than Asians and non-Hispanic whites.

Among women with a bachelor's degree, Hispanics earn the least

(median earnings of women aged 25 or older with a bachelor's degree who work full-time, year-round, by race and Hispanic origin, 2012)

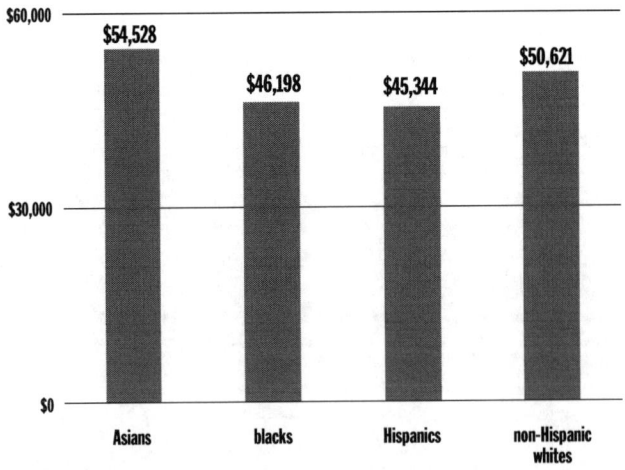

Table 3.37 Women Who Work Full-Time by Earnings and Education, 2012: Asian Women

(number and percent distribution of Asian women aged 25 or older who work full-time, year-round, by earnings and educational attainment, 2012; median earnings of women with earnings; women in thousands as of 2013)

| | total | less than 9th grade | 9th to 12th grade, no diploma | high school graduate | some college, no degree | associate's degree | bachelor's degree or more | | | | |
							total	bachelor's degree	master's degree	professional degree	doctoral degree
Asian women who work full-time	2,662	62	94	451	253	208	1,593	967	405	117	104
Under $5,000	13	0	0	5	4	0	4	4	0	0	0
$5,000 to $9,999	24	4	2	7	4	3	5	2	3	0	0
$10,000 to $14,999	89	6	27	36	2	2	15	15	0	0	0
$15,000 to $19,999	145	17	7	66	11	11	32	27	5	0	0
$20,000 to $24,999	229	18	23	74	30	20	63	44	13	4	3
$25,000 to $29,999	191	8	13	52	28	33	58	45	6	0	7
$30,000 to $34,999	185	3	7	53	32	10	80	72	8	0	0
$35,000 to $39,999	205	2	8	46	25	25	99	73	21	4	2
$40,000 to $44,999	176	2	3	27	25	12	107	72	23	4	8
$45,000 to $49,999	163	0	0	24	25	28	86	55	23	5	3
$50,000 to $54,999	164	0	0	22	22	14	105	78	20	5	3
$55,000 to $59,999	112	0	0	6	8	10	88	70	15	2	0
$60,000 to $64,999	146	0	2	6	24	10	104	67	25	8	5
$65,000 to $69,999	89	0	0	2	3	7	77	45	29	3	1
$70,000 to $74,999	93	0	0	6	2	3	82	38	31	1	14
$75,000 to $79,999	67	0	0	1	1	1	64	39	13	8	4
$80,000 to $84,999	71	0	0	2	2	3	64	36	18	0	10
$85,000 to $89,999	35	0	0	0	0	2	33	23	8	0	1
$90,000 to $94,999	67	0	0	2	0	0	65	32	24	4	5
$95,000 to $99,999	38	0	0	0	0	2	36	16	13	0	7
$100,000 or more	359	1	1	13	5	11	327	116	108	70	33
Median earnings	**$46,385**	–	**$21,607**	**$27,548**	**$37,356**	**$38,888**	**$61,522**	**$54,528**	**$71,139**	**$110,125**	**$81,033**

PERCENT DISTRIBUTION

| | total | less than 9th grade | 9th to 12th grade, no diploma | high school graduate | some college, no degree | associate's degree | bachelor's degree or more | | | | |
							total	bachelor's degree	master's degree	professional degree	doctoral degree
Asian women who work full-time	100.0%	100.0%	100.0%	100.0%	100.0%	100.0%	100.0%	100.0%	100.0%	100.0%	100.0%
Under $15,000	4.7	16.6	31.4	10.7	3.5	2.7	1.5	2.2	0.8	0.0	0.0
$15,000 to $24,999	14.0	57.1	31.8	31.1	16.2	15.3	6.0	7.3	4.4	3.6	2.8
$25,000 to $34,999	14.1	17.9	21.3	23.1	23.6	20.8	8.7	12.1	3.4	0.0	6.5
$35,000 to $49,999	20.4	6.2	12.2	21.6	29.6	30.9	18.3	20.7	16.6	10.6	11.7
$50,000 to $74,999	22.7	0.6	2.2	9.4	23.7	21.2	28.6	30.7	29.4	15.2	21.1
$75,000 to $99,999	10.4	0.0	0.3	1.2	1.2	3.6	16.4	15.1	18.7	11.0	26.4
$100,000 or more	13.5	1.6	0.8	3.0	2.1	5.5	20.5	12.0	26.8	59.6	31.4

Note: Asians are those who identify themselves as being of the race alone and those who identify themselves as being of the race in combination with other races. Earnings include wages and salary only. "–" means sample is too small to make a reliable estimate.
Source: Bureau of the Census, 2013 Current Population Survey Annual Social and Economic Supplement, Internet site http:// www.census.gov/hhes/www/cpstables/032013/perinc/toc.htm; calculations by New Strategist

Table 3.38 Women Who Work Full-Time by Earnings and Education, 2012: Black Women

(number and percent distribution of black women aged 25 or older who work full-time, year-round, by earnings and educational attainment, 2012; median earnings of women with earnings; women in thousands as of 2013)

	total	less than 9th grade	9th to 12th grade, no diploma	high school graduate	some college, no degree	associate's degree	bachelor's degree or more total	bachelor's degree	master's degree	professional degree	doctoral degree
Black women who work full-time	5,771	63	202	1,531	1,286	717	1,971	1,281	569	61	60
Under $5,000	18	0	0	7	4	5	2	2	0	0	0
$5,000 to $9,999	90	11	19	40	10	7	3	3	0	0	0
$10,000 to $14,999	281	18	32	122	53	31	24	23	1	0	0
$15,000 to $19,999	503	8	33	248	120	61	32	23	10	0	0
$20,000 to $24,999	649	8	53	245	184	85	75	61	9	2	2
$25,000 to $29,999	590	9	19	233	128	85	115	94	21	0	0
$30,000 to $34,999	686	4	21	193	222	92	154	122	27	2	4
$35,000 to $39,999	578	0	6	133	182	96	161	114	46	0	2
$40,000 to $44,999	437	1	7	84	87	61	198	156	33	3	6
$45,000 to $49,999	373	0	2	66	65	43	197	121	63	8	4
$50,000 to $54,999	318	2	0	41	68	36	171	105	54	4	8
$55,000 to $59,999	191	0	1	34	29	30	97	42	47	4	3
$60,000 to $64,999	222	2	2	23	46	22	128	94	29	0	4
$65,000 to $69,999	140	0	0	21	16	31	72	49	19	4	0
$70,000 to $74,999	140	0	0	6	25	7	103	60	32	5	5
$75,000 to $79,999	66	0	3	5	8	3	48	27	17	0	4
$80,000 to $84,999	103	0	0	9	8	9	77	44	30	0	4
$85,000 to $89,999	76	0	0	11	12	0	53	34	16	3	0
$90,000 to $94,999	52	0	0	4	5	3	40	24	14	0	2
$95,000 to $99,999	36	0	0	0	7	3	25	14	8	1	2
$100,000 or more	223	0	6	5	8	6	197	69	95	22	11
Median earnings	$35,383	–	$20,990	$26,534	$32,275	$34,176	$50,437	$46,198	$56,307	–	–

PERCENT DISTRIBUTION

	total	less than 9th grade	9th to 12th grade, no diploma	high school graduate	some college, no degree	associate's degree	bachelor's degree or more total	bachelor's degree	master's degree	professional degree	doctoral degree
Black women who work full-time	100.0%	100.0%	100.0%	100.0%	100.0%	100.0%	100.0%	100.0%	100.0%	100.0%	100.0%
Under $15,000	6.7	44.8	25.6	11.1	5.2	5.9	1.5	2.1	0.3	0.0	0.0
$15,000 to $24,999	20.0	26.0	42.2	32.2	23.6	20.3	5.4	6.6	3.3	3.1	3.7
$25,000 to $34,999	22.1	21.2	19.6	27.8	27.2	24.8	13.7	16.9	8.4	3.5	6.0
$35,000 to $49,999	24.1	1.3	7.0	18.5	26.0	27.9	28.2	30.6	24.9	19.3	18.5
$50,000 to $74,999	17.5	6.3	1.5	8.1	14.3	17.7	28.9	27.3	31.8	30.2	33.7
$75,000 to $99,999	5.8	0.0	1.3	1.9	3.0	2.5	12.3	11.1	14.8	6.7	20.3
$100,000 or more	3.9	0.4	2.8	0.3	0.6	0.9	10.0	5.4	16.6	37.1	17.8

Note: Blacks are those who identify themselves as being of the race alone and those who identify themselves as being of the race in combination with other races. Earnings include wages and salary only. "–" means sample is too small to make a reliable estimate.
Source: Bureau of the Census, 2013 Current Population Survey Annual Social and Economic Supplement, Internet site http:// www.census.gov/hhes/www/cpstables/032013/perinc/toc.htm; calculations by New Strategist

Table 3.39 Women Who Work Full-Time by Earnings and Education, 2012: Hispanic Women

(number and percent distribution of Hispanic women aged 25 or older who work full-time, year-round, by earnings and educational attainment, 2012; median earnings of women with earnings; women in thousands as of 2013)

	total	less than 9th grade	9th to 12th grade, no diploma	high school graduate	some college, no degree	associate's degree	bachelor's degree or more total	bachelor's degree	master's degree	professional degree	doctoral degree
Hispanic women who work full-time	5,372	496	538	1,546	920	592	1,279	898	302	44	36
Under $5,000	39	14	4	6	4	2	9	6	3	0	0
$5,000 to $9,999	103	20	20	32	12	5	14	14	0	0	0
$10,000 to $14,999	441	94	93	142	53	24	35	29	5	1	0
$15,000 to $19,999	672	132	136	235	79	48	42	38	3	2	0
$20,000 to $24,999	806	119	126	288	130	80	62	49	12	1	0
$25,000 to $29,999	583	56	62	205	114	59	86	80	5	1	0
$30,000 to $34,999	550	30	34	190	117	80	99	85	12	0	2
$35,000 to $39,999	441	17	30	138	109	60	87	61	26	0	0
$40,000 to $44,999	331	5	11	89	82	47	98	79	12	4	3
$45,000 to $49,999	280	7	11	47	46	47	122	79	40	1	1
$50,000 to $54,999	296	0	1	65	60	37	132	96	31	1	4
$55,000 to $59,999	121	0	2	26	23	19	51	31	14	4	2
$60,000 to $64,999	156	1	3	36	26	14	76	46	26	3	1
$65,000 to $69,999	81	0	0	6	14	33	28	20	6	2	0
$70,000 to $74,999	82	0	0	11	12	9	50	33	13	1	2
$75,000 to $79,999	67	0	1	9	12	6	39	20	15	4	0
$80,000 to $84,999	60	0	0	2	5	4	49	25	20	2	2
$85,000 to $89,999	22	0	0	3	1	1	17	14	3	0	0
$90,000 to $94,999	43	0	2	0	0	4	36	24	9	1	2
$95,000 to $99,999	9	0	0	0	2	1	7	5	2	0	0
$100,000 or more	188	0	2	17	18	11	141	63	47	17	14
Median earnings	$30,241	$19,388	$20,484	$26,330	$31,801	$34,657	$48,891	$45,344	$55,945	–	–

PERCENT DISTRIBUTION

Hispanic women who work full-time	100.0%	100.0%	100.0%	100.0%	100.0%	100.0%	100.0%	100.0%	100.0%	100.0%	100.0%
Under $15,000	10.9	26.0	21.8	11.6	7.5	5.3	4.5	5.4	2.5	3.2	0.0
$15,000 to $24,999	27.5	50.7	48.7	33.8	22.7	21.7	8.1	9.7	4.8	4.7	0.0
$25,000 to $34,999	21.1	17.4	17.9	25.5	25.1	23.5	14.5	18.4	5.5	3.2	6.1
$35,000 to $49,999	19.6	5.8	9.5	17.7	25.8	26.0	24.0	24.4	25.6	12.4	13.0
$50,000 to $74,999	13.7	0.2	1.1	9.3	14.8	19.0	26.4	25.2	29.8	24.7	27.3
$75,000 to $99,999	3.7	0.0	0.6	0.9	2.2	2.7	11.5	9.8	16.2	13.4	13.0
$100,000 or more	3.5	0.0	0.3	1.1	1.9	1.9	11.0	7.0	15.6	38.4	40.5

Note: Earnings include wages and salary only. "–" means sample is too small to make a reliable estimate.
Source: Bureau of the Census, 2013 Current Population Survey Annual Social and Economic Supplement, Internet site http://www.census.gov/hhes/www/cpstables/032013/perinc/toc.htm; calculations by New Strategist

Table 3.40 Women Who Work Full-Time by Earnings and Education, 2012: Non-Hispanic White Women

(number and percent distribution of non-Hispanic white women aged 25 or older who work full-time, year-round, by earnings and educational attainment, 2012; median earnings of women with earnings; women in thousands as of 2013)

	total	less than 9th grade	9th to 12th grade, no diploma	high school graduate	some college, no degree	associate's degree	bachelor's degree or more total	bachelor's degree	master's degree	professional degree	doctoral degree
Non-Hispanic white women who work full-time	27,369	85	529	6,282	4,374	3,717	12,382	7,785	3,612	452	533
Under $5,000	193	3	6	57	47	23	56	40	13	0	3
$5,000 to $9,999	279	3	23	92	42	20	99	83	15	1	0
$10,000 to $14,999	802	13	72	279	198	104	136	112	20	2	3
$15,000 to $19,999	1,308	10	93	499	292	192	222	178	35	5	4
$20,000 to $24,999	2,212	20	114	855	427	347	448	383	56	5	4
$25,000 to $29,999	2,367	6	84	909	510	354	505	410	77	10	8
$30,000 to $34,999	2,724	6	43	879	543	469	784	607	153	11	13
$35,000 to $39,999	2,580	4	21	730	530	352	942	707	207	10	18
$40,000 to $44,999	2,277	2	24	582	353	356	960	661	275	8	17
$45,000 to $49,999	1,881	5	19	316	304	310	927	572	312	11	32
$50,000 to $54,999	2,012	6	8	365	254	267	1,112	688	362	34	28
$55,000 to $59,999	1,029	0	0	176	117	123	612	392	199	12	9
$60,000 to $64,999	1,402	0	9	164	188	171	871	496	316	13	45
$65,000 to $69,999	827	0	0	64	107	123	533	321	168	16	28
$70,000 to $74,999	953	1	7	77	99	137	633	356	233	17	27
$75,000 to $79,999	652	0	0	45	34	62	511	321	140	24	26
$80,000 to $84,999	669	0	0	53	85	86	444	227	163	28	26
$85,000 to $89,999	313	0	0	13	39	34	228	113	94	5	16
$90,000 to $94,999	403	0	0	8	31	37	327	180	119	11	16
$95,000 to $99,999	240	0	1	11	28	31	170	90	61	11	7
$100,000 or more	2,250	5	6	108	149	120	1,862	850	594	215	204
Median earnings	**$41,647**	**$22,101**	**$22,791**	**$31,623**	**$35,914**	**$39,964**	**$54,995**	**$50,621**	**$60,915**	**$95,058**	**$80,395**

PERCENT DISTRIBUTION

	total	less than 9th grade	9th to 12th grade, no diploma	high school graduate	some college, no degree	associate's degree	bachelor's degree or more total	bachelor's degree	master's degree	professional degree	doctoral degree
Non-Hispanic white women who work full-time	100.0%	100.0%	100.0%	100.0%	100.0%	100.0%	100.0%	100.0%	100.0%	100.0%	100.0%
Under $15,000	4.7	22.4	19.1	6.8	6.6	3.9	2.4	3.0	1.3	0.8	1.1
$15,000 to $24,999	12.9	36.2	39.2	21.5	16.4	14.5	5.4	7.2	2.5	2.4	1.5
$25,000 to $34,999	18.6	14.1	23.9	28.5	24.1	22.1	10.4	13.1	6.4	4.8	3.9
$35,000 to $49,999	24.6	13.3	12.2	25.9	27.1	27.4	22.9	24.9	22.0	6.5	12.6
$50,000 to $74,999	22.7	8.4	4.4	13.5	17.5	22.1	30.4	28.9	35.4	20.5	25.6
$75,000 to $99,999	8.3	0.0	0.2	2.1	5.0	6.7	13.6	12.0	16.0	17.6	17.2
$100,000 or more	8.2	5.5	1.1	1.7	3.4	3.2	15.0	10.9	16.4	47.5	38.2

Note: Non-Hispanic whites are those who identify themselves as being of the race alone and not Hispanic. Earnings include wages and salary only.
Source: Bureau of the Census, 2013 Current Population Survey Annual Social and Economic Supplement, Internet site http:// www.census.gov/hhes/www/cpstables/032013/perinc/toc.htm; calculations by New Strategist

Among Women, Lawyers Earn the Most

Cashiers earn the least.

Among full-time workers, women earn 77 percent as much as men. There are many reasons for the earnings gap between women and men. On average, working men are older and have more job experience than working women. In addition, the average male worker has been better educated, although that is no longer the case in the younger age groups. The different career choices of men and women also contribute to the gap.

Among women who work full-time, lawyers earn the most, a median of $117,311 in 2012. Doctors earned a median of $111,891. Other high-paying occupations among women are CEO ($82,167) and engineer ($79,532). Among the 2.3 million women employed full-time as nurses, median earnings are a substantial $59,223. Women's earnings are lowest among chefs and cooks ($20,542) and cashiers ($19,165).

■ The earnings gap between women and men should shrink in the years ahead as better-educated women gain job experience.

Women's earnings vary by occupation

(median earnings of women aged 15 or older working full-time, year-round, by selected occupation, 2012)

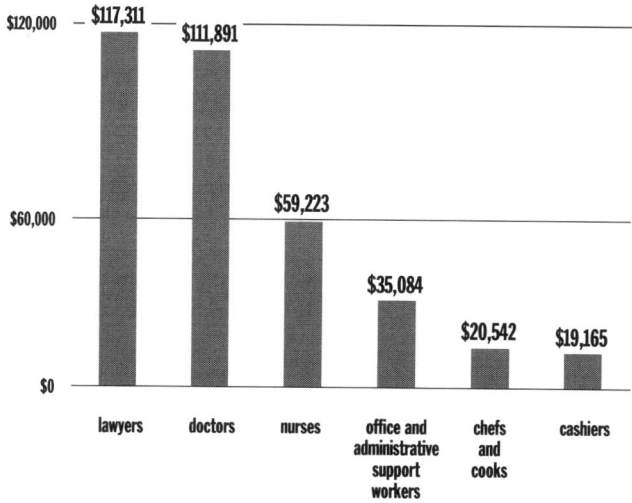

Table 3.41 Median Earnings of Women by Occupation, 2012

(number of women aged 15 or older who work full-time, year-round, and median earnings, by occupation of longest job held, 2012; women in thousands as of 2013)

	number with earnings	median earnings
TOTAL WOMEN WORKING FULL-TIME, YEAR-ROUND	**44,042**	**$37,791**
Management, science, and arts occupations	**20,517**	**51,304**
Management, business and financial operations occupations	8,255	52,438
Management occupations	5,177	55,719
Chief executives, general and operations managers	641	82,167
All other managers	4,535	52,078
Business and financial operations occupations	3,078	51,350
Business operations specialists	1,518	51,688
Financial specialists	1,560	51,128
Professional and related occupations	12,262	50,605
Computer and mathematical occupations	966	67,203
Computer scientists, analysts, programmers, engineers, and administrators	849	67,114
Mathematicians, statisticians, operations research, and other math occupations	105	67,314
Architecture and engineering occupations	326	66,232
Engineers	193	79,532
Life, physical, and social science occupations	447	61,119
Psychologists and sociologists	96	64,843
All other scientists	249	61,484
Science technicians	86	46,468
Community and social services occupations	1,131	41,364
Legal occupations	687	58,468
Lawyers, judges, and magistrates	277	117,311
Paralegals, legal assistants, and legal support workers	409	43,443
Education, training, and library occupations	3,798	44,159
Postsecondary teachers	380	60,192
All other teachers	2,817	45,683
Archivists, curators, museum technicians, librarians, and other technicians and assistants	601	22,723
Arts, design, entertainment, sports, and media occupations	747	44,724
Health care practitioner and technical occupations	4,161	55,583
Doctors	254	111,891
Nurses	2,295	59,223
All other health and technical occupations	1,613	47,416
Service occupations	**7,064**	**23,927**
Health care support occupations	1,807	26,624
Protective service occupations	494	42,215
Firefighters and police	140	66,239
All other protective service occupations	307	35,326
Food preparation and serving related occupations	1,576	20,739
Supervisors	211	26,963
Chefs and cooks	428	20,542
All other food preparation occupations	937	19,897
Building and grounds cleaning and maintenance occupations	1,116	21,078
Supervisors	127	30,110
All other maintenance occupations	989	20,681

	number with earnings	median earnings
Personal care and service occupations	2,072	$22,824
Supervisors	163	31,750
All other personal care and service occupations	1,908	22,070
Sales and office occupations	**13,581**	**32,991**
Sales and related occupations	4,131	30,495
Supervisors	1,434	33,632
Cashiers	834	19,165
Insurance sales agents	221	41,065
Real estate brokers and sales agents	252	35,689
All other sales and related occupations	1,389	31,432
Office and administrative support occupations	9,450	35,084
Supervisors	824	41,185
Postal workers	196	52,993
All other office and administrative support occupations	8,429	33,678
Natural resources, construction, and maintenance occupations	**362**	**31,678**
Farming, fishing, and forestry occupations	95	20,587
Farming, fishing, and forestry occupations, except supervisors	86	20,265
Construction and extraction occupations	98	27,494
Construction	93	27,348
Installation, maintenance, and repair occupations	169	42,773
All other installation, maintenance, and repair occupations, except supervisors	126	41,981
Production, transportation, and material moving occupations	**2,450**	**27,381**
Production occupations	1,622	27,324
Supervisors	126	39,761
All other production occupations	1,496	26,808
Transportation and material moving occupations	**828**	**27,511**
Auto, bus, truck, ambulance, taxi drivers	254	30,780
All other transportation occupations	506	25,852

Note: Number of workers does not add to total because only occupations with data on median earnings are shown. Earnings include wages and salary only.
Source: Bureau of the Census, 2013 Current Population Survey Annual Social and Economic Supplement, Internet site http://www.census.gov/hhes/www/cpstables/032013/perinc/toc.htm; calculations by New Strategist

Nearly Two-Thirds of Women Receive Wage or Salary Income

About one in four receives Social Security.

Wage or salary income is the only type received by the majority of women, with 65 percent earning wages or a salary in 2012. The second-most-common type of income is interest, received by 41 percent of women. Social Security ranks third at 24 percent. Among those with Social Security income, the median annual amount received was $11,475.

Hispanic women are most likely to receive wage or salary income. Seventy-two percent of Hispanic women had wage or salary income in 2012 versus 69 percent of Asian women, 67 percent of black women, and 63 percent of non-Hispanic white women. Twenty-eight percent of non-Hispanic white women receive Social Security income versus a smaller 20 percent of blacks and only 14 percent of Hispanics and Asians.

■ As the baby-boom generation retires, the proportion of women with Social Security and retirement income will rise.

Few women receive retirement income

(percentage of women aged 15 or older receiving income, by source of income, 2012)

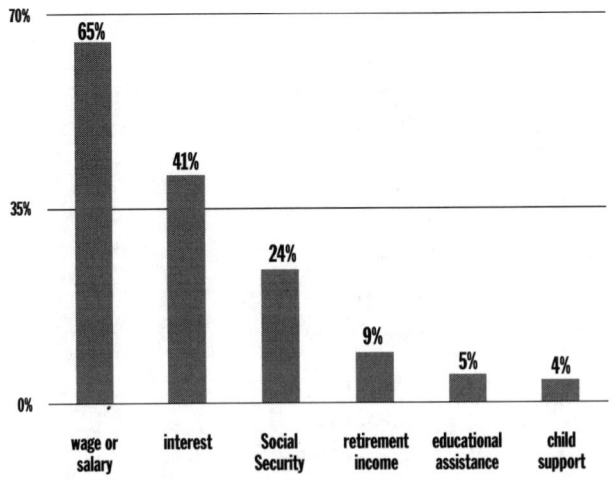

Table 3.42 Median Income of Women by Source of Income, 2012: Total Women

(number and percent of women aged 15 or older with income, and median income of those with income, 2012; women in thousands as of 2013)

	number	percent receiving	median income
Women with income	**109,383**	**100.0%**	**$21,520**
Earnings	74,188	67.8	26,882
Wage or salary	70,757	64.7	27,279
Nonfarm self-employment	4,796	4.4	10,652
Farm self-employment	730	0.7	1,865
Social Security	26,538	24.3	11,475
SSI (Supplemental Security)	3,450	3.2	7,972
Public Assistance	1,726	1.6	2,370
Veteran's benefits	585	0.5	12,123
Survivor's benefits	2,163	2.0	7,572
Disability benefits	781	0.7	10,319
Unemployment compensation	3,770	3.4	3,935
Worker's compensation	686	0.6	2,861
Property income	47,417	43.3	1,587
Interest	44,360	40.6	1,406
Dividends	14,513	13.3	1,698
Rents, royalties, estates, trusts	5,404	4.9	2,292
Retirement income	9,985	9.1	10,303
Company or union retirement	4,862	4.4	6,529
Federal government retirement	887	0.8	17,118
Military retirement	259	0.2	13,674
State or local government retirement	2,933	2.7	15,716
Railroad retirement	92	0.1	11,392
Annuities	354	0.3	6,737
IRA or Keogh, or 401(k)	392	0.4	6,954
Pension income	7,489	6.8	10,655
Company or union retirement	3,776	3.5	6,451
Federal government retirement	631	0.6	20,096
Military retirement	106	0.1	13,299
State or local government retirement	2,626	2.4	16,486
Railroad retirement	57	0.1	–
Annuities	117	0.1	9,771
Alimony	361	0.3	8,472
Child support	4,525	4.1	3,920
Educational assistance	5,810	5.3	4,945
Financial assistance from outside the household	1,562	1.4	3,931
Other income	530	0.5	1,715

Note: IRA and 401(k) income includes only withdrawals taken in the form of annuities. "–" means sample is too small to make a reliable estimate.
Source: Bureau of the Census, 2013 Current Population Survey Annual Social and Economic Supplement, Internet site http:// www.census.gov/hhes/www/cpstables/032013/perinc/toc.htm; calculations by New Strategist

Table 3.43 Median Income of Women by Source of Income, 2012: Asian Women

(number and percent of Asian women aged 15 or older with income, and median income of those with income, 2012; women in thousands as of 2013)

	number	percent receiving	median income
Asian women with income	**5,972**	**100.0%**	**$23,290**
Earnings	4,368	73.1	31,393
Wage or salary	4,131	69.2	31,993
Nonfarm self-employment	308	5.2	12,485
Farm self-employment	36	0.6	–
Social Security	818	13.7	10,268
SSI (Supplemental Security)	167	2.8	8,046
Public Assistance	36	0.6	–
Veteran's benefits	23	0.4	–
Survivor's benefits	60	1.0	–
Disability benefits	37	0.6	–
Unemployment compensation	160	2.7	4,911
Worker's compensation	31	0.5	–
Property income	2,709	45.4	1,513
Interest	2,528	42.3	1,373
Dividends	772	12.9	1,600
Rents, royalties, estates, trusts	302	5.1	2,160
Retirement income	249	4.2	11,213
Company or union retirement	108	1.8	10,086
Federal government retirement	19	0.3	–
Military retirement	12	0.2	–
State or local government retirement	67	1.1	–
Railroad retirement	0	0.0	–
Annuities	12	0.2	–
IRA or Keogh, or 401(k)	16	0.3	–
Pension income	154	2.6	11,475
Company or union retirement	86	1.4	8,624
Federal government retirement	11	0.2	–
Military retirement	3	0.1	–
State or local government retirement	47	0.8	–
Railroad retirement	0	0.0	–
Annuities	3	0.1	–
Alimony	5	0.1	–
Child support	99	1.7	4,032
Educational assistance	413	6.9	6,028
Financial assistance from outside the household	126	2.1	7,261
Other income	34	0.6	–

Note: IRA and 401(k) income includes only withdrawals taken in the form of annuities. Asians are those who identify themselves as being of the race alone and those who identify themselves as being of the race in combination with other races. "–" means sample is too small to make a reliable estimate.
Source: Bureau of the Census, 2013 Current Population Survey Annual Social and Economic Supplement, Internet site http://www.census.gov/hhes/www/cpstables/032013/perinc/toc.htm; calculations by New Strategist

Table 3.44 Median Income of Women by Source of Income, 2012: Black Women

(number and percent of black women aged 15 or older with income, and median income of those with income, 2012; women in thousands as of 2013)

	number	percent receiving	median income
Black women with income	**14,722**	**100.0%**	**$19,925**
Earnings	10,152	69.0	24,824
Wage or salary	9,911	67.3	25,046
Nonfarm self-employment	381	2.6	9,774
Farm self-employment	39	0.3	–
Social Security	2,912	19.8	10,596
SSI (Supplemental Security)	950	6.5	8,123
Public Assistance	573	3.9	2,540
Veteran's benefits	112	0.8	9,557
Survivor's benefits	191	1.3	6,016
Disability benefits	132	0.9	9,940
Unemployment compensation	781	5.3	3,782
Worker's compensation	114	0.8	4,496
Property income	3,274	22.2	1,461
Interest	3,019	20.5	1,365
Dividends	602	4.1	1,490
Rents, royalties, estates, trusts	323	2.2	2,109
Retirement income	1,117	7.6	11,286
Company or union retirement	543	3.7	8,058
Federal government retirement	143	1.0	15,880
Military retirement	24	0.2	–
State or local government retirement	309	2.1	15,865
Railroad retirement	4	0.0	–
Annuities	19	0.1	–
IRA or Keogh, or 401(k)	31	0.2	–
Pension income	852	5.8	12,173
Company or union retirement	447	3.0	8,716
Federal government retirement	105	0.7	24,275
Military retirement	8	0.1	–
State or local government retirement	266	1.8	16,807
Railroad retirement	2	0.0	–
Annuities	13	0.1	–
Alimony	20	0.1	–
Child support	946	6.4	3,072
Educational assistance	1,173	8.0	4,707
Financial assistance from outside the household	213	1.4	2,094
Other income	76	0.5	2723

Note: IRA and 401(k) income includes only withdrawals taken in the form of annuities. Blacks are those who identify themselves as being of the race alone and those who identify themselves as being of the race in combination with other races. "–" means sample is too small to make a reliable estimate.
Source: Bureau of the Census, 2013 Current Population Survey Annual Social and Economic Supplement, Internet site http:// www.census.gov/hhes/www/cpstables/032013/perinc/toc.htm; calculations by New Strategist

Table 3.45 Median Income of Women by Source of Income, 2012: Hispanic Women

(number and percent of Hispanic women aged 15 or older with income, and median income of those with income, 2012; women in thousands as of 2013)

	number	percent receiving	median income
Hispanic women with income	**13,689**	**100.0%**	**$16,725**
Earnings	10,293	75.2	20,369
Wage or salary	9,845	71.9	20,599
Nonfarm self-employment	560	4.1	10,781
Farm self-employment	26	0.2	–
Social Security	1,922	14.0	9,673
SSI (Supplemental Security)	618	4.5	7,562
Public Assistance	435	3.2	3,076
Veteran's benefits	39	0.3	–
Survivor's benefits	76	0.6	6,910
Disability benefits	85	0.6	9,025
Unemployment compensation	485	3.5	3,853
Worker's compensation	86	0.6	2,742
Property income	3,147	23.0	1,430
Interest	2,906	21.2	1,331
Dividends	535	3.9	1,591
Rents, royalties, estates, trusts	350	2.6	2,114
Retirement income	489	3.6	9,640
Company or union retirement	265	1.9	7,272
Federal government retirement	35	0.3	–
Military retirement	9	0.1	–
State or local government retirement	122	0.9	15,207
Railroad retirement	4	0.0	–
Annuities	8	0.1	–
IRA or Keogh, or 401(k)	11	0.1	–
Pension income	344	2.5	9,934
Company or union retirement	198	1.4	7,173
Federal government retirement	20	0.1	–
Military retirement	7	0.1	–
State or local government retirement	102	0.7	16,774
Railroad retirement	4	0.0	–
Annuities	5	0.0	–
Alimony	23	0.2	–
Child support	736	5.4	4,071
Educational assistance	905	6.6	3,946
Financial assistance from outside the household	190	1.4	2,937
Other income	58	0.4	–

Note: IRA and 401(k) income includes only withdrawals taken in the form of annuities. "–" means sample is too small to make a reliable estimate.
Source: Bureau of the Census, 2013 Current Population Survey Annual Social and Economic Supplement, Internet site http://www.census.gov/hhes/www/cpstables/032013/perinc/toc.htm; calculations by New Strategist

Table 3.46 Median Income of Women by Source of Income, 2012: Non-Hispanic White Women

(number and percent of non-Hispanic white women aged 15 or older with income, and median income of those with income, 2012; women in thousands as of 2013)

	number	percent receiving	median income
Non-Hispanic white women with income	**74,529**	**100.0%**	**$22,902**
Earnings	49,134	65.9	29,978
Wage or salary	46,660	62.6	30,353
Nonfarm self-employment	3,505	4.7	10,619
Farm self-employment	620	0.8	1,907
Social Security	20,692	27.8	11,843
SSI (Supplemental Security)	1,691	2.3	8,051
Public Assistance	666	0.9	2,110
Veteran's benefits	419	0.6	12,787
Survivor's benefits	1,818	2.4	7,684
Disability benefits	519	0.7	10,868
Unemployment compensation	2,330	3.1	3,933
Worker's compensation	455	0.6	2,639
Property income	38,051	51.1	1,620
Interest	35,681	47.9	1,419
Dividends	12,523	16.8	1,722
Rents, royalties, estates, trusts	4,399	5.9	2,348
Retirement income	8,078	10.8	10,131
Company or union retirement	3,945	5.3	6,316
Federal government retirement	677	0.9	17,926
Military retirement	211	0.3	13,806
State or local government retirement	2,415	3.2	15,748
Railroad retirement	84	0.1	16,181
Annuities	313	0.4	5,781
IRA or Keogh, or 401(k)	331	0.4	7,822
Pension income	6,116	8.2	10,357
Company or union retirement	3,047	4.1	6,221
Federal government retirement	488	0.7	20,002
Military retirement	91	0.1	13,060
State or local government retirement	2,194	2.9	16,354
Railroad retirement	51	0.1	–
Annuities	96	0.1	8,590
Alimony	311	0.4	8,825
Child support	2,750	3.7	4,168
Educational assistance	3,336	4.5	5,184
Financial assistance from outside the household	1009	1.4	4,438
Other income	342	0.5	1,561

Note: IRA and 401(k) income includes only withdrawals taken in the form of annuities. Non-Hispanic whites are those who identify themselves as white alone and not Hispanic. "–" means sample is too small to make a reliable estimate.
Source: Bureau of the Census, 2013 Current Population Survey Annual Social and Economic Supplement, Internet site http://www.census.gov/hhes/www/cpstables/032013/perinc/toc.htm; calculations by New Strategist

CHAPTER

4

Discretionary Income

In 2012, the average American household had $14,037 in discretionary income. This is money households could spend freely after paying their bills and buying necessities. In the aggregate, American households control $1.7 trillion in discretionary dollars.

Discretionary income is the money that remains for spending (or saving or paying down debt) after one has paid for all the necessary costs of living a middle-class lifestyle. Many businesses depend on discretionary dollars for sales and profits. This dependency makes discretionary income statistics important for marketers and other researchers. Despite this importance, however, discretionary income statistics can be hard to find because no government agency is charged with producing them. This chapter contains 2012 estimates of discretionary income produced by New Strategist's researchers.

Between 2007 and 2012, the amount of discretionary income available to the average household fell 2 percent, after adjusting for inflation—from $14,375 before the Great Recession to the $14,037 of 2012. This decline is not surprising. What is surprising is that the decline was not greater. Average household income, for example, fell 6 percent during those years. Disposable household income (the income that remains after taxes and mandatory withdrawals for retirement accounts) fell 5 percent. The reason for the relative stability in discretionary income is budget cutting, as many households reduced their spending on necessities in the wake of the Great Recession. One of the most important ways in which households cut their spending on necessities was by reducing housing expenses in the shift away from homeownership. The homeownership rate of 35-to-44-year-olds, for example, fell from 68 to 62 percent between 2007 and 2012. With more renters and fewer owners, the average household in the age group cut its spending on housing by 14 percent between 2007 and 2012, after adjusting for inflation.

Trends in Household Income and Spending, 2007 to 2012

(average annual income and spending of households, 2007 and 2012; in 2012 dollars)

	2012	2007	percent change
Average household income	$65,596	$69,862	−6.1%
Disposable income	54,920	57,601	−4.7
Discretionary income	14,037	14,375	−2.4
Average household spending	51,442	54,965	−6.4
Nondiscretionary spending	40,883	43,225	−5.4
Discretionary spending	10,559	11,740	−10.1

Note: Disposable income is what remains after taxes and manadatory withdrawals for retirement accounts.
Source: Calculations by New Strategist based on the Bureau of Labor Statistics' 2007 and 2012 Consumer Expenditure Surveys

Estimating Discretionary Income

New Strategist produced the estimates of discretionary income shown here in three steps. First we calculated disposable income—or take-home pay. We started with 2012 before-tax income data from the Bureau of Labor Statistics' Consumer Expenditure Survey. Disposable income is what remains after subtracting federal, state, and local income taxes; payroll taxes including FICA; and mandatory deductions from paychecks for retirement plans.

In step two, we examined consumer expenditures item by item to determine necessary household expenses. The Consumer Expenditure Survey is the only ongoing national survey of American household spending. It tracks the dollars Americans spend by detailed category of goods and services. By tagging necessities, we estimated nondiscretionary—or necessary—household spending.

In the third step, we subtracted necessary expenses from disposable income. The difference between necessary spending and disposable income is discretionary income. We calculated average and aggregate discretionary income for households by age of householder, household income, household type, race and Hispanic origin of householder, region of residence, and educational attainment of householder. Note that discretionary *income* is not the same as discretionary *spending*. Discretionary income is the money available to spend on discretionary items. Discretionary spending is the money households actually spend on discretionary items. In 2012, the average household spent $10,559 of its discretionary dollars, or 75 percent of its discretionary income. Discretionary spending was 10 percent lower in 2012 than in 2007, after adjusting for inflation. Many households are choosing to use their discretionary income to boost their savings or pay off debt.

Most major expenditure categories have a mixture of discretionary and necessary spending. A brief description of how we define various items by category follows, along with the discretionary share of spending in each category.

• **Food at home, 17 percent discretionary.** Most food-at-home items (groceries) are defined as necessary expenses with the exception of sweets and snack foods. Items such as prepared desserts, colas, ice cream, candy, etc. are deemed discretionary. Spending on groceries purchased on trips is also defined as discretionary.

• **Food away from home, 60 percent discretionary.** Meals at fast-food restaurants and employer and school cafeterias are tagged as necessary expenses. Meals at full-service restaurants are deemed discretionary. All snacks are identified as discretionary, as are restaurant meals on trips and catered affairs.

• **Alcoholic beverages, 100 percent discretionary.**

• **Housing and household operations, 7 percent discretionary.** We tag most housing expenses as necessary except for spending on "other lodging," which includes hotel and motel expenses. Also identified as discretionary are expenditures on housekeeping services, gardening and lawn care services, and items such as outdoor equipment (grills), decorative items for the home, and luggage. Computers and cell phone service are considered necessary expenses.

• **Apparel, 10 percent discretionary.** Costumes, dry cleaning expenses, watches, and jewelry are the only apparel items identified as discretionary.

• **Transportation, 8 percent discretionary.** Spending on "other vehicles" such as motorcycles and airplanes is identified as discretionary. Vehicle audio and video equipment as well as global positioning services and automobile clubs are also classified as discretionary. Any spending on transportation related to travel, such as vehicle rentals, airline fares, ship fares, and so on, is considered discretionary.

• **Health care, 1 percent discretionary.** Nonprescription vitamins are the only discretionary item in the health care category.

• **Entertainment, 100 percent discretionary.**

• **Personal care, 25 percent discretionary.** Cosmetics, perfume, and bath products are the only discretionary items in the personal care category.

• **Reading, 100 percent discretionary.**

• **Education, 15 percent discretionary.** The only discretionary items in the category are elementary and high school tuition and testing and tutoring services. We consider spending on college tuition to be a necessary expense in today's competitive economy.

• **Tobacco products and smoking supplies, 100 percent discretionary.**

• **Financial and miscellaneous products, 28 percent discretionary.** Discretionary expenses include lottery tickets, credit card memberships, and all cash gifts and charitable contributions. Also tagged as discretionary are voluntary contributions to retirement plans.

Entertainment is the discretionary item on which the average household spends the most (see table 4.1). Not only is entertainment one of the biggest household expenses overall, but we tagged the entire category as discretionary. In 2012, the average household spent $2,605 on entertainment. Spending on the number-two discretionary item, cash contributions to religious organizations, is considerably smaller at $734. Interestingly, two of the top-10 discretionary expenses are contributions—religious contributions is number two and cash gifts to people in other households (mostly family members) is number five. Eating at full-service restaurants is an important part of discretionary spending, dinner at full-service restaurants ranking third and lunch ranking 10th. Two travel categories also make the top-10 list—airline fares in seventh place and lodging in eighth place. The vices place highly among discretionary expenses, with alcoholic beverages in sixth place and tobacco in ninth place.

What Is Discretionary?

No definition of necessary expenses can be exact. All are likely to include at least some discretionary items, and some necessary items are probably included in discretionary spending as well. One reason for the overlap is that the categories of expenses in the Consumer Expenditure Survey can include both discretionary and necessary items.

Ultimately, defining basic expenses is subjective on the part of the consumer and a judgment call on the part of researchers. Some of the grocery spending we include as basic may be discretionary—for example buying an expensive steak in the grocery store. Others might argue that spending on fast food is discretionary, but many Americans would disagree. Fast-food meals have become a necessary expense for today's busy two-earner households.

Consumer Expenditure Survey data do not allow researchers to differentiate high-end homes, cars, or clothes from the bargain-basement variety. Consequently, some discretionary dollars are included in our calculations of necessary spending. For this reason, these estimates of discretionary income should be considered conservative.

Table 4.1 Top-10 Discretionary Expenditures, 2012

(amount spent by the average household on the 10 discretionary items on which the average household spends the most, 2012)

		average household spending
1.	Entertainment	$2,605.15
2.	Cash contributions to religious organizations	734.30
3.	Dinner at full-service restaurants	721.27
4.	Nonpayroll deposit to retirement plans	582.46
5.	Cash gifts	464.50
6.	Alcoholic beverages	451.16
7.	Airline fares	352.53
8.	Lodging on trips	341.61
9.	Tobacco products and smoking supplies	331.72
10.	Lunch at full-service restaurants	300.91

Source: Calculations by New Strategist based on the Bureau of Labor Statistics' 2012 Consumer Expenditure Survey

Discretionary Income Peaks in Late Middle Age

Householders aged 55 to 64 have the most discretionary income.

The average household had $14,037 in discretionary income in 2012. That sounds like a lot of money, but it amounts to just $38 per day per household for all spending on entertainment, pets, travel, charitable contributions, meals at sit-down restaurants, and snack food, among other items. Discretionary income was a higher $14,375 in 2007, after adjusting for inflation, but the 2 percent decline between 2007 and 2012 could be considered a modest drop given the severity of the Great Recession.

Overall, American households controlled $1.7 trillion discretionary dollars in 2012. Householders aged 55 to 64 have the largest share—26 percent. Households headed by 45-to-54-year-olds are not far behind, with 25 percent.

■ Average discretionary income per household member (average per capita) also peaks among householders aged 55 to 64—at $9,561 in 2012.

Discretionary income surpasses $20,000 among householders aged 55 to 64

(average discretionary income per household, by age of householder, 2012)

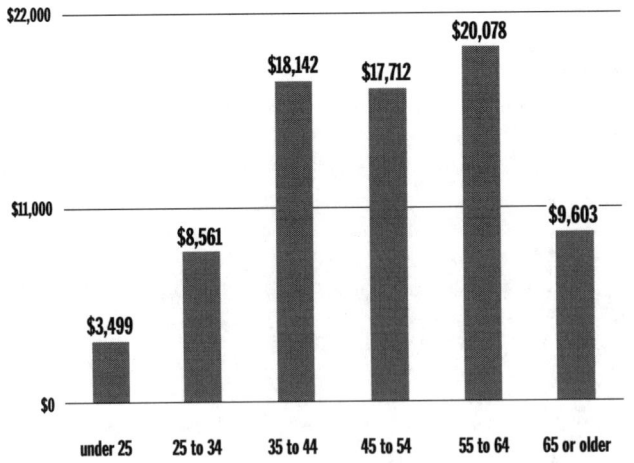

Table 4.2 Discretionary Income by Age of Householder, 2012

(number and percent distribution of total households, average before-tax household income, average discretionary income per household and per household member, aggregate discretionary income, and percent distribution of aggregate, by age of householder, 2012)

	total households		average before-tax household income	discretionary income			
	number (in 000s)	percent distribution		average per household	average per capita	aggregate (in millions)	percent distribution of aggregate
Total households	**124,416**	**100.0%**	**$65,596**	**$14,037**	**$5,615**	**$1,746,399**	**100.0%**
Under age 25	8,159	6.6	36,639	3,499	1,749	28,547	1.6
Aged 25 to 34	20,112	16.2	58,832	8,561	3,058	172,182	9.9
Aged 35 to 44	21,598	17.4	78,169	18,142	5,336	391,824	22.4
Aged 45 to 54	24,624	19.8	81,704	17,712	6,560	436,136	25.0
Aged 55 to 64	22,770	18.3	77,507	20,078	9,561	457,172	26.2
Aged 65 or older	27,154	21.8	44,713	9,603	5,649	260,757	14.9
Aged 65 to 74	14,993	12.1	53,521	12,340	6,855	185,006	10.6
Aged 75 or older	12,161	9.8	33,853	6,305	4,204	76,680	4.4

Note: For the definition of discretionary income, see chapter introduction. Per capita discretionary income is calculated by dividing average discretionary income per household by average household size. Aggregate discretionary income is calculated by multiplying average discretionary income per household by the number of households in the demographic segment.
Source: Calculations by New Strategist based on the Bureau of Labor Statistics' 2012 Consumer Expenditure Survey

More than 40 Percent of Households Have No Discretionary Income

The average household with an income below $40,000 has no discretionary dollars.

Discretionary income rises as household income increases. But 44 percent of households have no discretionary spending power. The average household with an income below $40,000 must spend all of its disposable income on necessities. Of course, many still find a few dollars for a movie, a meal at a full-service restaurant, cosmetics, or a six-pack of beer. That's because many lower income households spend more than they make. Family assistance, borrowing, and unreported income make up the difference.

Households with incomes between $40,000 and $49,999 had an average of $3,769 in discretionary income in 2012. The figure rises to a peak of $95,189 for households with incomes of $150,000 or more. Households with incomes of $150,000 or more control nearly half of the nation's $1.7 billion in discretionary dollars.

■ Discretionary income per capita peaks at $29,746 among households with incomes of $150,000 or more.

Households with incomes of $100,000 or more control 73 percent of discretionary dollars

(percent distribution of aggregate discretionary income by household income, 2012)

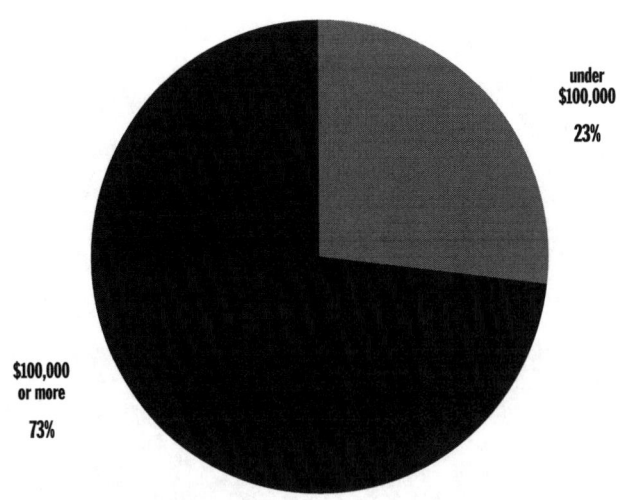

under
$100,000

23%

$100,000
or more

73%

Table 4.3 Discretionary Income by Household Income, 2012

(number and percent distribution of total households, average before-tax household income, average discretionary income per household and per household member, aggregate discretionary income, and percent distribution of aggregate, by household income, 2012)

	total households		average before-tax household income	discretionary income			
	number (in 000s)	percent distribution		average per household	average per capita	aggregate (in millions)	percent distribution of aggregate
Total households	**124,416**	**100.0%**	**$65,596**	**$14,037**	**$5,615**	**$1,746,399**	**100.0%**
Under $20,000	26,177	21.0	10,445	0	0	0	0.0
$20,000 to $39,999	28,041	22.5	29,593	0	0	0	0.0
$40,000 to $49,999	11,010	8.8	44,759	3,769	1,508	41,495	2.4
$50,000 to $69,999	17,972	14.4	59,283	8,458	3,253	152,012	8.7
$70,000 to $79,999	6,946	5.6	74,689	12,191	4,354	84,682	4.8
$80,000 to $99,999	10,977	8.8	88,974	16,870	5,817	185,183	10.6
$100,000 or more	23,293	18.7	171,910	55,082	17,213	1,283,027	73.5
$100,000 to $119,999	7,183	5.8	108,977	24,547	7,918	176,322	10.1
$120,000 to $149,999	6,947	5.6	132,318	33,507	10,471	232,776	13.3
$150,000 or more	9,162	7.4	251,270	95,189	29,746	872,120	49.9

Note: For the definition of discretionary income, see chapter introduction. Per capita discretionary income is calculated by dividing average discretionary income per household by average household size. Aggregate discretionary income is calculated by multiplying average discretionary income per household by the number of households in the demographic segment.
Source: Calculations by New Strategist based on the Bureau of Labor Statistics' 2012 Consumer Expenditure Survey

Married Couples Control Most Discretionary Income

Single-parent families have no extra money.

Married couples have the most discretionary income per household—an average of $22,599 in 2012 and well above the $14,037 of the average household. Couples without children at home had slightly less discretionary income than those with children. Single-parent families had no discretionary income in 2012.

A look at discretionary income per household member finds a different pattern. Couples without children at home—many of them empty-nesters—have the most discretionary income per capita, an average of $11,056 per household member. Married couples with children at home have a much smaller $5,927 in discretionary income per household member. People who live alone have $4,347 in per capita discretionary income available to them, almost as much as couples with preschoolers.

■ People who live alone account for 30 percent of households but control only 9 percent of discretionary dollars.

Married couples without children at home have the most discretionary income per household member

(average per capita discretionary income, by type of household, 2012)

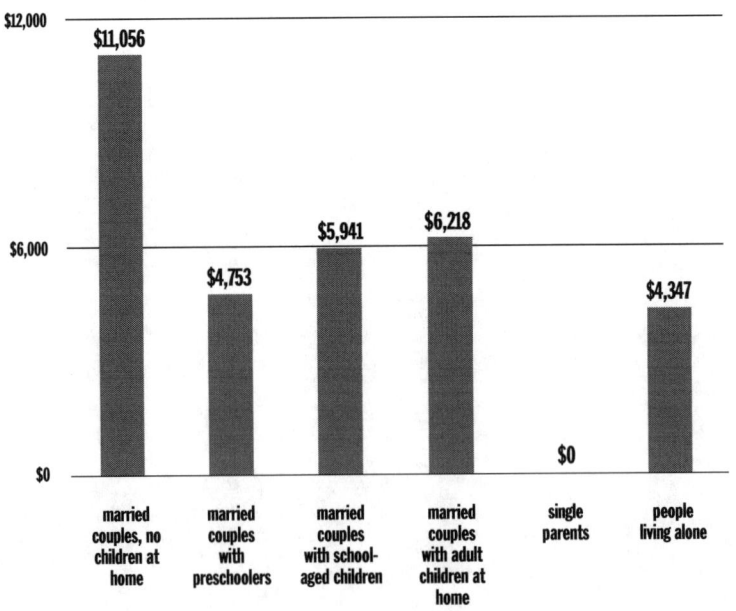

Table 4.4 Discretionary Income by Type of Household, 2012

(number and percent distribution of total households, average before-tax household income, average discretionary income per household and per household member, aggregate discretionary income, and percent distribution of aggregate, by type of household, 2012)

	total households		average before-tax household income	discretionary income			
	number (in 000s)	percent distribution		average per household	average per capita	aggregate (in millions)	percent distribution of aggregate
TOTAL HOUSEHOLDS	**124,416**	**100.0%**	**$65,596**	**$14,037**	**$5,615**	**$1,746,399**	**100.0%**
Married couples, total	**60,428**	**48.6**	**90,393**	**22,599**	**7,062**	**1,365,632**	**78.2**
Married couples without children at home	25,936	20.8	81,717	22,112	11,056	573,498	32.8
Married couples with children at home	29,252	23.5	98,104	23,117	5,927	676,215	38.7
Oldest child under age 6	5,676	4.6	85,200	16,636	4,753	94,426	5.4
Oldest child aged 6 to 17	14,797	11.9	100,698	24,954	5,941	369,245	21.1
Oldest child aged 18 or older	8,778	7.1	102,074	24,249	6,218	212,859	12.2
Single parent with children under age 18 at home	**6,524**	**5.2**	**34,194**	**0**	**0**	**0**	**0.0**
Single-person household	**36,942**	**29.7**	**34,102**	**4,347**	**4,347**	**160,605**	**9.2**

Note: Households by type do not add to total because not all household types are shown. For the definition of discretionary income, see chapter introduction. Per capita discretionary income is calculated by dividing average discretionary income per household by average household size. Aggregate discretionary income is calculated by multiplying average discretionary income per household by the number of households in the demographic segment.
Source: Calculations by New Strategist based on the Bureau of Labor Statistics' 2012 Consumer Expenditure Survey

Asian Households Have the Most Discretionary Income

Hispanic households have the least.

Asian households had the most discretionary income in 2012, an average of $22,586—61 percent more than the average household. Hispanic households had only $5,187 in discretionary dollars, 63 percent less than average. Non-Hispanic white households have considerably less discretionary income than Asians, at $16,423. Black households have substantially more discretionary income than Hispanics, at $8,388.

After adjusting for household size, the pattern remains the same. Asian households have the most discretionary income per capita ($8,066), followed by non-Hispanic white households ($7,140). Hispanic households have the least amount of discretionary income per capita (just $1,572).

■ Black households control a slightly larger share of aggregate discretionary income (7.5 percent) than Asian households (7.0 percent).

Hispanic households have the fewest discretionary dollars

(average discretionary income per household, by race and Hispanic origin of householder, 2012)

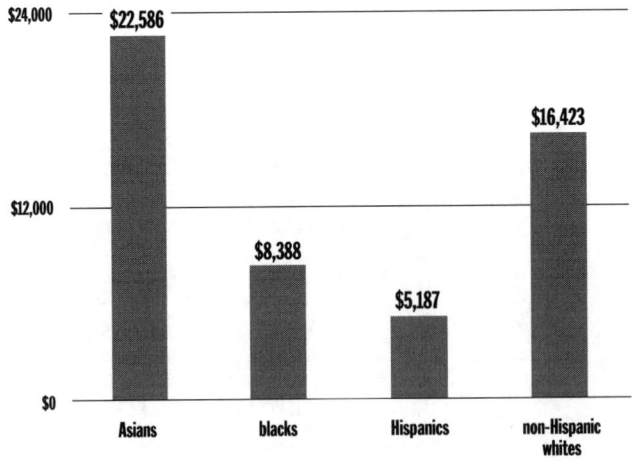

Table 4.5 Discretionary Income by Race and Hispanic Origin of Householder, 2012

(number and percent distribution of total households, average before-tax household income, average discretionary income per household and per household member, aggregate discretionary income, and percent distribution of aggregate, by race and Hispanic origin of householder, 2012)

	total households		average before-tax household income	discretionary income			
	number (in 000s)	percent distribution		average per household	average per capita	aggregate (in millions)	percent distribution of aggregate
Total households	**124,416**	**100.0%**	**$65,596**	**$14,037**	**$5,615**	**$1,746,399**	**100.0%**
Asian	5,393	4.3	86,156	22,586	8,066	121,804	7.0
Black	15,637	12.6	47,119	8,388	3,355	131,155	7.5
Hispanic	15,597	12.5	48,066	5,187	1,572	80,899	4.6
Non-Hispanic white and other	93,385	75.1	71,552	16,423	7,140	1,533,647	87.8

Note: Households by race and Hispanic origin do not add to total because of overlapping definitions. Asians and blacks include Hispanics and non-Hispanics who identify themselves as being of the respective race alone. Hispanics includes people of any race who identify themselves as Hispanic. "Other" includes people who identify themselves as non-Hispanic and as Alaska Native, American Indian, Asian (also included in the "Asian" row), Native Hawaiian or other Pacific Islander, and non-Hispanics reporting more than one race. For the definition of discretionary income, see chapter introduction. Per capita discretionary income is calculated by dividing average discretionary income per household by average household size. Aggregate discretionary income is calculated by multiplying average discretionary income per household by the number of households in the demographic segment.

Source: Calculations by New Strategist based on the Bureau of Labor Statistics' 2012 Consumer Expenditure Survey

Discretionary Income Is Highest in the Midwest

Households in the South have the smallest amount of discretionary income.

Discretionary income varies somewhat by region. Households in the Midwest have the largest amount of discretionary income, an average of $15,730 in 2012. Households in the Northeast follow closely, with $15,608 in discretionary income. Households in the South have the smallest amount of discretionary income—just $12,397.

On a per capita basis, households in the South and West also lag in discretionary income, with $4,959 per household member in the South and $5,314 per household member in the West. Households in the Northeast and Midwest have just over $6,500 in discretionary income per capita.

■ Because the South is the most populous region, it controls the largest share of discretionary income— 33 percent of the aggregate in 2012.

Discretionary income is higher in the Northeast than in the West

(average discretionary income per household, by age of householder, 2012)

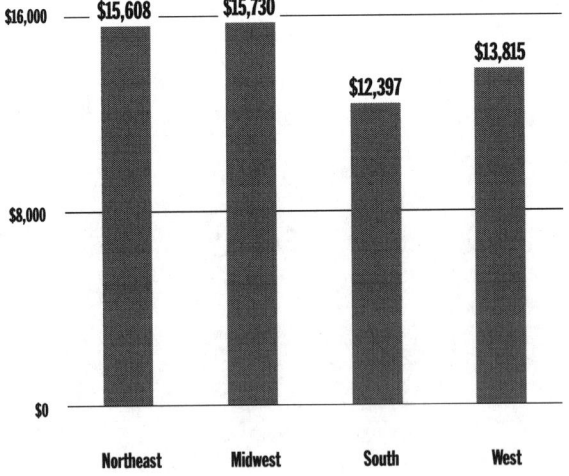

Table 4.6 Discretionary Income by Region of Residence, 2012

(number and percent distribution of total households, average before-tax household income, average discretionary income per household and per household member, aggregate discretionary income, and percent distribution of aggregate, by region, 2012)

| | total households | | average before-tax household income | discretionary income | | | |
	number (in 000s)	percent distribution		average per household	average per capita	aggregate (in millions)	percent distribution of aggregate
Total households	**124,416**	**100.0%**	**$65,596**	**$14,037**	**$5,615**	**$1,746,399**	**100.0%**
Northeast	22,459	18.1	72,036	15,608	6,503	350,543	20.1
Midwest	27,584	22.2	65,217	15,730	6,554	433,898	24.8
South	46,338	37.2	60,219	12,397	4,959	574,441	32.9
West	28,035	22.5	69,700	13,815	5,314	387,307	22.2

Note: For the definition of discretionary income, see chapter introduction. Per capita discretionary income is calculated by dividing average discretionary income per household by average household size. Aggregate discretionary income is calculated by multiplying average discretionary income per household by the number of households in the demographic segment.
Source: Calculations by New Strategist based on the Bureau of Labor Statistics' 2012 Consumer Expenditure Survey

The College Educated Control Most Discretionary Income

Those who did not go to college control few of the nation's discretionary dollars.

Households with any member who has a bachelor's degree controlled 61 percent of the nation's $1.7 trillion in discretionary income in 2012. Households whose most educated members went no further than high school controlled only 13 percent of aggregate discretionary income in 2012.

Discretionary income rises sharply with the educational attainment of household members. Households with a member who has a graduate degree had a substantial $34,212 in discretionary dollars available to them in 2012. The discretionary income available to households whose most educated member had a bachelor's degree was a smaller $22,854, still well above the all-household average of $14,037. For households whose most educated member was a high school graduate with no further education, discretionary income was just $7,488.

■ Discretionary income per capita also rises with educational attainment.

Discretionary income rises with education

(average discretionary income per household, by highest level of educational attainment of any household member, 2012)

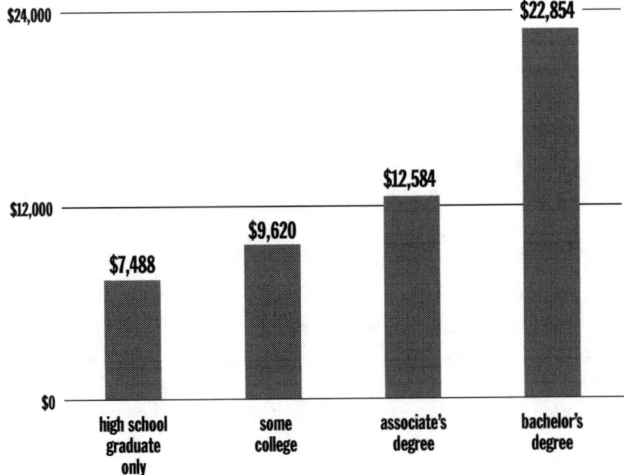

286   AMERICAN INCOMES

Table 4.7 Discretionary Income by Education of Householder, 2012

(number and percent distribution of total households, average before-tax household income, average discretionary income per household and per household member, aggregate discretionary income, and percent distribution of aggregate, by highest level of education of any household member, 2012)

	total households		average before-tax household income	discretionary income			
	number (in 000s)	percent distribution		average per household	average per capita	aggregate (in millions)	percent distribution of aggregate
Total households	**124,416**	**100.0%**	**$65,596**	**$14,037**	**$5,615**	**$1,746,399**	**100.0%**
Not a high school graduate	16,246	13.1	33,154	3,378	1,251	54,879	3.1
High school graduate only	31,022	24.9	47,221	7,488	2,995	232,278	13.3
Some college	25,623	20.6	55,987	9,620	4,009	246,504	14.1
Associate's degree	12,287	9.9	66,122	12,584	4,840	154,625	8.9
College graduate, total	39,238	31.5	99,667	27,031	11,263	1,060,624	60.7
Bachelor's degree only	24,798	19.9	89,438	22,854	9,522	566,732	32.5
Graduate degree	14,440	11.6	117,233	34,212	13,685	494,022	28.3

Note: For the definition of discretionary income, see chapter introduction. Per capita discretionary income is calculated by dividing average discretionary income per household by average household size. Aggregate discretionary income is calculated by multiplying average discretionary income per household by the number of households in the demographic segment.
Source: Calculations by New Strategist based on the Bureau of Labor Statistics' 2012 Consumer Expenditure Survey

Wealth

Every few years the federal government collects information about household assets, debt, and net worth through the Census Bureau's Survey of Income and Program Participation. The latest survey, taken in 2011, reveals the sharp decline in net worth caused by the Great Recession. Between 2005 and 2011, median household net worth fell by a steep 36 percent—to $68,828 after adjusting for inflation. Net worth fell in every age group, for every household type, and for every race and Hispanic origin group.

Meanwhile, household debt has been rising. Although the percentage of households in debt fell slightly over the 2000 to 2011 time period (from 74 to 69 percent), the median amount owed by the average household with debt increased by a substantial 37 percent, after adjusting for inflation. In 2011, the median debt of debtor households was $70,000.

Because of these financial problems, many Americans are rethinking retirement. The age at which workers expect to retire has climbed since 2007, according to the Retirement Confidence Survey, and retirement confidence has plunged.

■ Eighteen percent of households have no wealth, the figure being as high as 32 percent among householders under age 35.

■ A home is still the most valuable asset owned by the average American. In 2011, 65 percent of households were homeowners with a median of $80,000 in home equity.

■ The percentage of workers who expect to retire at age 65 or older grew from 57 to 68 percent between 2007 and 2013.

Net Worth Has Plunged

Householders aged 35 to 44 experienced the biggest decline in net worth.

Net worth is what remains when a household's debts are subtracted from its assets. The most valuable asset owned by the largest share of households is a house. As housing values climbed during the first half of the 2000s, so did net worth. By 2005, median household net worth exceeded $100,000. Then the housing bubble burst and the Great Recession set in. Median household net worth fell 36 percent between 2005 and 2011, to $68,828 after adjusting for inflation.

The median net worth of householders aged 35 to 44 fell by a steep 58 percent between 2005 and 2011—a larger decline than any other age group. Behind this decline was the fact that many were recent home buyers, who had purchased at the price peak and experienced the biggest decline in home equity as the housing market collapsed. Net worth fell the least among householders aged 65 or older, in large part because most were long-time homeowners who owned their homes free and clear.

■ Householders aged 65 or older have the highest net worth, with more than one in five having a net worth of at least $500,000.

Net worth fell sharply between 2005 and 2011

(median household net worth, 2005 and 2011; in 2011 dollars)

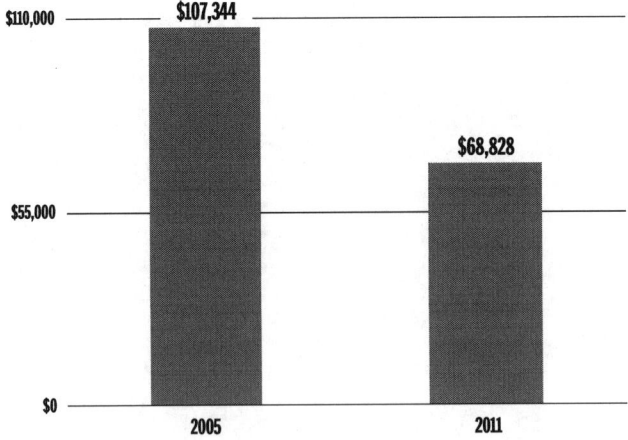

Table 5.1 Median Household Net Worth by Age of Householder, 2005 and 2011

(median net worth of households by age of householder, 2005 and 2011; percent change, 2005–11; in 2011 dollars)

	2011	2005	percent change
Total households	**$68,828**	**$107,344**	**–35.9%**
Under age 35	6,676	8,901	–25.0
Aged 35 to 44	35,000	84,044	–58.4
Aged 45 to 54	84,542	151,673	–44.3
Aged 55 to 64	143,964	207,778	–30.7
Aged 65 to 69	194,226	225,737	–14.0
Aged 70 to 74	181,078	233,746	–22.5
Aged 75 or older	155,714	184,512	–15.6

Source: Bureau of the Census, Wealth and Asset Ownership, Survey of Income and Program Participation, Internet site http://www.census.gov/people/wealth/; calculations by New Strategist

Table 5.2 Distribution of Net Worth by Age of Householder, 2011

(number of households, median net worth, and percent distribution of net worth, by age of householder, 2011)

	total households	under 35	35 to 44	45 to 54	55 to 64	65 or older
Total households	**118,689,091**	**22,876,706**	**21,741,098**	**25,494,745**	**22,328,534**	**26,248,007**
Median net worth	**$68,828**	**$6,676**	**$35,000**	**$84,542**	**$143,964**	**$170,516**

DISTRIBUTION OF HOUSEHOLDS BY NET WORTH

	total households	under 35	35 to 44	45 to 54	55 to 64	65 or older
Total households	**100.0%**	**100.0%**	**100.0%**	**100.0%**	**100.0%**	**100.0%**
Zero or negative	18.1	32.0	22.0	17.4	12.4	8.3
$1 to $4,999	9.1	15.4	10.2	7.6	6.3	6.6
$5,000 to $9,999	4.8	8.8	5.9	4.0	2.9	2.7
$10,000 to $24,999	6.6	10.9	7.8	5.7	4.8	4.1
$25,000 to $49,999	6.9	7.8	8.5	7.5	6.5	4.7
$50,000 to $99,999	10.4	9.8	10.8	11.1	10.0	10.4
$100,000 to $249,999	17.9	9.7	16.2	18.4	20.7	23.7
$250,000 to $499,999	12.6	3.6	10.2	14.1	15.2	19.0
$500,000 or more	13.5	2.0	8.3	14.2	21.2	20.6

Source: Bureau of the Census, Wealth and Asset Ownership, Survey of Income and Program Participation, Internet site http://www.census.gov/people/wealth/; calculations by New Strategist

Married Couples Have the Greatest Wealth

Female-headed households saw their net worth fall the most between 2005 and 2011.

Married couples had a median net worth (assets minus debts) of $139,024 in 2011, well above the $68,828 median for all households, according to the Census Bureau's Survey of Income and Program Participation. Male-headed households had a net worth of $27,310, and the net worth of female-headed households was $22,184.

Almost every age group by household type saw its median net worth fall sharply between 2005 and 2011, after adjusting for inflation. For the average household, median net worth fell 36 percent during those years. Married couples saw their net worth fall 29 percent, and the decline was an identical 29 percent for male-headed households. Among female-headed households, however, net worth fell by a larger 43 percent. The only exception to across-the-board declines in net worth occurred among male- and female-headed households with a householder under age 35, but their net worth increased by only hundreds of dollars.

Net worth rises with age regardless of household type. It peaks among married couples aged 65 or older at $284,790. Nearly one-third of elderly married couples have a net worth of $500,000 or more. In contrast, more than one-fourth of the youngest married couples have no wealth at all—meaning their debts are greater than their assets. Among male- and female-headed householders under age 35, the percentage with zero or negative net worth was a larger 32 and 40 percent, respectively.

■ Net worth exceeds $100,000 among married couples with a householder aged 35 or older and for male- and female-headed households with a householder aged 65 or older.

The net worth of married couples exceeds $100,000

(median household net worth by type of household, 2011)

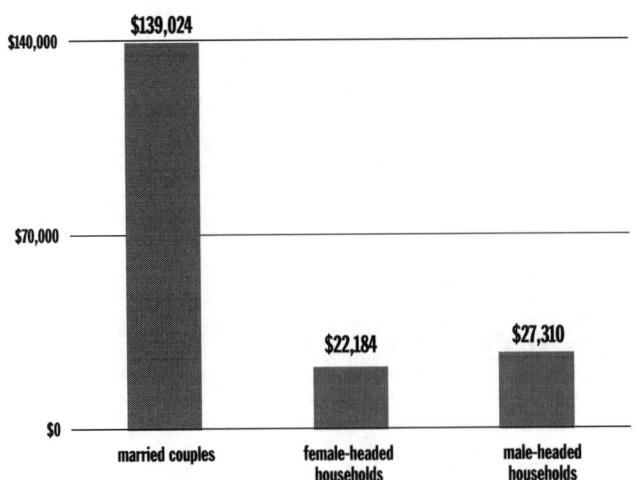

Table 5.3 Median Household Net Worth by Type of Household and Age of Householder, 2005 and 2011

(median household net worth by type of household and age of householder, 2005 and 2011; percent change, 2005–11; in 2011 dollars)

	2011	2005	percent change
TOTAL HOUSEHOLDS	**$68,828**	**$107,344**	**–35.9%**
Married couples	**139,024**	**194,742**	**–28.6**
Under age 35	19,526	36,292	–46.2
Aged 35 to 54	116,170	202,057	–42.5
Aged 55 to 64	239,847	335,825	–28.6
Aged 65 or older	284,790	338,648	–15.9
Female-headed households	**22,184**	**39,073**	**–43.2**
Under age 35	1,392	1,270	9.6
Aged 35 to 54	9,640	25,532	–62.2
Aged 55 to 64	61,879	90,906	–31.9
Aged 65 or older	104,000	143,826	–27.7
Male-headed households	**27,310**	**38,266**	**–28.6**
Under age 35	6,200	5,509	12.5
Aged 35 to 54	24,813	48,596	–48.9
Aged 55 to 64	55,718	85,188	–34.6
Aged 65 or older	130,000	146,577	–11.3

Source: Bureau of the Census, Wealth and Asset Ownership, Survey of Income and Program Participation, Internet site http:// www.census.gov/people/wealth/; calculations by New Strategist

Table 5.4 Distribution of Net Worth among Married-Couple Households by Age, 2011

(number of married-couple households, median net worth, and percent distribution of net worth, by age of householder, 2011; number of married couples in thousands)

	total couples	under 35	35 to 54	55 to 64	65 or older
Number of married couples	59,918	9,672	26,519	12,610	11,117
Median net worth	$139,024	$19,526	$116,170	$239,847	$284,790

DISTRIBUTION OF MARRIED-COUPLE HOUSEHOLDS BY NET WORTH

Total married couples	100.0%	100.0%	100.0%	100.0%	100.0%
Zero or negative	13.0	25.8	14.3	8.0	4.2
$1 to $4,999	5.3	10.6	5.3	3.3	2.8
$5,000 to $9,999	3.2	6.3	3.3	2.1	1.4
$10,000 to $24,999	5.6	11.0	5.7	3.5	3.0
$25,000 to $49,999	6.6	10.4	7.4	5.0	3.0
$50,000 to $99,999	9.9	12.3	10.8	8.0	7.8
$100,000 to $249,999	20.2	14.3	20.2	21.4	24.0
$250,000 to $499,999	16.5	5.9	16.5	18.7	23.2
$500,000 or more	19.9	3.5	16.5	30.1	30.6

Source: Bureau of the Census, Wealth and Asset Ownership, Survey of Income and Program Participation, Internet site http://www.census.gov/people/wealth/; calculations by New Strategist

Table 5.5 Distribution of Net Worth among Female-Headed Households by Age, 2011

(number of female-headed households, median net worth, and percent distribution of net worth, by age of householder, 2011; number of female-headed households in thousands)

	total female-headed households	under 35	35 to 54	55 to 64	65 or older
Number of female-headed households	35,522	7,132	11,592	5,882	10,915
Median net worth	$22,184	$1,392	$9,640	$61,879	$104,000

DISTRIBUTION OF FEMALE-HEADED HOUSEHOLDS BY NET WORTH

Total female-headed households	**100.0%**	**100.0%**	**100.0%**	**100.0%**	**100.0%**
Zero or negative	24.3	40.3	28.9	19.4	11.8
$1 to $4,999	13.4	21.5	14.0	9.5	9.5
$5,000 to $9,999	6.4	11.6	7.4	3.8	3.5
$10,000 to $24,999	6.8	9.8	7.3	5.9	4.8
$25,000 to $49,999	7.0	5.1	8.6	8.0	5.9
$50,000 to $99,999	10.9	5.5	11.4	13.1	12.7
$100,000 to $249,999	15.8	4.5	12.3	20.2	24.6
$250,000 to $499,999	9.0	1.2	6.0	11.1	16.2
$500,000 or more	6.3	0.5	4.1	9.0	11.0

Source: Bureau of the Census, Wealth and Asset Ownership, Survey of Income and Program Participation, Internet site http://www.census.gov/people/wealth/; calculations by New Strategist

Table 5.6 Distribution of Net Worth among Male-Headed Households by Age, 2011

(number of male-headed households, median net worth, and percent distribution of net worth, by age of householder, 2011; number of male-headed households in thousands)

	total male-headed households	under 35	35 to 54	55 to 64	65 or older
Number of male-headed households	23,249	6,073	9,125	3,837	4,215
Median net worth	$27,310	$6,200	$24,813	$55,718	$130,000

DISTRIBUTION OF MALE-HEADED HOUSEHOLDS BY NET WORTH

Total male-headed households	**100.0%**	**100.0%**	**100.0%**	**100.0%**	**100.0%**
Zero or negative	21.8	32.1	22.6	15.9	10.3
$1 to $4,999	12.5	15.9	12.5	11.1	8.7
$5,000 to $9,999	6.4	9.7	6.1	4.3	3.9
$10,000 to $24,999	8.7	11.8	8.9	7.6	5.0
$25,000 to $49,999	7.8	7.0	8.8	8.9	6.1
$50,000 to $99,999	11.0	10.9	10.9	11.8	10.9
$100,000 to $249,999	15.4	8.4	15.7	19.5	20.9
$250,000 to $499,999	8.3	2.7	8.3	10.1	14.9
$500,000 or more	8.1	1.4	6.3	10.7	19.2

Source: Bureau of the Census, Wealth and Asset Ownership, Survey of Income and Program Participation, Internet site http:// www.census.gov/people/wealth/; calculations by New Strategist

Non-Hispanic Whites Have the Highest Net Worth

Blacks and Hispanics have little wealth.

The median net worth (assets minus debts) of non-Hispanic white households was $110,500 in 2011, well above the $68,828 net worth of the average household. The median net worth of non-Hispanic white households exceeds the $89,339 of Asian households and is more than 10 times that of black or Hispanic households.

Between 2005 and 2011, net worth fell regardless of race or Hispanic origin. Hispanic households experienced the largest decline, their median net worth falling by an enormous 61 percent after adjusting for inflation. Non-Hispanic whites experienced the smallest decline, a 26 percent drop—well below the 36 percent loss recorded by the average household, according to the Census Bureau's Survey of Income and Program Participation.

■ The percentage of households with zero or negative net worth ranges from a low of 13.7 percent among non-Hispanic whites to a high of 33.5 percent among blacks.

Net worth of Asians is well above average

(median net worth of households by race and Hispanic origin of householder, 2011)

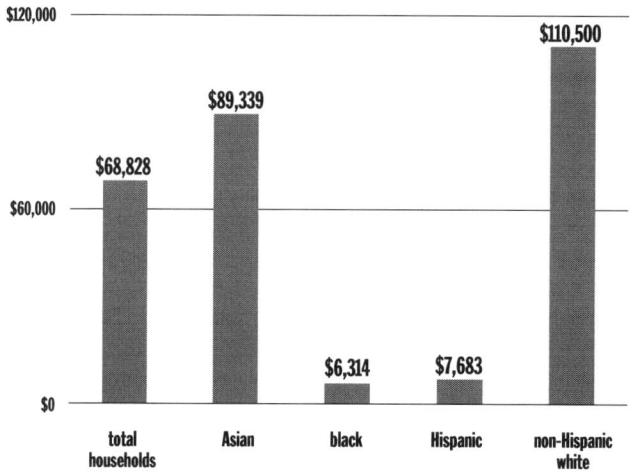

Table 5.7 Median Household Net Worth by Race and Hispanic Origin of Householder, 2005 and 2011

(median net worth of households by race and Hispanic origin of householder, 2005 and 2011; percent change, 2005–11; in 2011 dollars)

	2011	2005	percent change
Total households	**$68,828**	**$107,344**	**–35.9%**
Asian	89,339	175,890	–49.2
Black	6,314	12,684	–50.2
Hispanic	7,683	19,670	–60.9
Non-Hispanic white	110,500	150,132	–26.4

Note: Asians and blacks are those who identify themselves as being of the race alone. Non-Hispanic whites are those who identify themselves as being white alone and not Hispanic. Hispanics may be of any race.
Source: Bureau of the Census, Wealth and Asset Ownership, Survey of Income and Program Participation, Internet site http://www.census.gov/people/wealth/; calculations by New Strategist

Table 5.8 Distribution of Net Worth by Race and Hispanic Origin of Householder, 2011

(number of households, median net worth, and percent distribution of net worth, by race and Hispanic origin of householder, 2011)

	total households	Asian	black	Hispanic	non-Hispanic white
Total households	**118,689,091**	**3,939,591**	**15,056,795**	**14,099,126**	**83,245,166**
Median net worth	**$68,828**	**$89,339**	**$6,314**	**$7,683**	**$110,500**

DISTRIBUTION OF HOUSEHOLDS BY NET WORTH

	total households	Asian	black	Hispanic	non-Hispanic white
Total households	**100.0%**	**100.0%**	**100.0%**	**100.0%**	**100.0%**
Zero or negative	18.1	15.4	33.5	28.5	13.7
$1 to $4,999	9.1	9.0	14.6	16.5	6.8
$5,000 to $9,999	4.8	5.5	7.0	7.4	3.9
$10,000 to $24,999	6.6	6.6	7.9	8.4	6.0
$25,000 to $49,999	6.9	7.2	6.6	8.0	6.7
$50,000 to $99,999	10.4	8.2	9.0	9.9	10.8
$100,000 to $249,999	17.9	17.0	12.6	11.2	20.1
$250,000 to $499,999	12.6	13.8	5.6	6.1	15.1
$500,000 or more	13.5	17.3	3.3	3.9	16.9

Note: Asians and blacks are those who identify themselves as being of the race alone. Non-Hispanic whites are those who identify themselves as being white alone and not Hispanic. Hispanics may be of any race.
Source: Bureau of the Census, Wealth and Asset Ownership, Survey of Income and Program Participation, Internet site http://www.census.gov/people/wealth/; calculations by New Strategist

Homes Are the Most Important Asset

Home values plunged between 2005 and 2011, driving down net worth.

The automobile is the most commonly owned asset in the United States. Nearly 85 percent of households own at least one motor vehicle. The second most commonly owned asset is an interest-earning account at a financial institution (70 percent). A home is the third most commonly owned asset, with 65 percent of households owning a house. The nation's homeowners had a median of $80,000 in home equity (home value minus mortgage debt) in 2011. They had a median of $6,824 equity in their motor vehicles, and just $2,450 in their savings accounts.

Behind the higher net worth of older householders is their greater homeownership and home equity. Nearly 80 percent of householders aged 65 or older owned a home in 2011, with a median equity of $130,000. In contrast, only 37 percent of householders under age 35 were homeowners. Those owners had just $20,000 in home equity.

■ The median value of 401(k) retirement accounts peaks at $47,000 among householders aged 55 to 64.

Retirement accounts are modest, even among those approaching retirement age

(median value of 401(k) accounts owned by households, by age of householder, 2011)

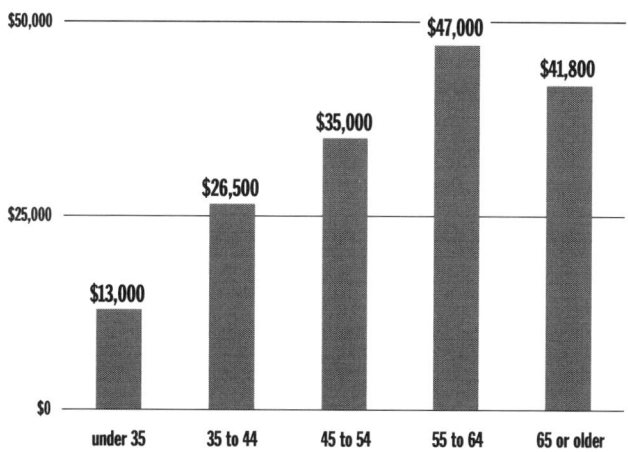

Table 5.9 Asset Ownership of Households by Age of Householder, 2011

(percent of households owning selected assets and median value or equity of assets for owners, by age of householder, 2011)

	total households	under 35	35 to 44	45 to 54	55 to 64	65 or older
PERCENT WITH ASSET						
Interest-earning asset at financial institution	69.8%	63.2%	68.6%	69.7%	73.3%	73.8%
Regular checking account	29.0	29.2	30.8	31.2	29.1	25.0
Stocks and mutal fund shares	19.6	11.3	16.4	19.4	24.3	25.4
Own business	13.8	10.6	15.6	18.3	17.1	8.0
Motor vehicles	84.7	81.5	87.5	86.9	87.8	80.2
Own home	65.3	36.7	61.3	70.4	76.7	78.9
Rental property	5.5	2.1	4.1	5.8	7.8	7.2
IRA or Keogh account	28.9	16.1	26.3	30.3	37.5	33.7
401(k) and thrift savings	42.1	39.2	52.5	52.6	48.7	20.2
MEDIAN VALUE OR EQUITY OF ASSET FOR OWNERS						
Interest-earning asset at financial institution	$2,450	$1,000	$1,500	$2,500	$3,700	$5,000
Regular checking account	600	500	500	528	700	800
Stocks and mutal fund shares	20,000	6,000	12,000	20,000	27,000	50,000
Own business (equity)	8,000	5,000	10,000	7,000	10,000	6,000
Motor vehicles (equity)	6,824	4,698	6,492	7,113	7,113	7,113
Own home (equity)	80,000	20,000	40,000	70,000	97,000	130,000
Rental property (equity)	180,000	70,000	98,000	165,000	200,000	240,000
IRA or Keogh account	34,000	10,000	23,000	34,000	48,000	52,000
401(k) and thrift savings	30,000	13,000	26,500	35,000	47,000	41,800

Source: Bureau of the Census, Wealth and Asset Ownership, Survey of Income and Program Participation, Internet site http:// www.census.gov/people/wealth/; calculations by New Strategist

Motor Vehicles Are the Most Commonly Owned Asset

A home is the second most commonly owned asset among married couples.

Most households, regardless of household type, own a motor vehicle. The figure ranges from a high of 93 percent among married couples to a low of 74 percent among female-headed households. Among married couples, a home is the second most common asset, owned by 79 percent. The median equity couples have in their home rises from a low of $20,000 among the youngest couples to a high of $150,000 among couples aged 65 or older.

Among male- and female-headed households, a savings account is the second most common asset, owned by 62 to 64 percent of female- and male-headed households, respectively. In third place is a home, with 52 percent of female-headed households and 51 percent of male-headed households being homeowners.

The majority of married couples have a 401(k) account, and those accounts have a median value of $40,000. A smaller 29 to 33 percent of female- and male-headed households have 401(k) accounts, respectively, with a median value of $15,000 for female-headed households and $20,000 for male-headed households.

■ Among asset owners, the equity held in rental property exceeds the value of all other assets. But few households own rental property—just 8 percent of couples and 3 to 4 percent of female- and male-headed households.

Homeownership is an important asset for most households

(percent of households that own a home by type of household, 2011)

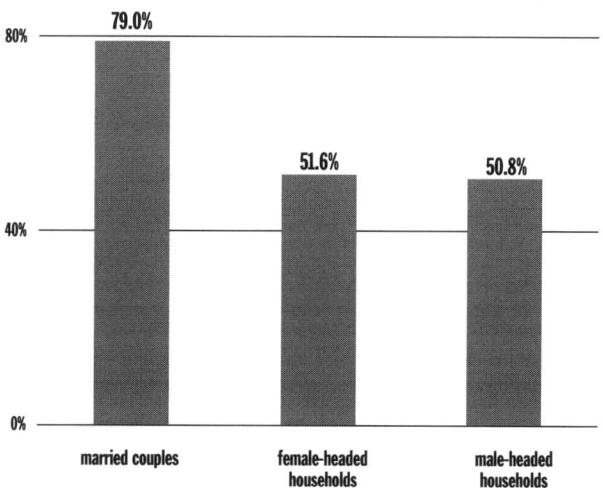

Table 5.10 Asset Ownership of Married-Couple Households by Age, 2011

(percent of total and married-couple households owning selected assets, and median value or equity of asset for owners, by age of married-couple householder, 2011)

	total households	married couples				
		under 35	35 to 44	45 to 54	55 to 64	65 or older
PERCENT WITH ASSET						
Interest-earning asset at financial institution	69.8%	76.9%	70.1%	76.0%	80.1%	81.3%
Regular checking account	29.0	30.8	32.1	32.5	29.4	26.9
Stocks and mutal fund shares	19.6	25.6	14.7	23.3	31.4	33.8
Own business	13.8	18.4	14.6	20.9	21.6	12.3
Motor vehicles	84.7	92.9	91.2	93.1	94.3	92.2
Own home	65.3	79.0	56.4	78.4	87.8	90.4
Rental property	5.5	7.5	3.9	6.6	10.1	10.2
IRA or Keogh account	28.9	36.6	21.3	34.9	44.8	44.8
401(k) and thrift savings	42.1	53.4	51.4	62.0	58.4	29.1
MEDIAN VALUE OR EQUITY OF ASSET FOR OWNERS						
Interest-earning asset at financial institution	$2,450	$4,000	$1,900	$3,320	$6,000	$8,000
Regular checking account	600	900	700	800	1,000	1,200
Stocks and mutal fund shares	20,000	25,000	6,619	19,000	32,000	65,000
Own business (equity)	8,000	10,000	10,000	10,000	10,000	8,000
Motor vehicles (equity)	6,824	8,485	5,986	8,657	10,226	9,445
Own home (equity)	80,000	85,000	20,000	69,000	118,000	150,000
Rental property (equity)	180,000	200,000	90,000	170,000	220,000	330,000
IRA or Keogh account	34,000	42,000	11,000	32,300	60,000	75,000
401(k) and thrift savings	30,000	40,000	17,000	40,000	58,000	50,000

Source: Bureau of the Census, Wealth and Asset Ownership, Survey of Income and Program Participation, Internet site http:// www.census.gov/people/wealth/; calculations by New Strategist

Table 5.11 Asset Ownership of Female-Headed Households by Age, 2011

(percent of total households and of female-headed households owning selected assets, and median value or equity of asset for owners, by age of female householder, 2011)

	total households	female-headed households				
		under 35	35 to 44	45 to 54	55 to 64	65 or older
PERCENT WITH ASSET						
Interest-earning asset at financial institution	69.8%	61.8%	51.8%	59.8%	66.2%	68.1%
Regular checking account	29.0	27.6	26.5	30.1	31.2	23.6
Stocks and mutal fund shares	19.6	12.6	5.4	10.2	14.9	18.5
Own business	13.8	6.8	5.9	9.4	9.1	3.3
Motor vehicles	84.7	74.5	71.8	78.8	79.8	68.8
Own home	65.3	51.6	18.9	47.6	64.5	70.4
Rental property	5.5	3.1	0.4	2.2	4.3	5.0
IRA or Keogh account	28.9	20.9	10.2	19.6	29.2	24.8
401(k) and thrift savings	42.1	28.7	27.4	39.3	38.8	12.9
MEDIAN VALUE OR EQUITY OF ASSET FOR OWNERS						
Interest-earning asset at financial institution	$2,450	$1,000	$500	$600	$1,100	$2,500
Regular checking account	600	305	202	280	400	500
Stocks and mutal fund shares	20,000	16,000	7,000	10,000	16,000	25,000
Own business (equity)	8,000	3,000	2,000	4,000	4,000	2,500
Motor vehicles (equity)	6,824	4,113	3,383	4,091	4,825	4,415
Own home (equity)	80,000	75,000	15,000	43,000	72,000	115,000
Rental property (equity)	180,000	139,000	–	90,000	150,000	155,000
IRA or Keogh account	34,000	20,140	6,500	19,000	30,000	30,000
401(k) and thrift savings	30,000	15,000	6,800	15,000	25,000	25,000

Note: "–" means sample is too small to make a reliable estimate.
Source: Bureau of the Census, Wealth and Asset Ownership, Survey of Income and Program Participation, Internet site http://www.census.gov/people/wealth/; calculations by New Strategist

Table 5.12 Asset Ownership of Male-Headed Households by Age, 2011

(percent of total households and of male-headed households owning selected assets, and median value or equity of asset for owners, by age of male-headed householder, 2011)

	total households	male-headed households				
		under 35	35 to 44	45 to 54	55 to 64	65 or older
PERCENT WITH ASSET						
Interest-earning asset at financial institution	69.8%	63.7%	65.3%	61.3%	61.7%	68.6%
Regular checking account	29.0	26.6	27.9	27.9	24.8	23.7
Stocks and mutal fund shares	19.6	14.7	12.9	12.9	15.5	20.8
Own business	13.8	12.8	9.7	15.7	14.6	9.2
Motor vehicles	84.7	79.1	77.5	80.8	78.8	77.8
Own home	65.3	50.8	26.4	54.2	59.2	70.5
Rental property	5.5	3.8	1.1	4.1	5.7	5.2
IRA or Keogh account	28.9	21.5	14.9	21.0	26.5	27.5
401(k) and thrift savings	42.1	33.4	33.7	42.1	31.6	15.7
MEDIAN VALUE OR EQUITY OF ASSET FOR OWNERS						
Interest-earning asset at financial institution	$2,450	$1,255	$800	$1,000	$1,700	$5,000
Regular checking account	600	600	700	500	500	1,000
Stocks and mutal fund shares	20,000	15,000	6,000	10,000	25,000	65,000
Own business (equity)	8,000	7,000	4,000	10,000	8,000	7,000
Motor vehicles (equity)	6,824	4,892	4,178	4,759	5,500	6,338
Own home (equity)	80,000	60,000	25,000	40,000	73,000	110,000
Rental property (equity)	180,000	100,000	–	65,000	100,000	160,000
IRA or Keogh account	34,000	25,000	7,759	20,000	36,427	51,000
401(k) and thrift savings	30,000	20,000	12,000	26,000	33,000	38,000

Note: "–" means sample is too small to make a reliable estimate.
Source: Bureau of the Census, Wealth and Asset Ownership, Survey of Income and Program Participation, Internet site http://www.census.gov/people/wealth/; calculations by New Strategist

Homeownership Boosts the Net Worth of Non-Hispanic Whites

The lower homeownership rate of blacks and Hispanics reduces their net worth.

Although Asians are equally as or more likely than non-Hispanic whites to own a variety of assets, there is one glaring deficit that makes all the difference: a home. Fully 73 percent of non-Hispanic whites own a home compared with a smaller 59 percent of Asians. In large part because of that difference, non-Hispanic whites have a higher net worth than Asians.

Blacks and Hispanics are less likely than the average household to own most assets, including a home. Only 44 percent of black and 47 percent of Hispanic households owned a home in 2011 compared with 65 percent of all households. Because housing equity accounts for the largest share of net worth, the lower homeownership rate of blacks and Hispanics largely explains their below-average net worth.

■ Among race and Hispanic origin groups, Hispanics are least likely to have any retirement assets.

Non-Hispanic whites have the highest rate of homeownership

(percent of households that own their home, by race and Hispanic origin, 2011)

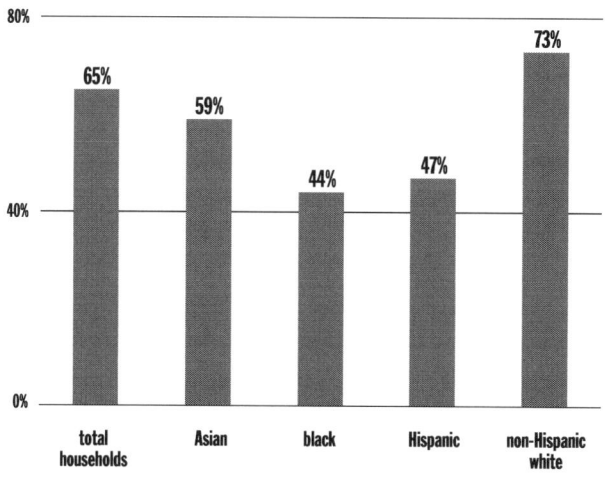

Table 5.13 Asset Ownership of Households by Race and Hispanic Origin of Householder, 2011

(percent of households owning selected assets and median value or equity of assets for owners, by race and Hispanic origin of householder, 2011)

	total households	Asian	black	Hispanic	non-Hispanic white
PERCENT WITH ASSET					
Interest-earning asset at financial institution	69.8%	77.7%	51.9%	53.6%	75.4%
Regular checking account	29.0	35.8	24.6	30.2	29.1
Stocks and mutal fund shares	19.6	22.6	6.4	4.3	24.5
Own business	13.8	15.2	7.4	11.5	15.3
Motor vehicles	84.7	84.2	70.5	77.3	88.3
Own home	65.3	58.7	43.8	47.2	72.6
Rental property	5.5	7.0	2.9	2.6	6.4
IRA or Keogh account	28.9	31.5	11.2	9.9	35.4
401(k) and thrift savings	42.1	50.0	31.7	25.8	46.4
MEDIAN VALUE OR EQUITY OF ASSET FOR OWNERS					
Interest-earning asset at financial institution	$2,450	$4,500	$500	$700	$3,250
Regular checking account	600	900	242	300	800
Stocks and mutal fund shares	20,000	19,000	4,750	8,000	24,000
Own business (equity)	8,000	6,000	2,000	2,000	10,000
Motor vehicles (equity)	6,824	7,839	3,916	5,267	7,113
Own home (equity)	80,000	120,000	50,000	47,000	85,000
Rental property (equity)	180,000	130,000	155,000	150,000	180,000
IRA or Keogh account	34,000	26,000	15,000	17,000	36,500
401(k) and thrift savings	30,000	38,000	12,000	15,000	35,000

Note: Asians and blacks are those who identify themselves as being of the race alone. Non-Hispanic whites are those who identify themselves as being white alone and not Hispanic. Hispanics may be of any race.
Source: Bureau of the Census, Wealth and Asset Ownership, Survey of Income and Program Participation, Internet site http://www.census.gov/people/wealth/; calculations by New Strategist

Most Households Are in Debt

The percentage of households with debt declined in most age groups between 2000 and 2011.

Sixty-nine percent of households have debt, owing a median of $70,000 in 2011. The median amount of debt owed by the average debtor household increased 37 percent between 2000 and 2011, after adjusting for inflation.

Householders aged 35 to 54 are most likely to be in debt, with 79 to 80 percent owing money. Debt declines with age, falling to a low of 44 percent among householders aged 65 or older.

Four types of debt are most common—home-secured debt such as mortgages (41 percent of households have this type of debt), credit card debt (38 percent), vehicle debt (30 percent), and "other debt"—a category that includes student loans (19 percent). Mortgages are the largest debt for the average household. The median amount owed by the average homeowner for home-secured debt was $117,000 in 2011. For householders under age 45, other debt exceeds vehicle and credit card debt.

■ Behind the 9 percentage point decline in the percentage of householders under age 35 with debt is the reluctance (or inability) of young adults to become homeowners.

Debt declines with advancing age

(median amount of debt owed by households by age of householder, 2011)

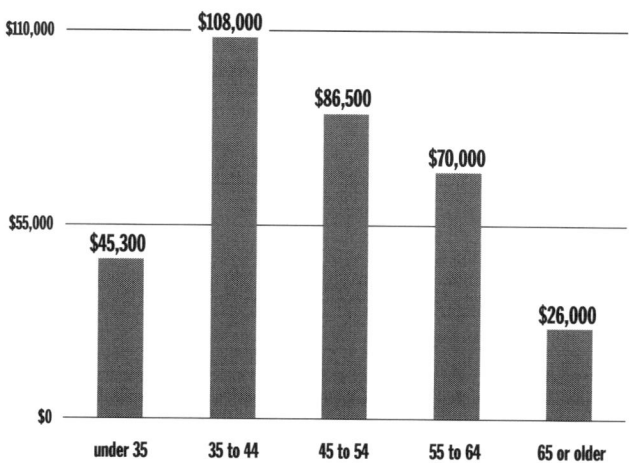

Table 5.14 Debt of Households by Age of Householder, 2000 and 2011

(percent of households with debt and median amount owed by those with debt, by age of householder, 2000 and 2011; percentage point and percent change, 2000–11; in 2011 dollars)

	2011	2000	percentage point change
PERCENT WITH DEBT			
Total households	**69.0%**	**74.2%**	**−5.2**
Under age 35	72.2	81.5	−9.3
Aged 35 to 44	79.6	85.5	−5.9
Aged 45 to 54	78.9	85.9	−7.0
Aged 55 to 64	73.0	76.8	−3.8
Aged 65 or older	44.4	41.0	3.4

	2011	2000	percent change
MEDIAN AMOUNT OWED			
Total households with debt	**$70,000**	**$50,971**	**37.3%**
Under age 35	45,300	40,240	12.6
Aged 35 to 44	108,000	86,650	24.6
Aged 45 to 54	86,500	63,445	36.3
Aged 55 to 64	70,000	42,654	64.1
Aged 65 or older	26,000	12,072	115.4

Source: Bureau of the Census, Wealth and Asset Ownership, Survey of Income and Program Participation, Internet site http://www.census.gov/people/wealth/; calculations by New Strategist

Table 5.15 Debt of Households by Type of Debt and Age of Householder, 2011

(percent of households with debt and median amount of debt for debtors, by age of householder, 2011)

	total households	under 35	35 to 44	45 to 54	55 to 64	65 or older
PERCENT WITH DEBT						
Total debt	**69.0%**	**72.2%**	**79.6%**	**78.9%**	**73.0%**	**44.4%**
Secured debt	55.3	53.4	66.3	67.2	60.9	31.3
Home debt	40.5	31.3	51.9	53.4	46.1	21.8
Business debt	4.1	3.2	4.3	5.8	5.5	2.0
Vehicle debt	30.4	37.7	38.8	35.0	29.4	13.5
Unsecured debt	46.2	52.5	54.2	52.0	47.2	27.8
Credit card debt	38.3	38.3	44.7	44.3	41.4	24.7
Loans	6.8	7.9	8.3	8.1	6.8	3.6
Other debt	18.6	31.3	22.9	20.5	15.0	5.4
MEDIAN AMOUNT OF DEBT FOR DEBTORS						
Total debt	**$70,000**	**$45,300**	**$108,000**	**$86,500**	**$70,000**	**$26,000**
Secured debt	91,000	76,500	128,500	99,000	85,000	50,000
Home debt	117,000	125,000	150,000	110,000	100,000	75,000
Business debt	25,000	20,000	20,000	25,000	30,000	25,000
Vehicle debt	10,000	10,000	10,000	11,000	10,000	9,000
Unsecured debt	7,000	9,700	8,400	8,000	6,000	3,450
Credit card debt	3,500	3,000	4,000	4,000	4,000	2,200
Loans	7,000	6,000	8,000	6,000	7,000	7,000
Other debt	10,000	13,000	12,000	10,000	8,688	4,000

Note: Secured debt is backed by collateral, unsecured debt is not. "Other debt" includes student loans and medical debt.
Source: Bureau of the Census, Wealth and Asset Ownership, Survey of Income and Program Participation, Internet site http://www.census.gov/people/wealth/; calculations by New Strategist

Married Couples Have the Biggest Debts

Couples aged 35 to 54 owe the most.

Most households, regardless of household type, are in debt. The figure ranges from a high of 80 percent among married couples to a low of 57 percent among female-headed households.

Four types of debt are most common: home-secured (mortgage), credit card, vehicle loans, and "other debt"—a category that includes student loans. Home-secured debt is the most common type among married couples (53 percent). For male- and female-headed households, credit card debt is most common (30 and 33 percent, respectively).

Married couples with debt owe the most money, a median of $99,000 in 2011. Female-headed households with debt owe a median of $30,000, and male-headed households with debt owe $45,900. Home-secured debt is the largest for the three types of households, and business debt ranks second—but few households own businesses. Other debt (much of it student loans) exceeds vehicle debt among male- and female-headed households.

■ Fewer than half of households have outstanding credit card debt, and the median amount owed by those with credit card debt ranges from $2,500 to $4,000.

Most households have debt, including female- and male-headed households

(percent of households with debt by type of household, 2011)

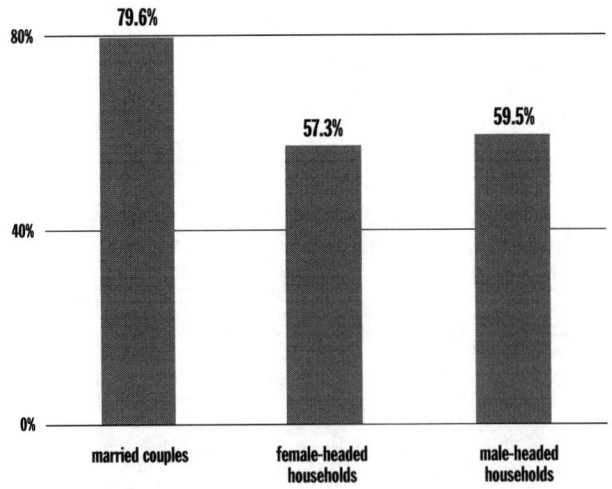

Table 5.16 Debt of Married-Couple Households by Type of Debt and by Age of Householder, 2011

(percent of total and married-couple households with debt, and median amount of debt for debtors, by age of married-couple householder, 2011)

	total households	married couples				
		under 35	35 to 44	45 to 54	55 to 64	65 or older
PERCENT WITH DEBT						
Total debt	**69.0%**	**79.6%**	**83.7%**	**87.4%**	**80.9%**	**55.9%**
Secured debt	55.3	68.6	71.1	77.9	70.4	41.8
Home debt	40.5	53.5	49.6	64.7	54.3	29.0
Business debt	4.1	5.9	4.9	6.8	7.1	3.1
Vehicle debt	30.4	38.9	50.0	44.6	36.0	19.2
Unsecured debt	46.2	53.4	59.2	59.6	52.7	34.4
Credit card debt	38.3	45.1	44.5	50.7	46.2	30.8
Loans	6.8	8.5	10.1	9.6	8.0	4.8
Other debt	18.6	21.4	35.5	24.3	17.2	6.8
MEDIAN AMOUNT OF DEBT FOR DEBTORS						
Total debt	**$70,000**	**$99,000**	**$100,000**	**$121,750**	**$85,500**	**$33,000**
Secured debt	91,000	110,000	111,000	128,500	92,500	57,178
Home debt	117,000	128,000	138,000	140,000	100,000	87,000
Business debt	25,000	25,000	20,500	25,000	26,000	25,000
Vehicle debt	10,000	11,000	11,000	12,000	10,600	10,000
Unsecured debt	7,000	8,000	10,000	9,000	6,900	4,000
Credit card debt	3,500	4,000	3,400	4,600	4,000	3,000
Loans	7,000	8,000	7,000	8,000	9,000	7,800
Other debt	10,000	10,000	13,000	10,900	10,000	2,700

Note: Secured debt is backed by collateral, unsecured debt is not. "Other debt" includes student loans and medical debt.
Source: Bureau of the Census, Wealth and Asset Ownership, Survey of Income and Program Participation, Internet site http:// www.census.gov/people/wealth/; calculations by New Strategist

Table 5.17 Debt of Female-Headed Households by Type of Debt and Age of Householder, 2011

(percent of total households and of female-headed households with debt, and median amount of debt for debtors, by age of female householder, 2011)

	total households	female-headed households				
		under 35	35 to 44	45 to 54	55 to 64	65 or older
PERCENT WITH DEBT						
Total debt	69.0%	57.3%	61.4%	69.4%	67.9%	36.1%
Secured debt	55.3	39.8	36.9	50.7	52.2	23.3
Home debt	40.5	26.1	15.3	35.4	38.5	16.6
Business debt	4.1	1.6	1.2	2.1	3.2	0.5
Vehicle debt	30.4	20.7	27.2	26.5	22.6	9.2
Unsecured debt	46.2	39.9	47.6	47.6	45.6	23.7
Credit card debt	38.3	32.5	33.6	38.1	40.7	21.5
Loans	6.8	4.7	5.6	6.2	4.9	2.5
Other debt	18.6	16.5	29.3	21.6	14.1	4.1
MEDIAN AMOUNT OF DEBT FOR DEBTORS						
Total debt	$70,000	$30,000	$18,000	$43,000	$47,500	$18,900
Secured debt	91,000	55,000	16,500	70,000	70,000	40,000
Home debt	117,000	90,000	107,000	100,000	90,000	60,000
Business debt	25,000	14,000	–	7,000	–	–
Vehicle debt	10,000	8,000	8,000	8,500	8,000	7,600
Unsecured debt	7,000	5,400	8,000	6,800	5,000	2,800
Credit card debt	3,500	2,500	2,000	3,000	3,000	2,000
Loans	7,000	5,000	5,000	5,000	5,000	7,000
Other debt	10,000	10,000	12,000	11,000	7,000	6,000

Note: Secured debt is backed by collateral, unsecured debt is not. "Other debt" includes student loans and medical debt.
"–" means sample is too small to make a reliable estimate.
Source: Bureau of the Census, Wealth and Asset Ownership, Survey of Income and Program Participation, Internet site http:// www.census.gov/people/wealth/; calculations by New Strategist

Table 5.18 Debt of Male-Headed Households by Type of Debt and Age of Householder, 2011

(percent of total households and of male-headed households with debt, and median amount of debt for debtors, by age of male householder, 2011)

	total households	male-headed households				
		under 35	35 to 44	45 to 54	55 to 64	65 or older
PERCENT WITH DEBT						
Total debt	**69.0%**	**59.5%**	**66.5%**	**67.8%**	**54.9%**	**35.6%**
Secured debt	55.3	44.6	44.5	54.8	42.9	24.4
Home debt	40.5	29.2	20.7	40.0	30.7	16.5
Business debt	4.1	3.4	2.9	4.2	3.5	2.5
Vehicle debt	30.4	23.2	30.2	26.8	18.4	9.8
Unsecured debt	46.2	37.5	47.6	40.9	31.9	20.6
Credit card debt	38.3	29.9	33.9	34.4	27.0	17.2
Loans	6.8	5.8	7.0	6.5	5.4	3.2
Other debt	18.6	14.7	26.9	13.6	8.8	5.0
MEDIAN AMOUNT OF DEBT FOR DEBTORS						
Total debt	**$70,000**	**$45,900**	**$27,000**	**$75,000**	**$44,209**	**$25,500**
Secured debt	91,000	75,000	28,000	96,000	68,000	55,000
Home debt	117,000	106,000	107,000	120,000	89,000	70,000
Business debt	25,000	25,000	–	25,000	–	–
Vehicle debt	10,000	9,000	9,200	9,000	8,000	8,000
Unsecured debt	7,000	7,000	9,500	7,500	5,800	4,000
Credit card debt	3,500	3,000	2,500	4,000	3,800	2,000
Loans	7,000	5,000	5,000	6,000	5,000	–
Other debt	10,000	12,000	16,000	10,000	7,477	6,500

Note: Secured debt is backed by collateral, unsecured debt is not. "Other debt" includes student loans and medical debt.
"–" means sample is too small to make a reliable estimate.
Source: Bureau of the Census, Wealth and Asset Ownership, Survey of Income and Program Participation, Internet site http://www.census.gov/people/wealth/; calculations by New Strategist

Asians Are Most Likely to Be in Debt

Asian households with debt owe more than other race and Hispanic-origin groups.

Asians are slightly more likely than non-Hispanic whites to be in debt, 72 versus 71 percent in 2011. The median amount of debt owed by Asian households is higher than the median owed by non-Hispanic whites: $108,000 versus $80,000. The reason for their greater debt is housing, with Asians owing a median of $190,000 in home debt compared with $117,000 owed by non-Hispanic whites. Behind the higher housing debt of Asians is their younger age and the fact that many live in California, where housing prices are relatively high.

Black households are less likely than average to be in debt—62 percent of black households versus 69 percent of all households. The same is true for Hispanics, with 63 percent of Hispanic households in debt. Among black and Hispanic households with debt, the median amount owed was $35,000 and $41,000, respectively, compared with $70,000 owed by the average household. The lower homeownership rate of blacks and Hispanics accounts for their smaller debts.

■ A substantial 21 percent of black households have "other debt," a category that includes student loans.

Households headed by blacks are least likely to be in debt

(percent of households with debt by race and Hispanic origin of householder, 2011)

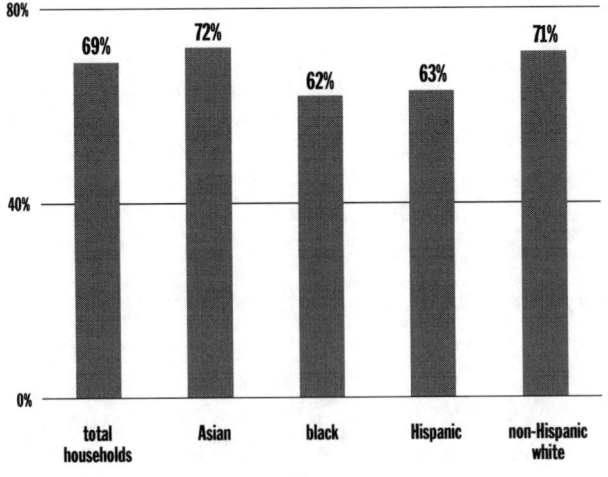

Table 5.19 Debt of Households by Type of Debt, Race, and Hispanic Origin of Householder, 2011

(percent of households with debt and median amount of debt for debtors, by race and Hispanic origin of householder, 2011)

	total households	Asian	black	Hispanic	non-Hispanic white
PERCENT WITH DEBT					
Total debt	**69.0%**	**72.2%**	**62.0%**	**63.3%**	**70.9%**
Secured debt	55.3	57.0	44.1	48.6	58.3
Home debt	40.5	43.8	29.0	31.7	44.0
Business debt	4.1	3.7	2.0	2.4	4.8
Vehicle debt	30.4	27.5	25.3	29.2	31.5
Unsecured debt	46.2	45.2	44.3	41.5	47.2
Credit card debt	38.3	40.4	35.1	34.3	39.4
Loans	6.8	5.0	6.4	5.8	7.1
Other debt	18.6	14.5	21.2	14.8	18.8
MEDIAN AMOUNT OF DEBT FOR DEBTORS					
Total debt	**$70,000**	**$108,000**	**$35,000**	**$41,000**	**$80,000**
Secured debt	91,000	160,000	60,000	77,000	97,500
Home debt	117,000	190,000	97,000	120,000	117,000
Business debt	25,000	–	18,000	12,000	25,000
Vehicle debt	10,000	11,000	9,000	10,000	10,000
Unsecured debt	7,000	7,000	6,800	5,000	7,470
Credit card debt	3,500	4,000	3,000	3,100	3,650
Loans	7,000	–	5,000	5,000	7,200
Other debt	10,000	14,000	10,000	8,000	10,800

Note: Secured debt is backed by collateral, unsecured debt is not. "Other debt" includes student loans and medical debt. Asians and blacks are those who identify themselves as being of the race alone. Non-Hispanic whites are those who identify themselves as being white alone and not Hispanic. Hispanics may be of any race. "–" means sample is too small to make a reliable estimate.
Source: Bureau of the Census, Wealth and Asset Ownership, Survey of Income and Program Participation, Internet site http://www.census.gov/people/wealth/; calculations by New Strategist

Retirement Worries Are Growing

Confidence in retirement readiness has dropped sharply since 2007.

Only 13 percent of workers are "very confident" in their ability to afford a comfortable retirement, according to the 2013 Retirement Confidence Survey. This figure is down from 27 percent who felt "very confident" in 2007—just before the Great Recession.

Reality may be dawning on many workers. Since 2007, the expected age of retirement has climbed. The percentage of workers who expect to retire at age 65 or older increased from 57 to 68 percent between 2007 and 2013. At the same time, the percentage expecting to retire before age 65 fell from 38 to 23 percent.

■ Only 17 percent of workers are very confident that they are doing a good job of saving for retirement, down from 26 percent who felt that way in 2007.

More than two-thirds of workers are not planning on an early retirement

(percentage of workers who expect to retire at age 65 or older, 2007 and 2013)

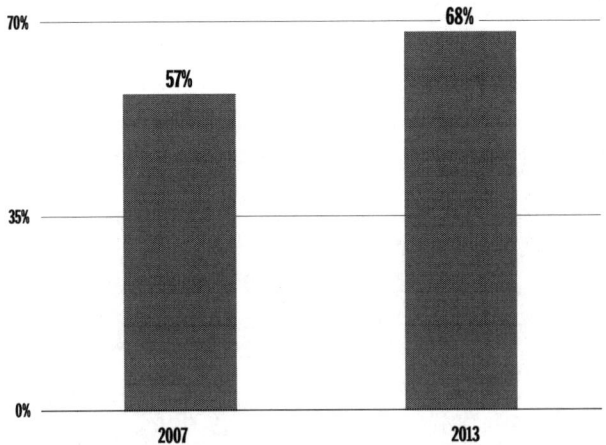

Table 5.20 Retirement Confidence, 2007 to 2013

(percent of workers aged 25 or older "very confident" in selected financial aspects of retirement, 2007 to 2013)

	2013	2010	2007
Very confident you will have enough money to live comfortably throughout your retirement	13%	16%	27%
Very confident you will have enough money to take care of basic expenses during retirement	25	29	40
Very confident you will have enough money to take care of medical expenses during retirement	14	12	20
Very confident you will have enough money to pay for long-term care during retirement	11	10	17
Very confident that the Social Security system will continue to provide benefits of at least equal value to the benefits received by retirees today	5	7	7
Very confident that the Medicare system will continue to provide benefits of at least equal value to the benefits received by retirees today	6	5	6
Very confident you are doing a good job of preparing financially for retirement	17	21	26

Source: Employee Benefit Research Institute, American Savings Education Council, and Mathew Greenwald & Associates, Inc., 2007, 2010, and 2013 Retirement Confidence Surveys, Internet site http://www.ebri.org/surveys/rcs/

Table 5.21 Expected Age of Retirement, 2007 and 2013

(responses of workers aged 25 or older to question about expected age of retirement, 2007 and 2013; percentage point change, 2007–13)

EXPECTED AGE OF RETIREMENT	2013	2007	percentage point change
Under age 60	9%	17%	–8
Aged 60 to 64	14	21	–7
Aged 65	25	27	–2
Aged 66 or older	36	24	12
Never retire	7	6	1
Don't know/refused	8	6	2
Before age 65	23	38	–15
Aged 65 or older*	68	57	11

* Includes "never retire."
Source: Employee Benefit Research Institute, American Savings Education Council, and Mathew Greenwald & Associates, Inc., 2007 and 2013 Retirement Confidence Surveys, Internet site http://www.ebri.org/surveys/rcs/

Table 5.22 Retirement Savings by Age, 2013

(percent distribution of workers aged 25 or older by savings and investments, not including value of primary residence, by age, 2013)

	total	25 to 34	35 to 44	45 to 54	55 or older
Total workers	**100.0%**	**100.0%**	**100.0%**	**100.0%**	**100.0%**
Less than $10,000	46	60	46	40	36
$10,000 to $24,999	11	15	12	11	7
$25,000 to $49,999	9	9	11	6	9
$50,000 to $99,999	10	8	10	13	8
$100,000 or more	24	9	21	30	42
$100,000 to $249,999	12	7	13	14	18
$250,000 or more	12	2	8	16	24

Source: Employee Benefit Research Institute, American Savings Education Council, and Mathew Greenwald & Associates, Inc., 2013 Retirement Confidence Survey, Internet site http://www.ebri.org/surveys/rcs/2013/

6

Poverty

Poverty rose sharply between 2000 and 2012 as the Great Recession destroyed businesses and jobs. In 2012, the poverty rate stood at 15.0 percent, up from 11.3 percent in 2000. The number of poor climbed by nearly 15 million during those years to 46 million in 2012.

The poverty population has changed, creating new obstacles to reducing the poverty rate. Until Social Security came to the rescue, the elderly were most likely to be poor. Today, children have a much higher poverty rate (21.8 percent) than the elderly (9.1 percent). Until single-parent families became such a significant presence among households, married couples accounted for most poor families. Today, female-headed families are the majority of families in poverty. Non-Hispanic whites once accounted for most of the poor. Today, most of the poor are Hispanic or black. Blacks once outnumbered Hispanics among the poor. Now poor Hispanics outnumber poor blacks.

■ Poverty rates will continue to remain high until jobs become plentiful again and single-parents decline as a share of families.

Poverty Trends

Women Head More than Half of the Nation's Poor Families

The share of poor families headed by women has exceeded 50 percent for decades.

In 2012, female-headed families accounted for the 50.3 percent majority of the nation's 9.5 million poor families. This proportion is little changed from the 51 percent of 2000. Married couples account for a smaller 39 percent of families below poverty level.

Men head few poor families, although the proportion has grown since 2000. Male-headed families accounted for about 11 percent of families in poverty in 2012, up from 8 percent in 2000.

■ The married-couple share of poor families has fallen slightly since 2000, when they were 41 percent of the total.

Married couples head a smaller share of poor families

(percent distribution of families in poverty by family type, 2000 and 2012)

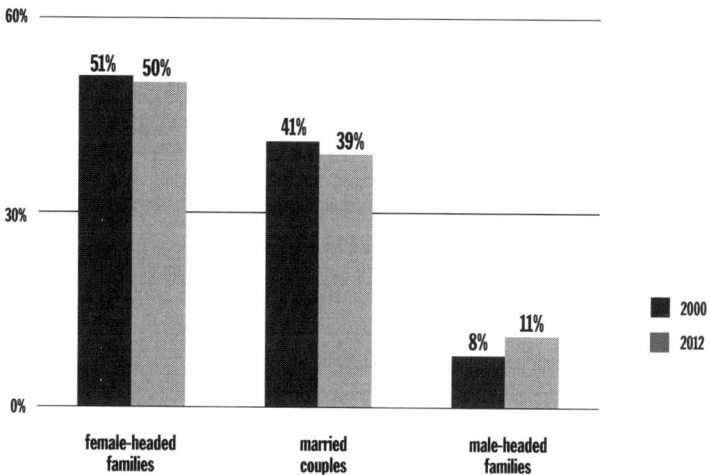

Table 6.1 Distribution of Families below Poverty Level by Family Type, 2000 to 2012

(number of families below poverty level and percent distribution by family type, 2000 to 2012; families in thousands as of the following year)

	total families in poverty		married couples	female householder, no spouse present	male householder, no spouse present
	number	percent			
2012	9,520	100.0%	38.9%	50.3%	10.7%
2011	9,497	100.0	38.5	51.5	10.0
2010	9,400	100.0	39.2	51.4	9.5
2009	8,792	100.0	38.8	50.5	10.7
2008	8,147	100.0	40.0	51.1	8.9
2007	7,623	100.0	37.4	53.5	9.1
2006	7,668	100.0	37.9	53.3	8.8
2005	7,657	100.0	38.4	52.8	8.7
2004	7,835	100.0	41.0	50.6	8.4
2003	7,607	100.0	40.9	50.7	8.4
2002	7,229	100.0	42.2	50.0	7.8
2001	6,813	100.0	40.5	50.9	8.6
2000	6,400	100.0	41.2	51.2	7.6

Source: Bureau of the Census, Current Population Surveys, Annual Social and Economic Supplement, Internet site http://www .census.gov/hhes/www/poverty/data/historical/families.html; calculations by New Strategist

Family Poverty Increased between 2000 and 2012

Black and Hispanic families are about equally likely to be poor.

Family poverty was significantly higher in 2012 than in 2000. A substantial 11.8 percent of the nation's families were poor in 2012, up from 8.7 percent in 2000. Poverty rates were higher in 2012 than in 2000 for every type of family.

The poverty rate has increased among families regardless of the race and Hispanic origin of householder. Among non-Hispanic white families, who are least likely to be poor, the poverty rate climbed from 5.4 to 7.1 percent between 2000 and 2012. Among black families, the poverty rate grew from 19.3 to 23.7 percent during those years. The increase was similar for Hispanic families.

■ The poverty rate among Hispanic married couples (16.6 percent) is much higher than the rate among black couples (9.7 percent).

Family poverty has grown since 2000 in every race and Hispanic origin group

(poverty rate of families by race and Hispanic origin of householder, 2000 and 2012)

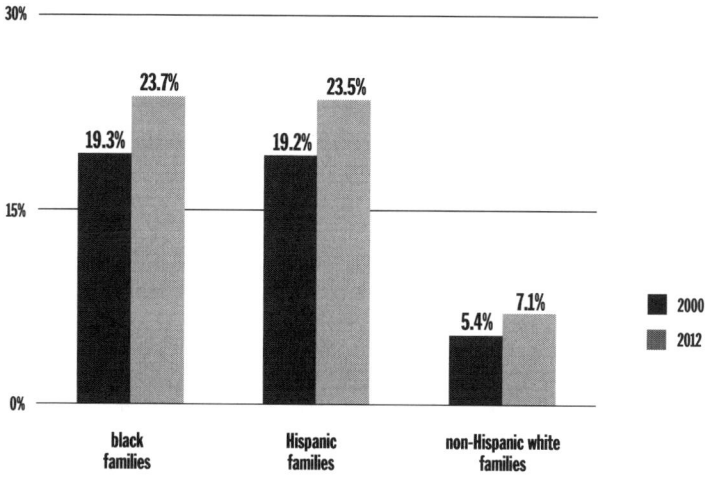

Table 6.2 Number and Percent of Families below Poverty Level by Family Type, 2000 to 2012: Total Families

(number and percent of families below poverty level by family type, 2000 to 2012; families in thousands as of the following year)

NUMBER IN POVERTY	total families in poverty	married couples	female householder, no spouse present	male householder, no spouse present
2012	9,520	3,705	4,793	1,023
2011	9,497	3,652	4,894	950
2010	9,400	3,681	4,827	892
2009	8,792	3,409	4,441	942
2008	8,147	3,261	4,163	723
2007	7,623	2,849	4,078	696
2006	7,668	2,910	4,087	671
2005	7,657	2,944	4,044	669
2004	7,835	3,216	3,962	657
2003	7,607	3,115	3,856	636
2002	7,229	3,052	3,613	564
2001	6,813	2,760	3,470	583
2000	6,400	2,637	3,278	485
POVERTY RATE				
2012	11.8%	6.3%	30.9%	16.4%
2011	11.8	6.2	31.2	16.1
2010	11.8	6.3	31.7	15.8
2009	11.1	5.8	29.9	16.9
2008	10.3	5.5	28.7	13.8
2007	9.8	4.9	28.3	13.6
2006	9.8	4.9	28.3	13.2
2005	9.9	5.1	28.7	13.0
2004	10.2	5.5	28.3	13.4
2003	10.0	5.4	28.0	13.5
2002	9.6	5.3	26.5	12.1
2001	9.2	4.9	26.4	13.1
2000	8.7	4.7	25.4	11.3

*Source: Bureau of the Census, Current Population Surveys, Annual Social and Economic Supplement, Internet site http://www
.census.gov/hhes/www/poverty/data/historical/people.html; calculations by New Strategist*

Table 6.3 Number and Percent of Families below Poverty Level by Family Type, 2002 to 2012: Asian Families

(number and percent of Asian families below poverty level by family type, 2002 to 2012; families in thousands as of the following year)

NUMBER IN POVERTY	Asian families in poverty	married couples	female householder, no spouse present	male householder, no spouse present
2012	409	245	115	49
2011	434	265	122	47
2010	379	232	115	32
2009	359	239	87	34
2008	356	254	76	26
2007	281	187	77	17
2006	272	183	61	27
2005	306	201	83	22
2004	243	150	54	39
2003	320	203	89	28
2002	218	137	51	30
POVERTY RATE				
2012	9.5%	7.2%	20.2%	14.2%
2011	10.0	7.7	21.4	14.0
2010	9.2	7.2	20.7	9.7
2009	9.6	8.0	18.0	12.3
2008	9.8	8.7	16.5	10.1
2007	8.1	6.8	17.0	7.0
2006	7.8	6.4	15.6	11.4
2005	9.1	7.5	20.0	8.8
2004	7.4	5.7	14.0	14.8
2003	10.0	7.9	23.5	11.8
2002	7.4	5.9	14.3	12.6

Note: Asians are those who identify themselves as being of the race alone and those who identify themselves as being of the race in combination with other races.
Source: Bureau of the Census, Current Population Surveys, Annual Social and Economic Supplement, Internet site http://www.census.gov/hhes/www/poverty/data/historical/index.html

Table 6.4 Number and Percent of Families below Poverty Level by Family Type, 2000 to 2012: Black Families

(number and percent of black families below poverty level by family type, 2000 to 2012; families in thousands as of the following year)

NUMBER IN POVERTY	black families in poverty	married couples	female householder, no spouse present	male householder, no spouse present
2012	2,439	458	1,707	274
2011	2,431	426	1,762	242
2010	2,403	407	1,738	257
2009	2,193	383	1,569	241
2008	2,112	365	1,580	167
2007	2,091	313	1,570	208
2006	2,041	356	1,506	180
2005	2,050	348	1,524	178
2004	2,082	386	1,538	158
2003	2,021	331	1,496	194
2002	1,958	340	1,454	165
2001	1,829	328	1,351	150
2000	1,686	266	1,300	120
POVERTY RATE				
2012	23.7%	9.7%	38.0%	24.8%
2011	24.2	9.4	39.3	24.2
2010	24.1	9.1	38.4	26.3
2009	22.7	8.6	36.8	24.9
2008	21.9	8.0	37.1	19.8
2007	22.0	7.0	37.2	25.1
2006	21.5	7.9	36.4	20.4
2005	22.0	8.2	36.2	21.3
2004	22.8	9.1	37.6	20.7
2003	22.1	7.8	36.8	24.1
2002	21.4	8.0	35.7	20.8
2001	20.7	7.8	35.2	19.4
2000	19.3	6.3	34.3	16.3

Note: Beginning in 2002, blacks are those who identify themselves as being of the race alone and those who identify themselves as being of the race in combination with other races.
Source: Bureau of the Census, Current Population Surveys, Annual Social and Economic Supplement, Internet site http://www.census.gov/hhes/www/poverty/data/historical/index.html

Table 6.5 Number and Percent of Families below Poverty Level by Family Type, 2000 to 2012: Hispanic Families

(number and percent of Hispanic families below poverty level by family type, 2000 to 2012; families in thousands as of the following year)

NUMBER IN POVERTY	Hispanic families in poverty	married couples	female householder, no spouse present	male householder, no spouse present
2012	2,807	1,238	1,266	303
2011	2,651	1,145	1,272	234
2010	2,739	1,221	1,270	248
2009	2,369	1,054	1,066	249
2008	2,239	1,078	1,007	154
2007	2,045	926	968	151
2006	1,922	903	881	139
2005	1,948	917	876	155
2004	1,953	934	872	147
2003	1,925	976	792	157
2002	1,792	927	717	148
2001	1,649	799	711	139
2000	1,540	772	664	104
POVERTY RATE				
2012	23.5%	16.6%	40.7%	21.7%
2011	22.9	15.9	41.2	18.4
2010	24.3	17.3	42.6	20.0
2009	22.7	16.0	38.8	23.0
2008	21.3	15.6	39.2	15.1
2007	19.7	13.4	38.4	15.3
2006	18.9	13.3	36.0	14.7
2005	19.7	13.8	38.9	15.9
2004	20.5	14.7	38.9	15.9
2003	20.8	15.7	37.0	17.3
2002	19.7	15.0	35.3	17.0
2001	19.4	13.8	37.0	17.0
2000	19.2	14.2	36.4	13.6

Source: Bureau of the Census, Current Population Surveys, Annual Social and Economic Supplement, Internet site http://www.census.gov/hhes/www/poverty/data/historical/people.html; calculations by New Strategist

Table 6.6 Number and Percent of Families below Poverty Level by Family Type, 2000 to 2012: Non-Hispanic White Families

(number and percent of non-Hispanic white families below poverty level by family type, 2000 to 2012; families in thousands as of the following year)

NUMBER IN POVERTY	non-Hispanic white families in poverty	married couples	female householder, no spouse present	male householder, no spouse present
2012	3,835	1,735	1,713	387
2011	3,955	1,787	1,766	403
2010	3,880	1,802	1,743	336
2009	3,797	1,697	1,701	399
2008	3,383	1,545	1,473	365
2007	3,184	1,388	1,489	308
2006	3,372	1,436	1,628	309
2005	3,285	1,450	1,537	298
2004	3,505	1,710	1,491	304
2003	3,270	1,575	1,455	241
2002	3,208	1,628	1,374	207
2001	3,051	1,477	1,305	270
2000	2,896	1,435	1,226	236
POVERTY RATE				
2012	7.1%	4.0%	23.4%	11.4%
2011	7.3	4.1	23.4	12.5
2010	7.2	4.1	24.1	11.0
2009	7.0	3.9	23.3	12.5
2008	6.2	3.5	20.7	11.9
2007	5.9	3.2	20.7	10.3
2006	6.2	3.2	22.0	10.6
2005	6.1	3.3	21.5	9.9
2004	6.5	3.9	20.8	10.5
2003	6.1	3.6	20.4	8.9
2002	6.0	3.7	19.4	7.7
2001	5.7	3.3	19.0	10.3
2000	5.4	3.2	17.8	9.2

Note: Beginning in 2002, non-Hispanic whites are those who identify themselves as being white alone and not Hispanic.
Source: Bureau of the Census, Current Population Surveys, Annual Social and Economic Supplement, Internet site http://www
.census.gov/hhes/www/poverty/data/historical/people.html; calculations by New Strategist

Many More Families with Children Are in Poverty

Since 2000, the poverty rate has climbed sharply for male- and female-headed families with children.

More than 18 percent of families with children under age 18 were poor in 2012. Between 2000 and 2012 the poverty rate for families with children climbed from 12.7 to 18.4 percent.

The poverty rate of female-headed families with children grew from 33.0 to 40.9 percent between 2000 and 2012. Among their male counterparts, the percentage point increase in the poverty rate was almost as great, the rate rising from 15.3 to 22.6 percent. Poverty also grew among married couples with children during the decade, but the increase was much smaller.

In 2012, Hispanic female-headed families with children had the highest poverty rate, at 48.6 percent. This figure was up from 42.9 percent in 2000. Similarly, the poverty rate of black female-headed families with children grew from 41.0 percent in 2000 to 46.8 percent in 2012. More than one in five Hispanic married couples with children are poor. Their black counterparts are much less likely to be poor, with a poverty rate of 12.5 percent.

■ Among families with children, the poverty rate is lowest for non-Hispanic white married couples (5.0 percent).

Poverty has grown among families with children

(poverty rate of families with children under age 18 by family type, 2000 and 2012)

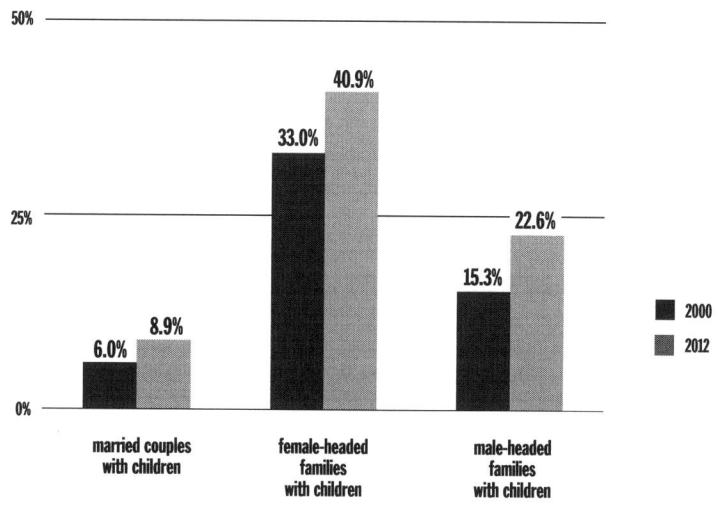

Table 6.7 Number and Percent of Families with Children below Poverty Level by Family Type, 2000 to 2012: Total Families with Children

(number and percent of families with related children under age 18 below poverty level by family type, 2000 to 2012; families in thousands as of the following year)

NUMBER IN POVERTY	total families with children in poverty	married couples	female householder, no spouse present	male householder, no spouse present
2012	7,063	2,246	4,099	717
2011	7,111	2,216	4,243	652
2010	7,145	2,309	4,163	673
2009	6,630	2,161	3,800	670
2008	6,104	1,989	3,645	471
2007	5,830	1,765	3,593	471
2006	5,822	1,746	3,615	461
2005	5,729	1,777	3,493	459
2004	5,819	1,903	3,477	439
2003	5,772	1,885	3,416	470
2002	5,397	1,831	3,171	395
2001	5,138	1,643	3,083	412
2000	4,866	1,615	2,906	345
POVERTY RATE				
2012	18.4%	8.9%	40.9%	22.6%
2011	18.5	8.8	40.9	21.9
2010	18.5	9.0	40.9	24.1
2009	17.1	8.3	38.5	23.7
2008	15.7	7.5	37.2	17.6
2007	15.0	6.7	37.0	17.5
2006	14.6	6.4	36.5	17.9
2005	14.5	6.5	36.2	17.6
2004	14.8	7.0	35.9	17.1
2003	14.8	7.0	35.5	19.1
2002	13.9	6.8	33.7	16.6
2001	13.4	6.1	33.6	17.7
2000	12.7	6.0	33.0	15.3

Source: Bureau of the Census, Current Population Surveys, Annual Social and Economic Supplement, Internet site http://www.census.gov/hhes/www/poverty/data/historical/people.html; calculations by New Strategist

Table 6.8 Number and Percent of Families with Children below Poverty Level by Family Type, 2002 to 2012: Asian Families with Children

(number and percent of Asian families with related children under age 18 below poverty level by family type, 2002 to 2012; families in thousands as of the following year)

NUMBER IN POVERTY	Asian families with children in poverty	married couples	female householder, no spouse present	male householder, no spouse present
2012	265	154	82	29
2011	287	168	92	27
2010	244	140	93	11
2009	238	153	64	21
2008	204	141	52	11
2007	178	109	65	4
2006	178	116	46	16
2005	189	121	54	14
2004	154	97	43	15
2003	199	121	66	12
2002	151	94	39	18
POVERTY RATE				
2012	11.8%	8.4%	27.5%	24.5%
2011	12.6	9.1	30.1	22.6
2010	11.3	8.0	29.1	10.7
2009	11.5	9.0	23.4	20.7
2008	10.5	8.8	21.4	12.5
2007	9.6	7.1	27.8	5.1
2006	9.5	7.3	23.8	19.2
2005	10.4	8.1	24.3	15.5
2004	8.4	6.3	19.5	15.4
2003	10.9	8.0	28.2	15.2
2002	9.2	6.9	21.0	21.1

Note: Asians are those who identify themselves as being of the race alone and those who identify themselves as being of the race in combination with other races.

Source: Bureau of the Census, Current Population Surveys, Annual Social and Economic Supplement, Internet site http://www.census.gov/hhes/www/poverty/data/historical/index.html

Table 6.9 Number and Percent of Families with Children below Poverty Level by Family Type, 2000 to 2012: Black Families with Children

(number and percent of black families with related children under age 18 below poverty level by family type, 2000 to 2012; families in thousands as of the following year)

NUMBER IN POVERTY	black families with children in poverty	married couples	female householder, no spouse present	male householder, no spouse present
2012	1,944	286	1,479	179
2011	1,951	272	1,532	148
2010	1,979	279	1,501	198
2009	1,787	259	1,365	163
2008	1,756	225	1,416	115
2007	1,706	194	1,385	128
2006	1,686	221	1,347	117
2005	1,679	213	1,335	131
2004	1,655	213	1,339	102
2003	1,698	210	1,341	146
2002	1,597	199	1,288	110
2001	1,524	205	1,220	99
2000	1,411	157	1,177	76
POVERTY RATE				
2012	32.1%	12.5%	46.8%	29.5%
2011	32.8	12.2	47.7	28.8
2010	33.6	12.7	47.1	40.0
2009	30.4	11.4	44.3	30.5
2008	29.6	9.8	44.4	25.5
2007	29.0	8.5	43.7	29.5
2006	28.1	9.1	43.3	25.8
2005	28.3	9.2	42.0	29.6
2004	28.6	9.3	43.3	25.3
2003	28.6	9.1	42.7	30.7
2002	27.2	8.5	41.3	26.3
2001	26.6	8.7	40.8	24.6
2000	25.3	6.7	41.0	21.7

Note: Beginning in 2002, blacks are those who identify themselves as being of the race alone and those who identify themselves as being of the race in combination with other races.
Source: Bureau of the Census, Current Population Surveys, Annual Social and Economic Supplement, Internet site http://www .census.gov/hhes/www/poverty/data/historical/index.html

Table 6.10 Number and Percent of Families with Children below Poverty Level by Family Type, 2000 to 2012: Hispanic Families with Children

(number and percent of Hispanic families with related children under age 18 below poverty level by family type, 2000 to 2012; families in thousands as of the following year)

NUMBER IN POVERTY	Hispanic families with children in poverty	married couples	female householder, no spouse present	male householder, no spouse present
2012	2,341	973	1,133	235
2011	2,265	916	1,159	189
2010	2,373	1,022	1,159	192
2009	2,004	876	945	183
2008	1,905	874	912	119
2007	1,759	766	881	112
2006	1,636	718	811	106
2005	1,651	771	777	102
2004	1,685	778	806	102
2003	1,629	789	713	127
2002	1,527	752	657	118
2001	1,405	646	645	115
2000	1,323	649	597	77
POVERTY RATE				
2012	30.1%	20.9%	48.6%	30.1%
2011	29.3	19.7	49.1	26.1
2010	30.9	21.8	50.5	27.8
2009	28.4	19.9	46.0	30.2
2008	26.8	18.9	46.6	22.0
2007	24.9	16.4	46.6	22.0
2006	23.4	15.6	42.5	22.8
2005	24.4	16.9	45.2	20.6
2004	25.5	17.8	46.0	20.4
2003	25.2	18.4	43.0	24.9
2002	24.1	17.7	41.4	23.6
2001	23.7	16.2	43.2	24.5
2000	23.3	16.8	42.9	18.4

Source: Bureau of the Census, Current Population Surveys, Annual Social and Economic Supplement, Internet site http://www.census.gov/hhes/www/poverty/data/historical/people.html; calculations by New Strategist

Table 6.11 Number and Percent of Families with Children below Poverty Level by Family Type, 2000 to 2012: Non-Hispanic White Families with Children

(number and percent of non-Hispanic white families with related children under age 18 below poverty level by family type, 2000 to 2012; families in thousands as of the following year)

NUMBER IN POVERTY	non-Hispanic white families with children in poverty	married couples	female householder, no spouse present	male householder, no spouse present
2012	2,510	820	1,415	274
2011	2,618	846	1,496	276
2010	2,573	872	1,447	253
2009	2,553	854	1,412	286
2008	2,201	738	1,246	217
2007	2,176	678	1,283	215
2006	2,296	683	1,405	208
2005	2,171	661	1,308	201
2004	2,294	800	1,287	207
2003	2,185	746	1,269	170
2002	2,088	781	1,170	137
2001	2,014	696	1,135	184
2000	1,940	709	1,058	173
POVERTY RATE				
2012	11.2%	5.0%	33.1%	16.3%
2011	11.7	5.2	33.0	17.3
2010	11.3	5.2	32.6	17.2
2009	10.8	4.9	31.7	18.5
2008	9.3	4.2	28.5	14.1
2007	9.2	3.8	29.2	13.2
2006	9.3	3.7	30.2	13.6
2005	8.8	3.6	29.2	13.1
2004	9.3	4.3	28.2	13.8
2003	8.9	4.0	28.1	12.5
2002	8.5	4.1	26.2	10.4
2001	8.1	3.6	25.7	13.4
2000	7.7	3.7	24.6	12.3

Note: Beginning in 2002, non-Hispanic whites are those who identify themselves as being white alone and not Hispanic.
Source: Bureau of the Census, Current Population Surveys, Annual Social and Economic Supplement, Internet site http://www
.census.gov/hhes/www/poverty/data/historical/index.html

Poverty Rate Has Increased since 2000

Poverty is higher among females than males.

The number of poor in the United States has expanded enormously since 2000, rising from 31.6 million to 46.5 million. The poverty rate was 15.0 percent in 2012, up from 11.3 percent in 2000. Behind the rise in poverty are the Great Recession and the slow economic recovery. The poverty rate in 2012 was only slightly below the 2010 post–Great Recession high of 15.1 percent.

Among males, 13.6 percent were poor in 2012—close to the all-time high for males of 14.0 percent in 2010, according to Census Bureau statistics collected since the 1960s. Among females, 16.3 percent were poor in 2012, up from 12.6 percent in 2000. Females accounted for 56 percent of the poor in 2012, a figure that has not changed much since 2000.

■ Females have a higher poverty rate than males because they are more likely to be raising children alone, which limits their ability to work full-time.

Poverty rate is still close to its post–Great Recession high

(percent of people who are poor, 2000 to 2012)

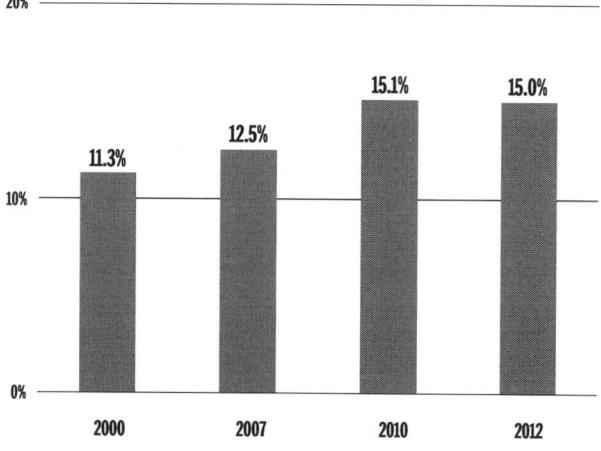

Table 6.12 Number and Percent of People below Poverty Level by Sex, 2000 to 2012

(number and percent of people below poverty level by sex, 2000 to 2012; people in thousands as of the following year)

NUMBER IN POVERTY	total people in poverty	females	males
2012	46,496	25,840	20,656
2011	46,247	25,746	20,501
2010	46,343	25,451	20,893
2009	43,569	24,094	19,475
2008	39,829	22,131	17,698
2007	37,276	20,973	16,302
2006	36,460	20,460	16,000
2005	36,950	21,000	15,950
2004	37,040	20,641	16,399
2003	35,861	20,078	15,783
2002	34,570	19,408	15,162
2001	32,907	18,580	14,327
2000	31,581	18,045	13,536
POVERTY RATE			
2012	15.0%	16.3%	13.6%
2011	15.0	16.3	13.6
2010	15.1	16.3	14.0
2009	14.3	15.6	13.0
2008	13.2	14.4	12.0
2007	12.5	13.8	11.1
2006	12.3	13.6	11.0
2005	12.6	14.1	11.1
2004	12.7	13.9	11.5
2003	12.5	13.7	11.2
2002	12.1	13.3	10.9
2001	11.7	12.9	10.4
2000	11.3	12.6	9.9

Source: Bureau of the Census, Current Population Surveys, Annual Social and Economic Supplement, Internet site http://www.census.gov/hhes/www/poverty/data/historical/people.html; calculations by New Strategist

A Growing Share of Poor People Are Aged 18 to 64

The elderly make up a smaller share of the poor than they did in 2000.

Most of the nation's 46 million poor are aged 18 to 64. In 2012, 57 percent of people in poverty were of working age, up from 53 percent in 2000. Children under age 18 are a smaller percentage of the poor than they once were, their share falling from 37 percent in 2000 to 35 percent in 2012. The elderly share of the poor declined from 11 to 8 percent during those years.

The poverty rate of the elderly has fallen since 2000, while the rate for people under age 65 has climbed. Among children, the poverty rate was 16.2 percent in 2000 and a much larger 21.8 percent in 2012. The poverty rate of people aged 18 to 64 grew from 9.6 to 13.7 percent during those years. At the same time, the poverty rate of people aged 65 or older fell from 9.9 to 9.1 percent.

■ Poverty rates among the elderly have fallen because a more educated and affluent generation has entered the age group.

Poverty rate has increased among people under age 65

(poverty rate of people by age, 2000 and 2012)

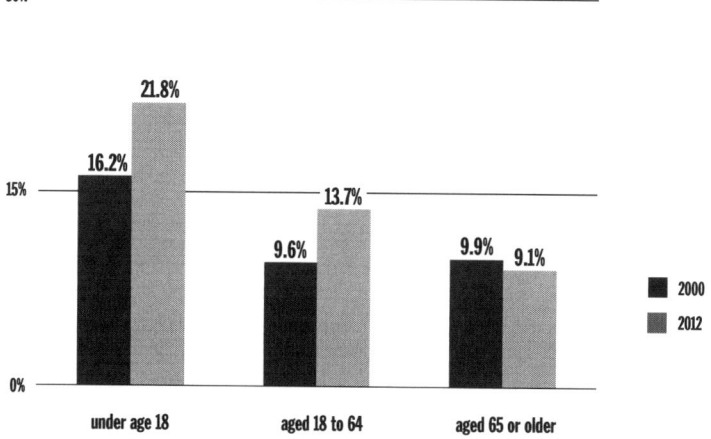

Table 6.13 Distribution of People below Poverty Level by Age, 2000 to 2012

(total number of people below poverty level and percent distribution by age, 2000 to 2012; people in thousands as of the following year)

	total people in poverty		under age 18	aged 18 to 64	aged 65 or older
	number	percent			
2012	46,496	100.0%	34.6%	57.0%	8.4%
2011	46,247	100.0	34.9	57.3	7.8
2010	46,343	100.0	35.1	57.2	7.7
2009	43,569	100.0	35.5	56.7	7.9
2008	39,829	100.0	35.3	55.5	9.2
2007	37,276	100.0	35.7	54.7	9.5
2006	36,460	100.0	35.2	55.5	9.3
2005	36,950	100.0	34.9	55.3	9.8
2004	37,040	100.0	35.2	55.5	9.3
2003	35,861	100.0	35.9	54.2	9.9
2002	34,570	100.0	35.1	54.6	10.3
2001	32,907	100.0	35.7	54.0	10.4
2000	31,581	100.0	36.7	52.8	10.5

Source: Bureau of the Census, Current Population Surveys, Annual Social and Economic Supplement, Internet site http://www .census.gov/hhes/www/poverty/data/historical/people.html; calculations by New Strategist

Table 6.14 Number and Percent of People below Poverty Level by Age, 2000 to 2012

(number and percent of people below poverty level by age, 2000 to 2012; people in thousands as of the following year)

NUMBER IN POVERTY	total people in poverty	under age 18	aged 18 to 64	aged 65 or older
2012	46,496	16,073	26,497	3,926
2011	46,247	16,134	26,492	3,620
2010	46,343	16,286	26,499	3,558
2009	43,569	15,451	24,684	3,433
2008	39,829	14,068	22,105	3,656
2007	37,276	13,324	20,396	3,556
2006	36,460	12,827	20,239	3,394
2005	36,950	12,896	20,450	3,603
2004	37,040	13,041	20,545	3,453
2003	35,861	12,866	19,443	3,552
2002	34,570	12,133	18,861	3,576
2001	32,907	11,733	17,760	3,414
2000	31,581	11,587	16,671	3,323
POVERTY RATE				
2012	15.0%	21.8%	13.7%	9.1%
2011	15.0	21.9	13.7	8.7
2010	15.1	22.0	13.8	8.9
2009	14.3	20.7	12.9	8.9
2008	13.2	19.0	11.7	9.7
2007	12.5	18.0	10.9	9.7
2006	12.3	17.4	10.8	9.4
2005	12.6	17.6	11.1	10.1
2004	12.7	17.8	11.3	9.8
2003	12.5	17.6	10.8	10.2
2002	12.1	16.7	10.6	10.4
2001	11.7	16.3	10.1	10.1
2000	11.3	16.2	9.6	9.9

Source: Bureau of the Census, Current Population Surveys, Annual Social and Economic Supplement, Internet site http://www.census.gov/hhes/www/poverty/data/historical/people.html; calculations by New Strategist

Non-Hispanic Whites Are a Minority of the Poor

Hispanics and blacks account for the majority of the poor.

Non-Hispanic whites were only 41 percent of the poverty population in 2012, down from 45 percent in 2000. The black share of the poor remained the same during those years, at 25 percent. In contrast, the Hispanic share of the poor grew from 25 to 29 percent. Only 4 percent of poor Americans are Asian.

During the past decade, the poverty rate of Asians, blacks, Hispanics, and non-Hispanic whites has increased. In 2012, the poverty rate of blacks (27.1 percent) was slightly greater than the Hispanic rate (25.6 percent). The poverty rate of Asians is much lower at 11.4 percent, and non-Hispanic whites have the lowest poverty rate at 9.7 percent.

■ Poverty will not decline significantly until jobs become more plentiful.

Poverty rate has grown in every racial and ethnic group

(poverty rate of people by race and Hispanic origin, 2000 and 2012)

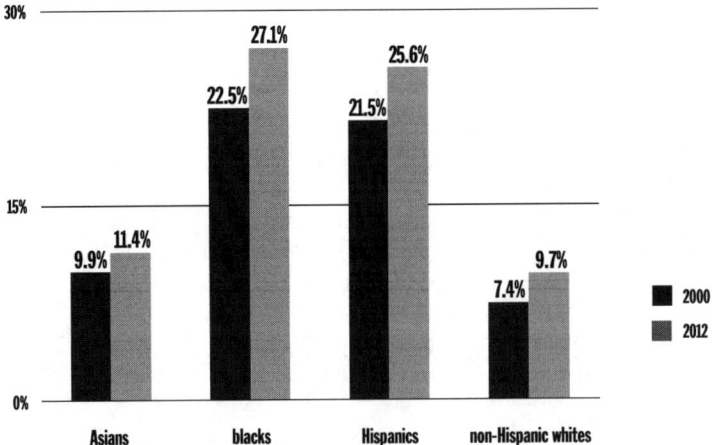

Table 6.15 Distribution of People below Poverty Level by Race and Hispanic Origin, 2000 to 2012

(total number of people below poverty level and percent distribution by race and Hispanic origin, 2000 to 2012; people in thousands as of the following year)

	total people in poverty		Asian	black	Hispanic	non-Hispanic white
	number	percent				
2012	46,496	100.0%	4.5%	25.4%	29.3%	40.7%
2011	46,247	100.0	4.7	25.4	28.6	41.5
2010	46,343	100.0	4.5	25.0	29.2	41.5
2009	43,569	100.0	4.4	24.3	28.3	42.5
2008	39,829	100.0	4.2	24.8	27.6	42.7
2007	37,276	100.0	3.9	25.9	26.5	43.0
2006	36,460	100.0	4.0	25.9	25.4	43.9
2005	36,950	100.0	4.1	25.8	25.4	43.9
2004	37,040	100.0	3.5	25.4	24.6	45.6
2003	35,861	100.0	4.3	25.4	25.2	44.3
2002	34,570	100.0	3.6	25.7	24.7	45.0
2001	32,907	100.0	3.9	24.7	24.3	46.4
2000	31,581	100.0	4.0	25.3	24.5	45.5

Note: Beginning in 2002, Asians and blacks are those who identify themselves as being of the race alone and those who identify themselves as being of the race in combination with other races. Non-Hispanic whites are those who identify themselves as being white alone and not Hispanic.

Source: Bureau of the Census, Current Population Surveys, Annual Social and Economic Supplement, Internet site http://www .census.gov/hhes/www/poverty/data/historical/people.html; calculations by New Strategist

Table 6.16 Number and Percent of People below Poverty Level by Race and Hispanic Origin, 2000 to 2012

(number and percent of people below poverty level by race and Hispanic origin, 2000 to 2012; people in thousands as of the following year)

NUMBER IN POVERTY	total people in poverty	Asians	blacks	Hispanics	non-Hispanic whites
2012	46,496	2,072	11,809	13,616	18,940
2011	46,247	2,189	11,730	13,244	19,171
2010	46,343	2,064	11,597	13,522	19,251
2009	43,569	1,901	10,575	12,350	18,530
2008	39,829	1,686	9,882	10,987	17,024
2007	37,276	1,467	9,668	9,890	16,032
2006	36,460	1,447	9,447	9,243	16,013
2005	36,950	1,501	9,517	9,368	16,227
2004	37,040	1,295	9,411	9,122	16,908
2003	35,861	1,527	9,108	9,051	15,902
2002	34,570	1,243	8,884	8,555	15,567
2001	32,907	1,275	8,136	7,997	15,271
2000	31,581	1,258	7,982	7,747	14,366
POVERTY RATE					
2012	15.0%	11.4%	27.1%	25.6%	9.7%
2011	15.0	12.3	27.5	25.3	9.8
2010	15.1	12.0	27.4	26.5	9.9
2009	14.3	12.4	25.9	25.3	9.4
2008	13.2	11.6	24.6	23.2	8.6
2007	12.5	10.2	24.4	21.5	8.2
2006	12.3	10.1	24.2	20.6	8.2
2005	12.6	10.9	24.7	21.8	8.3
2004	12.7	9.7	24.7	21.9	8.7
2003	12.5	11.8	24.3	22.5	8.2
2002	12.1	10.0	23.9	21.8	8.0
2001	11.7	10.2	22.7	21.4	7.8
2000	11.3	9.9	22.5	21.5	7.4

Note: Beginning in 2002, Asians and blacks are those who identify themselves as being of the race alone and those who identify themselves as being of the race in combination with other races. Non-Hispanic whites are those who identify themselves as being white alone and not Hispanic.
Source: Bureau of the Census, Current Population Surveys, Annual Social and Economic Supplement, Internet site http://www .census.gov/hhes/www/poverty/data/historical/people.html; calculations by New Strategist

Poverty Has Grown in Every Region

The number of poor in the West is second only to the South.

The South and West are home to nearly two-thirds of the nation's poor. The 41 percent plurality of the poor lives in the South, a figure that has been fairly stable over the past 12 years. Another 24 percent of the poor lives in the West, 19 percent in the Midwest, and 16 percent in the Northeast.

The poverty rate in the Northeast was higher in 2012 than at any time since 2000, at 13.6 percent. In the other three regions, poverty rates were down slightly from their post–Great Recession highs. The South has the highest poverty rate among regions, with 16.5 percent of its residents poor in 2012.

■ The Great Recession has hit the Midwest particularly hard, as many unemployed manufacturing workers joined the ranks of the nation's poor.

Poverty rate has grown the most in the Midwest

(poverty rate of people by region, 2000 and 2012)

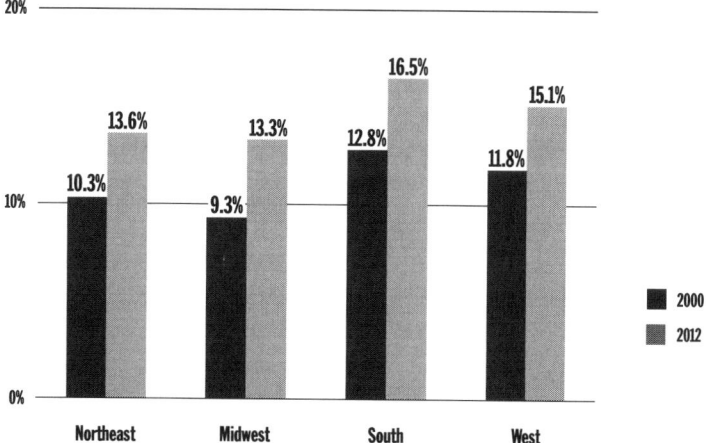

Table 6.17 Distribution of People below Poverty Level by Region, 2000 to 2012

(total number of people below poverty level and percent distribution by region, 2000 to 2012; people in thousands as of the following year)

	total people in poverty		Northeast	Midwest	South	West
	number	percent				
2012	46,496	100.0%	16.1%	19.0%	41.1%	23.8%
2011	46,247	100.0	15.6	19.9	39.7	24.7
2010	46,343	100.0	15.2	19.9	41.3	23.7
2009	43,569	100.0	15.3	20.1	40.4	24.2
2008	39,829	100.0	15.8	20.4	39.8	24.0
2007	37,276	100.0	16.5	19.4	41.6	22.5
2006	36,460	100.0	17.1	20.1	40.8	22.0
2005	36,950	100.0	16.5	20.1	40.2	23.2
2004	37,040	100.0	16.9	20.4	40.0	22.7
2003	35,861	100.0	16.9	19.3	40.6	23.2
2002	34,570	100.0	17.0	19.1	40.6	23.3
2001	32,907	100.0	17.3	18.1	41.1	23.5
2000	31,581	100.0	17.3	18.7	40.2	23.7

Source: Bureau of the Census, Current Population Surveys, Annual Social and Economic Supplement, Internet site http://www .census.gov/hhes/www/poverty/data/historical/people.html; calculations by New Strategist

Table 6.18 Number and Percent of People below Poverty Level by Region, 2000 to 2012

(number and percent of people below poverty level by region, 2000 to 2012; people in thousands as of the following year)

NUMBER IN POVERTY	total people in poverty	Northeast	Midwest	South	West
2012	46,496	7,490	8,851	19,106	11,049
2011	46,247	7,208	9,221	18,380	11,437
2010	46,343	7,038	9,216	19,123	10,966
2009	43,569	6,650	8,768	17,609	10,542
2008	39,829	6,295	8,120	15,862	9,552
2007	37,276	6,166	7,237	15,501	8,372
2006	36,460	6,222	7,324	14,882	8,032
2005	36,950	6,103	7,419	14,854	8,573
2004	37,040	6,260	7,545	14,817	8,419
2003	35,861	6,052	6,932	14,548	8,329
2002	34,570	5,871	6,616	14,019	8,064
2001	32,907	5,687	5,966	13,515	7,739
2000	31,581	5,474	5,916	12,705	7,485
POVERTY RATE					
2012	15.0%	13.6%	13.3%	16.5%	15.1%
2011	15.0	13.1	14.0	16.0	15.8
2010	15.1	12.9	14.0	16.8	15.3
2009	14.3	12.2	13.3	15.7	14.8
2008	13.2	11.6	12.4	14.3	13.5
2007	12.5	11.4	11.1	14.2	12.0
2006	12.3	11.5	11.2	13.8	11.6
2005	12.6	11.3	11.4	14.0	12.6
2004	12.7	11.6	11.7	14.1	12.5
2003	12.5	11.3	10.7	14.1	12.6
2002	12.1	10.9	10.3	13.8	12.4
2001	11.7	10.7	9.4	13.5	12.1
2000	11.3	10.3	9.3	12.8	11.8

Source: Bureau of the Census, Current Population Surveys, Annual Social and Economic Supplement, Internet site http://www .census.gov/hhes/www/poverty/data/historical/people.html; calculations by New Strategist

Naturalized Citizens Have the Lowest Poverty Rate

The poverty rate is highest among the foreign-born who are not citizens.

Native-born Americans had a poverty rate of 14.3 percent in 2012, slightly below the 15.0 percent rate among all U.S. residents. The poverty rate was a much higher 19.2 percent among the foreign-born population. But the poverty rate differs sharply among the foreign-born by citizenship status.

Naturalized citizens had a poverty rate of 12.4 percent in 2012, significantly lower than the rate among native-born Americans. The poverty rate of the foreign-born who are not citizens stood at 24.9 percent, double the rate among naturalized citizens. Since 2000, the poverty rate has increased in every citizenship category, the biggest increase occurring among the foreign-born who are not citizens.

■ The foreign-born account for 17 percent of the nation's poor.

Only 12 percent of naturalized citizens are poor

(poverty rate of U.S. residents by nativity and citizenship status, 2012)

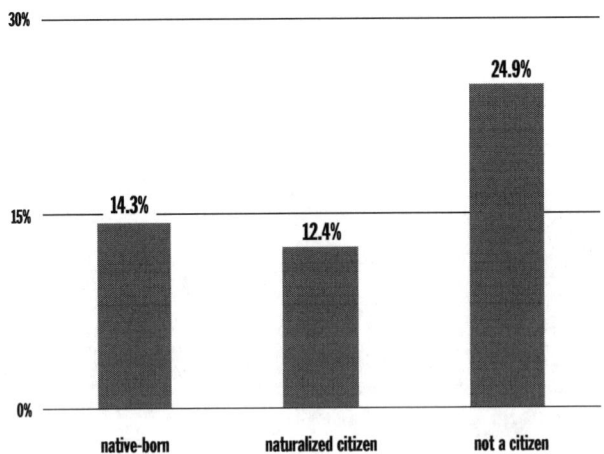

Table 6.19 Number and Percent of People below Poverty Level by Nativity Status, 2000 to 2012

(number and percent of people below poverty level by nativity status, 2000 to 2012; people in thousands as of the following year)

| | | | foreign-born | | |
NUMBER IN POVERTY	total people in poverty	native-born	total	naturalized citizen	not a citizen
2012	46,496	38,803	7,693	2,252	5,441
2011	46,247	38,661	7,586	2,233	5,353
2010	46,343	38,485	7,858	1,954	5,904
2009	43,569	36,407	7,162	1,736	5,425
2008	39,829	33,293	6,536	1,577	4,959
2007	37,276	31,126	6,150	1,426	4,724
2006	36,460	30,790	5,670	1,345	4,324
2005	36,950	31,080	5,870	1,441	4,429
2004	37,040	31,023	6,017	1,326	4,691
2003	35,861	29,965	5,897	1,309	4,588
2002	34,570	29,012	5,558	1,285	4,273
2001	32,907	27,698	5,209	1,186	4,023
2000	31,581	26,680	4,901	1,060	3,841
POVERTY RATE					
2012	15.0%	14.3%	19.2%	12.4%	24.9%
2011	15.0	14.4	19.0	12.5	24.3
2010	15.1	14.4	19.9	11.3	26.8
2009	14.3	13.7	19.0	10.8	25.1
2008	13.2	12.6	17.8	10.2	23.3
2007	12.5	11.9	16.5	9.5	21.3
2006	12.3	11.9	15.2	9.3	19.0
2005	12.6	12.1	16.5	10.4	20.4
2004	12.7	12.1	17.1	9.8	21.6
2003	12.5	11.8	17.2	10.0	21.7
2002	12.1	11.5	16.6	10.0	20.7
2001	11.7	11.1	16.1	9.9	19.7
2000	11.3	10.8	15.4	9.0	19.2

Source: Bureau of the Census, Current Population Surveys, Annual Social and Economic Supplement, Internet site http://www.census.gov/hhes/www/poverty/data/historical/people.html; calculations by New Strategist

Poverty Rate Has Increased in Most States since 2007

The number of poor also grew substantially in most states.

The poverty rate grew in all but two states between 2007 (when the Great Recession began) and 2012. Wyoming and Mississippi were the two states in which the poverty rate fell during those years. Only one state had a poverty rate that exceeded 20 percent in 2007 (Mississippi). By 2012, three additional states had a poverty rate above 20 percent: Arkansas, Louisiana, and New Mexico. In 2007, 19 states had a poverty rate below 10 percent. By 2012, only four states had a poverty rate of less than 10 percent. New Hampshire had the lowest poverty rate in 2012, at 8.1 percent.

Nationally, the number of poor grew 25 percent between 2007 and 2012, rising from 37 million to 46 million. The number of poor expanded by 73 percent in Nevada.

■ The sluggish economic recovery is keeping poverty rates high in most states.

Among the 50 states, Nevada experienced one of the biggest increases in its poverty rate between 2007 and 2012

(percent of Nevada residents who are poor, 2007 and 2012)

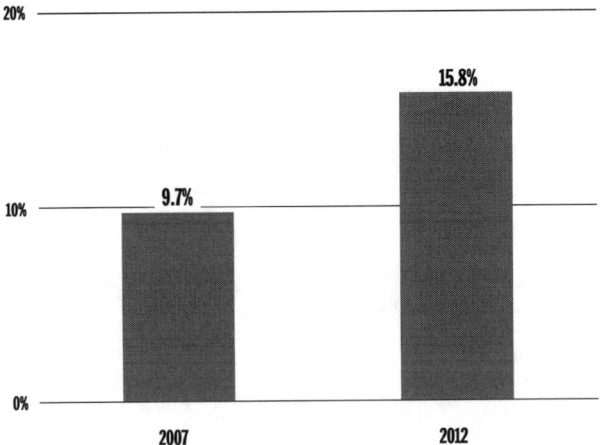

Table 6.20 Number of Poor by State, 2000 to 2012

(number of people below poverty level by state, 2000 to 2012; percent change for selected years; numbers in thousands)

	2012	2010	2007	2000	percent change 2007–12	percent change 2000–12
United States	**46,496**	**46,343**	**37,276**	**31,581**	**24.7%**	**47.2%**
Alabama	777	812	662	583	17.4	33.3
Alaska	70	87	51	47	37.4	49.1
Arizona	1,260	1,208	912	607	38.1	107.6
Arkansas	584	440	387	436	51.0	34.0
California	6,015	6,073	4,589	4,294	31.1	40.1
Colorado	613	615	478	425	28.2	44.2
Connecticut	363	303	309	258	17.4	40.6
Delaware	121	109	80	65	51.4	86.3
District of Columbia	116	118	104	84	11.9	38.6
Florida	2,926	3,006	2,250	1,754	30.1	66.8
Georgia	1,752	1,814	1,294	982	35.4	78.4
Hawaii	188	162	94	106	99.5	76.9
Idaho	229	213	149	162	54.0	41.6
Illinois	1,608	1,798	1,262	1,307	27.4	23.0
Indiana	964	1,041	740	513	30.2	87.8
Iowa	310	307	264	237	17.5	30.9
Kansas	397	400	319	213	24.4	86.3
Kentucky	776	754	653	502	18.9	54.6
Louisiana	944	949	673	750	40.3	25.9
Maine	170	164	142	128	19.9	33.1
Maryland	585	628	491	386	19.1	51.5
Massachusetts	743	711	707	618	5.1	20.2
Michigan	1,331	1,530	1,076	967	23.7	37.7
Minnesota	534	563	482	276	10.8	93.5
Mississippi	636	658	655	418	–3.0	52.1
Missouri	905	890	742	505	22.0	79.3
Montana	134	142	122	126	9.9	6.4
Nebraska	226	184	174	145	30.1	56.1
Nevada	433	446	250	180	73.2	140.5
New Hampshire	106	84	76	56	40.0	90.0
New Jersey	814	966	742	612	9.7	33.0
New Mexico	420	372	271	312	55.2	34.8
New York	3,328	3,062	2,757	2,604	20.7	27.8
North Carolina	1,652	1,633	1,423	1,000	16.1	65.2
North Dakota	79	82	57	65	38.2	21.2
Ohio	1,751	1,746	1,446	1,117	21.1	56.8
Oklahoma	668	603	476	503	40.3	32.7
Oregon	523	537	481	371	8.7	41.0
Pennsylvania	1,756	1,535	1,273	1,033	38.0	70.0

| | 2012 | 2010 | 2007 | 2000 | percent change | |
					2007–12	2000–12
Rhode Island	141	146	99	106	42.1%	32.7%
South Carolina	779	773	617	441	26.3	76.7
South Dakota	106	109	74	79	42.6	33.6
Tennessee	1,194	1,052	906	759	31.8	57.3
Texas	4,444	4,633	3,903	3,204	13.8	38.7
Utah	312	278	255	170	22.5	83.8
Vermont	69	67	61	60	12.8	14.6
Virginia	850	835	664	577	28.1	47.4
Washington	796	779	661	634	20.4	25.5
West Virginia	301	306	265	261	13.7	15.5
Wisconsin	640	567	601	493	6.5	29.9
Wyoming	56	53	56	52	–0.8	6.9

*Source: Bureau of the Census, Current Population Surveys, Annual Social and Economic Supplement, Internet site http://www
.census.gov/hhes/www/poverty/data/historical/people.html; calculations by New Strategist*

Table 6.21 Poverty Rate by State, 2000 to 2012

(percent of people below poverty level by state, 2000 to 2012; percentage point change for selected years)

	2012	2010	2007	2000	percentage point change 2007–12	percentage point change 2000–12
United States	**15.0%**	**15.1%**	**12.5%**	**11.3%**	**2.5**	**3.7**
Alabama	16.2	17.2	14.5	13.3	1.7	2.9
Alaska	10.0	12.5	7.6	7.6	2.4	2.4
Arizona	19.0	18.8	14.3	11.7	4.7	7.3
Arkansas	20.1	15.3	13.8	16.5	6.3	3.6
California	15.9	16.3	12.7	12.7	3.2	3.2
Colorado	11.9	12.3	9.8	9.8	2.1	2.1
Connecticut	10.3	8.6	8.9	7.7	1.4	2.6
Delaware	13.5	12.2	9.3	8.4	4.2	5.1
District of Columbia	18.4	19.5	18.0	15.2	0.4	3.2
Florida	15.3	16.0	12.5	11.0	2.8	4.3
Georgia	18.1	18.8	13.6	12.1	4.5	6.0
Hawaii	13.8	12.4	7.5	8.9	6.3	4.9
Idaho	14.4	13.8	9.9	12.5	4.5	1.9
Illinois	12.6	14.1	10.0	10.7	2.6	1.9
Indiana	15.2	16.3	11.8	8.5	3.4	6.7
Iowa	10.3	10.3	8.9	8.3	1.4	2.0
Kansas	14.0	14.5	11.7	8.0	2.3	6.0
Kentucky	17.9	17.7	15.5	12.6	2.4	5.3
Louisiana	21.1	21.5	16.1	17.2	5.0	3.9
Maine	12.8	12.6	10.9	10.1	1.9	2.7
Maryland	9.9	10.9	8.8	7.4	1.1	2.5
Massachusetts	11.3	10.9	11.2	9.8	0.1	1.5
Michigan	13.7	15.7	10.8	9.9	2.9	3.8
Minnesota	10.0	10.8	9.3	5.7	0.7	4.3
Mississippi	22.0	22.5	22.6	14.9	–0.6	7.1
Missouri	15.2	15.0	12.8	9.2	2.4	6.0
Montana	13.4	14.5	13.0	14.1	0.4	–0.7
Nebraska	12.2	10.2	9.9	8.6	2.3	3.6
Nevada	15.8	16.6	9.7	8.8	6.1	7.0
New Hampshire	8.1	6.5	5.8	4.5	2.3	3.6
New Jersey	9.3	11.1	8.7	7.3	0.6	2.0
New Mexico	20.4	18.3	14.0	17.5	6.4	2.9
New York	17.2	16.0	14.5	13.9	2.7	3.3
North Carolina	17.2	17.4	15.5	12.5	1.7	4.7
North Dakota	11.4	12.6	9.3	10.4	2.1	1.0
Ohio	15.4	15.4	12.8	10.0	2.6	5.4
Oklahoma	18.0	16.3	13.4	14.9	4.6	3.1
Oregon	13.5	14.3	12.8	10.9	0.7	2.6
Pennsylvania	13.9	12.2	10.4	8.6	3.5	5.3

	2012	2010	2007	2000	percentage point change	
					2007–12	2000–12
Rhode Island	13.6%	14.0%	9.5%	10.2%	4.1	3.4
South Carolina	16.7	16.9	14.1	11.1	2.6	5.6
South Dakota	12.8	13.6	9.4	10.7	3.4	2.1
Tennessee	18.6	16.7	14.8	13.5	3.8	5.1
Texas	17.0	18.4	16.5	15.5	0.6	1.5
Utah	11.0	10.0	9.6	7.6	1.4	3.4
Vermont	11.2	10.8	9.9	10.0	1.3	1.2
Virginia	10.6	10.7	8.6	8.3	2.0	2.3
Washington	11.6	11.6	10.2	10.8	1.4	0.8
West Virginia	16.7	16.8	14.8	14.7	1.9	2.0
Wisconsin	11.4	10.1	11.0	9.3	0.4	2.1
Wyoming	9.6	9.6	10.9	10.8	–1.3	–1.2

Source: Bureau of the Census, Current Population Surveys, Annual Social and Economic Supplement, Internet site http://www
.census.gov/hhes/www/poverty/data/historical/people.html; calculations by New Strategist

A Growing Share of the Poor Lives in the Suburbs

The share of the poor in nonmetropolitan areas has declined.

The poverty population is becoming increasingly suburban. In 2000, about 36 percent of the poor lived in the suburbs. By 2012, the suburbs were home to 39 percent of the poor. During those years, the percentage of the poor who live in the principal cities of metropolitan areas held steady at 42 to 43 percent. The percentage who live in nonmetropolitan areas fell from 22 to 18 percent.

Poverty rates climbed between 2000 and 2012 regardless of metropolitan status. In principal cities, the poverty rate grew from 16.3 to 19.7 percent. In nonmetropolitan areas, the poverty rate climbed from 13.4 to 17.7 percent. In the suburbs, the rate grew from 7.8 to 11.2 percent.

■ The largest share of the poor once lived in rural areas. Today, the suburbs are close to overtaking the central cities as home to the largest share of the poor.

Poverty rate has grown both inside and outside of metro areas

(percent of people who are poor by metropolitan status, 2000 and 2012)

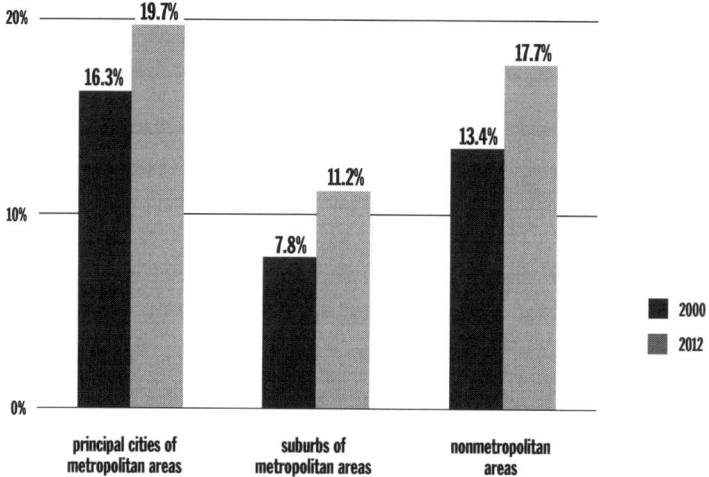

Table 6.22 Distribution of People below Poverty Level by Metropolitan Residence, 2000 to 2012

(total number of people below poverty level and percent distribution by metropolitan residence, 2000 to 2012; people in thousands as of the following year)

	total people in poverty		inside metropolitan areas			not in metropolitan area
	number	percent	total	inside principal cities	outside principal cities	
2012	46,496	100.0%	81.8%	42.9%	38.9%	18.2%
2011	46,247	100.0	82.6	43.3	39.3	17.4
2010	46,343	100.0	83.0	42.1	40.9	17.0
2009	43,569	100.0	81.8	41.9	39.9	18.2
2008	39,829	100.0	81.8	43.2	38.5	18.2
2007	37,276	100.0	80.3	42.9	37.4	19.7
2006	36,460	100.0	80.3	42.1	38.3	19.7
2005	36,950	100.0	81.5	43.2	38.2	18.5
2004	37,040	100.0	–	–	–	–
2003	35,861	100.0	79.1	40.6	38.5	20.9
2002	34,570	100.0	78.4	39.9	38.5	21.6
2001	32,907	100.0	77.3	40.7	36.6	22.7
2000	31,581	100.0	77.9	42.0	35.9	22.1

Note: Prior to 2005, "principal cities" were called "central cities" and defined somewhat differently. "–" means data are not available.
Source: Bureau of the Census, Current Population Surveys, Annual Social and Economic Supplement, Internet site http://www .census.gov/hhes/www/poverty/data/historical/people.html; calculations by New Strategist

Table 6.23 Number and Percent of People below Poverty Level by Metropolitan Residence, 2000 to 2012

(number and percent of people below poverty level by metropolitan residence, 2000 to 2012; people in thousands as of the following year)

		inside metropolitan areas			
NUMBER IN POVERTY	total people in poverty	total	inside principal cities	outside principal cities	not in metropolitan area
2012	46,496	38,033	19,934	18,099	8,463
2011	46,247	38,202	20,007	18,195	8,045
2010	46,343	38,466	19,532	18,933	7,877
2009	43,569	35,655	18,261	17,394	7,914
2008	39,829	32,570	17,222	15,348	7,259
2007	37,276	29,921	15,983	13,938	7,355
2006	36,460	29,283	15,336	13,947	7,177
2005	36,950	30,098	15,966	14,132	6,852
2004	37,040	–	–	–	–
2003	35,861	28,367	14,551	13,816	7,495
2002	34,570	27,096	13,784	13,311	7,474
2001	32,907	25,446	13,394	12,052	7,460
2000	31,581	24,603	13,257	11,346	6,978
POVERTY RATE					
2012	15.0%	14.5%	19.7%	11.2%	17.7%
2011	15.0	14.6	20.0	11.3	17.0
2010	15.1	14.9	19.8	11.9	16.5
2009	14.3	13.9	18.7	11.0	16.6
2008	13.2	12.9	17.7	9.8	15.1
2007	12.5	11.9	16.5	9.0	15.4
2006	12.3	11.8	16.1	9.1	15.2
2005	12.6	12.2	17.0	9.3	14.5
2004	12.7	–	–	–	–
2003	12.5	12.1	17.5	9.1	14.2
2002	12.1	11.6	16.7	8.9	14.2
2001	11.7	11.1	16.5	8.2	14.2
2000	11.3	10.8	16.3	7.8	13.4

Note: Prior to 2005, "principal cities" were called "central cities" and defined somewhat differently. "–" means data are not available.
Source: Bureau of the Census, Current Population Surveys, Annual Social and Economic Supplement, Internet site http://www.census.gov/hhes/www/poverty/data/historical/people.html; calculations by New Strategist

Many of the Poor Have Jobs

Nearly 3 million poor people work full-time, year-round.

Many people live in poverty despite having a job. In 2012, a substantial 34 percent of poor people aged 16 or older had a job. This figure is lower than in previous years because of the continuing high unemployment rate. The number of poor with a job climbed from 8.5 million in 2000 to nearly 11 million in 2012.

A substantial share of the poor has a full-time job, yet an income below the poverty line. In 2012, 9.1 percent of poor people worked full-time, year-round. This figure was lower than the nearly 12 percent in 2000 because of the rise in unemployment.

■ Falling wages for uneducated, low-skilled workers have boosted the number of working poor.

Number of poor people who work has grown

(number of poor people who work, 2000 and 2012)

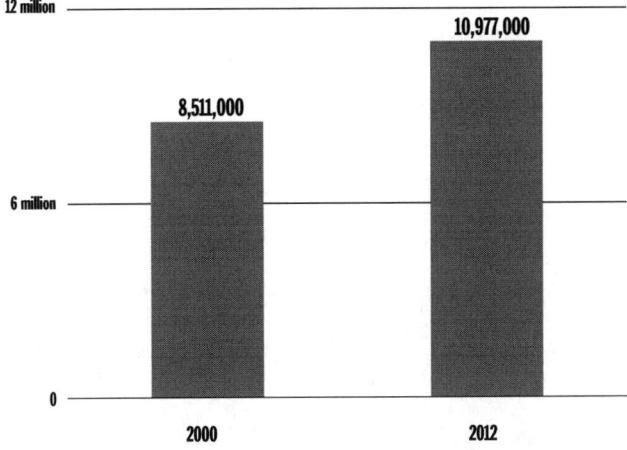

Table 6.24 People below Poverty Level by Work Status, 2000 to 2012

(number and percent distribution of people aged 16 or older below poverty level by work status, 2000 to 2012; people in thousands as of the following year)

NUMBER IN POVERTY	total people aged 16 or older in poverty	did not work	worked total	worked full-time, year-round
2012	31,933	20,956	10,977	2,904
2011	31,630	21,042	10,588	2,770
2010	31,731	20,989	10,742	2,640
2009	29,625	18,945	10,680	2,641
2008	27,216	17,131	10,085	2,754
2007	25,297	16,208	9,089	2,768
2006	24,896	15,715	9,181	2,906
2005	25,381	16,041	9,340	2,894
2004	25,256	15,872	9,384	2,891
2003	24,266	15,446	8,820	2,636
2002	23,601	14,647	8,954	2,635
2001	22,245	13,715	8,530	2,567
2000	21,080	12,569	8,511	2,439
PERCENT DISTRIBUTION				
2012	100.0%	65.6%	34.4%	9.1%
2011	100.0	66.5	33.5	8.8
2010	100.0	66.1	33.9	8.3
2009	100.0	63.9	36.1	8.9
2008	100.0	62.9	37.1	10.1
2007	100.0	64.1	35.9	10.9
2006	100.0	63.1	36.9	11.7
2005	100.0	63.2	36.8	11.4
2004	100.0	62.8	37.2	11.4
2003	100.0	63.7	36.3	10.9
2002	100.0	62.1	37.9	11.2
2001	100.0	61.7	38.3	11.5
2000	100.0	59.6	40.4	11.6

Source: Bureau of the Census, Current Population Surveys, Annual Social and Economic Supplement, Internet site http://www .census.gov/hhes/www/poverty/data/historical/people.html; calculations by New Strategist

Poverty, 2012

Few Households with Two Earners Are Poor

Single-earner households are much more vulnerable to poverty.

Two incomes can keep families out of poverty. Only 2.6 percent of families with two or more workers have incomes that place them below poverty level. The proportion ranges from just 1.4 percent among non-Hispanic white families to 7.4 percent of Hispanic families. But among families with only one worker, a larger 16.6 percent are poor.

Among married couples, poverty is practically nonexistent for those in which both husband and wife work full-time. But for married couples in which only the husband works full-time and the wife does not work, the poverty rate is as high as 15.1 percent among Hispanics.

■ The poverty rate of Hispanic families is relatively high because many are headed by householders with little education.

Poverty is less likely for families with two or more workers

(percent of families below poverty level by number of workers, 2012)

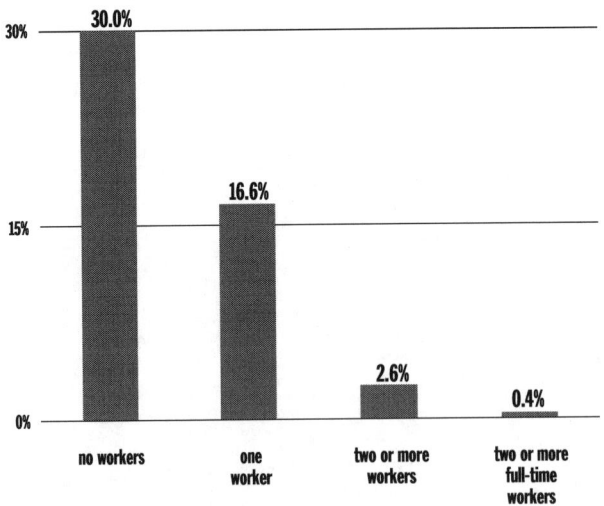

Table 6.25 Families below Poverty Level by Work Status, Race, and Hispanic Origin, 2012

(number and percent of families below poverty level by work status, race, and Hispanic origin, 2012; numbers in thousands)

NUMBER IN POVERTY	total families in poverty	Asians	blacks	Hispanics	non-Hispanic whites
Total families	**9,520**	**409**	**2,439**	**2,807**	**3,835**
With no workers	3,940	163	1,108	878	1,782
With one or more workers	5,581	246	1,330	1,929	2,053
One	4,531	193	1,126	1,506	1,670
Two or more	1,049	53	204	422	384
With one or more full-time, year-round workers	2,114	110	438	931	655
One	2,024	105	424	883	630
Two or more	90	5	14	47	24
POVERTY RATE					
Total families	**11.8%**	**9.5%**	**23.7%**	**23.5%**	**7.1%**
With no workers	30.0	43.4	57.6	61.2	19.2
With one or more workers	8.2	6.2	15.9	18.3	4.6
One	16.6	12.4	25.7	31.5	10.2
Two or more	2.6	2.2	5.1	7.4	1.4
With one or more full-time, year-round workers	3.8	3.2	6.9	11.1	1.8
One	5.9	5.2	9.8	16.1	2.8
Two or more	0.4	0.3	0.7	1.7	0.2

Note: Asians and blacks include those who identify themselves as being of the race alone and those who identify themselves as being of the race in combination with other races. Non-Hispanic whites are those who identify themselves as white alone and not Hispanic. Numbers do not add to total because not all races are shown and Hispanics may be of any race.
Source: Bureau of the Census, 2013 Current Population Survey Annual Social and Economic Supplement, Internet site http://www.census.gov/hhes/www/cpstables/032013/pov/toc.htm; calculations by New Strategist

Table 6.26 Married Couples below Poverty Level by Work Status, Race, and Hispanic Origin, 2012

(number and percent of married-couple families below poverty level by work status, race, and Hispanic origin, 2012; numbers in thousands)

NUMBER IN POVERTY	total families in poverty	Asians	blacks	Hispanics	non-Hispanic whites
Total married couples	**3,705**	**245**	**458**	**1,238**	**1,735**
With no workers	1,389	99	185	258	828
With one or more workers	2,316	146	273	980	907
Both husband and wife work	523	29	78	202	220
Wife works, husband does not work	378	29	58	85	196
Husband works, wife does not work	1,305	79	115	664	446
With one or more full-time, year-round workers	1,158	77	129	571	391
Both husband and wife work full-time, year-round	39	2	6	16	15
Wife works full-time, year-round, husband does not	216	18	44	83	73
Husband works full-time, year-round, wife does not	859	54	70	450	290
POVERTY RATE					
Total married couples	**6.3%**	**7.2%**	**9.7%**	**16.6%**	**4.0%**
With no workers	15.3	35.2	27.3	37.9	11.2
With one or more workers	4.6	4.7	6.8	14.5	2.5
Both husband and wife work	1.7	1.6	3.1	5.6	0.9
Wife works, husband does not work	8.2	11.1	11.3	18.7	5.9
Husband works, wife does not work	10.0	7.9	12.4	25.9	5.2
With one or more full-time, year-round workers	2.7	2.8	3.8	10.1	1.3
Both husband and wife work full-time, year-round	0.2	0.2	0.4	0.9	0.1
Wife works full-time, year-round, husband does not	3.6	4.9	6.6	11.2	1.7
Husband works full-time, year-round, wife does not	4.5	4.1	5.7	15.1	2.2

Note: Asians and blacks include those who identify themselves as being of the race alone and those who identify themselves as being of the race in combination with other races. Non-Hispanic whites are those who identify themselves as white alone and not Hispanic. Numbers do not add to total because not all races are shown and Hispanics may be of any race.
Source: Bureau of the Census, 2013 Current Population Survey Annual Social and Economic Supplement, Internet site http:// www.census.gov/hhes/www/cpstables/032013/pov/toc.htm; calculations by New Strategist

Table 6.27 Female-Headed Families below Poverty Level by Work Status, Race, and Hispanic Origin, 2012

(number and percent of female-headed families below poverty level by work status, race, and Hispanic origin, 2012; numbers in thousands)

NUMBER IN POVERTY	total families in poverty	Asians	blacks	Hispanics	non-Hispanic whites
Total female-headed families	**4,793**	**115**	**1,707**	**1,266**	**1,713**
With no workers	2,141	46	789	540	783
With one or more workers	2,652	69	917	726	930
One	2,376	61	821	629	851
Two or more	276	8	96	97	78
With one or more full-time, year-round workers	741	20	270	254	206
One	730	20	269	246	204
Two or more	12	0	2	8	2
POVERTY RATE					
Total female-headed families	**30.9%**	**20.2%**	**38.0%**	**40.7%**	**23.4%**
With no workers	67.5	–	76.4	84.5	54.7
With one or more workers	21.5	13.6	26.6	29.4	15.8
One	28.6	20.6	32.5	38.4	22.2
Two or more	6.9	3.8	10.4	11.7	3.8
With one or more full-time, year-round workers	9.0	5.4	11.9	15.2	5.2
One	10.9	7.5	14.0	18.4	6.4
Two or more	0.8	0.0	0.4	2.4	0.2

Note: Asians and blacks include those who identify themselves as being of the race alone and those who identify themselves as being of the race in combination with other races. Non-Hispanic whites are those who identify themselves as white alone and not Hispanic. Numbers do not add to total because not all races are shown and Hispanics may be of any race. "–" means sample is too small to make a reliable estimate.
Source: Bureau of the Census, 2013 Current Population Survey Annual Social and Economic Supplement, Internet site http://www.census.gov/hhes/www/cpstables/032013/pov/toc.htm; calculations by New Strategist

Table 6.28 Male-Headed Families below Poverty Level by Work Status, Race, and Hispanic Origin, 2012

(number and percent of male-headed families below poverty level by work status, race, and Hispanic origin, 2012; numbers in thousands)

NUMBER IN POVERTY	total families in poverty	Asians	blacks	Hispanics	non-Hispanic whites
Total male-headed families	**1,023**	**49**	**274**	**303**	**387**
With no workers	410	18	134	81	171
With one or more workers	612	32	140	222	217
One	519	22	121	181	190
Two or more	94	10	18	41	27
With one or more full-time, year-round workers	215	13	39	106	58
One	207	13	36	102	58
Two or more	8	0	4	4	0
POVERTY RATE					
Total male-headed families	**16.4%**	**14.2%**	**24.8%**	**21.7%**	**11.4%**
With no workers	46.8	–	63.0	69.6	33.9
With one or more workers	11.4	10.0	15.7	17.4	7.5
One	16.4	16.5	21.0	27.6	10.6
Two or more	4.3	5.3	5.9	6.7	2.4
With one or more full-time, year-round workers	5.2	4.9	6.1	10.5	2.6
One	6.6	7.7	6.9	15.2	3.3
Two or more	0.8	0.2	3.0	1.2	0.0

Note: Asians and blacks include those who identify themselves as being of the race alone and those who identify themselves as being of the race in combination with other races. Non-Hispanic whites are those who identify themselves as white alone and not Hispanic. Numbers do not add to total because not all races are shown and Hispanics may be of any race. "–" means sample is too small to make a reliable estimate.
Source: Bureau of the Census, 2013 Current Population Survey Annual Social and Economic Supplement, Internet site http://www.census.gov/hhes/www/cpstables/032013/pov/toc.htm; calculations by New Strategist

Poverty Rate Is Highest among Families in the South

Families in the Northeast and Midwest are least likely to be poor.

Fully 13.2 percent of families in the South live in poverty, a greater share than the 11.8 percent of all families who are poor and higher than the poverty rate in the other regions. Among families with children, the poverty rate in the South climbs to 20.3 percent. In every region, families headed by Hispanics and blacks have higher poverty rates than those headed by Asians or non-Hispanic whites.

Married couples have lower poverty rates than other family types regardless of region, race, or Hispanic origin. Behind their lower poverty rate is the fact that married-couple families are likely to have two or more earners in the household, which boosts incomes. Among Hispanic married couples, for example, the poverty rate peaks at 17.3 percent in the South. Among Hispanic female-headed families, the poverty rate peaks at a much larger 45.5 percent in the Midwest.

■ Hispanics have the highest poverty rate because of their relatively low educational attainment.

Among married couples in the South, Hispanics have the highest poverty rate

(percent of married-couple families below poverty level in the South, by race and Hispanic origin, 2012)

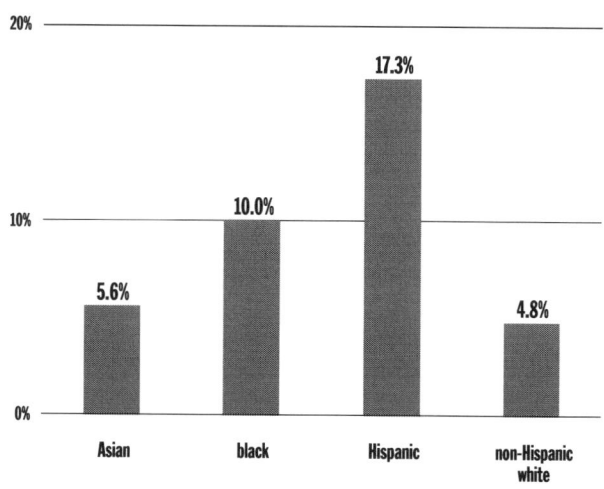

Table 6.29 Families below Poverty Level by Region, Race, and Hispanic Origin, 2012

(number and percent of families below poverty level by region, race, and Hispanic origin, 2012; numbers in thousands)

NUMBER IN POVERTY	total families in poverty	Asians	blacks	Hispanics	non-Hispanic whites
Total families	**9,520**	**409**	**2,439**	**2,807**	**3,835**
Northeast	1,491	94	427	464	604
Midwest	1,775	63	453	220	998
South	4,067	91	1,347	1,075	1,522
West	2,188	162	211	1,048	711
POVERTY RATE					
Total families	**11.8%**	**9.5%**	**23.7%**	**23.5%**	**7.1%**
Northeast	10.5	10.9	23.5	27.6	6.0
Midwest	10.2	12.6	26.3	22.1	7.1
South	13.2	8.9	23.3	23.6	7.9
West	11.9	8.3	21.6	22.2	6.8

Note: Asians and blacks include those who identify themselves as being of the race alone and those who identify themselves as being of the race in combination with other races. Non-Hispanic whites are those who identify themselves as white alone and not Hispanic. Numbers do not add to total because not all races are shown and Hispanics may be of any race.
Source: Bureau of the Census, 2013 Current Population Survey Annual Social and Economic Supplement, Internet site http:// www.census.gov/hhes/www/cpstables/032013/pov/toc.htm; calculations by New Strategist

Table 6.30 Families with Children below Poverty Level by Region, Race, and Hispanic Origin, 2012

(number and percent of families with related children under age 18 at home below poverty level by region, race, and Hispanic origin, 2012; numbers in thousands)

NUMBER IN POVERTY	total families in poverty	Asians	blacks	Hispanics	non-Hispanic whites
Total families with children	**7,063**	**265**	**1,944**	**2,341**	**2,510**
Northeast	1,112	68	329	385	418
Midwest	1,356	47	384	195	707
South	2,999	57	1,066	897	955
West	1,595	93	165	864	429
POVERTY RATE					
Total families with children	**18.4%**	**11.8%**	**32.1%**	**30.1%**	**11.2%**
Northeast	17.0	14.5	31.3	35.9	10.2
Midwest	16.8	16.5	36.5	29.3	11.7
South	20.3	10.4	31.6	30.8	12.1
West	17.5	9.8	28.6	27.6	9.9

Note: Asians and blacks include those who identify themselves as being of the race alone and those who identify themselves as being of the race in combination with other races. Non-Hispanic whites are those who identify themselves as white alone and not Hispanic. Numbers do not add to total because not all races are shown and Hispanics may be of any race.
Source: Bureau of the Census, 2013 Current Population Survey Annual Social and Economic Supplement, Internet site http://www.census.gov/hhes/www/cpstables/032013/pov/toc.htm; calculations by New Strategist

Table 6.31 Married Couples below Poverty Level by Region, Race, and Hispanic Origin, 2012

(number and percent of married-couple families below poverty level by region, race, and Hispanic origin, 2012; numbers in thousands)

NUMBER IN POVERTY	total families in poverty	Asians	blacks	Hispanics	non-Hispanic whites
Total married couples	**3,705**	**245**	**458**	**1,238**	**1,735**
Northeast	545	71	86	140	265
Midwest	613	38	61	91	405
South	1,579	45	276	510	744
West	968	91	35	497	320
POVERTY RATE					
Total married couples	**6.3%**	**7.2%**	**9.7%**	**16.6%**	**4.0%**
Northeast	5.3	9.9	11.2	16.5	3.3
Midwest	4.7	9.7	8.9	14.4	3.6
South	7.1	5.6	10.0	17.3	4.8
West	7.1	6.1	7.4	16.4	3.8

Note: Asians and blacks include those who identify themselves as being of the race alone and those who identify themselves as being of the race in combination with other races. Non-Hispanic whites are those who identify themselves as white alone and not Hispanic. Numbers do not add to total because not all races are shown and Hispanics may be of any race.
Source: Bureau of the Census, 2013 Current Population Survey Annual Social and Economic Supplement, Internet site http://www.census.gov/hhes/www/cpstables/032013/pov/toc.htm; calculations by New Strategist

Table 6.32 Married Couples with Children below Poverty Level by Region, Race, and Hispanic Origin, 2012

(number and percent of married-couple families with related children under age 18 at home below poverty level by region, race, and Hispanic origin, 2012; numbers in thousands)

NUMBER IN POVERTY	total families in poverty	Asians	blacks	Hispanics	non-Hispanic whites
Total married couples with children	**2,246**	**154**	**286**	**973**	**820**
Northeast	329	49	51	114	128
Midwest	361	31	48	71	202
South	942	27	165	397	357
West	614	46	22	391	133
POVERTY RATE					
Total married couples with children	**8.9%**	**8.4%**	**12.5%**	**20.9%**	**5.0%**
Northeast	7.7	12.6	14.0	22.4	4.2
Midwest	6.8	13.3	14.5	18.2	4.6
South	10.0	5.9	12.2	21.9	6.2
West	9.8	6.2	9.0	20.0	4.2

Note: Asians and blacks include those who identify themselves as being of the race alone and those who identify themselves as being of the race in combination with other races. Non-Hispanic whites are those who identify themselves as white alone and not Hispanic. Numbers do not add to total because not all races are shown and Hispanics may be of any race.
Source: Bureau of the Census, 2013 Current Population Survey Annual Social and Economic Supplement, Internet site http:// www.census.gov/hhes/www/cpstables/032013/pov/toc.htm; calculations by New Strategist

Table 6.33 Female-Headed Families below Poverty Level by Region, Race, and Hispanic Origin, 2012

(number and percent of female-headed families below poverty level by region, race, and Hispanic origin, 2012; numbers in thousands)

NUMBER IN POVERTY	total families in poverty	Asians	blacks	Hispanics	non-Hispanic whites
Total female-headed families	**4,793**	**115**	**1,707**	**1,266**	**1,713**
Northeast	809	16	296	275	293
Midwest	943	19	329	108	474
South	2,111	31	943	480	635
West	930	50	138	403	312
POVERTY RATE					
Total female-headed families	**30.9%**	**20.2%**	**38.0%**	**40.7%**	**23.4%**
Northeast	28.2	17.2	36.1	44.8	19.9
Midwest	30.7	–	40.2	45.5	24.5
South	33.0	24.5	38.1	41.9	24.3
West	29.5	17.0	37.4	36.3	23.9

Note: Asians and blacks include those who identify themselves as being of the race alone and those who identify themselves as being of the race in combination with other races. Non-Hispanic whites are those who identify themselves as white alone and not Hispanic. Numbers do not add to total because not all races are shown and Hispanics may be of any race. "–" means sample is too small to make a reliable estimate.
Source: Bureau of the Census, 2013 Current Population Survey Annual Social and Economic Supplement, Internet site http://www.census.gov/hhes/www/cpstables/032013/pov/toc.htm; calculations by New Strategist

Table 6.34 Female-Headed Families with Children below Poverty Level by Region, Race, and Hispanic Origin, 2012

(number and percent of female-headed families with related children under age 18 at home below poverty level by region, race, and Hispanic origin, 2012; numbers in thousands)

NUMBER IN POVERTY	total families in poverty	Asians	blacks	Hispanics	non-Hispanic whites
Total female-headed families with children	**4,099**	**82**	**1,479**	**1,133**	**1,415**
Northeast	685	12	252	236	250
Midwest	833	13	288	104	420
South	1,789	20	820	433	491
West	793	38	118	360	255
POVERTY RATE					
Total female-headed families with children	**40.9%**	**27.5%**	**46.8%**	**48.6%**	**33.1%**
Northeast	40.2	–	44.4	53.7	33.4
Midwest	40.9	–	49.1	52.3	34.8
South	42.1	–	46.8	50.3	31.7
West	38.9	26.5	47.0	43.3	32.9

Note: Asians and blacks include those who identify themselves as being of the race alone and those who identify themselves as being of the race in combination with other races. Non-Hispanic whites are those who identify themselves as white alone and not Hispanic. Numbers do not add to total because not all races are shown and Hispanics may be of any race. "–" means sample is too small to make a reliable estimate.

Source: Bureau of the Census, 2013 Current Population Survey Annual Social and Economic Supplement, Internet site http:// www.census.gov/hhes/www/cpstables/032013/pov/toc.htm; calculations by New Strategist

Table 6.35 Male-Headed Families below Poverty Level by Region, Race, and Hispanic Origin, 2012

(number and percent of male-headed families below poverty level by region, race, and Hispanic origin, 2012; numbers in thousands)

NUMBER IN POVERTY	total families in poverty	Asians	blacks	Hispanics	non-Hispanic whites
Total male-headed families	**1,023**	**49**	**274**	**303**	**387**
Northeast	137	8	45	49	46
Midwest	219	6	63	21	118
South	377	15	129	85	143
West	290	21	38	148	80
POVERTY RATE					
Total male-headed families	**16.4%**	**14.2%**	**24.8%**	**21.7%**	**11.4%**
Northeast	12.1	–	19.5	22.7	7.0
Midwest	17.5	–	29.3	16.2	13.9
South	16.7	19.0	24.3	18.7	12.1
West	18.2	12.7	28.6	24.9	11.5

Note: Asians and blacks include those who identify themselves as being of the race alone and those who identify themselves as being of the race in combination with other races. Non-Hispanic whites are those who identify themselves as white alone and not Hispanic. Numbers do not add to total because not all races are shown and Hispanics may be of any race. "–" means sample is too small to make a reliable estimate.
Source: Bureau of the Census, 2013 Current Population Survey Annual Social and Economic Supplement, Internet site http:// www.census.gov/hhes/www/cpstables/032013/pov/toc.htm; calculations by New Strategist

Table 6.36 Male-Headed Families with Children below Poverty Level by Region, Race, and Hispanic Origin, 2012

(number and percent of male-headed families with related children under age 18 at home below poverty level by region, race, and Hispanic origin, 2012; numbers in thousands)

NUMBER IN POVERTY	total families in poverty	Asians	blacks	Hispanics	non-Hispanic whites
Total male-headed families with children	**717**	**29**	**179**	**235**	**274**
Northeast	98	7	25	36	41
Midwest	162	3	47	20	85
South	269	11	82	66	108
West	188	8	25	113	41
POVERTY RATE					
Total male-headed families with children	**22.6%**	**24.5%**	**29.5%**	**30.1%**	**16.3%**
Northeast	18.7	–	21.2	28.1	14.1
Midwest	23.0	–	36.5	–	17.8
South	23.8	–	29.3	28.4	18.5
West	23.3	–	30.8	32.7	12.1

Note: Asians and blacks include those who identify themselves as being of the race alone and those who identify themselves as being of the race in combination with other races. Non-Hispanic whites are those who identify themselves as white alone and not Hispanic. Numbers do not add to total because not all races are shown and Hispanics may be of any race. "–" means sample is too small to make a reliable estimate.
Source: Bureau of the Census, 2013 Current Population Survey Annual Social and Economic Supplement, Internet site http://www.census.gov/hhes/www/cpstables/032013/pov/toc.htm; calculations by New Strategist

Poverty Rate Is Highest in Central Cities

The rate is lowest in the suburbs.

The percentage of families who live in poverty is higher in the principal (central) cities of metropolitan areas than outside principal cities (suburbs) or in nonmetropolitan areas. The poverty rate is higher for Hispanic and black families than for non-Hispanic white or Asian families. It is higher for families with children than for those without children.

The poverty rate peaks among black female-headed families with children who live in nonmetropolitan areas, where the rate is an enormous 62.2 percent. Their Hispanic counterparts are not far behind, with a poverty rate of 58.2 percent. The poverty rate among families with children bottoms out among non-Hispanic white married couples in the suburbs, with just 3.8 percent poor.

■ The poverty rate of families in nonmetropolitan areas is well above the national average, at 13.8 percent in 2012.

Among families with children, the poverty rate peaks among black female-headed families in nonmetropolitan areas

(highest and lowest poverty rate among families with children by race, Hispanic origin, and metropolitan residence, 2012)

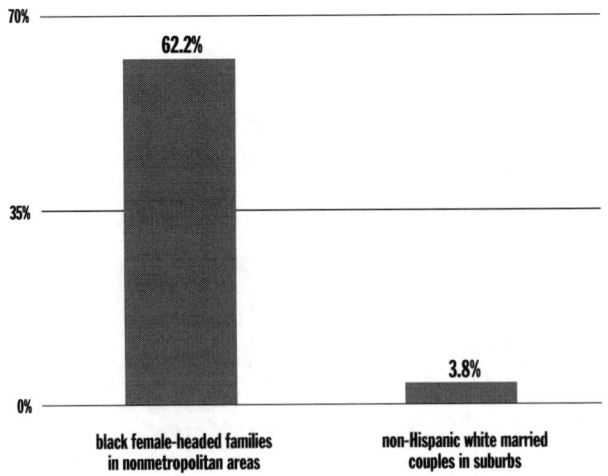

Table 6.37 Families below Poverty Level by Metropolitan Status, Race, and Hispanic Origin, 2012

(number and percent of families below poverty level by metropolitan status, race, and Hispanic origin, 2012; numbers in thousands)

NUMBER IN POVERTY	total families in poverty	Asians	blacks	Hispanics	non-Hispanic whites
Total families	**9,520**	**409**	**2,439**	**2,807**	**3,835**
Metropolitan	7,705	398	2,077	2,574	2,744
Inside principal cities	3,989	266	1,326	1,466	981
Outside principal cities	3,717	131	751	1,108	1,763
Not metropolitan	1,815	11	361	233	1,091
POVERTY RATE					
Total families	**11.8%**	**9.5%**	**23.7%**	**23.5%**	**7.1%**
Metropolitan	11.4	9.5	22.4	23.3	6.3
Inside principal cities	16.3	13.1	26.6	26.1	8.2
Outside principal cities	8.6	6.1	17.6	20.4	5.6
Not metropolitan	13.8	8.0	34.9	25.4	10.2

Note: Asians and blacks include those who identify themselves as being of the race alone and those who identify themselves as being of the race in combination with other races. Non-Hispanic whites are those who identify themselves as white alone and not Hispanic. Numbers do not add to total because not all races are shown and Hispanics may be of any race.
Source: Bureau of the Census, 2013 Current Population Survey Annual Social and Economic Supplement, Internet site http://www.census.gov/hhes/www/cpstables/032013/pov/toc.htm; calculations by New Strategist

Table 6.38 Families with Children below Poverty Level by Metropolitan Status, Race, and Hispanic Origin, 2012

(number and percent of families with related children under age 18 at home below poverty level by metropolitan status, race, and Hispanic origin, 2012; numbers in thousands)

NUMBER IN POVERTY	total families in poverty	Asians	blacks	Hispanics	non-Hispanic whites
Total families with children	**7,063**	**265**	**1,944**	**2,341**	**2,510**
Metropolitan	5,737	257	1,647	2,131	1,788
Inside principal cities	3,042	160	1,063	1,206	657
Outside principal cities	2,695	96	583	925	1,131
Not metropolitan	1,326	8	297	209	722
POVERTY RATE					
Total families with children	**18.4%**	**11.8%**	**32.1%**	**30.1%**	**11.2%**
Metropolitan	17.5	11.9	30.3	29.8	9.9
Inside principal cities	24.2	16.1	35.7	33.2	12.9
Outside principal cities	13.4	8.3	23.8	26.4	8.7
Not metropolitan	23.1	8.6	47.9	33.2	17.2

Note: Asians and blacks include those who identify themselves as being of the race alone and those who identify themselves as being of the race in combination with other races. Non-Hispanic whites are those who identify themselves as white alone and not Hispanic. Numbers do not add to total because not all races are shown and Hispanics may be of any race.
Source: Bureau of the Census, 2013 Current Population Survey Annual Social and Economic Supplement, Internet site http://www.census.gov/hhes/www/cpstables/032013/pov/toc.htm; calculations by New Strategist

Table 6.39 Married Couples below Poverty Level by Metropolitan Status, Race, and Hispanic Origin, 2012

(number and percent of married-couple families below poverty level by metropolitan status, race, and Hispanic origin, 2012; numbers in thousands)

NUMBER IN POVERTY	total families in poverty	Asians	blacks	Hispanics	non-Hispanic whites
Total married couples	**3,705**	**245**	**458**	**1,238**	**1,735**
Metropolitan	2,976	241	368	1,128	1,238
Inside principal cities	1,389	165	212	626	390
Outside principal cities	1,587	76	156	502	848
Not metropolitan	729	4	90	110	496
POVERTY RATE					
Total married couples	**6.3%**	**7.2%**	**9.7%**	**16.6%**	**4.0%**
Metropolitan	6.0	7.3	8.7	16.5	3.6
Inside principal cities	8.7	10.7	10.8	19.0	4.2
Outside principal cities	4.8	4.3	6.8	14.1	3.3
Not metropolitan	7.3	3.7	19.6	18.1	5.8

Note: Asians and blacks include those who identify themselves as being of the race alone and those who identify themselves as being of the race in combination with other races. Non-Hispanic whites are those who identify themselves as white alone and not Hispanic. Numbers do not add to total because not all races are shown and Hispanics may be of any race.
Source: Bureau of the Census, 2013 Current Population Survey Annual Social and Economic Supplement, Internet site http://www.census.gov/hhes/www/cpstables/032013/pov/toc.htm; calculations by New Strategist

Table 6.40 Married Couples with Children below Poverty Level by Metropolitan Status, Race, and Hispanic Origin, 2012

(number and percent of married-couple families with related children under age 18 at home below poverty level by metropolitan status, race, and Hispanic origin, 2012; numbers in thousands)

NUMBER IN POVERTY	total families in poverty	Asians	blacks	Hispanics	non-Hispanic whites
Total married couples with children	**2,246**	**154**	**286**	**973**	**820**
Metropolitan	1,838	151	230	880	576
Inside principal cities	923	97	133	494	202
Outside principal cities	915	55	97	386	375
Not metropolitan	408	2	57	93	244
POVERTY RATE					
Total married couples with children	**8.9%**	**8.4%**	**12.5%**	**20.9%**	**5.0%**
Metropolitan	8.5	8.6	11.0	20.6	4.3
Inside principal cities	12.5	12.2	14.0	23.9	5.6
Outside principal cities	6.4	5.6	8.6	17.5	3.8
Not metropolitan	11.1	–	26.9	23.5	8.3

Note: Asians and blacks include those who identify themselves as being of the race alone and those who identify themselves as being of the race in combination with other races. Non-Hispanic whites are those who identify themselves as white alone and not Hispanic. Numbers do not add to total because not all races are shown and Hispanics may be of any race. "–" means sample is too small to make a reliable estimate.
Source: Bureau of the Census, 2013 Current Population Survey Annual Social and Economic Supplement, Internet site http://www.census.gov/hhes/www/cpstables/032013/pov/toc.htm; calculations by New Strategist

Table 6.41 Female-Headed Families below Poverty Level by Metropolitan Status, Race, and Hispanic Origin, 2012

(number and percent of female-headed families below poverty level by metropolitan status, race, and Hispanic origin, 2012; numbers in thousands)

NUMBER IN POVERTY	total families in poverty	Asians	blacks	Hispanics	non-Hispanic whites
Total female-headed families	**4,793**	**115**	**1,707**	**1,266**	**1,713**
Metropolitan	3,878	107	1,466	1,159	1,227
Inside principal cities	2,163	69	974	674	492
Outside principal cities	1,715	38	492	485	735
Not metropolitan	915	7	241	107	486
POVERTY RATE					
Total female-headed families	**30.9%**	**20.2%**	**38.0%**	**40.7%**	**23.4%**
Metropolitan	29.4	19.9	36.5	40.0	20.9
Inside principal cities	35.1	21.9	39.9	41.9	26.0
Outside principal cities	24.4	17.0	31.3	37.6	18.5
Not metropolitan	40.1	–	50.9	51.1	33.5

Note: Asians and blacks include those who identify themselves as being of the race alone and those who identify themselves as being of the race in combination with other races. Non-Hispanic whites are those who identify themselves as white alone and not Hispanic. Numbers do not add to total because not all races are shown and Hispanics may be of any race. "–" means sample is too small to make a reliable estimate.
Source: Bureau of the Census, 2013 Current Population Survey Annual Social and Economic Supplement, Internet site http://www.census.gov/hhes/www/cpstables/032013/pov/toc.htm; calculations by New Strategist

Table 6.42 Female-Headed Families with Children below Poverty Level by Metropolitan Status, Race, and Hispanic Origin, 2012

(number and percent of female-headed families with related children under age 18 at home below poverty level by metropolitan status, race, and Hispanic origin, 2012; numbers in thousands)

NUMBER IN POVERTY	total families in poverty	Asians	blacks	Hispanics	non-Hispanic whites
Total female-headed families with children	**4,099**	**82**	**1,479**	**1,133**	**1,415**
Metropolitan	3,309	77	1,264	1,033	1,014
Inside principal cities	1,836	49	841	598	388
Outside principal cities	1,472	28	423	435	626
Not metropolitan	791	6	215	100	401
POVERTY RATE					
Total female-headed families with children	**40.9%**	**27.5%**	**46.8%**	**48.6%**	**33.1%**
Metropolitan	39.1	27.7	44.9	47.9	30.3
Inside principal cities	45.2	32.7	48.6	50.6	36.2
Outside principal cities	33.4	21.9	39.1	44.6	27.5
Not metropolitan	50.4	–	62.2	58.2	43.3

Note: Asians and blacks include those who identify themselves as being of the race alone and those who identify themselves as being of the race in combination with other races. Non-Hispanic whites are those who identify themselves as white alone and not Hispanic. Numbers do not add to total because not all races are shown and Hispanics may be of any race. "–" means sample is too small to make a reliable estimate.

Source: Bureau of the Census, 2013 Current Population Survey Annual Social and Economic Supplement, Internet site http://www.census.gov/hhes/www/cpstables/032013/pov/toc.htm; calculations by New Strategist

Table 6.43 Male-Headed Families below Poverty Level by Metropolitan Status, Race, and Hispanic Origin, 2012

(number and percent of male-headed families below poverty level by region, race, and Hispanic origin, 2012; numbers in thousands)

NUMBER IN POVERTY	total families in poverty	Asians	blacks	Hispanics	non-Hispanic whites
Total male-headed families	**1,023**	**49**	**274**	**303**	**387**
Metropolitan	852	49	243	287	279
Inside principal cities	437	32	140	166	99
Outside principal cities	415	17	103	121	180
Not metropolitan	171	0	31	16	108
POVERTY RATE					
Total male-headed families	**16.4%**	**14.2%**	**24.8%**	**21.7%**	**11.4%**
Metropolitan	16.0	14.8	24.3	22.1	10.2
Inside principal cities	19.4	18.7	24.2	23.2	12.3
Outside principal cities	13.6	10.8	24.5	20.9	9.4
Not metropolitan	18.7	–	29.6	16.5	16.4

Note: Asians and blacks include those who identify themselves as being of the race alone and those who identify themselves as being of the race in combination with other races. Non-Hispanic whites are those who identify themselves as white alone and not Hispanic. Numbers do not add to total because not all races are shown and Hispanics may be of any race. "–" means sample is too small to make a reliable estimate.
Source: Bureau of the Census, 2013 Current Population Survey Annual Social and Economic Supplement, Internet site http://www.census.gov/hhes/www/cpstables/032013/pov/toc.htm; calculations by New Strategist

Table 6.44 Male-Headed Families with Children below Poverty Level by Metropolitan Status, Race, and Hispanic Origin, 2012

(number and percent of male-headed families with related children under age 18 at home below poverty level by metropolitan status, race, and Hispanic origin, 2012; numbers in thousands)

NUMBER IN POVERTY	total families in poverty	Asians	blacks	Hispanics	non-Hispanic whites
Total male-headed families with children	**717**	**29**	**179**	**235**	**274**
Metropolitan	590	29	153	219	198
Inside principal cities	282	15	90	114	67
Outside principal cities	308	14	64	105	130
Not metropolitan	127	0	26	16	77

POVERTY RATE					
Total male-headed families with children	**22.6%**	**24.5%**	**29.5%**	**30.1%**	**16.3%**
Metropolitan	22.1	26.0	28.2	30.4	14.8
Inside principal cities	25.8	–	29.9	29.7	17.6
Outside principal cities	19.6	–	26.2	31.3	13.7
Not metropolitan	25.3	–	–	–	21.9

Note: Asians and blacks include those who identify themselves as being of the race alone and those who identify themselves as being of the race in combination with other races. Non-Hispanic whites are those who identify themselves as white alone and not Hispanic. Numbers do not add to total because not all races are shown and Hispanics may be of any race. "–" means sample is too small to make a reliable estimate.
Source: Bureau of the Census, 2013 Current Population Survey Annual Social and Economic Supplement, Internet site http://www.census.gov/hhes/www/cpstables/032013/pov/toc.htm; calculations by New Strategist

Non-Hispanic Whites Dominate the Elderly Poor

Minorities account for the majority of poor under age 55.

Among the nation's 46 million poor in 2012, only 41 percent were non-Hispanic white. Twenty-nine percent were Hispanic, 25 percent were black, and 4 percent were Asian.

The non-Hispanic white share of the poor rises fairly steadily with age. Among poor children, 30 percent are non-Hispanic white, 30 percent are black, and the largest share—37 percent—is Hispanic. The non-Hispanic white share of the poor becomes the majority in the 55-to-59 age group. Among poor people aged 75 or older, fully 63 percent are non-Hispanic white.

■ As the Hispanic population expands, it represents a growing share of the poor.

Non-Hispanic whites account for most of the elderly poor

(percent of people below poverty level who are non-Hispanic white, by age, 2012)

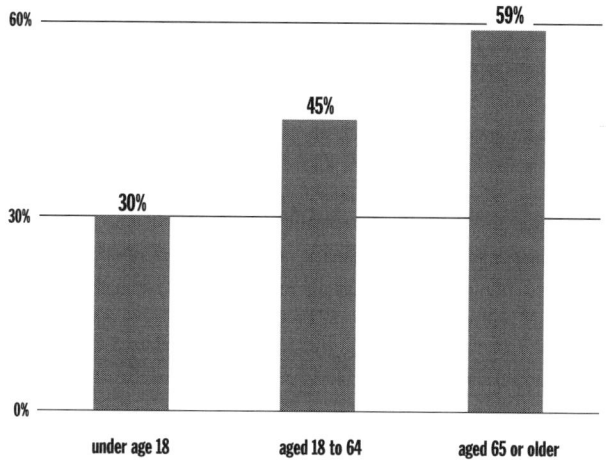

Table 6.45 People below Poverty Level by Age, Race, and Hispanic Origin, 2012

(number of people below poverty level and percent distribution of poor by age, race, and Hispanic origin, 2012; numbers in thousands)

NUMBER IN POVERTY	total people in poverty	Asians	blacks	Hispanics	non-Hispanic whites
Total people	**46,496**	**2,072**	**11,809**	**13,616**	**18,940**
Under age 18	16,073	570	4,815	5,976	4,782
Under age 5	4,953	154	1,509	1,898	1,425
Aged 5 to 17	11,121	416	3,305	4,079	3,357
Aged 18 to 64	26,497	1,291	6,265	6,977	11,833
Aged 18 to 24	6,117	360	1,493	1,614	2,608
Aged 25 to 34	6,633	318	1,575	2,032	2,727
Aged 35 to 44	4,960	213	1,137	1,650	1,946
Aged 45 to 54	4,675	235	1,132	971	2,270
Aged 55 to 59	2,230	78	547	378	1,209
Aged 60 to 64	1,882	87	381	332	1,074
Aged 65 or older	3,926	211	730	663	2,324
Aged 65 to 74	1,960	97	393	396	1,081
Aged 75 or older	1,965	114	337	267	1,243

PERCENT DISTRIBUTION OF POOR BY RACE AND HISPANIC ORIGIN

	total people in poverty	Asians	blacks	Hispanics	non-Hispanic whites
Total in poverty	**100.0%**	**4.5%**	**25.4%**	**29.3%**	**40.7%**
Under age 18	100.0	3.5	30.0	37.2	29.8
Under age 5	100.0	3.1	30.5	38.3	28.8
Aged 5 to 17	100.0	3.7	29.7	36.7	30.2
Aged 18 to 64	100.0	4.9	23.6	26.3	44.7
Aged 18 to 24	100.0	5.9	24.4	26.4	42.6
Aged 25 to 34	100.0	4.8	23.7	30.6	41.1
Aged 35 to 44	100.0	4.3	22.9	33.3	39.2
Aged 45 to 54	100.0	5.0	24.2	20.8	48.6
Aged 55 to 59	100.0	3.5	24.5	17.0	54.2
Aged 60 to 64	100.0	4.6	20.2	17.6	57.1
Aged 65 or older	100.0	5.4	18.6	16.9	59.2
Aged 65 to 74	100.0	4.9	20.1	20.2	55.2
Aged 75 or older	100.0	5.8	17.2	13.6	63.3

Note: Asians and blacks include those who identify themselves as being of the race alone and those who identify themselves as being of the race in combination with other races. Non-Hispanic whites are those who identify themselves as white alone and not Hispanic. Numbers do not add to total because not all races are shown and Hispanics may be of any race.
Source: Bureau of the Census, 2013 Current Population Survey Annual Social and Economic Supplement, Internet site http:// www.census.gov/hhes/www/cpstables/032013/pov/toc.htm; calculations by New Strategist

Poverty Rate Is Highest among Children

Black children are most likely to be poor.

Among the nation's children, more than one in five lives below the poverty level. The 21.8 percent poverty rate of children exceeds the 20.4 percent poverty rate of young adults. Poverty falls with age and bottoms out at 9.1 percent among people aged 65 or older. In every age group, poverty is greater among females than males.

Among black children, 36.7 percent are poor—a rate that exceeds the 33.8 percent among Hispanic children. A much smaller 12.5 percent of Asian and 12.3 percent of non-Hispanic white children are poor. The poverty rate among blacks and non-Hispanic whites is lowest among those aged 65 or older, at 18.3 and 6.8 percent, respectively. For Hispanics, the rate bottoms out among those aged 45 to 54, at 16.3 percent. Among Asians, 35-to-44-year-olds are least likely to be poor, at 7.4 percent.

■ Black children have a higher poverty rate than non-Hispanic whites because most are being raised by single mothers.

Poverty rate is highest among children

(percent of people below poverty level by age, 2012)

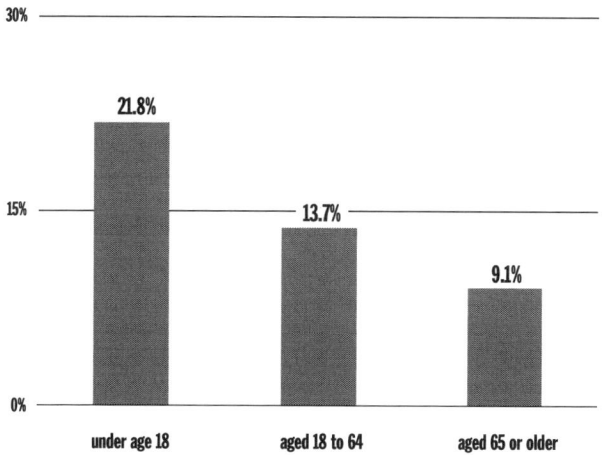

Table 6.46 People below Poverty Level by Age and Sex, 2012: Total People

(number and percent of people below poverty level by age and sex, 2012; numbers in thousands)

NUMBER IN POVERTY	total people in poverty	females	males
Total people	**46,496**	**25,840**	**20,656**
Under age 18	16,073	8,058	8,015
Under age 5	4,953	2,467	2,486
Aged 5 to 17	11,121	5,591	5,530
Aged 18 to 64	26,497	15,138	11,359
Aged 18 to 24	6,117	3,355	2,762
Aged 25 to 34	6,633	4,045	2,588
Aged 35 to 44	4,960	2,890	2,070
Aged 45 to 54	4,675	2,549	2,126
Aged 55 to 59	2,230	1,235	995
Aged 60 to 64	1,882	1,063	818
Aged 65 or older	3,926	2,643	1,282
Aged 65 to 74	1,960	1,196	764
Aged 75 or older	1,965	1,448	518

POVERTY RATE			
Total people	**15.0%**	**16.3%**	**13.6%**
Under age 18	21.8	22.3	21.3
Under age 5	25.1	25.5	24.7
Aged 5 to 17	20.6	21.1	20.1
Aged 18 to 64	13.7	15.4	11.9
Aged 18 to 24	20.4	22.5	18.2
Aged 25 to 34	15.9	19.3	12.4
Aged 35 to 44	12.4	14.3	10.5
Aged 45 to 54	10.8	11.5	10.0
Aged 55 to 59	10.7	11.5	9.9
Aged 60 to 64	10.7	11.3	10.0
Aged 65 or older	9.1	11.0	6.6
Aged 65 to 74	7.9	9.1	6.6
Aged 75 or older	10.6	13.3	6.7

Source: Bureau of the Census, 2013 Current Population Survey Annual Social and Economic Supplement, Internet site http://www.census.gov/hhes/www/cpstables/032013/pov/toc.htm; calculations by New Strategist

Table 6.47 People below Poverty Level by Age and Sex, 2012: Asians

(number and percent of Asians below poverty level by age and sex, 2012; numbers in thousands)

NUMBER IN POVERTY	total people in poverty	females	males
Total Asians	**2,072**	**1,148**	**925**
Under age 18	570	316	254
Under age 5	154	90	64
Aged 5 to 17	416	226	190
Aged 18 to 64	1,291	709	582
Aged 18 to 24	360	165	196
Aged 25 to 34	318	178	140
Aged 35 to 44	213	139	74
Aged 45 to 54	235	130	105
Aged 55 to 59	78	43	35
Aged 60 to 64	87	54	32
Aged 65 or older	211	122	89
Aged 65 to 74	97	55	42
Aged 75 or older	114	67	47
POVERTY RATE			
Total Asians	**11.4%**	**12.0%**	**10.8%**
Under age 18	12.5	13.5	11.4
Under age 5	11.8	13.4	10.0
Aged 5 to 17	12.8	13.6	12.0
Aged 18 to 64	10.8	11.3	10.3
Aged 18 to 24	19.2	17.7	20.6
Aged 25 to 34	10.6	11.5	9.7
Aged 35 to 44	7.4	9.1	5.5
Aged 45 to 54	10.1	10.4	9.7
Aged 55 to 59	7.7	7.7	7.7
Aged 60 to 64	10.6	11.7	9.1
Aged 65 or older	12.4	12.6	12.1
Aged 65 to 74	9.4	9.9	8.9
Aged 75 or older	16.9	16.3	18.0

Note: Asians are those who identify themselves as being of the race alone and those who identify themselves as being of the race in combination with other races.
Source: Bureau of the Census, 2013 Current Population Survey Annual Social and Economic Supplement, Internet site http:// www.census.gov/hhes/www/cpstables/032013/pov/toc.htm; calculations by New Strategist

Table 6.48 People below Poverty Level by Age and Sex, 2012: Blacks

(number and percent of blacks below poverty level by age and sex, 2012; numbers in thousands)

NUMBER IN POVERTY	total people in poverty	females	males
Total blacks	**11,809**	**6,614**	**5,195**
Under age 18	4,815	2,420	2,395
Under age 5	1,509	771	738
Aged 5 to 17	3,305	1,648	1,657
Aged 18 to 64	6,265	3,695	2,570
Aged 18 to 24	1,493	815	678
Aged 25 to 34	1,575	1,009	565
Aged 35 to 44	1,137	692	445
Aged 45 to 54	1,132	651	482
Aged 55 to 59	547	301	246
Aged 60 to 64	381	227	154
Aged 65 or older	730	499	230
Aged 65 to 74	393	239	154
Aged 75 or older	337	261	76

POVERTY RATE			
Total blacks	**27.1%**	**28.6%**	**25.4%**
Under age 18	36.7	37.7	35.8
Under age 5	41.0	43.0	39.1
Aged 5 to 17	35.1	35.7	34.5
Aged 18 to 64	23.7	25.7	21.2
Aged 18 to 24	29.5	31.1	27.8
Aged 25 to 34	26.2	31.2	20.4
Aged 35 to 44	20.9	23.1	18.2
Aged 45 to 54	20.2	21.3	18.9
Aged 55 to 59	22.4	22.5	22.3
Aged 60 to 64	19.7	19.7	19.6
Aged 65 or older	18.3	21.4	13.8
Aged 65 to 74	16.4	17.8	14.6
Aged 75 or older	21.1	26.3	12.6

Note: Blacks are those who identify themselves as being of the race alone and those who identify themselves as being of the race in combination with other races.
Source: Bureau of the Census, 2013 Current Population Survey Annual Social and Economic Supplement, Internet site http:// www.census.gov/hhes/www/cpstables/032013/pov/toc.htm; calculations by New Strategist

Table 6.49 People below Poverty Level by Age and Sex, 2012: Hispanics

(number and percent of Hispanics below poverty level by age and sex, 2012; numbers in thousands)

NUMBER IN POVERTY	total people in poverty	females	males
Total Hispanics	**13,616**	**7,355**	**6,260**
Under age 18	5,976	2,971	3,005
Under age 5	1,898	955	943
Aged 5 to 17	4,079	2,017	2,062
Aged 18 to 64	6,977	3,985	2,992
Aged 18 to 24	1,614	895	718
Aged 25 to 34	2,032	1,230	802
Aged 35 to 44	1,650	916	733
Aged 45 to 54	971	527	444
Aged 55 to 59	378	215	162
Aged 60 to 64	332	200	132
Aged 65 or older	663	400	263
Aged 65 to 74	396	223	173
Aged 75 or older	267	176	90
POVERTY RATE			
Total Hispanics	**25.6%**	**27.9%**	**23.4%**
Under age 18	33.8	34.5	33.2
Under age 5	37.1	38.1	36.2
Aged 5 to 17	32.5	33.0	32.0
Aged 18 to 64	21.6	25.1	18.3
Aged 18 to 24	25.6	29.1	22.2
Aged 25 to 34	23.6	30.0	17.9
Aged 35 to 44	21.6	24.3	19.0
Aged 45 to 54	16.3	17.7	14.9
Aged 55 to 59	17.5	19.4	15.5
Aged 60 to 64	21.0	24.0	17.8
Aged 65 or older	20.6	21.8	19.1
Aged 65 to 74	20.7	20.7	20.6
Aged 75 or older	20.6	23.4	16.7

Source: Bureau of the Census, 2013 Current Population Survey Annual Social and Economic Supplement, Internet site http://www.census.gov/hhes/www/cpstables/032013/pov/toc.htm; calculations by New Strategist

Table 6.50 People below Poverty Level by Age and Sex, 2012: Non-Hispanic Whites

(number and percent of non-Hispanic whites below poverty level by age and sex, 2012; numbers in thousands)

NUMBER IN POVERTY	total people in poverty	females	males
Total non-Hispanic whites	**18,940**	**10,711**	**8,229**
Under age 18	4,782	2,415	2,367
Under age 5	1,425	692	733
Aged 5 to 17	3,357	1,723	1,634
Aged 18 to 64	11,833	6,678	5,155
Aged 18 to 24	2,608	1,478	1,130
Aged 25 to 34	2,727	1,610	1,116
Aged 35 to 44	1,946	1,139	808
Aged 45 to 54	2,270	1,212	1,058
Aged 55 to 59	1,209	667	542
Aged 60 to 64	1,074	572	502
Aged 65 or older	2,324	1,618	706
Aged 65 to 74	1,081	674	406
Aged 75 or older	1,243	944	300

POVERTY RATE			
Total non-Hispanic whites	**9.7%**	**10.8%**	**8.6%**
Under age 18	12.3	12.8	11.9
Under age 5	14.5	14.3	14.6
Aged 5 to 17	11.6	12.2	11.0
Aged 18 to 64	9.7	10.8	8.5
Aged 18 to 24	15.6	18.0	13.4
Aged 25 to 34	11.3	13.4	9.2
Aged 35 to 44	8.2	9.5	6.8
Aged 45 to 54	7.8	8.2	7.3
Aged 55 to 59	8.0	8.7	7.3
Aged 60 to 64	8.2	8.3	8.0
Aged 65 or older	6.8	8.6	4.6
Aged 65 to 74	5.6	6.7	4.4
Aged 75 or older	8.3	10.8	4.8

Note: Non-Hispanic whites are those who identify themselves as being white alone and not Hispanic.
Source: Bureau of the Census, 2013 Current Population Survey Annual Social and Economic Supplement, Internet site http://www.census.gov/hhes/www/cpstables/032013/pov/toc.htm; calculations by New Strategist

Poverty Rate Varies by Family Status and Age

The largest share of the poor live in female-headed families.

Among the nation's 46 million poor, the 34 percent plurality lives in a female-headed family. A smaller 30 percent live in a married-couple family, and 27 percent are what the government calls "unrelated individuals"—meaning people who live alone or with nonrelatives.

The family status of the poor varies considerably by race and Hispanic origin. Among poor blacks, the 53 percent majority lives in a female-headed family. Among Hispanics, in contrast, 41 percent of the poor live in a married-couple family and a smaller 35 percent are in a female-headed family. Among poor non-Hispanic whites, the largest share is in the "unrelated individual" category (38 percent). Among poor Asians, the 46 percent who live in a married-couple family greatly outnumber those in other living situations.

■ Among all people aged 65 or older, the poverty rate is just 9.1 percent, but among unrelated individuals aged 65 or older the poverty rate is a higher 17.3 percent.

People who live alone or with nonrelatives account for a large share of the poor

(percent distribution of people living below poverty level by family status, 2012)

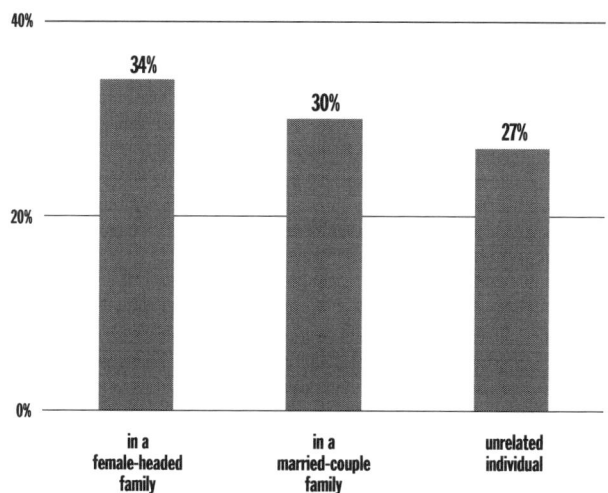

Table 6.51 People below Poverty Level by Age and Family Status, 2012: Total People

(number and percent of people in poverty, and percent distribution of people below poverty level by age and family status, 2012; numbers in thousands)

NUMBER IN POVERTY	total people in poverty	living in married-couple family	living in female-headed family	living in male-headed family	living in unrelated subfamily	unrelated individuals
Total people	46,496	14,177	15,957	3,065	740	12,558
Under age 18	16,073	5,462	8,692	1,336	440	144
Aged 18 to 24	6,117	1,114	1,916	407	57	2,623
Aged 25 to 34	6,633	1,972	2,094	382	127	2,057
Aged 35 to 44	4,960	1,839	1,453	314	73	1,281
Aged 45 to 54	4,675	1,419	890	310	36	2,020
Aged 55 to 59	2,230	645	338	102	4	1,140
Aged 60 to 64	1,882	652	199	69	2	959
Aged 65 or older	3,926	1,074	374	145	0	2,332
POVERTY RATE						
Total people	15.0%	7.5%	33.9%	17.4%	46.3%	22.4%
Under age 18	21.8	11.1	47.1	25.7	51.4	94.8
Aged 18 to 24	20.4	7.8	29.0	16.3	53.5	39.9
Aged 25 to 34	15.9	9.0	36.0	14.8	40.7	18.2
Aged 35 to 44	12.4	7.2	27.8	15.6	37.2	18.7
Aged 45 to 54	10.8	5.1	18.3	13.7	40.3	23.5
Aged 55 to 59	10.7	4.8	19.0	10.7	–	24.3
Aged 60 to 64	10.7	5.8	16.7	11.1	–	21.3
Aged 65 or older	9.1	4.3	11.9	10.1	–	17.3
PERCENT DISTRIBUTION OF POOR BY FAMILY STATUS						
Total people	100.0	30.5	34.3	6.6	1.6	27.0
Under age 18	100.0	34.0	54.1	8.3	2.7	0.9
Aged 18 to 24	100.0	18.2	31.3	6.7	0.9	42.9
Aged 25 to 34	100.0	29.7	31.6	5.8	1.9	31.0
Aged 35 to 44	100.0	37.1	29.3	6.3	1.5	25.8
Aged 45 to 54	100.0	30.4	19.0	6.6	0.8	43.2
Aged 55 to 59	100.0	28.9	15.2	4.6	0.2	51.1
Aged 60 to 64	100.0	34.6	10.6	3.7	0.1	51.0
Aged 65 or older	100.0	27.4	9.5	3.7	0.0	59.4

Note: "–" means sample is too small to make a reliable estimate.
Source: Bureau of the Census, 2013 Current Population Survey Annual Social and Economic Supplement, Internet site http://www.census.gov/hhes/www/cpstables/032013/pov/toc.htm; calculations by New Strategist

Table 6.52 People below Poverty Level by Age and Family Status, 2012: Asians

(number and percent of Asians in poverty, and percent distribution of Asians below poverty level by age and family status, 2012; numbers in thousands)

NUMBER IN POVERTY	total people in poverty	living in married-couple family	living in female-headed family	living in male-headed family	living in unrelated subfamily	unrelated individuals
Total Asians	**2,072**	**948**	**374**	**146**	**26**	**580**
Under age 18	570	331	167	47	12	13
Aged 18 to 24	360	56	58	30	6	211
Aged 25 to 34	318	128	39	20	4	128
Aged 35 to 44	213	108	41	18	0	46
Aged 45 to 54	235	132	31	17	2	53
Aged 55 to 59	78	34	12	7	0	25
Aged 60 to 64	87	39	14	2	2	30
Aged 65 or older	211	119	12	5	0	74
POVERTY RATE						
Total Asians	**11.4%**	**7.4%**	**21.3%**	**12.8%**	**29.1%**	**24.8%**
Under age 18	12.5	8.9	30.5	20.6	–	–
Aged 18 to 24	19.2	5.7	24.8	16.4	–	44.8
Aged 25 to 34	10.6	7.2	17.7	9.5	–	16.4
Aged 35 to 44	7.4	4.9	19.0	18.8	–	13.3
Aged 45 to 54	10.1	7.7	15.7	10.4	–	22.5
Aged 55 to 59	7.7	4.8	12.9	7.6	–	21.3
Aged 60 to 64	10.6	6.8	15.4	–	–	35.5
Aged 65 or older	12.4	10.4	7.6	5.2	–	25.7
PERCENT DISTRIBUTION OF POOR BY FAMILY STATUS						
Total Asians	**100.0**	**45.8**	**18.1**	**7.0**	**1.3**	**28.0**
Under age 18	100.0	58.1	29.3	8.2	2.1	2.3
Aged 18 to 24	100.0	15.6	16.1	8.3	1.7	58.6
Aged 25 to 34	100.0	40.3	12.3	6.3	1.3	40.3
Aged 35 to 44	100.0	50.7	19.2	8.5	0.0	21.6
Aged 45 to 54	100.0	56.2	13.2	7.2	0.9	22.6
Aged 55 to 59	100.0	43.6	15.4	9.0	0.0	32.1
Aged 60 to 64	100.0	44.8	16.1	2.3	2.3	34.5
Aged 65 or older	100.0	56.4	5.7	2.4	0.0	35.1

Note: Asians are those who identify themselves as being of the race alone and those who identify themselves as being of the race in combination with other races. "–" means sample is too small to make a reliable estimate.
Source: Bureau of the Census, 2013 Current Population Survey Annual Social and Economic Supplement, Internet site http://www.census.gov/hhes/www/cpstables/032013/pov/toc.htm; calculations by New Strategist

Table 6.53 People below Poverty Level by Age and Family Status, 2012: Blacks

(number and percent of blacks in poverty, and percent distribution of blacks below poverty level by age and family status, 2012; numbers in thousands)

NUMBER IN POVERTY	total people in poverty	living in married-couple family	living in female-headed family	living in male-headed family	living in unrelated subfamily	unrelated individuals
Total blacks	**11,809**	**1,951**	**6,220**	**845**	**131**	**2,663**
Under age 18	4,815	780	3,539	373	87	36
Aged 18 to 24	1,493	188	751	99	7	449
Aged 25 to 34	1,575	242	761	137	25	408
Aged 35 to 44	1,137	240	535	55	11	296
Aged 45 to 54	1,132	206	321	100	1	504
Aged 55 to 59	547	115	120	28	0	284
Aged 60 to 64	381	67	63	21	0	230
Aged 65 or older	730	113	129	32	0	456
POVERTY RATE						
Total blacks	**27.1%**	**11.6%**	**41.2%**	**25.7%**	**65.3%**	**32.6%**
Under age 18	36.7	15.3	52.3	34.2	69.6	–
Aged 18 to 24	29.5	12.6	34.9	21.6	–	47.4
Aged 25 to 34	26.2	12.3	40.7	28.4	–	24.8
Aged 35 to 44	20.9	10.4	33.2	14.6	–	26.3
Aged 45 to 54	20.2	8.6	24.4	26.2	–	34.0
Aged 55 to 59	22.4	10.4	28.9	19.4	–	36.7
Aged 60 to 64	19.7	8.1	19.9	18.2	–	33.8
Aged 65 or older	18.3	7.0	19.6	13.2	–	30.6
PERCENT DISTRIBUTION OF POOR BY FAMILY STATUS						
Total blacks	**100.0**	**16.5**	**52.7**	**7.2**	**1.1**	**22.6**
Under age 18	100.0	16.2	73.5	7.7	1.8	0.7
Aged 18 to 24	100.0	12.6	50.3	6.6	0.5	30.1
Aged 25 to 34	100.0	15.4	48.3	8.7	1.6	25.9
Aged 35 to 44	100.0	21.1	47.1	4.8	1.0	26.0
Aged 45 to 54	100.0	18.2	28.4	8.8	0.1	44.5
Aged 55 to 59	100.0	21.0	21.9	5.1	0.0	51.9
Aged 60 to 64	100.0	17.6	16.5	5.5	0.0	60.4
Aged 65 or older	100.0	15.5	17.7	4.4	0.0	62.5

Note: Blacks are those who identify themselves as being of the race alone and those who identify themselves as being of the race in combination with other races. "–" means sample is too small to make a reliable estimate.
Source: Bureau of the Census, 2013 Current Population Survey Annual Social and Economic Supplement, Internet site http://www.census.gov/hhes/www/cpstables/032013/pov/toc.htm; calculations by New Strategist

Table 6.54 People below Poverty Level by Age and Family Status, 2012: Hispanics

(number and percent of Hispanics in poverty, and percent distribution of Hispanics below poverty level by age and family status, 2012; numbers in thousands)

NUMBER IN POVERTY	total people in poverty	living in married-couple family	living in female-headed family	living in male-headed family	living in unrelated subfamily	unrelated individuals
Total Hispanics	**13,616**	**5,540**	**4,816**	**1,002**	**240**	**2,018**
Under age 18	5,976	2,514	2,822	455	156	29
Aged 18 to 24	1,614	480	566	154	13	400
Aged 25 to 34	2,032	841	582	124	41	444
Aged 35 to 44	1,650	803	430	109	19	289
Aged 45 to 54	971	418	196	84	8	265
Aged 55 to 59	378	126	96	25	2	129
Aged 60 to 64	332	134	43	16	0	140
Aged 65 or older	663	223	82	36	0	321
POVERTY RATE						
Total Hispanics	**25.6%**	**18.3%**	**42.8%**	**21.2%**	**57.2%**	**31.0%**
Under age 18	33.8	23.6	54.5	29.4	65.7	–
Aged 18 to 24	25.6	16.0	34.8	21.4	–	42.6
Aged 25 to 34	23.6	18.6	41.1	14.9	50.8	25.4
Aged 35 to 44	21.6	17.5	35.0	19.0	–	24.2
Aged 45 to 54	16.3	11.8	22.8	14.7	–	27.0
Aged 55 to 59	17.5	10.4	29.1	14.5	–	29.1
Aged 60 to 64	21.0	14.5	26.7	12.6	–	37.8
Aged 65 or older	20.6	12.6	17.8	18.6	–	40.7
PERCENT DISTRIBUTION OF POOR BY FAMILY STATUS						
Total Hispanics	**100.0**	**40.7**	**35.4**	**7.4**	**1.8**	**14.8**
Under age 18	100.0	42.1	47.2	7.6	2.6	0.5
Aged 18 to 24	100.0	29.7	35.1	9.5	0.8	24.8
Aged 25 to 34	100.0	41.4	28.6	6.1	2.0	21.9
Aged 35 to 44	100.0	48.7	26.1	6.6	1.2	17.5
Aged 45 to 54	100.0	43.0	20.2	8.7	0.8	27.3
Aged 55 to 59	100.0	33.3	25.4	6.6	0.5	34.1
Aged 60 to 64	100.0	40.4	13.0	4.8	0.0	42.2
Aged 65 or older	100.0	33.6	12.4	5.4	0.0	48.4

Note: "–" means sample is too small to make a reliable estimate.
Source: Bureau of the Census, 2013 Current Population Survey Annual Social and Economic Supplement, Internet site http://www.census.gov/hhes/www/cpstables/032013/pov/toc.htm; calculations by New Strategist

Table 6.55 People below Poverty Level by Age and Family Status, 2012: Non-Hispanic Whites

(number and percent of non-Hispanic whites in poverty, and percent distribution of non-Hispanic whites below poverty level by age and family status, 2012; numbers in thousands)

NUMBER IN POVERTY	total people in poverty	living in married-couple family	living in female-headed family	living in male-headed family	living in in unrelated subfamily	unrelated individuals
Total non-Hispanic whites	**18,940**	**5,701**	**4,655**	**1,030**	**352**	**7,202**
Under age 18	4,782	1,832	2,251	438	192	68
Aged 18 to 24	2,608	376	554	109	31	1,536
Aged 25 to 34	2,727	773	705	102	57	1,090
Aged 35 to 44	1,946	688	465	125	44	624
Aged 45 to 54	2,270	638	335	110	25	1,161
Aged 55 to 59	1,209	362	119	42	2	685
Aged 60 to 64	1,074	412	76	32	0	553
Aged 65 or older	2,324	620	150	71	0	1,483

POVERTY RATE						
Total non-Hispanic whites	**9.7%**	**4.5%**	**24.3%**	**12.0%**	**39.3%**	**18.6%**
Under age 18	12.3	6.2	36.5	18.2	41.6	–
Aged 18 to 24	15.6	4.3	21.1	9.6	–	36.8
Aged 25 to 34	11.3	5.7	30.5	9.3	31.9	15.4
Aged 35 to 44	8.2	4.2	20.9	12.6	38.1	15.0
Aged 45 to 54	7.8	3.2	13.6	9.5	–	19.9
Aged 55 to 59	8.0	3.5	12.7	7.7	–	20.6
Aged 60 to 64	8.2	4.6	12.5	10.2	–	16.7
Aged 65 or older	6.8	3.0	8.1	7.9	–	13.7

PERCENT DISTRIBUTION OF POOR BY FAMILY STATUS						
Total non-Hispanic whites	**100.0**	**30.1**	**24.6**	**5.4**	**1.9**	**38.0**
Under age 18	100.0	38.3	47.1	9.2	4.0	1.4
Aged 18 to 24	100.0	14.4	21.2	4.2	1.2	58.9
Aged 25 to 34	100.0	28.3	25.9	3.7	2.1	40.0
Aged 35 to 44	100.0	35.4	23.9	6.4	2.3	32.1
Aged 45 to 54	100.0	28.1	14.8	4.8	1.1	51.1
Aged 55 to 59	100.0	29.9	9.8	3.5	0.2	56.7
Aged 60 to 64	100.0	38.4	7.1	3.0	0.0	51.5
Aged 65 or older	100.0	26.7	6.5	3.1	0.0	63.8

Note: Non-Hispanic whites are those who identify themselves as being of the race alone and not Hispanic. "–" means sample is too small to make a reliable estimate.
Source: Bureau of the Census, 2013 Current Population Survey Annual Social and Economic Supplement, Internet site http:// www.census.gov/hhes/www/cpstables/032013/pov/toc.htm; calculations by New Strategist

Few College Graduates Are Poor

Many of the poor are high school dropouts.

In 2012, only 4.5 percent of the nation's college graduates had incomes that placed them below the poverty level. In contrast, 29.7 percent of high school dropouts were poor. Among the 24 million poor Americans aged 25 or older, fully 30 percent were high school dropouts and another 35 percent had no more than a high school diploma.

A college degree almost guarantees a life free of poverty—regardless of race or Hispanic origin. The proportion of college graduates who are poor ranges from 3.8 percent among non-Hispanic whites to 8.0 percent among Hispanics.

■ If the educational attainment of Hispanics grows, their poverty rate should fall.

Poverty rate declines as education increases

(percent of people aged 25 or older below the poverty level, by education, 2012)

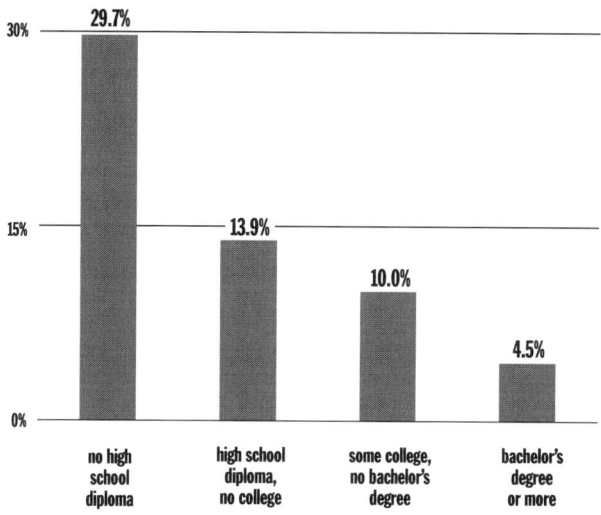

Table 6.56 People below Poverty Level by Education, Race, and Hispanic Origin, 2012

(number and percent of people aged 25 or older in poverty, and percent distribution of people below poverty level by educational attainment, race, and Hispanic origin, 2012; numbers in thousands)

NUMBER IN POVERTY	total people in poverty	Asians	blacks	Hispanics	non-Hispanic whites
Total people aged 25 or older	**24,306**	**1,142**	**5,501**	**6,025**	**11,550**
No high school diploma	7,275	265	1,680	3,082	2,318
High school diploma, no college	8,562	314	2,142	1,796	4,215
Some college, no bachelor's degree	5,520	212	1,283	798	3,159
Bachelor's degree or more	2,949	350	397	350	1,858
POVERTY RATE					
Total people aged 25 or older	**11.7%**	**9.7%**	**21.6%**	**20.7%**	**8.3%**
No high school diploma	29.7	23.3	44.3	31.3	23.4
High school diploma, no college	13.9	13.7	25.4	20.2	10.1
Some college, no bachelor's degree	10.0	10.1	16.9	13.2	8.1
Bachelor's degree or more	4.5	5.7	7.1	8.0	3.8
PERCENT DISTRIBUTION OF POOR BY EDUCATIONAL ATTAINMENT					
Total people aged 25 or older	**100.0**	**100.0**	**100.0**	**100.0**	**100.0**
No high school diploma	29.9	23.2	30.5	51.2	20.1
High school diploma, no college	35.2	27.5	38.9	29.8	36.5
Some college, no bachelor's degree	22.7	18.6	23.3	13.2	27.4
Bachelor's degree or more	12.1	30.6	7.2	5.8	16.1

Note: Asians and blacks are those who identify themselves as being of the race alone and those who identify themselves as being of the race in combination with other races. Non-Hispanic whites are those who identify themselves as white alone and not Hispanic. Numbers do not add to total because not all races are shown and Hispanics may be of any race.
Source: Bureau of the Census, 2013 Current Population Survey Annual Social and Economic Supplement, Internet site http://www.census.gov/hhes/www/cpstables/032013/pov/toc.htm; calculations by New Strategist

Many Young-Adult Workers Are Poor

Among 18-to-24-year-olds with a job, one in seven is poor.

While poverty rates are relatively low for people with jobs, a substantial number of workers are poor despite getting a paycheck. Among all workers aged 16 or older, 7.0 percent had incomes that placed them below poverty level in 2012. The poverty rate among workers is highest in the young-adult age group: 13.7 percent of 18-to-24-year-old workers are poor. Even among young adults who work full-time, 5.6 percent are poor. Many young adults earn minimum wage in entry-level jobs.

Hispanic workers are most likely to be poor. Nearly 14 percent of Hispanic workers live in poverty, including 7.5 percent of those with full-time jobs. Among non-Hispanic white workers with full-time jobs, only 1.5 percent are poor.

■ Hispanic workers have the highest poverty rate because of their low level of education.

Many Hispanics who work full-time are poor

(percent of full-time workers below poverty level, by race and Hispanic origin, 2012)

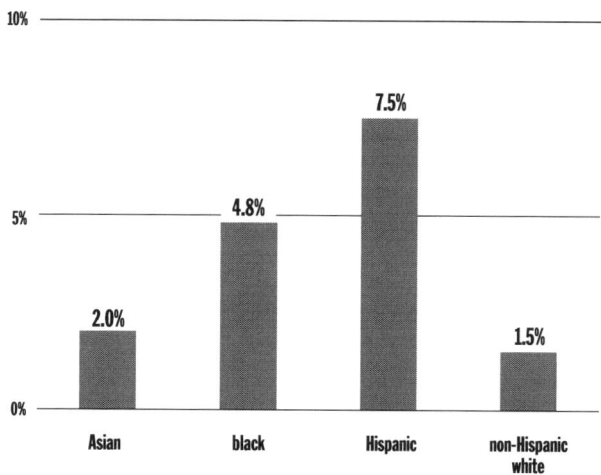

Table 6.57 Number and Percent of Workers below Poverty Level by Sex, Age, and Work Status, 2012: Total Workers

(number and percent of workers aged 16 or older below poverty level by sex, age, and work status, 2012; numbers in thousands)

	total workers		full-time, year-round workers	
	number	poverty rate	number	poverty rate
Total workers in poverty	**10,977**	**7.0%**	**2,904**	**2.8%**
Aged 16 to 17	135	7.6	4	–
Aged 18 to 24	2,634	13.7	359	5.6
Aged 25 to 34	3,239	9.6	958	4.1
Aged 35 to 54	3,831	5.7	1,298	2.6
Aged 55 to 64	968	3.7	252	1.4
Aged 65 or older	170	1.8	34	0.8
Male workers in poverty	**5,051**	**6.1**	**1,541**	**2.6**
Aged 16 to 17	53	6.1	0	0.0
Aged 18 to 24	1,176	11.9	182	4.8
Aged 25 to 34	1,400	7.7	475	3.5
Aged 35 to 54	1,877	5.3	730	2.5
Aged 55 to 64	467	3.5	140	1.4
Aged 65 or older	77	1.5	14	0.5
Female workers in poverty	**5,926**	**8.0**	**1,363**	**3.1**
Aged 16 to 17	82	9.0	4	–
Aged 18 to 24	1,457	15.5	177	6.6
Aged 25 to 34	1,839	11.8	482	4.9
Aged 35 to 54	1,954	6.2	567	2.6
Aged 55 to 64	501	4.0	113	1.3
Aged 65 or older	93	2.2	20	1.2

Note: "–" means data are not available.
Source: Bureau of the Census, 2013 Current Population Survey Annual Social and Economic Supplement, Internet site http://www.census.gov/hhes/www/cpstables/032013/pov/toc.htm; calculations by New Strategist

Table 6.58 **Number and Percent of Workers below Poverty Level by Sex, Age, and Work Status, 2012: Asian Workers**

(number and percent of Asian workers aged 16 or older below poverty level by sex, age, and work status, 2012; numbers in thousands)

	total workers		full-time, year-round workers	
	number	poverty rate	number	poverty rate
Total Asian workers in poverty	**460**	**5.0%**	**130**	**2.0%**
Aged 16 to 17	8	8.4	0	0.0
Aged 18 to 24	93	9.3	2	0.7
Aged 25 to 34	105	4.5	30	1.8
Aged 35 to 54	190	4.6	69	2.1
Aged 55 to 64	53	4.2	22	2.4
Aged 65 or older	12	3.4	7	3.1
Asian male workers in poverty	**222**	**4.6**	**77**	**2.1**
Aged 16 to 17	0	0.0	0	0.0
Aged 18 to 24	49	9.7	0	0.0
Aged 25 to 34	45	3.7	18	1.9
Aged 35 to 54	102	4.6	45	2.4
Aged 55 to 64	21	3.3	11	2.3
Aged 65 or older	5	2.7	3	2.7
Asian female workers in poverty	**238**	**5.4**	**53**	**1.9**
Aged 16 to 17	7	–	0	0.0
Aged 18 to 24	44	8.9	2	1.6
Aged 25 to 34	59	5.5	12	1.7
Aged 35 to 54	88	4.5	24	1.7
Aged 55 to 64	32	5.1	11	2.6
Aged 65 or older	7	4.3	3	3.5

Note: Asians are those who identify themselves as being of the race alone and those who identify themselves as being of the race in combination with other races. "–" means sample is too small to make a reliable estimate.
Source: Bureau of the Census, 2013 Current Population Survey Annual Social and Economic Supplement, Internet site http:// www.census.gov/hhes/www/cpstables/032013/pov/toc.htm; calculations by New Strategist

Table 6.59 Number and Percent of Workers below Poverty Level by Sex, Age, and Work Status, 2012: Black Workers

(number and percent of black workers aged 16 or older below poverty level by sex, age, and work status, 2012; numbers in thousands)

	total workers		full-time, year-round workers	
	number	poverty rate	number	poverty rate
Total black workers in poverty	**2,371**	**12.5%**	**577**	**4.8%**
Aged 16 to 17	28	15.1	0	0.0
Aged 18 to 24	591	21.0	81	9.1
Aged 25 to 34	750	16.7	187	6.5
Aged 35 to 54	803	9.7	255	4.1
Aged 55 to 64	179	7.2	50	2.8
Aged 65 or older	20	2.7	5	1.3
Black male workers in poverty	**890**	**10.0**	**202**	**3.4**
Aged 16 to 17	9	11.5	0	0.0
Aged 18 to 24	248	19.1	41	9.7
Aged 25 to 34	242	11.3	48	3.3
Aged 35 to 54	311	8.1	86	2.9
Aged 55 to 64	73	6.4	24	2.9
Aged 65 or older	7	2.0	2	0.9
Black female workers in poverty	**1,482**	**14.6**	**375**	**6.0**
Aged 16 to 17	19	17.7	0	0.0
Aged 18 to 24	343	22.6	40	8.5
Aged 25 to 34	508	21.6	138	9.7
Aged 35 to 54	493	11.1	168	5.2
Aged 55 to 64	105	7.9	26	2.8
Aged 65 or older	13	3.3	3	1.6

Note: Blacks are those who identify themselves as being of the race alone and those who identify themselves as being of the race in combination with other races.
Source: Bureau of the Census, 2013 Current Population Survey Annual Social and Economic Supplement, Internet site http:// www.census.gov/hhes/www/cpstables/032013/pov/toc.htm; calculations by New Strategist

Table 6.60 Number and Percent of Workers below Poverty Level by Sex, Age, and Work Status, 2012: Hispanic Workers

(number and percent of Hispanic workers aged 16 or older below poverty level by sex, age, and work status, 2012; numbers in thousands)

	total workers		full-time, year-round workers	
	number	poverty rate	number	poverty rate
Total Hispanic workers in poverty	**3,313**	**13.8%**	**1,158**	**7.5%**
Aged 16 to 17	31	14.9	0	0.0
Aged 18 to 24	692	18.0	130	8.7
Aged 25 to 34	1,037	15.8	373	8.6
Aged 35 to 54	1,307	12.5	582	7.7
Aged 55 to 64	187	8.1	70	4.3
Aged 65 or older	59	9.5	3	0.8
Hispanic male workers in poverty	**1,755**	**12.8**	**710**	**7.5**
Aged 16 to 17	18	15.5	0	0.0
Aged 18 to 24	337	15.8	87	9.2
Aged 25 to 34	534	13.6	226	8.2
Aged 35 to 54	747	12.5	359	7.9
Aged 55 to 64	94	7.4	37	3.9
Aged 65 or older	27	7.9	1	0.69
Hispanic female workers in poverty	**1,558**	**15.1**	**448**	**7.5**
Aged 16 to 17	14	14.2	0	0.0
Aged 18 to 24	355	20.7	43	7.8
Aged 25 to 34	504	18.9	148	9.2
Aged 35 to 54	561	12.4	222	7.5
Aged 55 to 64	93	9.0	34	4.8
Aged 65 or older	32	11.4	1	1.1

Source: Bureau of the Census, 2013 Current Population Survey Annual Social and Economic Supplement, Internet site http://www.census.gov/hhes/www/cpstables/032013/pov/toc.htm; calculations by New Strategist

Table 6.61 Number and Percent of Workers below Poverty Level by Sex, Age, and Work Status, 2012: Non-Hispanic White Workers

(number and percent of non-Hispanic white workers aged 16 or older below poverty level by sex, age, and work status, 2012; numbers in thousands)

	total workers		full-time, year-round workers	
	number	poverty rate	number	poverty rate
Total non-Hispanic white workers in poverty	**4,825**	**4.6%**	**1,062**	**1.5%**
Aged 16 to 17	67	5.2	4	–
Aged 18 to 24	1,259	10.9	143	3.8
Aged 25 to 34	1,358	6.7	376	2.6
Aged 35 to 54	1,509	3.4	403	1.2
Aged 55 to 64	556	2.8	119	0.8
Aged 65 or older	76	1.0	16	0.5
Non-Hispanic white male workers in poverty	**2,198**	**4.0**	**574**	**1.4**
Aged 16 to 17	25	3.9	0	0.0
Aged 18 to 24	537	9.1	56	2.5
Aged 25 to 34	597	5.5	186	2.2
Aged 35 to 54	714	3.1	248	1.3
Aged 55 to 64	287	2.8	80	1.0
Aged 65 or older	37	0.9	5	0.3
Non-Hispanic white female workers in poverty	**2,627**	**5.4**	**488**	**1.7**
Aged 16 to 17	42	6.5	4	–
Aged 18 to 24	721	12.8	87	5.7
Aged 25 to 34	761	8.0	190	3.1
Aged 35 to 54	795	3.9	156	1.1
Aged 55 to 64	270	2.8	40	0.6
Aged 65 or older	38	1.2	11	0.9

Note: Non-Hispanic whites are those who identify themselves as being white alone and not Hispanic. "–" means sample is too small to make a reliable estimate.
Source: Bureau of the Census, 2013 Current Population Survey Annual Social and Economic Supplement, Internet site http://www.census.gov/hhes/www/cpstables/032013/pov/toc.htm; calculations by New Strategist

Many of the Nonworking Poor Are Ill or Disabled

More than one in four say they did not work because of illness or disability.

Among the 21 million poor people aged 16 or older who were not in the labor force at any time in 2012, illness or disability was one of the most important reasons cited for not working. Twenty-seven percent gave this reason, including about half of those aged 55 to 64.

Twenty percent of the nonworking poor did not work because they were retired, including 77 percent of people aged 65 or older. Another 20 percent of the nonworking poor cited caring for home and family as the reason they did not work in 2012. Surprisingly few of the nonworking poor said they did not work in 2012 because they could not get a job—only 16 percent of poor men and 7 percent of poor women gave this as a reason.

■ As the population ages, illness and disability may become an even more important reason for keeping the poor out of the labor force.

Many of the poor are too sick to work

(percent distribution of poor people aged 16 or older who did not work by reason for not working, 2012)

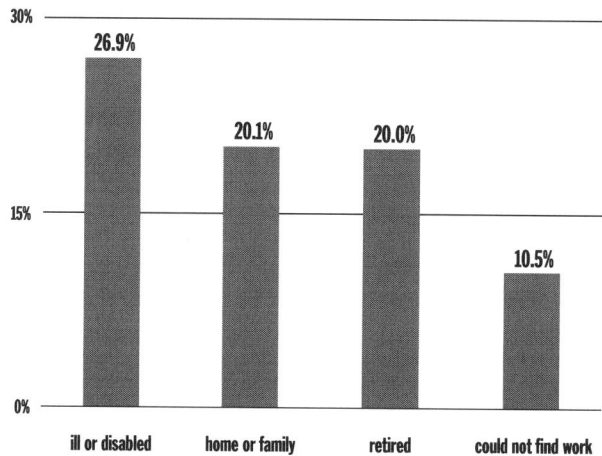

Table 6.62 People below Poverty Level by Reason for Not Working, 2012

(number of people aged 16 or older below poverty level who did not work and percent distribution by reason for not working, by sex and age, 2012; numbers in thousands)

| | did not work at all in 2012 | | | | | | |
| | total | | ill or disabled | retired | home or family | could not find work | school/other |
	number	percent					
Total people in poverty who did not work	**20,956**	**100.0%**	**26.9%**	**20.0%**	**20.1%**	**10.5%**	**22.4%**
Aged 16 to 17	1,376	100.0	2.3	0.8	2.5	2.3	92.1
Aged 18 to 24	3,483	100.0	7.6	1.5	19.3	12.7	58.9
Aged 25 to 34	3,394	100.0	17.9	2.3	40.1	15.7	23.9
Aged 35 to 54	5,805	100.0	43.0	4.6	28.9	15.6	8.0
Aged 55 to 64	3,144	100.0	49.0	29.2	11.6	7.9	2.3
Aged 65 or older	3,755	100.0	18.5	76.6	2.9	1.0	1.0
Total men in poverty who did not work	**8,304**	**100.0**	**30.1**	**18.4**	**7.2**	**15.8**	**28.5**
Aged 16 to 17	661	100.0	2.4	0.8	1.7	2.9	92.3
Aged 18 to 24	1,586	100.0	9.0	0.9	4.4	17.5	68.3
Aged 25 to 34	1,187	100.0	23.8	2.9	13.1	28.1	32.0
Aged 35 to 54	2,319	100.0	49.8	5.6	11.1	23.5	10.1
Aged 55 to 64	1,346	100.0	49.4	33.8	5.3	9.1	2.5
Aged 65 or older	1,205	100.0	20.0	74.0	2.7	1.4	1.8
Total women in poverty who did not work	**12,652**	**100.0**	**24.8**	**21.1**	**28.6**	**7.0**	**18.5**
Aged 16 to 17	716	100.0	2.2	1.0	3.2	1.8	91.6
Aged 18 to 24	1,898	100.0	6.5	2.0	31.8	8.7	50.9
Aged 25 to 34	2,206	100.0	14.7	1.9	54.7	9.1	19.6
Aged 35 to 54	3,485	100.0	38.5	3.9	40.7	10.4	6.6
Aged 55 to 64	1,797	100.0	48.7	25.7	16.3	7.1	2.2
Aged 65 or older	2,551	100.0	17.8	77.7	2.9	0.9	0.6

Source: Bureau of the Census, 2013 Current Population Survey Annual Social and Economic Supplement, Internet site http://www.census.gov/hhes/www/cpstables/032013/pov/toc.htm; calculations by New Strategist

Poverty Is Highest in the South

The poverty rate is lowest in the Midwest.

With 16.5 percent of its residents living below poverty level in 2012, residents of the South are most likely to be poor. In most age groups, the poverty rate in the South exceeds the rates in the other regions.

Among Asians, the poverty rate is highest in the Midwest at 14.7 percent. Among Hispanics, the poverty rate peaks at 29.1 percent in the Northeast. Among blacks, the highest poverty rate is in the Midwest, at 29.5 percent. The poverty rate among non-Hispanic whites is highest in the South at 10.5 percent.

■ The overall poverty rate is highest in the South partly because of the region's large black and Hispanic populations.

More than 16 percent of people who live in the South are poor

(percent of people below poverty level by region, 2012)

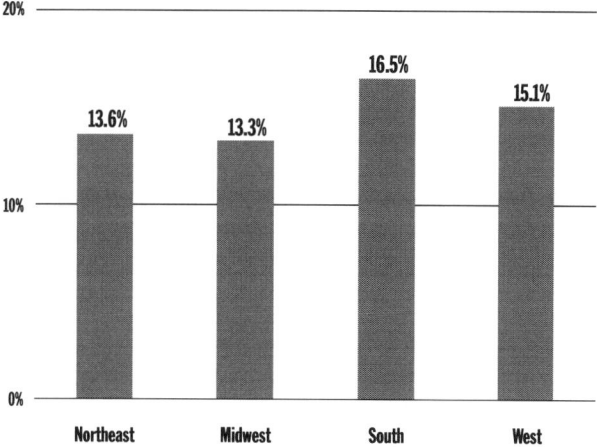

Table 6.63 People below Poverty Level by Age and Region, 2012

(number and percent of people in poverty, and percent distribution of people below poverty level by age and region 2012; numbers in thousands)

NUMBER IN POVERTY	total people in poverty	Northeast	Midwest	South	West
Total people	**46,496**	**7,490**	**8,851**	**19,106**	**11,049**
Under age 18	16,073	2,365	3,144	6,773	3,791
Aged 18 to 24	6,117	916	1,187	2,482	1,532
Aged 25 to 34	6,633	1,057	1,325	2,681	1,570
Aged 35 to 44	4,960	825	891	1,989	1,256
Aged 45 to 54	4,675	875	899	1,853	1,048
Aged 55 to 59	2,230	370	432	908	520
Aged 60 to 64	1,882	322	309	772	479
Aged 65 or older	3,926	760	664	1,648	853
POVERTY RATE					
Total people	**15.0%**	**13.6%**	**13.3%**	**16.5%**	**15.1%**
Under age 18	21.8	19.6	19.9	24.2	21.2
Aged 18 to 24	20.4	16.9	18.4	22.8	21.1
Aged 25 to 34	15.9	14.8	15.5	17.1	15.0
Aged 35 to 44	12.4	11.8	10.9	13.2	13.1
Aged 45 to 54	10.8	10.7	9.7	11.6	10.4
Aged 55 to 59	10.7	9.4	9.6	11.9	10.9
Aged 60 to 64	10.7	10.0	8.0	11.8	12.0
Aged 65 or older	9.1	9.4	6.8	10.2	9.2
PERCENT DISTRIBUTION OF POOR BY REGION					
Total people	**100.0**	**16.1**	**19.0**	**41.1**	**23.8**
Under age 18	100.0	14.7	19.6	42.1	23.6
Aged 18 to 24	100.0	15.0	19.4	40.6	25.0
Aged 25 to 34	100.0	15.9	20.0	40.4	23.7
Aged 35 to 44	100.0	16.6	18.0	40.1	25.3
Aged 45 to 54	100.0	18.7	19.2	39.6	22.4
Aged 55 to 59	100.0	16.6	19.4	40.7	23.3
Aged 60 to 64	100.0	17.1	16.4	41.0	25.5
Aged 65 or older	100.0	19.4	16.9	42.0	21.7

Source: Bureau of the Census, 2013 Current Population Survey Annual Social and Economic Supplement, Internet site http://www.census.gov/hhes/www/cpstables/032013/pov/toc.htm; calculations by New Strategist

Table 6.64 People below Poverty Level by Region, Race, and Hispanic Origin, 2012

(number and percent of people in poverty, and percent distribution of people below poverty level by region, race, and Hispanic origin, 2012; numbers in thousands)

NUMBER IN POVERTY	total people in poverty	Asians	blacks	Hispanics	non-Hispanic whites
Total people	**46,496**	**2,072**	**11809**	**13616**	**18,940**
Northeast	7,490	502	2077	2107	3,247
Midwest	8,851	334	2253	1211	4,974
South	19,106	440	6353	5055	7,154
West	11,049	797	1127	5243	3,565
POVERTY RATE					
Total people	**15.0%**	**11.4%**	**27.1%**	**25.6%**	**9.7%**
Northeast	13.6	14.3	26.8	29.1	8.6
Midwest	13.3	14.7	29.5	25.1	9.7
South	16.5	10.7	26.7	25.8	10.5
West	15.1	9.6	25.4	24.4	9.4
PERCENT DISTRIBUTION OF POOR BY RACE AND HISPANIC ORIGIN					
Total people	**100.0**	**4.5**	**25.4**	**29.3**	**40.7**
Northeast	100.0	6.7	27.7	28.1	43.4
Midwest	100.0	3.8	25.5	13.7	56.2
South	100.0	2.3	33.3	26.5	37.4
West	100.0	7.2	10.2	47.5	32.3

Note: Asians and blacks include those who identify themselves as being of the race alone and those who identify themselves as being of the race in combination with other races. Non-Hispanic whites are those who identify themselves as white alone and not Hispanic. Numbers do not add to total because not all races are shown and Hispanics may be of any race.
Source: Bureau of the Census, 2013 Current Population Survey Annual Social and Economic Supplement, Internet site http://www.census.gov/hhes/www/cpstables/032013/pov/toc.htm; calculations by New Strategist

Poverty Is High in Nonmetropolitan Areas

The poverty rate is highest in central cities.

Poverty in the nation's nonmetropolitan areas is not far below that of the central cities. In 2012, a substantial 17.7 percent of nonmetropolitan residents were poor, as were 19.7 percent of central (principal) city residents. In the suburbs, a smaller 11.2 percent of residents are poor. In some age groups, poverty in nonmetropolitan areas exceeds that in the central cities. By race and Hispanic origin, the poverty rate peaks at 40.7 percent among blacks who live in nonmetropolitan areas.

Among the nation's metropolitan areas with at least 1 million residents, the poverty rate is highest in Memphis at 19.9 percent in 2012, according to the Census Bureau's American Community Survey. The poverty rate is lowest in the Washington, D.C. metropolitan area, just 8.4 percent of its residents being poor.

■ Washington, D.C., is the only major metropolitan area in which the poverty rate is not in the double digits.

Poverty rate is lowest in the suburbs

(percent of people below poverty level by metropolitan residence, 2012)

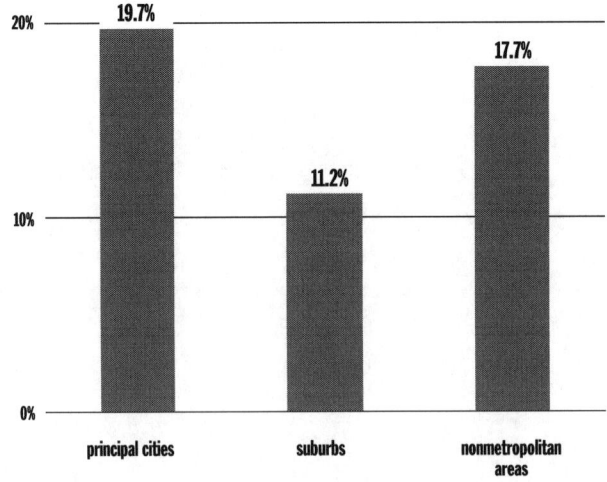

Table 6.65 People below Poverty Level by Age and Metropolitan Status, 2012

(number and percent of people in poverty, and percent distribution of people below poverty level by age and metropolitan status, 2012; numbers in thousands)

| | | inside metropolitan areas | | | |
NUMBER IN POVERTY	total people in poverty	total	inside principal cities	outside principal cities	not in metropolitan area
Total people	**46,496**	**38,033**	**19,934**	**18,099**	**8,463**
Under age 18	16,073	13,124	7,035	6,090	2,949
Aged 18 to 24	6,117	5,083	2,809	2,274	1,034
Aged 25 to 34	6,633	5,476	3,057	2,419	1,157
Aged 35 to 44	4,960	4,166	2,208	1,958	794
Aged 45 to 54	4,675	3,815	1,798	2,017	861
Aged 55 to 59	2,230	1,731	814	917	499
Aged 60 to 64	1,882	1,479	708	771	403
Aged 65 or older	3,926	3,159	1,506	1,653	767
POVERTY RATE					
Total people	**15.0%**	**14.5%**	**19.7%**	**11.2%**	**17.7%**
Under age 18	21.8	20.9	29.1	15.8	26.7
Aged 18 to 24	20.4	19.7	25.9	15.2	24.4
Aged 25 to 34	15.9	15.1	18.4	12.2	21.2
Aged 35 to 44	12.4	12.1	16.1	9.4	14.9
Aged 45 to 54	10.8	10.3	14.0	8.4	13.1
Aged 55 to 59	10.7	10.0	13.6	8.1	13.8
Aged 60 to 64	10.7	10.3	13.9	8.3	12.4
Aged 65 or older	9.1	9.0	12.5	7.2	9.4
PERCENT DISTRIBUTION OF POOR BY METROPOLITAN STATUS					
Total people	**100.0**	**81.8**	**42.9**	**38.9**	**18.2**
Under age 18	100.0	81.7	43.8	37.9	18.3
Aged 18 to 24	100.0	83.1	45.9	37.2	16.9
Aged 25 to 34	100.0	82.6	46.1	36.5	17.4
Aged 35 to 44	100.0	84.0	44.5	39.5	16.0
Aged 45 to 54	100.0	81.6	38.5	43.1	18.4
Aged 55 to 59	100.0	77.6	36.5	41.1	22.4
Aged 60 to 64	100.0	78.6	37.6	41.0	21.4
Aged 65 or older	100.0	80.5	38.4	42.1	19.5

Source: Bureau of the Census, 2013 Current Population Survey Annual Social and Economic Supplement, Internet site http:// www.census.gov/hhes/www/cpstables/032013/pov/toc.htm; calculations by New Strategist

Table 6.66 People below Poverty Level by Metropolitan Status, Race, and Hispanic Origin, 2012

(number and percent of people in poverty, and percent distribution of people below poverty level by metropolitan status, race, and Hispanic origin, 2012; numbers in thousands)

NUMBER IN POVERTY	total people in poverty	Asians	blacks	Hispanics	non-Hispanic whites
Total people	**46,496**	**2,072**	**11,809**	**13,616**	**18,940**
Metropolitan	38,033	2,010	10,045	12,501	13,911
Inside principal cities	19,934	1,315	6,444	7,200	5,261
Outside principal cities	18,099	695	3,601	5,301	8,650
Not metropolitan	8,463	62	1,765	1,115	5,029
POVERTY RATE					
Total people	**15.0%**	**11.4%**	**27.1%**	**25.6%**	**9.7%**
Metropolitan	14.5	11.5	25.6	25.4	8.8
Inside principal cities	19.7	15.5	30.0	28.7	11.2
Outside principal cities	11.2	7.7	20.3	21.9	7.8
Not metropolitan	17.7	9.8	40.7	28.9	13.5
PERCENT DISTRIBUTION OF POOR BY RACE AND HISPANIC ORIGIN					
Total people	**100.0**	**4.5**	**25.4**	**29.3**	**40.7**
Metropolitan	100.0	5.3	26.4	32.9	36.6
Inside principal cities	100.0	6.6	32.3	36.1	26.4
Outside principal cities	100.0	3.8	19.9	29.3	47.8
Not metropolitan	100.0	0.7	20.9	13.2	59.4

Note: Asians and blacks include those who identify themselves as being of the race alone and those who identify themselves as being of the race in combination with other races. Non-Hispanic whites are those who identify themselves as white alone and not Hispanic. Numbers do not add to total because not all races are shown and Hispanics may be of any race.
Source: Bureau of the Census, 2013 Current Population Survey Annual Social and Economic Supplement, Internet site http:// www.census.gov/hhes/www/cpstables/032013/pov/toc.htm; calculations by New Strategist

Table 6.67 People below Poverty Level by Metropolitan Area, 2012

(number and percent of people below poverty level in metropolitan areas with at least 1 million population, and rank of large metropolitan areas by poverty rate, 2012)

	number in poverty	poverty rate	poverty rate rank among metros
Atlanta–Sandy Springs–Marietta, GA	887,901	16.6%	12
Austin–Round Rock–San Marcos, TX	278,461	15.5	22
Baltimore–Towson, MD	303,704	11.3	47
Birmingham–Hoover, AL	186,891	16.8	11
Boston–Cambridge–Quincy, MA–NH	479,126	10.7	50
Buffalo–Niagara Falls, NY	157,407	14.2	34
Charlotte–Gastonia–Rock Hill, NC–SC	272,027	15.1	23
Chicago–Joliet–Naperville, IL–IN–WI	1,362,635	14.5	29
Cincinnati–Middletown, OH–KY–IN	313,902	14.9	27
Cleveland–Elyria–Mentor, OH	314,832	15.6	21
Columbus, OH	275,385	15.1	24
Dallas–Fort Worth–Arlington, TX	984,719	15.0	25
Denver–Aurora–Broomfield, CO	332,043	12.7	40
Detroit–Warren–Livonia, MI	740,712	17.4	6
Grand Rapids–Wyoming, MI	126,882	16.5	13
Hartford–West Hartford–East Hartford, CT	127,371	10.9	48
Houston–Sugar Land–Baytown, TX	1,005,192	16.4	14
Indianapolis–Carmel, IN	253,758	14.4	30
Jacksonville, FL	211,746	15.7	20
Kansas City, MO–KS	261,177	12.9	39
Las Vegas–Paradise, NV	323,075	16.4	15
Los Angeles–Long Beach–Santa Ana, CA	2,266,193	17.6	4
Louisville/Jefferson County, KY–IN	205,800	16.1	18
Memphis, TN–MS–AR	259,780	19.9	1
Miami–Fort Lauderdale–Pompano Beach, FL	993,904	17.5	5
Milwaukee–Waukesha–West Allis, WI	244,236	15.9	19
Minneapolis–St. Paul–Bloomington, MN–WI	352,560	10.7	51
Nashville-Davidson–Murfreesboro–Franklin, TN	229,686	14.3	32
New Orleans–Metairie–Kenner, LA	230,153	19.4	2
New York–Northern New Jersey–Long Island, NY–NJ–PA	2,785,196	14.8	28
Oklahoma City, OK	204,759	16.2	17
Orlando–Kissimmee–Sanford, FL	369,925	16.9	9
Philadelphia–Camden–Wilmington, PA–NJ–DE–MD	787,217	13.4	37
Phoenix–Mesa–Glendale, AZ	741,322	17.4	7
Pittsburgh, PA	279,386	12.1	43
Portland–Vancouver–Hillsboro, OR–WA	316,515	14.0	35
Providence–New Bedford–Fall River, RI–MA	209,423	13.6	36
Raleigh–Cary, NC	147,281	12.7	41
Richmond, VA	147,786	11.9	44

	number in poverty	poverty rate	poverty rate rank among metros
Riverside–San Bernardino–Ontario, CA	813,251	19.0%	3
Rochester, NY	146,943	14.4	31
Sacramento–Arden-Arcade–Roseville, CA	366,076	16.9	10
Salt Lake City, UT	146,232	12.7	42
San Antonio–New Braunfels, TX	378,226	17.3	8
San Diego–Carlsbad–San Marcos, CA	465,295	15.0	26
San Francisco–Oakland–Fremont, CA	522,229	11.9	45
San Jose–Sunnyvale–Santa Clara, CA	202,357	10.8	49
Seattle–Tacoma–Bellevue, WA	409,239	11.7	46
St. Louis, MO–IL	394,288	14.3	33
Tampa–St. Petersburg–Clearwater, FL	458,689	16.4	16
Virginia Beach–Norfolk–Newport News, VA–NC	212,979	13.1	38
Washington–Arlington–Alexandria, DC–VA–MD–WV	477,661	8.4	52

Source: Bureau of the Census, 2012 American Community Survey, Internet site http://factfinder2.census.gov/faces/nav/jsf/pages/index.xhtml; calculations by New Strategist

More than One-Third of Nation's Poor Live in Four States

Twelve states are home to more than 1 million poor people.

Thirty-six percent of poor Americans live in California, Texas, New York, or Florida. Other states with more than 1 million poor residents are Arizona, Georgia, Illinois, Michigan, North Carolina, Ohio, Pennsylvania, and Tennessee. Together, the 12 states with at least 1 million poor residents account for the 62 percent majority of the nation's poor.

Among the 50 states, the poverty rate is highest in Mississippi, at 22.0 percent in 2012. The poverty rate is lowest in New Hampshire, at 8.1 percent. The poverty rate is below 10 percent in only three other states: New Jersey, Maryland, and Wyoming.

■ The poverty rate is likely to remain high in most states until jobs become more plentiful.

Poverty rate is highest in Mississippi and lowest in New Hampshire

(percent of people in poverty in the states with the highest and lowest poverty rate, 2012)

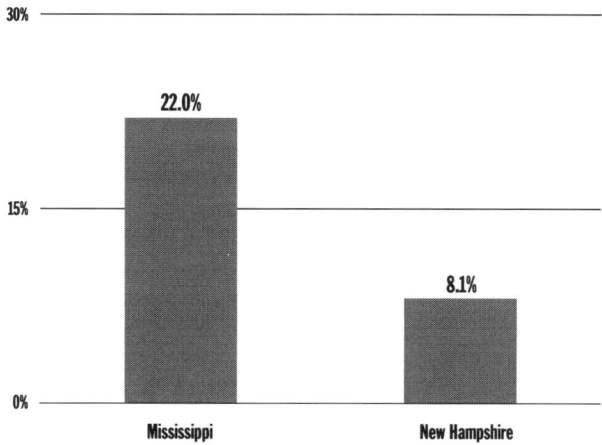

Table 6.68 People below Poverty Level by State, 2012

(number and percent of people below poverty level by state, and rank of states by poverty rate; number in poverty in thousands)

	number in poverty	poverty rate	poverty rate rank among states
United States	**46,496**	**15.0%**	–
Alabama	777	16.2	16
Alaska	70	10.0	46
Arizona	1,260	19.0	5
Arkansas	584	20.1	4
California	6,015	15.9	17
Colorado	613	11.9	36
Connecticut	363	10.3	44
Delaware	121	13.5	30
District of Columbia	116	18.4	7
Florida	2,926	15.3	20
Georgia	1,752	18.1	8
Hawaii	188	13.8	26
Idaho	229	14.4	23
Illinois	1,608	12.6	34
Indiana	964	15.2	22
Iowa	310	10.3	45
Kansas	397	14.0	24
Kentucky	776	17.9	10
Louisiana	944	21.1	2
Maine	170	12.8	33
Maryland	585	9.9	48
Massachusetts	743	11.3	40
Michigan	1,331	13.7	27
Minnesota	534	10.0	47
Mississippi	636	22.0	1
Missouri	905	15.2	21
Montana	134	13.4	31
Nebraska	226	12.2	35
Nevada	433	15.8	18
New Hampshire	106	8.1	51
New Jersey	814	9.3	50
New Mexico	420	20.4	3
New York	3,328	17.2	11
North Carolina	1,652	17.2	12
North Dakota	79	11.4	38
Ohio	1,751	15.4	19
Oklahoma	668	18.0	9
Oregon	523	13.5	29
Pennsylvania	1,756	13.9	25

	number in poverty	poverty rate	poverty rate rank among states
Rhode Island	141	13.6%	28
South Carolina	779	16.7	15
South Dakota	106	12.8	32
Tennessee	1,194	18.6	6
Texas	4,444	17.0	13
Utah	312	11.0	42
Vermont	69	11.2	41
Virginia	850	10.6	43
Washington	796	11.6	37
West Virginia	301	16.7	14
Wisconsin	640	11.4	39
Wyoming	56	9.6	49

Note: "–" means not applicable.
Source: Bureau of the Census, 2013 Current Population Survey Annual Social and Economic Supplement, Internet site http://www.census.gov/hhes/www/cpstables/032013/pov/toc.htm; calculations by New Strategist

Glossary

adjusted for inflation A dollar value that has been adjusted for the rise in the cost of living by use of the consumer price index.

age Classification by age is based on the age of the person at his/her last birthday.

American Community Survey The ACS is an on-going nationwide survey of 250,000 households per month, providing detailed demographic data at the community level. Designed to replace the census long-form questionnaire, the ACS includes more than 60 questions that formerly appeared on the long form, such as questions about language spoken at home, income, and education. ACS data are available for areas as small as census tracts.

American Housing Survey The AHS collects national and metropolitan-level data on the nation's housing, including apartments, single-family homes, and mobile homes. The Census Bureau conducts the nationally representative survey, with a sample of 55,000 homes, for the Department of Housing and Urban Development every other year.

American Indians American Indians include Alaska Natives unless those groups are shown separately.

American Time Use Survey Under contract with the Bureau of Labor Statistics, the Census Bureau collects ATUS information, revealing how people spend their time. The ATUS sample is drawn from U.S. households completing their final month of interviews for the Current Population Survey. One individual from each selected household is chosen to participate in the ATUS. Respondents are interviewed by telephone about their time use during the previous 24 hours.

Asian The term "Asian" includes Native Hawaiians and other Pacific Islanders unless those groups are shown separately.

baby boom Americans born between 1946 and 1964.

baby bust Americans born between 1965 and 1976. Also known as Generation X.

Behavioral Risk Factor Surveillance System The BRFSS is a collaborative project of the Centers for Disease Control and Prevention and U.S. states and territories. It is an ongoing data collection program designed to measure behavioral risk factors in the adult population aged 18 or older. All 50 states, three territories, and the District of Columbia take part in the survey, making the BRFSS the primary source of information on the health-related behaviors of Americans.

black The black racial category includes those who identified themselves as "black" or "African American."

Consumer Expenditure Survey The CEX is an ongoing study of the day-to-day spending of American households administered by the Bureau of Labor Statistics. The CEX includes an interview survey and a diary survey. The average spending figures shown are the integrated data from both the diary and interview components of the survey. Two separate, nationally representative samples are used for the interview and diary surveys. For the interview survey, about 7,500 consumer units are interviewed on a rotating panel basis each quarter for five consecutive quarters. For the diary survey, 7,500 consumer units keep weekly diaries of spending for two consecutive weeks.

consumer unit *(on spending tables only)* For convenience, the terms consumer unit and household are used interchangeably in the spending section of this book, although consumer units are somewhat different from the Census Bureau's households. A consumer unit includes all the related members of a household or any financially independent member of a household. A household may include more than one consumer unit.

Current Population Survey The CPS is a nationally representative survey of the civilian noninstitutional population aged 15 or older. It is taken monthly by the Census Bureau for the Bureau of Labor Statistics, collecting information from 60,000 households on employment and unemployment. In March of each year the survey includes the Annual Social and Economic Supplement, which is the source of most national data on the characteristics of Americans, such as educational attainment, living arrangements, and incomes.

disability The National Health Interview Survey

estimates the number of people aged 18 or older who have difficulty in physical functioning, probing whether respondents could perform nine activities by themselves without using special equipment. The categories are walking a quarter mile; standing for two hours; sitting for two hours; walking up 10 steps without resting; stooping, bending, kneeling; reaching over one's head; grasping or handling small objects; carrying a 10-pound object; and pushing/pulling a large object. Adults who reported that any of these activities was very difficult or they could not do it at all were defined as having physical difficulties.

dual-earner couple A married couple in which both the householder and the householder's spouse are in the labor force.

earnings A type of income, earnings is the amount of money a person receives from his or her job. *See also* Income.

employed All civilians who did any work as a paid employee or farmer/self-employed worker or who worked 15 hours or more as an unpaid farm worker or in a family-owned business during the reference period. All those who have jobs but are temporarily absent from their jobs due to illness, bad weather, vacation, labor management dispute, or personal reasons are considered employed.

expenditure The transaction cost including excise and sales taxes of goods and services acquired during the survey period. The full cost of each purchase is recorded even though full payment may not have been made at the date of purchase. Average expenditure figures may be artificially low for infrequently purchased items such as cars because figures are calculated using all consumer units within a demographic segment rather than just purchasers. Expenditure estimates include money spent on gifts for others.

family A group of two or more people (one of whom is the householder) related by birth, marriage, or adoption and living in the same household.

family household A household maintained by a householder who lives with one or more people related to him or her by blood, marriage, or adoption.

female/male householder A woman or man who maintains a household without a spouse present. May head family or nonfamily household.

foreign-born population People who are not U.S. citizens at birth.

full-time employment Full-time is 35 or more hours of work per week during a majority of the weeks worked.

full-time, year-round Indicates 50 or more weeks of full-time employment during the previous calendar year.

General Social Survey The GSS is a biennial survey of the attitudes of Americans taken by the University of Chicago's National Opinion Research Center. NORC conducts the GSS through face-to-face interviews with an independently drawn, representative sample of 1,500 to 3,000 noninstitutionalized people aged 18 or older who live in the United States.

generation X Americans born between 1965 and 1976. Also known as the baby-bust generation.

Hispanic Because Hispanic is an ethnic origin rather than a race, Hispanics may be of any race. While most Hispanics are white, there are black, Asian, American Indian, and even Native Hawaiian Hispanics.

household All the persons who occupy a housing unit. A household includes the related family members and all the unrelated persons, if any, such as lodgers, foster children, wards, or employees who share the housing unit. A person living alone is counted as a household. A group of unrelated people who share a housing unit as roommates or unmarried partners is also counted as a household. Households do not include group quarters such as college dormitories, prisons, or nursing homes.

household, race/ethnicity of Households are categorized according to the race or ethnicity of the householder only.

householder The householder is the person (or one of the persons) in whose name the housing unit is owned or rented or, if there is no such person, any adult member. With married couples, the householder may be either the husband or wife. The householder is the reference person for the household.

householder, age of The age of the householder is used to categorize households into age groups such as those used in this book. Married couples, for example, are classified according to the age of either the husband or wife, depending on which one identified him- or herself as the householder.

housing unit A housing unit is a house, an apartment, a group of rooms, or a single room occupied or intended for occupancy as separate living quarters. Separate living quarters are those in which the occupants do not live and eat with any other persons in the structure and that have direct access from the outside of the building or through a common hall that is used or intended for use by the occupants of another unit or by the general public. The occupants may be a single family, one person living alone, two or more families living together, or any other group of related or unrelated persons who share living arrangements.

Housing Vacancy Survey The HVS is a supplement to the Current Population Survey, providing quarterly and annual data on rental and homeowner vacancy rates, characteristics of units available for occupancy, and homeownership rates by age, household type, region, state, and metropolitan area. The Current Population Survey sample includes 60,000 occupied housing units and about 9,000 vacant units.

housing value The respondent's estimate of how much his or her house and lot would sell for if it were for sale.

iGeneration Americans born between 1995 and 2009.

immigrants Aliens admitted for legal permanent residence in the United States.

income Money received in the preceding calendar year by a person aged 15 or older from any of the following sources: earnings from longest job (or self-employment), earnings from jobs other than longest job, unemployment compensation, workers' compensation, Social Security, Supplemental Security income, public assistance, veterans' payments, survivor benefits, disability benefits, retirement pensions, interest, dividends, rents and royalties or estates and trusts, educational assistance, alimony, child support, financial assistance from outside the household, and other periodic income. Income is reported in several ways in this book. Household income is the combined income of all household members. Income of persons is all income accruing to a person from all sources. Earnings are the money a person receives from his or her job.

industry Refers to the industry in which a person worked longest in the preceding calendar year.

job tenure The length of time a person has been employed continuously by the same employer.

labor force The labor force tables in this book show the civilian labor force only. The labor force includes both the employed and the unemployed (people who are looking for work). People are counted as in the labor force if they were working or looking for work during the reference week in which the Census Bureau fields the Current Population Survey.

labor force participation rate The percent of the civilian noninstitutional population that is in the civilian labor force, which includes both the employed and the unemployed.

male householder *See* Female/Male Householder.

married couples with or without children under age 18 Refers to married couples with or without own children under age 18 living in the same household. Couples without children under age 18 may be parents of grown children who live elsewhere or they could be childless couples.

median The median is the amount that divides the population or households into two equal portions: one below and one above the median. Medians can be calculated for income, age, and many other characteristics.

median income The amount that divides the income distribution into two equal groups, half having incomes above the median, half having incomes below the median. The medians for households or families are based on all households or families. The median for persons are based on all persons aged 15 or older with income.

metropolitan statistical area To be defined as an MSA, an area must include a city with 50,000 or more inhabitants, or a Census Bureau–defined urbanized area of at least 50,000 inhabitants and a total metropolitan population of at least 100,000 (75,000 in New England). The county (or counties) that contains the largest city becomes the "central county" (counties), along with any adjacent counties that have at least 50 percent of their population in the urbanized area surrounding the largest city. Additional "outlying counties" are included in the MSA if they meet specified requirements of commuting to the central counties and other selected requirements of metropolitan character (such as population density and percent urban). In New England, MSAs are defined in terms of cities and towns rather than counties. For this reason, the concept of New England County Metropolitan Area is used to define metropolitan areas in the New England division.

millennial generation Americans born between 1977 and 1994.

mobility status People are classified according to their mobility status on the basis of a comparison between their place of residence at the time of the March Current Population Survey and their place of residence in March of the previous year. Nonmovers are people living in the same house at the end of the period as at the beginning of the period. Movers are people living in a different house at the end of the period from that at the beginning of the period. Movers from abroad are either citizens or aliens whose place of residence is outside the United States at the beginning of the period, that is, in an outlying area under the jurisdiction of the United States or in a foreign country. The mobility status for children is fully allocated from the mother if she is in the household; otherwise it is allocated from the householder.

National Health and Nutrition Examination Survey The NHANES is a continuous survey of a representative sample of the U.S. civilian noninstitutionalized population. Respondents are interviewed at home about their health and nutrition, and the interview is followed up by a physical examination that measures such things as height and weight in mobile examination centers.

National Health Interview Survey The NHIS is a continuing nationwide sample survey of the civilian noninstitutional population of the United States conducted by the Census Bureau for the National Center for Health Statistics. In interviews each year, data are collected from more than 100,000 people about their illnesses, injuries, impairments, chronic and acute conditions, activity limitations, and use of health services.

National Household Education Survey Sponsored by the National Center for Education Statistics, the NHES provides descriptive data on the educational activities of the U.S. population, including after-school care and adult education. The NHES is a system of telephone surveys of a representative sample of 45,000 to 60,000 households in the United States.

National Survey of Family Growth Sponsored by the National Center for Health Statistics, the NSFG is a periodic nationally representative survey of the civilian noninstitutionalized population aged 15 to 44. In-person interviews are completed with men and women, collecting data on marriage, divorce, contraception, and infertility. The 2006–10 survey updates previous NSFG surveys taken in 1973, 1976, 1988, 1995, and 2002.

National Survey on Drug Use and Health The NSDUH is an annual survey of a nationally representative sample of people aged 12 or older living in households, noninstitutional group quarters (such as college dorms), and military bases in the United States. It is the primary source of information about illegal drug use in the United States and has been conducted since 1971. Interviews are held in person and incorporate procedures (such as anonymity and computer-assisted interviewing) that will increase respondents' cooperation and willingness to report honestly about their illicit drug use behavior.

nonfamily household A household maintained by a householder who lives alone or who lives with people to whom he or she is not related.

nonfamily householder A householder who lives alone or with nonrelatives.

non-Hispanic People who do not identify themselves as Hispanic are classified as non-Hispanic. Non-Hispanics may be of any race.

non-Hispanic white People who identify their race as white and who do not indicate a Hispanic origin.

nonmetropolitan area Counties that are not classified as metropolitan areas.

occupation Occupational classification is based on the kind of work a person did at his or her job during the previous calendar year. If a person changed jobs during the year, the data refer to the occupation of the job held the longest during that year.

occupied housing units A housing unit is classified as occupied if a person or group of people is living in it or if the occupants are only temporarily absent—on vacation, for example. By definition, the count of occupied housing units is the same as the count of households.

outside principal city The portion of a metropolitan county or counties that falls outside of the principal city or cities; generally regarded as the suburbs.

own children Own children are sons and daughters, including stepchildren and adopted children, of the householder. The totals include never-married children living away from home in college dormitories.

owner occupied A housing unit is "owner occupied" if the owner lives in the unit, even if it is mortgaged or not fully paid for. A cooperative or condominium unit is "owner occupied" only if the owner lives in it. All other occupied units are classified as "renter occupied."

part-time employment Part-time is less than 35 hours of work per week in a majority of the weeks worked during the year.

percent change The change (either positive or negative) in a measure that is expressed as a proportion of the starting measure. When median income changes from $20,000 to $25,000, for example, this is a 25 percent increase.

percentage point change The change (either positive or negative) in a value that is already expressed as a percentage. When a labor force participation rate changes from 70 percent to 75 percent, for example, this is a 5 percentage point increase.

poverty level The official income threshold below which families and people are classified as living in poverty. The threshold rises each year with inflation and varies depending on family size and age of householder.

principal city The largest city in a metropolitan area is called the principal or central city. The balance of the metropolitan area outside the principal or central city is regarded as the "suburbs."

proportion or share The value of a part expressed as a percentage of the whole. If there are 4 million people aged 25 and 3 million of them are white, then the white proportion is 75 percent.

race Race is self-reported and can be defined in three ways. The "race alone" population comprises people who identify themselves as being of only one race. The "race in combination" population comprises people who identify themselves as being of more than one race, such as white and black. The "race, alone or in combination" population includes both those who identify themselves as being of one race and those who identify themselves as being of more than one race.

recession generation Americans born from 2010 to the present.

regions The four major regions and nine census divisions of the United States are the state groupings as shown below:
Northeast:
—New England: Connecticut, Maine, Massachusetts, New Hampshire, Rhode Island, and Vermont
—Middle Atlantic: New Jersey, New York, and Pennsylvania
Midwest:
—East North Central: Illinois, Indiana, Michigan, Ohio, and Wisconsin
—West North Central: Iowa, Kansas, Minnesota, Missouri, Nebraska, North Dakota, and South Dakota
South:
—South Atlantic: Delaware, District of Columbia, Florida, Georgia, Maryland, North Carolina, South Carolina, Virginia, and West Virginia
—East South Central: Alabama, Kentucky, Mississippi, and Tennessee
—West South Central: Arkansas, Louisiana, Oklahoma, and Texas
West:
—Mountain: Arizona, Colorado, Idaho, Montana, Nevada, New Mexico, Utah, and Wyoming
—Pacific: Alaska, California, Hawaii, Oregon, and Washington

renter occupied *See* Owner Occupied.

Retirement Confidence Survey The RCS—sponsored by the Employee Benefit Research Institute, the American Savings Education Council, and Mathew Greenwald & Associates—is an annual survey of a nationally representative sample of 1,000 people aged 25 or older. Respondents are asked a core set of questions that have been included in the survey since 1996, measuring attitudes and behavior toward retirement, as well as additional questions about current retirement issues.

rounding Percentages are rounded to the nearest tenth of a percent; therefore, the percentages in a distribution do not always add exactly to 100.0 percent. The totals, however, are always shown as 100.0. Moreover, individual figures are rounded to the nearest thousand without being adjusted to group totals, which are independently rounded; percentages are based on the unrounded numbers.

self-employment A person is categorized as self-employed if he or she was self-employed in the job held longest during the reference period. Persons who report self-employment from a second job are excluded, but those who report wage and salary income from a second job are included. Unpaid workers in family businesses are excluded. Self-employment statistics include only nonagricultural workers and exclude people who work for themselves in incorporated business.

sex ratio The number of men per 100 women.

suburbs *See* Outside Principal City.

Survey of Income and Program Participation The Survey of Income and Program Participation is a continuous, monthly panel survey of up to 36,700 households conducted by the Census Bureau. It is designed to measure the effectiveness of existing federal, state, and local programs and to measure economic well-being, including wealth, asset ownership, and debt.

unemployed Unemployed people are those who, during the survey period, had no employment but were available and looking for work. Those who were laid off from their jobs and were waiting to be recalled are also classified as unemployed.

white The white racial category includes many Hispanics (who may be of any race) unless the term "non-Hispanic white" is used.

Youth Risk Behavior Surveillance System The Centers for Disease Control created the YRBSS to monitor health risks being taken by young people at the national, state, and local level. The national survey is taken every two years based on a nationally representative sample of 16,000 students in 9th through 12th grade in public and private schools.

Bibliography

Bureau of Labor Statistics
   Internet site http://www.bls.gov/
   —2012 Consumer Expenditure Survey, Internet site http://www.bls.gov/cex/home.htm

Bureau of the Census
   Internet site http://www.census.gov/
   —2013 Current Population Survey, Annual Social and Economic Supplement, Internet site http://www.census.gov/hhes/www/income/data/
   —American Community Survey, Internet site http://factfinder2.census.gov/faces/nav/jsf/pages/index.xhtml
   —Historical Income Data, Current Population Survey Annual Social and Economic Supplements, Internet site http://www.census.gov/hhes/www/income/data/historical/index.html
   —Historical Poverty Tables, Current Population Survey Annual Social and Economic Supplements, Internet site http://www.census.gov/hhes/www/poverty/data/historical/index.html
   —*Income, Poverty, and Health Insurance Coverage in the United States: 2012*, Current Population Report P60-245, 2013, Internet site http://www.census.gov/hhes/www/income/
   —Wealth and Asset Ownership, Survey of Income and Program Participation, Internet site http://www.census.gov/people/wealth/

Employee Benefit Research Institute
   Internet site http://www.ebri.org/
   —Retirement Confidence Survey, Internet site http://www.ebri.org/surveys/rcs/

Index

401(k) (as asset)
  by age of householder, 300
  by household type, 302–304
  by race and Hispanic origin of householder, 306

age
  assets by, 300–304
  at retirement, expected, 317
  debt by, 308–309
  discretionary income by, 277
  household income by, 13, 47–81
  income quintile by, 37–39
  men's earnings by, 181–185
  men's income by, 139, 142–145, 159–163
  net worth by, 291–296
  poverty by, 338–339, 384–396, 400–408, 411
  retirement savings by, 318
  women's earnings by, 251–255
  women's income by, 205, 208–211, 229–233
aggregate income, 9
alimony
  source of men's income, 195–199
  source of women's income, 265–269
Asian households
  assets of, 306
  by income quintile, 37–39
  debt of, 315
  discretionary income of, 283
  in poverty
    by family type, 325, 331, 361–382
    by metropolitan residence, 375–382
    by number of earners, 361–364
    by region, 366–373
    historical, 325, 331
  income of
    by age, 48, 54, 60, 66, 72, 78
    by education, 113
    by household type, 42, 54, 60, 66, 72, 78, 90, 101, 107
    by number of earners, 84
    by presence of children, 90, 101, 107
    by region, 124–127
    historical, 17
  net worth of, 298
Asians
  earnings of
    by education, 187, 257
    by work status, 175, 245
    historical, 151, 217
    men, 151, 175, 187
    women, 217, 245, 257

  in poverty
    by age, 384, 387, 393, 401
    by educational attainment, 398
    by family status, 393
    by metropolitan status, 412
    by region, 409
    by sex, 387, 401
    by work status, 401
    historical, 341–342
  income of
    by age, 142, 160, 208, 230
    by region, 167, 237
    by source, 196, 266
    historical, 141–142, 207–208
    men, 141–142, 160, 164, 167, 196
    women, 207–208, 230, 234, 237, 266
assets
  by age of householder, 300
  by household type, 302–304
  by race and Hispanic origin of householder, 306
associate's degree. *See* Educational attainment.
Atlanta–Sandy Spring–Marietta, GA metropolitan
  area
  household income, 132–133
  people in poverty, 413–414
Austin–Round Rock–San Marcos TX metropolitan
  area
  household income, 132–133
  people in poverty, 413–414

bachelor's degree. *See* Educational attainment.
Baltimore–Towson, MD metropolitan area
  household income, 132–133
  people in poverty, 413–414
Birmingham–Hoover, AL metropolitan area
  household income, 132–133
  people in poverty, 413–414
black households
  assets of, 306
  by income quintile, 37–39
  debt of, 315
  discretionary income of, 283
  in poverty
    by family type, 326, 332, 361–382
    by metropolitan residence, 375–382
    by number of earners, 361–364
    by region, 366–373
    historical, 326, 332
  income of
    by age, 49, 55, 61, 67, 73, 79
    by education, 114
    by household type, 43, 55, 61, 67, 73, 79, 91, 102, 108
    by number of earners, 85
    by presence of children, 91, 102, 108
    by region, 124–127

historical, 17
net worth of, 298
blacks
  earnings of
    by education, 188, 258
    by work status, 176, 246
    historical, 151, 217
    men, 151, 176, 188
    women, 217, 246, 258
  in poverty
    by age, 384, 388, 394, 402
    by educational attainment, 398
    by family status, 394
    by metropolitan status, 412
    by region, 409
    by sex, 388, 402
    by work status, 402
    historical, 341–342
  income of
    by age, 143, 161, 209, 231
    by region, 168, 238
    by source, 197, 267
    historical, 141, 143, 207, 209
    men, 141, 143, 161, 164, 168, 197
    women, 207, 209, 232, 234, 238, 267
Boston–Cambridge–Quincy, MA–NH metropolitan
  area
  household income, 132–133
  people in poverty, 413–414
Buffalo–Niagara Falls, NY metropolitan area
  household income, 132–133
  people in poverty, 413–414
business debt
  by age of householder, 309
  by household type, 311–313
  by race and Hispanic origin of householder, 315
business equity (as asset)
  by age of householder, 300
  by household type, 302–304
  by race and Hispanic origin of householder, 306

central cities. *See* Metropolitan status.
Charlotte–Gastonia–Rock Hill, NC–SC
  metropolitan area
  household income, 132–133
  people in poverty, 413–414
checking account (as asset)
  by age of householder, 300
  by household type, 302–304
  by race and Hispanic origin of householder, 306
Chicago–Joliet–Naperville, IL–IN–WI
  metropolitan area
  household income, 132–133
  people in poverty, 413–414
child support
  source of men's income, 195–199

source of women's income, 265–269
Cincinnati–Middletown, OH–KY–IN metropolitan
  area
  household income, 132–133
  people in poverty, 413–414
Cleveland–Elyria–Mentor, OH metropolitan area
  household income, 132–133
  people in poverty, 413–414
college degree. *See* Educational attainment.
Columbus, OH metropolitan area
  household income, 132–133
  people in poverty, 413–414
credit card debt
  by age of householder, 309
  by household type, 311–313
  by race and Hispanic origin of householder, 315

Dallas–Fort Worth–Arlington, TX metropolitan
  area
  household income, 132–133
  people in poverty, 413–414
debt of households
  by age of householder, 308–309
  by household type, 311–313
  by race and Hispanic origin of householder, 315
Denver–Aurora–Broomfield, CO metropolitan area
  household income, 132–133
  people in poverty, 413–414
Detroit–Warren–Livonia, MI metropolitan area
  household income, 132–133
  people in poverty, 413–414
disability, as reason poor did not work, 406
disability benefits
  source of men's income, 195–199
  source of women's income, 265–269
discretionary household income, definition of,
  271–274
discretionary household spending, 271, 275
disposable household income, 271
dividends
  source of men's income, 195–199
  source of women's income, 265–269
doctoral degree. *See* Educational attainment.
dual-earner couples. *See* Households, married
  couple.

earners
  by household income quintile, 37–39
  household income by, 23, 83–87
  poverty rate by number of, 361–364
earnings. *See also* Males, earnings of; *and*
  Females, earnings of.
  as source of men's income, 195–199
  as source of women's income, 265–269
education debt
  by age of householder, 309

by household type, 311–313
by race and Hispanic origin of householder, 315
educational assistance
source of men's income, 195–199
source of women's income, 265–269
educational attainment
discretionary income by, 287
earnings by race and Hispanic origin, 187–190
earnings of men by, 153, 180–190
earnings of women by, 219, 250–260
household income by, 19, 112–116
people in poverty by, 398

families. *See* Households.
family, as reason poor did not work, 406
females. *See also* Households, female-headed; *and*
    Households, women living alone.
earnings of
    by age, 251–255
    as percent of men's earnings, 223
    by education, 219, 250–260
    by occupation, 221, 262–263
    by race and Hispanic origin, 217, 245–248,
        257–260
    by work status, 215, 244–248
    historical, 215–223
in poverty
    by age, 386–390, 400–406
    by race and Hispanic origin, 387–390,
        400–404
    by reason for not working, 406
    by work status, 400–404
    historical, 336
income of
    by age, 205, 208–211, 229–233
    by metropolitan status, 242
    by race and Hispanic origin, 207–211,
        230–234, 237–240
    by region, 213, 236–240
    by source, 265–269
    historical, 205–213
wives earning more than husbands, 225
foreign-born, in poverty, 347
full-time workers
    below poverty level, 357, 400–404
    earnings of, 149–155, 174–193, 215–223,
        244–263
    income of, 159–172, 229–242

Grand Rapids–Wyoming, MI metropolitan area
    household income, 132–133
    people in poverty, 413–414

Hartford–West Hartford–East Hartford, CT
    metropolitan area
    household income, 132–133

people in poverty, 413–414
Hispanic households
assets of, 306
by income quintile, 37–39
debt of, 315
discretionary income of, 283
in poverty
    by family type, 327, 333, 361–382
    by metropolitan residence, 375–382
    by number of earners, 361–364
    by region, 366–373
    historical, 327, 333
income of
    by age, 50, 56, 62, 68, 74, 80
    by education, 115
    by household type, 44, 56, 62, 68, 74, 80, 92,
        103, 109
    by number of earners, 86
    by presence of children, 92, 103, 109
    by region, 124–127
    historical, 17
net worth of, 298
Hispanics
earnings of
    by education, 189, 259
    by work status, 177, 247
    historical, 151, 217
    men, 151, 177, 189
    women, 217, 247, 259
in poverty
    by age, 384, 389, 395, 403
    by educational attainment, 398
    by family status, 395
    by metropolitan status, 412
    by region, 409
    by sex, 389, 403
    by work status, 403
    historical, 341–342
income of
    by age, 144, 162, 210, 232
    by region, 169, 239
    by source, 198, 268
    historical, 141, 144, 207, 210
    men, 141, 144, 162, 164, 169, 198
    women, 207, 210, 232, 234, 239, 268
homeownership status
    income quintile by, 37–39
    of households, 300–306
household income
    aggregate, share of, 9
    by age of householder, 13, 47–81
    by census division, 119–122
    by educational attainment, 19, 112–116
    by household size, 21
    by household type, 15, 25–27, 29, 41–45, 53–81,
        89–110

by metropolitan residence, 131–133
by number of earners, 23, 83–87
by presence of children, 25–27, 89–110
by quintile, 9, 37–39
by race and Hispanic origin, 17, 42–93,
    100–116, 124–127
by region, 31, 118–127
by state, 33–34, 129–130
by work experience of husband and wife, 29,
    95–98
discretionary by, 279
historical, 9–34
households, female-headed
assets of, 303
by income quintile, 37–39
debt of, 312
in poverty, 322–334, 363, 370–371, 379–380
income by age of householder, 59–63
income by presence of children, 26, 100–104
income by race and Hispanic origin, 42–45,
    60–63, 101–104
income, historical, 15, 26
net worth of, 295
people in poverty living in, 292–296
households, male-headed
assets of, 304
by income quintile, 37–39
debt of, 313
in poverty, 322–334, 364, 372–373, 381–382
income by age of householder, 65–69
income by presence of children, 27, 106–110
income by race and Hispanic origin, 42–45,
    66–69, 107–110
income, historical, 15, 27
net worth of, 296
people in poverty living in, 292–296
households, married couple
assets of, 302
by income quintile, 37–39
by work experience of husband and wife, 29,
    95–98
debt of, 311
discretionary income of, 281
in poverty, 322–334, 362, 368–369, 377–378
income by age of householder, 53–57
income by presence of children, 25, 89–93
income by race and Hispanic origin, 42–45,
    54–57, 90–93
income, historical, 15, 25, 29
net worth of, 294
people in poverty living in, 292–296
wives earning more than husbands, 225
households, men living alone
by age of householder, 77–81
by income quintile, 37–39
income by race and Hispanic origin, 42–45,

78–81
income, historical, 15
households, single-earner
by income quintile, 37–39
in poverty, 361–364
income by race and Hispanic origin, 83–87
income, historical, 23
households, single-parent, discretionary income
    of, 281
households, single-person, discretionary income of,
    281. See also Households, men living
    alone; and Households, women living alone.
households, two-earner
by income quintile, 37–39
income by race and Hispanic origin, 83–87
in poverty, 361–364
income, historical, 23
households, women living alone
by age of householder, 71–75
by income quintile, 37–39
income by race and Hispanic origin, 42–45,
    72–75
income, historical, 15
house (as asset). See also Mortgage debt and
    Homeownership status.
by age of householder, 300
by household type, 302–304
by race and Hispanic origin of householder, 306
Houston–Sugar Land–Baytown, TX metropolitan
    area
household income, 132–133
people in poverty, 413–414

Indianapolis–Carmel, IN metropolitan area
household income, 132–133
people in poverty, 413–414
interest-earning assets
by age of householder, 300
by household type, 302–304
by race and Hispanic origin of householder, 306
interest income
source of men's income, 195–199
source of women's income, 265–269
IRA (as asset)
by age of householder, 300
by household type, 302–304
by race and Hispanic origin of householder, 306

Jacksonville, FL metropolitan area
household income, 132–133
people in poverty, 413–414

Kansas City, MO–KS metropolitan area
household income, 132–133
people in poverty, 413–414

Las Vegas–Paradise, NV metropolitan area
  household income, 132–133
  people in poverty, 413–414
Los Angeles–Long Beach–Santa Ana metropolitan
  area
  household income, 132–133
  people in poverty, 413–414
Louisville–Jefferson County, KY–IN metropolitan
  area
  household income, 132–133
  people in poverty, 413–414

males. *See also* Households, male-headed; *and*
  Households, men living alone.
  earnings of
    by age, 181–185
    by education, 153, 180–190
    by occupation, 155, 192–193
    by race and Hispanic origin, 151, 175–178,
      187–190
    by work status, 149, 174–178
    historical, 149, 151, 153, 155
    relative to women's, 223
  in poverty
    by age, 386–390, 400–406
    by race and Hispanic origin, 387–390,
      400–404
    by reason for not working, 406
    by work status, 400–404
    historical, 336
  income of
    by age, 139, 142–145, 159–163
    by metropolitan status, 172
    by race and Hispanic origin, 141–145,
      160–164, 167–170
    by region, 147, 166–170
    by source, 195–199
    historical, 139–148
master's degree. *See* Educational attainment.
Medicare, attitude toward, 317
Memphis, TN–MS–AR metropolitan area
  household income, 132–133
  people in poverty, 413–414
men. *See* Males.
metropolitan status. *See also* individual
    metropolitan areas.
  families in poverty by, 375–382
  household income by, 131–133
  men's income by, 172
  people in poverty by, 354–355, 411–414
  women's income by, 242
Miami–Fort Lauderdale–Pompano Beach, FL
    metropolitan area
  household income, 132–133
  people in poverty, 413–414
Midwest. *See* Region.

Milwaukee–Waukesha–West Allis, WI
    metropolitan area
  household income, 132–133
  people in poverty, 413–414
Minneapolis–St. Paul–Bloomington, MN–WI
    metropolitan area
  household income, 132–133
  people in poverty, 413–414
mortgage debt
  by age of householder, 309
  by household type, 311–313
  by race and Hispanic origin of householder, 315
mutual fund ownership
  by age of householder, 300
  by household type, 302–304
  by race and Hispanic origin of householder, 306

Nashville-Davidson–Murfreesboro–Franklin, TN
    metropolitan area
  household income, 132–133
  people in poverty, 413–414
net worth of households
  by age of householder, 291
  by household type, 293–296
  by race and Hispanic origin of householder, 298
New Orleans–Metairie–Kenner, LA metropolitan
    area
  household income, 132–133
  people in poverty, 413–414
New York–Northern New Jersey–Long Island,
    NY–NJ metropolitan area
  household income, 132–133
  people in poverty, 413–414
nonmetropolitan areas. *See* Metropolitan status.
Northeast. *See* Region.

occupation
  men's earnings by, 155, 192–193
  women's earnings by, 221, 262–263
Oklahoma City, OK metropolitan area
  household income, 132–133
  people in poverty, 413–414
Orlando–Kissimmee–Sanford, FL metropolitan
    area
  household income, 132–133
  people in poverty, 413–414

part-time workers
  earnings of men, 149, 174–178
  earnings of women, 215, 244–248
pension
  source of men's income, 195–199
  source of women's income, 265–269
Philadelphia–Camden–Wilmington, PA–NJ–DE–
    MD metropolitan area

household income, 132–133
people in poverty, 413–414
Phoenix–Mesa–Glendale, AZ metropolitan area
household income, 132–133
people in poverty, 413–414
Pittsburgh, PA metropolitan area
household income, 132–133
people in poverty, 413–414
Portland–Vancouver–Hillsboro, OR–WA
metropolitan area
household income, 132–133
people in poverty, 413–414
poverty, families in
by family type, 322–334, 362–382
by metropolitan residence, 375–382
by number of earners, 361–364
by presence of children, 330–334, 367–373,
376–382
by race and Hispanic origin, 325–328, 331–334,
366–382
by region, 366–373
historical, 322–334
poverty, people in
by age, 338–339, 384–396, 400–408, 411
by citizenship status, 347
by educational attainment, 398
by family status, 292–296
by metropolitan area, 413–414
by metropolitan status, 354–355, 411–412
by race and Hispanic origin, 341–342, 384,
387–390, 393–404, 409, 412
by reason for not working, 406
by region, 344–345, 408–409
by sex, 336, 386–390, 400–406
by state, 349–352, 416–417
by work status, 357, 400–404
historical, 336–357
of the foreign-born, 347
principal cities. See Metropolitan status.
professional degree. See Educational attainment.
Providence–New Bedford–Fall River, RI–MA
metropolitan area
household income, 132–133
people in poverty, 413–414
public assistance
source of men's income, 195–199
source of women's income, 265–269

race and Hispanic origin. See individual groups.
Raleigh–Cary, NC metropolitan area
household income, 132–133
people in poverty, 413–414
region
discretionary income by, 285
families in poverty by, 366–373
household income by, 31, 118–127

men's income by, 147, 166–170
people in poverty by, 344–345, 408–409
women's income by, 213, 236–240
rental property (as asset)
by age of householder, 300
by household type, 302–304
by race and Hispanic origin of householder, 306
rents and royalties
source of men's income, 195–199
source of women's income, 265–269
retirement
as reason poor did not work, 406
attitude toward, 317
expected age of, 317
savings, 318
source of men's income, 195–199
source of women's income, 265–269
retirement accounts (as asset)
by age of householder, 300
by household type, 302–304
by race and Hispanic origin of householder, 306
Richmond, VA metropolitan area
household income, 132–133
people in poverty, 413–414
Riverside–San Bernardino–Ontario, CA metropolitan
area
household income, 132–133
people in poverty, 413–414
Rochester, NY metropolitan area
household income, 132–133
people in poverty, 413–414

Sacramento–Arden-Arcade–Roseville, CA
metropolitan area
household income, 132–133
people in poverty, 413–414
salaries. See Wages and salaries.
Salt Lake City, UT metropolitan area
household income, 132–133
people in poverty, 413–414
San Antonio–New Braunfels, TX metropolitan area
household income, 132–133
people in poverty, 413–414
San Diego–Carlsbad–San Marcos, CA metropolitan
area
household income, 132–133
people in poverty, 413–414
San Francisco–Oakland–Fremont, CA metropolitan
area
household income, 132–133
people in poverty, 413–414
San Jose–Sunnyvale–Santa Clara, CA metropolitan
area
household income, 132–133
people in poverty, 413–414
savings accounts (as asset)

by age of householder, 300
by household type, 302–304
by race and Hispanic origin of householder, 306
school, as reason poor did not work, 406
Seattle–Tacoma–Bellevue, WA metropolitan area
   household income, 132–133
   people in poverty, 413–414
self-employment
   source of men's income, 195–199
   source of women's income, 265–269
Social Security
   attitude toward, 317
   source of men's income, 195–199
   source of women's income, 265–269
South. *See* Region.
SSI (Supplemental Security Income)
   source of men's income, 195–199
   source of women's income, 265–269
St. Louis, MO–IL metropolitan area
   household income, 132–133
   people in poverty, 413–414
state
   household income by, 33–34, 129–130
   people in poverty by, 349–352, 416–417
stocks (as asset)
   by age of householder, 300
   by household type, 302–304
   by race and Hispanic origin of householder, 306
student debt
   by age of householder, 309
   by household type, 311–313
   by race and Hispanic origin of householder, 315
suburbs. *See* Metropolitan status.
survivors benefits
   source of men's income, 195–199
   source of women's income, 265–269

Tampa–St. Petersburg–Clearwater, FL metropolitan
   area
   household income, 132–133
   people in poverty, 413–414

unemployment, as reason poor did not work, 406
unemployment compensation
   source of men's income, 195–199
   source of women's income, 265–269
unrelated individuals, in poverty, 292–296

vehicles (as asset)
   by age of householder, 300
   by household type, 302–304
   by race and Hispanic origin of householder, 306
veterans benefits
   source of men's income, 195–199
   source of women's income, 265–269

Virginia Beach–Norfolk–Newport News, VA–NC
   metropolitan area
   household income, 132–133
   people in poverty, 413–414

wages and salaries
   source of men's income, 195–199
   source of women's income, 265–269
Washington–Arlington–Alexandria, DC–VA–MD–
   WV metropolitan area
   household income, 132–133
   people in poverty, 413–414
West. *See* Region.
White, non-Hispanic households
   assets of, 306
   by income quintile, 37–39
   debt of, 315
   discretionary income of, 283
   in poverty
      by family type, 328, 334, 361–382
      by metropolitan residence, 375–382
      by number of earners, 361–364
      by region, 366–373
      historical, 328, 334,
   income of
      by age, 51, 57, 63, 69, 75, 81
      by education, 116
      by household type, 45, 57, 63, 69, 75, 81, 93,
         104, 110
      by number of earners, 87
      by presence of children, 93, 104, 110
      by region, 124–127
      historical, 17
   net worth of, 298
White, non-Hispanics
   earnings of
      by education, 190, 260
      by work status, 178, 248
      historical, 151, 217
      men, 151, 178, 190
      women, 217, 248, 260
   in poverty
      by age, 384, 390, 396, 404
      by educational attainment, 398
      by family status, 395
      by metropolitan status, 412
      by region, 409
      by sex, 390, 404
      by work status, 404
      historical, 341–342
   income of
      by age, 145, 163, 211, 233
      by region, 170, 240
      by source, 199, 269
      historical, 141, 145, 207, 211

men, 141, 145, 163–164, 170, 199
women, 207, 211, 233–234, 240, 269
wives earning more than husbands, 225
women. *See* Females.
work status
earnings by, 149, 174–178, 215,
husband and wife, 29, 95–98
poverty status by, 357, 400–404
workers' compensation
source of men's income, 195–199
source of women's income, 265–269